Big Theories Revisited 2

Volume 12 in
Research on Sociocultural Influences on Motivation and Learning
Gregory Arief D. Liem, *Series Editor*
Dennis M. McInerney, *Founding Editor*

RESEARCH ON SOCIOCULTURAL INFLUENCES ON MOTIVATION AND LEARNING

Gregory Arief D. Liem, *Series Editor*
Dennis M. McInerney, *Founding Editor*

Big Theories Revisited 2

edited by

Gregory Arief D. Liem

National Institute of Education
Nanyang Technological University, Singapore

Dennis M. McInerney

The Australian Catholic University
The Education University of Hong Kong

INFORMATION AGE PUBLISHING, INC.
Charlotte, NC • www.infoagepub.com

Library of Congress Cataloging-in-Publication Data

A CIP record for this book is available from the Library of Congress
http://www.loc.gov

ISBN: 978-1-64113-268-8 (Paperback)
978-1-64113-269-5 (Hardcover)
978-1-64113-270-1 (ebook)

Printed in the United States of America

CONTENTS

SECTION III

WHO WANTS ME TO STUDY WELL, AND WHO CAN I DO IT WITH?

SECTION IV

HOW DO I REGULATE MY STUDIES, AND WHO CAN HELP ME DO IT?

SECTION V

ARE MY PEERS AND I MORE ALIKE, OR DIFFERENT, IN OUR SCHOOL MOTIVATION AND LEARNING?

CHAPTER 1

SOCIOCULTURAL PERSPECTIVES ON SCHOOL MOTIVATION, ENGAGEMENT, AND ACHIEVEMENT

Theory, Research, and Application

Gregory Arief D. Liem
Dennis M. McInerney

It takes a village to raise a child.
—African proverb

The school motivation of students is closely associated with the quality of their school engagement and achievement, as well as their well-being and flourishing in other important areas of life including "the psychological, cognitive, social, and physical qualities that students need to live a happy and fulfilling life" (Organization for Economic Cooperation and Development [OECD], 2017, p. 8). Identifying facilitating conditions of school motivation and their processes is thus a meaningful educational purpose, both in and of itself and as a pathway to the holistic development of young people. Although motivation appears to be a largely individual-level

Big Theories Revisited 2, pages 1–12
Copyright © 2018 by Information Age Publishing
All rights of reproduction in any form reserved.

phenomena, it is unequivocally social and societal in nature as well. As is implicit in the African adage quoted above, motivation does not develop in a contextual vacuum. Thus, educational policies and practices seeking to foster school motivation, and to understand its influence on engagement, achievement, and well-being, will be effective only when we, intentionally and systematically, take the sociocultural foundation of these psychological constructs into consideration.

In the initial edition of *Big Theories Revisited* (McInerney & Van Etten, 2004), motivation and engagement theorists were "challenged" to look into their models through a sociocultural lens. The volume was comprehensive in its coverage, comprising 13 chapters on major and contemporary (or "big") theories on motivation and engagement, including attribution theory, self-determination theory, personal investment theory, self-worth theory, expectancy-value theory, and self- and co-regulation models of learning. The volume has been well-received by the academic community, and it was particularly fruitful in prompting scholarly discussions and studies addressing issues pertinent to sociocultural influences on school motivation and engagement. This was objectively reflected by the large number of citations of its chapters in education and educational psychology periodicals, textbooks, edited books, and dissertations.

Significant advancement has been made in the theorizing, conceptualizing, and research on motivation and engagement constructs under such big theories since the publication of the volume more than a decade ago. In this second edition, we invited scholars to critically examine the "what" (factors) and "how" (processes) of sociocultural influences in relation to the key motivation and/or engagement construct(s) of their expertise. Whenever relevant, we also invited authors to illustrate the practicality of such theories in (cross-cultural, multicultural, or culture-specific) applied settings. As a point of departure, we specifically encouraged authors to address the following questions:

- What is the current status of the theoretical model and construct under focus particularly in understanding student motivation and engagement? What are the issues, debates and controversies about the theory? What are the conceptual, methodological, and practical contributions and challenges of the theory?
- To what extent have the theoretical model and construct been applied to understand motivation and engagement of students in different societies? What are the major cross-cultural, cross-ethnic, or between-gender findings documented in recent years? Are the construct, the model, and its key tenets cross-culturally applicable? Is the universal "etic" model sufficient, or is there a need to develop a culture-specific "emic" model?

- In what ways do sociocultural factors, ranging from the role of parents, family, teachers, and peers to that of the larger communal and societal milieus (e.g., education system characteristics, value and belief systems, national ideologies, economic development), influence student motivation and engagement? What is the role of gender and ethnic socialization in these processes? How, and to what extent, can these sociocultural factors be incorporated into the model such that student motivation and engagement processes can be better understood?

We made it clear to our contributors that we solicited new chapters rather than chapters with merely updated materials. As a result, this second edition puts together 16 chapters written by scholars who are known to be the authority in different areas of student motivation and engagement. Whereas some of the chapter topics covered in the initial edition are also part of this edition, some are new and provide fresh sociocultural angles on achievement-related processes and outcomes. Likewise, whereas some of the authors contributed to the earlier edition of the volume, many of them are different. What appears to be the same across the two editions is the scholarly distinction of the authors and the substantive rigor of the chapters in advancing our current understanding of this field of enquiry.

We organize the 16 chapters in this volume into five thematic sections. The first section consists of three chapters that focus on student motivation and engagement perspectives addressing the question, "Why and what do I want to achieve in my studies?" The second section comprises four chapters that focus on perspectives addressing the question, "How do I think and feel about myself and my studies? The three chapters in the third section focus on perspectives relevant to the following question, "Who wants me to study well, and who can I do it with? And the fourth section consists of four chapters that focus their discussions on addressing the question, "How do I regulate my studies, and who can help me do it?" As an interesting and stimulating contrast to the first four sections, the fifth section—"Are my peers and I more alike, or different, in our school motivation and learning?"—delves into standpoints that argue for cross-cultural similarities in achievement-related processes and outcomes. An overview of these chapters is provided below.

SECTION I: WHY AND WHAT DO I WANT TO ACHIEVE IN MY STUDIES?

The focus of authors in the first section is on the reasons and the aims of students' motivated behaviors, and how sociocultural contexts influence the adoption, expression, and regulation of their pursuit. In Chapter 2,

Reeve, Ryan, and Deci take both etic and emic approaches to better understand student motivation, and flourishing more generally, from the lens of self-determination theory. On the one hand, the theory operates based on three universal assumptions that individuals are naturally motivated due to their basic psychological needs, have inherent tendencies toward growth, and proactively engage the environment which may support or frustrate the satisfaction of their needs. On the other hand, the theory recognizes that sociocultural events (e.g., rewards, praises, goals, feedback) and expectations (e.g., norms, values, priorities, obligations) affect students' motivation. Importantly, the theory emphasizes the role of students' agency in the degree to which they are (or are not) open and ready to accept these social recommendations and cultural practices. In their conclusion, the authors highlight five unique contributions of SDT including its role as one of the culturally critical big theories of motivation in education.

Goal complex, or the connection between a reason and an aim of achievement-relevant pursuit, is a relatively nascent theoretical concept in achievement goal theory. In Chapter 3, Liem and Elliot make the case for the relevance of this concept to understanding the processes through which sociocultural factors influence the adoption of achievement goals. The authors distinguish two types of reasons prompting achievement goal adoption, distal and proximal. Unlike proximal reasons that mainly represent cross-culturally universal motive dispositions, the contents of distal reasons are formed through the internalization of culturally-shaped values, and hence they are likely to be socioculturally different. Integrating the hierarchical model of achievement motivation and the bioecological model of human development, Liem and Elliot then propose a taxonomy of sociodemographically- and sociocontextually-grounded distal reasons for goal adoption, and the mechanisms through which cultural expectations, norms, and prescriptions affect achievement goal adoption and regulation through their more immediate impact on distal reasons. The authors end by calling for cross-cultural research to examine the functional significance of both distal and proximal reasons in goal adoption and regulation.

In Chapter 4, King, Datu, and McInerney argue for personal investment (PI) theory as a useful framework for understanding achievement motivation in cross-cultural contexts. PI theory focuses on three key components of meaning—sense of self (who am I), perceived goals of behavior (what do I want), and facilitating conditions (what are my available options)—as critical for understanding student motivation. Unlike traditional motivation theories, PI theory puts a heavy emphasis on culture which is argued to play a powerful role in shaping these three components of meaning. Interestingly, the chapter also documents how PI researchers have uncovered cross-cultural similarities (etic) and differences (emic) in the three PI components based on studies with students from diverse sociocultural backgrounds. One of the key contributions of PI theory and researchers, as argued by the authors, is in its role to broaden the scope of student motivation research—often confined to Western settings—by including understudied populations. The chapter concludes with theoretical and empirical recommendations that could move PI theory forward.

SECTION II: HOW DO I THINK AND FEEL ABOUT MYSELF AND MY STUDIES?

The focus of chapters in the second section is on the cognitive and affective components of students' evaluation of their ability, tasks, and achievement striving more generally. These are represented in the theoretical concepts of expectancy for success, self-efficacy, and achievement emotions. Constructs or concepts similar to achievement-related reasons and goals (e.g., perceived utility of a task) focused on in the earlier section are also discussed here, suggesting the interconnected nature of these factors in student motivation. In Chapter 5, Tonks, Wigfield, and Eccles critically examine the current status of expectancy-value theory (EVT) positing that one's beliefs about expectation for success on a task and about the values of the task (in terms of interestingness, importance, utility, and cost) would contribute to one's motivation and engagement in such a task. The authors specifically highlight two new areas of EVT research emerging in the past 15 years. The first looks at the effectiveness of interventions designed to enhance students' valuing of school tasks, whereas the second centers on the expansion of the "cost" concept initially narrowly defined in terms of what one has to give up to do something that one chooses to do. As formally reflected in the "cultural milieu" box in its graphical representation, EVT is construed as a very relevant model to understanding sociocultural influences on achievement-related behaviors, particularly through the moderating role of sociocultural contexts in the development of subjective task values (more so than on success expectancy beliefs) and in the strength of the relations between the EVT components and persistence, choice, and performance. The authors conclude that the "presence" of EVT in the field of motivation in education has steadily increased over the last 15 years.

Self-efficacy has been consistently shown to affect students' persistence and performance in school. Academic self-efficacy and its development are therefore the focus of the two chapters in this section. In Chapter 6, DiBenedetto and Schunk provide an overview of recent research on self-efficacy in education. After differentiating self-efficacy from other similar constructs (ability beliefs, grit, intention, engagement, and self-determination), the authors review trends in self-efficacy research with discussions focusing on sociocultural influences (culture, gender, family, socioeconomic status) on self-efficacy development and on other issues such as measurement of self-efficacy, ways of using technology to develop self-efficacy (e.g., gaming), and self-efficacy in groups and nonacademic settings (e.g., mentoring relationships, bullying, terrorism). DiBenedetto and Schunk include throughout their chapter specific recommendations for future self-efficacy research in education, and suggestions on how self-efficacy principles can be applied to help develop and sustain a sense of agency in learners. Indeed, their chapter provides a rich and updated review of research on the role of self-efficacy in education, and beyond.

Complementary to the preceding chapter, in Chapter 7, Usher and Weidner provide a thoughtful discussion on how sociocultural processes influence self-efficacy development through the four primary sources of self-efficacy as hypothesized in Bandura's social-cognitive theory. These sources include mastery experience, vicarious experience, social persuasions, and physiological and affective states. Guided by the interesting and dynamic vignette of a hypothetical middle school student named Mia, Usher and Weidner paint a picture of how cultural identity, socialization, nationality, and other sociocultural processes might affect the ways in which learners interpret their academic experiences and assess their capabilities. They then provide a review of recent studies on sources of academic self-efficacy, particularly those that considered diverse sociocultural contexts and identities of learners. They highlight cultural similarities and differences in how students are exposed to various types of efficacy-relevant information, the interpretation rules students apply to this information, and the relative influence of this information on students' academic self-efficacy. Usher and Weidner also provide recommendations for how sociocultural processes can be better addressed methodologically in self-efficacy research. They close by recommending ways that researchers can use to broaden their assessment of the sources of self-efficacy and to better capture the range of efficacy-relevant information students weigh, both positive and negative.

In Chapter 8, Pekrun provides an overview of his control-value theory of achievement emotions (CVT) and a well-argued discussion on the influence of gender and sociocultural contexts on students' achievement emotions. CVT posits that achievement emotions are triggered by appraisals of control over, and the value of, achievement activities and their outcomes, and different types and combinations of control and value appraisals are thought to prompt different emotions. Given that appraisals are considered proximal antecedents, more distal individual and socio-contextual factors are thought to influence students' emotion by shaping their appraisals. Thus, CVT posits that the influence of these distal factors is mediated by students' control and value appraisals, and that any individual and socio-contextual factors shaping students' appraisals also influence their emotions. Pekrun concludes that the basic mechanisms linking students' appraisals and emotions are universal across genders, environments, and cultures. However, the contents, objects, frequency, and intensity of students' emotions differ widely as a function of social influences. As such, while acknowledging the relative universality of basic mechanisms, he believes that emotion theory and its related educational practice need to consider the uniqueness of emotions in different genders, social environments, and sociocultural as well as historical contexts.

SECTION III: WHO WANTS ME TO STUDY WELL, AND WHO CAN I DO IT WITH?

As noted earlier, academic endeavor is social in nature in terms of its facilitation, pursuit, and consequences. Students are motivated to study not only because of the encouragement by their parents and teachers, but also because they see it as a way to fulfill their responsibility to these people. Further, aside from the fact that group project is an ubiquitous component of assessment across curricular subjects and instructional methods, working with peers is a way of learning that many students like and choose to do on their own accord. Indeed, chapters in this section focus on these issues. In Chapter 9, Wentzel proposes a competence-in-context model to understand school motivation. The model predicts that social supports and motivational beliefs are related to classroom competence by way of pursuit of goals to achieve outcomes that are central to the learning process. These goals can reflect both academic and social outcomes, including displays of efforts to learn and understand subject matter and appropriate classroom behavior. Social provisions from teachers and peers in the form of clear expectations and opportunities for goal pursuit, instrumental help, emotional support and safety, and responsivity reflect potential contextual influences on student goal pursuit. The author asserts that, these provisions support goal pursuit by providing input concerning socially-valued goals that students should pursue, and facilitating positive motivational beliefs in the form of values, self-efficacy, control beliefs, perceived social expectations and belongingness. Wentzel believes that the model is unique in its perspective on competence-in-context for understanding motivation at school, and it extends more traditional views of classroom motivation by recognizing the role of social supports in facilitating student motivation and pursuit of appropriate classroom goals.

Next, in Chapter 10, Rubie-Davies, Webber, and Turner present a culturally responsive model of teacher expectation, a new big theory which integrates culturally responsive pedagogy, high expectation teaching, and school–family–community partnerships. Based on different perspectives of culturally responsive pedagogy, the authors examine the applicability of teacher expectation theory to improving Māori students' school performance. They point out that the culturally responsive pedagogy and high expectation teaching models place a heavier emphasis on the classroom and student-teacher relationships than they are on *whānau* (extended family), a cultural concept of particular importance for the Māori community. Without the inclusion of *whānau*, the authors argue, high expectations and culturally responsive pedagogy alone will not make a significant difference for Maori students. Their model shows us that school culture and attitudes towards certain ethnic communities need to change for high teacher expectations and culturally responsive pedagogy to positively impact the educational achievement of students from those communities.

In Chapter 11, Inns and Slavin focus on the effectiveness of cooperative learning with students from various cultural groups. They first provide a theoretical overview of cooperative learning which refers to a variety of teaching methods that require students to work together to help each other learn contents or complete projects. Although much research has shown positive effects of cooperative learning on achievement in many subject areas and grade levels, we "challenge" the authors to examine if these instructional methods apply to *all* students across different sociocultural backgrounds. As they critically examine, research in the United States has generally found the benefits of cooperative learning, including for African American and Hispanic students, consistent with their cultural orientations toward cooperation and communalism. Research in Asia with students from Confucian heritage culture (CHC) societies, however, has shown a more complex pattern of findings. Although achievement outcomes of cooperative learning are generally positive, some aspects of Asian culture, such as respect for and dependence on teachers rather than peers, may need to be taken into account in applications of cooperative learning in this tradition. Like the message by Rubie-Davies and her co-authors in the earlier chapter, Inns and Slavin's chapter reminds us that there is not such a thing as "one size fits all" as far as cross-cultural transfers of pedagogical principles and practices are concerned, regardless of how effective these principles and practices are proven to be in their culture of origin.

SECTION IV: HOW DO I REGULATE MY STUDIES, AND WHO CAN HELP ME DO IT?

The social foundation of academic endeavor, highlighted in the previous section, continues to be an important theme even in what appears to be individually-oriented constructs and processes like self-regulated learning. The recognition that students share the regulation of their learning with others especially teachers and peers (and even parents), both in person and through the technology, has received greater attention in recent days. This is indeed the focus of chapters in this section. In Chapter 12, Cleary, Kitsantas, Pape, and Slemp provide an overview of recent advances in social-cognitive theory and research examining the influence of sociocultural and socialization influences on the development of self-regulated learning skills in learners across various contexts. After briefly reviewing the basic tenets of social-cognitive theory, they use sociocultural principles to further understand the role of environment as delineated in Bandura's notion of reciprocal determinism. Central to their chapter is the exploration of the intersection of a three-phase model of self-regulated learning with a model of self-regulated learning skill acquisition that emphasizes different levels of social influence. Of particular interest are the different ways in which social-cognitive researchers have conceptualized and studied emulative or guided practice activities, and whether such findings are consistent across different cultures. Interestingly, the authors interweave an embedded case study—Jennifer and Desmond in Ms. Johnson's Algebra class—throughout the chapter and present two field-based studies to illustrate how socio-cognitive theory and research can be applied to authentic classroom contexts. The authors conclude their chapter by discussing important areas for future research and the potential need for blending social-cognitive theory with sociocultural perspectives.

Next, in Chapter 13, Perry, Mazabel, Dantzer, and Winne examine how theory and research on self-regulation and self-determination are evolving to reflect sociocultural perspectives on learning, and how these developments enrich and expand understandings of how self-regulation and self-determination can be promoted in complex teaching and learning environments. These authors first examine the two theories, with particular attention to recent advances that reflect an increasingly sociocultural examination of these two theories. They then describe a research–practice partnership in which they have engaged with an after school music education program. In this section, they underscore the sociocultural context that surrounds the program and its implications for how they have co-constructed research and practice with their partners. They close the chapter with notes highlighting implications for research and practice that derive from our work.

In line with the idea that individuals exist as part of the larger social and physical environment, in Chapter 14, McCaslin and Vriesema take a co-regulation perspective on academic behaviors. This perspective is one that describes how personal (e.g., disposition), social (e.g., relationships), and cultural (e.g., societal expectations) factors interact to influence student learning behaviors. Specifically, the authors describe the theories that influence their thinking, explain McCaslin's co-regulation perspective, and present three examples of their research that illustrate the co-regulation framework. Overall, this chapter provides evidence for the importance of understanding the relationships between the self, others, and society, and specifically asserts that students' personal histories yield differences in what they bring to an academic situation, in what and how they participate, and what that means for their sense of self. The authors conclude that the co-regulation model serves as a vehicle for research on cultural-social-personal dynamics.

In Chapter 15, Hickey and Andrews describe how the situative theories of motivation and engagement have evolved through refinements made on approaches to online instruction and assessment in courses for secondary, undergraduate, graduate, and open learners. The authors provide some historical context regarding situative approaches to motivation and summarize an empirical test of situated motivation. They then describe how the core set of educational design principles emerged across cycles of design-based research across several educational technologies, including online courses. The work of these authors has resulted in generalizable design principles for motivating productive forms of disciplinary engagement in online settings. The chapter then uses examples from a graduate-level learning sciences course to illustrate the current design principles and describe how they support engagement and achievement, while accommodating diversity in prior experience, current application context, and future goals. Hickey and Andrews end their chapter by putting forth the "next steps" to extend the application of situative theories of motivation and engagement.

SECTION V: ARE MY PEERS AND I MORE ALIKE, OR DIFFERENT, IN OUR SCHOOL MOTIVATION AND LEARNING?

Chapters in the previous sections have focused their discussions on sociocultural influences on motivation, learning, and achievement. Taking a reasonably contrasting view, the two chapters in this last section zoom in on the relative cross-cultural universality of the psychoeducational factors and processes. Although these chapters largely argue for the dynamic relations between motivation, engagement, and achievement through pancultural and evolutionary (or etic) lenses, they recognize the possible culture-specific (or emic) factors and processes influencing schooling outcomes. In Chapter 16, Sedikides delves into the panculturality of the need for positive feedback and its potency for motivation and learning. The author recognizes that, although feedback is the medium through which schools (e.g., teachers) inform students of their progress, its administration is often less effective than it is intended to be. In an effort to understand why, he focuses on the self-evaluation motives underlying the pursuit and reception of feedback, including self-enhancement, self-protection, self-assessment, and self-improvement. His reviews point to the apparent panculturality of the self-evaluation motives and their implications for student motivation and learning. In particular, university students—both in Western and East-Asian cultures—desire and solicit predominantly positive rather than accurate feedback, while finding positive feedback more satisfying and useful than improving feedback at least in the short run. These students also selectively forget negative feedback than accurate feedback, when it is targeted at them (rather than another person), and when it refers to important (rather than unimportant) aspects of their self-concept. The author ends by drawing implications for feedback-giving practices, and also by calling for research that moves beyond the East-West divide and adopts a more nuanced view of culture.

In Chapter 17, Martin provides a theoretical account on evolutionary educational psychology, as one line of evolutionary psychology theorizing that seeks to explain how evolved biases in learning and motivation influence students' capacity and motivation to learn and achieve. The author explains that evolutionary educational psychology is a predominantly cognitive perspective, and he understands that critical responses to it have identified a lack of detail on the interpersonal, sociocultural, and social aspects of achievement, motivation, learning, and instruction. Addressing these criticisms, Martin revisits and draws on the confluence of "classic" evolutionary, educational, and psychological theorizing to explore factors and processes relevant to student and classroom life. The chapter concludes by recognizing the presence of pan-human evolutionary factors and processes that operate to shape students' learning, as well as culture-specific adaptations of these factors and processes that operate for the student to achieve optimally in his/her specific context. To the extent that this is the case, the author asserts, evolutionary psychology applied to the classroom integrates both etic (universal) and emic (culture-specific) principles to inform how students learn and achieve.

CODA

If you want to go fast, walk alone. If you want to go far, walk together.
—African Proverb

We began this chapter with an African proverb, "It takes a village to raise a child," and applied it to understanding student educational development. As an overview of the present volume, this chapter has shown that school motivation, engagement, and achievement are not only a multicontextual experience involving the family, class, school, education system, community, and society where learners belong to, but also a multidimensional phenomenon encompassing the cognitive, behavioral, and emotional aspects of the learners. Indeed, it takes not only a whole 'village' but also a whole variety of contemporary theories to shed light on school motivation, engagement, and achievement.

As noted in the beginning of this chapter, we presented the contributing authors three overarching questions as a set of guidelines in putting together their thoughts and ideas into a sociocultural discussion on the motivation and/or engagement constructs of their expertise. We, the editors, are delighted that the authors have very competently addressed these questions in their respective chapters. Not only do we believe that you, the readers, will find many of your own questions answered, we also hope that this volume will spark many more focal questions in your mind as you read its chapters.

We are optimistic that the multitude of questions we pose, both current and forthcoming, will lead us to a deeper, clearer, and more integrated understanding of motivation, engagement, and achievement as a complex socioculturally-rooted psychological phenomenon. To this goal that we all share, another African proverb reminds us that efforts to address these questions can be effectively pursued only when we work together hand in hand, collaboratively, and in the spirit of learning from one another. Happy reading!

REFERENCES

McInerney, D. M., & Van Etten, S. (Eds.). (2004). *Big theories revisited.* Greenwich, CT: Information Age.

Organization for Economic Cooperation and Development. (2017). *PISA 2015 results (Volume III): Students' well-being.* Paris, France: Author.

SECTION I

WHY AND WHAT DO I WANT TO ACHIEVE
IN MY STUDIES?

CHAPTER 2

SOCIOCULTURAL INFLUENCES ON STUDENT MOTIVATION AS VIEWED THROUGH THE LENS OF SELF-DETERMINATION THEORY

Johnmarshall Reeve
Richard M. Ryan
Edward L. Deci

Imagine doing what many educational researchers do—visit a classroom, observe teacher–student interactions, and formulate some forecasts about these students' future motivation and learning. In a secondary school foreign language classroom, you might watch as the teacher (a) sets a challenging goal for students (e.g., learn 20 verbs on Monday, 20 nouns on Tuesday), (b) recommends some tried-and-true learning strategies (e.g., learn in pairs, prepare flashcards), (c) models what skill and expertise look like in this domain (e.g., play a YouTube video of native speakers), (d) encourages students to emulate those role models, (e) provides corrective feedback,

Big Theories Revisited 2, pages 15–40
Copyright © 2018 by Information Age Publishing
All rights of reproduction in any form reserved.

(f) aids students' self-control (e.g., suppress and override lesson-irrelevant temptations and distractions), and (g) evaluates students' learning.

The next day, you attend the same classroom and group of students, but this time a different teacher is present. She uses the former teacher's well-scripted lesson plan and implements all of the same self-regulatory strategies (e.g., goal setting, social modeling), but her way of relating to students is different. She listens carefully to what her students say, she seeks to understand what they want and need, and she uses flexible language, uttering words and phrases such as:

- "Okay"
- "Yes"
- "I understand"
- "Any suggestions?"
- "What do you want to work on the most?"
- "Do you think you can do this?"
- "Are you stuck anywhere?"
- "Do you think that was a good performance?"
- "What do you think it will take to improve?"

While the first teacher was a competent and effective teacher, there is something special about this second teacher and how her students respond to her and to the lesson. She is aware of her students' needs, preferences, and emotions. She is responsive to their engagement-disengagement signals, and she seems to be in synch, rather in conflict, with her students. Her students sense that she is "on their side." The students on this day show more enthusiasm and more initiative. Compared to yesterday, they are more attentive, they take more responsibility for their own learning, and they act more like agents and less like pawns. The teacher-student interactions are back-and-forth, rather than unilateral. Overall, you get the impression that students are engaged, are learning the language, and are happy.

SELF-DETERMINATION THEORY

Self-determination theory (SDT) is a macro-theory of motivation that seeks to explain how sociocultural conditions facilitate or undermine human engagement and flourishing (Ryan & Deci, 2017). As shown in Figure 2.1, SDT is rooted in a series of assumptions about the nature of human motivation and how social conditions affect it. The theory has been extended to offer a set of six mini-theories, the most recent of which is "relationships motivation theory" (Deci & Ryan, 2014). Across these mini-theories, SDT provides a comprehensive (i.e., "big") theory of motivation that is both of

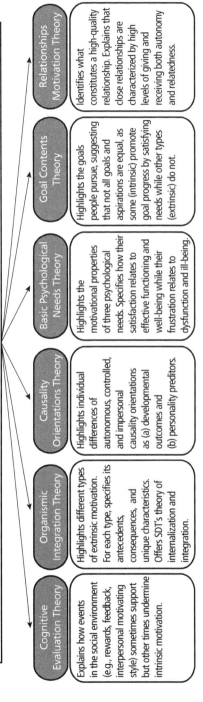

Self-Determination Theory

Meta-Theory
An approach to motivation that uses empirical methods to explain how sociocultural conditions facilitate and undermine flourishing.

Assumptions
1. **Intrinsic Activity:** Everyone possesses the three activity-generating psychological needs of autonomy, competence, and relatedness.
2. **Organismic Approach:** Everyone has inherent tendencies toward growth, integration, synthesis, and organization, though these inherent tendencies require environmental support for their development and actualization.
3. **Person-Environment Dialectic:** Person proactively engages the environment; environment offers regulations to internalize.

Mini-Theories
Each mini-theory addresses a different domain of motivation to explain particular motivational phenomena, including (from left to right in the six entries below) the effects of external events and social conditions, extrinsic motivation and internalization, self-determination in the personality, well-being, goals and life aspirations, and high-quality relationships.

Cognitive Evaluation Theory	Organismic Integration Theory	Causality Orientations Theory	Basic Psychological Needs Theory	Goal Contents Theory	Relationships Motivation Theory
Explains how events in the social environment (e.g., rewards, feedback, interpersonal motivating style) sometimes support but other times undermine intrinsic motivation.	Highlights different types of extrinsic motivation. For each type, specifies its antecedents, consequences, and unique characteristics. Offers SDT's theory of internalization and integration.	Highlights individual differences of autonomous, controlled, and impersonal causality orientations as (a) developmental outcomes and (b) personality preditors.	Highlights the motivational properties of three psychological needs. Specifies how their satisfaction relates to effective functioning and well-being while their frustration relates to dysfunction and ill-being.	Highlights the goals people pursue, suggesting that not all goals and aspirations are equal, as some (intrinsic) promote goal progress by satisfying needs while other types (extrinsic) do not.	Identifies what constitutes a high-quality relationship. Explains that close relationships are characterized by high levels of giving and receiving both autonomy and relatedness.

Figure 2.1   Self-determination theory's meta-theory, assumptions, and mini-theories.

scientific interest and educationally pragmatic. It acknowledges that student educational outcomes vary widely, and explains the conditions under which students sometimes thrive and flourish and other times suffer.

Theoretical Assumptions

As shown in the upper part of Figure 2.1, SDT is built on three key assumptions (Ryan & Deci, 2017). The first is the assumption of intrinsic activity, which assumes that students are naturally prone towards activity, engagement, and learning. This first assumption highlights the motivational importance of constructs such as intrinsic motivation and autonomous motivation. The second is an organismic framework that assumes that this growth-oriented nature is in active exchange with, and dependent upon, a nurturing environment. According to SDT, the educational environment can afford (or fail to provide) the resources students need to be engaged and well. Specifically, when environments are supportive of students' basic psychological needs for autonomy, competence, and relatedness, SDT predicts that students will thrive both cognitively and affectively. Yet when learning environments withhold supports for these basic needs, then the motivation and wellbeing of students both suffer. The classic plant metaphor applies here: Just as plants that receive water, sunshine, and nutritious soil thrive whereas those that do not suffer, students whose needs are satisfied will thrive whereas those without supports for experiencing autonomy, competence and relatedness will wither as learners. The third assumption is that of a person–environment dialectic. This assumption states that students proactively engage in their environment to secure resources, learn new information, discover new and more effective ways of functioning, internalize helpful ways of thinking and behaving, and create a more motivationally-supportive environment for themselves, while the environment in turn affords new and constructive ways of thinking and acting for individuals to internalize and incorporate into their self-structure.

We emphasize SDT's core assumptions for two reasons. First, most of the debates and controversies involving SDT occur at this level. The assumption of inherent activity, for instance, states that all human beings, irrespective of their age, gender, language, socioeconomic status, nationality, culture, ability level, special-needs status, or historical time period, possess the same three inherent psychological needs, whose satisfaction largely determines whether or not they thrive and flourish. The three psychological needs are those for autonomy (need to experience volition and self-endorsement in one's behavior), competence (need to experience effectance in one's interactions with the environment), and relatedness (need to experience warm, close, responsive, and reciprocal care in one's relationships). A great deal of cross-cultural research has been conducted to empirically test this assumption of universal psychological needs (Chirkov, Ryan, & Sheldon, 2011). For instance, one group of researchers tested if nationality (Belgium, China, Peru, United States) moderated the relation between adolescents' need satisfaction and well-being and also the relation between their need frustration and ill-being (Chen et al., 2015). In all four countries, extent of need satisfaction predicted extent of well-being and extent of need frustration predicted extent of ill-being, while nationality did not moderate either correlation. Alternatively, some educators reject the idea that all students benefit from autonomy need satisfaction, the pursuit of intrinsic goals, autonomy-supportive relationships with their teachers, and autonomy-supportive classroom environments more generally. Instead, these educators endorse the "match hypothesis," which is the belief that it is only students who have a strong autonomy orientation to begin with that benefit from autonomy, intrinsic goals, and autonomy support. For students with a strong control orientation, these educators suggest that control-oriented students benefit from external regulation, the pursuit of extrinsic goals, controlling relationships, and controlling classroom environments. There is very little, if any, evidence to support either the match hypothesis or the proposition that students benefit from intrapsychic or interpersonal control (Vansteenkiste, Lens, & Deci, 2006; Vansteenkiste, Timmermans, Lens, Soenens, & Van den Broeck, 2008). Nevertheless, this debate and controversy persists (e.g., Harackiewicz & Elliot, 1998; Sagiv & Schwartz, 2000). Because this is so, we readdress this issue in the chapter's second section.

Second, recent advances in research methods and statistical modelling have occurred since the publication of the first *Big Theories Revisited* volume (McInerney & Van Etten, 2004) that have made these difficult to test assumptions more accessible to empirical test. For instance, to establish the scientific credibility of the assumption that people have inherent psychological needs and intrinsic motivation, some researchers have undertaken a neuroscientific program of research that has essentially discovered the physical, neural basis of both psychological needs and intrinsic motivation (Lee & Reeve, 2013, 2017; Ryan & Di Domenico, 2017). In addition, the capacity to empirically test the assumption of a person–environment dialectic has been greatly facilitated by the introduction of sophisticated statistical approaches (e.g., multilevel structural equation modeling analyses with longitudinal data) that afford new opportunities to propose and test hypothesized models that feature reciprocal relations between students and their educational environment. For example, longitudinal data sets show that changes in students' motivation, engagement, and behavior affect longitudinal changes in teachers' classroom motivating styles, just as changes in teachers' motivating styles affect longitudinal changes in students' motivation, engagement, and behavior (Jang, Kim, & Reeve, 2016).

Even daily fluctuations in teacher need supports have been shown to foster corresponding daily changes in student interest (Tsai, Kunter, Lüdtke, Trautwein, & Ryan, 2008).

Mini-Theories

As shown in the lower part of Figure 2.1, SDT offers six mini-theories. Here, we simply introduce each mini-theory, identify its domain of application, and offer some related education-centric questions. A fuller account of each mini-theory can be found in other resources (Ryan & Deci, 2017; Vansteenkiste, Niemiec, & Soenens, 2010).

Cognitive Evaluation Theory

SDT's first mini-theory was cognitive evaluation theory, which was proposed to explain how any external event (e.g., a reward, a grade) might affect students' intrinsic motivation through its impact on experiences of autonomy, competence, and relatedness. The theory specifies how classroom conditions sometimes lead to the satisfaction of these needs (i.e., when offered in an autonomy-supportive and competence-informing way) and hence to intrinsic motivation, whereas at other times they lead to the frustration of basic needs (e.g., when offered in a behaviorally-controlling and incompetence-informing way) and hence to extrinsic motivation or amotivation. The theory explains how the same classroom events or structures can be offered in a ways that either support or undermine students' intrinsic motivation, including the supportive vs. undermining use of extrinsic rewards (Deci, Koestner, & Ryan, 1999), praise and positive feedback (Ryan, Mims, & Koestner, 1983), evaluations (Mouratidis, Lens, & Vansteenkiste, 2010), deadlines and goals (Mossholder, 1980), and competition (Reeve & Deci, 1996). Overall, cognitive evaluation theory explains how such environmental events affect students' psychological needs and, hence, functionally enhance or undermine intrinsic motivation. Questions that have been explained by the cognitive evaluation mini-theory include:

- What is the effect of an extrinsic reward on intrinsic motivation?
- How can teachers introduce a classroom event (e.g., an assessment, a goal) so that it will support, rather than undermine, students' intrinsic motivation?

Cognitive evaluation theory's range has been extended from its original focus on external events to interpersonal contexts more generally (e.g., classroom climate, teacher's motivating style). While external events represent direct and proximal influences on students' motivation, social contexts are more pervasive in their influence. One practical application of this research has been to specify (i.e., operationally define) what an autonomy-supportive climate or motivating style is, and also what a controlling climate or motivating style is. Autonomy support is an interpersonal tone of understanding that manifests itself through instructional behaviors such as taking the students' perspective, vitalizing their psychological needs during instruction, and providing explanatory rationales for requested behaviors and procedures (Reeve, 2016; Deci, Eghrari, Patrick, & Leone, 1994). Even tone of voice can affect perceived autonomy, and thus motivation (Zougkou, Weinstein, & Paulmann, 2017). These acts of autonomy-supportive instruction generally lead students to experience high need satisfaction and low need frustration (Cheon, Reeve, & Song, 2016). Guided by cognitive evaluation theory, formal autonomy-supportive intervention programs have been developed and implemented to show that (a) teachers can learn how to become more autonomy supportive (and less controlling) and (b) when they do then students and teachers alike both benefit in important ways, such as enhanced motivation and engagement for students and greater job satisfaction and teaching efficacy for teachers (Cheon, Reeve, Yu, & Jang, 2014; Cheon et al., 2016).

Organismic Integration Theory

Organismic integration theory proposes that motivated behaviors can be placed on a continuum of low to high autonomy. Organismic integration theory identifies different types of extrinsic motivation (i.e., external regulation, introjected regulation, identified regulation, integrated regulation), and it specifies the antecedents, consequences, and unique characteristics of each. This mini-theory also provides SDT's conceptualization of the developmental processes of internalization and personality/identity integration. In doing so, organismic integration theory explains how students can transform (i.e., accept and internalize) an originally externally-endorsed value or externally-requested behavior into a self-endorsed and authentically-held value or behavior. Overall, organismic integration theory describes distinct types of extrinsic motivation, and it explains under what conditions the most autonomous forms of extrinsic motivation (identified regulation, integrated regulation) are likely to emerge in the classroom. Questions that have been explained by the organismic integration mini-theory include:

- How can teachers motivate students to engage in and benefit from uninteresting but personally useful learning activities?
- Can students transform externally requested behaviors (e.g., clean your desk space) into self-endorsed, volitional behaviors?

Causality Orientations Theory

Causality orientations theory offers a personality perspective. It proposes that students acquire varying levels of three causality orientations (i.e., autonomous, controlled, impersonal) that reflect their beliefs about what forces routinely and reliably initiate and regulate their behavior. The mini-theory proposes that students tend to hold different relative strengths of these three causality orientations, and these individual differences help explain why autonomy-oriented students are inclined to be more productive and happy, even when in the same classroom or social context (i.e., because an autonomy orientation tends students toward autonomous motivation, a controlled orientation tends students toward controlled motivation, and an impersonal orientation tends students toward amotivation). The mini-theory further explains how causality orientations can be understood as developmental outcomes (e.g., students who have been continually subjected to controlling environments will tend to develop a controlled causality orientation) as well as individual difference predictors of students' educational outcomes (e.g., engagement, prosocial behavior). Causality orientations, largely being resultants of person–environment interactions over lifespan development, represent individual differences that are largely not captured by traditional personality trait measures such as the "Big Five" (Olesen, 2011). Overall, causality orientations theory adds a personality-developmental perspective to explain autonomous and controlled motivations. Questions that have been explained by the causality orientations mini-theory include:

- In the same classroom, why do some students interpret events and communications as controlling while other students interpret the same events and communications as autonomy supportive?
- Why are some students more self-determined than are other students?

Basic Psychological Needs Theory

Basic psychological needs theory highlights the motivational properties of the three universal needs of autonomy, competence, and relatedness. It explains how need satisfaction leads students toward effective functioning and well-being, and also how need frustration leads students toward dysfunction and ill-being. "Basic" suggests that psychological needs function as "essential nutrients" that allow students to experience good days, positive well-being, vitality, and flourishing (Ryan, 1995; Sheldon, Ryan, & Reis, 1996). For instance, empirical tests show that "what's satisfying about satisfying events" is an experience of autonomy, competence, or relatedness satisfaction, just as "what's unsatisfying about unsatisfying events" is an experience of autonomy, competence, and relatedness frustration (Sheldon, Elliot, Kim, & Kasser, 2001, p. 336; Jang, Reeve, Ryan, & Kim, 2009).

Overall, basic needs theory explains the ultimate source of students' intrinsic activity, adaptive functioning, and psychological well-being. Questions that have been explained by the basic needs mini-theory include:

- Are the psychological needs universal, or are they only western sociocultural constructions that do not predict wellness and engagement in eastern cultures?
- Why do students sometimes say, "I enjoyed today's class; it was a good, fun, and worthwhile class"?

Goal Contents Theory

Goal contents theory focuses on the content of the goals people are pursuing in their lives. It starts with the proposition that not all goals and aspirations are equally likely to satisfy basic needs or foster wellness. Some goals represent reliable paths toward autonomy, competence, and relatedness need-satisfying experiences, whereas other goals do not. That is, some goal pursuits afford students frequent and recurring opportunities to experience engagement-fostering and progress-enabling need satisfaction. These types of goals (e.g., the pursuit of personal growth or closer relationships) are referred to as intrinsic goals, because they generate intrinsic satisfaction. Extrinsic goals are those that when pursued or attained provide little or no opportunities for students to experience need satisfaction. In fact, these goals sometimes put students in the position of having to sacrifice their psychological need satisfactions in the pursuit of the extrinsic goal (e.g., "To become class valedictorian, I need to treat my classmates as my rivals"). Typical extrinsic goals are the pursuit of money, fame, power, or popularity, though in schools these goals often take on a feel of "educational materialism" (e.g., high test scores, getting into the best schools) rather than financial materialism. Overall, goal contents theory explains why some goals generate more satisfaction, engagement, and progress than do other goals. Questions that have been explained by the goal contents mini-theory include:

- Why do students fail to make progress on the goals they pursue?
- Can the same learning activity be reframed away from the pursuit of an extrinsic goal (make a high test score) into the pursuit of an intrinsic goal (develop a personal skill)?

Relationships Motivation Theory

Relationships motivation theory explains what constitutes a high-quality and deeply-satisfying interpersonal relationship. This mini-theory starts with the proposition that not all relationships afford experiences of relatedness need satisfaction. Relationships motivation theory explains that close, high-quality relationships are characterized by both the giving and the receiving of autonomy and relatedness satisfaction, and especially by the mutuality of autonomy and autonomy support. It further states that autonomy and relatedness satisfactions are not antithetical, though some socializing agents do pit autonomy satisfaction against relatedness satisfaction (e.g., conditional regard; Assor, Roth, & Deci, 2004). When relationship partners both give and receive autonomy support, the ensuing need satisfaction enables and facilitates greater relationship satisfaction, attachment security, and wellness (Deci, La Guardia, Moller, Scheiner, & Ryan, 2006). When relationship partners try to control and pressure one another, however, the ensuing need frustration contributes to relationship dysfunction, defensiveness, insecurity, ill-being, and relationship dissatisfaction. The mini-theory also addresses the dynamics of helping, arguing that only when help is experienced as volitionally offered does it have psychological benefits for the receiver (e.g., Weinstein & Ryan, 2010). The theory has application to the roles of teaching and mentoring, where attributions concerning helpers are salient (Wild, Enzle, & Hawkins, 1992). Overall, relationships motivation theory explains the core ingredients that underlie a deeply-satisfying interpersonal relationship. Questions that have been explained by the relationships motivation mini-theory include:

- Why do students feel close and secure with some teachers, but distant and defensive with other teachers?
- Is the giving of autonomy support as beneficial to the giver as the receipt of autonomy support is to the recipient?

ETIC AND EMIC SOCIOCULTURAL INFLUENCES

Any classroom observation makes it clear that teachers strive to affect change in their students. Teachers, for instance, introduce learning activities, utter praise, set goals, offer rewards, enforce rules, provide feedback, endorse values, and offer themselves or others as role models, and they do so typically to induce an educationally productive change in their students' thinking, feeling, or behaving. The same can be said for cultural influences, as cultures also affect change in students by establishing norms, setting expectations, prescribing attitudes toward authorities, legitimizing hierarchies, and promoting what is desirable and acceptable in terms of values, beliefs, priorities, roles, and duties. Self-determination theory has richly investigated how teacher-delivered and culturally endorsed events affect changes in students' motivation, engagement, development, and achievement. The repeated finding is that when students experience the sociocultural influence as a support to their autonomy, then it tends to promote autonomous motivation, active engagement, cultural competence, identity integration, and achievement, and the reason it is able to do this is because autonomy support allows students to become more open and ready to accept and deeply internalize the social recommendation as their own (Chirkov & Ryan, 2001; Chirkov, Ryan, Kim, & Kaplan, 2003; Downie, Koestner, El Geledi, & Cree, 2004; Roth, Assor, Niemiec, Ryan, & Deci, 2009).

The etic–emic distinction is often made in sociocultural investigations, with etic corresponding to constructs that are robust and generalizable across cultures and emic corresponding to constructs that are specific or unique to one particular culture (Kotlak, 2006). Some cross-cultural researchers suggest that the SDT findings of the benefits of autonomy satisfaction and autonomy support and the costs of autonomy frustration and interpersonal control are only emic. For instance, Ruth Chao argued, "For Asians, parental obedience and some aspects of strictness may be equated with parental concern, caring, or involvement. . . . For Asians, parental control may not always involve "domination" of children per se, but rather a more organizational type of control for the purpose or goal of keeping the family running more smoothly and fostering family harmony" (Chao, 1994, p. 1112). In other words, the concern is that some etic constructs and explanations may actually be only emic constructs and explanations, once they are put to rigorous cross-cultural test.

SDT is an etic scientific theory of basic psychological needs and human motivation, but it also recognizes that (a) cultures vary in the values and priorities they seek to transmit to their members and (b) different cultures can assign, within limits, different meanings to the same educational practices or styles they use to transmit their values. From its onset, a central proposition of SDT has been that any practice or communication has a *functional significance*, or a psychological meaning, to the person who is receiving that practice or communication. On average, students might experience a teacher-imposed rule (e.g., "clean up before you leave") as a controlling communication, but the meaning of the rule might be experienced by students quite differently. The functional significance for one student might be "this is a restriction to my personal freedom and choice" whereas for another it might be understood as "helpful guidance to achieve competent functioning." These represent different senses of internalization with respect to following the rule or practice.

The functional significance of a culturally-endorsed prescription or proscription to an individual affects the extent to which he or she is able to internalize it. When cultures use controlling methods, and individuals interpret the functional significance of the recommendation as controlling, then the quality of the individual's internalization will tend to be impoverished, conflicted, and unstable, as in the case of introjection or societal (external) regulation. Such introjected values tend to represent conflict-generating liabilities. When cultural socialization is characterized by autonomy-supportive methods, and individuals interpret the functional significance of the recommendation as autonomy supportive, then the quality of the individual's internalization will be heartfelt and self-transformative, as in the case of identification and integration. Such fully internalized values tend to represent assets for human flourishing.

As shown in the middle of Figure 2.2, these two concepts (functional significance, internalization) are important constructs to bridge together what is etic and what is emic in SDT. In making this bridge, the crucial question that determines the functional significance of any act of instruction is this: "Is the motivator trying to control me to get some specific outcome, or is he or she supporting my autonomy?" (Ryan & Deci, 2017, p. 164). For internalization, the crucial question is the extent to which there is an

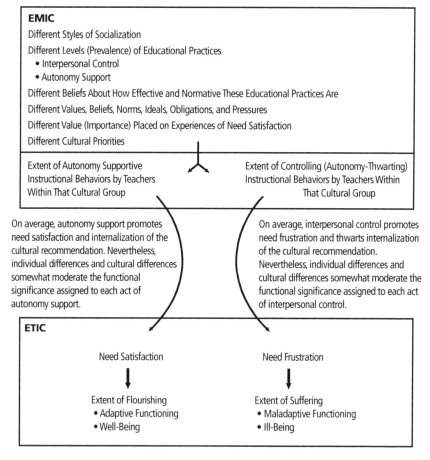

Figure 2.2 How the concept of functional significance integrates what is emic and what is etic in SDT.

experience of personal choice to accept the recommendation as one's own, because an experience of choice or volition is as closely linked to satisfaction and well-being as are experiences of autonomy, competence, and relatedness need satisfaction (Miller, Das, & Chakravarty, 2011).

What is etic in SDT (i.e., what is culturally universal) appears in the lower half of Figure 2.2. Psychological need satisfaction, when it occurs, has a very close positive relation to flourishing—to adaptive functioning (e.g., engagement, learning) and to well-being. That is, irrespective of the person's gender or nationality, any person who experiences autonomy satisfaction, competence satisfaction, and relatedness satisfaction gains the benefits of adaptive functioning and well-being (Chen et al., 2015; Chirkov, Ryan, & Willness, 2005; Jang, Kim, & Reeve, 2012; Jang et al., 2009; Taylor & Lonsdale, 2010). Similarly, psychological need frustration, when it occurs, has an equally close relation to suffering and ill-being. That is, any person who experiences autonomy frustration, competence frustration, and relatedness frustration suffers the costs of maladaptive functioning (e.g., disengagement, antisocial behavior) and ill-being (Chen et al., 2015; Sheldon, Elliot, Kim, & Kasser, 2001; Soenens, Park, Vansteenkiste, & Mouratidis, 2012; Wang, Pomerantz, & Chen, 2007). So, what is etic in SDT are the tight relations between need satisfaction and wellness and between need frustration and illness.

What is emic in SDT (i.e., what is culturally specific) appears in the upper half of Figure 2.2. Culture influences what people believe to be true, and culture influences what behaviors represent "best practices" regarding education (Oyserman & Lee, 2008). Cultures vary in teaching and parenting practices and cultures endorse different beliefs. For instance, collectivistic cultures show high rates of controlling teaching styles, and often embrace interpersonal control as both an effective and normative classroom practice (Reeve et al., 2014). Similarly, while Belgian and Chinese parents overlap considerably in their parenting styles, Chinese parents on average are more interpersonally controlling than Belgian parents (Wuyts, Chen, Vansteenkiste, & Soenens, 2015). Cultures also vary in their values, goals, priorities, and norms, as some cultures value group priorities and social expectations over personal interests while other cultures value the opposite (Miller et al., 2011). Some cultures push academic achievement as a single pathway to success in the society for young people, while other cultures are more materialistic (Dittmar, 2007).

Because of these between-culture differences, cultures vary in the value they place on an experience of need satisfaction (e.g., how important is it) and also on how much its members desire such an experience (Chen et al., 2015). These differences mean that cultures will display different levels of various educational practices (e.g., autonomy support, interpersonal control).

In some cultures, socializers may encourage students to interpret a specific event (e.g., directive command from a teacher) as being non-thwarting, or maybe even supportive. But there are meaningful limits as to how much room for interpretation there is, as there are some practices, such as harsh control, that cannot be re-interpreted as a functional support to one's autonomy. In that spirit, we provide below what we hear as the most common reinterpretations of interpersonal control (e.g., "harmful" is reinterpreted into "not so bad" or even somewhat beneficial), as voiced by authoritarian and hierarchical cultures, such as nations that embrace Confucian values (Chao, 1994), a "win at all costs" competitive ethos (Cheon, Reeve, Lee, & Lee, 2015), or an explicit hierarchy of command (e.g., the military; Ricks, 1997).

I strictly control your behavior	→ I know what is best for you.
I will monitor you	→ I am here to assure your success in life.
Control and domination	→ Involvement and engagement
I am tough, even harsh	→ I care
I constantly push and pressure you.	→ I am an ideal teacher or parent.

As a case in point, consider the Asian concept of *guan* (or training). In this socialization process, teachers and parents encourage students to see the functional significance of interpersonal "control and domination" as more benign "involvement and engagement." This is typically done by arguing that intrusive involvement is actually an expression of care, warmth, and sacrifice (Stewart, Bond, Kennard, & Zaman, 2002). While warm, supportive involvement does contribute constructively to students' motivation (via experiences of relatedness need satisfaction; Sparks, Dimmock, Lonsdale, & Jackson, 2016), we do not see the reinterpretation of "control" into "control + involvement" as a constructive process, even when it prompts students to partially "take in" guan-based educational assets such as a work-ethic, self-discipline, or a strong valuing of education. This is because the partial "taking in" process is fueled by guilt-inducing introjections that are rooted in an external causality rather than by volitional identifications and integrations (i.e., internalization). Introjected motivation can be seen as having its bright side in that it can motivate working hard and enacting a high level of self-control, but it also has its dark side in that it gives rise to equal measures of harshly-experienced anxiety, perfectionism, self-criticism, superficial learning strategies, and ill-being (Powers, Koestner, & Zuroff, 2007).

A second example can be seen in the Asian concept of *filial piety*, which is elevated respect (reverence) for one's parents, elders, and ancestors. When this value is communicated as care, support, and an attachment to wisdom and guidance, it tends to promote internalization and individual autonomy, but when this same value is communicated as duty and obligation, unquestioned obedience, and submission to authority, it tends to promote only introjection and external regulation (Pan, Gauvain, & Schwartz, 2013).

Sometimes socializers such as teachers or parents will use controlling methods, and they will attempt to justify their usage in terms of the student's "own good." But SDT suggests that this justification will be successful only to the extent that it is actually functioning as a support for autonomy, competence, or relatedness. Good intentions are not always enough to change this functional significance.

We realize that many cultures encourage reinterpretations of educators' controlling behaviors (e.g., "I strictly control your behavior, but I do so because I care and I know what is best for you."), but there are limits. One limit is that students across the globe generally benefit from autonomy support and generally suffer from teacher control, and this is the case even for students educated in China (Zhou, Ma, & Deci, 2009), Singapore (Lim & Wang, 2009), Korea (Jang et al., 2009), Taiwan (Hardre et al, 2006), Israel (Assor, Kaplan, Kanat-Maymon, & Roth, 2005), Brazil (Chirkov et al., 2005), Russia (Chirkov & Ryan, 2001), and Nigeria and India (Sheldon, Abad, & Omoile, 2009). Another limit is that people who are subjected to controlling instructional behaviors routinely experience a rather pronounced spike in physiological upset, such as a cortisol episode (Reeve & Tseng, 2011) or a secretory immunoglobulin (SlgA) reaction (Bartholomew, Ntoumanis, Ryan, & Thogersen-Ntoumani, 2011), both of which are rather unambiguous stress reactions.

The first author has been implementing teacher-focused autonomy-supportive intervention workshops in a hierarchical culture (South Korea) for the last 8 years (for an overview, see Reeve & Cheon, 2014). Collectively, these dozen experimentally-based, longitudinal studies reveal three core findings: (a) teachers in a hierarchical, Confucius culture can learn how to become more autonomy supportive and less controlling toward their students; (b) when these teachers become more autonomy supportive their students benefit in important and wide-ranging ways (e.g., need satisfaction, classroom engagement, conceptual learning, skill development, well-being, academic achievement); and (c) when teachers become more autonomy supportive they themselves benefit in important and wide-ranging ways (e.g., teaching efficacy, job satisfaction, and vitality during teaching). In one recent intervention study, Korean teachers randomly assigned into the experimental (intervention) group received a series of workshops to help them learn how to transform their existing controlling instructional behaviors into "structure-providing" (or competence-satisfying) instructional behaviors. For instance, teachers learned how to transform forcefully-imposed "extrinsic instructional goals" (e.g., make the top score) into "intrinsic instructional goals" (e.g., improve your skill) and to do so in an autonomy-supportive way (e.g., take the students' perspective, acknowledge any negative feelings, and provide an explanatory rationale for the requested effort). Korean secondary-grade teachers were able to teach in more "structured and autonomy-supportive" ways, and when they did their students benefited in terms of greater need satisfaction, lesser need frustration, greater engagement, and greater internalization (Cheon & Reeve, 2017).

FOUR CLASSIC SOCIOCULTURAL INFLUENCES, AS VIEWED THROUGH THE LENS OF SDT

Most big theories of motivation in education emphasize the importance of teacher-provided learning activities, expectations, goals, and regulatory style. In this section, we provide a SDT perspective of how these sociocultural influences can be presented to students in ways that support their autonomous (rather than their controlled) motivation.

Learning Activities

When teachers introduce a learning activity (e.g., watch a video, create a product, take a field trip), they can expect to see variation in how interesting and how important each student finds that learning activity to be. SDT principles can be applied to enhance the interest or importance of practically any learning activity. To vitalize interest (intrinsic motivation), teachers can introduce the learning activity in a way that involves and satisfies students' psychological needs. For instance, a teacher nurtures autonomy by giving students more say and self-direction during the learning activity (Jang, Reeve, & Halusic, 2016), a teacher nurtures competence by providing an optimal challenge and the progress-enabling guidance students need to master it (Lee & Reeve, 2017), and a teacher nurtures relatedness by creating opportunities for classmates to work together (La Guardia & Patrick, 2008). To vitalize a sense of importance, teachers can communicate the personal relevance of the learning activity as it relates to the students' own goals and concerns. In each case, the teacher presents the learning activity in a way that nurtures students' need satisfaction and, by doing so, enhances interest (Tsai et al., 2008) or importance (Jang, 2008).

Expectations

Most big theories of motivation emphasize the motivational pull of teacher expectations, although they sometimes use alternative terms such as goals, standards, rules, plans of action, or possible selves. The basic idea is that students are performing or behaving at a "present state" and the teacher then asks them to perform or behave at an "ideal state." Teachers then provide the guidance and scaffolding students need to adjust their performance or behavior to meet the high expectations. In SDT, as in most big theories of motivation, the above describes "competence support." But one unique contribution of SDT is the finding that competence support by itself is not enough, as it needs to be delivered in an autonomy-supportive way. So, before teachers present students with their expectations and standards, they might begin by taking the students' perspectives (e.g., "What are your goals? What would you like to do?"), then acknowledging their students' negative feelings (e.g., "Yes, this will be difficult; it will take a lot of extra work; I realize that I am asking you to do what you cannot yet do."), and finally by offering an explanatory rationale for the high expectations (e.g., "The reason that I am asking you to try to do this is to help you develop a new skill that may be quite useful to you."). In SDT, competence support represents good practice, but supporting students' competence and autonomy represents best practice (Koestner, Powers, Carbonneau, Milyavskaya, & Chua, 2012).

Goals

Goal is such a central concept in many big theories of motivation and in teachers' repertoire of classroom motivational strategies that we give it special attention here. The key point is that the positive effects of goals are often moderated by how much or how little students autonomously endorse them. Some teacher-provided goals are fully endorsed, feel authentic, and are wholeheartedly accepted, embraced, and owned by the student, whereas others feel artificial or socially manufactured and are taken on as social obligations without a sense of personal ownership. The former are those that reflect the student's interests, needs, values, and preferences, whereas the latter are those that neglect or even conflict with the student's autonomous motivations (Sheldon & Elliot, 1998, 1999). For those goals that are volitionally self-endorsed, their pursuit draws upon personal resources (e.g., psychological needs, autonomous motivation; Koestner, Otis, Powers, Pelletier, & Gagnon, 2008) that especially energize, direct, and sustain the goal pursuit (Sheldon & Elliot, 1999). The extent to which students in one nation or one cultural group might tend to volitionally self-endorse any one particular educational goal (e.g., "be admitted to the best university") may represent an important motivational difference between the nations or cultures.

Regulatory Styles

A fundamental premise of SDT is that the quality of a student's motivation matters as much as does its quantity. Motivation quality speaks to the question of "what type" of motivation the student has during a learning activity, while quantity speaks to the question of "how much" motivation the student has. Most big theories conceptualize motivation as a unitary construct that varies in its quantity (and the more, the better). But SDT research shows that students who are highly autonomously motivated (i.e., high in intrinsic motivation and identified regulation) show more positive outcomes than do students who are highly control motivated (i.e., high in introjected and external regulation; Ryan & Connell, 1989). For instance, after controlling for the amount of motivation students have for school, students who possess autonomous motivation show more positive educational outcomes, such as engagement and conceptual learning, than do students who possess controlled motivation (Ratelle, Guay, Vallerand, Larose, & Senecal, 2007; Wang, Morin, Ryan, & Liu, 2016). The instructional implication is the recommendation that teachers work not only to highly motivate their students but to vitalize and support their autonomous motivation in particular.

FIVE UNIQUE CONTRIBUTIONS OF SDT TO THE BIG THEORIES OF MOTIVATION

The big motivation theories of education, such as self-efficacy theory, expectancy-value theory, achievement goal theory, and all those represented in the current volume, collectively provide a sophisticated, comprehensive overview to explain the nature and dynamics of students' academic motivation. Among these theories, SDT provides five unique contributions.

SDT Uniquely Emphasizes Autonomy and Autonomy Support

Most big theories of motivation emphasize the motivational centrality of students' competence (e.g., self-efficacy, mastery motivation, mastery goals, or personal control beliefs). These theories do not include constructs such as intrinsic motivation, autonomy, or autonomy support. Yet, SDT argues that the psychological need for autonomy represents an essential psychological architecture of human nature and student motivation. That is, all students possess an engagement-fostering, growth-motivating, and interest-taking psychological need for autonomy, and this motivational asset is a universal endowment in all students. Recognizing the capacity of autonomy to energize and sustain students' high-quality learning, classroom engagement, adaptive functioning, healthy personality development, and psychological well-being, SDT researchers study the provision of autonomy support as the key sociocultural force that predicts variance in students' educational outcomes.

SDT Uniquely Identifies the Essential Elements That Define a High-Quality Relationship

Many big theories of motivation in education emphasize the importance of teachers establishing high-quality, caring, and responsive relationships with their students. A relationship that offers students' high and consistent levels of involvement, care, concern, and love supports students' motivation because it creates a sense of trust and security that allows students to open up to teachers to cooperate with them, accept their requests, and internalize their values and recommendations (i.e., a willingness to be influenced). This is because students have a sense of assurance that their teacher cares deeply about their welfare. In SDT, the above describes "relatedness support," and some SDT theorists (Sparks, Dimmock, Whipp, Lonsdale, & Jackson, 2015; Sparks et al., 2016) have carefully identified what teacher behaviors most allow students to experience such relatedness support, including individualized conversation, showing care, promoting cooperation and teamwork, and friendly communication. But, as made clear by relationships motivation theory, students cannot experience a high-quality teacher-student relationship if teachers' relatedness support is not also accompanied by autonomy support. Not only have SDT theorists conceptually and operationally defined what constitutes a high-quality relationship, they have further developed formal intervention programs to help teachers learn how to become more relatedness supportive (Sparks et al., 2015) and more autonomy supportive (Cheon et al., 2016).

SDT Uniquely Reminds Educators of Schooling's Twin Mission to Develop Happy, Productive Students

Practically, all SDT studies of student motivation include multiple dependent measures (student outcomes) to make sure that the sociocultural factors and motivational processes under study promote in students both high productivity (e.g., engagement, learning, achievement, skill development) and well-being (e.g., happiness, satisfaction, positive affect, self-esteem). This is because SDT understands the limits of hard-driving achievement that is void of experiences of personal satisfaction (e.g., perfectionism, introjection) as well as happy students who do not actually learn, do, or achieve anything (e.g., permissiveness, indulgence). Thus, SDT-based intervention programs seek to promote in students high-quality motivation (i.e., autonomous motivation, need satisfaction) that is capable of supporting both academic progress and psychological well-being.

SDT is Uniquely a Culturally Critical Theory

What is etic in SDT is the close relation between psychological need satisfaction and well-being (as well as between psychological need frustration and ill-being). That is, basic psychological need satisfaction is understood as good and beneficial for everyone. This proposition sounds like a value, but it is also a conclusion from the empirical literature. Because psychological need satisfaction leads to well-being, SDT is uniquely positioned to be a culturally critical theory—one that can be used to evaluate a culture or organization. All cultures—just like all relationships—feature both need-supportive and need-thwarting elements, but some cultures are over-weighted toward the latter. What SDT criticizes are those political, economic, and cultural systems that diminish, suppress, or outright crush people's opportunities for autonomy, competence development, and relatedness satisfaction. SDT is a theory that respects diversity across cultures, while it still embraces a deep respect for the autonomy of people within every culture. When a culture systematically thwarts individuals' autonomy, competence or relatedness, the implications for ill-being can be disastrous (Van Bergen & Saharso, 2016).

SDT Uniquely Recommends That Teachers Provide Support, Rather Than Influence

The subtitle of the present book features the phrase "sociocultural influence," and it therefore suggests that what effective teachers do is influence their students in positive, constructive ways. In schools, influence is a sociocultural process in which teachers, administrators, parents, and others get students to complete their homework, make high grades, and value prosocial behavior. Adopting an influence mindset, teachers wonder, "What can I do to increase my students' motivation and engagement?" Self-determination theory, in contrast, presumes that students are fully capable of motivating and engaging themselves. They do not need educators to motivate them (because they already have plenty of available high-quality motivation) but, instead, they need educators to understand them and to support the motivation they already have (e.g., intrinsic motivation, psychological needs, intrinsic goals, self-endorsed values). Adopting a support mindset, teachers wonder, "How can I create the conditions under which students can motivate themselves?" (Deci, 1995). So, looking through the lens of SDT, the teaching priority is not so much to provide "sociocultural influence" as it is to provide "support" for the motivation students already have.

CONCLUDING REMARKS

Sociocultural influences are ever-present in global classrooms. Their presence and potency put a theoretical burden on each big theory of motivation to explain how these social forces advance or interfere with the educational process—and with students' classroom motivation and engagement in particular. To serve this purpose, SDT offers an interconnected network of six mini-theories to explain basic motivational processes and to solve classroom problems. SDT further bridges the etic-emic distinction often made in sociocultural investigations of teaching practices and student motivation, and it uses the key concepts of internalization and functional significance to do so. In terms of improving educational practice, the chapter uses the lens of SDT to look closely at the four particular sociocultural influences of learning activities, expectations, goals, and regulatory styles. In the end, we celebrate how the big theories of motivation in education collectively provide a sophisticated understanding of students' academic motivation, but we further note that SDT offers five unique contributions, such as a strong emphasis on student autonomy and teacher autonomy support.

REFERENCES

Assor, A., Kaplan, H., Kanat-Maymon, Y., & Roth, G. (2005). Directly controlling teacher behaviors as predictors of poor motivation and engagement in girls and boys: The role of anger and anxiety. *Learning and Instruction, 15,* 397–413.

Assor, A., Roth, G., & Deci, E. L. (2004). The emotional costs of perceived parental conditional regard: A self-determination theory analysis. *Journal of Personality, 72,* 47–87.

Bartholomew, K. J., Ntoumanis, N., Ryan, R. M., & Thøgersen-Ntoumanis, C. (2011). Psychological need thwarting in the sport context: Assessing the darker side of athletic experience. *Journal of Sport & Exercise Psychology, 33,* 75–102.

Chao, R. K. (1994). Beyond parental control and authoritarian parenting style: Understanding Chinese parenting through the cultural notion of training. *Child Development, 65,* 1111–1119.

Chen, B., Vansteenkiste, M., Beyers, W., Boone, L., Deci, E., Van der Kaap-Deeder, J., ... Verstuyf, J. (2015). Basic psychological need satisfaction, need frustration, and need strength across four cultures. *Motivation and Emotion, 39,* 216–236.

Cheon, S. H., & Reeve, J. (2017). *Enhancing PE students' health goals and health self-concept: A teacher-focused intervention to support students' autonomy and intrinsic goal pursuit.* Manuscript submitted for publication.

Cheon, S. H., Reeve, J., Lee, J., & Lee, Y. (2015). Giving and receiving autonomy support in a high-stakes sport context: A field-based experiment during the 2012 London Paralympic Games. *Psychology of Sport and Exercise, 19,* 59–69.

Cheon, S. H., Reeve, J., & Song, Y.-G. (2016). A teacher-focused intervention to decrease PE students' amotivation by increasing need satisfaction and decreasing need frustration. *Journal of Sport and Exercise Psychology, 38,* 217–235.

Cheon, S. H., Reeve, J., Yu, T. H., & Jang, H.-R. (2014). The teacher benefits from giving autonomy support during physical education instruction. *Journal of Sport and Exercise Psychology, 36,* 331–346.

Chirkov, V. I., & Ryan, R. M. (2001). Parent and teacher autonomy-support in Russian and U.S. adolescents: Common effects on well-being and academic motivation. *Journal of Cross-Cultural Psychology, 32,* 618–635.

Chirkov, V. I., Ryan, R. M., & Sheldon, K. (Eds.). (2011). *Human autonomy in cross-cultural contexts: Perspectives on the psychology of agency, freedom, and well-being.* New York, NY: Springer.

Chirkov, V. I., Ryan, R. M., Kim, Y., & Kaplan, U. (2003). Differentiating autonomy from individualism and independence: A self-determination theory perspective on internalization of cultural orientations and well-being. *Journal of Personality and Social Psychology, 84,* 97–100.

Chirkov, V. I., Ryan, R. M., & Willness, C. (2005). Cultural context and psychological needs in Canada and Brazil: Testing a self-determination approach to internalization of cultural practices, identify, and well-being. *Journal of Cross-Cultural Psychology, 36,* 425–443.

Deci, E. L. (1995). *Why we do what we do: Understanding self-motivation.* New York, NY: Penguin Books.

Deci, E. L., Eghrari, H., Patrick, B. C., & Leone, D. R. (1994). Facilitating internalization: The self-determination theory perspective. *Journal of Personality, 62,* 119–142.

Deci, E. L., Koestner, R., & Ryan, R. M. (1999). A meta-analytic review of experiments examining the effects of extrinsic rewards on intrinsic motivation. *Psychological Bulletin, 125,* 627–668.

Deci, E. L., La Guardia, J. G., Moller, A. C., Scheiner, M. J., & Ryan, R. M. (2006). On the benefits of giving as well as receiving autonomy support: Mutuality in close friendships. *Personality and Social Psychology Bulletin, 32,* 313–327.

Deci, E. L., & Ryan, R. M. (2014). Autonomy and need satisfaction in close relationships: Relationships motivation theory. In N. Weinstein (Ed.), *Human motivation and interpersonal relationships: Theory, research and applications* (pp. 53–73). Dordrecht, Netherlands: Springer.

Dittmar, H. (2007). The costs of consumer culture and the "cage within": The impact of the material "good life" and "body perfect" ideals on individuals' identity and well-being. *Psychological Inquiry, 18,* 23–31.

Downie, M., Koestner, R., ElGeledi, S., & Cree, K. (2004). The impact of cultural internalization and integration on well-being among tricultural individuals. *Personality and Social Psychology Bulletin, 30,* 305–314.

Harackiewicz, J. W., & Elliot, A. J. (1998). The joint effects of target and purpose goals on intrinsic motivation: A mediational analysis. *Personality and Social Psychology Bulletin, 24*, 675–689.

Hardre, P. L., Chen, C., Huang, S., Chiang, C., Jen, F., & Warden, L. (2006). Factors affecting high school students' academic motivation in Taiwan. *Asia Pacific Journal of Education, 26*, 198–207.

Jang, H. (2008). Supporting students' motivation, engagement, and learning during an uninteresting activity. *Journal of Educational Psychology, 100*, 798–811.

Jang, H., Kim, E. J., & Reeve, J. (2012). Longitudinal test of self-determination theory's motivation mediation model in a naturally-occurring classroom context. *Journal of Educational Psychology, 104*, 1175–1188.

Jang, H., Kim, E.-J., & Reeve, J. (2016). Why students become more engaged or more disengaged during the semester: A self-determination theory dual-process model. *Learning and Instruction, 43*, 27–38.

Jang, H., Reeve, J., & Halusic, M. (2016). A new autonomy-supportive way of teaching that increases conceptual learning: Teaching in students' preferred ways. *Journal of Experimental Education, 84*, 686–701.

Jang, H., Reeve, J., Ryan, R. M., & Kim, A. (2009). Can self-determination theory explain what underlies the productive, satisfying learning experiences of collectivistically-oriented South Korean adolescents? *Journal of Educational Psychology, 101*, 644–661.

Koestner, R., Otis, N., Powers, T. A., Pelletier, L., & Gagnon, H. (2008). Autonomous motivation, controlled motivation, and goal progress. *Journal of Personality, 76*, 1201–1230.

Koestner, R., Powers, T. A., Carbonneau, N., Milyavskaya, M., & Chua, S. N. (2012). Distinguishing autonomous and directive forms of goal support: Their effects on goal progress, relationship quality, and subjective well-being. *Personality and Social Psychology Bulletin, 38*, 1609–1620.

Kotlak, C. (2006). *Mirror for humanity.* New York, NY: McGraw-Hill.

La Guardia, J. G., & Patrick, H. (2008). Self-determination theory as a fundamental theory of close relationships. *Canadian Psychology, 49*, 201–209.

Lee, W., & Reeve, J. (2013). Self-determined, but not non-self-determined, motivation predicts activations in the anterior insular cortex: An fMRI study of personal agency. *Social, Cognitive, and Affective Neuroscience, 8*, 538–545.

Lee, W., & Reeve, J. (2017). Identifying the neural substrates of intrinsic motivation during task performance. *Cognitive, Affective, and Behavioral Neuroscience, 17*, 939–953.

Lim, B. S. C., & Wang, C. K. J. (2009). Perceived autonomy support, behavioural regulations in physical education and physical activity intention. *Psychology for Sport and Exercise, 10*, 52–60.

McInerney, D. M., & Van Etten, S. (Eds.). (2004). *Big theories revisited.* Greenwich, CT: Information Age.

Miller, J. G., Das, R., & Chakravarthy, S. (2011). Culture and the role of choice in agency. *Journal of Personality and Social Psychology, 101*, 46–61.

Mossholder, K. W. (1980). Effects of externally mediated goal setting on intrinsic motivation: A laboratory experiment. *Journal of Applied Psychology, 65*, 202–210.

Mouratidis, A., Lens, W., & Vansteenkiste, M. (2010). How you provide corrective feedback makes a difference: The motivating role of communicating in an autonomy-supportive way. *Journal of Sport and Exercise Psychology, 32*, 619–637.

Olesen, M. H. (2011). General causality orientations are distinct from but related to dispositional traits. *Personality and Individual Differences, 51*, 460–465.

Oyserman, D., & Lee, S. W. S. (2008). Does culture influence what and how we think? Effects of priming individualism and collectivism. *Psychological Bulletin, 134*, 311–342.

Pan, Y., Gauvain, M., & Schwartz, S. J. (2013). Do parents' collectivistic tendency and attitudes toward filial piety facilitate autonomous motivation among young Chinese adolescents? *Motivation and Emotion, 37*, 701–711.

Powers, T. A., Koestner, R., & Zuroff, D. C. (2007). Self-criticism, goal motivation, and goal progress. *Journal of Social and Clinical Psychology, 26*, 826–840.

Ratelle, C. F., Guay, F., Vallerand, R. J., Larose, S., & Senecal, C. (2007). Autonomous, controlled, and amotivated types of academic motivation: A person-centered analysis. *Journal of Educational Psychology, 99*, 734–746.

Reeve, J. (2016). Autonomy-supportive teaching: What it is, how to do it. In W. C. Liu, J. C. K. Wang, & R. M. Ryan (Eds.), *Building autonomous learners: Perspectives from research and practice using self-determination theory* (pp. 129–152). Singapore, Singapore: Springer.

Reeve, J., & Cheon, H. S. (2014). An intervention-based program of research on teachers' motivating styles. In S. Karabenick & T. Urdan's (Eds.), *Advances in motivation and achievement: Motivational interventions* (Vol. 18, pp. 293–339). Bingley, England: Emerald Group.

Reeve, J., & Deci, E. L. (1996). Elements of the competitive situation that affect intrinsic motivation. *Personality and Social Psychology Bulletin, 22*, 24–33.

Reeve, J., & Tseng, C.-M. (2011). Cortisol reactivity to a teacher's motivating style: The biology of being controlled versus supporting autonomy. *Motivation and Emotion, 35*, 63–74.

Reeve, J., Vansteenkiste, M., Assor, A., Ahmad, I., Cheon, S. H., Jang, H., Kaplan, H., Moss, J. D., Olaussen, B. S., & Wang, C. K. J. (2014). The beliefs that underlie autonomy-supportive and controlling teaching: A multinational investigation. *Motivation and Emotion, 38*, 93–110.

Ricks, T. E. (1997). *Making the corps.* New York, NY: Scribner.

Roth, G., Assor, A., Niemiec, C. P., Ryan, R. M., & Deci, E. L. (2009). The emotional and academic consequences of parental conditional regard: Comparing conditional positive regard, conditional negative regard, and autonomy support as parenting practices. *Developmental Psychology, 45*, 1119–1142.

Ryan, R. M. (1995). Psychological needs and the facilitation of integrative processes. *Journal of Personality, 63*, 397–427.

Ryan, R. M., & Connell, J. P. (1989). Perceived locus of causality and internalization: Examining reasons for acting in two domains. *Journal of Personality and Social Psychology, 57*, 749–761.

Ryan, R. M., & Deci, E. L. (2017). *Self-determination theory: Basic psychological needs in motivation, development, and wellness.* New York, NY: Guilford Press.

Ryan, R. M., Mims, V., & Koestner, R. (1983). Relation of reward contingency and interpersonal context to intrinsic motivation: A review and test using cognitive evaluation theory. *Journal of Personality and Social Psychology, 45,* 736–750.

Sagiv, L., & Schwartz, S. H. (2000). Value priorities and subjective well-being: Direct relations and congruity effects. *European Journal of Social Psychology, 30,* 177–198.

Sheldon, K. M., Abad, N., & Omoile, J. (2009). Testing self-determination theory via Nigerian and Indian adolescents. *International Journal of Behavioral Development, 33,* 451–459.

Sheldon, K. M., & Elliot, A. J. (1998). Not all personal goals are personal: Comparing autonomous and controlled reasons as predictors of effort and attainment. *Personality and Social Psychological Bulletin, 24,* 546–557.

Sheldon, K. M., & Elliot, A. J. (1999). Goal striving, need-satisfaction, and longitudinal wellbeing: The self-concordance model. *Journal of Personality and Social Psychology, 76,* 482–497.

Sheldon, K. M., Elliot, A. J., Kim, Y., & Kasser, T. (2001). What is satisfying about satisfying events? Testing 10 candidate psychological needs. *Journal of Personality and Social Psychology, 80,* 325–339.

Sheldon, K. M., Ryan, R. M., & Reis, H. T. (1996). What makes for a good day?: Competence and autonomy in the day and in the person. *Personality and Social Psychology Bulletin, 22,* 1270–1279.

Soenens, B., Park, S. Y., Vansteenkiste, M., & Mouratidis, A. (2012). Perceived parental psychological control and adolescent depressive experiences: A cross-cultural study with Belgian and South Korean adolescents. *Journal of Adolescence, 35,* 261–272.

Sparks, C., Dimmock, J., Whipp, P., Lonsdale, C., & Jackson, B. (2015). "Getting connected": High school physical education teacher behaviors that facilitate students' relatedness support perceptions. *Sport, Exercise, and Performance Psychology, 4,* 219–236.

Sparks, C., Dimmock, J., Lonsdale, C., & Jackson, B. (2016). Modeling indicators and outcomes of students' perceived teacher relatedness support in high school physical education. *Psychology of Sport and Exercise, 26,* 71–82.

Stewart, S. M., Bond, M. H., Kennard, B. D., & Zaman, R. M. (2002). Does the Chinese construct of guan export to the West? *International Journal of Psychology, 37,* 74–82.

Taylor, I. M., & Lonsdale, C. (2010). Cultural differences in the relationships among autonomy support, psychological need satisfaction, subjective vitality, and effort in British and Chinese physical education. *Journal of Sport and Exercise Psychology, 32,* 655–673.

Tsai, Y.-M., Kunter, M., Lüdtke, O., Trautwein, U., & Ryan, R. M. (2008). What makes lessons interesting? The role of situational and individual factors in three school subjects. *Journal of Educational Psychology, 100,* 460–472.

Van Bergen, D. D., & Saharso, S. (2016). Suicidality of young ethic minority women with an immigrant background: The role of autonomy. *European Journal of Women's Studies, 23,* 297–311.

Vansteenkiste, M., Lens, W., & Deci, E. L. (2006). Intrinsic versus extrinsic goal contents in self-determination theory: Another look at the quality of academic motivation. *Educational Psychologist, 41*, 19–31.

Vansteenkiste, M., Niemiec, C. P., & Soenens, B. (2010). The development of the five mini-theories of self-determination theory: An historical overview, emerging trends, and future directions. In T. C. Urdan & S. A. Karabenick (Eds.), *Advances in motivation and achievement—The decade ahead: Theoretical perspectives on motivation and achievement* (Vol. 16A, pp. 105–165). London, England: Emerald Group.

Vansteenkiste, M., Timmermans, T., Lens, W., Soenens, B., & Van den Broeck, A. (2008). Does extrinsic goal framing enhance extrinsic goal oriented individuals' learning and performance? An experimental test of the match-perspective vs. self-determination theory. *Journal of Educational Psychology, 100*, 387–397.

Wang, J. C. K., Morin, A. J. S., Ryan, R. M., & Liu, W. C. (2016). Students' motivational profiles in the physical education context. *Journal of Sport and Exercise Psychology, 38*, 612–630.

Wang, Q., Pomerantz, E. M., & Chen, H. (2007). The role of parents' control in early adolescents' psychological functioning: A longitudinal investigation of United States and China. *Child Development, 78*, 1592–1610.

Weinstein, N., & Ryan, R. M. (2010). When helping helps: Autonomous motivation for prosocial behavior and its influence on well-being for the helper and recipient. *Journal of Personality and Social Psychology, 98*, 222–244.

Wild, T. C., Enzle, M. E., & Hawkins, W. L. (1992). Effects of perceived extrinsic versus intrinsic teacher motivation on student reactions to skill acquisition. *Personality and Social Psychology Bulletin, 18*, 245–251.

Wuyts, D., Chen, B., Vansteenkiste, M., & Soenens, B. (2015). Social pressure and unfulfilled dreams among Chinese and Belgian parents. *Journal of Cross-Cultural Psychology, 46*, 1150–1168.

Zhou, M., Ma, W. J., & Deci, E. L. (2009). The importance of autonomy for rural Chinese children's motivation for learning. *Learning and Individual Differences, 19*, 492–498.

Zougkou, K., Weinstein, N., & Paulmann, S. (2017). ERP correlates of motivating voices: Quality of motivation and time-course matters. *Social Cognitive and Affective Neuroscience, 12*, 1687–1700.

CHAPTER 3

SOCIOCULTURAL INFLUENCES ON ACHIEVEMENT GOAL ADOPTION AND REGULATION

A Goal Complex Perspective

Gregory Arief D. Liem
Andrew J. Elliot

The achievement goal perspective has been one of the "big" theories of academic motivation in the past 4 decades. Theoretical and conceptual work, supported by an accumulating body of empirical evidence, has attested to the importance of the achievement goals that students pursue (i.e., goal adoption) and of the implications of this goal pursuit for achievement-related processes and outcomes (i.e., goal regulation; see Elliot & Hulleman, 2017; Liem, Lau, & Cai, 2016 for reviews). While the centrality of achievement goals as a motivational construct has been studied across Eastern and Western societies, there has been speculation that sociocultural contexts may account for cross-cultural variability in the degree to which different goals are adopted and the degree to which regulatory processes and outcomes are associated with the pursuit of these goals (Dekker & Fischer, 2008; King & McInerney, 2014; Maehr & Nicholls, 1980; Zusho & Clayton, 2011).

Big Theories Revisited 2, pages 41–67

In this chapter, we seek to articulate the potential processes through which sociocultural contexts influence the adoption and regulation of achievement goals. We begin by providing a brief historical overview of different achievement goal models proffered in the literature. This overview is necessary to understand the connection between a reason (the "why") and a goal (the "what") that students pursue in academic settings. This reason–goal combination, also known as a "goal complex," is crucial to shed light on sociocultural influences on achievement goal adoption and regulation. To this end, we specifically distinguish distal from proximal reasons for goal adoption. Guided by the bioecological model of individual development (Bronfenbrenner, 1977, 1979, 1994), we then systematically identify personal, social, and contextual antecedents of achievement goals, while exploring their functional role as distal reasons through which sociodemographic and socio-contextual factors affect goal adoption. We end the chapter by calling for cross-cultural research that incorporates both distal and proximal reasons to better understand the influence of sociocultural factors on achievement goal adoption and regulation.

BRIEF HISTORICAL BACKGROUND
OF ACHIEVEMENT GOAL MODELS

Emerging in the 1980s, early achievement goal theorists agreed that achievement goals represent *purposes* that students hold for engaging in achievement relevant behaviors (Dweck, 1986; Maehr, 1989; Maehr & Nicholls, 1980; Nicholls, 1989). These pioneers proffered a dichotomous achievement goal model with *mastery* and *performance* goals as the two main types of goals. Mastery goals represent the purpose to *develop* competence, whereas performance goal reflect the purpose to *demonstrate* competence relative to that of others. This early model construed the two goals as approach motivation which orients students to attain desirable outcomes, and largely viewed mastery goals as more optimal for learning processes and outcomes than performance goals (see Elliot & Hulleman, 2017; Senko, 2016 for reviews).

In the late 1990s, Elliot and colleagues (Elliot 1999; Elliot & Harackiewicz, 1996; Elliot & McGregor, 2001) revised the dichotomous achievement goal model in two major ways. One of the revisions pertained to incorporation of the classic approach-avoidance dimension of motivation (Atkinson, 1957; McClelland, 1951) into the achievement goal conceptualization. This led to, first, the trichotomous achievement goal model (Elliot & Church, 1997) in which performance goals are divided into *performance-approach* and *performance-avoidance* goals and, subsequently, the 2 × 2 achievement goal model (Elliot & McGregor, 2001) in which mastery goals are bifurcated into *mastery-approach* and *mastery-avoidance* goals. Meta-analyses have shown that these goals are associated with distinct patterns of antecedents (e.g., achievement motives, implicit beliefs) and that, relative to avoidance goals, approach goals generally give rise to more adaptive affective, cognitive, and behavioral outcomes (see Baranick, Stanley, Bynum, & Lance, 2010; Lochbaum & Gottardy, 2015; Huang, 2012; Senko & Dawson, 2017).

Elliot, Murayama, and Pekrun (2011) subsequently proffered a 3×2 achievement goal model. This model separated mastery goals into *task-based* and *self-based* goals, resulting in task-approach, task-avoidance, self-approach, and self-avoidance goals. Students pursuing *task-approach* goals aim to do a task correctly, whereas those pursuing *task-avoidance* goals seek to avoid doing a task incorrectly. Students pursuing *self-approach* goals focus on attaining a level of competence better than their previous attainment, whereas those pursuing *self-avoidance* goals seek to avoid doing worse than that they have done previously. Analogous to performance-approach and performance-avoidance goals in the 2×2 model, *other-approach* and *other-avoidance* goals are the other two achievement goal constructs in the 3×2 model. Empirical work based on the 3×2 model to date has yielded relatively mixed and inconclusive patterns of the relations between the goals and their antecedents and consequences (see Elliot & Hulleman, 2017 for a review).

There are different meanings of the word "purpose" ("aim" and "reason"), and early achievement goal models conceptualized achievement goals as a combination of both of these meanings (and also other achievement-related concepts such as attributional tendencies, emotions, effort). In view of this, the second major revision of the achievement goal approach involved separation of these two goal components (Elliot & Thrash, 2001). This revision led to a more precise conceptual definition of achievement goals as cognitive representations of competence-focused *aims* that students seek to attain (Elliot & Murayama, 2008). As described earlier, the 3×2 achievement goal model posits that progress regarding competence-focused aims can specifically be evaluated with respect to *task-referenced,* *intrapersonal,* and *interpersonal* standards. Thus, the goal constructs operationalized in the measures based on the 3×2 model (Elliot et al., 2011), as well as the revised 2×2 model (Elliot & Murayama, 2008), comprise an aim only, rather than both an aim and a reason (see also Elliot & Hulleman, 2017) for a discussion of goal standards and goal standpoints).

GOAL COMPLEX: THE SYNERGY BETWEEN A REASON AND AN AIM OF GOAL PURSUIT

As noted above, current theorizing defines achievement goals as competence-focused aims or future end-states that students strive to attain or avoid

(Elliot & Murayama, 2008; Elliot et al., 2011). Reason, which was a component of achievement goals in the early conceptualizing of the construct, is now considered to be an antecedent of achievement goal adoption. The conceptual separation of aim and reason, and the theoretical relation between the two components, are depicted in the hierarchical model of achievement motivation (Elliot & Thrash, 2001). Specifically, reasons (the why) are conceptualized as an antecedent that gives rise to the energization of behavior, whereas achievement goals are conceptualized as aims (the what) that provide direction to the energized behavior.

These revisions of the achievement goal approach have brought us to the concept of "achievement goal complex," which refers to the synergy between an aim and its underlying reason in the pursuit of competence-based possibilities (Elliot & Thrash, 2001). As asserted by Elliot and Thrash (2001), "numerous goal complexes are possible in any given achievement setting, and each goal complex is likely to have a somewhat distinct predictive profile, even those possessing the same goal component" (p. 148). That is, it is conceivable that the same aim is "fueled" by a variety of reasons, and that the different aims may be instigated by the same reason. This reason and aim pairing (i.e., a goal complex) is believed to better clarify the nature of achievement goal regulatory processes than simply considering the reason or aim alone.

Aligned with the call for research in this area (Vansteenkiste, Lens, Elliot, Soenens, & Mouratidis, 2014), goal complex studies (e.g., Senko & Tropiano, 2016; Sommet & Elliot, 2017) have mainly focused on *autonomous* and *controlling* motivation as two broad types of motivational reasons derived from self-determination theory (SDT; Ryan & Deci, 2017). Theoretically, autonomous motivation comprises *intrinsic motivation* (i.e., doing something for its own sake) and *identified motivation* (i.e., doing something because of a personally valued meaning of the activity), whereas controlling motivation comprises *external motivation* (i.e., doing something to earn rewards and/or avoid punishments from the social environment) and *introjection motivation* (i.e., doing something to enhance self-worth and/or avoid shame or guilt). In other words, autonomous motivation refers to a psychological force that energizes an individual's behavior through the enjoyment of doing an activity and the fulfilment of personal meaning that the activity brings about, whereas controlling motivation refers to a psychological force that prompts an individual's behavior through the intention to attain or avoid positive or negative consequences and to meet internalized social expectations.

Research seeking to link achievement goals to non-SDT-based reasons to form goal complexes has also begun (see e.g., Hodis, Tait, Hodis, Hodis, & Scornavacca, 2016); this recent attempt has primarily focused on reasons grounded in self-presentation (i.e., to demonstrate ability or to avoid looking incompetent) and self-improvement (i.e., to develop ability or to avoid becoming incompetent) motives, two motivational underpinnings known to be antecedents of goal adoption (Elliot, 1999). From a goal content perspective, however, theorists agree that although the achievement goals that students seek to pursue focus them on academic competence, their adoption and pursuit are unequivocally social in nature (Dowson & McInerney, 2003; Elliot et al., 2016; Liem, 2016; Wentzel, 2000). This means that students are expected to navigate their academic trajectory by coordinating their academic goals with their (nonacademic competence) social goals such as social responsibility, social concern, social status, and social affiliation (Dowson & McInerney, 2003). Indeed, Senko and Tropiano (2016) asserted that social and academic goals may be arranged hierarchically such that social goals may serve as reasons for academic goals, and vice versa (cf. Wentzel, 2000).

Importantly, qualitative studies explicitly asking participants, "What are the reasons that you study?," have identified various reasons for students wanting to achieve in academic settings (e.g., Lee & Bong, 2016; Urdan & Mestas, 2006; see also Boekaerts, de Koning, & Vedder, 2006; Ford, 1992 for taxonomies of goals; and Splitter & McInerney, 2015 for a relevant discussion on reasons for motivated behaviors). As a study by Lee and Bong (2016) with Korean high school students showed, these reasons include more abstract, superordinate, and distant goals or concerns such as "to make my dream come true," "to earn money," "to get a better job or career," "to make my parents happy," "to fulfil my duty as a student," "to advance to the next school level," "to avoid lagging behind in society," "to avoid regret in the future," and "for my own well-being." These identity-, class-/school-, society-, happiness-, and future-oriented goals, along with the aforementioned social goals (Dowson & McInerney, 2003), have been relatively underexplored as the potential reasons for achievement goal adoption in the goal complex approach and the hierarchical model of achievement motivation.

Distal and Proximal Reasons

The hierarchical model of achievement motivation posits reasons as "the psychological starting point for action" (Elliot & Thrash, 2001, p. 144). Reasons have been primarily represented in constructs rooted in competence-based motive dispositions (i.e., achievement motive, fear of failure). Elliot and Church (1997), for instance, showed that the achievement motive positively predicted performance-approach and mastery-approach goals, whereas fear of failure positively predicted performance-approach and performance-avoidance goals. These reason-goal relationships point to the following goal complex possibilities: (a) students strive to learn because they anticipate the pride and joy of achievement, (b) students try to not perform worse than others because of their desire to avoid failure, and (c) students seek to outperform others because of both the anticipation of pride and joy upon achievement and their desire to avoid failure.

Aside from competence-based motives, the hierarchical model (Elliot, 1999; Elliot & Thrash, 2001) posits other motivational dispositions that may serve as reasons for achievement goal adoption. These include self-based (e.g., self-validation, self-protection, self-enhancement, and self-monitoring motives; fear of negative evaluation) and relationally-based (e.g., social affiliation and social approval motives; fear of rejection) variables. Like competence-based motives, self- and relationally-based motives can be conceptualized in terms of both approach and avoidance motivation (Atkinson, 1957). As shown by Hodis et al. (2016), the possible reasons that students strive to learn optimally (i.e., a task-approach goal), to improve (i.e., a self-based goal), or to outperform others (i.e., an other-approach goal) are in order to avoid failing to develop their potential (i.e., a self-improvement grounded reason) and/or to demonstrate their competence to others (i.e., a self-presentation grounded reason).

The hierarchical model (Elliot & Thrash, 2001) considers "hard wiring," chronically accessible, and enduring dispositional antecedents, such as sociodemographic factors (e.g., gender, ethnicity, religion, socioeconomic background) and socio-contextual factors (i.e., social, educational, and cultural settings such as parent-child interaction, classroom climate, assessment system, cultural values and beliefs), as antecedents of achievement goal adoption, rather than reasons per se. Thus, the range of reasons in the hierarchical model appears to be restricted to relatively enduring and affectively-based motivational dispositions, and precludes sociocultural antecedents that are more situational and contextual in nature. This conceptualizing prevents social goals, and by implication other socioculturally internalized values, norms, aspirations, expectations, beliefs, and (higher-order) goals, from being considered as reasons for the adoption of achievement goals.

That said, there is intuitive ground to believe that factors associated with sociodemographic background (gender, ethnicity) and those embedded in social, educational, and cultural contexts (parental expectation, classroom goal structure, societal norms, national ideologies) could also function as reasons for goal adoption. To illustrate, a student may try to perform better than others in his class because of one of the following reasons: his desire to fulfill his duty as a son, his dream to go to the prestigious school in town, or his wish to maintain a positive reputation in the class he belongs to (cf. Lee & Bong, 2016). These concerns about the parents' academic expectation, the broader goal of going to a good school, and the school climate are clearly motivational and capable of prompting students to adopt a certain achievement goal. Thus, it appears that the technical definition of reason in the initial articulation of the hierarchical model does not allow for other relevant constructs that are likely to function as instigators of achievement goal adoption to be considered as reasons. As the goal complex approach develops, therefore, the need to expand the reason concept has become more apparent.

In view of the multitude of constructs that can prompt achievement goal adoption, in the present chapter, we propose a broader and more inclusive conceptualization of reason. The expanded conceptualization is consistent with the relatively wide-ranging and encompassing lexical definition of reason, "a cause, explanation, or justification for an action or event" (Oxford Dictionaries, 2013). We believe taking a broader view of the reason concept advances goal complex research in two important ways. First, it allows us to classify reasons and to clarify their role in the sociocultural (contextual) processes of goal adoption and, second, it allows us to expand the content of reason and to explore other constructs that have not been previously considered. Each of these contributions is elaborated on below.

First, we make a conceptual distinction between proximal and distal reasons. A proximal reason represents the immediate psychological starting point of behavior. As discussed above, this type of reason has been empirically operationalized through such constructs as competence-, self-, and relationally-based desires and fears that directly instigate achievement goal adoption (e.g., Hodis et al., 2016). In contrast, a distal reason represents a broader class of constructs that influence achievement goal adoption. Distal reasons include such constructs as values, goals, aspirations, expectations, and beliefs that individuals acquire and integrate into their identity through socialization and internalization processes.

Although the two types of reasons share a functional role as the motivational impetus for achievement goal adoption, the processes associated with each type of reason are likely to show some differences. Unlike proximal reasons that immediately prompt achievement goal adoption, distal reasons prompt achievement goal adoption either directly, or indirectly through their more immediate impact on the activation of proximal reasons. To illustrate an indirect influence, the socioculturally-internalized belief that academic performance is in direct proportion to students' *face* (ego) and in-group (family) reputation (i.e., distal reason), commonly held by students with an interdependent self-construal (Markus, Kitayama, & Heimen, 1996), could give rise to a heightened concern about failure (i.e., a proximal reason) which would, in turn, lead to the adoption of performance-avoidance goals.

Second, the proximal-distal distinction brings us to the possibility of expanding the content of the reason concept not only by including a wide range of psychological constructs (e.g., values, aspirations, role- or identity-related prescriptions, expectations, and other [non-achievement] goals), but also considering these constructs in association with a broad range of sociocultural contexts (e.g., family, class, school, community, society). Further, we think that expansion of the construct applies to both distal and proximal reasons. That is, while prior work tended to conceptualize proximal reasons as relatively nonconscious, less accessible, and largely affectively-based constructs (Elliot & Thrash, 2001), we think that both proximal and distal reasons include constructs that may vary in their nature (cognitive, affective) and their relative consciousness and accessibility to individuals (see also Sommet, Elliot, & Sheldon, in press, for a similar perspective). As reflected in the example given earlier, the fear of failure regarding an upcoming examination (i.e., a proximal reason) and the desire to not let family down (i.e., a distal reason) are instigators of achievement goal adoption that students are cognitively aware of, chronically accessible, and temporally enduring in guiding the selection of the achievement goal one adopts. In this case in point, the proximal reason is closely associated with the education system that the student is in, and the distal reason is closely associated with his family setting and its socialization. Of course, reasons also likely emerge from other socialization contexts, and this is what we will discuss in the sections to follow.

Sociocultural Influences on Distal Reasons

Elliot and Thrash (2001) contended that the substantive contents of achievement goals are essentially the same across contexts. That is, regardless of educational and sociocultural settings, students pursuing a task-approach goal are those who seek to acquire a level of competence according to what is specified in the task evaluation rubric, students pursuing a self-approach goal are those who aim to attain a level of competence that is better than their previous performance, and students pursuing an other-approach goal are those who strive to attain a level of competence better than that of others. In this regard, examination scores or final grades are typically construed as indicators of academic competence across the majority of, if not all, education systems worldwide.

The number of conceivably distinct achievement goals is finite, and the number of possible proximal reasons is relatively large and includes all of the different dimensions of competence-, self-, and relationally-based constructs like desires, fears, hopes, worries, concerns, and thoughts. The number of possible substantive contents of distal reasons, however, is infinite. This is because, as discussed in this chapter, distal reasons originate from the various levels of personal, social, and contextual representations (e.g., sociodemographic factors, as well as family, classroom, school, community, societal, and cultural settings).

As an achievement goal functions as a channel through which its undergirding reason affects achievement-relevant behavior, the meaning and degree of endorsement of an achievement goal may differ according to the reason(s) it serves. By implication, the pursuit of an achievement goal may lead to different regulatory processes and outcomes when prompted by different reasons. It is the contents of the distal reasons that, we contend, are likely to be particularly contextually shaped and, therefore, socioculturally varied in the extent to which they are endorsed. These socioculturally-grounded reasons are then presumed to give rise to the different culture-specific meanings of achievement goal adoption and determine the degree to which the regulatory process of achievement goal pursuit is adaptive in a certain culture. Thus, just like achievement goals function as a channel through which proximal reasons influence achievement-relevant behavior, distal reasons may serve as a channel through which sociodemographic and socio-contextual antecedents affect goal adoption. In view of the multitude of sociodemographic and socio-contextual factors and of the values, beliefs, expectations, and goals associated with these factors, it is important to build a taxonomy classifying distal reasons in a specific and systematic way. To this end, we find the bioecological model of human development a useful framework from which to build a taxonomy of distal reasons of achievement goal adoption.

TAXONOMY OF DISTAL REASONS FOR ACHIEVEMENT GOAL ADOPTION

The bioecological model of human development (Bronfenbrenner 1977, 1979, 1994) has gained popularity in educational psychology research (Goodnow, 1992; Swick & Williams, 2006; Tudge, Mokrova, Hatfield, & Karnik, 2009), and has been used in furthering understanding of socio-contextual influences on motivation (e.g., Martin, Anderson, Bobis, Way, & Vellar, 2012). The model assumes that a student's psychobiological dispositions (gender, ethnicity, temperaments, traits) interact with his/her ecological environments in affecting his/her socioemotional development and, by implication, his/her academic motivation. The ecological environments can be specifically classified into five distinct but nested systems, namely the microsystem, mesosystem, exosystem, macrosystem, and chronosystem. Figure 3.1 shows a graphical representation of the model adapted in this chapter to identify and classify the potential demographically-, socially-, educationally-, and culturally-derived distal reasons for goal adoption. Complementary to Figure 3.1, Table 3.1 shows the classification of antecedents of achievement goals according to the hierarchical model of achievement motivation (Elliot, 1999; Elliot & Thrash, 2001) and its

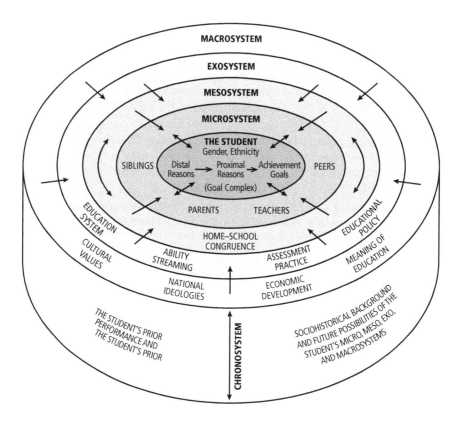

Figure 3.1 Systemic model of sociocultural influences on achievement goal adoption and regulation.

parallel classification based on the bioecological model of human development (Bronfenbrenner, 1977, 1979, 1994). The two models work hand in hand in guiding the development of the taxonomy. The more specific contents of the distal reasons potentially derived from students' personal or sociodemographic factors and each of the systems are discussed next.

Sociodemographically Grounded Distal Reasons

A host of sociodemographic and psychobiological factors have been conceptually posited and empirically found to influence achievement goal adoption or academic motivation in general (see Elliot, 1999; Elliot & Hulleman, 2017). Among these factors, gender and ethnicity are focused on in the present chapter because they are key sociocultural constructs that determine one's gender and ethnic identity (DeCuir-Gunby & Schutz, 2014;

TABLE 3.1 Taxonomy of Distal Reasons for the Adoption of Achievement Goals

| Broad Classification | Antecedents | | More Specific Variables | Examples of Approach- and Avoidance-oriented Distal Reasons Underlying Achievement Goal Adoption |
	Elliot's Hierarchical Model of Achievement Motivation	Bronfenbrenner's Bioecological Model of Human Development		
Individual	Sociodemographic and dispositional factors	Psychobiological factors	Gender	"…because I want to do what is expected of me as a … (male/female)." (approach) "…because I don't want to be different from my peers who are of the same sex." (avoidance)
			Ethnicity	"…because I want to live up to what my ethnic community expects of me." (approach) "…because I want to avoid the negative stereotype of students from my ethnicity." (avoidance)
Socio-contextual	Environmental contexts	Microsystem	Parents/family/ancestors	"…because I want to make my parents proud of me." (approach) "…because I don't want to disappoint my parents." (avoidance)
			Teachers	"…because I want to please and impress my teacher." (approach) "…because I don't want my teacher to think that I am dumb." (avoidance)
			Classmates/peers	"…because I want to maintain my friendships." (approach) "…because I don't want to be looked down upon by my peers." (avoidance)

(continued)

TABLE 3.1 Taxonomy of Distal Reasons for the Adoption of Achievement Goals (continued)

| Broad Classification | Antecedents | | More Specific Variables | Examples of Approach- and Avoidance-oriented Distal Reasons Underlying Achievement Goal Adoption |
	Elliot's Hierarchical Model of Achievement Motivation	Bronfenbrenner's Bioecological Model of Human Development		
Socio-contextual (continued)	Environmental contexts (continued)	Mesosystem	Home-school links	"…because my teacher and parents agree that this is what I should do." (approach) "…because I don't want to fall short of meeting the expectations set by my teacher and parents." (avoidance)
		Exosystem	Classroom and school contexts	"…because I want to maintain the reputation of my class/school." (approach) "…because I don't want to bring down the reputation of my class/school." (avoidance)
			Education system and its policies and practices	"…because I want to do well in the upcoming national examination." (approach) "…because I don't want to be placed in the lower-ability stream." (avoidance)
		Macrosystem	Cultural values, national ideologies, economic development	"…because I want to contribute to the society." (approach) "…because I don't want to be a burden to my country" (avoidance)
		Chronosystem	Past experiences and future possibilities	"…because I aspire to be a scientist in the future." (approach) "…because I don't want to repeat my history of failure." (avoidance)

Eccles, 2009; Graham & Taylor, 2002; Holder & Kessels, 2017; Hill & Lynch, 1983; Phinney, 1990) from which distal reasons for goal adoption are likely to emerge.

We believe gender and ethnicity are likely to prompt goal adoption through their impact on students' gender and ethnic identity. Gender and ethnic identity are presumed to function as distal reasons by providing the specific contents of such reasons through the process of the socialization of expectations, values, beliefs, norms, and broader goals associated with a certain gender and ethnicity. Various definitions of identity have been proffered in the literature. For example, Marcia (1980) defined identity as "an internal, self-constructed organization of drives, abilities, beliefs, and individual history" (p. 159) and, according to Waterman (1984), identity is "a clearly delineated self-definition comprised of those goals, values, and beliefs to which the person is unequivocally committed" (p. 331). Despite this definitional variability, theorists essentially agree that the contents, valence, and salience of the components of one's identity (e.g., expectations, values, goals) are acquired over time as a result of the individual's interactions with, and interpretations of experiences in, his or her sociocultural contexts (Eccles, 2009; Kaplan & Flum, 2010). This suggests that as a result of gender-role or ethnicity-role socialization, girls and boys or students of different ethnicities should acquire different patterns of beliefs not only about who they *are* and who they *would like* to become, but also who they *should* be and become according to the sociocultural expectations set by their gender or ethnicity (Hill & Lynch, 1983; Phinney, 1990).

Theorists also believe that self-identity functions as a motivational force that drives and leads individuals to engage in a certain activity and to pursue a certain outcome that is aligned with, or expected by, such an identity (Eccles, 2009; Kaplan & Flum, 2010). As clearly pointed out by Eccles (2009), "behavioral choices are a primary mechanism through which individuals enact their personal and collective/social identities and thus validate their identities" (p. 79). This implies that any identity-related expectation, both educational and non-educational, that comes (or does not come) with one's social role as a student who is of a certain gender or ethnic background, may serve as a distal reason for the student in selecting and pursuing an achievement goal.

As shown in Figure 3.2, sociodemographic factors (e.g., gender, ethnicity) are presumed to affect goal adoption in two interrelated ways. First, sociodemographic factors impact goal adoption through their more immediate influences on distal reasons which may then induce proximal reasons that foster achievement goal adoption (Mechanism 1). Second, sociodemographic factors impact goal adoption through their more immediate influences on distal reasons which directly prompt achievement goal adoption (Mechanism 2).

The mechanisms depicted in Figure 3.2 raise an interesting possibility: that any observed gender- or ethnic-related differences in achievement

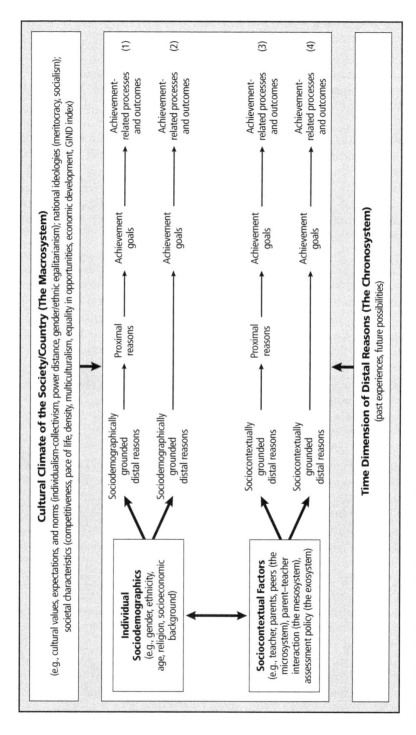

Figure 3.2 Sociocultural influences on achievement goal adoption and regulation: Four interrelated mechanisms.

goal endorsement (e.g., Eaton & Dembo, 1997; Sutantoputri & Watt, 2013; Theis & Fischer, 2017) may in part be attributable to gender- and ethnic-identity related differences in such distal reasons (cf. the expectancy-value model; Eccles, 2009). Indeed, gender differences in distal reason-relevant constructs have been observed. Eccles (2007), for example, found that the male American youth in her study saw becoming famous and making lots of money as more important than did their female counterparts. In contrast, the female youth viewed making sacrifices for one's family and helping others as more important than did the male youth.

Ethnic differences on similar constructs have also been observed. Liem and Kennedy (in press), for example, found that the Chinese Indonesian students in their study tended to place an important value on wealth-oriented future goals and saw schooling as a means toward economic gains; they did so more than their native Indonesian peers. In contrast, the native Indonesian students were more inclined to place a high value on society-oriented future goals and to construe schooling as a means toward developing skills and knowledge for purposeful future work than were their Chinese Indonesian peers. These findings (Eccles, 2007; Liem & Kennedy, in press) provide a reasonable ground to believe that the salient distal reasons triggering the activation of proximal reasons and, in turn, the adoption of achievement goals, may also be different across genders and ethnicities (cf. Kaplan & Maehr, 2000 seeking to explain the academic motivation of African American students).

At this point in our discussion, it is clear that distal reasons can and should be differentiated according to their motivational valences. Distal reasons, just like any other achievement-relevant motivational constructs (see Elliot, 1999), may orient individuals to attain desirable outcomes or avoid undesirable outcomes. Differentiating approach-oriented from avoidance-oriented distal reasons is crucial in understanding sociocultural influences on goal adoption and regulation, particularly because members of certain cultures, ethnicities, genders, and socioeconomic levels differ in the degree to which they endorse avoidance (relative to approach) motivation (see e.g., Chang, 1996; Markus, Kitayama, & Heimen, 1996). Further, these motivational orientations have been found to predict personal well-being differentially across cultures, with avoidance goals typically associated with maladaptive functioning among individualist persons, but not necessarily so (or not necessarily in the same way) among collectivist individuals (see Elliot, Chirkov, Kim, & Sheldon, 2001; Elliot et al., 2012).

Socio-Contextually Grounded Distal Reasons

As Figure 3.1 and Table 3.1 show, social and educational settings of students' academic development can be classified into the micro, meso, and

exosystems. These systems are more concretely represented by specific socializers interacting with, and educational policies and practices impinging
on, students. Socializing agents (parents, teachers, peers, the community)
in the micro and mesosystems, and institutional (educational) forces (curriculum, assessment mode, ability streaming) embedded in the exosystem,
are likely to prompt goal adoption in two interrelated ways. First, socio-
contextual factors embedded in the micro, meso, and exosystems impact
goal adoption through their influence on students' distal reasons which
then induce proximal reasons that directly inform the selection or adoption of achievement goals (Mechanism 3). Second, socio-contextual factors
impact goal adoption through their influence on students' distal reasons,
which directly prompt achievement goal adoption (Mechanism 4). Each of
the systems and their illustrative reasons are discussed below.

The Microsystem

This system represents an immediate setting of development that comprises people who have direct and mutually influential interactions with a
student (Bronfenbrenner, 1977, 1979, 1994). The people in the microsystem we specifically focus on here are parents, teachers, and peers/class-
mates who are empirically known to exert an influence on achievement
goal adoption or school motivation more generally (see Martin & Dowson,
2009 for a review).

Interestingly, studies with high-school students in collectivist cultures
(e.g., Jiang, Bong, & Kim, 2015; Liem et al., 2012; Nie & Liem, 2013) have
shown a "double-edged sword" effect of socially-derived academic motivation. This effect points to a pattern whereby students' desire to conform
(i.e., to match their attitudes and behaviors to those of the majority [peers]
or respected people [parents, teachers]) not only gives rise to their perceived support from teachers and peers but also induces their senses of
guilt toward and conflict with their parents. In turn, these perceived social
relationships, which are positive and negative in nature respectively, foster
students' adoption of both approach and avoidance achievement goals. Research evidence, however, shows that this may not be the case among older
students in individualist, culturally-Western societies (see e.g., Benita, Roth,
and Deci, 2014; Duchesne & Ratelle, 2010; Fletcher, Shim, & Wang, 2012).
Thus, research needs to clarify if the double-edged sword effect is also observed in younger Western students for whom individuality and uniqueness
(as opposed to conformity) are among the more strongly cultivated personal attributes (Triandis, 1995).

The above discussion leads us to believe that specific key persons in the
microsystem, alongside the social goals (e.g., social responsibility, social affiliation; Dowson & McInerney, 2003) that students carry into their academic endeavor, are likely to serve as a source of the formation of parent-,

teacher-, and peer-specific distal reasons for goal adoption (see Table 3.1). Clearly, future research needs to distinguish the social agents and to ascertain if different social agents in the students' microsystem of their achievement context (parents vs. teachers vs. peers) are linked to differential patterns of goal complex effects in different cultures.

The Mesosystem

This system represents a setting that involves the interactions between two social agents in a student's microsystem. In other words, "a mesosystem is a system of microsystem" (Bronfenrenner, 1994, p. 40). An example of the mesosystem is the interaction between a student's teachers and parents who discuss his slow progress and agree on the "remedial intervention" needed to help his studies.

The extent to which people (parents, siblings, teachers, peers, neighbors) in the student's microsystem are positive, supportive and, importantly, in agreement with each other, influence the student's school motivation and well-being (Arunkumar, Midgley, & Urdan, 1999; Kumar, 2006). This points to the possibility that the agreement (or lack thereof) between parents and teachers in the academic expectations, norms, values, and goals they socialize to students are likely to serve as distal reasons that directly foster students' achievement goal adoption (e.g., "I strive to master the class material because my parents and teacher agree that I have to pass the upcoming midterm exam"). There is reason to believe that the degree of agreement (or congruence) of the message communicated by teachers and parents is more potent in influencing student motivation than the individual message from just one of these social agents.

Bronfenbrenner (1979) stated, "Seldom is attention paid to a person's behavior in more than one setting or the ways in which the relation between settings can affect what happens within them" (p. 18). Four decades have passed since his remark, and it is certainly true today as far as the role of the mesosystem in school motivation is concerned. Clearly, the impact of parents–teacher dissonance on achievement goal adoption is an area that future research, including research on the goal complex approach, should focus on. However, the interactions between other people in the student's miscrosystem (parents and siblings, teachers and classmates, family and the community/the media) should not be overlooked either.

The Exosystem

This setting represents a context of development that the student does not have a direct influence on, but that impacts on the student's development both directly and indirectly through its bearings on the meso and microsystems. In the context of schooling, this system is represented by educational policies and practices implemented in the classroom, at the school, or in the education system that influences achievement-relevant processes and outcomes (e.g., curriculum, assessment mode, ability grouping). Figure 3.1 shows that the exosystem itself is assumed to be influenced by the cultural values, national ideologies, and economic development of the society where achievement pursuit takes place (i.e., the macrosystem).

Of particular relevance to the exosystem are the concept of mastery and performance goal structures, representing the degree to which the school or classroom emphasizes or nurture students' adoption of mastery or performance goals, respectively (Meece, Anderman, & Anderman, 2006; Skaalvik, Federici, Wigfield, & Tangen, 2017). As elaborated by Meece et al. (2006), goal structures comprise six dimensions of pedagogical principles and practices, including task, authority, recognition, grouping, evaluation, and time (i.e., the TARGET framework). In relation to goal complexes, educational policies and practices associated with the contextual dimensions specified in the TARGET framework, collectively or independently, may be construed as distal reasons when students are continuously socialized to the salient messages that these policies and practices convey (see Table 3.1).

The Macrosytem

This setting comprises characteristics of the broader cultural context that serves as a "blueprint" for the ways in which people and institutions in the more inner systems (exo, meso, and microsystems) operate and influence the student. Examples of the macrosystem include cultural values, social beliefs, national ideologies, economic development, and other country-level attributes. More specifically, countries around the world are known to differ in, *inter alia*, their cultural value dimensions (e.g., individualism vs. collectivism, large vs. small power distance, masculinity [competitive] vs. femininity [less competitive]); social axioms or beliefs about how the world functions (e.g., fate control, social cynicism, social complexity); national ideologies (e.g., meritocracy, socialism); and economic and other advancement opportunities that people are provided with (Hofstede, Hofstede, & Minkov, 2010; Leung, Bond et al., 2002; Maehr & Nicholls, 1980; Triandis, 1995). Interestingly, achievement goal researchers (Dekker & Fischer, 2008; King & McInerney, 2014; Senko & Tropiano, 2016; Zusho & Clayton, 2011) have speculated that the degree to which achievement goals are endorsed is linked to the cultural values of the countries the individual resides in.

As a cultural blueprint, however, societal attributes embedded in the macrosystem are more concretely manifested, and can be more directly observed, in the student's exosystem (e.g., the country's education system), mesosystem (e.g., how parents and teachers interact and are in agreement with each other), and microsystem (e.g., how parents and teachers as socializers of culture interact with the student). One pertinent example of the macrosystem is the meaning of education. The cross-culturally differential belief in the importance of education (or, educational qualifications!) leads to varying levels of commitment to education at the societal, school, family, and individual levels which, in turn give rise to distal reasons linked to the macro, exo, meso, and microsystems of the students.

Whilst the influence of culture on students' adoption of achievement goals is most likely to be mediated by the students' micro, meso, and exo-systems, culture might also inform the content of distal reasons directly associated with the societal or country-level attributes (see Table 3.1). An example is when a student strives to learn to achieve for one of the following reasons: "I love my country," "I want to be a good citizen," "I want to make my country a better place for its people," "I wish to contribute to society and nation building," or "I want to work for the betterment of society." In fact, Grouzet et al. (2005, p. 802) found that two personal life goals related to society at large, namely community feeling ("to improve the world through activism or generativity") and conformity ("to fit in with other people"), are strongly endorsed by young people in 15 countries, both Eastern (China, South Korea) and Western (Australia, the United States). How commonly, and to what extent, do these life aspirations serve as distal reasons, prompt proximal reasons, lead to achievement goal adoption, and affect achievement goal-relevant regulatory processes? These are some of the pivotal research questions that future research may focus on.

The Chronosystem

This setting represents the temporal dimension (changes or consistencies) of the aforementioned systems that influence student's academic development, including (change in) the adoption of achievement goals. These include the student's academic history (e.g., prior achievement goals, past schooling experience and performance) and what has happened or been happening in the student's microsystem (e.g., temporal steadiness of the achievement-relevant messages received by the student in his interactions with parents, teachers, peers, and siblings), mesosystem (e.g., stability of family structure), exosystem (e.g., changes in the education system that impact curricula and instructional and assessment practices), and macrosystem (e.g., a shift in cultural values, the increasingly pervasive use of technology in education).

Although the bioecological model seems to have mainly focused on the influence of sociohistorical (past) experiences on development, future possibilities are particularly important in understanding school motivation (see e.g., McInerney, 2004, for a discussion). In fact, many perspectives of school motivation construe motivation as a "future oriented" and "in anticipation" construct as much as a consequence of past and present experiences. Furthermore, future goals are seen as playing a pivotal role in giving a sense of meaning and direction to present activities which students choose to invest themselves in. McInerney, Marsh, and Yeung (2003), for example, showed that students' sense of purpose ("I want to do well at school so that I can have a good future") was associated with their mastery-goal-focused constructs, namely effort ("I work hard to try to understand new things at school") and task ("I like to see that I am improving in my schoolwork").

It is not surprising, therefore, that many of the distal reasons discussed above are related to *future* socio-contextually bound social and life aspirations, concerns, expectations, and goals, either immediate or further distant. The relations between the future and achievement goals have indeed been established, with mastery-based goals linked to career-, society-, and family-focused future goals, and performance-based goals linked to fame- and wealth-focused future goals (Lee, McInerney, Liem, & Ortiga, 2010). However, it has been recognized that individuals vary in their attention to the future, with younger children, females, and people from certain cultural backgrounds seemingly having a shorter time orientation perspective and being less articulate about their future goals than older individuals, males, and people from other cultural groups (Green & DeBacker, 2004; McInerney, McInerney, Baseley, & Ardington, 1998; Simons, Vanteenkiste, Lens, & Lacante, 2004). Thus, it is reasonable to assume that the degree to which distal reasons prompt proximal reasons and energize achievement goals would depend on, or be moderated by, students' age, gender, and cultural background.

OTHER NOTEWORTHY POINTS

Figure 3.2 also shows that the macrosystem not only affects the "contents" of distal reasons through their influence on the exo, meso, and microsystems (as well as the students' gender and ethnic identity), it may also moderate the strength of the link between a reason and an achievement goal (i.e., a goal complex) and the extent to which the achievement-relevant processes and outcomes resulting from this goal complex are adaptive. That is, consistent with the importance of considering the "need" and "press" interaction in understanding motivated behaviors (Murray, 1938), the link between a reason and a goal can be solidified or weakened, and the adaptiveness of the regulatory process associated with this goal complex can be enhanced or attenuated by societal affordances and constraints faced by students in the achievement contexts they experience.

For example, although some research has shown less than optimal implications of the goal of trying to outperform others (i.e., pursuing a performance-approach goal) in fulfilling the desire to demonstrate ability (i.e., a self-presentation motive grounded reason; see Hulleman, Schrager, Bodmann, & Harackiewicz, 2010; Senko & Dowson, 2016), the synergistic relation between this reason and aim may not necessarily be detrimental for learning and achievement for students in a competitive setting where their work is normatively graded. In fact, their desire to demonstrate their ability relative to peers, which guides them to adopt a performance-approach goal, is likely to be effective for learning and performance because the setting provides them the opportunities to realize their intention and to attain their goal. In contrast, the adaptive effects of students' intention to develop their potential (i.e., a self-development motive grounded reason) which guides them to learn as much as they could (i.e., adopting a mastery-approach goal; Hulleman et al., 2010) may be compromised in a competitive classroom environment, because this setting does not provide sufficient resources (e.g., time for studies, academic help, collaboration) for the students to realize their desire and attain their goal.

The conceptual separation of the two types of reason and their proposed relationships depicted in Figure 3.2 may also help clarify why students in certain cultures are more inclined to endorse a given proximal reason and motivational valence (e.g., achievement motive vs. fear of failure; social approval motive vs. fear of rejection) than those in others (see also McClelland's [1951] analogous discussion on the socialization of motives). The literature has documented that, relative to their Western counterparts, Asians are generally more avoidance oriented (e.g., Chang, 1996; Elliot et al., 2001; Elliot et al., 2012). Moreover, large-scale international studies like the Programme for International Student Assessment (PISA) have consistently demonstrated that, despite their superior achievement, East Asian students tend to be more anxious and have more self-doubt than their Western counterparts (see Organization for Economic Cooperation and Development [OECD], 2017). While it is undeniable that cultural dispositions such as self-criticism and self-abasement play a role in these East-West differences, one of the reasons for the paradox might also be that "Asian students show keen interest in others' evaluations and reactions towards themselves" (Stankov, 2010, p. 559), apparently suggesting that the interdependent self-construal of Asian students makes their desire to impress and seek approval from others (especially parents and teachers) more salient, leading to their heightened perceived achievement pressure, intensified anxiety and, as a result, lowered confidence. The interesting question arising is: Which, and to what extent do, socioculturally-bound distal reasons account for proximal reasons? This, too, is an avenue for future research.

CLOSING REMARKS

The goal complex approach holds promise for researchers and practitioners as it not only addresses the what but also the why of achievement goal pursuit. This nascent approach requires systematic identification of the potential reasons that may undergird the adoption of achievement goals. The present chapter addresses this by, first, distinguishing distal from proximal reasons for achievement goal adoption; second, integrating the hierarchical model of achievement motivation and bioecological model of human development in identifying sociodemographically- and socio-contextually-rooted distal reasons; and third, articulating the potential mechanisms by which sociodemographic and socio-contextual factors influence the formation of the distal reasons presumed to guide goal adoption. We end the chapter by calling for cross-cultural research to incorporate both distal and proximal reasons to better understand the role of sociocultural factors on achievement goal adoption and regulation. Ultimately, as the theme of this volume suggests, student motivation is a complex phenomenon deeply rooted in the sociocultural milieu which provides not only opportunities but also boundaries for achievement-related behaviors.

REFERENCES

Arunkumar, R., Midgley, C., & Urdan, T. (1999). Perceiving high or low home-school dissonance: Longitudinal effects on adolescent emotional and academic well-being. *Journal of Research on Adolescence, 9*(4), 441–466.

Atkinson, J. (1957). Motivational determinants of risk-taking behavior. *Psychological Review, 64*, 359–372.

Baranik, L. E., Stanley, L. J., Bynum, B. H., & Lance, C. E. (2010). Examining the construct validity of mastery-avoidance achievement goals: A meta-analysis. *Human Performance, 23*, 265–282.

Benita, M., Roth, G., & Deci, E. L. (2014). When are mastery goals more adaptive? It depends on experiences of autonomy support and autonomy. *Journal of Educational Psychology, 106*(1), 258–267.

Boekaerts, M., de Koning, E., & Vedder, P. (2006). Goal-directed behavior and contextual factors in the classroom: An innovative approach to the study of multiple goals. *Educational Psychologist, 41*, 33–51.

Bronfenbrenner, U. (1977). Toward an experimental ecology of human development. *American Psychologist, 32*, 515–531.

Bronfenbrenner, U. (1979). *The ecology of human development.* Cambridge, MA: Harvard University Press.

Bronfenbrenner, U. (1994). Ecological models of human development. In T. Husen & T. N. Postlethwaite (Eds.), *International encyclopedia of education* (2nd ed., Vol. 3, pp. 1643–1647). Oxford, England: Pergamon Press.

Chang, E. (1996). Cultural differences in optimism, pessimism, and coping: Predictors of subsequent adjustment in Asian American and Caucasian American college students. *Journal of Counseling Psychology, 43*, 113–123.

Dekker, S., & Fischer, R. (2008). Cultural differences in academic motivation goals: A meta-analysis across 13 societies. *The Journal of Educational Research, 102*(2), 99–110.

DeCuir-Gunby, J. T., & Schutz, P. A. (2014). Researching race within educational psychology contexts. *Educational Psychologist, 49*(4), 244–260.

Dowson, M., & McInerney, D. M. (2003). What do students say about their motivational goals? Towards a more complex and dynamic perspective on student motivation. *Contemporary Educational Psychology, 28*, 91–113.

Duchesne, S., & Ratelle, C. (2010). Parental behaviors and adolescents' achievement goals at the beginning of middle school: Emotional problems as potential mediators. *Journal of Educational Psychology, 102*(2), 497–507.

Dweck, C. S. (1986). Motivational processes affecting learning. *American Psychologist, 41*, 1040–1048.

Eaton, M. J., & Dembo, M. H. (1997). Differences in the motivational beliefs of Asian American and non-Asian students. *Journal of Educational Psychology, 89*(3), 433–440.

Eccles, J. S. (2007). Where are all the women? Gender differences in participation in physical science and engineering. In S. J. Ceci & W. M. Williams (Eds.), *Why aren't more women in science? Top researchers debate the evidence* (pp. 199–210). Washington, DC: American Psychological Association.

Eccles, J. S. (2009). Who am I and what am I going to do with my life? Personal and collective identities as motivators of action. *Educational Psychologist, 44*(2), 78–89.

Elliot, A. J. (1999). Approach and avoidance motivation and achievement goals. *Educational Psychologist, 34*, 149–169.

Elliot, A. J., Aldhobaiban, N., Kobeisy, A., Murayama, K., Goclowska, M. A., Lichtenfeld, S., & Khayat, A. (2016). Linking social interdependence preferences to achievement goal adoption. *Learning and Individual Differences, 50*, 291–295.

Elliot, A. J., Chirkov, V. I., Kim, Y., & Sheldon, K. N. (2001). A cross-cultural analysis of avoidance (relative to approach) personal goals. *Psychological Science, 12*(6), 505–510.

Elliot, A. J., & Church, M. A. (1997). A hierarchical model of approach and avoidance achievement motivation. *Journal of Personality and Social Psychology, 72*, 218–232.

Elliot, A. J., & Harackiewicz, J. M. (1996). Approach and avoidance achievement goals and intrinsic motivation: A mediational analysis. *Journal of Personality and Social Psychology, 70*(3), 461–475.

Elliot, A. J., & Hulleman, C. S. (2017). Achievement goals. In A. J. Elliot, C. S. Dweck, & D. S. Yeager (Eds.), *Handbook of competence and motivation: Theory and application* (2nd ed., pp. 43–60). New York, NY: Guilford.

Elliot, A. J., & McGregor, H. A. (2001). A 2 × 2 achievement goal framework. *Journal of Personality and Social Psychology, 80*, 501–519.

Elliot, A. J., & Murayama, K. (2008). On the measurement of achievement goals: Critique, illustration, and application. *Journal of Educational Psychology, 100*(3), 613–628.

Elliot, A. J., Murayama, K., & Pekrun, R. (2011). A 3 × 2 achievement goal model. *Journal of Educational Psychology, 103*, 632–648.

Elliot, A. J., Sedikides, C., Murayama, K., Tanaka, A., Thrash, T. M., & Mapes, R. (2012). Cross-cultural generality and specificity in self-regulation: Avoidance personal goals and multiple aspects of well-being in the U.S. and Japan. *Emotion, 12,* 1031–1040.

Elliot, A. J., & Thrash, T. M. (2001). Achievement goals and the hierarchical model of achievement motivation. *Educational Psychology Review, 13,* 139–156.

Elliot, A. J., & Thrash, T. M. (2002). Approach-avoidance motivation in personality: Approach and avoidance temperaments and goals. *Journal of Personality and Social Psychology, 54,* 5–12.

Fletcher, K. L., Shim, S. S., & Wang, C. (2012). Perfectionistic concerns mediate the relationship between psychologically controlling parenting and achievement goal orientations. *Personality and Individual Differences, 52,* 876–881.

Ford, M. E. (1992). *Motivating humans: Goals, emotions, and personal agency beliefs.* Newbury Park, CA: SAGE.

Goodnow, C. (1992). Strengthening the links between educational psychology and the study of social contexts. *Educational Psychologist, 27*(2), 177–196.

Graham, S., & Taylor, A. Z. (2002). Ethnicity, gender, and the development of achievement values. In A. Wigfield & J. S. Ecles (Eds.), *Development of achievement motivation* (pp. 121–146). San Diego, CA: Academic Press.

Green, B. A., & DeBacker, T. K. (2004). Gender and orientations toward the future: Links to motivation. *Educational Psychology Review, 16*(2), 91–120.

Grouzet, M. E., Ahuvia, A., Kim, Y., Ryan, R. M., Schmuck, P., Kasser, T., . . . & Sheldon, K. M. (2005). The structure of goal contents across 15 cultures. *Journal of Personality and Social Psychology, 89,* 800–816.

Hill, J. P., & Lynch, M. E. (1983). The intensification of gender-related role expectations during early adolescence. In J. Brooks-Gunn & A. Petersen (Eds.), *Girls at puberty: Biological and psychosocial perspectives* (pp. 201–228). New York, NY: Plenum.

Hodis, F. A., Tait, C., Hodis, G. M., Hodis, M. A., & Scornavacca, E. (2016). Analyzing student motivation at the confluence of achievement goals and their underlying reasons: An investigation of goal complexes. *Social Psychology of Education, 19,* 643–660.

Hofstede, G., Hofstede, G. J., & Minkov, M. (2010). *Cultures and organizations: Software of the mind* (3rd ed.). New York, NY: McGraw-Hill.

Holder, K., & Kessels, U. (2017). Gender and ethnic stereotypes in student teachers' judgments: A new look from a shifting standards perspective. *Social Psychology of Education, 20,* 471–490.

Huang, C. (2012). Discriminant and criterion-related validity of achievement goals in predicting academic achievement: A meta-analysis. *Journal of Educational Psychology, 104*(1), 48–73.

Hulleman, C. S., Schrager, S. M., Bodmann, S. M., & Harackiewicz, J. M. (2010). A meta-analytic review of achievement goal measures: Different labels for the same constructs or different constructs with similar labels? *Psychological Bulletin, 136,* 422–449.

Jiang, Y., Bong, M., & Kim, S. I. (2015). Conformity of Korean adolescents in their perceptions of social relationships and academic motivation. *Learning and Individual Differences, 40,* 41–54.

Kaplan, A., & Flum, H. (2010). Achievement goal orientations and identity formation styles. *Educational Research Review, 5,* 50–67.

King, R. B., & McInerney, D. M. (2014). Culture's consequences on student motivation: Capturing cross-cultural universality and variability through personal investment theory. *Educational Psychologist, 49*(3), 175–198.

Klassen, R. M. (2004). Optimism and realism: A review of self-efficacy from a cross-cultural perspective. *International Journal of Psychology, 39*(3), 205–230.

Kumar, R. (2006). Students' experiences of home-school dissonance: The role of school academic culture and perceptions of classroom goal structures. *Contemporary Educational Psychology, 31*, 253–279.

Lee, M., & Bong, M. (2016). In their own words: Reasons underlying the achievement striving of students in schools. *Journal of Educational Psychology, 108*(2), 274–294.

Lee, J. Q., McInerney, D. M., Liem, G. A. D., & Ortiga, Y. P. (2010). The relationship between future goals and achievement goal orientations: An intrinsic-extrinsic motivation perspective. *Contemporary Educational Psychology, 35*(4), 264–279.

Leung, K., Bond, M. H., de Carrasquel, S. R., Munoz, C., Hernández, M., Murakami, F., . . . & Singelis, T. M. (2002). Social axioms: The search for universal dimensions of general beliefs about how the world functions. *Journal of Cross-Cultural Psychology, 33*(3), 286–302.

Liem, G. A. D. (2016). Academic and social achievement goals: Their additive, interactive, and specialized effects on school functioning. *British Journal of Educational Psychology, 86*(1), 37–56.

Liem, G. A. D., & Kennedy, K. J. (in press). Democracy and young people's individual beliefs: Beyond democratic institutions in Indonesia. In M. Klicperova-Baker (Ed.), *Humanism and democracy across borders of countries and disciplines.* San Diego, CA: San Diego University Press.

Liem, G. A. D., Lau, W. K., & Cai, E. Y. L. (2016). Promoting mastery-approach goals to support the success of the "Teach Less Learn More" educational initiative. In W. C. Liu, J. C. K. Wang, & R. M. Ryan (Eds.), *Building autonomous learners: Perspectives from research and practice using self-determination theory* (pp. 277–302). Singapore, Singapore: Springer.

Liem, G. A. D., Martin, A. J., Porter, A., & Colmar, S. (2012). Sociocultural antecedents of achievement motivation and achievement: The role of values and achievement motives in achievement goals and academic performance. *Asian Journal of Social Psychology, 15*(1), 1–13.

Lochbaum, M., & Gottardy, J. (2015). A meta-analytic review of the approach-avoidance achievement goals and performance relationships in the sport psychology literature. *Journal of Sport and Health Science, 4*, 164–173.

Maehr, M. L. (1989). Thoughts about motivation. In C. Ames & A. Ames (Eds.), *Research on motivation in education* (Vol. 3, pp. 299–315). New York, NY: Academic Press.

Maehr, M. L., & Nicholls, J. G. (1980). Culture and achievement motivation: A second look. In N. Warren (Ed.), *Studies in cross-cultural psychology* (Vol. 2, pp. 221–267). New York, NY: Academic Press.

Marcia, J. E. (1980). Identity in adolescence. In J. Albeson (Ed.), *Handbook of adolescent psychology* (pp. 159–187). New York, NY: John Wiley.

Markus, H., Kitayama, S., & Heimen, R. (1996). Culture and 'basic' psychological principles. In C. Higgins & A. Kruglanski (Eds.), *Social psychology: Handbook of basic principles* (pp. 857–913). New York, NY: Guilford Press.

Martin, A. J., Anderson, J. Bobis, J., Way, J., & Vellar, R. (2012). Switching on and switching off in mathematics: An ecological study of future intent and disengagement among middle school students. *Journal of Educational Psychology, 104*(1), 1–18.

Martin, A. J., & Dowson, M. (2009). Interpersonal relationships, motivation, engagement, and achievement: Yields for theory, current issues, and educational practice. *Review of Educational Research, 79*, 327–365.

McClelland, D. (1951). *Personality.* Chicago, IL: Dryden.

McInerney, D. M. (2004). A discussion of future time perspective: Effects of time perspective on student motivation. *Educational Psychology Review, 16*(2),141–151.

McInerney, D. M., Marsh, H. W., & Yeung, A. (2003). Toward a hierarchical goal theory of school motivation. *Journal of Applied Measurement, 4*, 1–23.

McInerney, D. M., McInerney, V., Baseley, P., & Ardington, A. (1998, April). *Parents, peers, cultural values and school processes: What has most influence on motivating indigenous minority students' school achievement? A qualitative study.* Paper presented at the Annual Meeting of the American Educational Research Association, San Diego, CA.

Meece, J. L., Anderman, E. M., & Anderman, L. H. (2006). Classroom goal structure, student motivation, and academic achievement. *Annual Review of Psychology, 57*, 487–503.

Murray, H. (1938). *Explorations in personality.* New York, NY: Oxford University Press.

Nicholls, J. G. (1989). *The competition ethos and democratic education.* Cambridge, MA: Harvard University Press.

Nie, Y., & Liem, G. A. D. (2013). Extending antecedents of achievement goals: The double-edged sword effect of social-oriented achievement motive and gender differences. *Learning and Individual Differences, 23*, 249–255.

Organization for Economic Cooperation and Development. (2017). *PISA 2015 results—Volume III: Students' well-being.* Paris, France: Author.

Phinney, J. S. (1990). Ethnic identity in adolescents and adults: review of research. *Psychological Bulletin, 108*(3), 499–514.

Reason. (2013). In OxfordDictionaries.com. Retrieved from https://en.oxford dictionaries.com/definition/reason

Ryan, R. M., & Deci, E. L. (2017). *Self-determination theory: Basic psychological needs in motivation, development, and wellness.* New York, NY: Guilford Press.

Senko, C. (2016). Achievement goal theory: A story of early promises, eventual discords, and future possibilities. In K. Wentzel & D. Miele (Eds.), *Handbook of motivation at school* (2nd ed., pp. 75–95). New York, NY: Routledge.

Senko C., & Dawson, B. (2017). Performance-approach goal effects depend on how they are defined: Meta-analytic evidence from multiple educational outcomes. *Journal of Educational Psychology, 109*(4), 574–598.

Senko, C., & Tropiano, K. T. (2016). Comparing three models of achievement goals: Goal orientations, goal standards, and goal complexes. *Journal of Educational Psychology, 108*(8), 1178–1192.

Simons, J., Vanteenkiste, M., Lens, W., & Lacante, M. (2004). Placing motivation and future time perspective theory in a temporal perspective. *Educational Psychology Review, 16*(2), 121–139.

Skaalvik, E. M., Federici, R. A., Wigfield, A., & Tangen, T. N. (2017). Students' perceptions of mathematics classroom goal structures: Implications for perceived task values and study behavior. *Social Psychology of Education, 20,* 543–563.

Sommet, N., & Elliot, A. J. (2017). Achievement goals, reasons for goal pursuit, and achievement goal complexes as predictors of beneficial outcomes: Is the influence of goals reducible to reasons? *Journal of Educational Psychology, 109*(8), 1141–1162.

Sommet, N., Elliot, A. J., & Sheldon, K. M. (in press). The "what" and "why" of achievement motivation: Conceptualization, operationalization, and consequences of self-determination derived achievement goal complexes. In R. Robbins & O. John (Eds.), *Handbook of personality psychology: Theory and research* (4th ed.). New York, NY: Guilford Press.

Splitter, L. J., & McInerney, D. M. (2015). Motivation: A philosophical and psychological synthesis. In F. Guay, H. W. Marsh, D. M. McInerney, & R. Craven (Eds.), *Self-concept, motivation, and identity* (pp. 273–297). Charlotte, NC: Information Age.

Stankov, L. (2010). Unforgiving Confucian culture: A breeding ground for high academic achievement, test anxiety and self-doubt? *Learning and Individual Differences, 20*(6), 555–563.

Sutantoputri, N. W., & Watt, H. M. G. (2013). Attribution and motivation: Gender, ethnicity, and religion differences among Indonesian university students. *International Journal of Higher Education, 2*(1), 12–21.

Swick, K., & Williams, R. (2006). An analysis of Bronfenbrenner's bio-ecological perspective for early childhood educators: Implications for working with families experiencing stress. *Early Childhood Education Journal, 33,* 371–378.

Theis, D., & Fischer, N. (2017). Sex differences in the development of achievement goals in middle school. *Learning and Individual Differences, 57,* 170–177.

Triandis, H. (1995). Motivation and achievement in collectivist and individualist cultures. *Advances in Motivation and Achievement, 9,* 1–30.

Tudge, J. H. R., Mokrova, I., Hatfield, B. E., Karnik, R. B. (2009). Uses and misuses of Bronfenbrenner's bioecological theory of human development. *Journal of Family Theory & Review, 1,* 198–210.

Urdan, T., & Mestas, M. (2006). The goals behind performance goals. *Journal of Educational Psychology, 98*(2), 354–365.

Vansteenkiste, M., Lens, W., Elliot, A. J., Soenens, B., & Mouratidis, A. (2014). Moving the achievement goal approach one step forward: Toward a systematic examination of the autonomous and controlled reasons underlying achievement goals. *Educational Psychologist, 49*(3), 153–174.

Waterman, A. S. (1984). Identity formation: Discovery or creation? *Journal of Early Adolescence, 4,* 329–341.

Wentzel, K. R. (2000). What is it that I'm trying to achieve? Classroom goals from a content perspective. *Contemporary Educational Psychology, 25,* 105–115.

Zusho, A., & Clayton, K. (2011). Culturalizing achievement goal theory and research. *Educational Psychologist, 46*(4), 239–260.

CHAPTER 4

PERSONAL INVESTMENT THEORY

A Cross-Cultural Framework for the Study of Student Motivation

Ronnel B. King
Jesus Alfonso D. Datu
Dennis M. McInerney

The goal of this chapter is to give an overview of the theoretical underpinnings and empirical evidence for personal investment (PI) theory. To do so, we first present the historical backdrop against which PI theory emerged and then document its basic theoretical assumptions. Given the centrality of culture in PI theory, we examine this concept more closely and provide evidence of how PI researchers have examined motivation in diverse sociocultural contexts. We then move to mapping directions for future research as PI theory enters into its third decade. Finally, we reflect on how the complex perspective and the close attention to contextual (cultural) factors favored by PI researchers have enriched motivational theorizing.

Big Theories Revisited 2, pages 69–88

HISTORICAL BACKGROUND

Before the ascent of social-cognitive theories of achievement motivation (of which personal investment is a prime example) in the 1970s, the dominant paradigm for understanding achievement was rooted in the work of McClelland and Atkinson (Atkinson & Feather, 1966; McClelland, 1961) which we refer to in this chapter as the McClelland-Atkinson model. According to this model, one's motive to achieve is driven in large part by a stable personality trait called the Need for Achievement usually abbreviated as nAch. The McClelland-Atkinson model assumed that some individuals are higher in nAch than others. Although their model also took cognitive factors into account such as the perceived probability of success and incentive value (whether an individual values achievement in the relevant domain), the crucial variable was nAch. Researchers typically measured the nAch construct using projective responses to selected Thematic Apperception Test (TAT) cards.

Maehr and Braskamp (1986) proposed personal investment (PI) theory as an alternative to the then dominant McClelland-Atkinson paradigm. Perhaps one can understand PI theory more thoroughly by contrasting it with the McClelland-Atkinson model. There are three key differences between these competing theoretical perspectives. First, PI theory posits that motivation is not a global, stable personality trait that either one has or does not have. Rather motivation is the result of a complex decision-making process concerning where to invest one's resources and energy. These decisions are determined, in part, by three components—sense of self, perceived goals of behavior, and conditions either facilitating or inhibiting the achievement of goals (described in detail below). To illustrate the point, Maehr (1974) contrasted an economically disadvantaged African-American child who chooses to invest his energies in the basketball court rather than in schoolwork with a White middle-class child who devotes his efforts to excelling in school. The McClelland Atkinson model would view the former as deficient in nAch and the latter as high in nAch. In contrast, PI theory would argue that both the African-American kid and the White middle-class child may have equal levels of motivation but, because of a confluence of different factors (sense of self, perceived goals, facilitating conditions), have chosen different domains in which to invest their energy and resources.

Second, personal investment theory emphasizes that motivation is not entirely dependent on the students' personalities but is partly situationally determined (Maehr, 1974). This view empowers teachers to recognize the critical role they play in shaping student motivation and learning. The McClelland-Atkinson model was disempowering for teachers as Maehr (1974) eloquently stated:

Educators have yet another reason for not focusing exclusively on the role of personality in achievement. Such a focus may suggest that there is little or nothing that can be done by the teacher to foster an interest in achievement: If the child happens to possess it—of course, make the most of it—but what teacher can presume to initiate basic changes in personality? . . . [T]he teacher is left hanging with the question: But what do I do? (p. 210)

Third, PI theory is not an ethnocentric model of achievement motivation based upon the assumption of deficits in academic motivation. The McClelland-Atkinson model, in contrast, may give the impression that some cultural groups are more deficient than others; in essence it is a deficit model. The McClelland-Atkinson model was built on Weber's (2002) work on the protestant ethic. In some cultures that did not value the protestant ethic (at least in the academic domain), children had low achievement motivation. Assuming that the protestant work ethic and its associated concepts constitute the gold standard in determining the level of one's achievement motivation may be culturally biased. As Maehr (1978) wrote, "Most disturbing is the question of whether the whole theory of achievement motivation is hopelessly ethnocentric in nature" (p. 208).

Looking at its historical roots, one can see that PI theory from its inception was designed to be a cross-cultural theory of achievement motivation. It offers a useful antidote to the tendency to view other cultures as deficient in achievement motivation and provides an encouraging message to educators who are encouraged by the theory's more agentic stance on teacher influence and the power of situational factors.

PERSONAL INVESTMENT THEORY: THEORETICAL FOUNDATIONS AND EMPIRICAL EVIDENCE

All individuals possess resources such as knowledge, skills, time, and energy. However, individuals differ in terms of where they choose to invest themselves and their resources. For example, while Student A might choose to invest much of his time in playing computer games, Student B might be more keen to devote her energies to preparing for the final exams. Still another student might eschew academic activities altogether but dedicate himself to practicing doggedly for an upcoming sports competition. Personal investment theory is interested in answering the question ". . . when and how do individuals invest time, talent, and energy in a particular activity?"

As explained above, PI theory does not assume motivation to be a stable trait that either one has or does not have. On the contrary, it presupposes that individuals are motivated but this motivation can be directed towards different ends. It takes a decision-making approach towards human motivation and posits that the decision to invest oneself in an activity depends on three key components:

1. *Sense of self* (Who am I?)—Refers to the more or less organized collections of perceptions, beliefs, and feelings about who one is. Sense of self is multifaceted but includes elements such as one's belief in one's capability (positive self-concept) or lack thereof (negative self-concept).
2. *Perceived goals* (What do I want?)—Refers to reasons or purposes for engaging in a task. These goals include mastery, performance, social, and extrinsic goals.
3. *Facilitating conditions* (What are the available options?)—Refers to the social-contextual environment within which a person is situated that makes certain options more available and salient in contrast to other less appealing alternatives. Facilitating conditions include sociocultural norms, opportunities, and options that an individual perceives in a given situation. These include (but are not limited to) positive and negative influence from one's parents, teachers, and peers. It also includes affect and valuing towards school.

According to PI theory how individuals answer these three key questions helps explain where and how they invest themselves in different activities. We now discuss each of the dimensions of the theory with research examples. To measure these sense of self and the perceived goals of behavior, McInerney and his colleagues developed the Inventory of School Motivation (ISM; McInerney, Yeung, & McInerney, 2001) which has been successfully validated across numerous cultural groups. It measures four dimensions of sense of self namely: *sense of purpose* (the extent to which a student places importance on schooling for his or her future aspirations), *positive self-concept* (the degree to which a student espouses desirable feelings toward his or her academic skills), *negative self-concept* (the extent to which a student holds undesirable feeling toward his or her academic competencies), and *self-reliance* (the degree to which a student can autonomously perform school-related tasks). Studies have found that sense of purpose, positive self-concept, and self-reliance are all positively related to adaptive school outcomes (King, Ganotice, & McInerney, 2012).

In terms of perceived goals, personal investment researchers focus on four types of perceived goals: *mastery goal* (the extent to which a student espouses intrinsic academic goals), *performance goal* (the degree to which a student espouses competition and other-oriented motives), *social goal* (the extent to which a student espouses social affiliation and concern), and *extrinsic goal* (the degree to which a student espouses external rewards and praises). In general, research has found cross-cultural evidence for the existence of these four perceived goals and the relative adaptiveness of mastery-oriented goals universally (King, McInerney, & Nasser, 2017; McInerney, 2008). In contrast, the results associated with performance (King, 2016), social (Cheng & Lam, 2013), and extrinsic goals (King et al., 2017) seem to be more influenced by cultural factors. For example, Cheng and Lam found that social goals seemed to be more adaptive for students with an interdependent self-construal. A large-scale meta-analytic investigation by Hulleman, Schrager, Bodmann, and Harackiewicz (2010) found that performance goals seemed to be more adaptive in collectivist (as opposed to individualist) contexts probably because in collectivist cultures, one does not only need to master the academic tasks but also demonstrate it to others such as one's parents.

The third key component in PI theory refers to facilitating conditions. McInerney and his colleagues (McInerney, Dowson, & Yeung, 2005) developed the Facilitating Conditions Questionnaire to measure the impact of significant others (parents, teachers, and peers) as well as the affect and valuing of school on school motivation and engagement. These facilitating conditions are rooted in Maehr's (1984; see also Maehr & Braskamp, 1986) insight that actions are related to the possibilities that exist for them.

Significant others include parents, teachers, and peers. Studies have found that parent, teacher, and peer support are all important predictors of student motivation, engagement, and achievement, however, their particular salience is situation and culturally dependent (McInerney et al., 2005). McInerney et al. (2005) found that parent support, teacher support, valuing for school, positive affect towards school, and peer support were positively correlated with GPA, while negative peer influence and negative parental influence were both negatively correlated with GPA among Australian elementary and high school students (see also McInerney, 2008).

Facilitating conditions do not only include the role of significant others. PI theory stands out among other social-cognitive theories of achievement motivation for its focus on affect. This focus on the role of affect was inspired by Triandis' (1977, 1980) early theorizing that motivated behavior is not only determined by cognitive and social factors but by (a) how much students enjoy or dislike the behavior, (b) what consequences are seen to be connected with the behavior, and (c) how much these consequences are valued. In general, studies have found that students who enjoy school and who value schooling and the consequences of having a good education are more likely to be motivated in the school context. Most of the major motivational theories have neglected affect in their theoretical models although this trend is changing in the last couple of years with the ascent of studies on the role of emotions in achievement related pursuit (Pekrun, Goetz, Titz, & Perry, 2002). However, PI theory from its inception included affect and valuing of school as key factors influencing engagement in learning.

CULTURE

Researchers have defined culture in different ways. In this paper, we adopt Kitayama's (2002) system view of culture as a "dynamic system that is composed of many loosely organized, often causally connected elements-meanings, practices, and associated mental processes and responses" (p. 92). An important assumption of this system view of culture is that culture is both "in the head" in the form of psychological tendencies and predispositions as well as "out there" in the form of external realities and collective behavioral patterns.

The role of culture in shaping achievement motivation has always been a central theme in PI research from its inception (Maehr, 1974). Although most of the modern social-cognitive theories of achievement motivation accept the power of situational and contextual factors, these are rarely explicitly examined in most empirical studies. Many of the studies assume that the relationships among the key variables are universal across cultures and that the meaning of motivation is also invariant across cultures. In his seminal paper on culture and motivation, Maehr (1974) emphasized the importance of (a) contextual conditions in eliciting achievement motivation and (b) cultural relativity of the achievement motivation concept. Since then, PI researchers have been guided by these two key principles as they attempted to understand achievement motivation in diverse cultural contexts.

Across these studies, PI theorists have found key cross-cultural similarities and differences. The three dimensions of meaning-facilitating conditions, sense of self, perceived goals, and facilitating conditions. These three components are assumed to be universally important for facilitating student investment in academic tasks. However, the contents of each of these three components of meaning may be different for students in diverse sociocultural contexts. PI theory can be construed as a skeleton frame upon which researchers can hang their more detailed picture for the different cultures that they study. A diagrammatic representation of how to visualize the findings that could accrue from the use of a PI perspective is presented in Figure 4.1.

At the top of the diagram is "personal investment." Maehr (1974) eschewed too much focus on inner drives, processes, psychic energies, and predilections and recommended that personal investment be operationalized as actual behavioral patterns that manifest motivation. He identified three possible candidates: change in direction (choice), persistence, and performance.

Underpinning personal investment are the three components of meaning: sense of self, perceived goals, and facilitating conditions. These three components are assumed to be universally important (etic) for facilitating student investment in academic tasks. However, the contents of each of these three components of meaning may be different for students in diverse sociocultural contexts (emic).

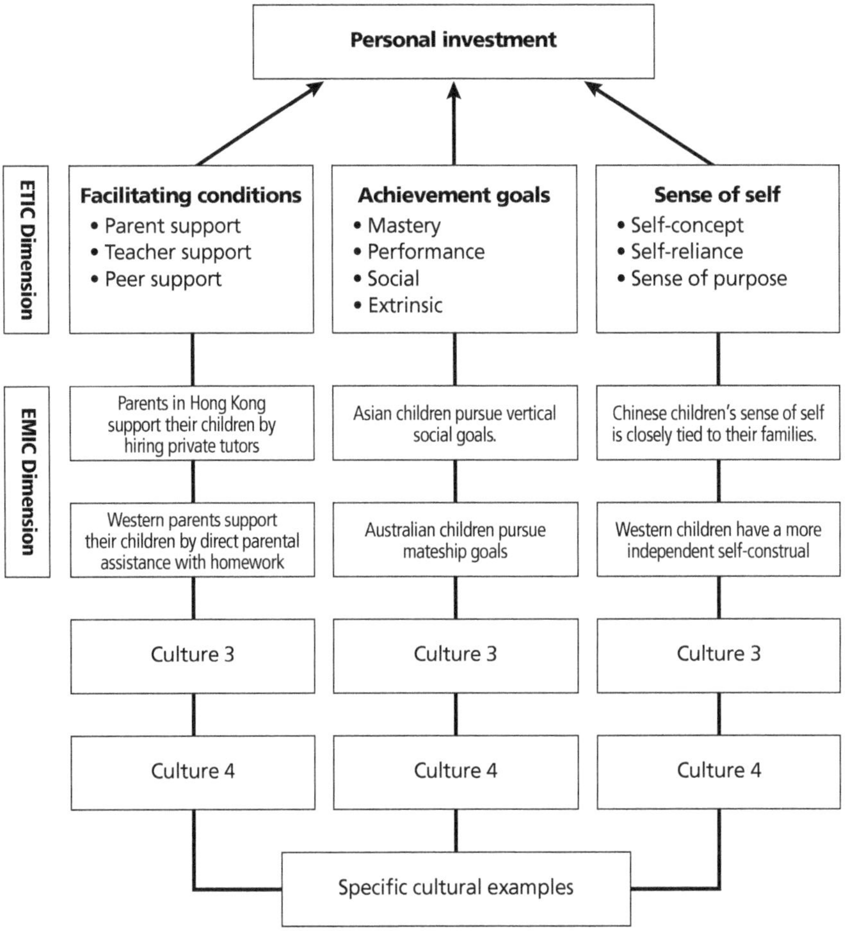

Figure 4.1 Personal investment theory as an integrative framework for etic and emic research. The etic dimension refers to cross-cultural universals and the emic dimension refers to the cultural particularities.

All individuals are embedded within cultural contexts, and they have a powerful role to play in shaping students' motivational processes. Cultures provide overarching goals and meanings for individuals embedded in them. One way that culture can influence motivation is by shaping students' attitudes towards the academic domain. For example, some cultures may put a relatively high value on academic success thus facilitating personal investment in academic endeavors. Other cultures, on the other hand, may foster relatively greater investment in other domains (sports, interpersonal relationships) rather than in the academic domain (Bernardo

& Ismail, 2010; Boehnke, 2008; Handel, Duan, Sutherland, & Ziegler, 2014; Oh et al., 2015).

Sociocultural contexts can also shape the content of the three dimensions of meaning posited in PI theory. What is salient under these three dimensions may be different for students in various cultural contexts. For example, under the facilitating conditions component, one could include filial piety and family obligation as sociocultural norms that could facilitate motivation for individuals in Chinese and other East Asian societies (Chen & Ho, 2012; Chen & Wong, 2014; Chow & Chu, 2007; Fuligni, 2001; Hui, Sun, Chow, & Chu; King & Ganotice, 2015). However, for Anglo-Americans and students in Western societies, filial piety and family obligation may not be salient motivators at least in the same way or to the same extent (Freeburg & Stein, 1996; Fuligni, Tseng, & Lam, 1999). Furthermore, in Confucian societies, there is the pervasive belief that effort is a part of the students' obligation, perhaps more strongly than in Western societies, and this belief could also have key implications for student learning (Chen, Fwu, Wei, & Wang, 2016; Fwu, Chen, Wei, & Wang, 2017; Fwu, Wang, Chen, & Wei, 2017; Li, 2002).

Under perceived goals of behavior, one could include mastery goals as a cross-culturally universal motivating factor. On the other hand, social goals, which pertain to striving to do well in order to fulfill social needs, may be more salient motivators in collectivist as opposed to individualistic contexts (King et al., 2017; King, McInerney, & Watkins, 2012, 2013). Another type of goal which may exhibit cross-cultural differences would be vertical goals. Vertical goals pertain to the goal of studying in order to please authority figures (Chen, Wang, Wei, Fwu, & Hwang, 2009). This goal may be a more effective motivator in Chinese settings than in Western contexts. Indeed, the impact of trying to please authority figures may backfire in Western contexts and lead to negative outcomes. Leondari and Gonida (2007) found that trying to please authority figures led to self-handicapping behaviors probably because such a goal was felt as externally imposed rather than autonomously endorsed.

In the context of the above, PI theory has helped generate key insights on the cross-cultural aspects of achievement motivation. Personal investment researchers have pioneered research among populations that are usually neglected in mainstream psychological research including Native American and Aboriginal Australian populations (Brickman, McInerney, & Martin, 2009; Magson et al., 2014; McInerney, 1995, 2012; McInerney & McInerney, 1996; McInerney & Swisher, 1995) alongside studies in Western populations (Korpershoek, Xu, Mok, McInerney, & Van der Werf, 2015; McInerney & Ali, 2006). They have also conducted work in East Asia (Mainland China, Hong Kong, Japan), Southeast Asia (Papua New Guinea, the Philippines, Singapore), Middle East (Qatar, Lebanon) Africa (South Africa), and Australia (Ganotice, Bernardo, & King, 2012, 2013; King, McInerney, & Watkins, 2012,

2013; Lee, McInerney, Liem, & Ortiga, 2010; McInerney, 2006, 2008; McInerney & Ali, 2006; McInerney, Hinkley, Dowson, & Van Etten, 1998; McInerney, Roche, McInerney, & Marsh, 1997; Nelson, O'Mara, McInerney, & Dowson, 2006; Suliman & McInerney, 2006; Watkins, McInerney, Akande, & Lee, 2003; Watkins, McInerney, & Boholst, 2003; Watkins, McInerney, & Lee, 2002).

While the results of these studies are too numerous to elaborate in detail, we focus on one of the key studies which highlighted the importance of looking at both etic (culturally universal) and emic (culturally specific) aspects of motivation. King, McInerney, and Nasser (2017) examined academic motivation across nine cultural groups (Anglo-Australian, Indigenous Australian, Hong Kong, Singapore, Philippines, Vietnam, Qatar, Lebanon, and Navajo). They used the three components of PI theory—sense of self, perceived goals, and facilitating conditions—to predict learning-related outcomes. They found that these three components predicted significant amounts of variance on the outcome variables but within each of these three components of meaning, differential patterns emerged. For example, mastery-oriented goals positively predicted engagement across all the nine cultural groups. However, social-oriented goals only positively predicted engagement in the collectivist cultures (e.g., Hong Kong, Singapore, Philippines) but not among the more individualistic Anglo-Australian students. Performance-oriented goals were positive predictors of engagement in Hong Kong which has one of the most competitive educational systems in the world but not among Anglo-Australians. The authors attributed these differential patterns of prediction to key cultural factors.

Figure 4.1 offers a useful heuristic for understanding the complex tapestry of factors that could lead to personal investment in different cultures. It highlights the importance of attending to both cross-cultural similarities and differences. Although students across diverse cultures are assumed to be influenced by facilitating conditions, perceived goals, and sense of self, the particular contents and specific manifestations of these dimensions may be different for students in different contexts. As further research is conducted using PI, more examples are found to populate the boxes in Figure 4.1 indicating universal as well as culture-specific components, thus providing a rich tapestry of similarities and differences across cultures.

THE FUTURE OF PERSONAL INVESTMENT THEORY

Personal investment theory has been in existence for three decades starting with the seminal publication of Maehr and Braskamp (1986). PI theory has been generative, helping researchers gain new insights and blaze new trails in understanding achievement motivation. However, as we enter the third decade of PI theory's existence, there is a need to reexamine how current developments in the mainstream motivational literature and cross-cultural psychology can provide new insights that can help upgrade PI theory's theoretical toolkit.

Incorporate the Approach-Avoidance Dimensions of Motivation

Motivational theorists have increasingly recognized that achievement motivation can be either approach-oriented (pursuing some desired end) or avoidance-oriented (avoiding an undesired end; Elliot, 2006; Elliot & Thrash, 2002). Achievement goal theorists have profitably applied the approach avoidance distinction to achievement goal research bifurcating both mastery and performance goals into their approach avoidance components. They found that approach and avoidance goals have very different effects on key learning outcomes (Elliot, 2006).

PI researchers can examine whether the incorporation of the approach-avoidance distinction would enrich their theorizing. While it is more straightforward to apply the distinction to mastery and performance goals (as these are the same goals that achievement goal theorists have investigated), extending the approach-avoidance distinction to social and extrinsic goals may be more challenging simply because of the lack of existing research.

Although we know of no existing study that examined approach-avoidance social goals from a PI perspective, researchers in cognate areas have found that avoidant types of social goals (e.g., wanting to hide one's social incompetence from others or wanting to avoid disapproval from authority figures) may have distinct effects from approach-oriented social goals (Ryan & Shim, 2006; Rudolph, Abaied, Flynn, Sugimura, & Agoston, 2011). For example, researchers have found that avoidance goals are more common in collectivist cultures and are not as maladaptive as they are in independent cultures (Elliot, Chirkov, & Kim, 2001).

Examine Both Domain-General and Domain-Specific Aspects of Personal Investment

PI researchers have mostly investigated motivation from a domain-general perspective. Not much research has been conducted on domain-specific motivational outcomes although there are some exceptions (e.g, Barnes, McInerney, & Marsh, 2005; Da Silva & McInerney, 2008; Da Silva, McInerney, McInerney, & Dowson, 2006; King & McInerney, 2014; Liem, McInerney, & Yeung, 2015). There is a need to examine potential cross-cultural differences in investment in different subjects. For example, students may be encouraged to invest themselves more in science and math in Culture A, while in Culture B students might be more encouraged to invest themselves in languages and arts.

Cultures clearly differ in the types of subjects they emphasize. For example, in the United Kingdom only .009% of the student population acquire degrees related to math and science. In India, the figure is much higher at .05%. There are also differences in terms of the number of hours spent studying math per year. In the Netherlands and Czech Republic, 84 to 90 hours per year are spent on math. The figure is much higher in Japan at 116 hours per year and in Hong Kong at 105 hours per year (Organization for Economic Cooperation and Development [OECD], 2014). These differential investments could be partly rooted in culture. PI researchers could extend their models to examine differences in the ways students invest themselves in diverse academic subjects.

Expand the Range of Cultures Examined

Although PI researchers have been pioneers in exploring cross-cultural issues, they have mostly operationalized culture in terms of nation or ethnicity. This phenomenon is common among most cross-cultural research in psychology and other intellectual disciplines. Cohen (2009) argued that there is a need to expand the range of cultures examined beyond the nation state or ethnicity. He wrote,

> Along with ethnicity or nationality, religion, region, and social class probably account for an especially large amount of variation in transmitted norms, values, beliefs, behaviors, and the like. These are important cultural influences. By studying these as cultures, psychologists can understand these domains better, as well as culture more broadly. (p. 195)

Recent work has shown that people from different socioeconomic classes have different values (Stephens, Markus, & Phillips, 2013). For the middle class, independent values are more important while those from lower social class backgrounds, interdependent values may be more emphasized. Research has found that first-generation students (who usually come from more disadvantaged socioeconomic backgrounds) feel alienated from the independent cultural values espoused by universities (Stephens, Townsend, Markus, & Phillips, 2012). When interdependent norms are highlighted, students from more disadvantaged economic backgrounds do better in school (Stephens, Fryberg, Markus, Johnson, & Covarrubias, 2012). Students from disadvantaged backgrounds also do better when they are made to feel that studying in college is part of who they are and not discordant with their sense of self (Stephens, Brannon, Markus, & Nelson, 2015).

Using a PI framework, Bernardo, Ganotice, and King (2015) examined how Filipino students from more disadvantaged socioeconomic backgrounds (operationalized as those who study in public high schools) compared with their middle-class peers (operationalized as those in private high schools) in terms of the three components of meaning in PI theory. They found that middle-class students had more positive facilitating conditions (parent support, teacher support, positive peer influence), more adaptive sense of self (sense of purpose, self-reliance, positive self-concept), and higher levels of goal striving (mastery goals, performance goals, social goals, and extrinsic goals) compared to those from more disadvantaged backgrounds.

PI researchers have conducted early work on how religion (McInerney, Davidson, Suliman, & Tremayne, 2006; McInerney, Dowson, & Yeung, 2005) and regional differences such as those between urban and rural areas (McInerney, 1988, 1991) could influence students' motivational outcomes. Much more needs to be done to flesh out how religious, socioeconomic, and regional differences are associated with students' investment in school.

Measure the Cultural Ingredient Responsible for Observed Cross-Cultural Differences

Early work in cross-cultural psychology has usually focused on making comparisons across two or three cultures. For example, researchers might compare the self-concept of Chinese and Americans. When they find that the self-concept of Americans is more trait-based while those of the Chinese is more role-based, they may attribute this to differences in individualism-collectivism. However, individualism-collectivism is often not measured explicitly but is assumed to be responsible for cross-cultural differences in self-concept. Although this type of research has greatly expanded our understanding of cross-cultural similarities and differences, more recent work has emphasized the need to measure the relevant cultural ingredient hypothesized to cause these cross-cultural differences.

Matsumoto and Yoo (2006) recommended the "unpackaging culture" approach which involves examining whether cultural differences in the target variable are mediated by other cultural-level variations (or cultural mediators). This approach involves regressing the target variable on culture (a dummy variable) and then on cultural mediators in a hierarchical regression analysis. Cultural differences can be verified by the significance of the coefficient in the first step of the hierarchical regression model. The role of the cultural model is assessed in the second step of the model. If the cultural mediators also have significant effects on the target variable and if the regression coefficient for culture becomes smaller compared to that in the first step, then it can be concluded that the cultural mediator accounts for the supposed cultural difference. This signifies "unpackaging" the effects of culture by identifying the specific cultural mediators hypothesized to account for this difference.

A good example of this approach was the study conducted by Bernardo and Ismail (2010). They wanted to understand why Malaysian and Filipino students differed in terms of the achievement goals they pursued: Malaysian students endorsed performance-approach goals more strongly compared to Filipino students, while Filipino students endorsed mastery goals more strongly. The researchers used the unpackaging approach and found that goal endorsement was linked to how students in different cultures perceived students with either mastery or performance-oriented profiles. In Malaysia, performance-oriented students were more well-liked and thought to have positive qualities. Students generally want to be friends with performance-oriented students. The opposite was found in the Philippines where it was mastery-oriented students who were perceived to be more likeable. The researchers were able to link achievement goal orientations with the contextual factors that may account for cross-national differences in espousing mastery and performance goals in Malaysia and Philippines.

Aside from unpackaging studies, another way to understand cross-cultural differences is to examine whether cultural variables moderate the relationships among theoretically-related constructs. Doing so allows researchers to have a more nuanced understanding of cross-cultural differences. Instead of just asserting that Culture A has more of variable X than Culture B (e.g., Chinese are more social goal-oriented compared to Americans), one can then say how certain cultural variables moderate the relationships among interrelated variables.

A good example of this approach was the study conducted by Cheng and Lam (2013). They wanted to understand under which circumstances social goals (which they defined as studying for the sake of authority figures) lead to maladaptive outcomes. They found that self-construal moderated the effects of social goals on avoidance behaviors and attitudes towards failure. For students with an independent self-construal, social goals led to higher levels of avoidance and lower willingness to improve after failure. The opposite was found for students with an interdependent self-construal.

In another study, King (2016) focused on the relationship of performance-avoidance goals with key learning outcomes. A meta-analytic study of achievement goal theory has found that performance-avoidance goals seem to be less harmful in Asian contexts as opposed to Western contexts, and this was attributed to differences in individualism-collectivism (Hulleman et al., 2010). However, none of the studies included in the meta-analysis actually included measures of individualism-collectivism. King (2016) measured individual-level collectivism (also called allocentrism) and found that collectivism moderated the effects of performance-avoidance goals on key learning outcomes. For individuals with higher levels of allocentrism, performance-avoidance goals were actually associated with higher levels of cognitive and meta-cognitive learning strategies.

Conduct More Qualitative Explorations

PI research and mainstream motivational research has thus far been dominated by quantitative approaches. There needs to be more research on the use of qualitative approaches in order to more deeply examine cultural variations in PI (e.g., McInerney & Liem, 2008; McInerney & McInerney, 2000; Nelson, McInerney, & Craven, 2005).

These initial qualitative explorations can also be followed by large-scale quantitative studies thereby complementing both etic and emic research approaches. An example of this approach was pioneered by Dowson and McInerney (2001, 2003). They criticized achievement goal theory's overemphasis on mastery and performance goals and conducted a qualitative study of students' motivational goals. They found other types of goals including social affiliation, social approval, social concern, social responsibility, social status, and work avoidance goals that students pursued. Sometimes, these goals loomed larger than mastery and performance goals. They then developed questionnaires to measure these goals and examined how these goals are associated with learning outcomes across different cultures (Dowson & McInerney, 2004; King & Watkins, 2011, 2012). This presents a good example of how qualitative research can enrich motivational theorizing.

CONCLUSION

In their review of PI research, Maehr and McInerney (2004) posed the question of whether the complex perspective offered by PI theory is justified. Compared to other mainstream theories of achievement motivation which usually focus on only one or two key variables, PI theory's focus on a wider range of variables may seem overly complex. When conducting research within the confines of a single culture (i.e., North American contexts), parsimonious theories may be adequate. However, when one starts encountering cultural "others," paradoxes that could not be explained easily by simple and elegant models start to emerge (see King & McInerney, 2014 for a documentation of these paradoxes). A more complex perspective—such as the one provided by PI theory—that takes into account a wider range of variables is needed to understand such phenomena.

REFERENCES

Atkinson, J. W., & Feather, N. T. (Eds.). (1966). *A theory of achievement motivation* (Vol. 66). New York, NY: Wiley.

Barnes, G., McInerney, D. M., & Marsh, H. W. (2005). Exploring sex difference in science enrolment intentions: An application of the general model of academic choice. *The Australian Educational Researcher, 32*, 1–23.

Bernardo, A. B. I., Ganotice, F. A., & King, R. B. (2015). Motivation gap and achievement gap between public and private high schools in the Philippines. *The Asia-Pacific Education Researcher, 24*, 657–667.

Bernardo, A. B. I., & Ismail, R. (2010). Social perceptions of achieving students and achievement goals of students in Malaysia and the Philippines. *Social Psychology of Education, 13*, 385–407.

Boehnke, K. (2008). Peer pressure: A cause of scholastic underachievement? A cross-cultural study of mathematical achievement among German, Canadian, and Israeli middle school students. *Social Psychology of Education, 11*, 149–160.

Brickman, S., McInerney, D. M., & Martin, A. J. (2009). Examining the valuing of schooling as a motivational indicator of American Indian students: Perspectives based on a model of future oriented motivation and self-regulation. *Journal of American Indian Education, 48*, 33–54.

Chen, S.-W., Fwu, B.-J., Wei, C.-F., & Wang, H.-H. (2016). High school teachers' beliefs about effort and their attitudes toward struggling and smart students in a Confucian society. *Frontiers in Psychology, 7*, 1366.

Chen, S. W., Wang, H. H., Wei, C. F., Fwu, B. J., & Hwang, K. K. (2009). Taiwanese students' self-attributions for two types of achievement goals. *The Journal of Social Psychology, 149*(2), 179–194.

Chen, W.-W., & Wong, Y.-L. (2014), What my parents make me believe in learning: The role of filial piety in Hong Kong students' motivation and academic achievement. *International Journal of Psychology, 49*, 249–256.

Chen, W.-W., & Ho, H.-Z. (2012), The relation between perceived parental involvement and academic achievement: The roles of Taiwanese students' academic beliefs and filial piety. *International Journal of Psychology, 47*, 315–324.

Cheng, R. W.-Y., & Lam, S.-F. (2013). The interaction between social goals and self-construal on achievement motivation. *Contemporary Educational Psychology, 38*, 136–148.

Chow, S.-Y., & Chu, M. H.-T. (2007). The impact of filial piety and parental involvement on academic achievement motivation in Chinese secondary school students. *Asian Journal of Counselling, 14*, 91–124.

Cohen, A. B. (2009). Many forms of culture. *American Psychologist, 64*, 194–204.

Da Silva, D., & McInerney, D. M. (2008). Motivational and self-goals of female students in contemporary Japan. In O. S. Tan, D. M. McInerney, A. D. Liem, & A-G. Tan (Eds.), *What the West can learn from the East: Asian perspectives on the psychology of learning and motivation—Research on multicultural education and international perspectives* (Vol. 7, pp. 191–216). Charlotte, NC.: Information Age.

Da Silva, D., McInerney, D. M., McInerney, V., & Dowson, M. (2006, July). *A multiple goal analysis of female Japanese university students' motivation.* Paper presented at the 4th Biennial SELF Conference, Ann Arbor, Michigan.

Dowson, M., & McInerney, D. M. (2001). Psychological parameters of students' social and work avoidance goals: A qualitative investigation. *Journal of Educational Psychology, 93,* 35–42.

Dowson, M., & McInerney, D. M. (2003). What do students say about their motivational goals? Towards a more complex and dynamic perspective on student motivation. *Contemporary Educational Psychology, 28,* 91–113.

Dowson, M., & McInerney, D. M. (2004). The development and validation of the Goal Orientation and Learning Strategies Survey (GOALS-S). *Educational and Psychological Measurement, 64,* 290–310.

Elliot, A. J. (2006). The hierarchical model of approach-avoidance motivation. *Motivation and Emotion,* 30, 111–116.

Elliot, A. J., Chirkov, V. I., Kim, Y., & Sheldon, K. M. (2001). A cross-cultural analysis of avoidance (relative to approach) personal goals. *Psychological Science, 12,* 505–510.

Elliot, A. J., & Thrash, T. M. (2002). Approach-avoidance motivation in personality: Approach and avoidance temperaments and goals. *Journal of Personality and Social Psychology,* 82, 804–818.

Freeburg, A. L., & Stein, C. H. (1996). Felt obligation towards parents in Mexican-American and Anglo-American young adults. *Journal of Social and Personal Relationships, 13,* 457–471.

Fuligni, A. J. (2001). Family obligation and the academic motivation of adolescents from Asian, Latin American, and European backgrounds. *New Directions for Child and Adolescent Development, 94,* 61–76.

Fuligni, A. J., Tseng, V., & Lam, M. (1999). Attitudes toward family obligations among American adolescents with Asian, Latin American, and European backgrounds. *Child Development, 70,* 1030–1044.

Fwu, B.-J., Chen, S.-W., Wei, C.-F., & Wang, H.-H. (2017). The mediating role of self-exertion on the effects of effort on learning virtues and emotional distress in academic failure in a Confucian context. *Frontiers in Psychology, 7,* 2047.

Fwu, B.-J., Wang, H.-H., Chen, S.-W., & Wei, C.-F. (2017). Feeling bad or being bad? The trapping effect of effort in academic failure in a Confucian cultural context. *Educational Psychology, 37,* 506–519.

Ganotice, F. A., Bernardo, A. B. I., & King, R. B. (2012). Testing the factorial invariance of the English and Filipino version of the inventory of school motivation with bilingual students in the Philippines. *Journal of Psychoeducational Assessment, 30,* 298–303.

Ganotice, F. A., Bernardo, A. B. I., & King, R. B. (2013). Adapting the facilitating conditions questionnaire (FCQ) for bilingual Filipino adolescents: Validating the English and Filipino versions. *Child Indicators Research, 6,* 237–256.

Handel, M., Duan, X., Sutherland, M., & Ziegler, A. (2014). Successful in science education and still popular: A pattern that is possible in China rather than in Germany or Russia. *International Journal of Science Education, 36,* 887–907.

Hui, E. K.-P., Sun, R. C.-F., Chow, S. S.-Y., & Chu, M. H.-T. (2011). Explaining Chinese students' academic motivation: Filial piety and self-determination. *Educational Psychology, 31,* 377–392.

Hulleman, C. S., Schrager, S. M., Bodmann, S. W., & Harackiewicz, J. M. (2010). A meta-analytic review of achievement goal measures: Different labels for the same constructs or different constructs with similar labels? *Psychological Bulletin, 136*, 422–449.

King, R. B. (2016). Is a performance-avoidance achievement goal always maladaptive? Not necessarily for collectivists. *Personality and Individual Differences, 99*, 190–195.

King, R. B., & Ganotice, F. A. (2015). Does family obligation matter for your motivation, engagement, and well-being? It depends on your self-construal. *Personality and Individual Differences, 86*, 243–248

King, R. B., Ganotice, F. A., & McInerney, D. M. (2012). Cross-cultural validation of the Sense of Self (SoS) Scale in Chinese and Filipino settings. *Child Indicators Research, 5*, 719–734.

King, R. B., & McInerney, D. M. (2014). Mapping changes in students' English and math self-concepts: A latent growth model study *Educational Psychology: An International Journal of Experimental Educational Psychology, 34*, 581–597.

King, R. B., McInerney, D. M., & Nasser, R. (2017). Different goals for different folks: A cross-cultural study of achievement goals across nine cultures. *Social Psychology of Education, 20*, 619–642.

King, R. B., McInerney, D. M., & Watkins, D. A. (2013). Examining the role of social goals in school: A study in two collectivist cultures. *European Journal of Psychology of Education, 28*, 1505–1523.

King, R. B., & Watkins, D. A. (2011). The reliability and validity of the Goal Orientation and Learning Strategies Survey (GOALS-S): A Filipino investigation. *The Asia Pacific Education Researcher, 20*, 579–594.

King, R. B., & Watkins, D. A. (2012). Cross-cultural validation of the five-factor structure of social goals. *Journal of Psychoeducational Assessment, 30*, 181–193.

Kitayama, S. (2002). Culture and basic psychological processes—Toward a system view of culture: Comment on Oyserman et al. (2002). *Psychological Bulletin, 128*, 89–96.

Korpershoek, H., Xu, J. K., Mok, M. M. C., McInerney, M. D., & Van der Werf, M. P. C. (2015). Testing the multidimensionality of the Inventory of School Motivation in a Dutch student sample. *Journal of Applied Measurement, 16*, 41–59.

Lee, J. Q., McInerney, D. M., Liem, G. A. D., & Ortiga, Y. Y. (2010). The relationship between future goals and achievement goal orientations: An intrinsic-extrinsic motivation perspective. *Contemporary Educational Psychology, 35*, 264–279.

Leondari, A., & Gonida, E. (2007). Predicting academic self-handicapping in different age groups: The role of personal achievement goals and social goals. *British Journal of Educational Psychology, 77*, 595–611.

Li, J. (2002). A cultural model of learning. *Journal of Cross-Cultural Psychology, 33*, 248–269.

Liem, G. A. D., McInerney, D. M., & Yeung, A. S. (2015). Academic self-concepts in ability streams: Considering domain specificity and same-stream peers. *Journal of Experimental Education, 83*, 83–89.

Maehr, M. L. (1974). Culture and achievement motivation. *American Psychologist, 29*(12), 887–896.

Maehr, M. L., & Braskamp, L. A. (1986). *The motivation factor: A theory of personal investment.* Lexington, MA: Lexington.

Maehr, M. L., & Lysy, A. (1978). Motivating students of diverse sociocultural backgrounds to achieve. *International Journal of Intercultural Relations, 2,* 38–70.

Maehr, M. L., & McInerney, D. M. (2004). Motivation as personal investment. In D. M. McInerney & S. Van Etten (Eds.), *Big theories revisited* (pp. 61–90). Greenwich, CT: Information Age.

Magson, N. R., Craven, R. G., Nelson, G. F., Yeung, A. S., Bodkin-Andrews, G. H., & McInerney, D. M. (2014). Motivation matters: Profiling indigenous and non-indigenous students' motivational goals. *The Australian Journal of Indigenous Education, 43,* 96–112.

Matsumoto, D., & Yoo, S. H. (2006). Toward a new generation of cross-cultural research. *Perspectives in Psychological Science, 1,* 234–250.

McClelland, D. C. (1961). *The achievement society.* Princeton, NJ: Von Nostrand.

McInerney, D. M. (1988). *The psychological determinants of motivation of urban and rural non-traditional Aboriginal students in school settings: A cross-cultural study.* (Unpublished doctoral dissertation). Sydney University, Sydney, Australia.

McInerney, D. M. (1991). Key determinants of motivation of urban and rural non-traditional Aboriginal students in school settings: Recommendations for educational change. *Australian Journal of Education, 35,* 154–174.

McInerney, D. M. (1995). Achievement motivation research and indigenous minorities: Can research be psychometric? *Cross-Cultural Research, 29,* 211–239.

McInerney, D. M. (2006). The motivational profiles and perceptions of schooling of Asian students in Australia. *Malaysian Journal of Learning and Instruction, 3,* 1–31.

McInerney, D. M. (2008). Personal investment, culture and learning: Insights into school achievement across Anglo, Aboriginal, Asian and Lebanese students in Australia. *International Journal of Psychology, 43,* 870–879.

McInerney, D. M. (2012). Conceptual and methodological challenges in multiple goal research among very remote Indigenous Australian students. *Applied Psychology: An International Review, 61*(4), 634–668.

McInerney, D. M., & Ali, J. (2006). Multidimensional and hierarchical assessment of school motivation: Cross-cultural validation. *Educational Psychology: An International Journal of Experimental Educational Psychology, 26,* 717–734.

McInerney, D. M., Davidson, N., Suliman, R., & Tremayne, B. (2000). Personal development, health and physical education in context: Muslim and catholic perspectives. *Australian Journal of Education, 44,* 26–42.

McInerney, D. M., Dowson, M., & Yeung, A. S. (2005). Inside culture and curriculum. Religious and sex differences among Arabic students' perceptions of personal development, health, and physical education. In D. M. McInerney & S. Van Etten (Eds.), *Focus on curriculum—Research on sociocultural influences on learning and motivation series* (Vol. 5, pp. 199–221). Greenwich, CT: Information Age.

McInerney, D. M., Hinkley, J., Dowson, M., & Van Etten, S. (1998). Aboriginal, Anglo, and immigrant Australian students' motivational beliefs about personal academic success: Are there cultural differences? *Journal of Educational Psychology, 90,* 621–629.

McInerney, D. M., & McInerney, V. (1996). Goals and school motivation: Aboriginal and Navajo perspectives. *SET Research Information for Teachers, SET 1,* 1–4.

McInerney, D. M., & McInerney, V. (2000, April). *A longitudinal qualitative study of school motivation and achievement.* Paper presented at the annual meeting of the American Educational Research Association, New Orleans, LA.

McInerney, D. M., Roche, L., McInerney, V., & Marsh, H. W. (1997). Cultural perspectives on school motivation: The relevance and application of goal theory. *American Educational Research Journal 34*, 207–236.

McInerney, D. M., Yeung, A., & Dowson, M. (2005). Facilitating conditions for school motivation: Construct validity and applicability. *Educational and Psychological Measurement, 65*, 1046–1066.

McInerney, D. M., Yeung, S. Y., & McInerney, V. (2001). Cross-cultural validation of the inventory of school motivation (ISM). *Journal of Applied Measurement, 2*, 134–152.

Nelson, G., McInerney, D. M., & Craven, R. (2005, November). *Education in developing countries: A qualitative study of student achievement in Papua and New Guinea.* Paper presented at AARE-International Education Research Conference, Parramatta, Australia.

Nelson, G. F., O'Mara, A. J., McInerney, D. M., & Dowson, M. (2006). Motivation in cross-cultural settings: A Papua New Guinea Psychometric Study. *International Education Journal, 7*, 400–409.

OECD. (2014). *Education at a glance 2014: OECD indicators.* Paris, France: Author.

Oh, H., Sutherland, M., Stack, N., Martin, M. M. B., Blumen, S., Nguyen, Q. A.,... & Ziegler, A. (2015). A cross-cultural study of possible iatrogenic effects of gifted education programs: Tenth graders perceptions of academically high performing classmates. *High Ability Studies, 26,* 152–166.

Triandis, H. C. (2002). Subjective culture, Unit 2. *Online Readings in Psychology and Culture.* Retrieved from https://scholarworks.gvsu.edu/orpc/vol2/iss2/6/

Pekrun, R., Goetz, T., Titz, W., & Perry, R. P. (2002). Academic emotions in students' self-regulated learning and achievement: A program of qualitative and quantitative research. *Educational Psychologist, 37*, 91–105.

Rudolph, K. D., Abaied, J. L., Flynn, M., Sugimura, N., & Agoston, A. M. (2011). Developing relationships, being cool, and not looking like a loser: Social goal orientation predicts children's responses to peer aggression. *Child Development, 82,* 1518–1530.

Ryan, A. M., & Shim, S. S. (2006). Social achievement goals: The nature and consequences of different orientations toward social competence. *Personality and Social Psychology Bulletin, 32,* 1246–1263.

Seaton, M., Marsh, H. W., & Craven, R. G. (2009). Earning its place as a pan-human theory: Universality of the big-fish-little-pond effect across 41 culturally and economically diverse countries. *Journal of Educational Psychology, 101,* 403–419.

Stephens, N. M., Brannon, T. N., Markus, H. R., & Nelson, J. E. (2015). Feeling at home in college: Fortifying school-relevant selves to reduce social class disparities in higher education. *Social Issues and Policy Review, 9,* 1–24.

Stephens, N., Fryberg, S., Markus, H. R., Johnson, C., & Covarrubias, R. (2012). Unseen disadvantage: How American universities' focus on independence undermines the academic performance of first-generation college students. *Journal of Personality and Social Psychology, 102,* 1178–1197.

Stephens, N. M., Markus, H. R., & Phillips, L. T. (2014). Social class culture cycles: How three gateway contexts shape selves and fuel inequality. *Annual Review of Psychology, 65,* 611–634.

Stephens, N. M., Townsend, S. S., Markus, H. R., & Phillips, L. T. (2012). A cultural mismatch: Independent cultural norms produce greater increases in cortisol and more negative emotions among first-generation college students. *Journal of Experimental Social Psychology, 48,* 1389–1393.

Suliman, R., & McInerney, D. M (2006). Motivational goals and school achievement: Lebanese-background students in south western Sydney. *Australian Journal of Education, 50,* 242–264.

Watkins, D., Adair, J., Akande, A., Cheng, C., Fleming, J., Ismail, M., . . . & McInerney, D. M. (1998). Cultural dimensions, gender, and the nature of self-concept: A fourteen country study. *International Journal of Psychology, 33,* 17–31.

Watkins, D., McInerney, D. M., Akande, A., & Lee, C. (2003). An investigation of ethnic differences in the motivation strategies for learning of students in desegregated South African schools. *Journal of Cross-Cultural Psychology, 34,* 189–194.

Watkins, D., McInerney, D.M., & Boholst, F. (2003). The reliability and validity of the inventory of school motivation: A Filipino investigation. *The Asia-Pacific Education Researcher, 12,* 87–100.

Watkins, D., McInerney, D. M., & Lee, C. (2002). Assessing the school motivation of Hong Kong students. *Psychologia, 45,* 144–154.

Weber, M. (2002). *The Protestant ethic and the spirit of capitalism, 3rd revision.* Los Angeles, CA: Roxbury.

Zusho, A., & Clayton, R. (2011). Culturalizing achievement goal theory and research. *Educational Psychologist, 46,* 239–260.

SECTION II

HOW DO I THINK AND FEEL ABOUT MYSELF
AND MY STUDIES?

CHAPTER 5

EXPECTANCY-VALUE THEORY IN CROSS-CULTURAL PERSPECTIVE

What Have We Learned in the Last 15 Years?

Stephen M. Tonks
Allan Wigfield
Jacquelynne S. Eccles

We introduced Jason in the 2004 version of this chapter, as a way to introduce the major constructs from expectancy-value theory (EVT) on which we focused in that chapter, and in the current one. Jason is a student starting 12th grade, his last year of high school, which means he had to decide which elective classes to take during his senior year. Ultimately, he made his decisions based on how well he expected to do in the classes available to him, his sense of the usefulness of the classes for his future endeavors, and his interest in the classes. He chose a history course because of an interest he developed in a previous engaging history class. And he chose an advanced math course because it would be useful to him in his chosen field

Big Theories Revisited 2, pages 91–115
Copyright © 2018 by Information Age Publishing
All rights of reproduction in any form reserved.

of engineering, would strengthen his university applications, and would help him be ready for the engineering curriculum in college. Jason also expected to do well in these two courses based on his previous performance. In addition, Jason weighed the costs of taking these two advanced academic courses in his final year as opposed to less challenging courses offered at his high school. Taking these courses would mean that Jason could not work as many hours at a part-time job, thus giving up income. He also would have to do more studying, meaning less time for socializing and participating in some fun extracurricular activities. In the end, Jason decided (after talking it over with his parents) that the costs did not outweigh his interest and the utility he saw in the history and math courses.

Jason's decision-making process shows how individuals' expectancies and values influence their choices of activities, in this case elective coursework during high school. This example captures some of the important constructs and principles of EVT. At the broadest level, EVT attempts to account for individuals' choices of and performance on activities they do. We focus in this chapter primarily on the contemporary expectancy-value model developed by Eccles, Wigfield, and their colleagues (Eccles, 1993, 2005, 2009; Eccles-Parsons et al., 1983; Wigfield & Eccles, 1992, 2000, 2002), and particularly focus on three constructs from the model that have received the most research attention: *beliefs about ability, expectancies for success,* and *achievement task values.* After reviewing research done over the last 15 years in Western cultures on the development of individuals' ability beliefs, expectancies and values, we discuss intervention work done during that time span focusing on how to increase students' valuing of different academic subjects, especially STEM subjects. We then turn to a discussion of cultural influences on expectancies and values, different research approaches used in cross-cultural research on these constructs, and findings from studies done in different countries and cultures since the first edition of this book was published.

EXPECTANCY-VALUE THEORY

Expectancy-value theory has a long history in the achievement motivation field (see Weiner, 1992; Wigfield & Eccles, 1992 for historical overviews). The expectancy and value constructs themselves initially were defined by theorists such as Lewin (1938) and Tolman (1932). John Atkinson (1957, 1964) developed the first formal expectancy-value model in an attempt to explain different kinds of achievement related behaviors, such as striving for success, choice among achievement tasks, and persistence. He postulated that resultant achievement motivation is a mathematical function of individuals' motives to approach success and avoid failure, expectancies (or probabilities) for success and failure, and incentive values for succeeding or avoiding failure. Atkinson defined expectancies for success as individuals' subjective understanding of the ratio of their previous successes to the number of times they attempted the task. He defined incentive value as the relative attractiveness of succeeding on a given achievement task; mathematically, he assumed that it equals one minus one's expectancy for success. Thus, for Atkinson, individuals' incentive values relate inversely to their expectancies for success. He and his colleagues did an extensive body of research on individuals' achievement strivings under different probabilities for success (see Atkinson, 1964; Wigfield & Eccles, 1992, for further discussion).

Modern Expectancy-Value Theories

Modern expectancy-value theories (e.g., Eccles, 1987, 1993; Eccles-Parsons et al., 1983; Feather, 1982, 1988; Wigfield, 1994; Wigfield & Eccles, 1992, 2000, 2002) and related theories such as Pekrun's (2006) control-value theory are based in Atkinson's (1957, 1964) work in that they link achievement or performance, persistence, and choice most directly to individuals' expectancy-related and task value beliefs. However, they differ from Atkinson's theory in several ways, as described next.

Eccles and Colleagues' Expectancy-Value Model
Eccles and her colleagues developed and tested an expectancy-value model of achievement-related performance and choices (e.g., Eccles, 1993; Eccles-Parsons et al., 1983; Eccles & Wigfield, 1995; Meece, Wigfield, & Eccles, 1990; Wigfield, 1994; Wigfield & Eccles, 1992, 2000, 2002). They elaborated the definitions of each construct proposed by Atkinson (1957, 1964), and also studied a variety of socialization and cultural influences on the development of each. Eccles and her colleagues have focused on how individuals' expectancies and values, and the variables influencing them, influence their choices of achievement activities, persistence on them, and performance. They initially developed the model to help explain gender differences in mathematics-related beliefs and choices of mathematics-related courses and majors. They broadened the model to other activity areas, most notably sport and physical skill activities (e.g., Eccles & Harold, 1991).

Figure 5.1 depicts a recent version of this model. We first see on the far right of the model that individuals' expectancies and values directly influence their performance and task choice. Expectancies and values themselves are influenced by individuals' task-specific beliefs such as perceptions of ability, perceptions of the difficulty of different tasks, and individuals' goals and self-schema, along with their affective memories for different

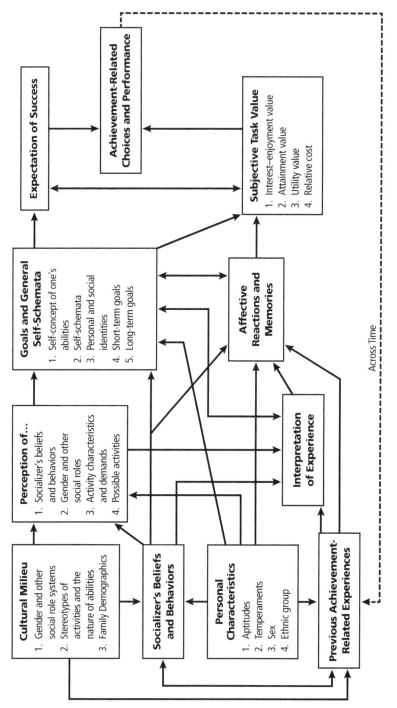

Figure 5.1   Eccles expectancy value model of achievement choices.

achievement-related events. These beliefs, goals, and affective memories are influenced by individuals' perceptions of other peoples' attitudes and expectations for them, and by their own interpretations of their previous achievement outcomes. Children's perceptions and interpretations are influenced by a broad array of social and cultural factors. These include socializers' (especially parents and teachers) beliefs and behaviors, their specific achievement experiences and aptitudes, and the cultural milieu in which they live.

Eccles and her colleagues' research provides support for many of the postulates of the model. To summarize briefly the major findings, they found that individuals' expectancies for success and valuing of different academic subjects predict their performance in these subjects and their choices of whether to continue taking them. Children's expectancies for success and valuing of achievement are influenced by their previous performance and their beliefs about their ability. Parents' and teachers' beliefs about students predict students' own expectancies and values. Variations in classroom environments influence children's expectancies and values in positive and negative ways. Finally, there are gender differences in children's beliefs and values about different activities that tend to conform to gender stereotypes about the activities, although these gender differences have lessened over time, especially in math (see Eccles, 1993; Eccles-Parsons et al., 1983; Eccles, Wigfield, & Schiefele, 1998; Wigfield & Eccles, 1992, 2000; Wigfield et al., 2015; Wigfield, Tonks, & Klauda, 2016, for review).

Because Eccles-Parsons and colleagues (1983) originally designed their model to explain a sociocultural phenomenon, we believe it is particularly well suited for a cultural analysis of motivation and activity choices. We expect that cultural differences in a wide array of activity and behavioral choices, particularly in the achievement domain, reflect cultural differences in success expectations and subjective task value-related beliefs. These differences themselves likely result from cultural differences in the wide range of social experiences that shape human development. The work Eccles, Wigfield, and colleagues have done on gender within the United States provides comprehensive examples of just how these cultural processes can work (see Eccles, 1993; Eccles-Parsons et al., 1983; Wigfield & Eccles, 2002, Wigfield et al., 2015, for reviews). This work shows that parents differentially socialize their sons and daughters' expectancies and values in different activity domains, resulting in children's expectancies, values, and activity choices indeed differing across gender.

Defining the Expectancy, Ability Belief, and Value Constructs

Eccles and colleagues defined expectancies for success as children's beliefs about how well they will do on an upcoming task (e.g., How well do you think you will do in math next year?). They distinguished conceptually expectancies for success from the individual's beliefs about ability. Ability beliefs refer to children's evaluations of their competence or ability, both in terms of their assessments of their own ability and also how they think they compare to other students. To return to our vignette, Jason's beliefs about his ability in different subjects come from many years' experience with them and reflect his assessment of his current skills in these subjects. His expectancies refer to how he thinks he will do in the future in the next level of these subjects, and he bases his expectancies primarily on his beliefs about his ability in a given subject area. Although conceptually distinct, these two constructs relate to each other strongly and positively (e.g., Eccles & Wigfield, 1995; Eccles, Wigfield, Harold, & Blumenfeld, 1993).

Turning to children's valuing of different activities, Eccles-Parsons et al. (1983) proposed that there are four main influences on individuals' overall valuing of a given activity: attainment value or importance, intrinsic value, utility value or usefulness of the task, and the cost of doing the task (see Eccles-Parsons et al., 1983; Wigfield & Eccles, 1992; Wigfield, Rosenzweig, & Eccles, 2017, for detailed discussion). Building on Battle's (1965, 1966) work on attainment value, Eccles-Parsons et al. defined attainment value as the importance of doing well on a given task. Attainment value incorporates identity issues; tasks are important when individuals view them as central to their own sense of themselves, or allow them to express or confirm important aspects of self (see also Eccles, 2005, 2009).

Intrinsic value is the enjoyment one gains from doing the task. This component is similar in certain respects to notions of intrinsic motivation and interest (see Renninger, 2000; Ryan & Deci, 2016; Schiefele, 2009), but it is important to acknowledge that these constructs come from different theoretical traditions. When children intrinsically value an activity they often become deeply engaged in it and can persist at it for a long time.

Utility value or usefulness refers to how a task fits into an individual's future plans, for instance, taking a math class to fulfill a requirement for a science degree. In certain respects, utility value is similar to extrinsic motivation, because when doing an activity out of utility value the activity is a means to an end rather than an end in itself (see Ryan & Deci, 2016). However, the activity also could tie to some important goals that the person holds deeply, such as attaining a certain occupation. In this sense, utility value also ties to personal goals and sense of self.

With respect to the relations of expectancies and values, as noted earlier, Atkinson (1957, 1964) posited that individuals' expectancies and values are inversely related. The implication of his proposal is that individuals value most tasks on which it is difficult for them to succeed. By contrast, in their research done in classroom and other achievement settings, Eccles and colleagues have found that students' expectancies, attainment value, intrinsic value, and utility value all relate positively (e.g., Eccles & Wigfield, 1995;

Eccles et al., 1993; Jacobs, Lanza, Osgood, Eccles, & Wigfield, 2002; Wigfield et al., 1997). That is, students value tasks at which they believe they can succeed.

Another influence on an individual's overall task value is the perceived cost of an activity, which Eccles-Parsons et al. (1983) defined as what the individual has to give up to do a task (e.g., Do I do my math homework or call my friend?), as well as the anticipated effort one will need to put into task completion. Is working this hard to get an A in math worth it? Eccles-Parsons et al. emphasized that cost is especially important to choice. Choices are influenced by both negative and positive task characteristics and all choices are assumed to have costs associated with them because one choice often eliminates other options. If Jason, from the above scenario, follows his inclinations and chooses to pursue an engineering major once he enters college, then he will not be able to pursue other possible majors.

Since the writing of this chapter for the first edition, there has been a great deal of work on the cost aspect of the model, with the work being done in the United States and Germany primarily. Notably, researchers have proposed and developed measures of different kinds of costs that can impact choice: opportunity cost (how doing one thing means that other things can't be done), effort cost (is the amount of effort needed to succeed on the task worth it), and psychological cost, or whether engaging in the activity will cause too much stress (e.g., Gaspard, Häfner, Parrisius, Trautwein, & Nagengast, 2017). These and other costs (economic costs; social costs) all can influence individuals' overall valuing of an activity, and thus impact the choices they make (see Barron & Hulleman, 2015; Wigfield et al., 2017, for further discussions).

Jason's choices of which classes to take reflect these different aspects of value and influences on his valuing of different classes. He chose a math class primarily because of its potential usefulness to him, as he plans to be an engineer. By contrast, he chose the advanced history course primarily because he likes history, rather than because it is useful to him. Sometimes these choices can reflect more than one aspect of value; in fact, Jason enjoys math to a degree and so his choice of a math class reflects both interest and usefulness. In addition, he is not overly concerned with the "costs" of taking these courses. Thus, the influence of an individual's valuing of an activity on the choice to pursue it or not is a complex process.

Culture and the Expectancy-Value Model:
Some General Considerations

Like gender-role socialization, the processes associated with many different dimensions of cultural socialization influence the ways in which members of cultural groups see themselves as well as the goals and values they develop for their lives. More specifically, experiences in the different types of learning environments in different cultures around the world should strongly influence students' expectancies and values in different subject areas, and their choices of activities to pursue. Finally, cultures and countries vary greatly in the opportunities they provide for children to try different types of activities as well as in the range of activities made available and salient to various individuals living in the cultural group, and various groups of children, such as boys and girls. Each of these processes should lead to both cultural group differences and within culture individual differences in expectancies, ability beliefs, and subjective task values.

At an even more basic level, cultures differ in the extent to which individuals have "choice" over such achievement-related behaviors as educational focus, careers, and leisure activities. Western cultures pride themselves on allowing individuals to make these choices for themselves, even though children's activity choices still continue to be heavily socialized by parents and peers in these Western cultures (see Jacobs & Eccles, 2000). Other cultures place less emphasis on individual choice, particularly individual choice based on maximizing self-fulfillment and self-actualization. For example, in interviews with young professionals in China, Eccles (J. Eccles, personal communication, August 17, 2003) found that career choices were based much more on the needs of the community for particular types of skills than on the needs of the individual to find a job that maximized the fit of one's occupation with one's talents and interests. In most cases, an individual's occupation was determined for them by their community, or by the state. Similarly, in interviews with Japanese students, Eccles (J. Eccles, personal communication, August 17, 2003) found that choices about future occupations were based more on the quality of the company than on the fit of the particular job category with the individual's talents and interests. In this case, the individuals were given more power to select their future occupation; but the criteria for their choices were quite different from the criteria advocated in vocational counseling in the United States.

Does this mean that the expectancy value model is not a useful theoretical tool for such cultures? No—but it does mean that we need to consider the full complexity of the Eccles et al. model and include both its cultural as well as its psychological components in studies of these influences. We need to pay particular attention to the sociocultural forces that underlie individual differences in expectancies, ability beliefs and subjective task values, as well as the relative predictive power of each of these constructs for the various achievement-related choices available to the individuals. In the interviews with Chinese and Japanese individuals just discussed the subjective value of various occupation categories was based on more communal considerations than is typical amongst European-American adolescents. In addition, the relevance of ability beliefs for choice should be less critical in many Asian children and adolescents than it is for European-American children and adolescents. These hypotheses, however, have not been fully tested. We turn next to a discussion of the research on the development of children's expectancies and values in Western cultures, and then turn to cross-cultural research on this topic.

RESEARCH ON EXPECTANCIES AND VALUES
IN WESTERN CULTURE

In the previous version of this chapter we reviewed work on the development of children's ability beliefs, expectancies for success, and achievement values, their relations to performance and choice, and how children of different ages may understand these constructs differently (see also Eccles, 2005; Wigfield, 1994; Wigfield & Eccles, 1992; Wigfield et al., 2015; Wigfield et al., 2016). In this section we briefly revisit that work, and discuss findings from the work done on these issues over the last 15 years. We also discuss work on motivation interventions; such work has increased dramatically in the last decade.

Changes in the Mean Levels of Expectancies and Values

Generally, researchers have found that children's competence beliefs and expectancies for success for different tasks decline across the elementary school years and into the middle school years (see Eccles et al., 1998; Wigfield et al., 2015 for reviews). To illustrate, cross-sectional and longitudinal studies of children's competence beliefs in a variety of academic and non-academic done in the United States and Australia show that these beliefs decline (e.g., Eccles et al., 1993; Marsh, 1989; Wigfield et al., 1997). These declines, particularly for math, often continue into and through secondary school (Eccles-Parsons et al., 1983; Jacobs et al., 2002). Researchers looking at changes in the mean level of children's values generally show that children value certain academic tasks less as they get older (Eccles et al., 1998; Jacobs et al., 2002; Wigfield et al., 1997; Wigfield et al., 2015).

Over the last 15 years, various researchers have found somewhat different (and more complex) patterns in these changes (see Wigfield et al., 2015), but the negative trend still dominates most of the findings. For instance, Archambault, Eccles, and Vida (2010) found seven different trajectories of change in students' competence beliefs in reading. Although these trajectories generally indicated declines in children's reading competence beliefs, they were markedly different and some showed increases across the high school years. Students whose literacy competence beliefs declined most strongly included boys and lower-SES students.

The negative changes in children's expectancy-related beliefs and achievement values found in the United States have been explained in two ways. One explanation involves children's growing sophistication at understanding, interpreting, and integrating the evaluative feedback they receive. They also engage in more social comparison with their peers, particularly once they begin school. These processes help children to become more accurate or realistic in their self-assessments, leading some to become relatively more negative about their ability and also about how much they value different achievement activities (see Wigfield, Eccles, & Pintrich, 1996). Returning to our example of Jason, he began school thinking he was quite good at many different activities. From the feedback he received and his comparisons with others, he began to realize he had stronger skills in some areas than others. Although his sense of competence declined to a degree, Jason was a good student especially in math and science, and so continued to believe he could do well in these and other areas. Thus he was willing to continue to take additional math courses.

The second explanation has to do with changes in classroom and school environments and conditions. In the United States, as children move through school, school environments often change in ways that make evaluation more salient and competition between students more likely. As high-stakes assessments became more prevalent in the United States, especially in the era of the No Child Left Behind Act (2002), such practices increased. This focus on evaluation, performance, and competence make it more likely for some children's expectancies and values to decline as they go through school (e.g., see Eccles & Midgley, 1989; Wigfield et al., 1996; Wigfield et al., 2015). These kinds of changes are characteristic of certain cultural approaches to schooling. In cultures outside the United States, such changes in school environments may or may not occur, which has implications for how children's expectancies and values may change in these different cultures. One example is Germany, where between-school tracking based on children's performance on aptitude measures begins as early as fifth grade, likely exacerbating differences in children's ability beliefs in the different tracks. To date, there still has been very little research on how educational practices in schools in different cultures and countries impact children's developing expectancies and values.

Relations of Expectancies and Values to Performance and Choice

Why should we be concerned about these negative mean-level changes? As noted earlier, in research done primarily in the United States individuals' expectancies for success and subjective values have been found to directly predict their achievement outcomes, including their performance, persistence, and choices of which activities to do (e.g., Eccles 1993; Eccles-Parsons et al., 1983; Eccles et al., 1998). Empirical support for these proposed linkages has been found in longitudinal studies of children ranging in age from 6 to 18. Even when level of previous performance is controlled, students' ability beliefs strongly predict their performance in different domains, including math, reading and sport. Students' subjective task values predict both intentions and actual decisions to keep taking mathematics and English and to engage in sports. The relations appear in children as young as first grade, although the relations strengthen across age (Eccles-Parsons et al., 1983; Eccles & Harold, 1991; Meece et al., 1990; see also Eccles et al., 1998; Wigfield et al., 2015 for detailed reviews). That students' ability beliefs and values are declining across the school years likely means that many opt out of certain subject areas as they perceive they lack ability in them, or lose interest in them. To deal with these issues researchers have developed intervention programs to foster students' valuing of different subject areas; we discuss that work next.

Intervening to Enhance Students' Achievement Values

Over the last 10 years a variety of researchers have developed interventions to enhance students' valuing of different academic subjects, notably in the STEM areas (see Harackiewicz, Tibbetts, Canning, & Hyde, 2014; Rosenzweig & Wigfield, 2016; Wigfield et al., 2017, for reviews). Researchers have focused on increasing students' valuing of different subjects because as noted earlier students' task values influence their choices of whether to continue taking courses in different subject areas, and (in college) their choices of whether to major in certain subject areas. Intervention researchers primarily have developed brief, social psychologically based interventions (see Yeager & Walton, 2011) that include only a few sessions that do not last a long time. By and large results of this work show that these interventions do enhance students' utility value and interest in the subject of focus in the study, and also student achievement. For instance, Hulleman and Harackiewicz (2009) and Hulleman, Godes, Hendricks, and Harackiewicz (2010) conducted experiments in which they had one group of high school or college students write a brief essay, either once in the lab or in class every three or four weeks, about the relevance of what they were learning to their lives. A control group completed an unrelated task, such as summarizing what they learned (students were either learning science, psychology or a new mental math technique). Results showed that (relative to the control group) the intervention boosted students' utility value and interest in the topics they were learning, as well as their achievement; however, the effects were stronger for students who started with low expectations for their performance.

In a laboratory study, Canning and Harackiewicz (2015) found that directly communicating utility value information to low-confidence students undermined their math performance and interest. However, when these students received this information *and* generated their own examples of utility value, they performed better and were more interested in the math technique than when they only generated their own examples. They also found that low-confidence students preferred to read examples of how utility value that connected to their everyday life versus to their careers or academics. Harackiewicz, Rozek, Hulleman, and Hyde (2012) targeted high school students' utility value by intervening with their parents. Parents were randomly assigned to treatment and control groups; treatment parents received brief materials a few times over 2 years on how to help their children make decisions about their futures; the materials emphasized the importance of math and science. Students whose parents received the materials took significantly more math and science courses than did those in the control group. Further, mothers' perceived utility value of math and science partially mediated these effects. Interestingly, though, follow up analyses of this data done by Rozek, Hyde, Svoboda, Hulleman, and Harackiewicz (2015) showed that the intervention only improved course taking for lower achieving boys and higher achieving girls.

Finally, some researchers have targeted several aspects of students' achievement values. Gaspard et al. (2015) designed an intervention program focused on achievement values (called MoMa) focused on enhancing ninth grade students' math utility value. They implemented in 25 German high schools a 1-hour intervention either encouraging students to write a brief essay connecting math to their lives, or asking them to read and respond to quotations from fellow students about the relevance of math. The study utilized a cluster randomized control design. Compared to a waiting control condition, students in both intervention conditions reported higher utility value for math, but effects were stronger in the quotation condition than the essay condition. Also, even though the intervention focused on utility value, students in the quotation condition also reported higher perceptions of intrinsic and attainment value (but not lower perceptions of cost) than students in the control group. Female students benefited from the intervention more than males on some measures.

In sum, interventions focused on enhancing students' valuing of achievement in different areas and also their actual achievement have successfully done so in studies done in the United States and Europe since the publication of the first edition of this volume, even when the interventions are relatively brief. Far less of this kind of work has been done in non-Western cultures. We turn next to cross-cultural research on students' developing expectancies and values.

CROSS-CULTURAL RESEARCH ON EXPECTANCIES AND VALUES

As noted in our chapter in the previous edition, the definition of cross-cultural research is complex; see Poortinga (1997) for an informative discussion of what cross-cultural research means in psychological research. As in our chapter for the first edition we use this term to mean research comparing individuals who live in different countries/cultures, rather than subgroups living within one country and focus on this kind of cross-cultural research on individuals' expectancies and values in this section. In addition to this distinction, much has been written about the distinction between etic and emic research in cross-cultural research, and which approach is more appropriate (e.g., Bempechat & Drago-Severson, 1999; Berry, 1989; Poortinga, 1997).

An *etic* approach to cross-cultural research assumes that constructs have the same meaning across cultures (Bempechat & Drago-Severson, 1999; Berry, 1989). For example, an etic model of expectancies and values would assume that students of all cultures interpret these constructs in the same way, or that these are universal constructs. When testing such a model, researchers might look for cross-cultural similarities and differences in the strength to which math expectancies and values predict math achievement. A goal of this approach might be to develop a universal expectancy-value model, which would have applicability across cultures.

In contrast, an *emic* approach assumes that constructs take on different meanings in different cultures (Bempechat & Drago-Severson, 1999; Berry, 1989). An emic model is culture-specific and cannot be generalized to other cultures. Researchers using this approach might address the meanings of expectancies and values within one specific culture by employing qualitative methods such as interviews and ethnographies to capture how individuals living in a given culture express these meanings. The end product of such research would be a detailed characterization of the construct meanings and their relations to performance and choice within the specific context. Cross-cultural work of both of these types has been done within the expectancy-value framework, although most extant work has taken an etic approach. This work includes studies of the factor structure of individuals' expectancies and values, age differences in them, and how they relate to performance and choice. By contrast, emic work on EVT focuses on the meaning of these constructs in different cultures.

The Factor Structure of Ability Beliefs and Values in Different Cultures

Over the last 15 years, researchers have examined in different countries the factor structures of students' ability beliefs, using versions of Marsh's (1989) Self-Description Questionnaire (SDQ), which measures students' perceptions of ability. One of Marsh's major findings is that children and adolescents' perceptions of ability are quite domain specific; Eccles and her colleagues also have found this with their measures of expectancies and values (e.g., Eccles et al., 1993). Studies examining the factor structures of individuals' responses to the SDQ in various countries find quite similar factor structures to those Marsh's found originally in Australia. For example, Leung, Marsh, Craven, and Abduljabbar (2015) found measurement invariance in the factor structures of the SDQ for secondary students (SDQII) among Chinese and Australian students. Also, investigations of the PSDQ (a measure of physical self-concept; Marsh & Redmayne, 1994) and the PSDQ-Short showed similar factor structures in Australia and Spain (Tomás, Marsh, González-Romá, Valls, & Nagengast, 2014), Finland (Haapea, Haverinen, Honkalampi, Kuittinen, & Räty, 2016), and France, (Maïano, Morin, & Mascret, 2015). These results indicate that children and adolescents' ability beliefs have similar factor structures in different countries, as measured by these questionnaires.

Given the similarity in factor structure in children's ability beliefs across cultures it might be argued that the construct does not vary in different cultures. One problem with drawing this conclusion is that the questionnaire measures used in these studies do not get at children's understandings of what their ability is. Instead, children respond to investigator-generated items, which were first developed in the west. Interview methods are necessary for the purpose of assessing whether the actual meaning of a construct like sense of ability or subjective values differ across cultures. We return to this point below.

Regarding work that examines the factor structures of students' subjective task values, Trautwein et al. (2013) note that comparing the underlying structures of students' value beliefs is difficult in general, because the operationalization of value beliefs varies widely from study to study, and because studies often include too few value items. While we know of no work comparing factor structure across cultures, recently researchers have begun examining factor structures of value beliefs in non-U.S. cultures. For example, Gaspard et al. (2017) investigated the factor structure of value beliefs in German students, Grades 5 through 12, using a newly developed measure that taps multiple facets of the value constructs from EVT. Their measure included intrinsic value, four facets of utility value, two facets of attainment value, and three facets of cost, and the researchers found support for a nine-factor model. An important next step is to test their measure and its factor structure across different cultures and languages.

We emphasize that values, more so than ability beliefs, may be influenced by culture, as values seem inherently influenced by culture. Parents and institutions within a given culture have the major responsibility to teach their children values of different kinds, including the value of academics. Given this, perhaps the factor structure of children's subjective values may vary more across cultures than the factor structure of children's ability beliefs. To address this issue, researchers should compare the factor structures of students' values across cultures and languages of test items, looking for measure invariance as well as similarities and differences in how the items are interpreted and understood by participants. In addition, interviews with students from different cultures about the different types of values would yield valuable information of how they differ from culture to culture.

Mean Differences in Individuals' Expectancies and Values Across Cultures

Researchers have examined how students' expectancies and values differ across culture as well as change over time in those cultures. We discuss that work next.

Cultural Differences in Expectancy and Ability Beliefs

There has been relatively little work of late comparing ability beliefs in different countries. In one study, Marsh et al. (2013) used data from the Trends in International Mathematics and Science Study (TIMSS) 2007 to compare self-concepts of ability (SCA; similar to both ability beliefs and expectancies in EVT) of high school students in four Middle Eastern countries (Saudi Arabia, Jordan, Oman, and Egypt) and four Anglo countries (United States, Australia, England, and Scotland). They showed that the students from the Middle East had higher SCAs than did those in the Anglo countries. This study expands cross-cultural research on SCA beyond previous studies that mostly compared self-concepts in the United States and Australia to countries in East Asia. An important next step in similar research is investigating specific cultural factors that might produce the differences found across cultures.

Cultural Differences in Achievement Values

Researchers initially examining this issue in different cultures looked primarily at differences across cultures in children's interest in different school-related activities, one of the components of task value in the expectancy-value model; we discussed this work in more detail in our chapter in the first edition of this book. Results of this work present a somewhat mixed picture, with some studies showing differences across cultures favoring Asian students in their interest in math compared to American students (e.g., Stevenson et al., 1990), and others showing few such differences (Henderson, Marx, & Kim, 1999).

As discussed above, research in the West has shown that students' values for academic activities tend to decrease with age (Wigfield et al., 2015). In the last 15 years, some research on age differences in subjective values has been done outside the United States and Australia. Gaspard et al. (2017) found evidence supporting the often-observed decline (in studies done in the United States) in students' values, in their cross-sectional study of German adolescents, Grades 5 to 12. Although they generally found that students' values for different domains decreased with age, there were differences related to domain and specific value facets. For example, in English, the typical trend of decreasing with age held for intrinsic value, importance of achievement, utility for school, and utility for job, as well as cost increasing with age. However, in biology, values were highest in the lower grades, lowest in the middle grades, and then higher in the upper grades. Work such as this should continue in diverse countries, to better understand the development of students' values. Further, this etic approach should be supplemented with emic work looking at the nature of subjective values in different cultures, and how these values may change across development.

Relations of Expectancies and Values to Performance and Choice in Different Cultures

Over the last 15 years, some work has been done across cultures relating expectancies and values to outcome such as performance and choice. Nagengast et al. (2011) used data from the 2006 Programme for International Student Assessment (PISA) to look at whether students' SCAs and enjoyment in science (representing intrinsic task value) predicted extracurricular activities and career aspirations in science among high school students from 57 countries. Students' science SCAs positively predicted career aspirations in all 57 countries and extracurricular science activities in all but one country. Also, enjoyment of science positively predicted both career aspirations and extracurricular activities in all 57 countries. The researchers also found that the interaction of science SCA and enjoyment significantly, albeit weakly, predicted the outcomes variables. By the authors' judgment, this study provided "the strongest support for the cross-national generalizability of EVT predictions ever undertaken" (p. 1064). Indeed, we know of no other study that has tested relationships from EVT in so many countries.

Pursuing similar secondary analysis studies using international databases could yield further fruitful findings.

Liem and Chua (2013) demonstrated a unique application of EVT in the domain of civic education with junior high and senior high school students in Indonesia. The researchers tested a model in which students' expectancies and values concerning their civic education class mediated the relationship between background factors (demographic and academic) and civic education targeted outcomes. Results showed that although expectancy and value beliefs together played a mediating role, students' valuing of civics education was a stronger predictor of many outcomes such as society-oriented future goals, awareness of good citizenship, and perceived utility of schools to foster civic qualities. Interestingly, ethnic minority students in the sample (primarily of Chinese background) reported lower valuing of civic education than did ethnic majority (native Indonesian background). Older students reported lower valuing than did younger students, supporting work discussed above on how students' ability beliefs and values decrease across age.

Recently, Dietrich, Viljaranta, Moeller, and Kracke (2017) investigated how German university students' expectancies and values predicted their effort in different college classes. They found that students reported expending more effort on tasks for which their expectancies or values were high compared to low. Additionally, when students had high expectancies and intrinsic, attainment and utility values for specific topics in an educational psychology course (e.g., knowledge acquisition or motivation), they also expended more effort. A final finding was students with higher values invested more effort than those with lower values.

Differences in the Meaning of the Ability and Value Constructs Across Cultures

Most of the work just reviewed takes the etic approach to cross-cultural research, in that the expectancy-value measures used in the studies were initially developed in western cultures and then given to children in other cultures, and comparisons made of the responses. The factor analytic studies perhaps can be considered a mixture of the etic and emic approaches (see also McInerney, 1995). Some researchers have taken an emic approach by examining the meaning of the expectancy/ability belief construct in different cultures; we discuss that work next.

In our chapter in the first edition of this volume, we discussed work by Holloway (1988) and others showing cultural differences in the meaning of ability. We could find no studies done over the last 15 years building on this earlier emic work, which is unfortunate, and so we just mention some key points from the earlier work here. The earlier work showed that Asian and American children differ in the extent to which they see effort and ability working together, with Asian children seeing them as more closely related. In Japan, social and intellectual abilities also are seen as more closely tied together.

This work on the differences in the meaning of ability across cultures has important implications for EVT. Recall that one important finding in expectancy-value research is that individuals' expectancies for success and ability beliefs predict their performance. We reviewed some evidence earlier suggesting these links hold in other cultures as well (although that research is scant). However, the *interpretation* of these findings across cultures may vary, given the differences in the meaning of ability in different cultures. Beliefs about ability may predict performance in different cultures, but we should not necessarily assume that children view ability in the same way in these cultures. Further, in cultures where effort appears a more important explanation for success than ability such as appears to be the case for Asian cultures, perhaps links between student effort and outcomes would be stronger than those between students' expectancies for success and outcomes.

To date, there has been little research on how the meaning of the values construct may vary across cultures. Hufton, Elliott, and Illushin (2002) found that Russian students did not appear to view the values of tasks in terms of the components of task value identified by Eccles and her colleagues. These findings suggest conceptualization of values varies across cultures, but they are preliminary. As we noted earlier we believe it is quite possible that culture may impact values even more than conceptions of ability, as a major cultural obligation is the socialization of children's values, both broadly and more specifically defined. In our chapter in the first edition we conjectured how the different value components may be influenced by cultural beliefs, such as the nature of identity, the relative importance of social roles and group membership, and the tolerance of the culture for engaging in activities outside of culturally accepted roles (e.g., what is appropriate for males and females to do in a given culture). These issues still have not been systematically studied, unfortunately.

We continue to believe that emic research on these and other related topics would help us understand cross-cultural differences in some of the important relations posited in the expectancy-value model. As noted earlier, in research done in the West, children's ability beliefs directly predict their performance, and values directly predict their intentions and choices of activities. We reviewed above cross-cultural research on how children's ability-related beliefs relate to their performance. Researchers now need to assess the relations of values to intentions and choice in other cultures. Having an understanding of what the different subcomponents of values mean to children in different cultures would be very beneficial for interpreting the results of these studies, particularly if the relations were different from those found in the studies done in the west. We turn next to some specific suggestions for future research on expectancies and values in different cultures.

SUGGESTIONS FOR FUTURE RESEARCH ON CHILDREN'S EXPECTANCIES AND VALUES

It is important to reiterate that Eccles and colleagues' EVT model was developed originally to address a sociocultural phenomenon, gender differences in mathematics-related performance and choice, and so it is particularly well suited for a cultural analysis of motivation and activity choices. Having said that, there is a great deal of research that needs to be done to assess the model cross-culturally.

Returning to the model in Figure 5.1, based on the work reviewed here, and in our chapter in the previous edition, it is clear that the links proposed in the model between ability and expectancy beliefs and task values to performance and choice are found in tests of the model in other cultures. However, much more work is needed to look more carefully at whether the strength of these relations varies across cultures. One reason this may occur could be the differences in how the different constructs are defined across cultures, which, as we have seen, does occur.

To understand clearly what the linkages mean, emic work needs to be done to investigate how individuals in different countries define and understand the crucial constructs in the model, before examining linkages among them. Some work on differences in the understanding of ability across cultures has been done, so we suggest that such work on possible cultural differences in the understanding of task values is especially important to do. Once these crucial constructs are cross-culturally better understood, their links to performance and choice can be examined.

It is quite possible that additional constructs need to be included in the model for it to account more fully for cultural influences. One example is in the socializers' beliefs and behaviors block, a set of constructs posited and shown to relate directly to children's own beliefs, values, and choices (see Simpkins, Fredricks, & Eccles, 2015). We need a better understanding of how socializers' beliefs and behaviors focused on their children's achievement vary across cultures, and differentially relate to children's own beliefs and achievement behaviors. An example of this is teachers' behavior. As discussed above, work in the United States shows that changes in students' expectancies and values are due in part to changes in teachers' instructional and assessment practices that occur across the school years, most notably after the transition to middle school. Whether and how these instructional changes occur in other cultures and how they impact children's developing expectancies and values is an important topic for research.

The "cultural milieu" block (see Figure 5.1) clearly is another place where additional constructs/variables need to be added. That block focuses on two major things, gender role stereotypes and cultural stereotypes about activities. These likely are important things to consider in all cultures, but other aspects of the cultural milieu should be added to this block. For example, particularly salient aspects of the cultural milieu include the overall value the culture places on education, the culture's view on providing children many choices and opportunities to engage in different activities versus controlling those choices, school organization and structure and how they change across the school years, and the economic opportunities more education provides. To date there is little work outside the United States on how such aspects of the larger societal fabric in different countries impacts children's developing expectancies, values, performance on different activities, and choices of which to pursue. We noted above that we define cross-cultural to mean research comparing individuals who live in different countries. But what constitutes a "different enough" country to use the cross-cultural moniker? For example, are Germany and Australia culturally different enough from the United States to call research cross-cultural when comparing findings to those from the United States? Indeed, much of the recent work furthering EVT in areas such as interventions and expansion of the value construct is being done in Germany (e.g., Gaspard et al., 2015; Gaspard et al., 2017).

In addition, as cross-cultural work on these and other topics in EVT proceed we think that it would be quite informative for authors to consider in their discussions how culture and language apply to and impact the findings. To illustrate, consider the finding from Gaspard et al.'s (2015) study that high school students reported higher utility for daily life and higher utility for job regarding their English classes than did younger students. The researchers' explanation was as follows: "These findings are in line with the global use of English, its omnipresence in the media, and the high relevance for career opportunities in general. Students might become increasingly aware of the relevance of English as they reflect on their futures and expand their horizons during adolescence" (p. 80). This explanation likely applies most directly to students in countries where English is a primary second language (such as Germany). Researchers doing similar work in other cultures where English is not the primary second language may find quite different results and so reach different conclusions. We encourage researchers to discuss the role that culture and language play in students' motivation when doing cross-cultural research within the EVT framework, and to explain their findings accordingly.

CONCLUSION

In this chapter, we focused on Eccles and colleagues' contemporary EVT model and summarized research that has been done over the last 15 years on the nature and development of children's ability beliefs, expectancies for success, and achievement task values. We believe the importance and "presence" of EVT in the field of motivation has increased over that time, and will continue to do so moving forward. During the last 15 years two areas of research based in EVT received increased attention. The first is work in Western cultures looking at how interventions designed to enhance students' valuing of achievement increases both their motivation for and achievement in different areas, particularly STEM subject areas. We look forward to extensions of this work to other cultures. The second is work on the perceived cost of engaging in different activities; this construct had been relatively neglected in research on EVT. The notion of "cost" may vary greatly across cultures, and so we also look forward to research on this construct in different cultures. We believe new cross-cultural research on these two topics, the other topics we mentioned in the previous section, and on other topics in addition to those we discussed will shed further light on the model's applicability in different cultural settings around the world.

REFERENCES

Archambault, I., Eccles, J. S., & Vida, M. N. (2010). Ability self-concepts and subjective value in literacy: Joint trajectories from grades 1 through 12. *Journal of Educational Psychology, 102*, 804–816.

Atkinson, J. W. (1957). Motivational determinants of risk taking behavior. *Psychological Review, 64*, 359–372.

Atkinson, J. W. (1964). *An introduction to motivation*. Princeton, NJ: Van Nostrand.

Barron, K. E., & Hulleman, C. S. (2015). Expectancy-value-cost model of motivation. In J. S. Eccles & K. Salmela-Aro (Eds.), *International encyclopedia of social and behavioral sciences: Motivational psychology* (2nd ed.). New York, NY: Elsevier.

Battle, E. (1965). Motivational determinants of academic task persistence. *Journal of Personality and Social Psychology, 2*, 209–218.

Battle, E. (1966). Motivational determinants of academic competence. *Journal of Personality and Social Psychology, 4*, 534–642.

Bempechat, J., & Drago-Severson, E. (1999). Cross-national differences in academic achievement: Beyond etic conceptions of children's understandings. *Review of Educational Research, 69*, 287–314.

Berry, J. W. (1989). Imposed etics-emics-derived etics: The operationalization of a compelling idea. *International Journal of Psychology, 24*, 721–735.

Canning, E. A., & Harackiewicz, J. M. (2015). Teach it, don't preach it: The differential effects of directly-communicated and self-generated utility value information. *Motivation Science, 1*(1), 47–71.

Dietrich, J., Viljaranta, J., Moeller, J., & Kracke, B. (2017). Situational expectancies and task values: Associations with students' effort. *Learning and Instruction, 17*, 53–64.

Eccles, J. S. (1987). Gender roles and women's achievement-related decisions. *Psychology of Women Quarterly, 11*, 135–172.

Eccles, J. S. (1993). School and family effects on the ontogeny of children's interests, self-perceptions, and activity choice. In J. Jacobs (Ed.), *Nebraska Symposium on Motivation, 1992: Developmental perspectives on motivation* (pp. 145–208). Lincoln, NE: University of Nebraska Press.

Eccles, J. S. (2005). Subjective task values and the Eccles et al. model of achievement related choices. In A. J. Elliott & C. S. Dweck (Eds.), *Handbook of competence and motivation* (pp. 105–121). New York, NY: Guilford.

Eccles, J. S. (2009). Who am I and what am I going to do with my life? Personal and collective identities as motivators of action. *Educational Psychologist, 44*, 78–89. doi:10.1080/00461520902832368

Eccles, J. S., & Harold, R. D. (1991). Gender differences in sport involvement: Applying the Eccles' expectancy-value model. *Journal of Applied Sport Psychology, 3*, 7–35.

Eccles, J. S., & Midgley, C. (1989). Stage/environment fit: Developmentally appropriate classrooms for early adolescents. In R. Ames & C. Ames (Eds.), *Research on motivation in education* (Vol. 3, pp. 139–181). New York, NY: Academic Press.

Eccles, J. S., & Wigfield, A. (1995). In the mind of the achiever: The structure of adolescents' academic achievement related-beliefs and self-perceptions. *Personality and Social Psychology Bulletin, 21*, 215–225.

Eccles, J. S., Wigfield, A., Harold, R., & Blumenfeld, P. B. (1993). Age and gender differences in children's self- and task perceptions during elementary school. *Child Development, 64*, 830–847.

Eccles, J. S., Wigfield, A., & Schiefele, U. (1998). Motivation to succeed. In W. Damon (Series Ed.) & N. Eisenberg (Vol. Ed.), *Handbook of child psychology* (5th ed., Vol. 3, pp. 1017–1095). New York, NY: Wiley.

Eccles-Parsons, J. S., Adler, T. F., Futterman, R., Goff, S. B., Kaczala, C. M., Meece, J. L., & Midgley, C. (1983). Expectancies, values, and academic behaviors. In J. T. Spence (Ed.), *Achievement and achievement motivation* (pp. 75–146). San Francisco, CA.: W. H. Freeman.

Feather, N. T. (1982). Expectancy-value approaches: Present status and future directions. In N. T. Feather (Ed.), *Expectations and actions: Expectancy-value models in psychology* (pp. 395–420). Hillsdale, NJ: Erlbaum.

Feather, N. T. (1988). Values, valences, and course enrollment: Testing the role of personal values within an expectancy-value framework. *Journal of Educational Psychology, 80*, 381–391.

Gaspard, H., Dicke, A., Flunger, B., Brisson, B., Hafner, I., Nagengast, B., & Trautwein, U. (2015). Fostering adolescents' value beliefs for mathematics with a relevance intervention in the classroom. *Developmental Psychology, 51*(9), 1226–1240.

Gaspard, H., Häfner, I., Parrisius, C., Trautwein, U., & Nagengast, B. (2017). Assessing task values in five subjects during secondary school: Measurement structure and mean level differences across grade level, gender, and academic subject. *Contemporary Educational Psychology, 48,* 67–84.

Haapea, I., Haverinen, K., Honkalampi, K., Kuittinen, M., & Räty, H. (2016). The factor structure and reliability of the short form of the physical self-description questionnaire in a Finnish adolescent athlete sample. *International Journal of Sport and Exercise Psychology, 14,* 1–17.

Harackiewicz, J. M., Rozek, C. S., Hulleman, C. S., & Hyde, J. S. (2012). Helping parents motivate adolescents in mathematics and science: An experimental test of a utility-value intervention. *Psychological Science, 23,* 899–906.

Harackiewicz, J. M., Tibbetts, Y., Canning, E. A., & Hyde, J. S. (2014). Harnessing values to promote motivation in education. In S. Karabenick and T. Urdan (Eds.), *Advances in motivation and achievement* (Vol. 18, pp. 71–105). Bingley, England: Emerald Group.

Henderson, B. B., Marx, M. H., & Kim, Y. C. (1999). Academic interests and perceived competence in American, Japanese, and Korean children. *Journal of Cross-Cultural Psychology, 30,* 32–50.

Holloway, S. D. (1988). Concepts of ability and effort in Japan and the United States. *Review of Educational Research, 58,* 327–345.

Hufton, N., Elliott, J. G., & Illushin, L. (2002). Achievement motivation across cultures: Some puzzles and their implications for future research. *New Directions for Child and Adolescent Development, 96,* 65–85.

Hulleman, C. S., Godes, O., Hendricks, B. L., & Harackiewicz, J. M. (2010). Enhancing interest and performance with a utility value intervention. *Journal of Educational Psychology, 102,* 880–895.

Hulleman, C. S., & Harackiewicz, J. M. (2009). Promoting interest and performance in high school science classes. *Science, 326,* 1410–1412.

Jacobs, J. E., & Eccles, J. S. (2000). Parents, task values, and real-life achievement choices. In C. Sansone & J. M. Harackiewicz (Eds.), *Intrinsic and extrinsic motivation: The search for optimal motivation and performance* (pp. 405–439). San Diego, CA: Academic Press.

Jacobs, J. E., Lanza, S., Osgood, D. W., Eccles, J. S., & Wigfield, A. (2002). Changes in children's self-competence and values: Gender and domain differences across grades one through twelve. *Child Development, 73,* 509–527.

Leung, K. C., Marsh, H. W., Craven, R. G., & Abduljabbar, A. S. (2015). Measurement invariance of the self-description questionnaire II in a Chinese sample. *European Journal of Psychological Assessment, 32,* 128–139.

Lewin, K. (1938). *The conceptual representation and the measurement of psychological forces.* Durham, NC: Duke University Press.

Liem, G. A. D., & Chua, B. L. (2013). An expectancy-value perspective of civic education motivation, learning, and desirable outcomes. *Educational Psychology: An International Journal of Experimental Educational Psychology, 33*(3), 276–306.

Maïano, C., Morin, A. J., & Mascret, N. (2015). Psychometric properties of the short form of the physical self-description questionnaire in a French adolescent sample. *Body image, 12,* 89–97.

Marsh, H. W. (1989). Age and sex effects in multiple dimensions of self-concept: Preadolescence to early adulthood. *Journal of Educational Psychology, 81,* 417–430.

Marsh, H. W., Abduljabbar, A. S., Abu-Hilal, M. M., Morin, A. J. S., Abdelfattah, F., Leung, K. C., . . . Parker, P. (2013). Factorial, convergent, and discriminant validity of TIMSS math and science motivation measures: A comparison of Arab and Anglo-Saxon countries. *Journal of Educational Psychology, 105*, 108–128.

Marsh, H. W., & Redmayne, R. S. (1994). A multidimensional physical self-concept and its relations to multiple components of physical fitness. *Journal of Sport and Exercise Psychology, 16*(1), 43–55.

McInerney, D. M. (1995). Achievement motivation and indigenous minorities: Can research be psychometric? *Cross-Cultural Research, 29*, 211–239.

Meece, J. L., Wigfield, A., & Eccles, J. S. (1990). Predictors of math anxiety and its consequences for young adolescents' course enrollment intentions and performances in mathematics. *Journal of Educational Psychology, 82*, 60–70.

Nagengast, B., Marsh, H. W., Scalas, L. F., Xu, M. K., Hau, K.-T., & Trautwein, U. (2011). Who took the "x" out of expectancy-value theory?: A psychological mystery, a substantive-methodological synergy, and a cross-national generalization. *Psychological Science, 22*, 1058–1066.

No Child Left Behind Act of 2001, P.L. 107-110, 20 U.S.C. § 6319 (2002).

Pekrun, R. (2006). The control-value theory of achievement emotions: Assumptions, corollaries, and implications for education and practice. *Educational Psychology Review, 18*, 315–341.

Poortinga, Y. H. (1997). Towards convergence? In J. W. Berry, Y. H. Poortinga, & J. Pandey (Eds.), *Handbook of cross-cultural psychology: Theory and method* (Vol. 1, pp. 347–387). Boston, MA: Allyn & Bacon.

Renninger, K. A. (2000). Individual interest and its implications for understanding intrinsic motivation. In C. Sansone & J. M. Harackiewicz (Eds.), *Intrinsic and extrinsic motivation: The search for optimal motivation and performance* (pp. 373–404). San Diego, CA: Academic Press.

Rosenzweig, E. Q., & Wigfield, A. (2016). STEM motivation interventions for adolescents: A promising start, but farther to go. *Educational Psychologist, 51*, 146–163.

Rozek, C. S., Hyde, J. S., Svoboda, R. C., Hulleman, C. S., & Harackiewicz, J. M. (2015). Gender differences in the effects of a utility-value intervention to help parents motivate adolescents in mathematics and science. *Journal of Educational Psychology, 107*(1), 195–206.

Ryan, R. M., & Deci, E. L. (2016). Facilitating and hindering motivation, learning, and well-being in schools: Research and observations from self-determination theory. In K. R. Wentzel & D. B. Miele (Eds.), *Handbook of motivation at school* (2nd ed., pp. 96–119). New York, NY: Routledge.

Schiefele, U. (2009). Situational and individual interest. In K. R. Wentzel & A. Wigfield (Eds.), *Handbook of motivation at school* (pp. 197–222). New York, NY: Routledge.

Simpkins, S. D., Fredricks, J. A., & Eccles, J. S. (2015). The role of parents in the ontogeny of achievement-related motivation and behavioral choices. *Monographs of the Society for Research in Child Development, 80* (2), 1–169.

Stevenson, H. W., Lee, S. Y., Chen, C., Stigler, J. W., Hsu, C. C., & Kitamura, S. (1990). Contexts of achievement: A study of American, Chinese, and Japanese children. *Monographs of the Society for Research in Child Development, 55* (Serial No. 221).

Tolman, E. C. (1932). *Purposive behavior in animals and men.* New York, NY: Appleton-Century-Crofts.

Tomás, I., Marsh, H. W., González-Romá, V., Valls, V., & Nagengast, B. (2014). Testing measurement invariance across Spanish and English versions of the physical self-description questionnaire: An application of exploratory structural equation modeling. *Journal of Sport and Exercise Psychology, 36,* 179–188.

Trautwein, U., Nagengast, B., Marsh, H. W., Gaspard, H., Dicke, A. -L., Lüdtke, O., & Jonkmann, K. (2013). Expectancy-value theory revisited. From expectancy-value theory to expectancy-valueS theory? In D. M. McInerney, H. W. Marsh, R. G. Craven, & F. Guay (Eds.), *Theory driving research: New wave perspectives on self-processes and human development* (pp. 233–249). Charlotte, NC: Information Age.

Weiner, B. (1992). *Human motivation: Metaphors, theories, and research.* Newbury Park, CA: SAGE.

Wigfield, A. (1994). Expectancy-value theory of achievement motivation: A developmental perspective. *Educational Psychology Review, 6,* 49–78.

Wigfield, A., & Eccles, J. (1992). The development of achievement task values: A theoretical analysis. *Developmental Review, 12,* 265–310.

Wigfield, A., & Eccles, J. S. (2000). Expectancy-value theory of motivation. *Contemporary Educational Psychology, 25,* 68–81.

Wigfield, A., & Eccles, J. S. (2002). The development of competence beliefs, expectancies for success, and achievement values from childhood through adolescence. In A. Wigfield & J. S. Eccles (Eds.), *Development of achievement motivation* (pp. 91–120). San Diego, CA: Academic Press.

Wigfield, A, Eccles, J. S., Fredricks, J., Simpkins, S. Roeser, R., & Schiefele, U. (2015). Development of achievement motivation and engagement. In R. Lerner (Series Ed.) and M. Lamb (Vol. Ed.), *Handbook of child psychology and developmental science* (7th ed., Vol. 3, pp. 657–700). New York, NY: Wiley.

Wigfield, A., Eccles, J. S., & Pintrich, P. R. (1996). Development between the ages of eleven and twenty-five. In D. C. Berliner and R. C. Calfee (Eds.), *The handbook of educational psychology* (pp. 148–185). New York, NY: MacMillan.

Wigfield, A., Eccles, J. S., Yoon, K. S., Harold, R. D., Arbreton, A., Freedman-Doan, C., & Blumenfeld, P. C. (1997). Changes in children's competence beliefs and subjective task values across the elementary school years: A three-year study. *Journal of Educational Psychology, 89,* 451–469.

Wigfield, A., Rosenzweig, E. Q., & Eccles, J. S. (2017). Achievement values. In A. J. Elliot, C. S. Dweck, & D. S. Yeager (Eds.), *Handbook of competence and motivation* (2nd ed., pp. 116–134). New York, NY: Guilford.

Wigfield, A., Tonks, S., & Klauda, S. L. (2016). Expectancy-value theory. In K. R. Wentzel & D. Miele (Eds.), *Handbook of motivation in school* (2nd ed., pp. 55–74). New York, NY: Routledge.

Yeager, D. S., & Walton, G. M. (2011). Social-psychological interventions in education: They're not magic. *Review of Educational Research, 81,* 267–301.

CHAPTER 6

SELF-EFFICACY IN EDUCATION REVISITED THROUGH A SOCIOCULTURAL LENS

Maria K. DiBenedetto
Dale H. Schunk

Educators are faced with myriad challenges as increasing numbers of students struggle with poverty and classroom sociocultural norms that often differ from those found in students' countries of origins. Many students also grapple with issues of sexual identity, bullying, and the pressures accompanying social media, which have become an integral part of youth and mainstream culture. Bandura's (2016) social-cognitive theory presents an agentic view of the learner as one who has "intentional influence over one's functioning and over the course of events by one's actions" (p. 4). By helping students develop a sense of personal agency, educators can positively influence learners' motivation, learning, and achievement—in and out of school—and their capability to deal effectively with sociocultural challenges.

Big Theories Revisited 2, pages 117–140
Copyright © 2018 by Information Age Publishing
All rights of reproduction in any form reserved.

This chapter addresses social-cognitive theory and the role of *self-efficacy*, a key component of agency, defined as one's perceived capabilities to plan and implement actions to reach personal goals (Bandura, 1986, 1997). Our particular focus in this chapter is on the sensitivity of self-efficacy to various sociocultural influences. We begin by establishing theoretical clarity by providing a conceptual framework of self-efficacy and distinguishing it from other constructs. We next cover the importance of self-efficacy for self-regulated learning. The chapter concludes with a discussion of current research trends and recommendations including the measurement of self-efficacy, sociocultural influences on self-efficacy, uses of technology to build self-efficacy, and self-efficacy in group and nonacademic settings.

Social-cognitive theory has been widely tested in various contexts and cultures involving diverse learners, and the principles of the theory have received much cross-cultural empirical validation (Bandura, 1997). This review makes it clear that the theory is universally applicable but that the operation of social cognitive variables—including self-efficacy—can be affected by sociocultural factors. In this chapter we discuss the theory in this universal sense and indicate areas of sociocultural influence. We recommend further research to explore individual and collective differences in self-efficacy due to sociocultural variables.

ESTABLISHING THEORETICAL CLARITY

It is important to establish theoretical clarity because other psychological constructs bear some similarity to self-efficacy. In this section we explain the conceptual framework of self-efficacy and distinguish it from other similar constructs.

Conceptual Framework

Self-efficacy is situated in Bandura's (1986) social-cognitive theory, which postulates that individuals' functioning involves reciprocal interactions between personal (e.g., cognitions, feelings, skills), behavioral (e.g., strategy use, help-seeking, actions), and environmental (e.g., classrooms, homes, gyms) factors. In the visual arts classroom, for example, a student's interest, skill, and value in creating art (personal), the classroom with art supplies and a supportive teacher (environment), and the strategy of visual imagery to create her sketch (behavioral), interact with each other to create a final drawing (DiBenedetto & Garrett, in press). Self-efficacy plays a critical role in empowering learners to feel as if they have control over outcomes through goal-directed behavior (Schunk & DiBenedetto, 2016).

Self-efficacy is present during each of the reciprocal interactions in the triadic model and can affect choice, effort, persistence, and achievement (Schunk & Pajares, 2004). These outcomes, in turn, empower individuals to alter their cognitive, emotional, and motivational processes, to increase their behavioral competencies, and to adjust their environmental conditions to make these conducive to goal achievement (Schunk & DiBenedetto, 2016).

Self-efficacy beliefs are acquired from knowledge about a particular task and what is needed to complete the task (Zimmerman, Schunk, & DiBenedetto, 2015). Bandura (1997) hypothesized that this knowledge is generated from four sources: enactive mastery accomplishments, vicarious experiences, forms of social persuasion, and physiological and affective indices. Enactive mastery accomplishments constitute the most robust source because they provide learners with authentic evidence of their capability to succeed. Accomplishments require learners to adapt and adjust to different circumstances, and repeated successes in doing so can enhance self-efficacy. Teachers who provide students with opportunities to learn and perform successfully likely build students' self-efficacy for future similar tasks (Zimmerman & DiBenedetto, 2008).

Vicarious experiences occur through observing models (Bandura, 1997). Each of us, in everyday life, observes others succeed, stumble, or fail in completing tasks. These observations can affect self-efficacy beliefs depending on attributes of the models such as whether they are perceived as similar to the observers, competent, and capable of coping with challenging situations. Self-efficacy can be raised when observers visualize themselves performing at the same competency level, which underscores the critical role of competent peers. Forms of social persuasion also can raise self-efficacy. A coach telling a batter that he can get a hit is likely to motivate and mobilize him to succeed. The belief the coach has in the batter will have an influential effect on the batter's self-efficacy if the batter perceives the coach as credible, knowledgeable, and aware of his players' talents. Social persuasion by respected teachers can be a significant motivator for students who struggle with self-doubts as long as the students are capable of performing successfully (Schunk & DiBenedetto, 2016).

Physiological and affective symptoms also can affect self-efficacy (Bandura, 1997). Students who experience anxiety or sweating when taking an exam may have low self-efficacy for success whereas students who feel calm and anticipate performing well are likely to have higher self-efficacy for achievement. Physiological and affective indicators provide information if learners self-monitor these reactions. The information provided can be diagnostic and used to help reduce impairment of performance by providing feedback to the learners allowing them to gain control of the learning event, thus increasing their sense of agency (Zimmerman, Schunk, & DiBenedetto, 2017).

Distinctions of Self-Efficacy From Other Constructs

In the first edition of this volume, Schunk and Pajares (2004) distinguished self-efficacy from *ability beliefs*. Beliefs learners have about the capability to accomplish something are different from perceptions about abilities, which are considered to be innate characteristics or traits (Galton, 1979). Ability beliefs have been found to be related to students' expectations for success (Wigfield, Tonks, & Klauda, 2016); however, cross cultural studies comparing students in the United States, China, and Japan, have found differences in ability beliefs. Students in the United States are more likely to attribute performance to ability than effort (Schunk, Meece, & Pintrich, 2014). In addition, older students tend to perceive ability to have a more important role in achievement than do younger students; but attributing performance to ability minimizes the influence of agency on outcomes. Learners who believe their performance will not change much as a function of their behavior are less likely to expand effort or use effective strategies, potentially leading to negative consequences (Schunk, 2012).

Grit is defined as "perseverance and passion for long-term goals" (Duckworth, Peterson, Matthews, & Kelly, 2007, p. 1087). Learners who have grit do not give up when faced with challenges or setbacks. They continue working towards their long-term goals, keeping them in focus, learning from their mistakes, and maintaining stamina in their passionate pursuit of their goals (Duckworth & Gross, 2014). In a meta-analysis of 584 effect sizes for over 65,000 individuals, Credé, Tynan, and Harms (2016) found that while there is a relationship between grit and academic performance, these effect sizes are modest in comparison to other well-known predictors of academic achievement.

Like students with grit, those who are self-efficacious set personal goals that are specific, challenging, and long reaching (Bandura, 1997). But self-efficacy also leads to other productive outcomes. Efficacious students set proximal goals to help them achieve their long-term goals and use feedback from their environment to make adjustments to their behaviors (Pajares, 1997). They work harder and persist longer when they encounter difficulties. Setting proximal goals enhances self-efficacy because attaining short-term goals provides information to learners about their learning progress (Schunk & DiBenedetto, 2016). Self-efficacy beliefs also relate to better self-monitoring, time planning and management, strategy use, and self-evaluations, which are skills required for successful self-regulated learning (Zimmerman & Schunk, 2011). Unlike grit, decades of research have demonstrated the power of self-efficacy beliefs with a variety of learners and contexts such as health and disease prevention, sports and physical education, music education and performance, science, mathematics, reading, writing, technology, mentoring, career training, and family and work settings (Bandura, 1997; Bembenutty,

Cleary, & Kitsantas, 2013; Pajares & Urdan, 2006; Zimmerman & Schunk, 2011). Lastly, grit is hypothesized to be a personality characteristic (Credé et al., 2016), whereas self-efficacy beliefs are specific to tasks and formulated from information from various sources.

Another construct that is conceptually similar to self-efficacy is *intention*. Intentions refer to the goals or outcomes that individuals plan to pursue, whereas self-efficacy beliefs are perceived capabilities for attaining those goals or outcomes. Self-efficacy is differentiated from intention in that students may intend to learn but if they do not believe in their capability to do so, they will not exert effort and persist. Bandura (1997) indicates that "intentions are essentially equivalent to proximal goals" (p. 285). Proximal goals provide learners with the opportunity to evaluate themselves as they progress towards goal attainment. This feedback can strengthen learners' self-efficacy and motivate them to continue (Zimmerman et al., 2015). Intentional goal-directed activities and goal attainments can foster and build self-efficacy. If learners do not feel self-efficacious, they may not work diligently towards reaching their goals. Feedback from successfully attaining proximal goals can help trigger a sense of self-efficacy for realizing larger intentions (goals).

One line of research has examined implementation intentions (Wieber, Odenthal, & Gollwitzer, 2010). Implementation intentions are plans learners have about how to deal with situations that might arise while working towards goal attainment. Implementation intentions have been shown to affect performance under certain self-efficacy conditions. In a study where college students worked on difficult cognitive tasks, Weiber et al. (2010) found that when self-efficacy was low to medium, implementation intentions did not improve performance; however, when self-efficacy was high, holding implementation intentions improved students' performance. In a similar study with high school students, researchers found that those who set goal intentions for solving mathematical problems had improved performances when self-efficacy was taken into account (Bayer & Gollwitzer, 2007). It seems that self-efficacy can serve to strengthen implementation intentions.

Engagement in a learning context is hypothesized to be important for its potential impact on learning and achievement, although it has not been consistently defined (Skinner, 2016). One definition refers to engagement as the interest, effort, attention, involvement, and connections students have with classrooms, teachers, peers, and schoolwork (Marks, 2000; Skinner, 2016). There are three facets of engagement: cognitive, behavioral, and motivational/affective (Linnenbrink & Pintrich, 2003; Skinner, 2016). Cognitive engagement refers to students' beliefs about their ability to learn, as well as whether students are actively thinking about what they are learning. It includes creative thinking, strategy use, and critical thinking skills. Behavioral engagement refers to actions that the teacher can observe such as effort, persistence, hard work, and help-seeking. Motivational/affective engagement refers to students' feelings about their peers, teacher, classroom and school. It also includes how students feel about the academic task or schoolwork. Are they motivated to perform well, are they interested in what they are learning about, and do they value the activity?

Unlike engagement, self-efficacy beliefs are present *before, during,* and *after* learning events. Students must feel some level of self-efficacy to be motivated to actively participate in learning. Researchers have shown that students who hold high self-efficacy beliefs about their schoolwork are more likely to be engaged (Linnenbrink & Pintrich, 2003). They use deeper processing strategies and are more thoughtful, metacognitive, and reflective compared to students with lower self-efficacy beliefs. Students with higher self-efficacy are more likely to be behaviorally engaged by using self-regulatory strategies such as elaborating, organizing content and study materials, and seeking help when needed. They also exert greater effort and are more persistent than students with lower self-efficacy. Self-efficacy beliefs are closely linked to motivational/affective engagement. Bandura (1997) suggests that students who feel competent about completing an activity are more likely to develop interest and value in the activity. Negative feelings and anxiety are likely to stem from debilitating self-efficacy beliefs. Students who do not feel competent are likely to react defensively and attribute performance to uncontrollable factors such as low ability (Zimmerman, 2011), and thus be less engaged in the task.

Self-determination theory suggests individuals are innately intrinsically motivated by three basic needs of competence, autonomy, and relatedness (Ryan & Deci, 2016). The need for competence is driven by intrinsic motivation, which leads individuals to seek challenging situations in which they can use different strategies and manipulate their environment to accomplish something they value. Autonomy refers to the need of individuals to feel as if they can make their own decisions and exercise control over what they do. Relatedness involves the need to feel connected to others and to develop strong bonds that last over time.

Self-efficacy is most similar to the psychological need of competence. Competence results from an intrinsic feeling a person has when accomplishing a challenging task, whereas self-efficacy is the belief that individuals have about their capability to engage in the behaviors needed to do the task (Ryan & Deci, 2016). One of the critical features of self-determination theory is that tasks must be challenging such that learners will feel intrinsic value upon completion. While an athlete may feel self-efficacious about his capability to swim 100 yards, if this task is easy for him to accomplish he will not feel intrinsically rewarded or competent upon doing so. One of the similarities shared with self-efficacy is that as children develop and interact with their environment, their intrinsic motivation and self-efficacy

TABLE 6.1   Differentiating Self-Efficacy From Other Motivational Constructs

Construct	Definition	Examples
Self-Efficacy	Belief in one's capability to perform at a designated level	I believe I am capable of dancing in this ballet without making any errors.
Ability Beliefs	Belief in one's innate skills or traits	I have always been a poor math student; just like my mom, I can't do math!
Grit	Passion and perseverance for a long-term goal	I am going to be the best baseball player that ever lived and nothing will stop me.
Intention	Goal or outcome that an individual plans to pursue	I plan to learn how to calculate percentages so that I can calculate a 20% sale discount on the pair of shoes I want to buy.
Engagement	Cognitive, behavioral, and motivational/affective involvement during an activity	I am really involved in my science class because I love doing experiments and solving science problems.
Competence	A basic psychological need driven by intrinsic motivation	I need to keep practicing this music piece because music is a part of who I am, and I love the way it sounds and the way I feel when I play it perfectly.

become differentiated towards specific domains (e.g., mathematics, science, sports; Schunk, 2012). While each of the needs described above has been examined in educational settings, social-cognitive theory emphasizes the influence of task-specific self-efficacy beliefs on one's academic achievement and performance. Table 6.1 provides a summary of the motivational constructs discussed in this section.

SELF-EFFICACY FOR SELF-REGULATED LEARNING AND PERFORMANCE

In addition to its role in motivation and achievement, self-efficacy is an important process during self-regulated learning. As the popularity of self-regulated learning in education has grown, researchers have increasingly explored the role of self-efficacy (Usher & Schunk, 2018). *Self-regulated learning* refers to one's self-generated feelings, thoughts, and behaviors directed towards goal attainment (Zimmerman, 2000). A social-cognitive model postulates that self-regulated learning involves three cyclical phases: forethought, performance, and self-reflection (Zimmerman, 2000). The forethought phase takes place prior to the learning event and involves students' motivational beliefs such as interest, outcome expectations, and goal orientations; and task analysis processes such as goal orientation and strategic planning. The performance phase takes place during the learning event and is influenced by the processes in the forethought phase. Students engage in self-observational processes such as self-monitoring and metacognition, and self-control processes such as imagery, self-instruction, attention focusing, and help-seeking. In the self-reflection phase students reflect upon their learning and form self-judgments and self-reactions. Self-judgments involve evaluating one's performance against a personal standard set in the forethought phase and then attributing the outcome to one or more attributions (perceived causes), such as strategy use, effort, ability, or luck. Students react to their performance, which includes adaptive or defensive responses based on how satisfied they are with the outcomes. The cycle is dynamic, as individuals move through each of the three phases. They experience thoughts, feelings, and physiological reactions that may cause changes in future actions.

Self-efficacy has been shown to be a critical motivational source in each of the three phases (Schunk & DiBenedetto, 2016). Individuals who feel self-efficacious to learn set higher learning goals, persist when challenges arise, reflect upon their performances and make adaptations as needed. An interview with tennis champion Serena Williams after she won her 23rd Grand Slam tournament, provides an example of a self-regulated individual who felt self-efficacious in the face of extreme pressure and challenges as she describes what was going through her mind as she tried to beat her sister, Venus, in the 2017 Australian Open: "She started to make her comeback. She started to serve really well . . . So, I was just really like . . . Stay focused. Get there. You got this. You gotta relax . . . You can close this out . . . You can serve this out." (Tennis, 2017).

Self-efficacy develops initially from external sources as it progresses through four developmental levels of self-regulated learning until these feelings and beliefs become internalized (Schunk & Zimmerman, 1997). At the observational level, social models such as coaches, teachers, and peers provide information on how to perform a task and how to engage in forethought phase processes (Schunk & DiBenedetto, 2016; White & DiBenedetto, 2015). At the emulation level, learners begin to practice the observed behaviors as they replicate what was modeled and begin to feel self-efficacious about being able to perform an identical task. During the self-control level, self-efficacy begins to internalize as learners independently perform tasks similar to the one originally modeled. In the self-regulation level, learners are self-efficacious in their capability to make adjustments and adaptations to complete tasks that may be different from the original task observed (Schunk & DiBenedetto, 2014). The levels are also dynamic in that if a student does not grasp the information at a level beyond observation, the student may go back to a previous level for further observations and practice (Bembenutty, White, & DiBenedetto, 2016).

We should expect that sociocultural influences could affect students' self-efficacy for self-regulated learning. For example, a distinction often is drawn between cultures that are more individualistic (stressing individual accomplishments) and collectivist (stressing group accomplishments). It may be that the idea of self-regulated learning is more compatible with beliefs of individuals in individualistic cultures, which could lead to higher self-efficacy for self-regulated learning for students from these cultures compared with students in collectivist cultures. We discuss these sociocultural differences in greater depth later in this chapter.

TRENDS IN SELF-EFFICACY RESEARCH

As documented in the chapter in the earlier edition of this volume (Schunk & Pajares, 2004), experimental research studies show that self-efficacy predicts and affects performance and achievement in diverse contexts. In the remainder of this chapter, we address four important current trends in self-efficacy research with recommendations for further research: measurement of self-efficacy including calibration; sociocultural influences on self-efficacy; technology uses to build self-efficacy; and self-efficacy in group and nonacademic settings.

Measurement of Self-Efficacy

Dynamic Assessment

Self-efficacy continues to be measured primarily using *self-report instruments*. Bandura (2005) contended that the construction of reliable and valid self-efficacy scales is dependent on knowledge about the specific domain. The scale should include gradations of challenges needed to perform the task successfully and the scales should be constructed after piloting open-ended questions that assess the challenges in completing the task. Researchers have found significant and positive relationships between self-efficacy and achievement when the self-efficacy measures closely align with the criterion task (Aguayo, Herman, Ojeda, & Flores, 2011). While self-report measures are easy to administer and analyze and are cost effective, there are several concerns about using forced response questionnaires that limit their usefulness. Surveys rely on learners' memories, limit the information obtained, and may result in responses that make learners appear more attractive to the investigator (Bandura, 1997; Perry & Rahim, 2011).

Self-efficacy also has been measured using the *structured interview*. Structured interviews and hypothetical scenarios were used by Zimmerman and Martinez-Pons (1986) to assess high school students' self-regulated learning. Advantages of using structured interviews are that they provide opportunities for the interviewees to elaborate, clarify, and describe their thoughts and feelings (Wolters, Benzon, & Arroyo-Giner, 2011). Disadvantages include: a reliance on participants' memories and ability to articulate responses; increased time, effort, and cost in collecting and analyzing data; and concerns about protecting self-images.

In recent years, researchers have begun to use more dynamic assessments of self-efficacy, which better capture its capacity to change rapidly as learners develop skills. One such dynamic assessment is *think alouds*, which involve participants verbally reporting their thoughts, feelings, and behavior while performing a task (Wolters et al., 2011). Participants are audio or video recorded and there is little, if any, interference from the investigator. Greene, Moos, Azevedo, and Winters (2008) used think alouds to assess students' self-regulatory processes when studying the circulatory system. An advantage of using think alouds is that they provide rich information on the internal thoughts and feelings of the participants. Drawbacks include the distractions involved in talking aloud as one works, and the interference that may have on performance.

Another recent trend for assessing self-efficacy is using a *microanalytic methodology* which involves asking participants specific questions targeting motivational and self-regulated learning processes while students are engaged in a learning activity (Zimmerman et al., 2017). Participants may be audio or video recorded as they complete a task, but one difference from a think aloud is that the investigator will ask the participants questions related to the processes being examined during the actual learning event rather than leaving participants to simply vocalize their thoughts. The microanalytic methodology has been used in athletic (Cleary & Zimmerman, 2001; Kitsantas & Zimmerman, 2002), academic (DiBenedetto & Zimmerman, 2010), and clinical (Schunk & DiBenedetto, 2014) settings. DiBenedetto and Zimmerman (2013) established construct and predictive validity of microanalysis with high school juniors on a science learning task and found it to have greater predictive validity in comparison to a previously established self-efficacy for learning survey.

Microanalytic assessments provide opportunities for diagnostic interventions. Cleary and colleagues, for example, have used the microanalytic methodology with ethnically diverse and academically at-risk adolescents in urban middle and high schools (Cleary & Platten, 2013; Cleary, Velardi, & Schnaidman, 2016). Their findings suggest that microanalysis can provide insight into students' self-regulation, as well as identify areas for teacher intervention. One disadvantage is that the microanalytic methodology is labor intensive and time consuming. A significant advantage is that the information provided is real time rather than retrospective as with surveys and is richer and more comprehensive than surveys. By using specific questions during the learning event, researchers can ask participants to explain their actions, which are an advantage over the think aloud methodology where participants are verbally reporting what they are doing without much direction or intervention.

Sociocultural variables have the potential to affect assessment measures. For example, in some cultures, talking aloud while working may not be culturally appropriate or may seem awkward and thus impact the validity of the think-aloud assessment. Students from some cultural backgrounds may not feel comfortable using self-report measures. Interviews may prove problematic for students from cultures that do not value open sharing of information. And research has shown cultural differences in the accuracy of self-efficacy judgments (Chiu & Klassen, 2010; Klassen, 2004). Children from Western cultures tend to be more optimistic in their judgments; those from Eastern cultures more modest. With respect to gender, boys often are more optimistic about their self-efficacy than are girls, particularly in mathematics (Pajares, 2002). Given the evidence that sociocultural variables can influence self-efficacy judgments, more research on these variables is needed to provide better insight into interpretation of results.

Calibration

An important area of self-efficacy research is its calibration, or consistency with performance. Errors in calibration may reflect a *judgment bias*, or direction of judgment error, and an *accuracy bias*, which refers to the magnitude of the student's judgment error (Chen & Zimmerman, 2007). Researchers have investigated students' calibration by examining their responses to questions about self-efficacy and comparing these responses to their performance scores. In a microanalytic study, DiBenedetto and Zimmerman (2010) examined ethnically diverse high school juniors' self-efficacy for learning and performance by having students study a passage on tornadoes and then take a test. The passage included information about how a tornado is formed, how to calculate the power of a tornado using the Fujita scale, and how to protect oneself from an oncoming tornado. Participants were either at-risk, average, or high-achieving science students. Findings revealed that high-achieving students underestimated their self-efficacy for learning and performing well on the tornado knowledge test, whereas at-risk students overestimated their self-efficacy for learning and performing well. An important implication from these findings is that the consequence of inaccurate self-appraisals can affect behavior. Students who underestimate their capability to perform well may spend additional time and effort studying, thus ultimately achieving higher. Students who overestimate their capability to perform well may exert less effort and time needed to study, thus resulting in lower grades than anticipated. Inaccurate assessments of capabilities may hinder the quality and quantity of studying and ultimately achievement (Zimmerman et al., 2015).

Sociocultural variables can potentially lead to self-efficacy bias (Schunk & Pajares, 2009). With respect to school culture, students who can perform at higher levels but intentionally perform at lower levels may do so to fit in with peers or the school environment and to avoid being socially isolated. Research also shows that students may lack calibration even before school work begins. In a study conducted by DiBenedetto and Bembenutty (2013), college students enrolled in an ethnically diverse urban college's interme-diate level biology courses were assessed on their self-efficacy at the begin-ning and end of the semester. Students had higher levels of self-efficacy at the start of the semester than at the end and these end of semester self-effi-cacy levels were better calibrated with their final grades than the initial self-efficacy scores. This suggests that as students receive feedback from their performances, teachers, and peers, they may become more calibrated with their achievement.

Researchers have identified cultural differences in self-efficacy judg-ments and calibration. In a cross-national study examining mathematics calibration, Taiwanese and U.S. middle school students were asked self-efficacy questions for solving mathematical problems with increasing diffi-culty (Chen & Zimmerman, 2007). Students' self-efficacy in both groups decreased as the problems became more difficult while their calibration bias scores increased. This means that as the problems became more challeng-ing, students tended to overestimate their capability to solve the problems correctly. In addition, while students' calibration scores increased with prob-lem difficulty, the Taiwanese students were slightly more calibrated than the U.S. students, particularly on the intermediate problems. The Taiwanese stu-dents had significantly higher mathematical scores and were more accurate in their self-efficacy judgments. The results suggest that the U.S. students may be less in touch with their capabilities, a result supported by other cross-cultural studies showing U.S. students to be more optimistic (Klassen, 2004). This study highlights the need for additional research to determine how cross-cultural differences may affect self-efficacy and calibration.

Sociocultural Influences on Self-Efficacy

Culture

McInerney (2008) describes culture as one's beliefs and value systems which have an influence on motivation and learning. In a recent research review, McInerney and King (2018) found that most studies do not use cul-ture, race, or ethnicity as independent variables; rather, countries outside of the United States accept self-regulation processes and variables such as self-efficacy as part of a theoretical framework and examine these processes within different learning contexts. McInerney and King discuss the challenge with finding studies that examine cultural influences on core theoretical constructs that have been primarily established in the United States.

As mentioned earlier, a cultural dimension that has been explored widely in self-efficacy research is individualism and collectivism. Individualistic cultures tend to stress independence and individual initiative, whereas collectivist cultures emphasize group identity and "we" consciousness (Klassen, 2004). The United States and western European countries are high in individualism, whereas Asian cultures tend to be more collectivist. Researchers comparing these cultures typically find that individuals from collectivist cultures judge self-efficacy lower than do those from more individualistic cultures including when performances are equivalent or higher. Further, lower self-efficacy beliefs are typically better calibrated with actual performances (Klassen, 2004). These results suggest that collectivist cultures may promote modesty in self-efficacy judgments. They also raise the issue of whether collective efficacy (discussed later) may be a better predictor of performance in these cultures than individual self-efficacy (Klassen, 2004).

Bandura (1997) stated that labels such as individualistic and collectivist can lead to misleading generalizations. He cited an example of how in parts of East Asia some people follow Confucianism while others follow Buddhism. Even though both groups are from a collectivist society, they differ significantly from one another on values and customs. Self-efficacy beliefs are multifaceted and complex and he cited the work of Earley (1993, 1994) as evidence of the universality of self-efficacy beliefs. Bandura indicated that while self-efficacy beliefs are personal, they are influenced by a number of factors, including one's sociocultural background.

To illustrate these cultural differences, we contrast post-victory responses of persons from different cultures. Sergio Garcia, born in Spain, won a top golf tournament in the world after years of competing and being so close to winning but never doing it. These are his words in one of his first interviews after winning the 2017 Masters: "I think life has a purpose for all of us. And for me, it was mentally now. And I'm glad it was because of all the things that happened throughout my career. I think I learned so much. And it helped me grow up not only as a golfer but as a person. I think it made this victory taste even better" (CBS News, 2017). An American or European, such as Masters winner Garcia who is from an individualistic culture, may be more self-efficacious when he feels he has more control over his personal actions.

In contrast, persons from collectivist societies may feel more self-efficacious when they believe they can work with others for the betterment of the group. Immediately after winning the 2017 Indianapolis 500 car race, Takuma Sato stated, "Unbelievable feeling; I cannot thank enough the whole team. Look at these guys" (as he points to his team members huddling close by; Pittamiglio, 2017). Rather than discussing strategies he used or challenges he faced, he first recognized the work of his teammates.

Classrooms have students from myriad cultural backgrounds. While self-efficacy beliefs may be universal, the challenge for educators is to understand that students' values, beliefs, and sociocultural experiences can affect self-efficacy beliefs. The impact of political upheavals and immigration may further complicate this picture. McInerney and King (2018) suggest a need for more cross-cultural studies examining the potential culture-specific influences on learning, performance, and self-regulation.

Gender

Many researchers have investigated the role of gender on self-efficacy beliefs but primarily in academic settings and with a focus on disciplines that are historically male or female (Meece & Painter, 2008). For example, Pajares and Valiante (2001) investigated differences in self-efficacy beliefs for writing and found that middle school girls had higher self-efficacy beliefs than boys even though there were no performance differences. Girls tend to have lower self-efficacy beliefs for learning mathematics and science than boys (Zimmerman & Martinez-Pons, 1990). Gender differences in self-efficacy beliefs seem to begin around the middle school years (Schunk & Pajares, 2004), which may arise due to social conformity and the socialization of skills based on the belief that boys and girls have biological predispositions (Butler & Hasenfratz, 2017).

A recent direction is a focus on teachers' perceptions. Teachers have been shown to believe boys have greater mathematical abilities than girls and that girls have to work harder to succeed. Riegle-Crumb and Humphries (2012) examined high school teachers' stereotypical perceptions of students' ability to perform mathematics. They used data from the Educational Longitudinal Study of 2002 (ELS), which consisted of a national survey of high school students. As part of the study, the investigators asked the teachers of the ELS students to indicate whether their students were in mathematics classes that were too easy, appropriate, or too difficult. Teachers tended to rate boys as enrolled in classes that were too easy for them compared to girls, even after controlling for grades and test scores.

The challenge with these and similar findings is that they can lead to gender disparities in career trajectories (Bandura, 1997). Women's self-efficacy beliefs about career choices are influenced by early experiences with teachers, peers, mastery experiences, cultural values and expectations, social media, and families. Sex role stereotyping can hinder the choices girls make in deciding which classes to take in college and careers to ultimately pursue (DiBenedetto & Bembenutty, 2013). To the extent that girls underestimate and boys overestimate their self-efficacy in mathematics, calibration of self-efficacy with performance will be affected. Researchers should continue to explore methods of self-efficacy assessment that minimize such biases.

Families and SES

Families have the earliest effect on children's self-efficacy beliefs (Pomerantz, Cheung, & Qin, 2012). Parents who provide warm, supportive environments that encourage mastery experiences foster self-efficacy beliefs in their children (Schunk & DiBenedetto, 2016). As children see parents and siblings cope with challenges, use strategies, persist, and apply effort in times of difficulty, they learn from these observations how to handle similar situations, which fosters self-efficacy beliefs.

Homes that include resources and assets such as books, games, technology, and opportunities to visit museums, take trips, and provide exposure to successful models stimulate curiosity and intellectual development (DiBenedetto & Bembenutty, 2013; Schunk & Pajares, 2009). Families with members who are well educated and have wide social connections are likely to emphasize education to their children and to enroll them in programs (e.g., tutoring, camps, school, and after school programs) that foster their self-efficacy and learning (Schunk & DiBenedetto, 2016). Family SES and parental involvement can affect students' motivation and learning.

Families are also sources of cultural influence. Children learn from their families the prevailing cultural values that are expressed in multiple ways. Whether parents stress individual accomplishments or group/collective performance should be conveyed often (Chiu & Klassen, 2010). An important area for future research is to examine the process whereby cultural values learned from families manifest themselves in children's self-efficacy judgments.

Technology Uses to Build Self-Efficacy

Much research related to technology and self-efficacy has focused on measuring students' self-efficacy for using computers (Joo, Bong, & Choi, 2000). A literature review of computer-based learning environments (CBLEs) examined relationships between computer self-efficacy, self-regulated learning processes, and performance outcomes, and found three significant outcomes (Moos & Azevedo, 2009). The first is that there are both behavioral factors (e.g., familiarity with being in a CBLE) and psychological factors (e.g., positive attitude and curiosity about being in a CBLE) that are positively related to computer self-efficacy. Second, computer self-efficacy is positively related to self-regulated processes such as navigational strategies and metacognition. Third, computer self-efficacy is related to learning outcomes.

A new area of inquiry is game-based learning. Video gaming can be used to increase and sustain motivation and interest, and help students make connections to real-life situations (Foster, 2008). Video games are different from traditional simulations that have been used extensively in science education. Simulations provide learners with opportunities to use manipulatives, engage in problem-based learning activities, and participate in discovery learning, yet they may not sustain student interest beyond the classroom. Video games capture learners' attention, are fun and exciting to play, often involve cognitive flexibility and the ability to strategize, are familiar to many youngsters, and can be developed to target learning goals. Good instructional games can take advantage of learners' attention by allowing them to identify with avatars that represent the players or other characters (i.e., a marine biologist), which helps boost intrinsic interest in the learning.

A growing body of research focuses on the impact of gaming on science self-efficacy and science learning. In one study, 100 fifth-grade students played a three-dimensional online game called Crystal Island (Meluso, Zheng, Spires, & Lester, 2012). Students were administered pre- and post-tests and results indicated there were significant gains in science content learning and self-efficacy. Ketelhut (2007) examined seventh graders' science self-efficacy for gathering data in a virtual environment, and found an increase in science self-efficacy and performance. A meta-analysis found that interactive simulations and video games resulted in improved cognitive gains and achievement compared with traditional classroom instruction (Vogel et al., 2006). These findings offer much promise for the role of gaming to build self-efficacy.

The role that technology may play in the development of self-efficacy in various settings (e.g., CBLEs, gaming, online social media) should be subject to sociocultural influences. Children from families with higher SES are more likely to have exposure and access to technology at a young age as compared to children of lower SES. Consequently, high SES children may feel more self-efficacious and motivated to use technology than their lower-SES counterparts. It seems possible that individualistic cultures may place greater emphasis on accomplishments using technology whereas collectivist cultures may instead put more stress on information sharing. Research has shown that girls may be less likely to choose opportunities for computer science compared with boys (Master, Cheryan, & Meltzoff, 2016). Family socialization on the importance of using computers is another cultural variable that impacts technology use (Ortiz, Green, & Lim, 2011). An important area for future self-efficacy research will be to determine how various sociocultural factors may influence students' self-efficacy and technology use.

Self-Efficacy in Group and Nonacademic Settings

Most self-efficacy research has been done with individuals, but as this chapter suggests, collective self-efficacy may be a better predictor of performance in certain cultural contexts. *Collective efficacy* refers to the self-efficacy of a group, team, or larger social entity. It is not simply the sum of the self-efficacy of the individual members but rather the group's perceptions of their capabilities for producing desired outcomes. Relative to individual self-efficacy, there is much less research on collective efficacy, yet the latter holds promise as a valid predictor of performance among individuals in more collectivistic environments. Given the current educational emphasis on group projects, cooperative learning, and problem-based learning, we recommend that investigating collective efficacy be a research priority.

To test the generality of self-efficacy as a predictor of motivation and learning, more research is needed on self-efficacy in nonacademic settings such as health, mentoring, bullying, and even terrorism. Schwarzer and Luszczynska (2015), for example, looked at cross-cultural studies on self-efficacy as a predictor, mediator, and moderator of dietary behaviors, exercise, dental care, sunscreen usage, managing diabetes, and worksite health. They distinguish different types of self-efficacy for health behavior change: *action self-efficacy* that predicts intentions and involves planning, *coping self-efficacy* that involves the link between the planning and behavior, and *recovery self-efficacy* that involves the maintenance of the behavior. Understanding how well the different types of self-efficacy helps predict health behavior change such as eating more fruits and vegetables, increasing physical activities, flossing one's teeth regularly, and managing stress at work, contributes to the self-efficacy literature and has implications for practice.

Mentoring relationships also can enhance mentees' self-efficacy (Schunk & Mullen, 2013). Mentors are models who show how tasks are completed and what proficiency levels are required for successful completion of tasks. They demonstrate self-regulation and how to cope in challenging situations. Through the development of self-regulated competency, mentors can foster mentees' self-efficacy and help them become independent, adaptable, and self-directed (DiBenedetto & White, 2013), but further research is needed on mentoring variables that may impact self-efficacy, such as characteristics of mentors that may appeal to mentees.

Unfortunately, in today's volatile times, dealing with cyberbullying, terrorism, and morality issues are concerns most educators are not prepared to deal with and are ones our younger generations will grapple with for most of their lives. Bandura (2016) discusses how self-efficacy beliefs come into play in bullying. According to Bandura, bullying is socially situated, meaning it takes place in a social setting involving victims, bullies, and bystanders. Bystanders may not intervene unless they feel self-efficacious to do so without getting harmed themselves.

Terrorists are self-efficacious in their beliefs about their ability to effect change (Bandura, 2016). They are not poor, lost, and confused individuals who have a low sense of self-efficacy. Rather, youngsters who are nourished in self-efficacy in their formative years feel empowered to lead militant acts and it is those individuals who present the most danger. The leaders of al Qaeda, and the hijackers on the September 11th planes, came from wealthy, educated families. Research comparing terrorists with non-terrorists has not identified differences in emotional stability (Abrahms, 2008). Additional research will help us better understand the operation of self-efficacy in these and other nonacademic contexts.

CONCLUSION

Since the first edition of this *volume* there have been many exciting developments in self-efficacy research and practice including in the areas of theoretical differentiation, assessment, and calibration. In particular, newer methods for real-time assessment of self-efficacy offer promise in understanding its dynamic role in predicting outcomes. The influence that various sociocultural factors may exert on self-efficacy has been increasingly demonstrated, and there is a clear need for further self-efficacy research in diverse learning environments—in and out of school. Self-efficacy's prominent role in individual and collective settings will likely lead researchers to continue to study self-efficacy with great interest globally.

REFERENCES

Abrahms, M. (2008). What terrorists really want: Terrorist motives and counterterrorism. *International Security, 32*(4), 78–105.

Aguayo, D., Herman, K., Ojeda, L., & Flores, L. Y. (2011). Culture predicts Mexican American's college self-efficacy and college performance. *Journal of Diversity in Higher Education, 4*, 79–89.

Bandura, A. (1986). *Social foundations of thought and action.* Upper Saddle River, NJ: Prentice Hall.

Bandura, A. (1997). *Self-efficacy: The exercise of control.* New York, NY: Freeman.

Bandura, A. (2005). Guide for creating self-efficacy scales. In F. Pajares & T. Urdan (Eds.), *Self-efficacy beliefs of adolescents* (pp. 307–338). Greenwich, CT: Information Age.

Bandura, A. (2016). *Moral disengagement: How people do harm and live with themselves.* New York, NY: Worth.

Bayer, U. C., & Gollwitzer, P. M. (2007). Boosting scholastic test scores by willpower: The role of implementation intentions. *Self and Identity, 6,* 1–19.

Bembenutty, H., Cleary, T., & Kitsantas, A. (2013). *Applications of self-regulated learning across diverse disciplines: A tribute to Barry J. Zimmerman.* Charlotte, NC: Information Age.

Bembenutty, H., White, M. C., & DiBenedetto, M. K. (2016). Applying social cognitive theory in the development of self-regulated competencies throughout K–12 grades. In A. A. Lipnevich, P. Preckel, & R. D. Roberts (Eds.), *Psychosocial skills and school systems in the 21st Century: Theory, research, and applications* (pp. 215–239). New York, NY: Springer.

Butler, R., & Hasenfratz, L. (2017). Gender and competence motivation. In A. Elliot, C. Dweck, & D. Yeager (Eds.), *Handbook of competence and motivation* (2nd ed., pp. 489–511). New York, NY: Guilford Press.

CBS News (2017, April 11). *Sergio Garcia on Masters victory: "I was just screaming."* Retrieved from: http://www.cbsnews.com/news/masters-sergio-garcia-win-champion-augusta-golf/

Chen, P., & Zimmerman, B. J. (2007). A cross-national comparison study on the accuracy of self-efficacy beliefs of middle-school mathematics students. *The Journal of Experimental Education, 75*(3) 221–244.

Chiu, M. M., & Klassen, R. M. (2010). Relations of mathematics self-concept and its calibration with mathematics achievement: Cultural differences among fifteen-year-olds in 34 countries. *Learning and Instruction, 20,* 2–17.

Cleary, T. J., & Platten, P. (2013). Examining the correspondence between self-regulated learning and academic achievement: A case study analysis. *Education Research International, 2013*(Article ID 272560), 18 pages. doi:10.1155/2013/272560

Cleary, T. J., Velardi, B., & Schnaidman, B. (2016, April). *Effects of a Self-Regulated Empowerment Program (SREP) on middle school students' strategic skills and mathematics achievement.* Paper presented at the annual meeting of the American Educational Research Association, Washington, DC.

Cleary, T. J., & Zimmerman, B. J. (2001). Self-practice by experts, non-experts, and novices. *Journal of Applied Sport Psychology, 13,* 61–82.

Credé, M., Tynan, M. C., & Harms, P. D. (2016). Much ado about grit: A meta-analytic synthesis of grit literature. *Journal of Personality and Social Psychology,* 1–20.

DiBenedetto, M. K., & Bembenutty, H. (2013). Within the pipeline: Self-regulated learning, self-efficacy, and socialization among college students in science courses. *Learning and Individual Differences, 23,* 218–224.

DiBenedetto, M. K., & Garrett, M. A. (in press). The art of self-regulated learning: Teaching the visual arts. In M. K. DiBenedetto (Ed.), *Connecting self-regulated learning and performance with instruction across high school content areas.* Dordrecht, Netherlands: Springer.

DiBenedetto, M. K., & White, M. C. (2013). Applying the model of development of self-regulatory competence to mentoring. In H. Bembenutty, T. Cleary, & A. Kitsantas, (Eds.), *Applications of self-regulated learning across diverse disciplines: A tribute to Barry J. Zimmerman* (pp. 445–472). Charlotte, NC: Information Age.

DiBenedetto, M. K., & Zimmerman, B. J. (2010). Differences in self-regulatory processes among students studying science: A microanalytic investigation. *The International Journal of Educational and Psychological Assessment, 5*(1), 2–24.

DiBenedetto, M. K., & Zimmerman, B. J. (2013). Construct and predictive validity of microanalytic measures of students' self-regulation of science learning. *Learning and Individual Differences, 26*, 30–41.

Duckworth, A. L., & Gross, J. J. (2014). Self-control and grit: Related but separable determinants of success. *Current Directions in Psychological Science, 23*, 319–325.

Duckworth, A. L., Peterson, C., Matthews, M. D., & Kelly, R. D. (2007). Grit: Perseverance and passion for long-term goals. *Journal of Personality and Social Psychology, 92*, 1087–1101.

Earley. P. C. (1993). Supervisors and shop stewards as sources of contextual information in goal setting: A comparison of the United States with England. *Journal of Applied Psychology, 71*, 111–117.

Earley, P. C. (1994). Self or group? Cultural effects of training on self-efficacy and performance. *Administrative Science Quarterly, 39*, 89–117.

Foster, A. (2008). Games and motivation to learn science: Personal identity, applicability, relevance and meaningfulness. *Journal of Interactive Learning Research, 19*(4), 597–614.

Galton, F., Sir (1979). *Hereditary genius: An inquiry into its laws and consequences.* London, England: Julian Friedman. (Originally published in 1869)

Greene, J. A., Moos, D. C., Azevedo, R., & Winters, F. I. (2008). Exploring differences between gifted and grade-level students' use of self-regulatory processes with hypermedia. *Computers & Education, 50*, 1069–1083.

Joo, Y. J., Bong, M., & Choi, H. J. (2000). Self-efficacy for self-regulated learning, academic self-efficacy, and internet self-efficacy in web-based instruction. *Educational Research Technology and Development, 48*(2), 5–17.

Ketelhut, D. J. (2007). The impact of student self-efficacy on scientific inquiry skills: An exploratory investigation in River City, a multi-user virtual environment. *The Journal of Science Education and Technology, 16*(1), 99–111.

Kitsantas, A., & Zimmerman, B. J. (2002). Comparing self-regulatory processes among novel, non-expert, and expert volleyball players: A microanalytic study. *Journal of Applied Sport Psychology, 14*, 91–105.

Klassen, R. M. (2004). Optimism and realism: A review of self-efficacy from a cross-cultural perspective. *International Journal of Psychology, 39*, 205–230.

Linnenbrink, E. A., & Pintrich, P. R. (2003). The role of self-efficacy beliefs in student engagement and learning in the classroom. *Reading & Writing Quarterly, 19*, 119–137.

Marks, H. M. (2000). Student engagement in instructional activity: Patterns in the elementary, middle, and high school years. *American Educational Research Journal, 37*, 153–184.

Master, A., Cheryan, S., & Meltzoff, A. N. (2016). Computing whether she belongs: Stereotypes undermine girls' interest and sense of belonging in computer science. *Journal of Educational Psychology, 108*, 424–437.

McInerney, D. M. (2008). The motivational roles of cultural differences and cultural identity in self-regulated learning. In D. H. Schunk & B. J. Zimmerman

(Eds.), *Motivation and self-regulated learning: Theory, research, and applications* (pp. 369–400). New York, NY: Erlbaum.

McInerney, D. M., & King, R. (2018). Culture and self-regulation in educational contexts. In D. H. Schunk & J. A. Greene (Eds.), *Handbook of self-regulation of learning and performance* (2nd ed., pp. 485–502). New York, NY: Routledge.

Meece, J. L., & Painter, J. (2008). Gender, self-regulation, and motivation. In D. H. Schunk & B. J. Zimmerman (Eds.), *Motivation and self-regulated learning: Theory, research, and applications* (pp. 339–368). New York, NY: Erlbaum.

Meluso, A., Zheng, M., Spires, H. A., & Lester, J. (2012). Enhancing 5th graders science content knowledge and self-efficacy through game-based learning. *Computers & Education, 59*, 497–504.

Moos, D. C., & Azevedo, R. (2009). Learning with computer-based learning environments: A literature review of computer self-efficacy. *Review of Educational Research, 79*, 576–600.

Ortiz, R. W., Green, T., & Lim, H. J. (2011). Families and home computer use: Exploring parent perceptions of the importance of current technology. *Urban Education, 46*(2), 202–215.

Pajares, F. (1997). Self-efficacy beliefs in achievement settings. Review of educational research. In M. Maehr & P. R. Pintrich (Eds.), *Advances in motivation and achievement* (Vol. 10, pp. 1–49). Greenwich, CT: JAI Press.

Pajares, F. (2002). Gender and perceived self-efficacy in self-regulated learning. *Theory into Practice, 41*(2), 116–25.

Pajares, F., & Urdan, T. (2006). *Self-efficacy beliefs of adolescents*. Greenwich, CT: Information Age.

Pajares, F., & Valiante, G. (2001). Gender differences in writing motivation and achievement of middle school students: A function of gender orientation? *Contemporary Educational Psychology, 26*, 366–381.

Perry, N. E., & Rahim, A. (2011). Studying self-regulated learning in classrooms. In B. J. Zimmerman, & D. H. Schunk (Eds.), *Handbook of self-regulation of learning and performance* (pp. 122–136). New York, NY: Routledge.

Pittamiglio, E. (2017, May 25). *Takuma Sato wins 101st running of the Indianapolis 500 (Indy 500)* [Online video]. Retrieved from https://www.youtube.com/watch?v=S0UC1Rqf1gE

Pomerantz, E. M., Cheung, C. S. S., & Qin, L. (2012). Relatedness between children and parents: Implications for motivation. In R. M. Ryan (Ed.), *The Oxford handbook of human motivation* (pp. 335–349). Oxford, England: Oxford University Press.

Riegle-Crumb, C., & Humphries, M. (2012). Exploring bias in math teachers' perceptions of ability by gender and race/ethnicity. *Gender and Society, 26*(2), 290–322.

Ryan, R. M., & Deci, E. L. (2016). Facilitating and hindering motivation, learning, and well-being in schools: Research and observations from self-determination theory. In K. R. Wentzel & D. B. Miele (Eds.), *Handbook of motivation at school* (2nd ed., pp. 96–119). New York, NY: Routledge.

Schwarzer, R., & Luszczynska, A. (2015). Self-beliefs and self-regulation in health behavior change. In F. Guay, R. Craven, H. Marsh, & D. M. McInerney (Eds.),

Self-concept, motivation and identity: Underpinning success with research and practice (pp. 201–224). Charlotte, NC: Information Age.

Schunk, D. H. (2012). Social cognitive theory. In K. R. Harris, S. Graham, & T. Urdan (Eds.), *APA educational psychology handbook, Vol. 1: Theories, constructs, and critical issues* (pp. 101–123). Washington, DC: American Psychological Association.

Schunk, D. H., & DiBenedetto, M. K. (2014). Academic self-efficacy. In M. J. Furlong, R. Gilman, & E. S. Huebner (Eds.), *Handbook of positive psychology in schools* (pp. 115–521). New York, NY: Routledge.

Schunk, D. H., & DiBenedetto, M. K. (2016). Self-efficacy theory in education. In K. R. Wentzel & D. Miele (Eds.), *Handbook of motivation at school* (2nd ed., pp. 34–54). New York, NY: Routledge.

Schunk, D. H., Meece, J. L., & Pintrich, P. R. (2014*). Motivation in education: Theory, research, and applications* (4th ed.). Boston, MA: Pearson Education.

Schunk, D. H., & Mullen, C. A. (2013). Toward a conceptual model of mentoring research: Integration with self-regulated learning. *Educational Psychology Review, 25*(3), 361–389.

Schunk, D. H., & Pajares, F. (2004). Self-efficacy in education revisited: Empirical and applied evidence. In D. M. McInerney & S. VanEtten (Eds.), *Big theories revisited* (pp. 115–138). Greenwich, CT: Information Age.

Schunk, D. H., & Pajares, F. (2009). Self-efficacy theory. In K. R. Wentzel & A. Wigfield (Eds.), *Handbook of motivation at school* (pp. 35–53). New York, NY: Routledge.

Schunk, D. H., & Zimmerman, B. J. (1997). Social origins of self-regulatory competence. *Educational Psychologist, 32*, 195–208.

Skinner, E. A. (2016). Engagement and disaffection as central to processes of motivational resilience and development. In K. R. Wentzel & D. B. Miele (Eds.), *Handbook of motivation at school* (2nd ed., pp. 145–168). New York, NY: Routledge.

Tennis, D. (2017, May 25). *Serena Williams championship interview|Australian Open 2017* [Online video]. Retrieved from https://www.youtube.com/watch?v=zX07W0XeeDs

Usher, E. L., & Schunk, D. H. (2018). Social cognitive theoretical perspective of self-regulation. In D. H. Schunk & J. A. Greene (Eds.), *Handbook of self-regulation of learning and performance* (2nd ed., pp. 19–35). New York, NY: Routledge.

Vogel, J. J., Vogel, D. S., Cannon-Bowers, J., Bowers, C. A., Muse, K., & Wright, M. (2006). Computer gaming and interactive simulations for learning: A meta-analysis. *Journal of Educational Computing Research, 34*(3), 229–243.

White, M. C., & DiBenedetto, M. K. (2015). *Self-regulation and the common core: Application to ELA standards.* New York, NY: Routledge.

Wieber, F., Odenthal, G., & Gollwitzer, P. (2010). Self-efficacy feelings moderate implementation intention effects. *Self and Identity. 9*, 177–194.

Wigfield, A., Tonks, S. M., & Klauda, S. L. (2016). Expectancy-value theory. In K. R. Wentzel & D. B. Miele (Eds.), *Handbook of motivation at school* (2nd ed., pp. 55–74). New York, NY: Routledge.

Wolters, C. A., Benzon, M. B., & Arroyo-Giner, C. (2011). In B. J. Zimmerman & D. H. Schunk (Eds.), *Handbook of self-regulation of learning and performance* (pp. 298–312). New York, NY: Routledge.

Zimmerman, B. J. (2000). Attaining self-regulation: A social cognitive perspective. In M. Boekaerts, P. R. Pintrich, & M. Zeidner (Eds.), *Handbook of self-regulation* (pp. 13–39). San Diego, CA: Academic Press.

Zimmerman, B. J. (2011). Motivational sources and outcomes of self-regulated learning and performance. In B. J. Zimmerman & D. H. Schunk (Eds.), *Handbook of self-regulation of learning and performance* (pp. 49–64). New York, NY: Routledge.

Zimmerman, B. J., & DiBenedetto, M. K. (2008). Mastery learning and assessment: Students and teachers in an era of high stakes testing. *Psychology in the Schools, 45*(3), 206–216.

Zimmerman, B. J., & Martinez-Pons, M. (1986). Development of a structured interview to assess student use of self-regulated learning strategies. *American Educational Research Journal, 23*(4), 614–628.

Zimmerman, B. J., & Martinez-Pons, M. (1990). Student differences in self-regulated learning: Relating grade, sex, and giftedness to self-efficacy and strategy use. *Journal of Educational Psychology, 82*, 51–59.

Zimmerman, B. J., & Schunk, B. J. (2011). *Handbook of self-regulation of learning and performance*. New York, NY: Routledge.

Zimmerman, B. J., Schunk, B. J., & DiBenedetto, M. K. (2015). A personal agency view of self-regulated learning: The role of goal setting. In F. Guay, R. Craven, H. Marsh, & D. McInerney (Eds.), *Self-concept, motivation and identity: Underpinning success with research and practice* (pp. 83–224). Charlotte, NC: Information Age.

Zimmerman, B. J., Schunk, B. J., & DiBenedetto, M. K. (2017). Role of self-efficacy and related beliefs in self-regulation of learning and performance. In A. Elliot, C. Dweck, & D. Yeager (Eds.), *Handbook of competence and motivation* (2nd ed., pp. 83–114). New York, NY: Guilford Press.

CHAPTER 7

SOCIOCULTURAL INFLUENCES ON SELF-EFFICACY DEVELOPMENT

Ellen L. Usher
Brianna L. Weidner

Mia settled into her math class during the first week of middle school. Her teacher, Mr. Anderson, announced that class would begin with a 30-minute test to assess students' background knowledge. Mia automatically began to think about her math capabilities. *Can I do well on this? Thirty minutes is a long time. Can I concentrate? Can I solve the types of problems that middle school students are expected to solve?* With these questions came a flurry of memories. Mia's thoughts then moved to the math class she was in. Maybe it wasn't by chance that she was placed in Mr. Anderson's class. Her eyes scanned the students around her. They briefly met her teacher's gaze. As she silently self-assessed, a math test appeared on her desk. Time to begin.

This academic setting is familiar enough. A teacher wishes to assess his students' ability level in math. He might naively assume that how students perform on his exam will directly reflect their elementary school preparation. But this would be too simple. A basic premise of this chapter is that

Big Theories Revisited 2, pages 141–164
Copyright © 2018 by Information Age Publishing
All rights of reproduction in any form reserved.

students, by their own psychological power to self-reflect, are in part key influencers of their own behavior. As Mia reflects on her past and present experiences and the contextual and situational factors around her, she comes to view herself as more or less capable of a solid performance. A wise teacher and parent knows that Mia's own thoughts and feelings can also sway her performance.

We will revisit Mia's experience throughout this chapter, which focuses on the development of self-efficacy in academic contexts. In doing so, we build on Dale Schunk and Frank Pajares's (2004) chapter in the previous *Big Theories* volume (McInerney & Van Etten, 2004), which reviewed compelling evidence that learners' self-efficacy, their beliefs about their academic capabilities, predict not only their academic performance but the amount of effort they put forth and how long they persist. Research over the past two decades has continued to show the power of self-efficacy in guiding human performance in diverse domains, such as learning, teaching, healthcare, sports, the workplace, civic engagement, and in the arts. Reviews and meta-analyses have shown that, in educational settings, students' with higher self-efficacy do better academically, are more skilled at regulating their own behaviors and emotions, and are more motivated to learn (e.g., Klassen & Usher, 2010; Richardson, Abraham, & Bond, 2012; Williams & Williams, 2010). Nevertheless, the level of self-efficacy that students report has been shown to differ across cultural contexts, which may signify that students form their self-efficacy differently according to their sociocultural background and local context (Klassen, 2004b; Lee, 2009; Oettingen & Zosuls, 2006). In this chapter we pursue the logical questions that follow from these findings: Where does self-efficacy come from? Do students develop their self-efficacy in similar ways? Do they rely on similar sources of ability information in different sociocultural conditions?

We begin by situating self-efficacy and its hypothesized sources within Bandura's (1986, 1997) social cognitive model of triadic reciprocality. As did Bandura, we emphasize how sociocultural context might affect individuals' interpretations of information from various sources, which in turn vary in their relative influence on individuals' self-appraisals. We also examine the theorized processes or mechanisms responsible for variation in how learners' self-efficacy develops. We consider the methodological approaches that have been used to examine cultural variations in the formation of self-efficacy in diverse contexts and reveal key findings from this research. We highlight limitations in this body of research and raise questions for researchers interested in a deeper understanding of the role that culture plays in self-efficacy development. We close by evaluating the contribution of research on the sources of self-efficacy to educational practice.

SOCIOCOGNITIVE INFLUENCES ON SELF-EFFICACY DEVELOPMENT

Bandura's (1986) social cognitive theory contends that all human functioning can be explained through the reciprocal influence of behavioral, environmental, and personal (e.g., cognitive, biological, motivational) factors. From this view, learners are not simply shaped by reinforcements or punishments from their environment but are also able to influence their own educational trajectories through their personal capacities. These personal capacities include the ability to self-reflect, to forecast the future, to learn vicariously, and to regulate one's life in the face of varying environmental demands. As a consequence, people are not just products of their environment, but producers of them (Bandura, 1997). Through their self-reflective evaluations and self-set standards, people can monitor and guide their own behavior. Bandura (2016) has contended that *self-efficacy*, or one's perceived capabilities to achieve desired goals, "is the foundation of human aspirations, motivation, and accomplishments" (p. 5). Those who view themselves as capable of achieving the outcomes they desire typically ensure their own success through perseverant effort. Those beset with self-doubt tend to withdraw from challenging pursuits (Bandura, 1997).

To understand the importance of self-efficacy, we must first consider what it means to be an "efficacious" or effective learner. Certainly, a student must be able to read and understand the learning content. But many other skills support reading and learning, such as selecting appropriate study techniques, minimizing distractions, and managing one's time (Usher & Schunk, 2018). Cognitive skills are also required, such as parsing out relevant information and making meaningful connections that facilitate retrieval. Effective learners must then be able to demonstrate what they have learned in a variety of ways (e.g., on tests, in writing, through projects, orally). Last but not least, learning involves the effective navigation of complex social and emotional landscapes. Without the efficacy to manage one's emotions, learning would be impaired. In short, students form beliefs about their efficacy for all these skills, and the pathways to developing one's self-efficacy in any particular domain may differ markedly.

In the chapter's opening story about Mia, we see a swirl of thoughts the young learner has, any of which might affect Mia's math performance. If Mia were simply a product of her environment, we would have no reason to attribute any causal power to her self-beliefs and emotions. But a social-cognitive view contends that Mia's performance will depend partly on her environmental circumstances and partly on her own cognitive and affective processes, including her self-efficacy (Pajares & Usher, 2008). As we will see next, both internal and external events influence what Mia will believe herself capable of.

SOURCES OF SELF-EFFICACY: DEFINING FEATURES

Bandura (1997) hypothesized that people rely on four primary sources of information when judging what they can do: their own past performance, the modeled actions of others, evaluative social messages, and their own physiological and affective states. None of these sources of information is guaranteed to raise or lower self-efficacy; their influence on self-efficacy depends on numerous contextual and individual factors, which we discuss below. Furthermore, it might appear that some sources of information (e.g., one's past performance) are exclusively internal to the individual; however, their influence cannot be divorced from the social contexts in which they occur (Bandura, 1997).

Enactive Experience

People tend to look to their own direct experience when judging their capabilities. When her math teacher announced a test during the first week of school, Mia's thoughts immediately went to her past experiences with math. Most often, successful past performances provide a strong boost to one's sense of efficacy (Usher & Pajares, 2008). But under certain circumstances, apparent successes do little to change self-efficacy and may even undermine it. For example, if one's success was claimed with little effort or with too much help from others, it provides little capability-related information (Bandura, 1997). Generally speaking, however, perceived mastery experience in a domain typically raises self-efficacy; perceived failures or missteps lower it.

Vicarious Experience

Individuals also look to the performances of others as sources of information about their own capabilities. Seeing how Ian, her fifth-grade friend and competitor, strategizes and solves math problems makes Mia feel more certain that she could tackle problems in a similar way. Teachers and parents can model skills that raise students' self-efficacy. Observing others can also lower self-efficacy, such as when one sees an esteemed classmate struggle. The degree to which social models influence self-efficacy depends in part on how similar the observer feels to the model. "The greater the assumed similarity, the more persuasive are the models' successes and failures" (Bandura, 1997, p. 87). The social environment often provides ability-related information. For example, in a learning environment where success is primarily defined in terms of one's performance relative to others, social comparisons become an important source of self-efficacy. Underperforming compared to one's classmates can have a devastating psychological effect, whereas surpassing others can provide a boost to one's confidence. As with other sources of information, the ultimate influence of vicarious experience on self-efficacy depends on numerous factors, including comparative standards set both internally (e.g., whom one chooses as a model) and externally (e.g., what is emphasized by one's sociocultural environment).

Social Persuasion

"You've almost got this. You can do it," cheered Mia's third-grade teacher, Ms. Juven, when Mia became frustrated with multiplication. Such persuasive messages can help learners maintain a belief in their own efficacy when academic work becomes tough. On the contrary, expressions that convey doubt about a person's capabilities can undermine self-efficacy. Social evaluations from respected members of one's community might carry particular influence. Careful framing of evaluative feedback in terms of one's personal progress can sustain a sense of efficacy (Bandura, 1997). Harsh criticism can lead to discouragement, whereas constructive critique can convince people of their own efficacy to reach their goals. Social messages are only persuasive to the extent that they are interpreted as such. Students can readily see through effusive or nonspecific praise, which can backfire and have the opposite effect on students' self-efficacy. A struggling student whose teacher frequently says, "Good job!" might come to believe his teacher gives him extra encouragement because he lacks ability.

Physiological and Affective States

Often in the background of one's life is an awareness of one's general affective and physiological state. In any given situation, individuals predict and adjust to their incoming sensations, and they use situational cues and past experience to make meaning of their feelings (Barrett, 2017). In turn, these perceived physiological and affective states can influence how capable individuals view themselves in given situations. Sweaty palms and racing heart at the start of a timed writing assignment could be viewed as signs of personal deficiency. The same arousal might signify to another student that she is ready to meet the challenge. In physical endeavors, the association between bodily states and self-efficacy might be more readily apparent. Feeling her body become tense when her teacher announced a math test might have prompted Mia to conclude that she could not perform well, but by conjuring up a pleasant memory, Mia could calm herself before she begins. As with external information, one's internal physical and emotional states influence self-efficacy according to how the individual perceives and interprets them.

SOCIAL COGNITIVE PROCESSING IN SELF-EFFICACY DEVELOPMENT: THE ROLE OF CULTURE

Let us now consider how culture can influence self-efficacy development. From a sociocognitive perspective, a host of cognitive, behavioral, and environmental processes are involved in a student's exposure to, perception of, and interpretation of efficacy-relevant information (see Figure 7.1). These processes can be relevant at one or more points during self-efficacy development. Before Mia entered Mr. Anderson's class, she had formulated a sense of herself as a math student, and she had tendencies to pay attention to certain features of her learning environment. She might also have been socialized to believe that some people are good at math. We could say that Mia arrived in sixth grade with certain socio-cognitive predispositions that made her hyperaware of some things and dismissive of others.

Situational and cultural factors also cue individuals to perceive certain information (and in turn to perceive themselves) in distinct ways. Oyserman

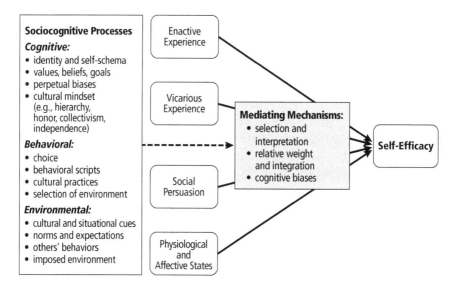

Figure 7.1 Sociocognitive influences on self-efficacy development. A host of sociocognitive processes are involved in the perception, activation, and selection of efficacy-relevant information. The ultimate influence of the four informational sources on learners' academic self-efficacy depends on these processes and a mediating cognitive mechanisms.

(2017) has suggested that these cues are "particular to a society, time, and place" (p. 437) and activate one's "cultural mindset," which carries with it certain goals and rules for how to interpret life's ambiguities. Cultural mindsets (e.g., collectivistic, individualistic, honor) have been shown to differ in how they affect learners' self-construal (Kitayama & Uskul, 2011). For example, Klassen (2004b) found that self-efficacy was lower among individuals from collectivistic cultures than from individualistic cultures. However, self-efficacy was equally or more predictive of performance in collectivistic cultures than in individualistic cultures. These findings do not indicate that self-efficacy "is a culturally bound Western construct that operates only as an *imposed etic* in non-Western cultural settings" (Klassen, 2004b, p. 225). Self-efficacy is still as relevant for individuals in collectivistic cultures who may prioritize their group's accomplishments because "without a resilient sense of self, people are easily overwhelmed by adversities in their attempts to improve their group life through collective effort" (Bandura, 1997, p. 32).

Researchers have argued that learners with a collectivistic mindset tend to view the self as interdependent and define the self in relation to the social positions of others (Kitayama & Uskul, 2011; Stephens, Markus, & Phillips, 2014). From this perspective, self-efficacy might be "determined by and contingent on the thoughts, feelings, and actions of others" (Chang et al., 2011, p. 121) rather than by one's own performance accomplishments. People with an individualistic mindset, on the other hand, are more apt to process information in terms of a self that is independent of the thoughts and actions of others. A review of cross-cultural research showed that Chinese and other Asian students whose national cultures are oriented toward collectivism place higher value on information obtained from hierarchically superior others (e.g., parents, teachers) than do students from Western cultures (Chang et al., 2011).

Personal value systems, in addition to broader cultural norms and expectations, can influence the ways in which people perceive and interpret the sources of self-efficacy. The same "objective" source of information may boost the self-efficacy of one student, yet leave another unaffected. The degree to which efficacy-relevant events change a learner's self-efficacy depends on a number of mediating processes including situational factors (where and under what conditions an event took place) and internal factors (personal standards and goals). To an average-ability American student attending an average-performing suburban high school, earning a B on an exam might raise self-efficacy. To a German adolescent attending the selective *gymnasium*, earning a similar grade (e.g., a 2+) might be devastating. As they interpret their experiences, students use different rules for weighting and integrating efficacy-related information based on their own unique experiences, identity, and context.

The social cognitive perspective does not position culture as a categorical "lens" through which self-efficacy information is perceived. This is because "cultures are diverse and dynamic social systems, not static monoliths" (Bandura, 2002, p. 269). Wide variation exists within and between cultures, and people's cognitive appraisal of cultural information varies. Students are likely to "engage with and get shaped by more than one culture" in different ways (Morris, Chiu, & Liu, 2015, p. 634). Imagine, for instance, a 16-year-old Latina student from rural South Carolina who has just received her teacher's critical comments on her Advanced Placement English composition paper. How might the student's own cultural identity affect the meaning she makes of her teacher's feedback? This depends in part on which identity is salient to her and which is made salient by her learning context (and the interaction of the two). She might see herself as a girl, southerner, Latina, immigrant, non-native English speaker, or an outsider. She might see herself as gifted, advanced, and skilled. How she ultimately interprets the feedback and revises her writing self-efficacy will depend on a complex set of processes that cannot be reduced to one interpretive lens. She, like all humans, is polycultural (belonging to many cultural groups), and her self-assessment will be situated in her local learning context.

The point we wish to make is that students' knowledge, experiences, identity, and sense of self can be influenced by how they make meaning of their many cultural memberships and by how their cultural memberships are viewed by others in their social environment. Cultural influences on self-efficacy development must therefore be considered as socially constructed (i.e., situated) and as subject to change (i.e., dynamic).

Research on the Sources of Self-Efficacy in Diverse Sociocultural Contexts

We now turn our attention to recent research investigating the sources of self-efficacy. In what contexts have researchers studied self-efficacy development? What have they found? We refer readers to Usher and Pajares (2008) for a review of earlier work in this area, which concluded with a call for additional studies that would better "capture the personal, social, situational, and temporal conditions under which students cognitively process and appraise their beliefs and experiences" (p. 784). We use this call as a framework for describing studies on the sources of self-efficacy that have been conducted in the past decade and emphasize how this body of work highlights the role of sociocultural context.

General Overview and Findings

Recent studies on the sources of academic self-efficacy have typically focused on STEM-related subjects (most often math). Fewer have focused on self-efficacy for general learning or language-based subjects such as reading, writing, or language acquisition. Most have featured middle school or university students as subject groups of interest, although several studies have examined elementary and high school students. The largest number of studies reviewed were conducted in Asian contexts such as China, Korea, and Taiwan with fewer studies conducted in the United States, Europe, Australia, and the Middle East.

Diverse methodological techniques have allowed for a clearer picture of how self-efficacy develops across samples and contexts. Pattern-centered approaches have helped detect trends in students' exposure to and perceptions of diverse sources of information (e.g., Chen & Usher, 2013). Such approaches allow for a more holistic view of how students combine and interpret multiple sources of ability-related information. Some efforts have been made to examine the development of self-efficacy longitudinally. For instance, preliminary evidence from Australian elementary school students shows that the effect of the sources on reading and math self-efficacy decreases as measurement of the sources and self-efficacy becomes more temporally displaced (Phan, 2012). A promising meta-analysis by van Dinther, Dochy, and Seegers (2011) provided a summary of factors related to academic self-efficacy in post-secondary settings, and noted that intervention research based in social cognitive theory and designed to increase students' self-efficacy could be a valuable tool for colleges and universities.

Regardless of their methodological approach, researchers have continued to report that mastery experience is typically the most influential source of self-efficacy (Butz & Usher, 2015; Fong & Krause, 2014; Joët, Usher, & Bressoux, 2011; Kiran & Sungur, 2012; Lin, Fong, & Wang, 2017; Lin & Tsai, 2017; van Dinther et al., 2011). This finding is consistent across age groups, national contexts, and domains. Mastery experience was unrelated to self-efficacy in only one study, which was conducted in an asynchronous online college algebra course, suggesting that in specific contexts, other sources of information may become more salient to students' self-efficacy (Hodges & Murphy, 2009).

Social Models and Messengers

Despite the known power of direct mastery experiences on self-efficacy, new ways of measuring other types of efficacy information have revealed important patterns in how students interpret the experiences and feedback of others. For example, Chan and Lam (2008) examined the role of social models in a competitive and non-competitive writing task. In a competitive condition, students were told that they would be placed in groups based on their ability to write metaphors and similes. In a noncompetitive condition, no groupings were used. Students in the competitive condition reported lower self-efficacy after being exposed to a proficient vicarious model than did those in the noncompetitive environment. This study demonstrates one way in which instructional framing might affect self-efficacy development. In competitive learning environments (e.g., teachers who promote high achievement via "leaderboards"; schools that post public rankings or admit only top-performing students), exposure to more successful others might lower rather than raise observers' self-efficacy. A similar phenomenon has been documented as the big-fish-little-pond effect: Learning alongside peers with higher average achievement can lower students' academic self-concept (see Marsh, Martin, Yeung, & Craven, 2017).

Some researchers have hypothesized that the potency of socially-conferred ability-information depends on the role or status of the people with whom learners interact. Sources of self-efficacy measures that distinguish between peers, family, and teachers as vicarious models and feedback providers have shown that not all sources are equally influential. For example, Ahn, Bong, and Kim (2017) found that, among Korean high school and college students, only social persuasions from teachers (and not from parents or peers) significantly predicted self-efficacy in math. In the domain of learning English, only vicarious experiences from teachers (and not from parents or peers) significantly predicted self-efficacy. Subsequent research has also shown that students who see their teachers as credible place more value on the feedback they receive from them (Won, Lee, & Bong, 2017).

Societal norms and cultural dispositions may lead individuals to place more weight on feedback and modeling from certain individuals. One study explored the social sources of middle school students' self-efficacy in math using data gathered in Korea, the Philippines, and the United States (Ahn, Usher, Butz, & Bong, 2015). Students in the United States and the Philippines tended to report more vicarious experience and social persuasion than did Korean students, regardless of whether the source was peers, parents, or teachers. Furthermore, U.S. students reported higher self-efficacy than did other students, likely reflecting a self-enhancement orientation characteristic of individuals in Western versus Eastern contexts (Heine & Hamamura, 2007).

However, distinct patterns emerged in the structural relationship between these variables. For Korean adolescents, social messages from family members were more strongly associated with math self-efficacy than for Filipino or American students. For the latter two groups, feedback from peers was also significantly related to self-efficacy. Researchers have suggested that in Korean culture, social support from parents may be particularly important for students' self-efficacy (Bong, Hwang, Noh, & Kim, 2014). Teachers were the only significant vicarious influence on self-efficacy in all three contexts, pointing to the importance of math teachers' modeling as a source of middle school students' self-efficacy across cultures.

These studies demonstrate that students perceive some social information differently in different cultural contexts. The results also show that, even within one national context (i.e., Korea), the relative predictive strength of social information on learners' math self-efficacy may differ for younger and older students. For instance, feedback from family members was a relevant source of self-efficacy for middle school students but not for high school and college students. Perhaps as students grow older and math content becomes more difficult, they rely less on family members and more on their teachers who have more expertise in a given subject area (Ahn et al., 2017).

Some evidence suggests that family structure can also influence how individuals learn to process and weigh socially-conferred information. Lin et al. (2017) found that in China, children who had no siblings (i.e., only children) reported fewer influential vicarious experiences than did those with siblings. Only children also relied more on self-regulatory strategies when discussing their self-efficacy to learn. Other sociocultural dynamics (e.g., power distance, family emphasis, religion) that have not yet been extensively explored in self-efficacy research might also affect how students perceive and interpret socially-conferred information (i.e., vicarious experience and social persuasions) when forming their self-efficacy.

Identity and Self-Efficacy Development

In this section we highlight research efforts that have focused on one or more aspects of students' sociocultural identities and their association with self-efficacy development. As we have acknowledged, identities are multifaceted and polycultural, so we urge readers to consider this while reading about research efforts that have focused on identity more narrowly.

Gender

Researchers have often considered gender in students' perception and interpretation of efficacy information, particularly in math and science. The quantitative evidence for gender differences is mixed. Some findings in the United States point to no differences in the sources of self-efficacy, even in traditionally male-dominated fields such as science (Britner & Pajares, 2006; Chen & Usher, 2013). However, Kiran and Sungur (2012) found that girls reported higher anxiety for science than did boys, even though their science self-efficacy did not differ. In France, elementary school girls reported fewer mastery experiences, less positive feedback, and higher anxiety than did boys in math but not in language (Joët et al., 2011). Cultural gender norms likely play a role in how girls and boys perceive their experiences and develop their self-efficacy. As Joët et al. (2011) noted, socialization practices in France might have resulted in differential treatment by parents and teachers in traditionally male-dominated subjects such as math. These social norms and practices could account for why girls lagged behind boys in their confidence in math but not in French.

We want to emphasize that even when students' reports indicate no group differences in self-efficacy, the pathways to self-efficacy may be different. Usher and Pajares (2008) suggested that more complex methodological approaches, such as mixed methods designs, might reveal how sociocultural factors influence self-efficacy development. In one such investigation in the United Kingdom, no significant gender differences emerged among elementary and middle school students' science self-efficacy when quantitative approaches were used; however, data from student interviews revealed distinct variation in the types of experiences girls and boys described as most influential to their self-efficacy (Webb-Williams, 2017). Girls consistently underestimated their science performance, and they placed greater emphasis on social comparisons and nonverbal cues than did their male peers. A similar pattern was found in the responses written by over 2,500 middle school students to the question, "What makes you feel more confident in math/reading?" (Butz & Usher, 2015). Girls described social persuasions as sources of their self-efficacy significantly more often than did boys, and this was the case in both math and reading. Likewise, when interviewed about their careers and self-efficacy in science, technology, engineering, and math (STEM), women focused more on vicarious experiences and social persuasions, whereas men attributed their high self-efficacy to mastery experience and personal attributes (Zeldin, Britner, & Pajares, 2008). Female undergraduate engineering majors were more likely than men to report that their parents or other close family members were most influential as social models (Usher, Mamaril, Li, Economy, & Kennedy, 2015).

Cultural Heritage Class, and Power

Comparatively less research has described the patterns of self-efficacy development among learners as a function of their racial and ethnic heritage, social class, or the power/privilege conferred (or not) by these distinctions. For example, Canadian adolescents of South Asian descent reported greater exposure to vicarious models and positive social messages in math than did their Anglo Canadian counterparts (Klassen, 2004a). Klassen suggested that this might reflect an other-oriented trend in self-efficacy development for students from non-Western cultures compared to a self-oriented trend for students from dominant Western cultural groups. Such findings might reflect how students' identity and social positionality within the broader culture can influence how they view their accomplishments and those of people around them. Students may develop differing ideas of what it means to be competent and successful according to their social class and the models to whom they have been exposed (Stephens, Dittmann, & Townsend, 2017).

Those belonging to groups of lower or marginalized stature may give more credence to evaluations from people in power. In the United States, some evidence suggests that African American students rely more on social persuasions than do White American students (Usher, 2009; Usher & Pajares, 2006). This is noteworthy given the evidence that U.S. teachers (most of whom are White) hold lower expectations of ethnic minority students than they do of White students (Tenenbaum & Ruck, 2007). Teachers' lower expectations are likely conveyed through overt and covert messages. Moreover, students who perceive that their teachers are biased or discriminatory perform worse academically (Brown, 2017). One redress has been to emphasize culturally-relevant teaching approaches that promote students' self-efficacy (e.g., Kelley, Siwatu, Tost, & Martinez, 2015). For example, Hispanic adolescents along the Mexican-U.S. border who felt that their teachers used practices that were inclusive of their home culture reported higher academic self-efficacy and demonstrated higher school performance (Chun & Dickson, 2011). Another approach has been to examine how to deliver critical feedback to students in ways that support their self-efficacy. In a series of experiments with seventh-grade students, Yeager et al. (2014) found that teacher feedback that conveyed both high standards and a sense of assurance was most effective for increasing students' persistence at a writing task. This effect was particularly strong among African American students who reported a greater sense of mistrust in their teachers.

As we have noted, research on the sources of self-efficacy has been conducted in Asia, North America, and Europe, and most has focused on the experiences of students living in densely-populated areas. Less is known about how academic self-efficacy develops among students in less developed areas of the world. Even within the same national context, self-efficacy and its sources can differ according to learners' cultural heritage, socioeconomic status, and position of power/privilege. More research is needed to investigate the self-efficacy development of students from understudied groups, including those from low-income backgrounds, first-generation college students, those with disabilities, or those who are otherwise disenfranchised. Researchers should consider self-efficacy development at the intersection of these diverse identities as well (Rosenthal, 2016).

Other Factors Related to Self-Efficacy Development

Students may derive information about their academic capabilities from factors related to the sources of self-efficacy Bandura (1997) hypothesized. Such factors include students' self-regulatory skills, motivational beliefs (e.g., autonomy), and classroom processes. For example, Lin et al. (2017) examined undergraduate students' journal entries about what made them feel more or less confident in school and found that students consistently described help availability, self-regulation, and interest as relevant to their capability beliefs. Similar patterns have been found for middle school students, whose open-ended responses described how their teachers' instruction style made them feel more or less certain of their own efficacy in math and reading (Butz & Usher, 2015).

Other evidence suggests that students' motivational orientations indirectly affect self-efficacy by influencing one or more of the four hypothesized sources. For example, undergraduate computer science students in Thailand who perceived their learning content to be meaningful and their instructor to be autonomy supportive also perceived more social persuasions, greater exposure to models, and less adverse physiological arousal, which in turn affected their computer science self-efficacy (Srisupawong, Koul, Neanchaleay, Murphy, & Francois, 2017). Perceived autonomy support was also a significant source of math self-efficacy among middle school math students in the United States (Collins, Usher, & Butz, 2015). Other research has shown that students who have a learning goal orientation (as opposed to a performance goal orientation) perceive negative feedback without suffering any loss to their self-efficacy (Dahling & Ruppel, 2016). Additional work is needed to examine how motivational beliefs, dispositions, and orientations might affect how efficacy-relevant information is perceived and weighted. This preliminary evidence suggests that factors in the learning environment can be altered to support students' self-efficacy by influencing the way students interpret efficacy-related experiences.

ADVANCING RESEARCH ON SELF-EFFICACY DEVELOPMENT

We have now described recent revelations about how the sources of self-efficacy operate in diverse contexts. However, research on these sources is still relatively young. In this section, we provide recommendations for further research on self-efficacy development.

Expanding Research to Less Explored Domains and Populations

As we have noted, self-efficacy research has focused primarily on the learning domains of math and science. We found considerably less or no research on the sources of self-efficacy in disciplines such as social sciences (e.g., history, geography), language acquisition, reading, and oral communication. Certain informational sources may be more relevant in certain domains of learning. For example, social interaction is essential when learning to speak a new language. Therefore, two or more sources of efficacy information (e.g., social persuasion and mastery experience) may need to be jointly investigated if they are not empirically separable in such contexts.

Nor have researchers explicitly investigated how learners develop their beliefs about their efficacy in areas known to support learning such as self-regulation, creativity, problem solving, and executive control. Efficacy beliefs in these domains have been shown to predict academic performance (e.g., Caprara et al., 2008; Hoffman & Schraw, 2008; Schunk & Usher, 2011). Examining the sources of self-efficacy in these understudied areas could help inform instructional practices that target not only new academic content but also the subprocesses that make learning that content possible. For example, researchers examining self-efficacy in the domain of writing would naturally ask students about their writing-related experiences. (Surely, one's perceived efficacy as a writer will be most sensitive to experiences in writing-related activities.) But given that competence in a subject like writing is undergirded by a complex set of subskills (e.g., attention regulation, language proficiency, time management), any experience that affects learners' perceived efficacy in these subareas could also affect self-efficacy in the broader domain. As a result, researchers might consider examining the relationship between subskill development (e.g., time management), self-efficacy for using subskills (e.g., for managing one's time), and domain-level self-efficacy (e.g., writing self-efficacy).

A lingering consideration for self-efficacy researchers is whether certain efficacy-relevant events that take place in one domain of activity affect self-efficacy in another domain of activity. Let's return to Mia, our chapter's protagonist. Mia was socially insecure and isolated in her early elementary years until Grade 5, when her class took a 3-day camping excursion to a remote forest. There, Mia realized how much others depended on her, and, together with her peers, Mia accomplished physical and social feats that she never thought possible. It was the trip of a lifetime. Mia's mom could not believe how much her disposition had changed. When Mia returned to school, her teacher noticed that she was much more confident in her academic capabilities. Might this transformative experience have affected Mia's self-efficacy in her academic pursuits? How? Anecdotal evidence seems to suggest that such psychologically-transformative experiences are possible, such as when the first-time marathoner has a renewed sense of efficacy for repairing his broken relationship, or when the former smoker who kicked her bad habit now feels capable of returning to school. We do not mean to suggest a hierarchical nature of self-efficacy beliefs, such as has been shown in self-concept research (Marsh et al., 2017). Instead, we raise the possibility that a self-transcendent experience in one area (e.g., overcoming great adversity) could change one's self-efficacy in another. Future work should address the impact of such transcendent experiences on students' self-efficacy across contexts.

Understanding How Learners Select and Weigh Efficacy-Relevant Information

Throughout the chapter we have alluded to the importance of identifying individual differences (e.g., construal biases) and contextual factors (e.g., instructional framing) that explain why people exposed to the same information differentially attend to it when judging what they can do. Construal biases, many of which operate outside of conscious awareness, are influenced by the norms and expectations of one's social or cultural group(s). For instance, in certain collectivistic cultures (e.g., East Asia), self-construal tends to be more modest and self-critical than in individualistic (e.g., United States) cultures, which promote self-enhancement and differentiation (Kurman, 2003). Some collectivistic cultures emphasize the value of sacrificing personal needs for group needs (i.e., horizontal collectivism), which could lead students to minimize the importance of their own performance accomplishments and maximize harmony within their group (Klassen, 2004b; Shavitt, Torelli, & Riemer, 2010). Such an orientation could also promote an overcritical view of one's self, particularly when one's performances do not meet the goals and expectations of the social group (Lee, Aaker, & Gardner, 2000). Conversely, some vertically-structured, individualistic cultures prize one's performance relative to others (i.e., competition), which might make social comparative experiences more salient in self-efficacy development (Shavitt et al., 2010).

Researchers investigating the influence of culture should be cautious about using students' nationality or cultural group alone as a proxy for self-construal. This approach assumes that people "behave like weathervanes, constantly shifting direction to conform to whatever momentary social influence happen[s] to impinge upon them" (Bandura, 1991, p. 249). From a social cognitive perspective, cognitive mechanisms mediate the effect of culture on the self-system (Kitayama & Uskul, 2011). Therefore, measures of self-construal may hold more explanatory power in predicting beliefs and behavior (Cross, Hardin, & Gercek-Swing, 2011).

Investigating how construal biases, rules, and cognitive selection processes influence self-efficacy development will require more complex research designs. Experimental techniques, which have been scarce in self-efficacy research, can be used to activate cultural mindsets that guide how individuals process information, and thereby enable researchers "to observe the consequences of disruptions to [individuals'] . . . values, norms, and meaning-making schemas" (Oyserman, 2017, pp. 439–440). Researchers might first take a more focused approach by investigating how cultural mindsets, and other factors, affect how learners weigh and interpret information from a single source of self-efficacy. For example, understanding how students make sense of their direct experiences might involve an investigation of any number of contextual features, such as learners'

> preconceptions of their capabilities, the perceived difficulty of the tasks, the amount of effort they expend, the amount of external aid they receive, the circumstances under which they perform, the temporal pattern of their successes and failures, and the way these enactive experiences are cognitively organized and reconstructed in memory. (Bandura, 1997, p. 81)

By experimentally manipulating these factors in different sociocultural and learning settings, researchers could begin to identify patterns in how self-efficacy develops among learners with different cultural orientations.

Considering the Valence of Efficacy-Relevant Information

Most research on self-efficacy development has focused on factors that raise self-efficacy. Whether researchers have used survey items ("People tell me that I am good at math.") or interview questions ("What has happened to make you more confident in math?"), most have attempted to understand how mastery experience, vicarious experience, and social persuasion *promote* self-efficacy and how adverse physiological and affective states *undermine* it. Each hypothesized source, however, can convey both positive and negative information about a person's efficacy. Initial evidence from our own lab has shown that, when given an open-ended opportunity to describe how they feel when doing engineering work, undergraduate engineering majors were about equally as likely to describe positive and negative affect; however, women were significantly more likely than men to describe negative affect (Usher et al., 2015). These findings suggest that (a) students' perceptions of efficacy-raising and efficacy-lowering events might vary, and (b) that these perceptions might be influenced by sociocultural factors.

Some evidence has shown a relationship between cultural background and students' attentional or "regulatory" focus (i.e., whether an individual is focused on the *approach* or *promotion* pursuit of ideals or on the *avoidance* or *prevention* of losses). For example, Lee et al. (2000) found that undergraduate students from the United States and China who held more independent self-construals (or who were experimentally primed to do so) were more likely to perceive promotion-focused information as more important to their self-esteem than were prevention-focused students, who tended to view the self as interdependent with others. Prevention-focused students viewed failure information as more salient to the self.

Similar findings have been reported in goal orientation research. Individuals from collectivistic countries (Russia, Korea, Japan) were more likely to adopt avoidance goals, whereas those from individualistic cultures (United States) were more likely to adopt approach goals (Elliot, Chirkov, Kim, & Sheldon, 2001; Hamamura, Meijer, Heine, Kamaya, & Hori, 2009). Although people from collectivistic backgrounds tended to pay greater attention to negative self-relevant information, this regulatory focus did not seem detrimental to their subjective well-being (Elliot et al., 2001). This body of work implies that research on self-efficacy development should consider how positive and negative efficacy-relevant information might be differently interpreted by students with different cultural backgrounds or self-construals and, in turn, how and whether these perceptions differently affect self-efficacy.

More diverse methodologies can begin to address these questions. Consider, for instance, how survey questions might target both positive and negative experiences (see Figure 7.2). Suppose 12-year-old Mia, responding to the statements on the right side of the figure (i.e., those that reflect typical self-efficacy-raising experiences), indicates that she often does well on math assignments but that people rarely tell her she is good at math. This is quite a typical scenario in sources of self-efficacy research. Mastery experience wins the day. But now suppose we give Mia the set of statements on the left (i.e., those that reflect self-efficacy-lowering experiences). She indicates that people often tell her that she is bad at math. We now have

Figure 7.2 Assessing the valence of potential sources of self-efficacy. Sample survey items to assess both positive (right) and negative (left) efficacy-relevant experiences and their hypothesized influence on self-efficacy.

a more complex picture of Mia's efficacy-relevant experiences. The point here is that how and what researchers ask about the sources of self-efficacy can influence the conclusions they reach. Method and measures matter.

IMPLICATIONS

Mr. Anderson's eyes roamed his math class. He noticed how nervous some students looked as he distributed the test. He calmly instructed students to pause.

> I want to tell you that this little exercise is going to be fun. Don't worry if you do not know the answers. That will help me understand how I can teach you this year. If you feel nervous, that's ok. Don't worry. We will learn a lot this year in math, and I am here to help you.

As Mr. Anderson smiled at Mia, she felt immediately relieved and began her work.

Not all teachers will be as comforting as Mr. Anderson, but all could benefit from understanding where self-efficacy comes from and how their actions might influence the learners in their care. As Stephens et al. (2014) aptly observed, "selves are highly contingent on their supporting sociocultural contexts" (p. 613). What features of the sociocultural context support students' self-efficacy? First, ensuring that students can progress at a manageable pace can help instill a sense of mastery. Second, teachers can frame their instruction and feedback in ways that convey a belief that students are capable. In cultural contexts where high interdependence is salient, students may be even more attuned to social messages. Teachers and parents can also facilitate students' exposure to proficient social models to whom students feel similar. Models who demonstrate perseverant effort through difficulties can boost observers' self-efficacy. Monitoring the psychological environment of their classroom, as Mr. Anderson did, can help teachers minimize factors that undermine self-efficacy.

Perhaps critical to effective teaching is an awareness of one's implicit biases that can be conveyed to learners with different identities. One study revealed that, even when boys and girls reported similar sources of self-efficacy, their parents and teachers were more likely to attribute girls' successes to hard work and effort and boys' successes to innate ability (Usher, 2009). Subtle cues can have long-term effects on students' self-efficacy and subsequent performances and choices. Teachers and parents can also help learners reflect on the meaning they give to messages in their broader cultural environment when judging their own capabilities. For a detailed list of additional recommendations to practitioners for how to support students' self-efficacy development, we refer readers to an excellent chapter by Pajares (2006).

Bandura (2016) emphasized that the capacity for self-influence places learners in a position of being *agents* of their own development. We have tried to show in this chapter that beliefs about one's personal efficacy do not develop in a vacuum. "Thinking occurs in culture, and culture structures what seems obvious, normative, and real" (Oyserman, 2017, p. 443). The influence of any experience therefore depends on people's sociocognitive constructions, which are affected by their geographical, social, and cultural locations.

REFERENCES

Ahn, H. S., Bong, M., & Kim, S. (2017). Social models in the cognitive appraisal of self-efficacy information. *Contemporary Educational Psychology, 48,* 149–166.

Ahn, H. S., Usher, E. L., Butz, A. R., & Bong, M. (2016). Cultural differences in the understanding of modelling and feedback as sources of self-efficacy information. *British Journal of Educational Psychology, 86*(1), 112–136.

Bandura, A. (1986). *Social foundations of thought and action: A social cognitive theory.* Englewood Cliffs, NJ: Prentice Hall.

Bandura, A. (1991). Social cognitive theory of self-regulation. *Organizational Behavior and Human Decision Processes, 50,* 248–287.

Bandura, A. (1997). *Self-efficacy: The exercise of control.* New York, NY: Freeman.

Bandura, A. (2002). Social cognitive theory in cultural context. *Applied Psychology: An International Review, 151,* 269–290. doi: 10.1111/1464-0597.00092

Bandura, A. (2016). *Moral disengagement: How people do harm and live with themselves.* New York, NY: Worth.

Barrett, L. F. (2017). The theory of constructed emotion: An active inference account of interoception and categorization. *Social Cognitive and Affective Neuroscience, 12,* 1–23.

Bong, M., Hwang, A., Noh, A., & Kim, S. (2014). Perfectionism and motivation of adolescents in academic contexts. *Journal of Educational Psychology, 106,* 711–729.

Britner, S. L., & Pajares, F. (2006). Sources of science self-efficacy beliefs of middle school students. *Journal of Research in Science Teaching, 43,* 485–499.

Brown, C. B. (2017). *Discrimination in childhood and adolescence: A developmental intergroup approach.* New York, NY: Routledge.

Butz, A. R., & Usher, E. L. (2015). Salient sources of self-efficacy in reading and mathematics. *Contemporary Educational Psychology, 42,* 49–61.

Caprara, G. V., Fida, R., Vecchione, M., Del Bove, G., Vecchio, G. M., Barbaranelli, C., & Bandura, A. (2008). Longitudinal analysis of the role of perceived self-efficacy for self-regulated learning in academic continuance and achievement. *Journal of Educational Psychology, 100*(3), 525–534.

Chan, J. C., & Lam, S. (2008). Effects of competition on students' self-efficacy in vicarious learning. *British Journal of Educational Psychology, 78,* 95–108.

Chang, L., Mak, M. C. K., Li, T., Wu, B. P., Chen, B. B., & Lu, H. J. (2011). Cultural adaptations to environmental variability: An evolutionary account of East-West differences. *Educational Psychology Review, 23*(1), 99–129.

Chen, J. A., & Usher, E. L. (2013). Profiles of the sources of science self-efficacy. *Learning and Individual Differences, 24*, 11–21.

Chun, H., & Dickson, G. (2011). A psychoecological model of academic performance among Hispanic adolescents. *Journal of Youth and Adolescence, 40*, 1581–1594.

Collins, J. S., Usher, E. L., & Butz, A. R. (2015, April). *Examining students' perceived autonomy support as a source of self-efficacy in mathematics.* Poster session presented at the Annual Meeting of the American Education Research Association, Chicago, IL.

Cross, S. E., Hardin, E. E., & Gercek-Swing, B. (2011). The what, how, why, and where of self-construal. *Personality and Social Psychology Review, 15*(2), 142–179.

Dahling, J. J., & Ruppel, C. L. (2016). Learning goal orientation buffers the effects of negative normative feedback on test self-efficacy and reattempt interest. *Learning and Individual Differences, 50*, 296–301.

Elliot, A. J., Chirkov, V. I., Kim, Y., & Sheldon, K. M. (2001). A cross-cultural analysis of avoidance (relative to approach) personal goals. *Psychological Science, 12*, 505–510.

Fong, C. J., & Krause, J. M. (2014). Lost confidence and potential: A mixed methods study of underachieving college students' sources of self-efficacy. *Social Psychology of Education, 17*, 249–268.

Hamamura, T., Meijer, Z., Heine, S. J., Kamaya, K., & Hori, I. (2009). Approach-avoidance motivation and information processing: A cross-cultural analysis. *Personality and Social Psychology Bulletin, 35*, 454–462.

Heine, S. J., & Hamamura, T. (2007). In search of East Asian self-enhancement. *Personality and Social Psychology Review, 11*(1), 4–27.

Hodges, C. B., & Murphy, P. F. (2009). Sources of self-efficacy beliefs of students in a technology-intensive asynchronous college algebra course. *Internet and Higher Education, 12*, 93–97.

Hoffman, B., & Schraw, G. (2009). The influence of self-efficacy and working memory capacity on problem-solving efficiency. *Learning and Individual Differences, 19*(1), 91–100.

Joët, G., Usher, E. L., & Bressoux, P. (2011). Sources of self-efficacy: An investigation of elementary school students in France. *Journal of Educational Psychology, 103*(3), 649–663.

Kelley, H. M., Siwatu, K. O., Tost, J. R., & Martinez, J. (2015). Culturally familiar tasks on reading performance and self-efficacy of culturally and linguistically diverse students. *Educational Psychology in Practice, 31*(3), 293–313.

Kiran, D., & Sungur, S. (2012). Middle school students' science self-efficacy and its sources: Examination of gender difference. *Journal of Science Education and Technology, 21*(5), 619–630.

Kitayama, S., & Uskul, A. K. (2011). Culture, mind, and the brain: Current evidence and future directions. *Annual Review of Psychology, 62*(1), 419–449.

Klassen, R. M. (2004a). A cross-cultural investigation of the efficacy beliefs of South Asian immigrant and Anglo Canadian nonimmigrant early adolescents. *Journal of Educational Psychology, 96*, 731–742.

Klassen, R. M. (2004b). Optimism and realism: A review of self-efficacy from a cross-cultural perspective. *International Journal of Psychology, 39*(3), 205–230.

Klassen, R. M., & Usher, E. L. (2010). Self-efficacy in educational settings: Recent research and emerging directions. In T. C. Urdan & S. A. Karabenick (Eds.), *Advances in motivation and achievement: The decade ahead: Theoretical perspectives on motivation and achievement* (Vol. 16A, pp. 1–33). Bingley, England: Emerald.

Kurman, J. (2003). Why is self-enhancement low in certain collectivist cultures? *Journal of Cross-Cultural Psychology, 34*, 496–510.

Lee, A. Y., Aaker, J. L., & Gardner, W. L. (2000). The pleasures and pains of distinct self-construals: The role of interdependence in regulatory focus. *Journal of Personality and Social Psychology, 78*, 1122–1134.

Lee, J. (2009). Universals and specifics of math self-concept, math self-efficacy, and math anxiety across 41 PISA 2003 participating countries. *Learning and Individual Differences, 19*, 355–365.

Lin, S., Fong, C. J., & Wang, Y. (2017). Chinese undergraduates' sources of self-efficacy differ by sibling status, achievement, and fear of failure along two pathways. *Social Psychology of Education.* Advance online publication. doi:10.1007/s11218-017-9367-0

Lin, T., & Tsai, C. (2017). Differentiating the sources of Taiwanese high school students' multidimenstional science learning self-efficacy: An examination of gender differences. *Research in Science Education.* Advanced online publication. doi:10.1007/s11165-016-9579-x

Marsh, H. W., Martin, A. J., Yeung, A. S., & Craven, R. G. (2017). Competence self-perceptions. In C. S. Dweck, A. Elliot, & D. S. Yeager (Eds.), *Handbook of competence and motivation* (2nd ed., pp. 85–115). New York, NY: Guilford Press.

McInerney, D. M., & Van Etten, S. (Eds.). (2004). *Big theories revisited.* Greenwich, CT: Information Age.

Morris, M. W., Chiu, C.-Y., & Liu, Z. (2015). Polycultural psychology. *Annual Review of Psychology, 66*, 631–659.

Oettingen, G., & Zosuls, K. M. (2006). Culture and self-efficacy in adolescents. In F. Pajares & T. Urdan (Eds.), *Adolescence and education: Self-efficacy beliefs of adolescents* (Vol. 5, pp. 245–265). Greenwich, CT: Information Age.

Oyserman, D. (2017). Culture three ways: Culture and subcultures within countries. *Annual Review of Psychology, 68*, 435–463.

Pajares, F. (2006). Self-efficacy during childhood and adolescence: Implications for teachers and parents. In F. Pajares & T. Urdan (Eds.), *Adolescence and education: Self-efficacy beliefs of adolescents* (Vol. 5, pp. 339–367). Greenwich, CT: Information Age.

Pajares, F., & Usher, E. L. (2008). Self-efficacy, motivation, and achievement in school from the perspective of reciprocal determinism. In M. Maehr, T. C. Urdan, & S. Karabenick (Eds.), *Advances in motivation and achievement: Social psychological perspectives* (Vol. 5, pp. 391–423). Bingley, England: Emerald.

Phan, H. P. (2012). The development of English and mathematics self-efficacy: A latent growth curve analysis. *Journal of Educational Research, 105*, 196–209.

Richardson, M., Abraham, C., & Bond, R. (2012). Psychological correlates of university students' academic performance: A systematic review and meta-analysis. *Psychological Bulletin, 138*(2), 353–387.

Rosenthal, L. (2016). Incorporating intersectionality into psychology: An opportunity to promote social justice and equity. *American Psychologist, 71*, 474–485.

Schunk, D. H., & Pajares, F. (2004). Self-efficacy in education revisited: Empirical and applied evidence. In D. M. McInerney & S. V. Etten (Eds.), *Research on sociocultural influences on motivation and learning: Big theories Revisited* (Vol. 4, pp. 115–138). Greenwich, CT: Information Age.

Schunk, D. H., & Usher, E. L. (2011). Assessing self-efficacy for self-regulated learning. In B. J. Zimmerman & D. H. Schunk (Eds.), *Handbook of self-regulation of learning and performance* (pp. 282–297). New York, NY: Routledge.

Shavitt, S., Torelli, C. J., & Riemer, H. (2010). Horizontal and vertical individualism and collectivism: Implications for understanding psychological processes. In M. Gelfand, C. Y. Chiu, & Y. Y. Hong (Eds.), *Advances in culture and psychology* (pp. 309–350). New York, NY: Oxford University Press.

Srisupawong, Y., Koul, R., Neanchaleay, J., Murphy, E., & Francois, E. J. (2017). The relationship between sources of self-efficacy in classroom environments and the strength of computer self-efficacy beliefs. *Education and Information Technologies.* Advanced online publication. doi:10.1007/s10639-017-9630-1

Stephens, N. M., Dittmann, A. G., & Townsend S. S. M. (2017). Social class and models of competence: How gateway institutions disadvantage working-class Americans and how to intervene. In C. S. Dweck, A. Elliot, & D. S. Yeager (Eds.), *Handbook of competence and motivation* (2nd ed., pp. 529–546). New York, NY: Guilford Press.

Stephens, N. M., Markus, H. R., & Phillips, L. T. (2014). Social class culture cycles: How three gateway contexts shape selves and fuel inequality. *Annual Review of Psychology, 65*, 611–634.

Tenenbaum, H. R., & Ruck, M. D. (2007). Are teachers' expectations different for racial minority than for European American students? A meta-analysis. *Journal of Educational Psychology, 99*(2), 253–273.

van Dinther, M., Dochy, F., & Segers, M. (2011). Factors affecting students' self-efficacy in higher education. *Educational Research Review, 6*(2), 95–108.

Webb-Williams, J. (2017). Science self-efficacy in the primary classroom: Using mixed methods to investigate sources of self-efficacy. *Research in Science Education.* Advance online publication. doi: 10.1007/s11165-016-9592-0

Williams, T., & Williams, K. (2010). Self-efficacy and performance in mathematics: Reciprocal determinism in 33 nations. *Journal of Educational Psychology, 102*(2), 453–466.

Won, S., Lee, S., & Bong, M. (2017). Social persuasions by teachers as a source of student self-efficacy: The moderating role of perceived teacher credibility. *Psychology in the Schools, 54*, 532–547.

Usher, E. L. (2009). Sources of middle school students' self-efficacy in mathematics: A qualitative investigation of student, teacher, and parent perspectives. *American Educational Research Journal, 46*, 275–314.

Usher, E. L., Mamaril, N. A., Li, C. R., Economy, D. R., & Kennedy, M. S. (2015). Sources of self-efficacy in undergraduate engineering. *Proceedings of the 2015 ASEE Annual Conference and Exposition*, Seattle, WA.

Usher, E. L., & Pajares, F. (2006). Sources of academic and self-regulatory efficacy beliefs of entering middle school students. *Contemporary Educational Psychology*, *31*, 125–141.

Usher, E. L., & Pajares, F. (2008). Sources of self-efficacy in school: Critical review of the literature and future directions. *Review of Educational Research*, *78*, 751–796.

Usher, E. L., & Schunk, D. H. (2018). Social cognitive theoretical perspective of self-regulation. In D. H. Schunk & J. A. Greene (Eds.), *Handbook of self-regulation of learning and performance* (2nd ed., pp. 19–35). New York, NY: Routledge.

Yeager, D. S., Purdie-Vaughns, V., Garcia, J., Apfel, N., Brzustoski, P., Master, A., ... Cohen, G. L. (2014). Breaking the cycle of mistrust: Wise interventions to provide critical feedback across the racial divide. *Journal of Experimental Psychology: General*, *143*, 804–824.

Zeldin, A. L., Britner, S. L., & Pajares, F. (2008). A comparative study of the self-efficacy beliefs of successful men and women in mathematics, science, and technology careers. *Journal of Research in Science Teaching*, *45*, 1036–1058.

CHAPTER 8

CONTROL-VALUE THEORY

A Social-Cognitive Approach
to Achievement Emotions

Reinhard Pekrun

Success and failure in educational settings shape students' careers and developmental trajectories. The overarching impact of educational achievement in a modern, meritocratic society implies that achievement fulfils a basic requisite for the arousal of intense emotion—success and failure in education are highly important to the individual student, to the extent that they influence completion versus dropout, employment versus unemployment, affluence versus poverty, and health versus disease. Consequently, situations that contribute to educational accomplishment arouse a multitude of different emotions, such as enjoyment, hope, pride, relief, anger, anxiety, shame, frustration, boredom, and hopelessness.

Furthermore, these emotions are not just mere epiphenomena of success and failure. Rather, they can strongly impact students' performance as well as psychological and physical well-being. Consider, for example, the last time you took an important exam. You may have hoped for success, feared failure, or felt desperate because you were unprepared, but it

Big Theories Revisited 2, pages 165–190
Copyright © 2018 by Information Age Publishing

is unlikely that you felt emotionally indifferent. Moreover, your emotional arousal likely affected your motivation, concentration, and strategies used for studying—even if you were unaware of these developments. Similarly, think of the last time you worked on some project. Depending on the goals and tasks involved, you may have enjoyed working on it or felt bored, experienced a sense of flow or frustration about never-ending obstacles, felt proud of the outcome or ashamed of lack of accomplishment. Again, these emotions likely had profound effects on your involvement in the project, motivation to persist, and strategies for approaching the tasks involved.

Research on these achievement emotions has begun to flourish over the past 15 years, but is in a fragmented state. Different traditions of research pertain to test anxiety (Zeidner, 1998), to the attributional antecedents of achievement emotions (Graham & Taylor, 2014), and to achievement emotions experienced in specific settings, such as education, work, and sports (see e.g., Ashkanasy & Humphrey, 2011; Pekrun & Linnenbrink-Garcia, 2014). To better integrate research in this field, conceptual frameworks are needed that are suited to synthesize the multitude of emerging findings. The control-value theory of achievement emotions (CVT; Pekrun, 2000, 2006; Pekrun & Perry, 2014) seeks to provide such a framework. The theory integrates propositions from previous accounts of achievement emotions, including attributional theories (Graham & Taylor, 2014), models of stress-related achievement emotions (e.g., Folkman & Lazarus, 1985), expectancy-value approaches to emotions (Pekrun, 1992a; Turner & Schallert, 2001), and theories of test anxiety (see Zeidner, 1998). Sharing common basic assumptions, these various approaches are complementary rather than mutually exclusive, making it possible to integrate their assumptions.

The CVT also seeks to expand existing assumptions. Specifically, previous theories have focused on explaining emotions related to achievement outcomes (i.e., success and failure). For example, attributional theories have considered the role of causal attributions of achievement for emotions that are triggered by success and failure, such as pride, shame, gratitude, and anger (Graham & Taylor, 2014). In contrast, emotions related to achievement activities, such as studying or attending class, have been neglected. The control-value theory seeks to explain these activity-related emotions as well. The excitement when starting a challenging course, boredom experienced during a monotonous lecture, or anger felt when task demands seem unreasonable are examples of activity-related emotions.

In this chapter, I provide an overview of the CVT, with a specific focus on the influence of gender and contextual factors considered in the theory. I first introduce the concept of achievement emotion used. Next, I provide a summary of basic propositions, which pertain to the appraisal antecedents of achievement emotions and to their functions for learning and performance. These propositions have immediate implications for the influence of more distal individual antecedents as well as the sociocultural context, which I discuss next. Specifically, I address the role of gender and students' social environments in the classroom and beyond. In conclusion, I highlight the relative universality of achievement emotions across academic domains, genders, and cultural contexts.

CONCEPT OF ACHIEVEMENT EMOTION

Emotions are commonly defined as multifaceted phenomena that comprise various component processes, including subjective feelings, cognitions, motivational tendencies, physiological processes, and expressive behavior (Shuman & Scherer, 2014). For example, a student experiencing pre-exam anxiety may feel uneasy and nervous (affective component), worry about possible failure (cognitive component), want to flee the impending exam situation (motivational component), have sweaty palms (physiological component), and display an anxious facial expression (expressive component).

Achievement emotions are defined as emotions that relate to achievement activities (e.g., studying) or achievement outcomes (success and failure; see Table 8.1). As such, it is possible to distinguish between outcome-related and activity-related achievement emotions. In the three-dimensional emotion taxonomy that is part of the CVT (Pekrun, 2006), the differentiation of activity versus outcome emotions pertains to the *object focus* of achievement emotions. In addition, as emotions more generally, achievement emotions can be grouped according to their *valence* and to the degree of *activation* implied (Table 8.1). In terms of valence, positive emotions can be distinguished from negative emotions, such as enjoyment (pleasant) versus anxiety (unpleasant). In terms of activation, physiologically activating emotions

TABLE 8.1	**A Three-Dimensional Taxonomy of Achievement Emotions**				
	Positive[a]		**Negative**[b]	
Object Focus	**Activating**	**Deactivating**	**Activating**	**Deactivating**
Activity	Enjoyment	Relaxation	Anger Frustration	Boredom
Outcome/ Prospective	Hope Joy[c]	Relief[c]	Anxiety	Hopelessness
Outcome/ Retrospective	Joy Pride Gratitude	Contentment Relief	Shame Anger	Sadness Disappointment

[a] Positive = pleasant emotion
[b] Negative = unpleasant emotion
[c] Anticipatory joy/relief

can be distinguished from deactivating emotions, such as excitement (activating) versus contentment (deactivating).

Many emotions in academic settings are seen as achievement emotions, since they relate to activities and outcomes that are typically judged according to competence-based standards of quality. However, not all of the emotions triggered in academic settings are achievement emotions. For example, topic emotions related to the contents of learning materials, epistemic emotions such as surprise, curiosity, and confusion, as well as social emotions frequently occur in these same settings. Achievement emotions can overlap with other categories of emotion, as in social achievement emotions such as admiration, envy, or contempt related to the success and failure of others.

Research has documented that the achievement emotions organized in the three-dimensional taxonomy are experienced frequently in academic settings. In a series of interview studies with high school and university students, we found that anxiety was the emotion reported most often, constituting 15–27% of all emotional episodes reported across academic situations (attending class, studying, and taking tests; e.g., Spangler, Pekrun, Kramer, & Hofmann, 2002). This prevalence of anxiety corroborates the importance of test anxiety research. However, the vast majority of emotions reported pertained to emotion categories other than anxiety, with episodes of enjoyment, satisfaction, hope, pride, relief, anger, boredom, and shame reported frequently as well.

BASIC PROPOSITIONS: THE ROLE OF CONTROL AND VALUE APPRAISALS

Emotions can be caused and modulated by numerous individual factors, including situational perceptions, cognitive appraisals, neurohormonal processes, physiological feedback from autonomic nervous system activity, and sensory feedback from facial, gestural and postural expression (Barrett, Lewis, & Haviland-Jones, 2016). Among these factors, appraisals of situational demands and personal competences likely play a major role in the arousal of achievement emotions. Specifically, the control-value theory proposes that *perceived control* and *perceived values* are most important. Succinctly stated, the theory posits that achievement emotions are induced when the individual feels in control of, or out of control of, achievement activities and outcomes that are subjectively important.

Perceived control pertains to the perceived controllability of achievement-related actions and outcomes, as implied by causal expectations (self-efficacy expectations and outcome expectancies), causal attributions of achievement, and competence appraisals (e.g., self-concepts of ability). Perceived value relates to the subjective importance of these activities and outcomes. These appraisals can pertain to characteristic of achievement activities themselves (intrinsic values) or to their instrumental value for obtaining outcomes (extrinsic values).

By focusing on these appraisals, the CVT integrates propositions from previous theories of achievement emotions, as noted earlier. Furthermore, by considering outcome expectancies and values, it shares assumptions with expectancy-value theories of motivation (e.g., Wigfield & Eccles, 2000). In fact, the original starting point for creating the CVT were my attempts to construct a generalized expectancy-value theory that integrated perspectives from traditional expectancy-value theories (Heckhausen, 1991; Raynor, 1982; Vroom, 1964) with Bandura's self-efficacy approach (Pekrun, 1983, 1988, 1993). As a side product, I used the principles of expectancy-value theory to also explain anxiety (expectancy-value theory of anxiety; Pekrun, 1983, 1988, 1992a). The CVT incorporates propositions from the expectancy-value theory of anxiety and expands them to explain a broader range of emotions.

By focusing on perceived control and value, the CVT also shares assumptions with other appraisal theories of emotion (e.g., Scherer, 2009). Specifically, the constructs of perceived control and value integrate several dimensions from traditional approaches to appraisals (perceived control: power, control, agency; perceived value: goal relevance, goal congruency, intrinsic pleasantness, normative significance; Scherer, Schorr, & Johnstone, 2001).

Outcome Emotions

Different control and value appraisals are assumed to instigate different achievement emotions (Table 8.1). *Prospective, anticipatory joy,* and *hopelessness* are expected to be triggered when there is high perceived control (joy) or a complete lack of control (hopelessness), respectively. For example, a student who believes she has prepared well for an exam may feel joyous about the prospect of receiving a good grade. Conversely, a student who believes he is incapable of mastering the exam may experience hopelessness. *Hope* and *anxiety* are instigated when there is uncertainty about control, the attentional focus being on anticipated success in the case of hope, and on anticipated failure in the case of anxiety. A student who is unsure about being able to master an important exam may hope for success, fear failure, or both.

Retrospective joy and *sadness* are considered control-independent emotions which immediately follow perceived success and failure, further cognitive elaboration being unnecessary. In contrast, *disappointment* and *relief* depend on the perceived match between expectations and the actual outcome. Disappointment is aroused when anticipated success does not occur, and relief when anticipated failure does not occur. Finally, *pride, shame, gratitude,* and *anger* are thought to be induced by causal attributions of success and failure to oneself or others, respectively. For example, a sports student who wins an important race will feel pride provided that he attributes the victory to his own ability or effort. Conversely, losing an important race can induce shame if attributed to lack of ability or effort.

Furthermore, the theory posits that these outcome emotions also depend on the subjective importance of the outcome, implying that they are a joint function of perceived control and value. For instance, a student should feel worried if she judges herself incapable of mastering the learning material (low controllability) in an important course (high value). In contrast, if she feels that she is able to learn the material (high controllability), or is indifferent about the course (low value), her anxiety should be low.

Activity Emotions

The theory proposes that *enjoyment* of achievement activities depends on a combination of positive competence appraisals and positive appraisals of the intrinsic value of the action (e.g., studying) and its reference object (e.g., learning material). For example, a student is expected to enjoy learning if he feels competent to meet the demands of the task and values the learning material. If he feels incompetent, or is disinterested in the material, studying is not enjoyable. *Anger* and *frustration* are aroused when the intrinsic value of the activity is negative (e.g., when working on a difficult project is perceived as taking too much effort). Finally, *boredom* is experienced when the activity lacks any intrinsic incentive value.

Empirical Evidence

Empirical studies confirm that perceived control over achievement relates positively to students' enjoyment, hope, and pride, and negatively to their anger, anxiety, shame, hopelessness, and boredom (for a summary of findings, see Pekrun & Perry, 2014). Furthermore, research has shown that the perceived value of achievement relates positively to both positive and negative achievement emotions except boredom, indicating that the importance of success and failure amplifies these emotions. For boredom, negative links with value have been found, corroborating that boredom is reduced when individuals value achievement (e.g., Pekrun, Goetz, Daniels, Stupnisky, & Perry, 2010). Finally, studies have confirmed that control and value interact in the arousal of achievement emotions, with positive emotions being especially pronounced when both control and value are high, and negative emotions being pronounced when value is high but control is lacking (e.g., Goetz, Frenzel, Stoeger, & Hall, 2010; Lauerman, Eccles, & Pekrun, 2017).

FUNCTIONS FOR LEARNING AND ACHIEVEMENT

Research has shown that emotions can profoundly influence a broad range of cognitive and behavioral processes (Barrett, Lewis, & Haviland-Jones, 2016; Clore & Huntsinger, 2007). For students' academic achievement, effects on attention, motivation, use of learning strategies, and self-regulation of learning may be most important, as depicted in the cognitive-motivational model of emotion effects that is part of the CVT (Pekrun, 1992b, 2006). As for *positive emotions*, activating emotions like enjoyment of learning focus students' attention on learning, promote their motivation to learn, and facilitate use of deep learning strategies and self-regulation. As such, these emotions are thought to have positive effects on students' achievement. In contrast, positive emotions that do not relate to learning, such as an adolescents' first romantic emotions, can draw attention away, reduce academic effort, and lower overall performance. Similarly, deactivating positive emotions, like relief and relaxation, may not always have positive effects on achievement.

As for *negative emotions*, activating emotions, such as anxiety, anger, or confusion, distract attention and reduce interest, intrinsic motivation, and deep learning, but they can strengthen extrinsic motivation to avoid failure. For example, if you are afraid of failing an impending exam, you may be highly motivated to invest effort in order not to fail. As such, the effects of these emotions on learning outcomes can be variable. Deactivating negative emotion such as hopelessness and boredom, on the other hand, generally undermine attention, motivation, and strategy use, suggesting that they uniformly impair achievement. If you are bored by a lecture, your mind starts wandering, you cannot focus your attention anymore on the lecture, your motivation to continue is undermined, and when you are tested on the contents, your memories of the material will remain poor.

Links between emotions and achievement outcomes have been best researched for students' achievement anxiety (Hembree, 1988; Zeidner, 1998), but recent studies have also addressed emotions other than anxiety. Across studies, positive emotions such as enjoyment of learning, hope, and pride typically correlated positively with students' grades and test scores at school. For negative emotions such as anxiety, anger, shame, hopelessness, and boredom, correlations were negative (Pekrun & Stephens, 2012). Furthermore, there also is longitudinal evidence demonstrating that students' emotions impact their achievement. Longitudinal investigations of students' achievement anxiety found that anxiety had negative effects on achievement outcomes over the years while controlling for prior achievement (Meece, Wigfield, & Eccles, 1990; Pekrun, 1992a; Steinmayr, Credel, McElvany, & Wirthwein, 2016). In a recent investigation of students' emotions in mathematics (Pekrun, Lichtenfeld, Marsh, Murayama, & Goetz, 2017), we found that math-related enjoyment and pride had positive effects on grades and test scores in math across 5 years during secondary school, whereas anger, anxiety, shame, hopelessness, and boredom had negative effects, while controlling for the influence of prior achievement, gender, intelligence, and family socioeconomic status. This evidence confirms that emotions influence students' achievement, over and above the impact of other variables such as cognitive ability, gender, and socioeconomic background.

THE INFLUENCE OF GENDER, SOCIAL ENVIRONMENTS, AND CULTURAL CONTEXT

To the extent that cognitive appraisals are proximal determinants of achievement emotions, more distal individual antecedents, such as goals, beliefs, cognitive abilities, or gender should affect these emotions by first influencing appraisals (Figure 8.1; Pekrun, 2006). Similarly, social environments and the broader sociocultural context should influence these emotions through shaping the emotion-arousing appraisals. As such, the CVT implies that gender and social environments should influence students' emotions by affecting their control and value appraisals.

Gender

The influence of students' gender has primarily been examined for their emotions in mathematics. The evidence shows that female students report higher levels of negative emotions in this domain, such as math anxiety, shame, and hopelessness, compared with boys (Frenzel, Pekrun, & Goetz, 2007a). For example, in the 2012 cycle of the Programme for International Student Assessment (PISA) which focused on mathematics, average math anxiety was significantly higher for females in 56 of the 65 participating countries (Organization for Economic Cooperation and Development [OECD], 2013). Female students also report lower positive emotions, such as enjoyment of math (Frenzel, Pekrun, & Goetz, 2007a). This is consistent with the gender differences in students' performance in mathematics—on an average, girls receive lower test scores in mathematics than boys, and they are especially underrepresented among high-achieving students in math (OECD, 2016).

Why are girls more afraid of math than boys, and why do they enjoy math less? The CVT offers an answer. Girls and boys not only differ in

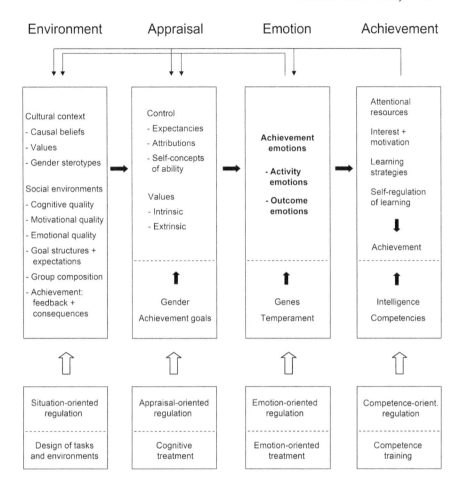

Figure 8.1   Basic propositions of the control-value theory of achievement emotions.

their math emotions; they also differ in their control and value appraisals in mathematics. Specifically, even if average performance is similar, female students report lower perceived control and competence in mathematics, likely due to socially shared gender stereotypes about math-related competencies and the lack of competent female role models in math. This difference in perceived control provides an explanation for the differences in emotions (Frenzel et al., 2007). Together, female students' doubts in their competence and lack of enjoyment in math contribute to their lack of interest in the science, technology, engineering, and mathematics (STEM) subjects and related career decisions, which partly explains the underrepresentation of females in many STEM-related occupations that involve mathematics as a major component.

Gender differences are also found for other academic domains and for domain-general constructs of achievement emotion. Similar to differences in math anxiety, average scores for general achievement anxiety are higher for female than for male students (Hembree, 1988; Zeidner, 1998). For example, in the PISA 2015 assessments, schoolwork-related anxiety was significantly higher for girls in all of the 55 countries that participated in the assessment of this variable (OECD, 2017). In contrast, girls may enjoy language-related activities more than boys do. For example, reading for enjoyment was reported more frequently by girls in 64 out of 65 countries participating in the PISA 2009 assessments (OECD, 2010).

However, a few words of caution are in order. First, although these gender differences were observed across countries and in many studies, they only describe the average student—they hold for the mean in the population but may not describe the single student. Within any given group of students, the variation of emotions among girls, and among boys, may be much larger than the differences between girls and boys. Second, the observed differences do not follow a simple plus–minus pattern—there are exceptions to the rule that female students report more negative and less positive emotions. For example, whereas girls typically report more anxiety, shame, and hopelessness in mathematics, boys have sometimes been found to report higher levels of anger and boredom than girls in this domain (Pekrun et al., 2017). Finally, it may even be that girls *report* different levels of emotions but do not differ much from boys in the emotions they *actually experience*. Similar to individual differences in actual emotions, differences in self-report may also be due to differences in self-appraisals—if you believe you are not capable of solving problems in a given domain, you would also not believe you enjoy working on such problems (Goetz, Bieg, Lüdtke, Pekrun, & Hall, 2013).

Social Environments

Similar to the role of individual antecedents such as gender, the impact of social environments is also thought to be mediated by individual control and value appraisals. Variables in the environment that affect these appraisals should influence the resulting emotions as well. According to the CVT, the following groups of factors may be relevant for a broad variety of achievement emotions (Figure 8.1).

Cognitive Quality

The cognitive quality of classroom instruction and social environments as defined by their structure, clarity, and potential for cognitive stimulation likely has a positive influence on students' perceived control and the perceived value of academic tasks, thus positively influencing their achievement emotions. When teachers provide clear explanations and well-structured examples, students can enjoy learning. In addition, the level of demands in the classroom and relative difficulty of tasks is critically important. Task difficulty impacts the likelihood of successful performance, thus influencing perceived control over task performance and all of the emotions that depend on perceived control as discussed earlier. For example, if the very first questions on an exam are too difficult and cannot be answered, perceived control can decrease to the extent that a student starts to panic or even resigns and does not complete the exam. Furthermore, the match between demands and competences can influence perceived task value, thus also influencing emotions. If demands slightly exceed current competencies, the task can be perceived as a challenge that can be enjoyable. In contrast, if the demands are too high (over-challenge) or too low (under-challenge), the incentive value of a task may be reduced to the extent that boredom is experienced (Csikszentmihalyi, 1975; Pekrun et al., 2010).

Motivational Quality

Teachers, parents, and peers deliver messages conveying information about the controllability and value of academic tasks, thus influencing students' emotions. For example, perceived control can be influenced by attributing a student's achievement to specific causes. Telling students that their failures are due to lack of ability can reduce the students' sense of control and prompt shame and anxiety; in contrast, attributing failure to lack of effort or study strategies helps students to uphold positive expectations and experience hope and confidence. Similarly, perceived value can be influenced by explaining the relevance of learning materials and educational attainment (Harackiewicz, Tibbetts, Canning, & Hyde, 2014). However, increasing perceived importance can boost not only positive emotions but negative emotions as well—as noted, greater value amplifies all types of emotion (except for boredom). Specifically, reminding students of the importance of successful performance on tests and exams is a double-edged sword—"fear appeals" can exacerbate students' anxiety (Putwain, Remedios, & Symes, 2015).

More indirect ways to increase value include use of learning materials that relate to students' interests. In addition, learning environments that fulfill students' needs for autonomy and social relatedness can help increase the perceived value of learning and foster positive activity-related emotions. For example, learning environments that support cooperation should help students fulfill their needs for social relatedness, thus making working on academic tasks more enjoyable. Environments supporting autonomy can increase perceived control and, by meeting needs for autonomy, the value of related achievement activities (Tsai, Kunter, Lüdtke, & Trautwein, 2008). However, these beneficial effects likely also depend on the match between individual competences and needs for academic autonomy, on the one hand, and the affordances of these environments, on the other. In case of a mismatch, loss of control and negative emotions could result.

Emotional Quality

Emotions can be directly transmitted to others by means of nonverbal communication. Displays of emotion conveyed by facial, gestural, and postural expression provide information about an individual's emotional state. These signals can be automatically mimicked by others so that the others experience the same emotion. Such "emotional contagion" (Hatfield, Cacioppo, & Rapson, 1994) likely plays a major role in daily classroom interaction, with emotions being transmitted from teachers to students, from students to teachers, and among classmates. As such, through emotional contagion, teachers can directly influence the mood in the class, provided that they display rather than suppress their emotions. In fact, a few studies suggest that teachers' enjoyment can strongly facilitate students' enjoyment of class and that this process is mediated through teachers' displayed enthusiasm for teaching (Frenzel, Becker-Kurz, Pekrun, Goetz, & Lüdtke, 2017; Frenzel, Goetz, Lüdtke, Pedurn, & Sutton, 2009). In addition, emotional contagion can involve observational learning: Watching how others enjoy solving a problem demonstrates that problem solving can be enjoyable, which can facilitate students' adoption of positive academic values.

Goal Structures and Social Expectations

Different standards for evaluating achievement imply different goal structures (Johnson & Johnson, 1974; Murayama & Elliot, 2009; Roseth, Johnson, & Johnson, 2008). In *individualistic goal structures* (alternatively called mastery goal structures), achievement is based on absolute (task mastery) or individual standards (individual improvement over time). Importantly, in these structures, the achievement of any individual student is independent from the achievement of other students. In contrast, *competitive goal structures* (alternatively called performance goal structures) are based on normative standards, which define a student's achievement relative to the achievement of other students. Under such a definition, individual achievement is dependent on the achievement of others. Not everybody can succeed in terms of outperforming others, and the (normative) success of some students comes at the cost of failure for others. Finally, in *cooperative goal structures*, individual achievement is a positive function of the achievement of others—the better the contributions of each student, the better the achievement of the whole group.

These goal structures define opportunities for experiencing success and perceiving control, thus influencing control-dependent emotions. Specifically, competitive goal structures imply, as noted, that some individuals have to experience failure, thus inducing negative outcome emotions such as anxiety and hopelessness in these individuals (Pekrun, Elliot, & Maier, 2006). Similarly, the demands implied by an important other's unrealistic expectancies for achievement can lead to negative emotions resulting from reduced subjective control. For example, if parents hold overly high aspirations for their children's academic success, they can reduce children's sense of control to meet their parents' expectations, which can prompt anxiety and ultimately prevent the very attainment that parents had hoped for in the first place (Murayama, Pekrun, Suzuki, Marsh, & Lichtenfeld, 2016).

Composition of Student Groups

The ability level of the classroom determines the likelihood of performing well relative to one's classmates. All else being equal, chances for performing well relative to others are reduced when being in a high-achieving class, thus students' perceived control and competence tend to be reduced as well. In contrast, being in a low-achieving class offers more chances to be successful, enabling a sense of competence (Marsh, 1987, calls this the "big-fish-little-pond effect"—all other things being equal, it may be preferable to be a "big fish" in a "little pond" rather than a relatively small fish in a big pond of high achievers). Due to these effects on perceived control, positive emotions such as enjoyment can be reduced, and negative emotions such as anxiety exacerbated, when a student is in a high-achieving class (Pekrun, Murayama, Marsh, Goetz, & Frenzel, 2018). Other things being equal, individual students' anxiety has, in fact, been found to be higher in high-ability classrooms than in low-ability classrooms (Preckel, Zeidner, Goetz, & Schleyer, 2008).

The negative effects of membership in a high-achieving classroom pose a conundrum for educators. Placing students in high-ability classes provides them with peers who are role models for cognitive development and can provide cognitive stimulation. However, these possible benefits need to be weighed against the psychosocial costs of such a placement, including the risk for a reduction of self-confidence, decrease in positive emotions, and increase in negative emotions. Furthermore, it may be that the possible beneficial effects on learning do not even occur: When controlling for measurement error and pre-existing differences, the effects of class-average achievement on individual achievement can be negative as well (Dicke et al., in press), implying that being in a high-achieving class neither benefits a student's emotions nor their cognitive learning.

Feedback and Consequences of Achievement

Success can strengthen perceived control, and cumulative failure undermines control. In environments involving frequent assessments, performance feedback is likely of primary importance for the arousal of achievement emotions. In addition, the consequences of success and failure are important, since they affect the instrumental value of achievement. Positive outcome emotions (e.g., hope for success) can be increased if success produces beneficial long-term outcomes (e.g., future career opportunities), provided sufficient contingency between one's own efforts, success, and these outcomes. Negative consequences of failure (e.g., unemployment), on the other hand, may increase achievement-related anxiety and hopelessness (Pekrun, 1992a). As such, high-stakes testing is likely to amplify students' test-related emotions and to exacerbate their negative emotions if failure cannot be avoided.

Cultural Context

According to the CVT, to the extent that emotion-generating appraisals and social environments vary across cultures, achievement emotions should vary as well. In cultures that emphasize the importance of hard work and focus on (controllable) effort rather than (uncontrollable) ability as an explanation for achievement, perceptions of control should be facilitated, thus promoting positive and reducing negative achievement emotions. In cultures that emphasize the intrinsic value of learning, positive activity emotions such as enjoyment of learning should be promoted. Alternatively, when the importance of achievement is foregrounded, outcome emotions such as hope and anxiety should be prompted. Furthermore, cultures can influence emotions by shaping students' immediate social environments. For example, if classroom environments differ across cultures in terms of quality of instruction, classroom goal structures, and procedures of assessment, students' emotions should be influenced accordingly.

Within any given cultural context, these different influences can be congruent, but they can also represent opposing forces that can be balanced in different ways. In the latter case, it is more difficult to predict the resulting frequency and intensity of emotions. For example, if the importance of avoiding failure is emphasized and coupled with ability attributions and high levels of competition, it is to be expected that negative outcome emotions such as anxiety and shame are exacerbated. In contrast, if failure avoidance is emphasized but coupled with effort attributions and cooperation among students (a pattern that has been described for East Asian countries; see, e.g., Kumar & Maehr, 2007), the net effect on students' emotions is difficult to predict.

Cross-cultural research confirms that students' appraisals and social environments can vary across countries representing different cultures. Most studies focused on comparing East Asian countries (specifically Japan, Korea, and China) with Western countries. Hypotheses were derived from descriptions of East Asian cultures as Confucian-heritage, collectivistic, and favoring interdependent self-construal, versus Western cultures as Christian-heritage, individualistic, and favoring independent self-construal (e.g., Hofstede, 1986). Based on such a view, it has been hypothesized that East Asian students value education more; favor effort attributions of achievement over ability attributions and are more ready to adopt an incremental conception of intelligence; prefer to defer to authority and conform with rules imposed by parents and teachers; and tend to cooperate rather than compete with peers (e.g., Kumar & Maehr, 2007; Lee, 1996). Accordingly, classroom environments in East Asian countries have been described as involving steeper hierarchies and a large power distance between teachers and students; higher conformity of students with both teachers and peers; as well as more collaboration and less competition among classmates, relative to classroom environments in Western countries (Leung, 2001; Liem, Martin, Nair, Bernardo, & Prasetya, 2009).

Early studies conducted in the 1960s to 1990s found some support for these predictions (Choi, Nisbett, & Norenzayan, 1999; Stevenson & Stigler, 1992; also see Liem et al., 2009; Reeve et al., 2014). However, most of these studies used small convenience samples of students and failed to establish equivalence of measurement instruments across countries. In contrast, the recent large-scale PISA studies considered measurement equivalence and included representative samples. The results cast doubt on the earlier findings. Students' perceived control, attributions of failure to the self, achievement motivation, and perceived instrumental value of mathematics as well as the instructional climate in classrooms did not systematically differ between East Asian and Western countries (OECD, 2013, 2017). For example, in the PISA 2015 assessment, scores for achievement motivation were significantly higher than the OECD average in the Korean, Hong Kong, and mainland China samples, but lower in Japan and Macao and not significantly different from the OECD average in the Taipei sample (OECD, 2017).

As such, it may well be that some of the hypothesized differences in appraisals and social environments represent culture myths rather than reality—conceptions of culture derived from the writings of Eastern and Western philosophers and education theorists may not be representative of everyday cultural practices (also see Voronov & Singer, 2000; Watkins & Biggs, 2001). It may also be that some of these differences existed in the past but vanish today due to the pressures of globalization in the "late modern age" (Giddens, 1991; also see Juan, Qin, & Park, 2013).

However, despite these possible trends towards universal harmonization of cultural beliefs and structures of education, students' emotions still differ across cultural contexts. For example, in a study by Frenzel, Thrash, Pekrun, and Goetz (2007), we investigated Chinese and German students' emotions in mathematics, using the Achievement Emotions Questionnaire-Mathematics (AEQ-M; Pekrun et al., 2011) after establishing cross-cultural measurement equivalence. The Chinese students reported higher levels of enjoyment, pride, anxiety, and shame, whereas the German students reported higher levels of anger. The findings are consistent with existing evidence that anger is more avoided in collectivistic cultures, as compared with individualistic cultures (e.g., Grimm, Church, Katigbak, & Reyes, 1999). They also are consistent with the PISA assessments that found particularly high levels of math and science anxiety in East Asian students (OECD, 2004, 2013, 2017), and extend these findings to achievement emotions other than anxiety.

RELATIVE UNIVERSALITY OF ACHIEVEMENT EMOTIONS

All things being equal, scientists prefer parsimonious explanations over more complex ones. From such a perspective, explaining local phenomena by use of universal, generalizable laws should be preferable to "local theories" (Schibeci & Grundy, 1987) that apply to only a limited number of local phenomena in specific sociohistorical contexts. However, while universal laws offer the advantage of explaining many phenomena (provided they are valid), it may be that they do not describe any of these phenomena in sufficient depth, implying that there may be a trade-off between parsimony and depth of explanation. Furthermore, there may be phenomena for which universal laws do not apply at all, so that describing them makes it necessary to construct a locally-specific set of laws or descriptive guidelines. Accordingly, where should the science of emotions be located on the continuum from universal (or nomothetic or etic) to local (or idiographic or emic)? Is it more appropriate to describe these emotions by general laws purportedly true for all humans, or to describe them in a way that is specific for sociohistorical contexts; for nations, institutions, and communities within these contexts; for different genders; or even for single individuals? This question is far from trivial. There is no all-or-none answer that would give clear priority for either of the two perspectives for all affective phenomena, and it likely cannot be answered by only considering normative criteria defining good science, or simply by theoretical speculation about the usefulness of different paradigms. Rather, the answer likely depends on the phenomenon under consideration, and can only be reached by means of empirical investigation and empirically grounded construction of theories.

For achievement emotions, the answer suggested by the CVT is that principles of *relative universality* hold (Pekrun, 2009). These principles integrate universal and local perspectives. Using a universal perspective, the theory is built on the premise that basic functional mechanisms of emotion are universal within our species. As such, the theory proposes that the principles linking achievement emotions with their antecedents and outcomes are universal across individuals, academic domains, genders, and cultures. For example, the proposed connections between specific control and value appraisals, on the one hand, and different emotions, on the other, are thought to be of a general nature. However, universality of functional mechanisms notwithstanding, the objects, frequencies, and process parameters (such as intensity and duration) of achievement emotions are expected to differ widely, due to differences in individual dispositions, developmental trajectories, achievement settings, and sociocultural contexts. For example, whereas the same proximal antecedents are assumed for female and male students' achievement emotions, the frequency and intensity of these emotions may well differ between genders, as noted earlier.

To understand relative universality, it is important to note that mean levels and relations of variables are logically and statistically independent. Even if mean levels (or other distributional parameters) of variables differ, the relations between the variables can be the same across groups. Based on the CVT, we have investigated principles of relative universality for the achievement emotions experienced by students across academic domains, genders, and cultures. The findings support relative universality of these emotions.

Academic Domains

In traditional approaches, an underlying assumption was that achievement emotions are generalized across situations and task domains. Specifically, in test anxiety research, most studies regarded this emotion as a general personality trait predisposing individuals to experience anxiety whenever confronted with an evaluative situation (Zeidner, 1998). However, research on achievement-related perceived control and values has suggested that these variables are organized in domain-specific ways (e.g., self-concepts of ability, self-efficacy, and task values; Bong, 2001). By implication, it can be assumed that emotions other than anxiety should also show domain specificity (i.e., they should differ across domains).

In a series of studies, we found evidence corroborating this assumption. For example, in a study by Goetz, Frenzel, Pekrun, Hall, and Lüdtke (2007), we used measures derived from the Achievement Emotions Questionnaire (Pekrun, Goetz, Frenzel, Barchfeld, & Perry, 2011) to analyze 8th and 11th grade students' enjoyment, pride, boredom, anger, and anxiety experienced in mathematics, physics, German, and English. As expected, the findings showed that mean levels of emotions differed across domains. Students reported more enjoyment and pride, and less boredom, in English than in the other three subjects, and less anger and anxiety in both English and German, as compared with mathematics and physics. In addition, there were substantial differences between individual students in the domain-related emotion scores, as indicated by low correlations across domains. With the exception of correlations between emotions in the adjacent domains of mathematics and physics, and in the adjacent domains of German and English, all coefficients were below $r = .35$ in the Grade 8 sample, and below $r = .20$ in the Grade 11 sample. These findings show that students' emotional experiences can be quite different across academic domains.

However, domain specificity notwithstanding, the interrelations of these emotions and their links with academic achievement proved to be similar across domains. In all four domains, enjoyment and pride showed substantial positive intercorrelations, as did boredom, anger, and anxiety. All correlations between the two positive emotions, on one hand, and the three negative emotions, on the other hand, were substantially negative in all four domains. Furthermore, the correlations of enjoyment and pride with students' academic achievement were consistently positive within all four domains, and the correlations of the negative emotions with achievement were consistently negative. Overall, combined with the domain specificity of distributional parameters, the generalizability of these functional relations supports principles of relative universality across academic domains.

Genders

As described earlier, girls and boys can differ considerably in their emotions in subjects such as mathematics. Nevertheless, it appears that the relations of these emotions with appraisals and achievement do not differ between genders. For example, Frenzel et al. (2007) explored gender differences in five mathematics emotions (enjoyment, pride, anxiety, hopelessness, and shame) in a representative sample of over 2,000 German students in Grade 5. In addition, students' perceived control and value as well as their math achievement were assessed. Students' competence beliefs in mathematics ("I am a good student in mathematics") were used as an indicator of perceived control, and the intrinsic value of this domain ("Mathematics is my favorite subject") as well as the value of achievement in the domain ("It is very important for me to get good grades in mathematics") as indicators of perceived values.

The findings suggest that there were clear differences between the math emotions reported by the two genders. Female students reported less enjoyment and pride in math, and more anxiety, hopelessness, and shame, even after controlling for prior achievement. These differences were congruent with the differences found for control- and value-related beliefs. Girls had lower scores for competence beliefs and domain value, whereas the scores for achievement value in mathematics did not differ. The findings of mediational analysis corroborated that gender was a significant predictor of all five emotions. After additionally including the competence belief and value variables in the regression equation, however, gender was no longer a significant predictor of pride, anxiety, hopelessness, and shame, and remained only a weak predictor of enjoyment, thus indicating substantial mediation of gender effects on the emotions by control and value appraisals. Supporting the CVT, this pattern of links corroborates that students' emotions can be explained by their appraisals, and that gender differences in these emotions are largely mediated by differences in appraisals.

In addition, the equivalence of relationships between appraisals and emotions across genders was explored by multigroup structural equation modeling. The findings showed that these relationships were largely equivalent. For each of the five emotions, the appraisal-emotion relationships had the same sign, were equally significant, and had similar size across genders. In sum, these findings indicate that there are substantial differences between the math emotions experienced by female and male students, with female students showing a debilitating pattern of lower enjoyment and pride, combined with higher anxiety, hopelessness, and shame. Nevertheless, the links between these emotions and students' appraisals were demonstratively equivalent for female and male students, thus corroborating assumptions on the relative universality of relations between appraisals and emotions across genders.

Cultural Contexts

In another series of studies, we investigated whether relative universality holds for students' emotions across cultural contexts. Some of these studies pertained to differences across Western cultures (e.g., Muis et al., 2015; Pekrun, Elliot, & Maier, 2006; Pekrun, Vogl, Muis, & Sinatra, 2017); in others, we included student samples from Western and Asian cultures. The findings indicate substantial differences of achievement across cultures. For example, as described earlier, Chinese and German students' math emotions differed substantially in the study by Frenzel et al. (2007). In contrast to mean-level differences, however, the relationships of these emotions with students' causal attributions of achievement, their math achievement, and parental expectations were reasonably similar across countries in this study.

In both samples, students' perceived control, as indicated by high ability attributions for success in mathematics, correlated positively with their enjoyment and pride, and negatively with their anxiety, anger, and shame. Lack of control, as indicated by attributions of failure to lack of ability, correlated negatively with enjoyment and pride, and positively with the negative emotions. Furthermore, expectations by parents that their child was able to do well in mathematics correlated positively with the two positive emotions, and negatively with the three negative emotions, in both samples. Finally, enjoyment and pride correlated positively, and anger, anxiety, and shame negatively, with students' math achievement in both samples.

This pattern of findings is consistent with recent PISA findings. As noted earlier, mean scores for mathematics anxiety, domain-general achievement anxiety, and science enjoyment differed substantially across countries in the PISA 2012 and 2015 assessments. These mean-level differences notwithstanding, the relations with students' performance were remarkably consistent. In the PISA 2012 assessment, students' anxiety and achievement in math correlated negatively in all of the 64 participating countries, and all of these correlations but one were significant (OECD, 2013). Similarly, in the PISA 2015 assessment, students' schoolwork-related anxiety showed negative correlations with their science performance in 52 of 55 countries participating in the assessment of anxiety (OECD, 2016). The robustness of relations with achievement also extends to positive emotions. The PISA 2015 assessment included students' enjoyment of science, based on items adapted from the Achievement Emotions Questionnaire (Pekrun et al., 2011). The relation between students' enjoyment and performance in science was positive in all of the 68 countries for which this relation was examined.

In sum, these results are consistent with the propositions of the CVT regarding the role of appraisals and the relations between emotions and achievement, as described earlier. The findings suggest that there can be substantial differences in levels of achievement emotions across cultures. At the same time, however, the functional relations of these emotions with their presumed antecedents and outcomes seem to be equivalent across cultures, thus again supporting principles of relative universality. Given the representativeness of samples and cross-cultural equivalence of measures in the PISA assessments, the substantial cross-country variation of emotions scores in these assessments, coupled with the robust uniformity of their relations with performance, is especially impressive and underscores the validity of relative universality assumptions.

CONCLUSIONS

Achievement emotions are critically important for students' educational careers and their psychological and physical well-being alike. The CVT offers an integrative theoretical account of the origins and functions of these emotions. The basic propositions of the theory pertain to the appraisal antecedents of achievement emotions and their effects on students' learning and performance. The available evidence confirms that students' control and value appraisals are prime determinants of their emotions, and that these emotions, in turn, impact students' attention, motivation to learn, use of learning strategies, and academic achievement. From the prime role of appraisals for the arousal of achievement emotions, it follows that gender, social environments, and culture influence these emotions by shaping students' appraisals. For these functional relations with individual and sociocultural antecedents as well as learning outcomes, the theory proposes universality across genders and sociocultural contexts while also positing that the contents and distributions of achievement emotions can vary widely. The available evidence supports such "relative universality" of achievement emotions, making it possible to explain these emotions parsimoniously while acknowledging their wide variation and uniqueness in individual students, genders, and sociocultural and historical contexts.

Much of the evidence, however, is based on samples from Western countries. More research using samples across multiple cultural contexts around the world is needed to more fully explore antecedents, outcomes, and the proposed relative universality of students' emotions. Furthermore, most of the few existing cross-cultural studies on achievement emotions were not well suited to infer valid conclusions about differences between cultures. Several requirements must be met to reach such conclusions. First, measures are needed that are culture-sensitive. Second, sensitivity notwithstanding, they need to be sufficiently equivalent across cultures to allow comparisons (Parker, Dowson, & McInerney, 2007). Within a confirmatory factor analysis framework, metric invariance is considered sufficient to compare relations between variables across cultures, whereas scalar invariance is required to compare parameters of distributions such as average levels of an emotion (e.g., Steenkamp & Baumgartner, 1998; for alternative approaches, see e.g., OECD, 2017; Carter, Kotrba, & Lake, 2014). Third, representative samples are needed. There is a dearth of studies meeting either of the three requirements, let alone all three of them (for an exception, see the recent PISA assessments cited earlier; e.g., OECD, 2017).

Finally, future research on the influence of gender, social environments, and cultural context also needs to consider study designs that make it possible to infer causal conclusions. To date, most of the existing studies used cross-sectional designs and correlational analysis. Using such a design to examine, for example, the influence of parental aspirations on students' test anxiety leaves it open whether any observed relations are caused by effects of aspirations on anxiety, effects of students' anxiety on their parents' wishes, third variables, or any combination of these possibilities. Longitudinal and experimental designs will be needed to disentangle the temporal and causal ordering of sociocultural variables and students' emotions.

REFERENCES

Ashkanasy, N. M., & Humphrey, R. H. (2011). Current emotion research in organizational behavior. *Emotion Review, 3,* 214–224.

Barrett, F. L., Lewis, M., & Haviland-Jones, J. M. (Eds.). (2016). *Handbook of emotions* (4th ed.). New York, NY: Guilford.

Bong, M. (2001). Between- and within-domain relations of academic motivation among middle and high school students: Self-efficacy, task value and achievement goals. *Journal of Educational Psychology, 93,* 23–34.

Carter, N. T., Kotrba, L. M., & Lake, C. J. (2014). Null results in assessing survey score comparability: Illustrating measurement invariance using item response theory. *Journal of Business Psychology, 29,* 205–220.

Choi, I., Nisbett, R. E., & Norenzayan, A. (1999). Causal attribution across culture: Variation and universality. *Psychological Bulletin, 125,* 47–63.

Clore, G. L., & Huntsinger, J. R. (2007). How emotions inform judgment and regulate thought. *Trends in Cognitive Sciences, 11,* 393–399.

Csikszentmihalyi, M. (1975). *Beyond boredom and anxiety.* San Francisco, CA: Jossey-Bass.

Dicke, T., Marsh, H. W., Parker, P. D., Pekrun, R., Guo, J., & Televantou, I. (in press). Effects of school-average achievement on individual self-concept and achievement: Unmasking phantom effects masquerading as true compositional effects. *Journal of Educational Psychology.*

Folkman, S., & Lazarus, R. S. (1985). If it changes it must be a process: Study of emotion and coping during three stages of a college examination. *Journal of Personality and Social Psychology, 48,* 150–170.

Frenzel, A. C., Becker-Kurz, B., Pekrun, R., Goetz, T., & Lüdtke, O. (2017). Emotion transmission in the classroom revisited: A reciprocal effects model of teacher and student enjoyment. *Journal of Educational Psychology.* Advance online publication. doi:10.1037/edu0000228

Frenzel, A. C., Goetz, T., Lüdtke, O., Pekrun, R., & Sutton, R. (2009). Emotional transmission in the classroom: Exploring the relationship between teacher and student enjoyment. *Journal of Educational Psychology, 101,* 705–716.

Frenzel, A. C., Pekrun, R., & Goetz, T. (2007). Girls and mathematics—A "hopeless" issue? A control-value approach to gender differences in emotions towards mathematics. *European Journal of Psychology of Education, 22,* 497–514.

Frenzel, A. C., Thrash, T. M., Pekrun, R., Goetz, T. (2007). Achievement emotions in Germany and China: A cross-cultural validation of the Academic Emotions Questionnaire-Mathematics (AEQ-M). *Journal of Cross-Cultural Psychology, 38,* 302–309.

Giddens, A. (1991). *Modernity and self-identity: Self and society in the late modern age.* Redwood City, CA: Stanford University Press.

Goetz, T., Frenzel, A. C., Pekrun, R., Hall, N. C., & Lüdtke, O. (2007). Between- and within-domain relations of students' academic emotions. *Journal of Educational Psychology, 99,* 715–733.

Goetz, T., Bieg, M., Lüdtke, O., Pekrun, R., & Hall, N. C. (2013). Do girls really experience more anxiety in mathematics? *Psychological Science, 24,* 2079–2087.

Goetz, T., Frenzel, A. C., Stoeger, H., & Hall, N. C. (2010). Antecedents of everyday positive emotions: An experience sampling analysis. *Motivation and Emotion, 34*, 49–62.

Graham, S., & Taylor, A. Z. (2014). An attributional approach to emotional life in the classroom. In R. Pekrun & L. Linnenbrink-Garcia (Eds.), *Handbook of emotions in education* (pp. 96–119). New York, NY: Taylor & Francis.

Grimm, S. D., Church, A. T., Katigbak, M. S., & Reyes, J. A. S. (1999). Self-described traits, values, and moods associated with individualism and collectivism. *Journal of Cross-Cultural Psychology, 30*, 466–500.

Harackiewicz, J. M., Tibbetts, Y., Canning, E. A., & Hyde, J. S. (2014). Harnessing values to promote motivation in education. In S. Karabenick & T. Urdan (Eds.), *Advances in motivation and achievement* (Vol. 18, pp. 71–105). Bingley, England: Emerald.

Hatfield, E., Cacioppo, J. T., & Rapson, R. L. (1994). *Emotional contagion.* New York, NY: Cambridge University Press.

Heckhausen, H. (1991). *Motivation and action.* Berlin, Germany: Springer.

Hembree, R. (1988). Correlates, causes, effects, and treatment of test anxiety. *Review of Educational Research, 58*, 47–77.

Hofstede, G. (1986). Cultural differences in teaching and learning. *International Journal of Intercultural Relations, 10*, 301–320.

Johnson, D. W., & Johnson, R. T. (1974). Instructional goal structure: Cooperative, competitive or individualistic. *Review of Educational Research, 4*, 213–240.

Juang, L. P., Qin, D. B., & Park, I. J. K. (2013). Deconstructing the myth of the "tiger mother": An introduction to the special issue on tiger parenting, Asian-heritage families, and child/adolescent well-being. *Asian American Journal of Psychology, 4*, 1–6.

Kumar, R., & Maehr, M. L. (2007). Cultural interpretations of achievement motivation: A situated perspective. F. Salili (Ed.), *Culture, motivation and learning: A multicultural perspective* (pp. 43–66). Charlotte, NC: Information Age.

Lauerman, F., Eccles, J. S., & Pekrun, R. (2017). Why do children worry about their academic achievement? An expectancy-value perspective on elementary students' worry about their mathematics and reading performance. *ZDM Mathematics Education, 49*, 339–354.

Lee, W. O. (1996). The cultural context for Chinese learners: Conceptions of learning in the Confucian tradition. In D. Watkins & J. Biggs (Eds.), *The Chinese learner: Cultural, psychological and contextual influences* (pp. 25–41). Camberwell, Australia: Australian Council for Educational Research.

Leung, F. K. S. (2001). In search of an East Asian identity in mathematics education. *Educational Studies in Mathematics, 47*, 35–51.

Liem, G. A. D., Martin, A. J., Nair, E., Bernardo, A. B. I., & Prasetya, P. H. (2009). Cultural factors relevant to secondary school students in Australia, Singapore, the Philippines and Indonesia: Relative differences and congruencies. *Australian Journal of Guidance and Counselling, 19*, 161–178.

Marsh, H. W. (1987). The big-fish-little-pond effect on academic self-concept. *Journal of Educational Psychology, 79*, 280–295.

Meece, J. L., Wigfield, A., & Eccles, J. S. (1990). Predictors of math anxiety and its influence on young adolescents' course enrollment intentions and performance in mathematics. *Journal of Educational Psychology, 82,* 60–70.

Muis, K. R., Pekrun, R., Sinatra, G. M., Azevedo, R., Trevors, G., Meier, E., & Heddy, B. (2015). The curious case of climate change: Testing a theoretical model of epistemic beliefs, epistemic emotions, and complex learning. *Learning and Instruction, 39,* 168–183.

Murayama, K., Pekrun, R., Suzuki, M., Marsh, H. W., & Lichtenfeld, S. (2016). Don't aim too high for your kids: Parental over-aspiration undermines students' learning in mathematics. *Journal of Personality and Social Psychology, 111,* 166–179.

Murayama, K., & Elliot, A. J. (2009). The joint influence of personal achievement goals and classroom goal structures on achievement-relevant outcomes. *Journal of Educational Psychology, 101,* 432–447.

Organization for Economic Cooperation and Development. (2004). *Learning for tomorrow's world: First results from PISA 2003.* Paris, France: Author.

Organization for Economic Cooperation and Development. (2010). *PISA 2009 results (Volume 3): Learning to learn—student engagement, strategies and practices.* Paris, France: Author.

Organization for Economic Cooperation and Development. (2013). *PISA 2012 results (Volume 3): Ready to learn. Students' engagement, drive and self-beliefs.* Paris, France: Author.

Organization for Economic Cooperation and Development. (2016). *PISA 2015 results (Volume 1): Excellence and equity in education.* Paris, France: Author.

Organization for Economic Cooperation and Development. (2017). *PISA 2015 results (Volume 3): Students' well-being.* Paris, France: Author.

Parker, P., Dowson, M., & McInerney, D. (2007). Standards for quantitative research in diverse sociocultural contexts. In D. McInerney, S. Van Etten, & M. Dowson (Eds.), *Standards in education* (pp. 315–330). Charlotte, NC: Information Age.

Pekrun, R. (1983). *Schule und Persönlichkeitsentwicklung* [Personality development at school]. Frankfurt, Germany: Lang.

Pekrun, R. (1988). *Emotion, Motivation und Persönlichkeit* [Emotion, motivation, and personality]. München, Germany: Psychologie Verlags Union.

Pekrun, R. (1992a). Expectancy-value theory of anxiety: Overview and implications. In D. G. Forgays, T. Sosnowski, & K. Wrzesniewski (Eds.), *Anxiety: Recent developments in self-appraisal, psychophysiological and health research* (pp. 23–41). Washington, DC: Hemisphere.

Pekrun, R. (1992b). The impact of emotions on learning and achievement: Towards a theory of cognitive/motivational mediators. *Applied Psychology: An International Review, 41,* 359–376.

Pekrun, R. (1993). Facets of students' academic motivation: A longitudinal expectancy-value approach. In M. Maehr & P. Pintrich (Eds.), *Advances in motivation and achievement* (Vol. 8, pp. 139–189). Greenwich, CT: JAI Press.

Pekrun, R. (2000). A social-cognitive, control-value theory of achievement emotions. In J. Heckhausen (Ed.), *Motivational psychology of human development* (pp. 143–163). Oxford, England: Elsevier Science.

Pekrun, R. (2006). The control-value theory of achievement emotions: Assumptions, corollaries, and implications for educational research and practice. *Educational Psychology Review, 18,* 315–341.

Pekrun, R. (2009). Global and local perspectives on human affect: Implications of the control-value theory of achievement emotions. In M. Wosnitza, S. A. Karabenick, A. Efklides, & P. Nenniger (Eds.), *Contemporary motivation research: From global to local perspectives* (pp. 97–115). Cambridge, MA: Hogrefe.

Pekrun, R., Elliot, A. J., & Maier, M. A. (2006). Achievement goals and discrete achievement emotions: A theoretical model and prospective test. *Journal of Educational Psychology, 98,* 583–597.

Pekrun, R., Goetz, T., Daniels, L. M., Stupnisky, R. H., & Perry, R. P. (2010). Boredom in achievement settings: Control-value antecedents and performance outcomes of a neglected emotion. *Journal of Educational Psychology, 102,* 531–549.

Pekrun, R., Goetz, T., Frenzel, A. C., Barchfeld, P., & Perry, R. P. (2011). Measuring emotions in students' learning and performance: The Achievement Emotions Questionnaire (AEQ). *Contemporary Educational Psychology, 36,* 36–48.

Pekrun, R., Lichtenfeld, S., Marsh, H. W., Murayama, K., & Goetz, T. (2017). Achievement emotions and academic performance: Longitudinal models of reciprocal effects. *Child Development, 88,* 1653–1670.

Pekrun, R., & Linnenbrink-Garcia, L. (Eds.). (2014). *International handbook of emotions in education.* New York, NY: Taylor & Francis.

Pekrun, R., Murayama, K., Marsh, H. W., Goetz, T., & Frenzel, A. C. (2018). *Happy fish in little ponds: Testing a compositional effects model of achievement and emotion.* Manuscript submitted for publication.

Pekrun, R., & Perry, R. P. (2014). Control-value theory of achievement emotions. In R. Pekrun & L. Linnenbrink-Garcia (Eds.), *International handbook of emotions in education* (pp. 120–141). New York, NY: Taylor & Francis.

Pekrun, R., & Stephens, E. J. (2012). Academic emotions. In K. R. Harris, S. Graham, T. Urdan, J. M. Royer, & M. Zeidner (Eds.), *APA educational psychology handbook* (Vol. 2, pp. 3–31). Washington, DC: American Psychological Association.

Pekrun, R., Vogl, E., Muis, K. R., & Sinatra, G. M. (2017). Measuring emotions during epistemic activities: The epistemically-related emotion scales. *Cognition and Emotion, 31,* 1268–1276.

Preckel, F., Zeidner, M., Goetz, T., & Schleyer, E. J. (2008). Female "big fish" swimming against the tide: The "big-fish-little-pond effect" and gender-ratio in special gifted classes. *Contemporary Educational Psychology, 33,* 78–96.

Putwain, D. W., Remedios, R., & Symes, W. (2015). Experiencing fear appeals as a challenge or a threat influences attainment value and academic self-efficacy. *Learning and Instruction, 40,* 21–28.

Raynor, J. O. (1982). Future orientation, self-evaluation, and achievement motivation: Use of an expectancy-value theory of personality functioning and change. In N. T. Feather (Ed.), *Expectations and actions: Expectancy-value models in psychology* (pp. 97–124). Hillsdale, NJ: Erlbaum.

Reeve, J., Vansteenkiste, M., Assor, A., Ahmad, I., Cheon, S. H., Jang, H., . . . Wang, C. K. J. (2014). The beliefs that underlie autonomy-supportive and controlling teaching: A multinational investigation. *Motivation and Emotion, 38,* 93–110.

Roseth, C. J., Johnson, D. W., & Johnson, R. T. (2008). Promoting early adolescents' achievement and peer relationships: The effects of cooperative, competitive, and individualistic goal structures. *Psychological Bulletin, 134*, 223–246.

Scherer, K. R. (2009). The dynamic architecture of emotion: Evidence for the component process model. *Cognition and Emotion, 23*, 1307–1351.

Scherer, K. R., Schorr, A., & Johnstone, T. (Eds.). (2001). *Appraisal processes in emotion.* Oxford, England: Oxford University Press.

Schibeci, R. A., & Grundy, S. (1987). Local theories. *Journal of Educational Research, 81*, 91–96.

Shuman, V., & Scherer, K. R. (2014). Concepts and structures of emotions. In R. Pekrun & L. Linnenbrink-Garcia (Eds.), *International handbook of emotions in education* (pp. 13–35). New York, NY: Taylor & Francis.

Spangler, G., Pekrun, R., Kramer, K., & Hofmann, H. (2002). Students' emotions, physiological reactions, and coping in academic exams. *Anxiety, Stress, and Coping, 15*, 413–432.

Steenkamp, J.-B. E. M., & Baumgartner, H. (1998). Assessing measurement invariance in cross-national consumer research. *Journal of Consumer Research, 25*, 78–90.

Steinmayr, R., Crede, J., McElvany, N., & Wirthwein, L. (2016). Subjective well-being, test anxiety, academic achievement: Testing for reciprocal effects. *Frontiers in Psychology, 6*, 1994. doi:10.3389/fpsyg.2015.01994

Stevenson, H. W., & Stigler, J. W. (1992). *The learning gap: Why our schools are failing and what we can learn from Japanese and Chinese education.* New York, NY: Summit Books.

Tsai, Y.-M., Kunter, M., Lüdtke, O., & Trautwein, U. (2008). What makes lessons interesting? The role of situational and individual factors in three school subjects. *Journal of Educational Psychology, 100*, 460–472.

Turner, J. E., & Schallert, D. L. (2001). Expectancy-value relationships of shame reactions and shame resiliency. *Journal of Educational Psychology, 93*, 320–329.

Voronov, M., & Singer, J. A. (2001). The myth of individualism-collectivism: A critical review. *Journal of Social Psychology, 142*, 461–480.

Vroom, V. H. (1964). *Work and motivation.* New York, NY: Wiley.

Watkins, D. A., & Biggs, J. B. (2001). The paradox of the Chinese learner and beyond. In D. A. Watkins & J. B. Biggs (Eds.), *Teaching the Chinese learner: Psychological and pedagogical perspectives* (pp. 3–23). Hong Kong, China: The University of Hong Kong.

Wigfield, A., & Eccles, J. S. (2000). Expectancy–value theory of achievement motivation. *Contemporary Educational Psychology, 25*, 68–81.

Zeidner, M. (1998). *Test anxiety: The state of the art.* New York, NY: Plenum.

SECTION III

WHO WANTS ME TO STUDY WELL,
AND WHO CAN I DO IT WITH?

CHAPTER 9

A COMPETENCE-IN-CONTEXT APPROACH TO UNDERSTANDING MOTIVATION AT SCHOOL

Kathryn Wentzel

Central to many definitions of competence is the notion that successful adaptation within social contexts requires meeting multiple demands that reflect personal interests as well as those of the social group. Therefore, becoming a competent and well-adjusted student is a multifaceted and complex process that involves the achievement of goals that are valued and interesting to the student as well as those that are valued by teachers and peers. Accomplishing these goals should result in effective social integration into classroom life, as well as in positive developmental outcomes for the student. Examples of goals that promote social integration are those that result in the smooth functioning of the social group (e.g., displays of appropriate classroom behavior) and are reflected in levels of social approval and positive interpersonal relationships and interactions; self-related goals are those reflecting the development of intrinsic and idiosyncratic

Big Theories Revisited 2, pages 193–212
Copyright © 2018 by Information Age Publishing
193

interests, a healthy sense of identity, and emotional well-being (Bronfen-brenner, 1989; Ford, 1992).

This "competence within context" perspective can be found in the work of several theorists (e.g., Bronfenbrenner, 1989; see also Eccles & Midgley, 1989; Ford, 1992; Maehr & Braskamp, 1986), who further suggest that com-petence is a product of personal attributes that facilitate successful goal pursuit and contextual supports. In the current chapter, personal attributes are discussed with regard to motivational beliefs that support goal choice and goal pursuit. These include values associated with the accomplishment of specific tasks, beliefs about abilities to achieve task-related outcomes, and beliefs about control and autonomy associated with goal choice and goal pursuit. Pursuit of goals also is likely to be motivated by the degree to which students perceive their teachers and peers as providing essential supports. Social supports believed to play an integral role in student goal setting provide opportunities for the accomplishment of personal goals, such as to make friends or to learn algebra, but also define the appropriate parameters of these accomplishments so that they contribute to the socially-valued outcomes, such as establishing friendship groups that are socially inclusive rather than exclusive and engaging in instructional activities dur-ing math class.

In short, a full appreciation of how and why students thrive or fail to thrive at school requires an understanding of the multiple goals that stu-dents, their peers, and their teachers bring to the classroom, and the per-sonal characteristics and social supports that are available to facilitate their achievement. However, this appreciation necessitates coming to terms with fundamental questions central to the education of children: (a) What are our educational goals for children that define their success? and (b) How can we, as adults and educators, support successful pursuit of these mul-tiple goals? In the following sections, these questions will be addressed with discussions of educational goals that are universally valued, with a specific focus on socially-valued outcomes reflecting behavioral competence; the motivational attributes that facilitate student goal pursuit; and the contex-tual supports that contribute to successful goal pursuit. Although the pre-dominant perspective of this chapter is based on Western theorizing and empirical research, the overarching goal is to highlight ways in which this perspective is applicable to non-Western as well as Western groups.

CLASSROOM COMPETENCE
AND SOCIALLY VALUED GOALS

What are goals, and what are the classroom-specific goals that competent students pursue? A basic tenet of motivational theories is that people have personal goals and that these goals can be powerful motivators of behavior (see e.g., Austin & Vancouver, 1996). Personal goals (i.e., What do I want to do?) determine the focus and direction of behavior. The content of goals (e.g., Ford, 1992) directs efforts toward specific outcomes (e.g., to learn algebra), and goal standards (e.g., Bandura, 1986) define acceptable levels of accomplishment (e.g., to learn enough algebra to pass the exam). Goal orientations (Maehr & Zusho, 2009) focus on specific reasons for achievement striving, such as to develop skills (e.g., task mastery) or to prove ability (e.g., performing better than others).

In this chapter, I focus on the content of goals, or *what* it is that a student wants to achieve. This definition is adopted to parallel definitions of educational objectives for students that also reflect *what* it is that others want students to accomplish at school. With regard to these latter sets of goals, public schools in the United States were initially developed with an explicit function of educating children to become healthy, moral, and economically productive citizens. Since then, social outcomes in the form of moral character, conformity to social rules and norms, cooperation, and positive styles of social interaction have been promoted consistently as goals for students to achieve (see Wentzel, 1991a, for a review). Internationally, educational policies reflect a similar focus on social responsibility and citizenship (see Organisation for Economic Co-operation and Development, n.d.). Reflecting these educational objectives, social outcomes relevant to schooling have been studied most often with respect to adherence to social rules and expectations reflecting cooperation, respect for others, and positive forms of group participation that govern social interaction in the classroom and more broadly in civil society. More specifically, the development of students' prosocial and responsible behavior has been the focus of empirical research (see Wentzel, 2013) and the target of positive behavior intervention programs in the United States and in other Western and non-Western countries (e.g., Freeman et al., 2016).

The importance of behavioral competence for understanding students' success at school is borne out in research on U.S. students. First, behaving in prosocial and responsible ways has been related consistently and positively to healthy relationships with teachers and peers (Wentzel, 2013). Teachers' preferences for students are based in large part on students' social behavior in the classroom. Elementary school teachers report preferences for students who are cooperative, conforming, cautious, and responsible; in the middle school grades, teachers describe their "ideal" students in part, as sharing, helpful, and responsive to rules (see Wentzel, 2013 for a review). Likewise, students who are socially accepted by their peers tend to be highly cooperative, helpful, and sociable; children with close friends at school also tend to enjoy these positive characteristics (Rubin, Bukowski, & Bowker, 2015). Second, these behavioral competencies appear to contribute to academic accomplishments at school. Correlational studies indicate that tendencies to be prosocial and empathic, prosocial interactions with peers, appropriate classroom conduct, and compliance have been related positively to intellectual outcomes in the elementary- and secondary-school years (see Wentzel, 2013 for a review). Interventions that teach children appropriate social behavior have led to significant and stable gains in academic achievement (e.g., Freeman et al., 2016).

Although the exact nature of what constitutes "appropriate behavior" is likely to differ across individuals, contexts and cultures, it is reasonable to assume that students who are behaviorally competent are more likely to earn higher grades for several reasons. On the one hand, behaving in prosocial and socially-responsible ways includes conforming to rules for social conduct but also to rules and conventions for completing learning activities. Following procedures for accomplishing academic tasks and adopting dictate specific standards for performance are certain to result in higher levels of performance. Students who behave appropriately also are likely to be appreciated by teachers and peers, leading to more academic help and assistance (see Wentzel, 2013). Engaging in socially-valued behavior in the classroom can also free students from social distractions and result in more focused attention and engagement in instructional activities.

In addition to its focus on behavioral comportment as an important outcome of schooling, a competence-in-context perspective also has implications for understanding the basic underpinnings of student motivation. For example, pursuit of goals to be prosocial and responsible also has been is related positively to healthy relationships with teachers and peers as well as to academic accomplishments (Wentzel, 2013). For the most part, these relations are mediated by students' displays of prosocial and socially-responsible behavior at school (Wentzel, 1991b, 1994). Therefore, an additional, critical question for understanding the role of context in promoting student success is: What leads students to pursue socially-valued goals in the first place? In the following section, a process model of motivational decision-making based on contextual as well as personal inputs that was developed to address this question is described.

PROCESS MODEL OF MOTIVATIONAL DECISION-MAKING AND CLASSROOM COMPETENCE

If the situational demands of the classroom require children to pursue and accomplish specific goals in order to be competent and well-adjusted students, explanatory models of classroom competence must consider personal and social factors that facilitate goal pursuit. A model depicting such factors is presented in Figure 9.1. Based on social developmental

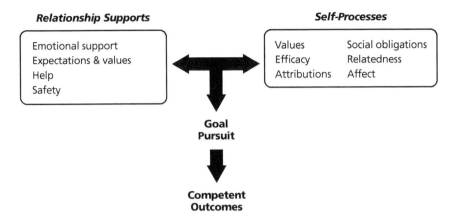

Figure 9.1 Process model of motivation and classroom contextual supports.

(e.g., Wentzel, 2015) and motivational (see Wentzel & Miele, 2016) perspectives, this model suggests that specific social, psychological, and affective processes regulate the extent to which students will actively pursue goals. The model predicts that social supports and motivational beliefs are related to classroom competence by way of pursuit of goals to achieve outcomes that are central to the learning process. These goals can reflect many outcomes, including displays of appropriate classroom behavior and efforts to learn and understand subject matter.

As depicted in the Figure 9.1, social provisions in the form of clear expectations and opportunities for goal pursuit, instrumental help, emotional support, and safety and responsivity reflect potential contextual influences on student goal pursuit. In part, these provisions support goal pursuit by providing input into socially-valued goals (including those valued by the larger culture) and facilitating positive motivational beliefs in the form of values, efficacy, control beliefs, perceived social expectations and belongingness. In this section, these motivational beliefs will be described first, followed by a discussion of ways in which social-contextual support might influence these beliefs and goal pursuit.

Motivational Beliefs Underlying Goal Pursuit

Motivation is commonly described as a set of interrelated beliefs about the self that explain the initiation, direction, intensity, persistence, and quality of behavior. The identification of motivational beliefs is particularly important when using a goal content perspective in that knowing which outcomes a student is trying to achieve does not offer insight into why they are trying to achieve them. Therefore, students' beliefs that underlie goal pursuit are potentially important self-processes for explaining the extent of students' efforts to achieve classroom goals. Most Western theorizing describes motivational beliefs as reflecting a range of concerns about personal goals, including which outcomes are personally desirable, values associated with goal attainment, and perceptions of ability, causality and control; in school settings, these beliefs typically are studied in relation to academic tasks and activities (see Wentzel & Miele, 2016). As described by numerous theorists (e.g, Bandura, 1986; Ryan & Deci, 2000; Weiner, 1992; Wigfield & Eccles, 2000), these beliefs inform a set of questions relevant for motivational decision-making that combine to explain why students might be motivated to pursue some goals but not others: (a) What do I want to do?; (b) Is doing this important and enjoyable?; (c) Can I do it?; and (d) What causes success and failure? The answers to these questions reflect beliefs about goals and values (Questions 1 and 2), ability (Question 3), and causality and control (Question 4).

As noted earlier, personal goals—What do I want to do?—determine the focus and direction of behavior, and represent the outcomes that students wish to achieve and accomplish at school. In turn, decisions to pursue these goals can be influenced by personal values concerning the perceived costs and benefits of goal accomplishment, the importance and long-term utility of goal achievement, and the intrinsic pleasure of engaging in goal-directed behavior (Wigfield & Eccles, 2000). In other words, values answer the question: Is doing this important and enjoyable? Students' beliefs about their abilities ("Can I do it?") also can influence what they choose to do and why they persist at certain activities and not others (Bandura, 1986; Schunk & Pajares, 2009). Positive beliefs about competence, or self-efficacy beliefs, can motivate engagement in tasks, whereas negative perceptions reflecting uncertainty about one's ability can result in disengagement (Bandura, 1986; Schunk & Pajares, 2009). Beliefs about causality and control provide students with a lens for interpreting past events and with a basis for developing expectations for the future (e.g., What causes success and failure?). These beliefs are reflected in causal attributions for success or failure (e.g., Graham & Williams, 2009; Weiner, 1992) and in personal theories or mindsets about if and how ability can change (e.g., Dweck & Master, 2009). Beliefs concerning autonomy and self-determination also have been studied in this regard (Ryan & Deci, 2001). To the extent that goals are perceived as self-determined, goal-directed behavior is experienced as freely chosen and emanating from one's self.

The universality of these self-processes for understanding student motivation has been argued theoretically (e.g., Bandura, 1989; Ryan & Deci, 2000) but has yet to be established empirically. However, of particular interest for understanding motivation from a competence-in-context perspective is the notion that students can also be motivated by beliefs reflecting social concerns that emanate from social interactions, contextual cues, and culturally-transmitted communications (see Ford, 1992; Wentzel, 2004; Wentzel & Brophy, 2013). These include beliefs about moral or social obligations to others and beliefs concerning interpersonal belongingness and emotional connectedness. Acknowledgement of these beliefs suggests that two additional questions are relevant for understanding motivational decision-making: (e) What am I supposed to do? and (f) Does anybody care if I do it? The addition of these beliefs allows for a broader conceptualization of motivation that incorporates Western notions of an ideal student as one who is a task-oriented, personally efficacious and autonomous learner with broader sociocultural ideals of one who is a relationship-oriented, socially-skilled, and interdependent learner. This recognition of contextual influences implies that sensitivity to social cues and values makes an additive and positive contribution to the set of beliefs that influence motivational decision making. Evidence to support this approach comes from work on coordinated task and social goal pursuit in relation to academic outcomes (e.g., Boekarts, 2009; Cooper & Jayatilaka, 2006; Liem, 2016; Wentzel, 1993).

With regard to the question—What am I supposed to do?—goal-related decision-making can be influenced by social expectations that define socially-valued goals, that is, what it is that others expect and want you to do in a given situation. This focus on socially-valued goals is based on the assumption that pursuit of these goals is a critical aspect of situational, and even broader cultural, competence. However, it is important to note that socially-valued goals can be task-related (e.g., to learn algebra) as well as social (e.g., to make new friends). In addition, goals are often described as being pursued for strictly social or extrinsic reasons (e.g., to please others or to avoid punishment), or for their own sake without the need for external prompts or rewards. Self-determination theory further defines these latter reasons as either reflecting the internalization of a goal, that is, an acquired value attached to goal attainment (identified reasons) or intrinsic interest in the process of achieving a goal (e.g., Ryan, 1993). In the current formulation, pursuit of socially-valued goals is discussed in terms of an internalized or intrinsic orientation towards responsibility to social relationships and groups. As such, it is considered as a separate component of motivation beliefs that is based on a sense of personal obligation.

At least two explanations have been offered for the development of these latter beliefs. First, proponents of an internalization perspective suggest that socially-derived values are first experienced as extrinsic constraints to one's sense of personal autonomy (Ryan & Deci, 2000). These values eventually become viewed as emanating from one's self through processes of socialization. In this case, they have become an important and valued part of an individual's self-system and identity (see also Cziksentmihalyi & Naka-mura, 1989). Second, as described by theorists who take a broader cultural psychology approach (e.g., Markus & Kitayama, 2003), these beliefs can also reflect a socially-motivated orientation based on the notion that the individual is part of a collective and interdependent social system. As part of this system, an individual experiences a sense of well-being when able to satisfy social obligations and contribute to the well-being of others. Both of these approaches will be discussed in a following section that describes socialization processes and mechanisms of influence.

Students' decisions to pursue goals also can be motivated by beliefs concerning the nature of their relationships with others (Question 6: "Does anybody care if I do it?). Few would argue that the need to belong and to experience a sense of relatedness with others is a powerful motivator of behavior. In addition, it has been described as a universal need that is important for positive human functioning across cultures (see Baumeister & Leary, 1995). When positive, these beliefs reflect feelings that one is a valued and integral member of a relationship or of a larger social group (Connell & Wellborn, 1991). In turn, motivation to engage in a socially-valued activity is more likely to occur if students believe that others care about them and want them to engage in activities that reflect group goals and promote the ongoing cohesion of the group. Beliefs that "someone cares" are central to understanding the role of interpersonal relationships with teachers and classmates in motivating students to engage academically and socially at school (Wentzel, 2009a, 2009b).

Social Processes That Support Positive Motivational Beliefs

Although a full review of the literature is beyond the scope of this article, these motivational beliefs appear to interact as a system to promote and sustain goal-directed behavior in academic (e.g., Ford, 1992) as well as social domains (e.g., prosocial behavior; Wentzel, 2004), and each has been related to a range of positive school-related outcomes (see Wentzel & Miele, 2016). Although beyond the scope of this chapter, the effectiveness of these belief systems in promoting positive outcomes also requires the emotional energy and will to engage in goal pursuit and to stay on task until goals are accomplished (see Ford, 1992; Pekrun, 2009; Weiner, 1992).

Of central concern for the current chapter is that these motivational beliefs have roots in the social interactions and relationships that students enjoy with others. The left-hand portion of Figure 9.1 suggests that students will engage in socially-valued goal pursuit when they perceive their relationships with their teachers and peers as providing specific supports that can promote goal attainment by way of motivational beliefs (Ford, 1992; see also Wentzel, 2004). These supports can be defined along four dimensions: Clear communication of expectations for achievement such that information is provided concerning what is expected and valued in the classroom; instrumental help to achieve these valued outcomes; emotional nurturance and caring such that students are made to feel like a valued member of the group; and a safe classroom environment that allows students to pursue goals in a secure, nonthreatening environment. Although the present discussion is focused on classroom teachers and peers, it is reasonable to expect that these same provisions can emanate from broader community or culturally-defined groups in their roles as educators.

A full description of these classroom supports can be found elsewhere (see Wentzel, 2009a, 2009b). However, the following illustrates their potential contributions to students' motivational beliefs and goal pursuit. First, it is reasonable to assume that students will pursue their personal goals and those valued by teachers to the extent teachers communicate clearly and consistently their values and expectations concerning classroom behavior and performance. These practices create a climate of interpersonal trust and fairness that promotes students' willingness to listen to teacher communications and adopt their behavioral and learning goals and values. In addition, teachers play the central role of transmitting knowledge and training students in academic subject areas. They do so by providing children with instrumental help in the form of information and advice, modeled behavior, and instructional experiences that facilitate learning.

With respect to motivational beliefs, clear communication and instrumental help in the form of direct instruction and modeling are powerful mechanisms whereby students learn what is expected of them and how to go about meeting those expectations. They provide input concerning goals, values, and social expectations for academic performance and social behavior (i.e., What am I supposed to do? Is this important and enjoyable to do?), and standards against which judgments of personal efficacy can be made (i.e., Can I do this?). These mechanisms also can result in the development of skills and abilities that bolster one's sense of efficacy and positive beliefs about control over the learning process (see Schunk & Parajes, 2009). Reinforcements and rewards from teachers and peers are additional and important sources of information concerning socially-valued goals, values, and perceptions of ability and control. These social cues convey to students the potential affective and interpersonal consequences if they do not behave or perform as expected.

Finally, levels of emotional closeness, security and safety associated with teacher–student relationships can play a causal role in the development of a range of positive motivational outcomes in children. In general, motivation to engage in socially-valued activities is more likely to occur if students believe that others care about them and want them to participate. Beliefs that others care about you also have added motivational benefit in that students will be more likely to pay attention to social cues concerning what they should be doing and to adopt an ongoing commitment to promoting the ongoing cohesion and smooth functioning of the group (Connell & Wellborn, 1991). Being socially accepted or rejected can also have a powerful impact on the opportunities students will have to interact with others to derive benefits from direct instruction and modeling. An additional aspect of teachers' emotional support is reflected in their efforts to protect students' physical well-being. In this regard, teachers can play a central role in creating classrooms that are free of peer harassment and in alleviating the negative effects of harassment once it has occurred (Olweus & Limber, 2009).

BEYOND THE CLASSROOM: INTERNALIZATION AND IDENTITY DEVELOPMENT

Recognizing that goal pursuit can be informed by social expectations raises the question of what leads students to pursue goals for their own sake without the need for external prompts or rewards. If specific socialization experiences promote the development of these social orientations, how does this influence occur? Two approaches to answering these questions will be offered here. The first suggests that specific parenting styles promote the internalization of adult values. The second approach takes a broader perspective based on identity development and approaches to self-definition that are embedded in cultural belief systems. This approach focuses on the development of culture-specific identities in which self-construals reflect autonomous desires to honor social and moral obligation to social relationships and groups.

Internalization and Parenting Styles

Internalization is a process whereby individuals move from experiencing social expectations and norms as externally imposed and controlling to a belief that one values social expectations as part of a personal identity motivated by autonomy and choice (e.g., Deci & Ryan, 1991). In Western cultures, scholars have proposed that authoritative approaches to parenting and parent–child interactions are most effective in promoting the internalization of adult and societal norms and values (e.g., Baumrind, 1971). These approaches reflect consistent enforcement of rules, expectations for self-reliance and self-control, solicitation of children's opinions and feelings, and expressions of warmth and approval. A more specific model of influence proposed by Ryan (1993; see also Grolnick, Friendly, & Bellas, 2009) recognizes the importance of parenting styles similar to those identified by Baumrind and speaks directly to the issue of why children adopt and internalize socially-valued goals. Ryan argues that within the context of a secure parent–child relationship in which caregivers provide contingent feedback, nurturance, and developmentally-appropriate structure and guidance, young children develop a generalized positive sense of social relatedness, personal competence, and autonomy when presented with new experiences and challenges. These positive aspects of self-development then support the internalization of socially-prescribed goals and values, that is, "the transformation of external controls and regulations into internal ones" (Ryan, 1993, p. 29).

Ryan's (1993) perspective on parent socialization implies that students' orientations toward achieving socially-valued outcomes in the classroom might be part of an overarching or more global motivational system derived from early socialization experiences. A growing literature supports a conclusion that parent socialization processes can have an impact on children's motivation to achieve in contexts outside the home (see Rowe, Ramani, & Pomerantz, 2016 for a review). Of interest, however, is that researchers also have demonstrated that the affective climate created by interactions with teachers and peers can promote adherence to expectations and norms that are valued within classroom settings (e.g., Wentzel, Russell, & Baker, 2016), and that these values can become stronger over time (e.g., Kindermann, 2007). Although these findings do not negate a parenting-internalization model, they suggest that at a minimum, emotional support from teachers and classmates can create a context wherein the effects of parenting are strengthened. However, the possibility that internalization can occur as a result of these classroom-based supports should not be discounted.

Identity Development and Social Self-Construals

Beyond parenting practices believed to promote internalization of adult goals and values, researchers also have acknowledged the role of family and cultural belief systems in promoting the development of a child's social identity. In contrast to theorists who often claim that goals to achieve social approval or social conformity are extrinsically motivated, a cultural psychology perspective (e.g., Miller, 1997) posits that individuals can pursue these goals for intrinsic or autonomous reasons. They propose that involvement with others and keeping social commitments can be inherently enjoyable (Gore, Cross, & Kanagawa, 2009), and a sense of personal well-being can arise from satisfying social role obligations and expectations (Miller, Das, & Chakravarthy, 2011). Often, these socially-motivated orientations are described as emanating from cultural beliefs concerning duty to others, such as the concept of dharma (Miller, 1997, p. 5) or filial piety (Ikels, 2004). Miller (1997) also characterizes these social orientations as reflecting a morality of care (see e.g., Gilligan, 1982) in which meeting the needs of others is integral to one's personal identity.

In contrast to notions of self-determination and personal agency (Deci & Ryan, 1991), Markus and Kitayama (2003) describe underlying reasons for socially-oriented behavior as being motivated by a sense of conjoint agency; this occurs when personal interests and those of close others become integrated, being experienced most often by individuals who value group harmony and interdependence. Researchers have documented that in children from non-Western cultures, this form of agency can promote positive forms of engagement to a greater extent than a sense of agency based on self-determination and personal choice (Miller et al., 2011). These findings have been explained in terms of qualitative differences in identity and self-construals: One student might think of herself as an independent, autonomous self when engaging in a task, whereas another student might see herself as an interdependent, autonomous self. The former student is likely to be motivated by an inner self that is believed to be distinct from others and independent of context, whereas the latter student is likely to be motivated by an inner self believed to be inseparable from others and from social contexts (Miller, 1997; Miller et al., 2011).

In contrast to work on parenting, less work has been done to clarify processes that explain how these socially-oriented identities develop. However, the notion of family obligation has been studied extensively as an example of interdependence and socially-oriented motivation, and it appears to vary across cultures and groups. Family obligation is typically defined as reflecting identification with the family group, and "serves to structure and provide meaning to children's motivation and behaviors..." (Fuligni, Alvarez, Bachman, & Ruble, 2005; p. 262). A sense of family obligation has been reported most often by students from Asian (Fuligni & Zhang, 2004; Gore et al., 2009; King & Ganotice, 2016; King, Ganotice, & Watkins, 2014; Rudy, Sheldon, Awong, & Tan, 2007) and Latin American (Cooper & Jayatilaka, 2006; Telzer, Tsai, Gonzales, & Fuligni, 2015) cultures, and members of minority and immigrant groups in the United States (Fuligni et al., 2005). In these samples, family obligation has been related to positive values for education (Fulingi, 2001; Fuligni & Zhang, 2004; King & Ganotice, 2016) and levels of academic engagement (Cooper & Jayatilaka, 2006; Fuligni et al., 2005; Liem, 2016; Rudy et al., 2007), and has been associated with adaptive forms of learning to a greater extent than in Western cultures (Gore et al., 2009; King et al., 2014). This work suggests that beyond models of parenting and family–school connections, researchers need to acknowledge the importance of family and culture in providing children a lens through which they interpret the expectations and opportunities for goal attainment that are provided by teachers and peers.

CONCLUSION

In this chapter, I presented a competence-in-context perspective on motivation that is based on two broad premises. First, a recognition of context and culture requires a focus on the goals that parents, educators, and society would like and expect children to achieve at school, and the implication of these socially-valued objectives for student goal setting. A central point is that if we are to understand children's competence at school, multiple outcomes and levels of influence must be acknowledged: What kinds of goals and needs does the individual child bring to the classroom, and which goals do teachers and peers (as well as the broader community and culture) expect students to achieve? Second, this perspective suggests that student motivation and engagement reflects decisions based on criteria associated with socially-valued goals as well as those associated with task-related engagement and mastery. Therefore, students must gain knowledge about the social expectations, rules, and norms of broader social contexts (e.g., classrooms, schools, communities), choose to adhere to those that will bring success, and coordinate these social challenges with personal interests and goals if they are to be successful at school.

The model of motivational decision-making described in this chapter focuses on the interactive role of contextual supports and self-beliefs in motivating goal pursuit. In turn, goal pursuit is assumed to predict classroom competence. This model is useful in its perspective on competence-in-context and it extends more traditional views of classroom motivation to include concerns about socially-valued goals and a sense of belongingness. Several important issues, however, remain for further study. First, greater focus on development and testing of theoretical models that explain links between pursuit of socially-valued social goals (e.g., to behave prosocially and responsibly) and academic achievement is needed. As described in previous sections, it is likely that pursuit of prosocial and social responsibility goals is related to academic outcomes for several reasons, including their influence on behavioral outcomes that contribute to the creation of positive social and instructional environments conducive to learning, and those that contribute directly to cognitive gains. Positive relations also might reflect the possibility that students are rewarded for their social efforts with good grades (or vice versa). These pathways of influence need to be explored systematically if we are to have significant theoretical advances in the field. At a more global level, a better understanding of what it means to behave prosocially and responsibly across contexts and cultures, and why differing instantiations of these behaviors support academic success is needed.

Related questions concern how students coordinate their own social and academic goals with those promoted within individual classrooms. Taking a broader sociocultural perspective, some students might want to achieve multiple goals but not perceive adequate opportunities to do so because their personal goals do not match those of teachers and classmates. In this case, they might disengage because they are overwhelmed with competing, incongruent goals across family, peer, and classroom contexts (Phelan, Davidson, & Cao, 1991). For example, studies of adolescent peer groups have documented that African-American youth might face disproportionate levels of conflict between parental and peer values, with the potential to have a negative impact on academic achievement (Steinberg, Dornbusch, & Brown,1992). Students who come to school with strong motives to behave cooperatively rather than competitively (e.g., Kagan & Madsen, 1971) might develop a generalized belief that the demands of reward structures focused on individual accomplishments are antagonistic to their socially-oriented identities.

Similarly, students might also value certain goals over others based on their gender, race, and ethnicity. For instance, girls are more likely to try to behave prosocially than are boys (Wentzel, 1989, 1991b, 1994), and students of Hispanic descent often pursue cooperative goals more often than Caucasian students (Kagan & Madsen, 1971). In short, adopting a competence-in-context perspective can provide researchers with a rich description of the multiple goals that students try to achieve but also a basis for understanding person–environment fit as it relates to classrooms and schools (Eccles, 1993). More in-depth examination of which goals students are trying to achieve and the degree to which these goals are compatible across multiple contexts is necessary to fully understand students' overall success and adjustment at school.

In addition, we often assume that students understand how they are supposed to behave and what it is they are supposed to accomplish while at school. However, for some students these expectations are not always immediately obvious. In particular, young children who are just beginning school and students who are raised in cultures with dissimilar goals and values to those espoused by American educational institutions might need explicit guidance with respect to the school-related goals they are expected to achieve at school (Ogbu, 1985). In addition, teachers vary in the degree to which they are perceived as socially supportive and caring by their students (Wentzel, 1994, 1997). In this regard, perceived discrimination in the form of differential access to resources as well as stereotyped judgments can pose threats to a student's emotional security and safety; in turn, these threats can result in alienation and disengagement from the social and academic life of the classroom (Crocker, Major, & Steele, 1998; Weinstein, 2002).

Subjective beliefs concerning support from classmates and teachers are likely to reflect to some degree cultural and familial expectations and belief systems (see e.g., Fordham & Ogbu, 1986; Okagaki & Sternberg, 1993; Phelan et al., 1991). Indeed, beliefs such as what it means to "care," what it means to be a friend, or what an appropriate teacher–student or peer relationship should entail are likely to vary as a function of race, gender, neighborhood, and family background (see e.g., Valenzuela & Dornbusch, 1994). These various definition imply that the more explicit and clearly defined we can make the social expectations of school contexts, the more likely students will at least understand the goals they are expected to achieve.

It is important to note, however, that some students reject socially-valued goals outright. It is likely that other students merely comply with social expectations and present the impression that they are interested in achieving what is required when in fact, they are not (see Juvonen, 1996; Sivan, 1986). Some students, however, are likely to be committed to achieving these goals, having internalized socially-valued goals or developed self-construals based on notions of interdependence and social responsibility. Therefore, identifying the precise socialization experiences—within the family and at school—that lead to these fundamentally different orientations toward learning remains a significant challenge to the field.

Finally, at a theoretical level, continued focus and elaboration of constructs relating to socially-motivated orientations also is needed. Similar ideas have been described by proponents of regulatory fit (Higgins, 2008) in terms of a prevention focus to goal setting; individuals who adopt this focus are believed to pursue goals in order to fulfill social responsibilities and obligations. Researchers are beginning to explore the relevance of culture and context for understanding this socially-oriented phenomenon (e.g., Kurman & Hui, 2012; Zhang & Mittal, 2007) but more work needs to be done. In addition, greater focus on the role of belongingness and group identity as a motivational construct is warranted. It is clear that these aspects of social relationships are critical to positive adaptation and school success in all cultures (e.g., Baumeister & Leary, 1995), although models of motivation in western cultures tend to focus almost exclusively on individualistic constructs such as personal efficacy and self-determination. Therefore, further examination of constructs of belongingness, social inclusion (e.g., Dovidio, Gaertner, Hodson, Houlette, & Johnson, 2005), and collective agency (Markus & Kitayama, 1991), as they interact with more individualistic self-beliefs is certain to yield more robust and powerful explanations of motivation at school.

REFERENCES

Austin, J. T., & Vancouver, J. B. (1996). Goal constructs in psychology: Structure, process, and content. *Psychological Bulletin, 120,* 338–375.

Bandura, A. (1986). *Social foundations of thought and action: A social cognitive theory.* Englewood Cliffs, NJ: Prentice-Hall.

Baumeister, R. F., & Leary, M. R. (1995). The need to belong—Desire for interpersonal attachments as a fundamental human motivation. *Psychological Bulletin, 117,* 497–529.

Baumrind, D. (1971). Current patterns of parental authority. *Developmental Psychology Monograph, 4*(1, Pt.2), 1–103.

Boekarts, M. (2009). Goal-directed behavior in the classroom. In K. R.Wentzel & A. Wigfield (Eds.), *Handbook of motivation at school* (pp. 105–122). New York, NY: Taylor Francis.

Bronfenbrenner, U. (1989). Ecological systems theory. In R. Vasta (Ed.), *Annals of child development* (Vol. 6, pp. 187–250). Greenwich, CT: JAI.

Connell, J. P., & Wellborn, J. G. (1991). Competence, autonomy, and relatedness: A motivational analysis of self-system processes. In M. R. Gunnar & L. A. Sroufe (Eds.), *Self processes and development: The Minnesota symposia on child development* (Vol. 23; pp. 43–78). Hillsdale, NJ: Erlbaum.

Cooper, R., & Jayatilaka, B. (2006). Group creativity: The effects of extrinsic, intrinsic, and obligation motivations. *Creativity Research Journal, 18,* 153–172.

Crocker, J., Major, B., & Steele, C. (1998). Social stigma. In D. M. Gilbert, S. T. Fiske, & G. Lindzey (Eds.), *The handbook of social psychology.* New York, NY: McGraw Hill.

Csikszentmihalyi, M., & Nakamura, J. (1989). The dynamics of intrinsic motivation: A study of adolescents. In C. Ames & R. Ames (Eds.), *Research on motivation in education: Goals and cognitions* (pp. 45–71). New York, NY: Academic Press.

Deci, E. L., & Ryan, R. M. (1991). A motivational approach to self: Integration in personality. In R. A.Dienstbier (Ed.), *Nebraska Symposium on Motivation: Perspectives on motivation* (Vol. 38, pp. 237–288). Lincoln, NE: University of Nebraska Press.

Dovidio, J. F., Gaertner, S. L., Hodson, G., Houlette, M. A., & Johnson, K. M. (2005). Social inclusion and Exclusion: Recategorization and the perception of intergroup boundaries. In D. Abrams, M. Hogg, & J. Marques (Eds.), *The social psychology of inclusion and exclusion.* (pp. 245–264). New York, NY: Psychology Press.

Dweck, C. S., & Master, A. (2009). Self-theories and motivation: Students' beliefs about intelligence. In K. Wentzel & A. Wigfield (Eds.), *Handbook of motivation at school* (pp. 123–140). New York, NY: Routledge.

Eccles, J. (1993). School and family effects on the ontogeny of children's interests, self-perceptions, and activity choices. In J. Jacobs (Ed.), *Developmental perspectives on motivation: Nebraska symposium on motivation* (Vol. 40, pp. 145–208). Lincoln, NE: University of Nebraska Press.

Eccles, J. S., & Midgley, C. (1989). Stage-environment fit: Developmentally appropriate classrooms for young adolescents. In C. Ames & R. Ames (Eds.),

Research on motivation in education (Vol. 3, pp. 139–186). New York, NY: Academic Press.

Ford, M. E. (1992). *Motivating humans: Goals, emotions, and personal agency beliefs.* Newbury Park, CA: SAGE.

Fordham, S., & Ogbu, J. U. (1986). Black students' school success: Coping with "the burden of 'acting white.'" *The Urban Review, 18*, 176–206.

Freeman, J., Simonsen, B., McCoach, B., Sugai, G., Lombardi, A., & Horner, R. (2016). Relationship between school-wide positive behavior interventions and supports and academic, attendance, and behavior outcomes in high schools. *Journal of Positive Behavior Interventions, 18*(1), 41–51.

Fuligni, A. (2001). Family obligation and the academic motivation of adolescents from Asian, Latin American, and European Backgrounds. *New Directions for Child and Adolescent Development, 94*, 61–75.

Fuligni, A. J., Alvarez, J., Bachman, M., & Ruble, D. (2005). Family obligation and the academic motivation of young children from immigrant families. In C. Cooper, C. Coll, W. Bartko, H. Davis, & C. Chatman (Eds.), *Developmental pathways through middle childhood: Rethinking contexts and diversity as resources* (pp. 261–282). Mahwah, NJ: Erlbaum.

Fuligni, A., & Zhang, W. (2004). Attitudes toward family obligation among adolescents in contemporary urban and rural china. *Child Development, 75*, 180–192.

Gilligan, C. (1982). *In a different voice: Psychological theory and women's development.* Cambridge, MA: Harvard University Press.

Gore, J. S., Cross, S. E, & Kanagawa, C. (2009). Acting in our interests: Relational self-construal and goal motivation across cultures. *Motivation and Emotion, 33*(1), 75–87.

Graham S., & Williams, C. (2009). An attributional approach to motivation in school. In K. Wentzel & A. Wigfield (Eds.), *Handbook of motivation at school* (pp. 11–34). New York, NY: Routledge.

Grolnick, W., Friendly, R. W., & Bellas, V. (2009). Parenting and children's motivation at school. In K. Wentzel & A. Wigfield (Eds.), *Handbook of motivation at school* (pp. 279–300). New York, NY: Routledge.

Higgins, E. T. (2008). Culture and personality: Variability across universal motives as the missing link. *Social and Personality Psychology Compass, 2*, 608–634.

Ikels, C. (2004). *Filial piety: Practice and discourse in contemporary East Asia.* Stanford, CA: Stanford University Press.

Juvonen, J. (1996). Self-presentation tactics promoting teacher and peer approval: The function of excuses and other clever explanations. In J. Juvonen & K. R. Wentzel (Eds.), *Social motivation: Understanding children's school adjustment* (pp. 43–65). New York, NY: Cambridge University Press.

Kagan, S., & Madsen, M. C. (1971). Cooperation and competition of Mexican, Mexican-American, and Anglo-American children of two ages under four instructional sets. *Developmental Psychology, 5*, 32–39.

Kindermann, T. A. (2007). Effects of naturally-existing peer groups on changes in academic engagement in a cohort of sixth graders. *Child Development, 78*, 1186–1203.

King, R. B., & Ganotice, F. (2015). Does family obligation matter for students' motivation, engagement, and well-being? It depends on your self-construal. *Personality and Individual Differences, 86,* 243–2488.

King, R. B., Ganotice, F. A., & Watkins, D. A. (2014). A cross-cultural analysis of achievement and social goals among Chinese and Filipino students. *Social Psychology of Education, 17*(3), 439–455.

Kurman, J., & Hui, C. (2012). Cultural regulatory fit and strategies for coping with unsuccessful outcomes. *European Journal of Social Psychology, 42*(4), 482–489.

Liem, G. A. D. (2016). Academic and social achievement goals: Their additive, interactive, and specialized effects on school functioning. *British Journal of Educational Psychology, 86*(1), 37–56.

Markus, H., & Kitayama, S. (2003). Culture, self, and the reality of the social. *Psychological Inquiry, 14*(3–4), 277–283.

Maehr, M. L., & Braskamp, L. A. (1986). *The motivation factor: A theory of persona investment.* Lexington, MA: Heath.

Maehr, M. L., & Zusho, A. (2009). Achievement goal theory: The past, present, and future. In K. Wentzel & A. Wigfield (Eds.), *Handbook of motivation at school* (pp. 77–104). New York, NY: Routledge.

Miller, J. G. (1997). Cultural conceptions of duty: Implications for motivation and morality. In D. Munro, J. E. Schumaker, & S. C. Carr (Eds.), *Motivation and culture* (pp. 178–192). New York, NY: Routledge.

Miller, J. G., Das, R., & Chakravarthy, S. (2011). Culture and the role of choice in agency. *Journal of Personality and Social Psychology, 101,* 46–61.

Ogbu, J. U. (1985). Origins of human competence: A cultural-ecological perspective. *Child Development, 52,* 413–429.

Okagaki, L., & Sternberg, R. J. (1993). Parental beliefs and children's school performance. *Child Development, 64*(1), 36–56.

Olweus, D., & Limber, S. P. (2009). The olweus bullying prevention program: Implementation and evaluation over two decades. In S. R. Jimerson, S. M. Swearer, & D. L. Espelage (Eds.), *Handbook of bullying in schools: An international perspective* (pp. 377–402). New York, NY: Routledge.

Organisation for Economic Co-operation and Development. (2017). *Policy advice and implementation.* Retrieved from https://oecd.org/education/policyadvice.htm

Pekrun, R. (2009). Emotions at school. In K. R.Wentzel & A. Wigfield (Eds.), *Handbook of motivation at school* (pp. 575–604). New York, NY: Taylor Francis.

Phelan, P., Davidson, A. L., & Cao, H. T. (1991). Students' multiple worlds: Negotiating the boundaries of family, peer, and school cultures. *Anthropology and Education Quarterly, 22,* 224–250.

Rowe, M., Ramani, G., & Pomerantz, E. (2016). Parental involvement and children's motivation and achievement: A domain-specific perspective. In K. Wentzel & D. Miele (Eds.), *Handbook of motivation at school* (2nd ed. pp. 459–476). Mahwah, NJ: Erlbaum.

Rubin, K. H., Bukowski, W., & Bowker, J. C. (2015). Children in peer groups. In M. Bornstein, T. Leventhal, & R. Lerner (Eds.), *Handbook of child psychology and developmental science: Ecological settings and processes* (pp. 175–222). New York, NY: John Wiley & Sons.

Rudy, D., Sheldon, K. M., Awong, T., & Tan, H. H. (2007). Autonomy, culture, and well-being: The benefits of inclusive autonomy. *Journal of Research in Personality, 41*(5), 983–1007.

Ryan, R. M. (1993). Agency and organization: Intrinsic motivation, autonomy, and the self in psychological development. In J. Jacobs (Ed.), *Nebraska symposium on motivation:* (Vol. 40, pp. 1–56). Lincoln, NE: University of Nebraska Press.

Ryan, R. M., & Deci, E. L. (2000). Self-determination theory and the facilitation of intrinsic motivation, social development, and well-being. *American Psychologist, 55(1),* 68–78.

Schunk, D., & Pajares, F. (2009). Self-efficacy theory. In K. R.Wentzel & A. Wigfield (Eds.), *Handbook of motivation at school* (pp. 35–54). New York, NY: Taylor Francis.

Sivan, E. (1986). Motivation in social constructivist theory. *Educational Psychologist, 21,* 209–233.

Steinberg, L., Dornbusch, S., & Brown, B. (1992). Ethnic differences in adolescent achievement: An ecological perspective. *American Psychologist, 47*(6), 723–729.

Telzer, E., Tsai, K., Gonzales, N., & Fuligni, A. (2015). Mexican American adolescents' family obligation values and behaviors: Links to internalizing symptoms across time and context. *Developmental Psychology, 51,* 75–86.

Valenzuela, A., & Dornbusch, S. M. (1994). Familism and social capital in the academic achievement of Mexican origin and Anglo adolescents. *Social Science Quarterly, 75,* 18–36.

Weiner, B. (1992). *Human motivation: Metaphors, theories and research.* Newbury Park, CA: SAGE.

Weinstein, R. S. (2002). *Reaching higher: The power of expectations in schooling.* Cambridge, MA: Harvard University Press.

Wentzel, K. R. (1989). Adolescent classroom goals, standards for performance, and academic achievement: An interactionist perspective. *Journal of Educational Psychology, 81,* 131–142.

Wentzel, K. R. (1991a). Social and academic goals at school: Achievement motivation in context. In M. Maehr and P. Pintrich (Eds.), *Advances in motivation and achievement* (Vol. 7, pp. 185–212). Greenwich, CT: JAI.

Wentzel, K. R. (1991b). Relations between social competence and academic achievement in early adolescence. *Child Development, 62,* 1066–1078.

Wentzel, K. R. (1993). Social and academic goals at school: Motivation and achievement in early adolescence. *Journal of Early Adolescence, 13,* 4–20.

Wentzel, K. R. (1994). Relations of social goal pursuit to social acceptance, classroom behavior, and perceived social support. *Journal of Educational Psychology, 86,* 173–182.

Wentzel, K. R. (1997). Student motivation in middle school: The role of perceived pedagogical caring. *Journal of Educational Psychology, 89,* 411–419.

Wentzel, K. R. (2004). Understanding classroom competence: The role of social-motivational and self-processes. In R. Kail (Ed.), *Advances in child development and behavior* (Vol. 32, pp. 213–241). New York, NY: Elsevier.

Wentzel, K. R. (2009a). Students' relationships with teachers as motivational contexts. In K. Wentzel & A. Wigfield (Eds.), *Handbook of motivation at school* (pp. 301–322). Mahwah, NJ: Erlbaum.

Wentzel, K. R. (2009b). Peer relationships and motivation at school. In K. Rubin, W. Bukowski, & B. Laursen (Eds.), *Handbook on peer relationships* (pp. 531–547). New York, NY: Guilford.

Wentzel, K. R. (2013). School adjustment. In W. Reynolds & G. Miller (Eds.), *Handbook of psychology: Educational Psychology* (Vol. 7, pp. 235–258). New York, NY: Wiley.

Wentzel, K. R. (2015). Socialization in school settings. In J. Grusec & P. Hastings (Eds.), *Handbook of social development* (2nd ed., pp. 251–275). New York, NY: Guilford.

Wentzel, K. R., & Brophy, J. (2013). *Motivation to learn* (3rd ed.). New York, NY: Taylor Francis.

Wentzel, K. R., & Miele, D. (2016). *Handbook of motivation at school* (2nd ed.). New York, NY: Taylor Francis.

Wentzel, K. R., Russell, S., & Baker, S. A. (2016). Emotional support and expectations for behavior from peers, teachers, and parents: Predictors of adolescent competence at school. *Journal of Educational Psychology, 108*, 242–255.

Wigfield, A., & Eccles, J. (2000). Expectancy-value theory of achievement motivation. *Contemporary Educational Psychology, 25*, 68–81.

Zhang, Y., & Mittal, V. (2007). The attractiveness of enriched and impoverished options: Culture, self-construal, and regulatory focus. *Personality and Social Psychology Bulletin, 33*, 588–598.

CHAPTER 10

MĀORI STUDENTS FLOURISHING IN EDUCATION

High Teacher Expectations, Cultural Responsiveness and Family–School Partnerships

Christine M. Rubie-Davies
Melinda Webber
Hana Turner

This chapter discusses the cultural appropriateness of teacher expectation theory to the Māori context. Māori theoretical models of culturally appropriate pedagogical practice are compared to teacher expectation theory in order to explore the likely responsiveness of teacher expectation theory to the teaching of Māori students. In addition, it has been argued (Macfarlane, Webber, Cookson-Cox, & McRae, 2014) that in order for Māori to be successful in school, there need to be strong links between the school and the community. Therefore, this chapter also discusses whether the theory of school-community relationships has relevance to culturally responsive practice. The "big theory" promulgated in this chapter is that although high

Big Theories Revisited 2, pages 213–235
Copyright © 2018 by Information Age Publishing

expectations for students do increase achievement, they are not enough to interrupt the negative impact of societal racism and negative academic stereotypes, on Māori student achievement. From a Māori world-view, *whānau* (extended family) are a critical factor to Māori student success and the Māori child is unlikely to see themselves as an individual or independent of their *whānau*. Therefore, even if a teacher has high expectations for an individual child, if they ignore or minimize the role of the child's *whānau* in their learning, the child will be negatively impacted. Hence, this chapter brings together theoretical perspectives pertaining to culturally responsive practice, high expectation teaching, and *whānau* engagement to produce one overarching or big theory that is theorized as being key to lifting Māori achievement.

Teacher Expectation Theory and Relevance for Māori Students

Teacher expectations are the beliefs that teachers hold about the likely future success of their students. Teacher expectation theory developed from an early experiment (Rosenthal & Jacobson, 1968) in which experimentally induced high expectations for some students resulted in academic gains for those students. This led researchers to develop theoretical understandings within the field focused on the premise that teachers have high expectations for some students and low for others. In relation to teacher expectation theory, a more productive line of inquiry, and one which is relevant to Māori students, is the research that relates specifically to teacher variables; the beliefs and practices of particular teachers associated with their expectations and which have been shown to have positive benefits for students, for example, the work of Weinstein (2002) or Rubie-Davies (2015). This research offers clues as to how teachers can increase all students' opportunities to learn and how they can motivate and engage students through the learning experiences that they provide. The current chapter will closely examine how the beliefs and practices of high expectation teachers align with Māori cultural beliefs and values. It will link expectation theory with that of culturally responsive practice within the New Zealand context and will present a new model of culturally responsive high expectation teaching. Therefore, this chapter argues that school-wide cultural change is required whereby teachers and other school administrators actively communicate high expectations of Māori students by protecting and affirming Māori identity, culture, and worldview, genuinely engaging with Māori *whānau* and community, and ensuring that Maori *whānau* have opportunities to genuinely participate in decision-making about their children's education. Interspersed throughout the chapter are the views of successful Māori secondary school students[1] about what contributes to their success and how their beliefs align with the culturally responsive theoretical model of teaching that we present. The second half of the chapter will focus on the theoretical underpinnings of school–community partnerships that have relevance for Māori. The discussion will focus on the importance of schools engaging *whānau* in the education of Māori. It will argue that education is a collective responsibility involving students, teachers, *whānau*, and community.

High Expectation Teachers

Rubie-Davies (2015) has theorized three core principles underlying the beliefs and practices of high expectation teachers (those who have high expectations for all students) who, overall, have large positive effects on student achievement and psychosocial outcomes. The three core principles are: implementing heterogeneous grouping and challenging learning experiences for all students, developing a positive class climate, and implementing goal setting (involving the development of student engagement, motivation, and autonomy, coupled with teacher feedback and monitoring of student progress). There is evidence (Rubie-Davies & Rosenthal, 2016) that the practices of high expectation teachers benefit Māori students but, from a sociocultural perspective, it is worth discussing more deeply the applicability of the high expectation principles for Māori in order to determine their cultural relevance and likelihood of improving student outcomes. At the same time, the findings related to culturally responsive teaching (CRT) for Māori are worth considering for their alignment with the beliefs and values of high expectation teachers.

Culturally Responsive Teaching

CRT is a methodology focused on raising achievement and improving the schooling experiences of indigenous and minority group students who have, historically, not been well-served by the education system, and, as a result, underachieve compared to students from the dominant ethnic group. CRT has been defined as connecting with students "to and through their personal and cultural strengths, their intellectual capabilities, and their prior accomplishments" (Gay, 2010, p. 26). Using students' ethnic and cultural backgrounds for context, CRT provides learning opportunities that are relevant, that build on ideas that students are already familiar with (i.e., their funds of knowledge), and which makes academic content easier for students to understand and master (Gay, 2010).

In their review of the international literature on culturally responsive schooling for indigenous American Indian and Alaskan Native youth, Castagno and Brayboy (2008) argued that despite 40 years of research promoting the benefits of CRT, very little had changed in teachers' practice. In many cases, CRT was "too easily reduced to essentializations, meaningless generalizations, or trivial anecdotes—none of which result in systemic, institutional, or lasting changes to schools serving indigenous youth" (p. 942). For CRT to truly be of benefit to students, Ladson-Billings (1995) identified that academic success and cultural competence were fundamental. It is not enough to "merely make them 'feel good'" (Ladson-Billings, 1995, p. 160), students must also achieve well at school. Cultural competence occurs when students attain proficiency in both their own and in the school's culture, without forsaking one for the other. In the New Zealand context, cultural competence for Māori has been encapsulated in the phrase "Māori achieving academic success *as* Māori" (Durie, 2001; Ministry of Education, 2013) which is when schools and teachers promote Māori culture and values positively so students are able to achieve success at school, but can do so in a way that does not come at a cost to their Māori identity and beliefs (Macfarlane et al., 2007). As one high achieving Māori student said ". . . succeeding academically is of no benefit if you haven't succeeded in every other aspect of life, for example, spiritually, emotionally, mentally, physically and for a Māori student, most importantly, culturally . . . "

The final aspect of CRT is the mutually-respectful relationships teachers form with parents, extended family and members of their local school community. Teachers need to know their local community and to be authentically involved in local events. The relationship must also be reciprocal with family and community members included in decision-making and regarded as valued members of the school (Castagno & Brayboy, 2008).

Models of Culturally Responsive Teaching

Within New Zealand, two theoretical models of CRT have been proposed (Bishop & Berryman, 2006; Macfarlane, 2004). At the heart of both models is the concept of teacher–student relationships in their broadest sense. Māori students learn best when teachers form strong culturally acknowledging relationships with them (Bishop & Berryman, 2006). The first model, the educultural wheel, was developed by Macfarlane (2004) and has at its center *pūmanawatanga* or the tone, pulse and morale of the classroom. The core of the classroom supports students as culturally located beings and provides an environment for learning in a collaborative and supportive atmosphere. The outer edges of the wheel are characterized by *manaakitanga, rangatiratanga, kotahitanga* and *whanaungatanga.* These terms are defined below.

Manaakitanga can be defined as an ethic of care. Teachers show that they care for every student by, for example, creating culturally safe classrooms, in which individual identity is acknowledged and supported, and by interacting with students in appropriate culturally supportive ways. *Rangatiratanga* relates to teacher effectiveness through the ways in which teachers interact with students both verbally and nonverbally and also through the types of learning experiences that they provide for students. However, *rangatiratanga* also means self-determination and, hence, stresses the need for teachers to create independent, culturally located autonomous beings who have learned how to learn. *Kotahitanga* concerns the ethic of bonding, of creating classrooms where there is unity and strong teacher–student and peer relationships being built. Shared support and care are paramount. The final aspect of the educultural wheel is *whanaungatanga,* which is about building relationships through shared experiences and working together. In the classroom, *whanaungatanga* relates to students supporting their peers to also attain success.

The second theoretical model of culturally responsive pedagogy, developed by Bishop and Berryman (2006), was implemented into several New Zealand secondary schools resulting in marked increases in Māori student achievement (Bishop & Berryman, 2010). The model consists of six culturally responsive practices, two of which, *manaakitanga* and *kotahitanga* are also found in Macfarlane's model. The additional constructs are *mana motuhake, ngā whakapiringatanga, wānanga,* and *ako* (defined below).

Mana motuhake relates to teachers showing that they care about student performance. Culturally responsive teachers develop students' personal and group identity and autonomy. *Ngā whakapiringatanga* concerns effective management of classrooms whereby teachers create culturally safe environments in which they implement practices based on sound pedagogical knowledge and innovative teaching designed to enhance student engagement and motivation. *Wānanga* involves teachers sharing knowledge with students during supportive interactions. *Ako,* a word which means "teach" and "learn" refers to the idea that students learn from teachers and teachers learn from students. In Bishop and Berryman's (2006) theoretical model, it refers to teachers employing a range of strategies in order to promote effective learning and to strengthen their relationships with students. The incorporation of the concepts that encompass CRT are summarized in Figure 10.1 and show how all the concepts are related to the core principle of *Pūmanawatanga.*

The diagram emphasizes the interrelationships of the theoretical models of both Macfarlane (2004) and Bishop and Berryman (2006) to demonstrate how their key concepts can be integrated into a culturally responsive

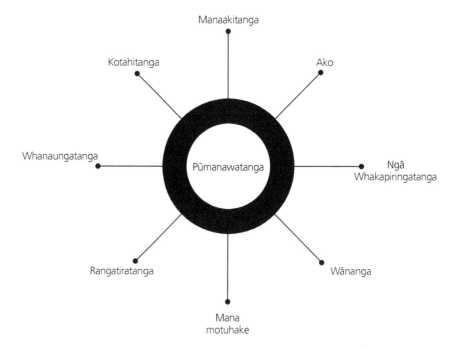

Figure 10.1 A culturally responsive model of teaching combining the important concepts of both Macfarlane's (2004) and Bishop and Berryman's (2006) models to show how teachers can support Māori academic success.

theoretical model of teaching applicable to Māori. The following sections will examine the degree to which high expectation teaching practices can be considered culturally responsive for Māori in relation to Figure 10.1. Additionally, high achieving Māori students' perceptions of academic success and effective teaching will be incorporated to demonstrate how each of the CRT constructs relates to student success.

Mixed-Ability Grouping and Learning Experiences

The first principle of high expectation teaching proposed by Rubie-Davies (2015) relates to students working in mixed and flexible forms of grouping rather than ability grouping. Ability grouping creates a hierarchy which may lead to students befriending those in their groups and, very often not working with, or forming relationships with, others in the classroom (Rubie-Davies, 2015). Overall, students in higher level groups receive more advanced opportunities to learn that enable them to progress rapidly whereas the learning of those in lower level groups is constrained through low level tasks (Rubie-Davies, 2017).

In high expectation classrooms, students are seated in mixed ability groupings. Ability is not made salient and students frequently work together on activities in a variety of groupings. Learning experiences have tasks and materials containing lower level tasks through to very high level tasks, but students choose the activities they want to engage in and often choose who they work with. Hence, all students are exposed to high-level, challenging activities. Additionally, when students complete tasks, they are expected to help and support each other. Thus, at the center of every high expectation classroom is *pūmanawatanga* or the creation of the heart and pulse of the class where student morale is key to learning.

Further, high expectation teachers deliver learning through the use of highly effective teaching practices, for example, the careful explanation of concepts (Bohn, Roehrig, & Pressley, 2004), making links to prior knowledge (Topping & Ferguson, 2005), and providing regular feedback on achievement of skills (Hattie, 2009), all of which lead to accelerated learning (Rubie-Davies, 2015). The utilization of mixed ability grouping and effective teaching practices relate closely to *rangatiratanga* (self-determination) whereby high expectation teachers are creating a learning platform that will enable students to become self-managing learners.

For academically successful Māori students, *rangatiratanga* was associated with working hard, driving their own learning, putting time and effort into studying, and possessing a good work ethic. One student explained that "an academically successful secondary school student is someone who is willing to put in endless hours of hard work to extend their knowledge beyond the level required." Behavioral engagement, which included attending school and classes regularly, was also perceived as important for academic success. Students did not "*wag* [truant] classes," they listened to teachers and peers, and were attentive during lessons.

Moreover, students completed homework regularly, attended extra classes, taught themselves new concepts, and wrote trial essays to prepare for assessments. Their success relied on additional work outside of class time, and students were willing to sacrifice their social lives in order to do well. High achieving Māori students were also well organized and punctual, ". . . time management is usually really good, as well as their ability to prioritize tasks effectively."

Ideal teachers who enacted rangatiratanga were passionate, enthusiastic, excited, energetic, and had a genuine love of their subject, which they passed onto their students: "My best teacher is so passionate about what she teaches which excites her and makes her happy . . . she loves it so much that she wants you to love it too!" Ideal teachers also arrived to class on time and had well-organized lessons.

High expectation teachers manage student behavior positively, a further core element of effective teaching (Topping & Ferguson, 2005). They use preventive techniques to ensure that students are engaged, feel valued, and the learning experiences are exciting and challenging. These factors together mean that students are engaged and motivated and, consequently, behavioral issues are minimized. Students feel secure and cared about within such an environment. This idea of creating a well-managed learning environment is evident in the concept of *ngā whakapiringatanga* in Figure 10.1. From a theoretical standpoint, ideal teachers for Māori students manage behavior through setting boundaries, clear expectations, and a sense of authority. Students appreciated classes where the environment was conducive to learning: "[My teacher] isn't what I would call strict, but she is professional and doesn't put up with any mischief. She likes everyone to be listening and actively willing to learn."

Ako, (referred to earlier as both teaching and learning), also relates to effective teaching practice. High expectation teachers teach effectively but, through their relationships with students, also learn which strategies most successfully engage students and help them learn. They adjust the ways they teach and introduce new methods to increase student progress. High achieving Māori students reported that ideal teachers used innovative and engaging strategies to make classes fun and enjoyable. One student said, "My best teacher provides a variety of different sources for us to learn from: online, through quizzes, [and] competitions as well as hands-on activities." Moreover, students liked practical lessons balanced with theory. Theoretical lessons ensured students had study notes for when they came to revise for examinations, and practical lessons, such as science experiments and hands-on activities, not only provided the application of theory-to-practice, they were fun and social ways to learn.

High expectation teachers value their students' background and endeavor to learn more about Māori students' culture, language, and the local community, *hapū* (sub-tribes) and *iwi* (tribes), practices which have been shown to result in classrooms that have a sense of community (Weinstein, 2002). Further, high expectation teachers engage in power-sharing by promoting student autonomy and encouraging student decision-making.

A Positive Class Climate

High expectation teachers create a warm, supportive classroom environment where, as has been stated above, behavior is managed positively and where students and their culture are respected. Although class climate research shows that students make gains in classes where the climate is positive (e.g., Pianta, Hamre, & Allen, 2012), theoretical models of class climate do not tend to include responsiveness to culture as a core element, whereas teacher expectation models do (see Rubie-Davies, 2015; Weinstein,

2002). High expectation teachers make positive links with students' *whānau* by having regular contact to communicate positive student behavior and academic progress. They meet with parents outside of school and attend community events. They learn about their students' cultural backgrounds, invite parents in to share their knowledge and some teachers learn *te reo* Māori (Māori language). Students know that their teacher cares for them as culturally-located beings (Rubie-Davies, 2015). Moreover, in their efforts to create a classroom community, high expectation teachers foster strong peer–peer relationships. Students understand that they are expected to support and care for each other. Collaboration and cooperation are core elements of high expectation classrooms. All of these key tenets fostered by high expectation teachers relate strongly to *whanaungatanga, manaakitanga,* and *kotahitanga.*

Research has shown that teachers must support the academic and emotional needs of Māori students in order for them to learn (Macfarlane, Glynn, Cavanagh, & Bateman, 2007). High expectation teachers expend effort in creating classrooms where teacher–student and student–student relationships are premised on care and respect—engendering *manaakitanga.* For Māori students, being known "as Māori" is important and they appreciate teachers who have an understanding of Māori knowledge and customs, and of students' connection to their *whānau, hapū,* and *iwi* (Macfarlane et al., 2014). One student said her best teacher was ". . . completely understanding of the different social and cultural backgrounds that the students come from and encourages us to try and incorporate these aspects of our lives into our school work." Another student explained: ". . . she comes from our community, knows how we grew up, and connects with the people we live around on a cultural level."

Whanaungatanga is also a central premise in high expectation classrooms. Building strong classroom relationships creates a positive and supportive classroom climate (Rubie-Davies, 2015). For Māori, success is not an individual pursuit, it is collective; therefore, success involves and benefits everyone in the group (Bevan-Brown, 1999). For example, "Doing well means not bragging, and encouraging and helping other students you know are struggling" (Macfarlane et al., 2014, p. 91).

Ideal teachers for Māori students who enacted *whanaungatanga* were approachable, friendly, personable, and made students feel welcome in their classrooms. One student said his teacher, "has a good relationship with his students so they all feel comfortable around him. This allows them to take further risks and ask more questions." Academically successful students and teachers enjoyed both social- and achievement-related interactions: "[We] can have a laugh, but he gets us through all assessments."

Because high expectation teachers endeavor to create a classroom community, there is a sense of unity in the classroom (*kotahitanga*). Students need to feel secure in their own identity and culturally safe within classrooms (Macfarlane, 2004). Academically successful students referred to teachers who bonded with their classes and built a sense of community. For example, "Not only is he a great teacher, but he is a cool guy to talk to. Our class keeps up a regular banter with him and we have our own inside jokes." Other students said their teachers treated them as if they were respected peers. One said, "She speaks to us as grown-ups and not in a way that makes us feel like we're Year 9 again [first year of secondary school]."

Bishop and Berryman (2006) defined kotahitanga as teachers providing students with feedback and informing them of their next learning steps. Academically successful Māori students were "open to criticism" and "willing to be corrected" so that they could "...learn from their mistakes." In another study (Macfarlane et al., 2014), a key characteristic of high achieving Māori students was humility; the ability to accept feedback and criticism graciously, even if it was sometimes difficult to hear. *Kotahitanga* is a core theoretical construct within a model of CRT for Māori because it implies that everyone must be "on the same page" and collectively committed to Māori student achievement.

Clear Learning Goals

The third high expectation principle of goal setting involves students working with their teachers, deciding on next steps in their learning. However, goal setting in high expectation classrooms includes other components such as teacher monitoring and feedback. Because students have considerable responsibility for their learning (*rangatiratanga*) in high expectation classrooms, their teachers monitor student learning closely and provide feedback in relation to their goals. Students clearly understand what they have mastered and what their next skills are. The setting of goals promotes student autonomy, engagement, and motivation (Morisano, 2012). Because students exercise choice in relation to their learning experiences, and all learning experiences are challenging and designed to promote learning, student engagement and motivation is increased (Martin, 2013). In high expectation classrooms, students understand that everyone is expected to succeed and that teachers and peers will provide the supports necessary to help all students achieve their goals.

When setting goals with students, teachers meet individually with students to openly discuss progress, to assess what has been learned, and to jointly agree on the next steps. Joint goal setting and interacting effectively with students relates to the concept of *wānanga*. For academically successful students, an important part of their learning was engaging in dialogic discussions (Bishop & Berryman, 2006). Such discussions included students asking teachers questions and having the work explained: "An academically successful secondary student is not afraid to admit she or he does not understand something because she or he will always find a way forward." Consequently, ideal teachers for Māori provided clear explanations of what students had to learn (and why), and were willing and able to answer their questions. They also provided worked examples, and pointed out obstacles and difficulties to avoid. One student said teachers, "... having solid knowledge about the topic and being able to answer any question that we ask makes me confident in my learning." Academically successful Māori students set goals related to their short-term school success as well as to medium or long-term plans such as getting into university or future career plans.

Students in the classes of high expectation teachers make large learning gains (Rubie-Davies, 2015) because teachers care about student performance (*mana motuhake*). Teachers work alongside students to ensure that learning experiences are interesting and are contributing to their achievement gains. They provide clear feedback to students and they set goals with students that are meaningful to them. All these pedagogical practices encompass closely the concept of *mana motuhake.*

For academically successful Māori students, *mana motuhake* was demonstrated through self-motivation, competitiveness, and wanting to prove that Māori can achieve as well as, or better than, others. For example, students were "spurred to beat the *Pākehā* [non-Māori of European descent]" (Mitchell & Mitchell, 1988, p. 6). Often though, for Māori, competitiveness was internal. As one student explained, high achievers "strive not to be better than anyone else, but to be better than the person they were yesterday."

For some students, the motivation to achieve at school came from a desire to improve their personal circumstances such as "the drive to want to do better in life and not have to live in poverty." Another student said, "... people need to have qualifications in order to have a good life; otherwise they may not have all the opportunities [in life] that they possibly could have." Students were not, however, willing to accept mediocrity, with one stating, "... they should strive for greatness and not just be happy to pass or accept what they are given."

Perseverance and resilience were also values held by successful Māori students: "An academically successful secondary school student has the mind-set to strive and continue on when it feels like completing an assignment is too difficult." Another student said, "... [they] never give up or say I can't." Students who were resilient did not "... let failure hold them down" or "... let setbacks disappoint them." One student advised that academically successful students needed to be able to "... have a positive attitude to be able to deal with problems faced in both school and at home [and have faith that] things will get better..."

When ideal teachers of Māori students enacted *mana motuhake*, they demonstrated they had high expectations and were focused on student learning and success. Teachers continually challenged and pushed students to improve or maintain their high results in the national qualifications. One student said, "[My teacher] truly believes that each and every one of us can achieve great things and this helps us all believe this about ourselves." Teachers took responsibility for student achievement and were constantly focused on students' next steps in their learning. For example, "She keeps track of mistakes you have made so she can check if you have learned from your mistake; if not she comes and re-explains how to do it correctly."

Bringing High Expectations and Māori Values Together

As has been shown, high expectation teachers structure their classrooms around the core principles considered necessary for Māori students to succeed: *whanaungatanga, kotahitanga, manaakitanga, ngā whakapiringatanga, rangatiratanga, ako, wānanga,* and *mana motuhake.* They teach in culturally responsive ways. These core principles can be found to varying degrees in Māori theoretical models of learning (e.g., Bishop & Berryman, 2006; Macfarlane, 2004) and when applied in classrooms have been shown to enable success not just for Māori students but for all students (Bishop & Berryman, 2010; Rubie-Davies & Rosenthal, 2016). It is also worth stressing that although the culturally responsive concepts have been separated out as relating to the key areas of high expectation teaching (grouping and learning experiences, class climate, and goal setting), these concepts overlap. For example, one reason that high expectation teachers work with mixed ability grouping is to foster student relationships. This practice also decreases the salience of achievement levels which increases student engagement and motivation. Goal setting which focuses on the skills that students need to learn next, promotes student engagement and motivation, which, in turn, creates a collegial and supportive class environment (Rubie-Davies, 2015). Thus, in the same way that the concepts designed to promote CRT are integrated and related to each other, so, too, are the high expectation practices interrelated. Figure 10.2 demonstrates how the culturally responsive concepts relate to high expectation teaching. For example, although ako relates to the way that high expectation teachers effectively provide for student learning, *ako* also relates to the strong emotionally and academically supportive relationships that high expectation teachers form with all their students. Figure 10.2 also shows that high expectation principles coupled with CRT is likely to increase student success more than one approach alone. Hence, this figure provides a theoretical model incorporating the constructs of both high expectation teaching and CRT to show how they

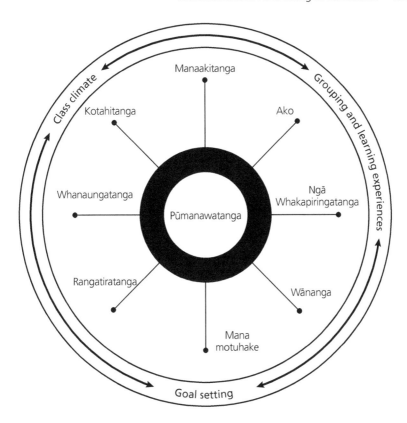

Figure 10.2 A model showing how high expectation teaching principles integrated with culturally responsive teaching would lead to greater Māori academic success.

could be integrated into a big theory of culturally adaptive practice for Māori students.

THE CRITICAL LEVER FOR MĀORI STUDENT SUCCESS: WHĀNAU-SCHOOL PARTNERSHIPS

In an early school effectiveness study, Edmonds (1979) theorized that although school-initiated parental involvement did not significantly affect student achievement in poorer schools, parent-initiated involvement did. Edmonds (1979) suggested that researchers needed to look more closely at the nature of involvement exercised by parents, in the hope that it might be an effective instrument for positive change. Nearly four decades later, we know that attention to improved relationships must go beyond the student–teacher dyad to include positive learning-focused relationships with Māori students' *whānau* and wider community (Bishop & Berryman, 2006; Bonne & Hotere-Barnes, 2015; Macfarlane et al., 2014). In fact, teachers who are serious about accelerating the learning of Māori students must understand that the critical lever for positive change is authentic *whānau*-school partnerships. Such a partnership must actively provide a counter to negative societal stereotypes that posit Māori as uneducable, low achievers, and academically disengaged. Rather, the authors of this chapter theorize that when schools and teachers hold high expectations for Māori *whānau*/community involvement and actively invite their participation in decision-making and co-teaching activities related to their children's learning, the partnerships result in improved student attendance, *whānau* involvement in learning, and student achievement. As such, schools must cultivate a climate in which *whānau* feel comfortable to initiate involvement in their children's education and should provide them with the appropriate opportunities to do so.

In their report on schools' progress in promoting success for Māori students, the Education Review Office (ERO, 2010) observed that in the most effective schools:

> ... parents and *whānau* were actively involved in the school and in students' learning. *Whānau* had a sense of connectedness and had a voice in determining the long-term direction of the school. The school ensured that ongoing opportunities for this partnership were encouraged, in order to find out and respond to the aspirations and expectations of parents and *whānau*. (p. 18)

The New Zealand Ministry of Education (2013) describes effective *whānau*-community-school relationships as starting "with the understanding that Māori children and students are connected to *whānau* and should not be viewed or treated as separate, isolated, or disconnected" (p. 18). Parents and *whānau* should *always* be involved in conversations about their children and their learning. Enhanced cultural connections through engagement with Māori *whānau* can provide important opportunities for Maori students' learning, particularly the development of cultural identity and a sense of belonging that contributes to well-being. Nevertheless, engagement between *whānau*, communities, and schools needs to be constructive and strengths-focused, because

> [f]or many *whānau*, contact with school only occurs when there is a crisis or a problem, or funds to raise ... Parents are often placed in a defensive position which all too often leads to a deteriorating relationship with school. The crisis approach to *whānau* involvement is not one that will induce a sense of *whānau* enthusiasm for learning or for education. While it is important that parents are kept informed of difficulties, it is more important that parents are also able to work with schools to identify potential and then to jointly construct pathways that will enable promise to be realized. (Durie, 2006, p. 10)

Whānau are a critical lever in the educational well-being of Māori students in education (Macfarlane et al., 2014). Therefore, teachers must ensure that Māori students' cultural engagement and ethnic identities are enriched by their experiences at school and their engagement and success is an integrated, school-wide and *whānau*/community informed activity (Hall, Hornby, & Macfarlane, 2015). Genuine *whānau* involvement in schools is critical because "students learn more and succeed at higher levels when home, school, and community work together to support students' learning and development" (Epstein & Sanders, 2006, p. 87).

Further, *whānau* should participate in decision-making about the best ways to be involved in their children's education rather than schools defining and restricting the terms of their involvement in schools. Webber (2012) has argued that the educative process for Māori must include *whānau* participation in terms of designing culturally responsive curriculum material that simultaneously strengthens students' cultural connections, increases their cultural competence, and improves their academic motivation to learn and succeed. Of particular importance in this regard is the work of Epstein (2008), from the United States, who identified six types of parent and community involvement in schools that led to improved student achievement. The six types of parental involvement endorsed by Epstein (2008) relate to Macfarlane's (2004) and Bishop and Berryman's (2006) models of culturally responsive pedagogy and core Māori values but have not yet been integrated into a big theory to explain relations between *whānau* engagement and culturally responsive pedagogy.

Epstein (2007) recommended activities focused on (a) strengthening parental skills in relating to their children, by designing interventions to help family and community members support children's learning at home and school (*manaakitanga, ngā whakapiringatanga*); (b) establishing clear lines of communication between school and families through, for example, after-school workshops or meetings focusing on a curriculum area, student behavior, or well-being—where children could attend with their parents (*kotahitanga, mana motuhake*); (c) promoting both family engagement and enhanced efficacy of family and community members by, for example, training parents and teachers to work as collaborators with complementary responsibilities for raising student achievement (*rangatiratanga*); (d) enhancing the learning relationship between parents and children by, for example, using local elders and resources in classroom programs so that students have a living understanding of their culture (*ako*); (e) inviting and honoring family and community stakeholders' input into long-term strategic decision-making and engaging them in developing culturally responsive whole-school initiatives to lift student achievement (*wānanga*); and (f) drawing upon the resources of the wider community to strengthen school programs and enhance student success, by incorporating family and community knowledge into curriculum and teaching (*whanaungatanga*). It is clear that effective *whānau* community–school partnerships occur in mutually-beneficial community and cultural contexts, not in isolation.

Additionally, a number of themes in Hall et al.'s (2015) research, also align with the values outlined in Macfarlane's (2004) and Bishop and Berryman's (2006) thematic frameworks and suggest that effective schools must engage with *whānau* in ways that matter to Māori communities themselves. *Rangatiratanga* was identified as a key factor for enabling family involvement, especially when the school principal was seen to actively advocate for things Māori, and *te reo* (Māori language) and *tikanga* (Māori customs) were prioritized, visible, and integrated into the whole school community. *Kotahitanga* was mentioned as important in terms of schools persistently reaching out to *whānau*, consulting with, and ensuring that *whānau* voice was sought and heard, and their knowledge and expertise was being drawn upon by the school. *Whanaungatanga* was premised on schools sustaining strong connections with *whānau* and being flexible and supportive about working with them. Enacting *whanaungatanga* ensured relationships between the school and *whānau* were fostered, bidirectional, and conducted with respect. Finally, Hall et al. (2015) described *manaakitanga* as central to teachers caring for Māori students' learning, and recognizing, fostering, and nurturing their individual strengths. *Manaakitanga* occurred when learning was engaging and purposeful and Māori students' specific learning needs were being met and extended. It is evident that to maximize the relationship between schools and Māori families and communities, *whānau* need to be part of determining both the relationships and the ways of engagement.

Building relationships and taking a strengths-based approach to interactions with Māori students and their *whānau* are key factors to Māori students enjoying and achieving educational success (Ministry of Education, 2013). Māori *whānau* engagement in schools depends on *whānau* being treated with dignity and respect, on school and classroom programs adding to *whānau* practices (not opposing them), on sharing structured and specific home-teaching strategies (rather than general advice), and on supportive group opportunities as well as opportunities for one-to-one involvement in their children's education (especially informal contact).

The New Zealand research indicates that when schools develop educationally powerful connections with *whānau* and Māori communities there is potential to significantly improve learning outcomes for Māori students (Berryman, Ford, & Egan, 2015). Alton-Lee, Robinson, Hohepa, and Lloyd (2009) examined the impact of *whānau*–school collaboration on student achievement and found that certain kinds of school and *whānau* connections and interventions can have large positive effects on the academic and social outcomes of Māori students. Three examples of connections that made the largest positive difference were a joint parent/*whānau* and school intervention, teacher-designed interactive homework with *whānau*, and the incorporation of *whānau* and community funds of knowledge (Alton-Lee et al., 2009). These findings show that strengthening *whānau* engagement around students' learning can improve Māori students' academic outcomes.

Significant positive effects have also consistently been found in the international research when schools have fostered family involvement effectively, including improved student achievement in mathematics (Sheldon, Epstein, & Galinda, 2010), writing (Wylie & Argo-Kemp, 2004), reading (Hughes & Kwok, 2007), and vocabulary (Wen, Bulotsky-Shearer, Hahs-Vaughn, & Korfmacher, 2012); improved parent and student confidence to participate in the school context, especially in communities with high populations of low-income and minority families (Lee & Bowen, 2006; Webber, McKinley, & Rubie-Davies, 2016); and improved student attendance, which is a perennial challenge in schools located in urban settings with high transience among *whānau* (Epstein & Sheldon, 2002). Other positive school-related outcomes related to increased *whānau* involvement include improved cognitive performance (Phillipson & Phillipson, 2012), lower rates of high school dropout and higher grade completion (Barnard, 2004), prevention of behavior problems (McNeal, 1999), and a decrease in truancy (Epstein & Sheldon, 2002). It is evident that engaging *whānau* and communities in education requires good quality education and effective and meaningful ways of working in partnership. The effect of *whānau* involvement in education is wide-ranging, not simply affecting academic outcomes but also influencing social-psychological attributes, including motivation and self-regulation (Gonzalez-DeHass, Willems, & Doan Holbein, 2005)

CONCLUSION

Teachers of Māori students who hold high expectations believe that although students' backgrounds may vary, every one of them can learn. Their practice is characterized by high expectations, situated within a wider dynamic of culturally responsive practice (Bishop & Berryman, 2006; Macfarlane, 2004) and respect for Māori students and their *whānau* (Bishop & Berryman, 2006). Additionally, the inclusion of *whānau* aspirations for their children has been identified as a critical factor in the well-being of Māori students (Bonne & Hotere-Barnes, 2015). Another important point is the need to re-frame power relationships so that Māori parents' engagement in their children's education is valued by more teachers and school leaders.

Therefore, schools and teachers must ensure that *whānau* expectations are articulated, acknowledged, and acted upon, in order for Māori success and potential to be realized in classrooms. Appreciating Māori students, *whānau*, and their social and cultural contexts must become an integral part of the beliefs and values of high expectation teachers in order to improve the outcomes of Māori students. The inclusion of *whānau*-school partnerships is reflected in our final theoretical model showing the culturally responsive values that need to underpin teaching, the practices of high expectation teachers that improve learning, and the necessary partnership with *whānau* if Māori students are to flourish in our education system.

This chapter has brought together three theoretical perspectives in relation to enabling the success of Māori students. First, at the classroom level, the research on high expectation teachers is relevant. The theoretical arguments suggest that teachers need to not only have high expectations of all their students, but they need to enact their instructional and emotional supports in culturally sensitive ways. Second, the practices of high expectation teachers align closely with the Māori values proposed in culturally responsive models of teaching and which are suggested as being supportive of Māori student success (Bishop & Berryman, 2006; Macfarlane, 2004). Third, it is suggested in this chapter that a crucial aspect in the success of Māori students is the partnership with *whānau*. This is the aspect of the culturally responsive model that we have presented (Figure 10.3) that currently is missing from most schools. Although high expectation teachers teach in culturally responsive ways and have a positive impact on their Māori students' academic, social, and emotional outcomes (Rubie-Davies, 2015), they often work in isolation within schools. Schools are communities, too, and it is essential that schools firstly, promote high expectation teaching, secondly incorporate Māori values into classroom and school structures, and thirdly, actively reach out to *whānau* to engage them in their children's schooling. High expectation teaching, the incorporation of Māori values into teaching, and the active engagement of *whānau* will lead to all Māori students flourishing in education.

The proposed theoretical model, our big theory incorporating culturally responsive practices, high expectation teaching, and school–family–community partnerships is likely to have general applicability in other cultural contexts where there are indigenous and minority students—particularly those where the students come from collectivist cultures. In a quasi-experimental study (Weinstein & Worrell, 2016), in a high school based on high expectation principles, the achievement of African American and Latino/a students has increased considerably, meaning that almost all graduate with an offer to a 4-year university and having completed five university-level courses in high school. Further, a key element of that program was connections with *whānau* and involving them in lifting their children's achievement. Families worked in partnership with the school. However, to our knowledge, the program of Weinstein and Worrell (2016) did not incorporate culturally responsive theoretical constructs into their high school.

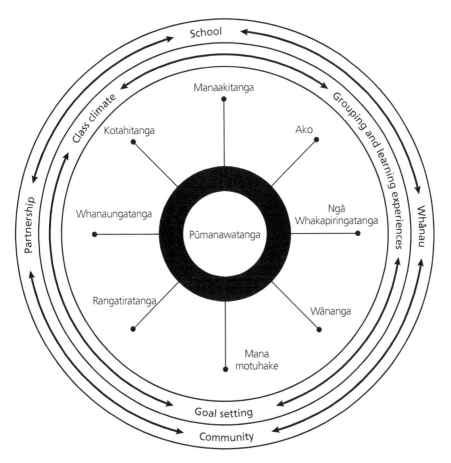

Figure 10.3 A final model demonstrating that core culturally responsive principles together with high expectation principles and a school–*whānau*–community partnership is likely to contribute most to Māori academic success.

In New Zealand, some of the core elements of the culturally responsive component of our big theory have been implemented into some secondary schools and have been found to lift not just the achievement of Māori students but also that of other students from collectivist cultures such as Pasifika students (Bishop & Berryman, 2010). Hence, there is some basis for including these elements into our theoretical model and for believing that these constructs have applicability in practice. Whether the core elements of our big theory would be applicable in other cultural contexts, though, is currently a philosophical debate worth having. Researchers would need to consider the degree to which the core cultural constructs within our theoretical model have applicability to specific other contexts. We believe strongly that our theoretical model, if applied in New Zealand classrooms, would result in not only improved academic achievement for Māori students but would also likely increase their motivation and engagement in schooling, and reduce truanting and school dropout.

NOTE

1. Unless otherwise indicated, all student quotes have been extracted from the following database: Turner, H. (2017). The attributes of high achieving secondary school students and their teachers. *figshare.* Retrieved from https://doi.org/10.17608/k6.auckland.5466595.v2

REFERENCES

Alton-Lee, A., Robinson, V., Hohepa, M., & Lloyd, C. (2009). Creating educationally powerful connections with family, whānau, and communities. In V. Robinson, M. Hohepa, & C. Lloyd (Eds.), *School leadership and student outcomes: Identifying what works and why* (pp. 142–170). Wellington, New Zealand: Ministry of Education.

Barnard, W. M. (2004). Parent involvement in elementary school and educational attainment. *Children and Youth Services Review, 26,* 39–62.

Berryman, M., Ford, T., & Egan, M. (2015). Developing collaborative connections between schools and Māori communities. *SET: Research Information for Teachers, 3,* 18–25.

Bevan-Brown, J. (1999). Special abilities: A Maori perspective, implications for catering for gifted children from minority cultures. *Gifted Education International, 14,* 86–96.

Bishop, R., & Berryman, M. (2006). *Culture speaks: Cultural relationships and classroom learning.* Wellington, New Zealand: Huia.

Bishop, R., & Berryman, M. (2010, May). *Te Kotahitanga: Culturally responsive professional development for teachers.* Paper presented at the Annual Meeting of the American Educational Research Association, Denver, CO.

Bohn, C. M., Roehrig, A. D., & Pressley, M. (2004). The first days of school in the classrooms of two more effective and four less effective primary-grades teachers. *The Elementary School Journal, 104,* 269–287.

Bonne, L., & Hotere-Barnes, A. (2015). English-medium schools engaging whānau: Building relationships, creating spaces. *SET: Research Information for Teachers, 3,* 26–34.

Castagno, A. E., & Brayboy, B. M. J. (2008). Culturally responsive schooling for indigenous youth: A review of the literature. *Review of Educational Research, 78,* 941–993.

Durie, M. (2006). *Whānau, education and Māori potential* [Hui Taumata Mātauranga presentation]. Retrieved from: http://www.massey.ac.nz/massey/fms/Te%20

Mata%20O%20Te%20Tau/Publications%20-%20Mason/HTML%20Charcode .pdf

Durie, M. (2001, March). *A framework for considering Māori educational advancement.* Keynote speech presented at the first Hui Taumata Mātauranga, Taupo, New Zealand.

Edmonds, R. (1979). Effective schools for the urban poor. *Educational Leadership, 37,* 15–23.

Education Review Office. (2010). *Promoting success for Māori students: Schools' progress.* Wellington, New Zealand: Education Review Office.

Epstein, J. (2008). Improving family and community involvement in secondary schools. *The Education Digest, 73,* 9–12.

Epstein, J., & Sanders. M. (2006). Prospects for change: Preparing educators for school, family, and community partnerships. *Peabody Journal of Education, 81,* 81–120.

Epstein, J. L., & Sheldon, S. B. (2002). Present and accounted for: Improving student attendance through family and community involvement. *Journal of Educational Research, 95,* 308–318.

Gay, G. (2010). *Culturally responsive teaching: Theory, research, and practice.* New York, NY: Teachers College Press.

Gonzalez-DeHass, A. R., Willems, P. P., & Doan Holbein, M. F. (2005). Examining the relationship between parental involvement and student motivation. *Educational Psychology Review, 17,* 99–123.

Hall, N., Hornby, G., & Macfarlane, S. (2015). Enabling school engagement for Māori families in New Zealand. *Journal of Child and Family Studies, 24,* 3038–3046.

Hattie, J. (2009). *Visible learning: A synthesis of over 800 meta-analyses relating to achievement,* London, England: Routledge.

Hughes, J., & Kwok, O. (2007). Influence of student-teacher and parent–teacher relationships on lower achieving readers' engagement and achievement in the primary grades. *Journal of Educational Psychology, 99,* 39–51.

Ladson-Billings, G. (1995). But that's just good teaching! The case for culturally relevant pedagogy. *Theory into Practice, 34,* 159–165.

Lee, J. S., & Bowen, N. K. (2006). Parent involvement, cultural capital, and the achievement gap among elementary school children. *American Educational Research Journal, 43,* 193–218.

Macfarlane, A. (2004). *Kia hiwa ra! Listen to culture.* Wellington, New Zealand: New Zealand Council for Educational Research.

Macfarlane, A., Glynn, T., Cavanagh, T., & Bateman, S. (2007). Creating culturally safe schools for Māori students. *The Australian Journal of Indigenous Education, 36,* 65–76.

Macfarlane, A., Webber, M., Cookson-Cox, C., & McRae, H. (2014). *Ka Awatea: An iwi case study of Māori students' success.* Christchurch, New Zealand: University of Canterbury.

Martin, A. J. (2013). Goal setting and personal best goals. In J. Hattie & E. Anderman (Eds.), *International Guide to Student Achievement* (pp. 356–358). London, England: Routledge.

McNeal, R. (1999). Parental involvement as social capital: Differential effectiveness on science achievement, truancy and dropping out. *Social Forces, 78,* 117–144.

Ministry of Education. (2013). *Ka Hikitia, Accelerating Success.* Wellington, New Zealand. Retrieved from http://www.minedu.govt.nz/theMinistry/PolicyAnd-Strategy/KaHikitia.aspx

Mitchell, H. A., & Mitchell, M. J. (1988). *Profiles of Maori pupils with high marks in School Certificate English and mathematics: Report to Research and Statistics Division, Department of Education.* Wellington, New Zealand: New Zealand Council for Educational Research.

Morisano, D. (2012). Goal setting in the academic arena. In E. A. Locke & G. P. Latham (Eds), *New Developments in goal setting and task performance* (pp. 495–506). London, England: Routledge.

Phillipson, S., & Phillipson, S. N. (2012). Children's cognitive ability and their academic achievement: The mediation effects of parental expectations. *Asia Pacific Review, 13,* 495–508.

Pianta, R. C., Hamre, B. K., & Allen, J. P. (2012). Teacher–student relationships and engagement: conceptualizing, measuring, and improving the capacity of classroom interactions. In S. L. Christenson, A. L. Reschly, & C. Wylie (Eds.). *Handbook of research on student engagement* (pp. 365–386). New York, NY: Springer.

Rosenthal, R., & Jacobson, L. (1968). *Pygmalion in the classroom: Teacher expectation and pupils' intellectual development.* New York, NY: Holt, Rinehart and Winston.

Rubie-Davies, C. M. (2017). *Teacher expectations in education.* London, England: Routledge.

Rubie-Davies, C. M. (2015). *Becoming a high expectation teacher: Raising the bar.* London, England: Routledge.

Rubie-Davies, C. M., & Rosenthal, R. (2016). Intervening in teachers' expectations: A random effects meta-analytic approach to examining the effectiveness of an intervention. *Learning and Individual Differences, 50,* 83–92.

Sheldon, S., Epstein, J., & Galinda, C. (2010). Not just numbers: Creating a partnership climate to improve mathematics proficiency in schools. *Leadership Policy in Schools, 9,* 27–48.

Topping, K., & Ferguson, N. (2005). Effective literacy teaching behaviors. *Research in Reading, 28,* 125–143.

Turner, H. (2017). The attributes of high achieving secondary school students and their teachers. *figshare.* Retrieved from https://doi.org/10.17608/k6.auckland.5466595.v2

Webber, M. (2012). Identity matters: The role of racial-ethnic identity for Maori students in multiethnic secondary schools. *SET: Research Information for Teachers, 2,* 20–25.

Webber, M., McKinley, E., & Rubie-Davies, C. (2016). Making it personal: Academic counseling with Maori students and their families. *Contemporary Educational Psychology, 47,* 51–60.

Weinstein, R. S. (2002). *Reaching higher: The power of expectations in schooling.* Cambridge, MA: Harvard University Press.

Weinstein R. S., & Worrell F. C. (Eds.). (2016). *Achieving college dreams: How a university-charter district partnership created an early college high school.* New York, NY: Oxford University Press.

Wen, X., Bulotsky-Shearer, R. J., Hahs-Vaughn, D., & Korfmacher, J. (2012). Head start program quality: Examination of classroom quality and parent involvement in predicting children's vocabulary, literacy, and mathematics achievement trajectories. *Early Childhood Research Quarterly, 27,* 640–653.

Wylie, C., & Arago-Kemp, V. (2004). *Whaia te iti Kahurangi: NZCER evaluation final report.* Wellington, New Zealand: Te Rūnanga o Ngāti Porou & the Ministry of Education.

CHAPTER 11

COOPERATIVE LEARNING

Theoretical Foundations
and Relevance Across Cultures[1]

Amanda J. Inns
Robert E. Slavin

Cooperative learning refers to instructional methods in which teachers organize students into small groups, which then work together to help one another learn academic content. Cooperative learning methods are extensively researched and under certain well-specified conditions are known to significantly improve student achievement in most subjects and grade levels. However, there remains considerable debate about the theoretical basis for achievement outcomes of cooperative learning. This chapter reviews and integrates evidence on the theoretical mechanisms relating to learning outcomes of cooperative learning, and presents evidence on the most widely used practical applications of cooperative methods. The chapter concludes with examining the use of cooperative learning in diverse contexts to explore the relevance of cooperative learning across cultures.

Cooperative learning methods vary widely in their details. Group sizes may be from two to several. Groups may work on projects or reports, or they may

Big Theories Revisited 2, pages 237–266
Copyright © 2018 by Information Age Publishing

help each other master basic or advanced skills. Group members may have individual roles or tasks, or they may all have the same task. Groups may be evaluated or rewarded based on group performance or the average of individual performances, or they may simply be asked to work together. Increasingly, cooperative learning is integrated with technology—infused instruction.

In one form or another, cooperative learning has been used and studied in every major subject, with students from preschool to college, and in all types of schools. Cooperative learning is used at some level by hundreds of thousands of teachers.

There have been hundreds of studies of cooperative learning focusing on a wide variety of outcomes, including academic achievement in many subjects, second language learning, attendance, behavior, intergroup relations, social cohesion, acceptance of classmates with disabilities, and attitudes toward subjects (see Gillies, 2014; Johnson & Johnson, 1998; Rohrbeck, Ginsburg-Block, Fantuzzo, & Miller, 2003; Roseth, Johnson, & Johnson, 2008; Slavin, 1995, 2013a; Webb, 2008b). Reviews of research on a wide variety of innovations in curriculum, technology, and professional development have consistently found certain forms of cooperative learning to be among the most effective of all strategies for elementary and secondary reading (Slavin, Cheung, Groff, & Lake, 2008; Slavin, Lake, Chambers, Cheung, & Davis, 2009) and mathematics (Slavin & Lake, 2008; Slavin, Lake, & Groff, 2009), especially for students with low socioeconomic status (Dietrichson, Bøg, Filges, & Klint Jørgensen, 2017).

Although there is a fair consensus among researchers about the positive effects of cooperative learning on student achievement, there remains controversy about why and how cooperative learning methods affect achievement and, most importantly, under what conditions cooperative learning has these effects. Different groups of researchers investigating cooperative learning effects on achievement begin with different assumptions and conclude by explaining the achievement effects of cooperative learning in quite different theoretical terms. In earlier work, Slavin (1995, 2010a, 2013b, 2015) identified motivationalist, social cohesion, cognitive-developmental, and cognitive-elaboration as the four major theoretical perspectives on the achievement effects of cooperative learning.

THEORETICAL PERSPECTIVES

Motivational Perspectives

Motivational perspectives on cooperative learning posit that task motivation is the most important part of the process, believing that the other processes are driven primarily by motivation. From a motivationalist perspective (e.g., Johnson & Johnson, 1998; Slavin, 1995, 2009, 2013a), cooperative incentive structures create a situation in which the only way group members can attain their own personal goals is if the group is successful. Therefore, to meet certain personal goals, group members must both help their group mates do whatever enables the group to succeed, and, perhaps even more importantly, to encourage their group mates to exert maximum efforts. In other words, rewarding groups based on group performance (or the sum of individual performances) creates an interpersonal reward structure in which group members will give or withhold social reinforcers (e.g., praise, encouragement) in response to group mates' task-related efforts.

The motivationalist critique of traditional classroom organization holds that the competitive grading and informal reward system of the traditional classroom creates peer norms opposing academic efforts (see Coleman, 1961). Since one student's success decreases the chances that others will succeed, students are likely to express norms that high achievement is for "nerds" or "teachers' pets." However, by having students work together toward a common goal, they may be motivated to express norms favoring academic achievement, to reinforce one another for academic efforts.

Not surprisingly, motivational theorists build group rewards into their cooperative learning methods. In methods developed at Johns Hopkins University (Slavin, 1994, 1995), students can earn certificates or other recognition if their average team scores on quizzes or other individual assignments exceed a preestablished criterion. Methods developed by David and Roger Johnson (1998; Johnson, Johnson, & Holubec, 2008) and their colleagues at the University of Minnesota often give students grades based on group performance, which is defined in several different ways. The theoretical rationale for these group rewards is that if students value the success of the group, they will encourage and help one another to achieve.

Considerable empirical evidence from practical applications of cooperative learning in elementary and secondary schools supports the motivationalist position that group rewards are essential to the effectiveness of cooperative learning, with one critical qualification. Use of group goals or group rewards enhances the achievement outcomes of cooperative learning if and only if the group rewards are based on the individual learning of all group members (McMaster & Fuchs, 2002; Rohrbeck et al., 2003; Sencibaugh & Sencibaugh, 2016; Slavin, 1995, 2009, 2010b; Webb, 2008a). Most often, this means that team scores are computed based on average scores on quizzes which all teammates take individually, without teammate help, or based on ratings of individual contributions to a group product, as when each student contributes a chapter to a group report.

Social Cohesion Perspective

A theoretical perspective somewhat related to the motivational viewpoint holds that the effects of cooperative learning on achievement are strongly mediated by the cohesiveness of the group. The quality of the group's interactions is thought to be largely determined by group cohesion. In essence, students will engage in the task and help one another learn because they identify with the group and want one another to succeed. This perspective is similar to the motivational perspective in that it emphasizes primarily motivational rather than cognitive explanations for the instructional effectiveness of cooperative learning. However, motivational theorists hold that students help their group mates learn primarily because it is in their own interests to do so. Social cohesion theorists, in contrast, emphasize the idea that students help their group mates learn because they care about the group. A hallmark of the social cohesion perspective is an emphasis on team building activities in preparation for cooperative learning, and processing or group self-evaluation during and after group activities. Social cohesion theorists have historically tended to downplay or reject the group incentives and individual accountability held by motivationalist researchers to be essential. They emphasize, instead, that the effects of cooperative learning on students and on student achievement depend substantially on the quality of the group's interaction (Battistich, Solomon, & Delucchi, 1993; Johnson & Johnson, 2008; Webb, 2008b).

Cohen and Lotan's (2014) work, as well as that of Shlomo and Yael Sharan (Sharan & Sharan, 1992) and Elliot Aronson and his colleagues (Aronson, Blaney, Stephan, Sikes, & Snapp, 1978), may be described as social cohesiveness theories. Cohen and Lotan (2014), Aronson et al. (1978), and Sharan and Sharan (1992) all prescribe forms of cooperative learning in which students take on individual roles within the group, which Slavin (1983, 2014a) calls *task specialization methods.*

In Aronson et al.'s (1978) Jigsaw method, students study material on one of four or five topics distributed among the group members. They meet in *expert groups* to share information on their topics with members of other teams who had the same topic, and then take turns presenting their topics to the team. In Sharan and Sharon's (1992) Group Investigation method, groups take on topics within a unit studied by the class as a whole, and then further subdivide the topic into tasks within the group. The students investigate the topic together and ultimately present their findings to the class. Cohen and Lotan's (2014) Finding Out/Descubrimiento program has students play different roles in discovery-oriented science activities.

One main purpose of the task specialization used in Jigsaw, Group Investigation, and Finding Out/Descubrimiento is to create interdependence among group members. In the Johnsons' methods, a somewhat similar form of interdependence is created by having students take on roles as "checker," "recorder," "observer," and so on. The idea is that if students value their groupmates and are dependent on one another, they are likely to encourage and help one another to succeed.

There is some empirical evidence that the achievement effects of cooperative learning depend on social cohesion and the quality of group interactions (Battistich et al., 1993; Johnson & Johnson, 2008; Webb, 2008a). The achievement outcomes of cooperative learning methods that emphasize task specialization are less clear. Research on the original form of Jigsaw has not generally found positive effects of this method on student achievement (Arslan, 2016; Hänze & Berger, 2007; Moreno, 2009; Slavin, 1995; Souvignier & Kronenberger, 2007). In contrast, there is evidence that when it is well implemented, Group Investigation can significantly increase student achievement (Mitchell, Montgomery, Holder, & Stuart, 2008; Sharan & Shachar, 1988). In studies of at least four weeks' duration, the Johnsons' (1998) methods have not been found to increase achievement more than individualistic methods unless they incorporate group rewards (in this case, group grades) based on the average of group members' individual quiz scores (see Slavin, 1995). Studies of forms of Jigsaw that have added group rewards to the original model have found positive achievement outcomes (Gambari & Yusuf, 2016; Mattingly & Van Sickle, 1991).

Research on practical classroom applications of methods based on social cohesion theories provide inconsistent support for the proposition that building cohesiveness among students through team building alone (i.e., without group incentives) will enhance student achievement. In general, methods which emphasize team building and group process but do not provide specific group rewards based on the learning of all group members are no more effective than traditional instruction in increasing achievement (Slavin, 1995), although these methods may be effective if group rewards are added to them (Huber & Huber, 2008).

Cognitive Perspectives

The major alternative to the motivationalist and social cohesiveness perspectives on cooperative learning, both of which focus primarily on group norms and interpersonal influence, is the cognitive perspective. The cognitive perspective holds that interactions among students will in themselves increase student achievement for reasons that have to do with mental processing of information rather than with motivations. Cooperative methods developed by cognitive theorists involve neither the group goals that are the cornerstone of the motivationalist methods nor the emphasis on building group cohesiveness characteristic of the social cohesion methods. However, there are several quite different cognitive perspectives, as well as some that are similar in theoretical perspective, but have developed on largely parallel tracks. The two most notable of these are described in the following sections—developmental perspectives and cognitive elaboration perspectives.

Developmental Perspective

One widely researched set of cognitive theories is the developmental perspective (e.g., Damon, 1984; Johnson & Johnson, 2015). The fundamental assumption of the developmental perspective on cooperative learning is that interaction among children around appropriate tasks increases their mastery of critical concepts. Vygotsky (Cole, John-Steiner, Scribner, & Souberman, 1978) defines the zone of proximal development as "...the distance between the actual developmental level as determined by independent problem solving and the level of potential development as determined through problem solving under adult guidance *or in collaboration with more capable peers*" (p. 86, emphasis added). In his view, collaborative activity among children promotes growth because children of similar ages are likely to be operating within one another's proximal zones of development, modeling in the collaborative group behaviors more advanced than those they could perform as individuals.

Similarly, Piaget (1926) held that social-arbitrary knowledge—language, values, rules, morality, and symbol systems—can only be learned in interactions with others. Peer interaction is also important in logical-mathematical thought in disequilibrating the child's egocentric conceptualizations and in providing feedback to the child about the validity of logical constructions.

There is a great deal of empirical support for the idea that peer interaction can help nonconservers become conservers. Many studies have shown that when conservers and nonconservers of about the same age work collaboratively on tasks requiring conservation, the nonconservers generally develop and maintain conservation concepts (see Bell, Grossen, & Perret-Clermont, 1985; Psaltis & Duveen, 2006, 2007). From the developmental perspective, the effects of cooperative learning on student achievement would be largely or entirely due to the use of cooperative tasks, not necessarily cooperative goals. In this view, opportunities for students to discuss, to argue, and to present and hear one another's viewpoints are the critical element of cooperative learning with respect to student achievement.

Despite considerable support from theoretical and laboratory research, there is little empirical evidence from classroom experiments conducted over meaningful time periods that pure cooperative methods, which depend solely on interaction, produce higher achievement (Sills, Rowse, & Emerson, 2016). However, it is likely that the cognitive processes described by developmental theorists are important mediating variables that can help explain the positive outcomes of effective cooperative learning methods (Slavin, 1995).

Cognitive Elaboration Perspective

A cognitive perspective on cooperative learning quite different from the developmental viewpoint is one which might be called the cognitive elaboration perspective. Research in cognitive psychology has long held that if information is to be retained in memory and related to information already in memory, the learner must engage in some sort of cognitive restructuring, or elaboration, of the material (Callender & McDaniel, 2009; Schunk, 2012; Wittrock, 1986). One of the most effective means of elaboration is explaining the material to someone else. Research on peer tutoring has long found achievement benefits for the tutor as well as the tutee (Calhoon, Al Otaiba, Cihak, King, & Avalos, 2007; Devin-Sheehan, Feldman, & Allen, 1976; Mathes, Torgesen, & Allor, 2001; Rohrbeck et al., 2003; Thurston, Tymms, Merrell, & Conlin, 2012; Van Keer, 2004). In such methods, students take roles as recaller and listener. They read a section of text, and then the recaller summarizes the information while the listener corrects any errors, fills in any omitted material, and helps think of ways both students can remember the main ideas. The students switch roles on the next section.

In terms of the empirical evidence for this perspective, Dansereau and his colleagues (O'Donnell, 1996, 2006) have found in a series of brief studies that college students working on structured cooperative scripts can learn technical material or procedures better than can students working alone. While both the recaller and the listener learned more than did students working alone, the recaller learned more (O'Donnell & Dansereau, 1992). This mirrors both the peer tutoring findings and the findings of Webb (2008b), who discovered that the students who gained the most from cooperative activities were those who provided elaborated explanations to others. In this research as well as in Dansereau's, students who received elaborated explanations learned more than those who worked alone, but not as much as those who served as explainers. Studies of Reciprocal Teaching, in which students learn to formulate questions for each other, have generally supported its positive effects on student achievement (O'Donnell & Dansereau, 2000; Palincsar, Brown, & Martin, 1987; Rosenshine & Meister, 1994; Spörer, Brunstein, & Kieschke, 2009).

Integrated Model

The alternative perspectives on cooperative learning may be seen as complementary, not contradictory. For example, motivational theorists would not argue that the cognitive theories are unnecessary. Instead, they assert that motivation drives cognitive process, which in turn produces learning (Slavin, 1995, 2013a). They would argue that it is unlikely over the long haul that students would engage in the kind of elaborated explanations found by Webb (2008) and others to be essential to profiting from cooperative activity without a goal structure designed to enhance motivation. Similarly, social cohesion theorists might hold that the utility of extrinsic incentives must lie in their contribution to group cohesiveness, caring, and pro-social norms among group members, which could in turn affect cognitive processes.

A simple path model of cooperative learning processes, adapted from Slavin (1995), is diagrammed in Figure 11.1. It depicts the main functional relationships among the major theoretical approaches to cooperative learning.

Figure 11.1 begins with a focus on group goals or incentives based on the individual learning of all group members. That is, the model assumes that motivation to learn and to encourage and help others to learn activates cooperative behaviors that will result in learning. This would include both task motivation and motivation to interact in the group. In this model, motivation to succeed leads to learning directly, and also drives the behaviors and attitudes that lead to group cohesion, which in turn facilitates the types of group interactions that yield enhanced learning and academic achievement. The relations are conceived to be reciprocal, such that as task motivation leads to the development of group cohesion, group cohesion may in turn reinforce and enhance task motivation. By the same token, the cognitive processes may become intrinsically rewarding and lead to increased task motivation and group cohesion.

Each aspect of the diagrammed model is well represented in the theoretical and empirical cooperative learning literature. All have well established rationales and some supporting evidence.

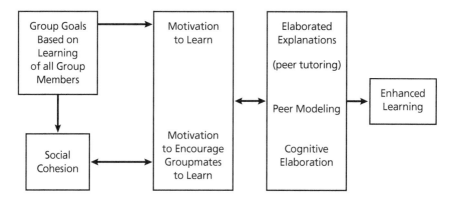

Figure 11.1 Integration of theoretical perspectives on cooperative learning effects on learning.

Reconciling the Four Perspectives

The model shown in Figure 11.1 illustrates how group goals might operate to enhance the learning outcomes of cooperative learning. Provision of group goals based on the individual learning of all group members might affect cognitive processes directly, by motivating students to engage in peer modeling, cognitive elaboration, or practice with one another. Group goals may also lead to group cohesiveness, increasing caring and concern among group members and making them feel responsible for one another's achievement, thereby motivating students to engage in cognitive processes that enhance learning.

Finally, group goals may motivate students to take responsibility for one another independently of the teacher, thereby solving important classroom organization problems and providing increased opportunities for cognitively appropriate learning activities. Scholars whose theoretical orientations de-emphasize the utility of extrinsic rewards attempt to intervene directly on mechanisms identified as mediating variables in the model described earlier. For example, social cohesion theorists intervene directly on group cohesiveness by engaging in elaborate team building and group processing training. Cognitive theorists would hold that the cognitive processes that are essential to any theory relating cooperative learning to achievement can be created directly, without the motivational or affective changes discussed by the motivationalist and social cohesion theorists.

From the perspective of the model diagrammed in Figure 11.1, starting with group goals and individual accountability permits students in cooperative learning groups to benefit from the full range of factors that are known to affect cooperative learning outcomes. While group goals and individual accountability may not always be absolutely necessary, to ignore them would be to ignore the tool with the most consistent evidence of positive effects on student achievement.

PRACTICAL APPLICATIONS OF COOPERATIVE LEARNING

Research and development over the years have led to the creation and evaluation of several practical approaches to cooperative learning. The most widely used and extensively researched of these programs are described in the following sections.

Cooperative learning methods fall into two main categories. One set, *Structured Team Learning*, involves rewards to teams based on the learning progress of their members, and individual accountability, which means that team success depends on individual learning, not group products. A second set,

Informal Group Learning Methods, includes methods more focused on social dynamics, projects, and discussion than on mastery of well-specified content.

Structured Team Learning Methods

Student Team Learning

Student Team Learning (STL) techniques were developed and researched at Johns Hopkins University (see Slavin, 1994, 1995). More than half of all experimental studies of practical cooperative learning methods involve STL methods.

All cooperative learning methods share the idea that students work together to learn and are responsible for one another's learning as well as their own. STL methods also emphasize the use of team goals and team success, which can only be achieved if all members of the team learn the objectives being taught. That is, in STL the students' tasks are not to *do* something as a team but to *learn* something as a team.

Four elements are central to all STL methods: *team rewards, individual opportunities, individual accountability,* and *equal opportunities* for success. Using STL techniques, teams earn certificates or other team rewards if they achieve above a designated criterion. *Individual accountability* means that the team's success depends on the individual learning of all team members. This focuses the activity of the team members on explaining concepts to one another and making sure that everyone on the team is ready for a quiz or other assessment that they will take without teammate help. *Equal opportunities for success* means that students contribute to their teams by improving over their past performances. This ensures that high, average, and low achievers are equally challenged to do their best and that the contributions of all team members will be valued.

Four principal student learning methods have been extensively developed and researched. Two are general cooperative learning methods adaptable to most subjects and grade levels: Student Team Achievement Divisions (STAD) and Teams–Games–Tournament (TGT). The remaining two are comprehensive curriculums designed for use in particular subjects at particular grade levels: Team Assisted Individualization (TAI) for mathematics in Grades 2–6 and Cooperative Integrated Reading and Composition (CIRC) for reading and writing instruction in Grades 3–8. Success for All (SFA), a comprehensive school reform model, utilizes cooperative learning in the form of CIRC in Grades 2–8. However, it also incorporates several additional elements, so its effects cannot be ascribed to cooperative learning alone. Descriptions of each of the five student learning methods can be found in Table 11.1.

TABLE 11.1   Descriptions of Student Team Learning Approaches

Description	Supporting Evidence
Student Teams–Achievement Divisions (STAD)	
Students are assigned to four-member learning teams mixed in performance level, sex, and ethnicity. The teacher presents a lesson, and the students work within their teams to make sure that all team members have mastered the lesson. Finally, all students take individual quizzes on the material, at which time they may *not* help one another. Students' quiz scores are compared to their own past averages, and points are awarded based on the degree to which students can meet or exceed their own earlier performances. These points are then summed to form team scores, and teams that meet certain criteria earn certificates or other rewards.	Barbato (2000); Mevarech (1985); Reid (1992); Slavin & Karweit (1984); Stevens & Slavin (1995b)
Teams–Games–Tournament (TGT)	
Uses teacher presentations and teamwork as well as weekly tournaments. In these, students compete with members of other teams to contribute points to their team score. Students compete at three-person tournament tables against others with a similar past record in mathematics. A procedure changes table assignments to keep the competition fair. The winner at each tournament table brings the same number of points to his or her team, regardless of which table it is; this means that low achiever (competing with other low achievers) and high achievers (competing with other high achievers) have equal opportunity for success. High performing teams earn certificates or other forms of team rewards.	Stevens & Slavin (1995b)
Team Assisted Individualization (TAI)	
Uses four-member mixed ability learning teams and certificates for high-performing teams and combines cooperative learning with individualized instruction. Specifically designed to teach mathematics to students in Grades 3–6. Students enter an individualized sequence according to a placement test and then proceed at their own rates. In general, team members work on different units. Teammates check each others' work against answer sheets and help one another with any problems. Final unit tests are taken without teammate help and are scored by student monitors. Each week, teachers total the number of units completed by all team members and give certificates or other team rewards to teams that exceed a criterion score based on the number of final tests passed, with extra points for perfect papers and completed homework.	Slavin & Karweit (1985); Stevens & Slavin (1995b)
Cooperative Integrated Reading and Composition (CIRC)	
A comprehensive program for teaching reading and writing in the upper elementary grades. All students are assigned to teams composed of two pairs from two different reading groups. While the teacher is working with one reading group, the paired students in the other groups are working on a series of cognitively engaging activities. Students work as a total team to master main idea and other comprehension skills. Students follow a sequence	Stevens & Durkin (1992); Stevens, Madden, Slavin, & Farnish (1987); Stevens & Slavin, (1995a, 1995)

(continued)

TABLE 11.1 Descriptions of Student Team Learning Approaches (cont.)	
Description	Supporting Evidence
of teacher instruction, team practice, team pre-assessments, and quizzes. That is, students do not take the quiz until their team-mates have determined that they are ready. Certificates are given to teams based on the average performance of all team members on all reading and writing activities.	
Success for All (SFA)	
A whole-school reform model for elementary and middle schools focused primarily on reading. It makes extensive use of cooperative learning, including incorporating a form of CIRC in Grades 2–8.	Borman et al. (2007); Quint, Zhu, Balu, Rappaport, & DeLaurentis (2015); Rowan, Camburn, Correnti, & Miller (2007); Slavin, Madden, Chambers, & Haxby (2009)

Peer-Assisted Learning Strategies

Peer-Assisted Learning Strategies (PALS) is a dyadic learning approach in which pairs of children take turns as teacher and learner. The children are taught simple strategies for helping each other, and are rewarded based on the learning of both members of the pair. Research on PALS in elementary and middle school math and reading has found positive effects of this approach on student achievement outcomes, (e.g., Calhoon, 2005; Calhoon, Al Otaiba, Greenberg, King, & Avalos, 2006; Fuchs, Fuchs, & Karns, 2001; Fuchs, Fuchs, Kazdan, & Allen, 1999; Mathes & Babyak, 2001). Positive effects of a similar program called Classwide Peer Tutoring (Greenwood, Delquadri, & Hall, 1989) have also been found, and another similar approach has been found to be effective in two Belgian studies (Van Keer & Verhaeghe, 2005, 2008).

IMPROVE

IMPROVE (Mevarech, 1985) is an Israeli mathematics program that uses cooperative learning strategies similar to those used in STAD but also emphasizes teaching of metacognitive skills and regular assessments of mastery of key concepts and re-teaching of skills missed by many students. Studies of IMPROVE have found positive effects on the mathematics achievement of elementary and middle school students in Israel (Kramarski, Mevarech, & Lieberman, 2001; Mevarech & Kramarski, 1997).

Informal Group Learning Methods

Jigsaw

Jigsaw was originally designed by Elliot Aronson and his colleagues (1978). In Aronson's Jigsaw method, students are assigned to six-member teams to work on academic material that has been broken down into sections. For example, a biography might be divided into early life, first accomplishments, major setbacks, later life, and impact on history. Each team member reads his or her section. Next, members of different teams who have studied the same sections meet in expert groups to discuss their sections. Then, the students return to their teams and take turns teaching their teammates about their sections. Since the only way students can learn sections other than their own is to listen carefully to their teammates, they are motivated to support and show interest in one another's work.

Slavin (1994) developed a modification of Jigsaw and then incorporated it in the STL family of programs. In this method, called Jigsaw II, students work in four- or five-member team as in TGT and STAD. Instead of each student being assigned a particular section of text, all students read a common narrative, such as a book chapter, a short story, or a biography. However, each student receives a topic (such as "climate" in a unit on France) on which to become an expert. Students with the same topics meet in expert groups to discuss them, after which they return to their teams to teach what they have learned to their teammates. Then, students take individual quizzes, which result in team scores based on the improvement score system of STAD. Teams that meet preset standards earn certificates. Jigsaw is used primarily in social studies and other subjects where learning from text is important (Mattingly & Van Sickle, 1991).

Learning Together

David and Roger Johnson at the University of Minnesota developed the Learning Together models of cooperative learning (Johnson & Johnson, 1998). The methods they have researched involve students working on assignments in four- or five-member heterogeneous groups. The groups hand in a single product (such as a worksheet) and receive praise and rewards based on the group product. Their methods emphasize team-building activities before students begin working together and regular discussions within groups about how well they are working together. Numerous brief experiments, all less than four weeks, have shown positive effects of these approaches (see Johnson & Johnson, 1998; Roseth et al., 2008).

Group Investigation

Group Investigation, developed by Shlomo Sharan and Yael Sharan (1992) at the University of Tel-Aviv, is a general classroom organization plan in which students work in small groups using cooperative inquiry, group discussion, and cooperative planning and projects. In this method, students form their own two- to six-member groups. After choosing subtopics from a unit being studied by the entire class, the groups further break their subtopics into individual tasks and carry out the activities necessary to prepare group reports. Each group then makes a presentation or display to communicate its findings to the class. A study in Israel by Sharan and Shachar (1988) found positive effects of Group Investigation on achievement in language and literature.

Computer-Supported Collaborated Learning

A new development in the field of cooperative learning has been the integration of technology with cooperative or collaborative learning, referred to as computer-supported collaborative learning (CSCL) This approach "begins with learning (and thus needs a pedagogy), that occurs with others (and thus needs to be social), and that takes place through/is facilitated by computers (and thus makes use of technology)" (Kirschner & Erkens, 2013, p. 2). For many, CSCL has much to offer, and may present solutions to many challenges in cooperative work, such as offering new ways to communicate or support for structuring their cooperative processes (Jeong & Hmelo-Silver, 2016). While currently the evidence supports face-to-face cooperative approaches over online strategies (Johnson & Johnson, 2013), there may be ways that technology can be effectively incorporated into cooperative learning through activities such as simulations, WebQuests, or joint writing (Johnson & Johnson, 2014).

COOPERATIVE LEARNING IN DIVERSE CULTURAL CONTEXTS

Cooperative learning has been studied in many countries and cultural contexts. It is important to understand how cooperative methods interact with cultural contexts and norms, especially beyond the mainstream Western cultures where they were mostly developed. This will be accomplished by first looking at the impact of cooperative learning on African American and Hispanic students in the United States, then at the effectiveness of cooperative learning in Asian countries.

African American and Hispanic Students

African American and Hispanic students tend to be underserved by the American education system despite continued reform efforts. One explanation is that both African American and Hispanic children bring their own culture to school that conflicts with the traditional American school experience (Good, Masewicz, & Vogel, 2010; Hale, 1986). Among the themes of African American culture that are distinct from the mainstream U.S. culture is communalism (Boykin, 1983). This unique culture is what helps shape African American students preferred learning styles, and may explain why African American students are particularly motivated and responsive to the interdependence and group work found in cooperative learning (Boykin, 1994). Similarly, Hispanic families promote the value of collectivism and provide a home environment that encourages and supports cooperation (Carger, 1996). Hispanic students may experience less cultural dissonance between home and school when schools embrace cooperative learning. So while cooperative learning is widely accepted as a universally effective practice in the United States, African American and Hispanic students are more likely to have family structures and cultural backgrounds that develop prosocial orientations, making them able to maximize learning in cooperative settings.

The belief that African American and Hispanic students specifically thrive in cooperative learning situations has not only been postulated; it has been examined empirically. In a qualitative study of African American males in a rural elementary school, Wilson-Jones and Caston (2004) found that all students preferred cooperative learning over other methods of instruction and that group work was more likely to lead to their academic success. Park (2001) explored the preferred learning styles of students of diverse backgrounds in secondary schools and found that students of Mexican-American backgrounds preferred group learning over individual approaches. The relevance of cooperative learning approaches to their specific cultural background should make African American and Hispanic students more engaged and motivated in those environments.

The evidence moves beyond stated preferences to behavior. Even at an early age, African American children at a day-care center were more likely to ask for help from their peers than from teachers, particularly for academic help (Watkins, 2002). The only times that adults were sought out were for social help, such as for bathroom visits or shoe-tying. In a study of preschool students attending Head Start (Strand, Pula, & Downs, 2015), students from Spanish-speaking Hispanic backgrounds were more likely to make cooperative choices than White students. From their first formal educational experiences, African American and Hispanic children tend to be already oriented toward cooperation and peer assistance.

Academic outcomes also improve for African American and Hispanic students under cooperative learning conditions. In a study comparing academic vocabulary use for African American students learning in collaborative group work, direct instruction, or a control condition, the students working in groups showed higher levels of productive academic vocabulary, likely due to greater use of the vocabulary during their group discussions (Chizhik, 2001). The increased opportunities to practice likely contributed to the improved outcomes.

Improved outcomes in other content areas have also been shown. Hispanic students in Texas were taught social studies using either cooperative learning or traditional teaching methods (Lampe, Rooze, & Tallent-Runnels, 1996). After the 12-week unit had concluded, students in the cooperative learning classes performed substantially better than the students in the traditional classes (ES = +0.91). Similar results were found in a 4-week study of eighth grade algebra students (Bunrasi, 2012); students receiving cooperative learning lessons outperformed students in the traditional lesson (ES = +0.24). Studies such as these show that a variety of cooperative learning strategies can have a positive impact on the participating Hispanic students.

In another example, Rohrbeck, Ginsburg-Block, Fantuzzo, and Miller (2003) conducted a meta-analysis of peer-assisted learning (PAL). While the overall meta-analysis showed positive impacts of PAL (ES = +0.33), the impact was even higher in studies with high numbers of African American and Hispanic students (ES = +0.51). It appears that for minority students, these group-work strategies were more effective than for the non-minority students.

While evidence supports the assertion that African American and Hispanic students are more responsive to and benefit more from cooperative learning, some evidence exists to the contrary. For example, in a study of high school African American students in high school social studies classes, students were instructed using either a traditional lecture method, or using the Jigsaw II strategy (Ross, Seaborn, & Wilson, 2002). There were no differences between the groups at posttest. The short duration of the study means the results should be interpreted with caution. However, one teacher, in explaining why she thought her students struggled with the cooperative learning approach, said:

> I think a lot of these kids are not trained early on to work in groups. It seems like they have been in school settings that taught them to do as you are told, stay in your seat and probably included a lot of busy work and handouts, things that they did not need group help with. It is not that they cannot do the work; I think it is because they have not been trained to do it. (Ross et al., 2002, p. 705)

This may point to another explanation for the lack of impact of cooperative learning in some studies. Students who have not previously experienced cooperative learning may not be able to take full advantage of it. However, students can be taught how to function successfully in cooperative learning groups. Webb and Farivar (1994) compared cooperative learning including training in academic helping skills with a cooperative learning-only condition. The results demonstrated that with the additional training, African American and Hispanic students were more likely to give help to their peers and have higher academic outcomes. So while culture may predispose African American and Hispanic students to cooperative strategies, they may still require training to maximize cooperative learning benefits (Slavin, 2014b).

Confucian Heritage Culture Students

While cooperative learning is widely accepted in Western societies, how might it work in Asian cultures? Some might assert that because Eastern societies tend to be more collectivist, they will readily adopt cooperative learning; others have argued that cooperative learning may not be readily applied in Eastern cultures (Hofstede, 2005; Phuong-Mai, Terlouw, & Pilot, 2005; Thanh, 2014), particularly Confucian heritage culture (CHC) countries.

CHC is a concept that describes a unique cultural pattern of countries that have a history of Confucian values. These countries include China, Korea, Japan, Vietnam, and Hong Kong (Chen & Liu, 2017). A closer look at CHC countries is especially relevant because their cultural context has had a deep influence on schooling, such that educational reforms from other cultures may not immediately transfer effectively (Carless, 2010; Kennedy, Chan, Fok, & Yu, 2008; Phuong-Mai et al., 2005; Thanh, 2014). They can vary along five different dimensions: power distance, individualism–collectivism, masculinity–femininity, uncertainty avoidance, and short-term orientation–long-term orientation (Hofstede, 2005). Phuong-Mai, Terlouw, and Pilot (2005) have detailed how Hofsted's dimensions of culture apply in these CHC contexts, as well as the complications this presents for cooperative learning. The three most relevant dimensions will be briefly summarized before examining the existing literature.

Power Distance

In CHC countries, power distance is quite high (Hofstede, 2005), and continues to hold in the school settings, where the teacher is the absolute authority. Classes are quiet, as students listen to the teacher, who functions as a "sage on the stage" (Morrison, 2014). Students work on their own to understand what the teacher presented, and may wait to ask questions until outside of class, where many teachers prefer to answer individual questions (Shi, 2006). Because of the role of the teacher as the ultimate authority in the classroom, their feedback is prized above all others, so that students prefer to receive feedback from the teacher rather than their peers (Hu & Lam, 2010). This contradicts the premise of cooperative learning, where students are learning from each other. The shift of power from held solely by the teacher to shared among peers may present a dilemma for CHC students in cooperative learning groups.

Individualism-Collectivism

CHC countries tend to have low levels of individualism and higher levels of collectivism. These students would be expected to have strong group affiliation and prioritize group needs. However, the distinction is not as simple as it appears; individualism and collectivism are often presented as opposites, but in reality are separate constructs. Furthermore, a simple view of collectivism argues that students would prefer and thrive in groupwork. However, the concept of harmony is also important in CHC countries, which may encourage students to avoid conflict and confrontation. These are important in cooperative learning, as students question and criticize each other to push their learning. A preference for peaceful group interactions will not necessarily lead to effective cooperative learning.

Uncertainty Avoidance

CHC countries with high levels of uncertainty avoidance may struggle in learning situations that are not highly structured or well-defined. However, this conflicts with many cooperative learning approaches, which often include open-ended tasks and less formal guidance.

With a deeper look at CHC values and how they interact with the needs of cooperative learning, a complicated picture emerges of how cooperative learning might mesh or clash with the students' culture. The research literature reflects this complicated understanding of how cooperative learning works in CHC countries.

Research on Cooperative Learning in CHC Countries

There have been several substantial reviews of cooperative learning in CHC contexts. Thanh, Gillies, and Renshaw (2008) conducted a review of cooperative learning strategies in classroom settings that took place in Asian contexts. The review included 14 studies covering primary, secondary, and college level students and diverse subjects such as English, math, and social studies. These studies examined mixed cooperative learning approaches as well as those described earlier such as STAD, Jigsaw, and Group Investigations. The authors coded whether each study had positive, negative, or null effects. While 50% of the studies reported positive outcomes, others found null or even negative effects. The review supports a belief that cooperative learning is not universally effective across CHC learning environments.

An additional important finding was that the authors reported a frequent mismatch between the participants' culture and cooperative learning as a barrier to effective use of the strategy, even in studies that reported positive outcomes. For example, both Lee, Chew, Ng, and Hing (1999) and Hassim et al. (2004) reported positive effects of the cooperative learning approaches used, but also reported difficulty implementing the strategies because some students wouldn't cooperate, possibly due to a preference for individual achievement or focus on individual competition. Given the mixed results of the studies and the reported conflicts between cooperative learning and the cultural context, the review concludes that cooperative learning may require adaptation to be effective in Asian contexts.

In a meta-analysis of studies of in-person cooperative learning around the globe, Kyndt et al. (2013) found a significant overall positive effect of cooperative learning (ES = +0.54). In further analysis, the authors found a significant effect of culture. Non-Western cultures, including Asian countries were found to have higher impacts of cooperative learning than Western countries, showing that not only can cooperative learning work in collectivist contexts such as CHC countries, but it might be more effective.

In an attempt to update the Thanh et al. review (2008), Chen and Liu (2017) examined the effect of cooperative learning on achievement in CHC countries in studies published since 2007. Using the same selection criteria as Thanh (2008), they found 39 additional studies covering primary, secondary, and college students. The review was more geographically diverse, covering a wider selection of CHC countries. Studies were coded as having positive, negative, or null achievement effects. The results showed that 33 of the 39 studies had positive findings, with only 5 studies having null or negative results.

The authors then combined the studies identified in their review with those from the earlier review (Thanh et al., 2008) for a more complete understanding of cooperative learning in CHC countries. This analysis led to a finding that more of the recent studies have been conducted at the college level, with those studies more likely to find positive effects. The authors explained this as a difference in the context between college and basic education. Those teaching in colleges may have more flexibility and are less concerned with high-stakes tests, while secondary schools teachers are concerned with preparing students for important examinations and thus resist changes to their instruction that they believe may have negative consequences on that preparation (Law et al., 1999)

The authors proposed one reason for the dramatic increase in effectiveness of cooperative learning in CHC contexts could be due to changes in students' familiarity with cooperative learning. Because cooperative learning was growing over this period, the studies in the earlier review that found negative or null effects may have been the first attempts to implement cooperative learning in that school. Teachers and students were both unfamiliar with the process and it was possibly poorly implemented, which was reflected in the lack of positive impacts. These students are now older, in college, and have been exposed to cooperative learning for a longer period of their life. Teachers have also had more time to become accustomed to this approach. That increased time to acclimate could result in the positive effects that are demonstrated in the more recent studies.

Another possible explanation for the shift in efficacy of cooperative learning is local changes in schooling and policy. Educational reforms have spread across CHC nations, often pushing those school systems to more Western approaches including cooperative learning (Thanh, 2014). These changes have often been driven by changes to the economy and what is needed for a success in the future (Ng & Renshaw, 2009). These top-level policy changes have filtered down and have caused changes in expectations for what schools should look like at the local level, possibly changing teachers' beliefs and behaviors to better support cooperative learning approaches.

In any case, the review documents the growth of research on cooperative learning in CHC countries, as well as bringing to light more positive evidence supporting its use. The review demonstrated that cooperative learning was "largely applicable" for CHC students (Chen & Liu, 2017, p. 84).

These reviews of cooperative learning paint a picture of cooperative learning as feasible in non-Western contexts, including CHC countries, though success is not guaranteed. The positive findings demonstrate the possibility that cooperative learning could be one way to improve educational outcomes in CHC countries. On the other hand, the negative results of some studies show that cooperative learning programs developed in the West may not be immediately universal, and cultural conflicts are possible. The application of cooperative learning in these countries is quite complicated (Yang, Badger, & Yu, 2006). Adapting cooperative learning to the local context may be necessary. They also serve as a reminder that culture is not static; the CHC contexts are changing, making cooperative learning more relevant today than it was in the past.

Adapting Cooperative Learning to Local Conditions

The bulk of the research on cooperative learning in CHC countries is simply assessing whether the strategy or program works. In one example, Tan, Sharan, and Lee (2007) compare the impact of Group Investigation with traditional classroom instruction for eighth grade students in Singapore. The results showed no differences between the two groups. Importantly, their study also included a questionnaire to get student's impressions of the program. These questionnaires revealed that students had positive perceptions of the program, from enjoying it, enjoying working with friends, and learning new skills. However, the negative responses revealed the clashes with the CHC cultural context. Students preferred teachers to provide the information, rather than find it themselves or depend on peers to produce it. They believed they would learn better from the teacher, which reflects that belief in the teacher as the ultimate authority, and students should sit and absorb the knowledge dispensed by the teacher. Second, students were concerned that they couldn't adequately prepare for examinations using this method because it took more time and they may not cover all of the topics. Only a teacher could fully prepare them for the all-important tests they needed to take.

These perceptions are important and illustrate how one cooperative learning approach didn't perfectly mesh with CHC context. Yet these objections are not insurmountable. They suggest the need to adapt cooperative learning to local contexts, without compromising the core of the program. Pham and Renshaw (2015) actually illustrate how this process could occur. They worked with teachers and students in Vietnam to implement STAD in history and geography classes. They took a three phase approach, where in the first phase, STAD was introduced and implemented as is. Then they gathered information on how students and teachers were responding to the program, to identify what wasn't working. Students identified two main problems: mixed-ability groups and unfair work distribution were problems. The issue with mixed-ability groups has been noted in other studies of cooperative learning in CHC contexts, while the unfair workloads are difficult to address when group harmony is a prized value; students are unlike to directly raise the issue in order to allow all members to "save face." Adjustments were developed, so that groups were reorganized into friendship groups, and a group leader was assigned who could mediate issues such as students not contributing fully. These were two adaptations that fit the local cultural context, and still allowed students to work together meaningfully.

In the second phase, STAD was implemented with these adjustments and again, information on the process was collected at the end. This time, issues with the teachers were identified, so that teachers had to change their behavior to better fit the cooperative learning approach. This included helping students with guided questions to reach deeper understanding, as well as reorganizing how teachers responded to student questions. Again, these were locally-developed solutions that continued to push the group toward better implementation of cooperative learning in a culturally acceptable way during the third phase of the study. Students and teachers were able to more effectively use STAD with these culturally appropriate adaptations. Pham and Renshaw have laid out a practical way to adapt Western-developed cooperative learning strategies for effective use in CHC schools.

There are numerous cultural and institutional constraints that could require adaptation of cooperative learning. Some challenges just may take time for students to become more familiar or comfortable, similar to how Hispanic and African American students needed to be actively taught how to function in cooperative groups. Other challenges will require alterations

TABLE 11.2 Challenges to Cooperative Learning Components in Confucian Heritage Culture (CHC) Contexts

Cooperative Learning Component	Challenge in CHC Schools
Rewards	Some may see it as unfair that all students get the same grade, regardless of contribution.
Group Formation	Mixed-ability groups may be uncomfortable due to emphasis on long-term friendships and family relationships.
Communication	Explicit statements of feelings and direct communication may be sacrificed in order to "save face." Challenging or criticizing others will occur less often.
Leadership	Groups may expect a leader or third-party to manage the group members.
Time	Students may need to spend more time getting to know each other and building trust and understanding before beginning tasks.
Teacher Role	Teachers will need to alter their role from "sage on the stage."
Activity Structure	Students may expect more detailed and formal task procedures. Less defined activities may be undesirable.

of the cooperative learning strategies, such as in the version of STAD developed in Vietnam (Pham & Renshaw, 2015). While these problems and solutions will need to be identified and addressed locally, an initial list of challenges to cooperative learning that could require adaptation is listed in Table 11.2.

Without question, culture has an impact on how cooperative learning is enacted and how students benefit. The differences across groups that are evident in the literature may be related to how well cooperative learning methods mesh with existing cultural norms and values. Given these differences, cooperative learning strategies may require adaptation, but the broad idea is relevant across contexts and could serve to improve educational outcomes for all students once adapted for local constraints.

NOTE

1. This chapter incorporates content from Slavin (2017) and Slavin (2000).

REFERENCES

Aronson, E., Blaney, N., Stephan, C., Sikes, J., & Snapp, M. (1978). *The Jigsaw classroom.* Beverly Hills, CA: SAGE.

Arslan, A. (2016). Effect of Jigsaw I technique on teaching Turkish grammar. *Educational Research and Reviews, 11*(8), 635–641.

Barbato, R. A. (2000). *Policy implications of cooperative learning on the achievement and attitudes of secondary school mathematics students* (Doctoral dissertation). Retrieved from ProQuest Dissertations and Theses. (UMI No. 9975337)

Battistich, V., Solomon, D., & Delucchi, K. (1993). Interaction processes and student outcomes in cooperative learning groups. *The Elementary School Journal, 94*(1), 19–32.

Bell, N., Grossen, M., & Perret-Clermont, A.-N. (1985). Peer conflict and psychological growth. In M. W. Berkowitz (Ed.), *Peer conflict and psychological growth* (pp. 41–54). San Francisco, CA: Jossey-Bass.

Borman, G. D., Slavin, R. E., Cheung, A. C. K., Chamberlain, A. M., Madden, N. A., & Chambers, B. (2007). Final reading outcomes of the national randomized field trial of "Success for All." *American Educational Research Journal, 44*(3), 701–731.

Boykin, A. W. (1983). The academic performance of Afro-American children. In J. T. Spence (Ed.), *Achievement and achievement motives: Psychological and sociological approaches* (pp. 324–337). San Francisco, CA: W.H. Freeman.

Boykin, A. W. (1994). Afrocultural expression and its implications for schooling. In E. Hollins, J. King, & W. Hayman (Eds.), *Teaching diverse populations: Formulating a knowledge base* (pp. 243–273). Albany: State University of New York Press.

Bunrasi, J. B. T. (2012). *Algebra I achievement of eighth grade Mexican American students using cooperative learning versus traditional instruction* (Doctoral dissertation). Retrieved from ProQuest Dissertations and Theses. (UMI No. 3522382)

Calhoon, M. B. (2005). Effects of a peer-mediated phonological skill and reading comprehension program on reading skill acquisition for middle school students with reading disabilities. *Journal of Learning Disabilities, 38*(5), 424–433.

Calhoon, M. B., Al Otaiba, S., Cihak, D., King, A., & Avalos, A. (2007). Effects of a peer-mediated program on reading skill acquisition for two-way bilingual first-grade classrooms. *Learning Disability Quarterly, 30*(3), 169–184.

Calhoon, M. B., Al Otaiba, S., Greenberg, D., King, A., & Avalos, A. (2006). Improving reading skills in predominantly Hispanic title 1 first-grade classrooms: The promise of Peer-Assisted Learning Strategies. *Learning Disabilities Research & Practice, 21*(4), 261–272.

Callender, A. A., & McDaniel, M. A. (2009). The limited benefits of rereading educational texts. *Contemporary Educational Psychology, 34*(1), 30–41.

Carger, C. L. (1996). *Of borders and dreams: A Mexican-American experience of urban education.* New York, NY: Teachers College Press.

Carless, D. (2010). *From testing to productive student learning: Implementing formative assessment in Confucian heritage settings.* New York, NY: Routledge.

Chen, Q., & Liu, Y. (2017). The impact of cooperative learning on CHC students' achievements and its changes over the past decade. *International Journal of Higher Education, 6*(2), 75–88.

Chizhik, A. W. (2001). Equity and status in group collaboration: Learning through explanations depends on task characteristics. *Social Psychology of Education, 5*(2), 179–200.

Cohen, E. G., & Lotan, R. A. (2014). *Designing groupwork: Strategies for the heterogeneous classroom.* New York, NY: Teachers College Press.

Cole, M., John-Steiner, V., Scribner, S., & Souberman, E. (Eds.). (1978). *L. S. Vygotsky: Mind in society: Mind in society development of higher psychological processes.* Cambridge, MA: Harvard University Press.

Coleman, J. S. (1961). *The adolescent society.* New York, NY: Free Press of Glencoe.

Damon, W. (1984). Peer education: The untapped potential. *Journal of Applied Developmental Psychology, 5*(4), 331–343.

Devin-Sheehan, L., Feldman, R. S., & Allen, V. L. (1976). Research on children tutoring children: A critical review. *Review of Educational Research, 46*(3), 355–385.

Dietrichson, J., Bøg, M., Filges, T., & Klint Jørgensen, A.-M. (2017). Academic interventions for elementary and middle school students with low socioeconomic status: A systematic review and meta-analysis. *Review of Educational Research, 87*(2), 243–282.

Fuchs, L. S., Fuchs, D., & Karns, K. (2001). Enhancing kindergartners' mathematical development: Effects of Peer-Assisted Learning Strategies. *The Elementary School Journal, 101*(5), 495–510.

Fuchs, L. S., Fuchs, D., Kazdan, S., & Allen, S. (1999). Effects of Peer-Assisted Learning Strategies in reading with and without training in elaborated help giving. *The Elementary School Journal, 99*(3), 201–219.

Gambari, I. A., & Yusuf, M. O. (2016). Effects of computer-assisted Jigsaw II cooperative learning strategy on physics achievement and retention. *Contemporary Educational Technology, 7*(4), 352–367.

Gillies, R. M. (2014). Cooperative learning: Developments in research. *International Journal of Educational Psychology, 3*(2), 125–140.

Good, M. E., Masewicz, S., & Vogel, L. (2010). Latino English language learners: Bridging achievement and cultural gaps between schools and families. *Journal of Latinos & Education, 9*(4), 321–339.

Greenwood, C. R., Delquadri, J. C., & Hall, R. V. (1989). Longitudinal effects of classwide peer tutoring. *Journal of Educational Psychology, 81*(3), 371–383.

Hale, J. E. (1986). *Black children: Their roots, culture, and learning styles.* Baltimore, MD: Johns Hopkins University Press.

Hänze, M., & Berger, R. (2007). Cooperative learning, motivational effects, and student characteristics: An experimental study comparing cooperative learning and direct instruction in 12th grade physics classes. *Learning and Instruction, 17*(1), 29–41.

Hassim, M. H., Mohd, K. A., Mohd, A. H., Khairiyah, M. Y., Hassan, S., & Esa, M. (2004, December). *Enhancing learning through cooperative learning: UTM experience.* Paper presented at Conference on Engineering Education. Kuala Lumpur, Malaysia.

Hofstede, G. H. (2005). *Cultures and organizations: Software of the mind* (2nd ed.). New York, NY: McGraw-Hill.

Hu, G., & Lam, S. T. E. (2010). Issues of cultural appropriateness and pedagogical efficacy: Exploring peer review in a second language writing class. *Instructional Science, 38*(4), 371–394.

Huber, G. L., & Huber, A. A. (2008). Structuring group interaction to promote thinking and learning during small group learning in high school settings.

In R. M. Gillies, A. Ashman, & J. Terwel (Eds.), *The teacher's role in implementing cooperative learning in the classroom* (pp. 110–131). New York, NY: Springer.

Jeong, H., & Hmelo-Silver, C. E. (2016). Seven affordances of computer-supported collaborative learning: How to support collaborative learning? How can technologies help? *Educational Psychologist, 51*(2), 247–265.

Johnson, D. W., & Johnson, F. P. (2013). *Joining together: Group theory and group skills* (11th ed.). Boston, MA: Allyn & Bacon.

Johnson, D. W., & Johnson, R. T. (1998). *Learning together and alone: Cooperative, competitive, and individualistic learning* (5th ed.). Boston, MA: Allyn & Bacon.

Johnson, D. W., & Johnson, R. T. (2008). Social interdependence theory and cooperative learning: The teacher's role. In R. B. Gillies, A. F. Ashman, & J. Terwel (Eds.), *The teacher's role in implementing cooperative learning in the classroom*. Boston, MA: Springer.

Johnson, D. W., & Johnson, R. T. (2014). Using technology to revolutionize cooperative learning: An opinion. *Frontiers in Psychology, 5,* Article 1156.

Johnson, D. W., & Johnson, R. T. (2015). Theoretical approaches to cooperative learning. In R. Gillies (Ed.), *Collaborative learning: Developments in research and practice* (pp. 17–46). New York, NY: Nova.

Johnson, D. W., Johnson, R. T., & Holubec, E. (2008). *Cooperation in the classroom* (8th ed.). Edina, MN: Interaction Book.

Kennedy, K. J., Chan, J. K. S., Fok, P. K., & Yu, W. M. (2008). Forms of assessment and their potential for enhancing learning: conceptual and cultural issues. *Educational Research for Policy and Practice, 7*(3), 197–207.

Kirschner, P. A., & Erkens, G. (2013). Toward a framework for CSCL research. *Educational Psychologist, 48*(1), 1–8.

Kramarski, B., Mevarech, Z. R., & Lieberman, A. (2001). Effects of multilevel versus unilevel metacognitive training on mathematical reasoning. *Journal of Educational Research, 94*(5), 292–300.

Kyndt, E., Raes, E., Lismont, B., Timmers, F., Cascallar, E., & Dochy, F. (2013). A meta-analysis of the effects of face-to-face cooperative learning. Do recent studies falsify or verify earlier findings? *Educational Research Review, 10,* 133–149.

Lampe, J. R., Rooze, G. E., & Tallent-Runnels, M. (1996). Effects of cooperative learning among Hispanic students in elementary social studies. *The Journal of Educational Research, 89*(3), 187–191.

Law, N. W. Y., Yuen, A. H. K., Chan, C. K. K., Yuen, J. K. L., Pan, N. F. C., Lai, M., & Lee, V. S. L. (1999). New experiences, new epistemology, and the pressures of change: The Chinese learner in transition. In C. K. K. Chan & N. Rao (Eds.), *Revisiting the Chinese learner: Changing contexts, changing education* (pp. 89–132). Hong Kong: Springer.

Lee, C. K.-E., Chew, J., Ng, M., & Hing, T. S. (1999, April). *Teachers' use of cooperative learning in their classrooms: case studies of four elementary school teachers.* Paper presented at the American Educational Research Association, Montreal.

Mathes, P. G., & Babyak, A. E. (2001). The effects of Peer-Assisted Learning Strategies for first-grade readers with and without additional mini-skills lessons. *Learning Disabilities Research & Practice, 16*(1), 28–44.

Mathes, P. G., Torgesen, J. K., & Allor, J. H. (2001). The effects of Peer-Assisted Learning Strategies for first-grade readers with and without additional computer-assisted instruction in phonological awareness. *American Educational Research Journal, 38*(2), 371–410.

Mattingly, R. M., & Van Sickle, R. L. (1991). Cooperative learning and achievement in social studies: Jigsaw II. *Social Education, 55*(6), 392–395.

McMaster, K. N., & Fuchs, D. (2002). Effects of cooperative learning on the academic achievement of students with learning disabilities: An update of Tateyama-Sniezek's review. *Learning Disabilities Research & Practice, 17*, 107–117.

Mevarech, Z. R. (1985). The effects of cooperative mastery learning strategies on mathematics achievement. *The Journal of Educational Research, 78*(6), 372–377.

Mevarech, Z. R., & Kramarski, B. (1997). IMPROVE: A multidimensional method for teaching mathematics in heterogeneous classrooms. *American Educational Research Journal, 34*(2), 365–394.

Mitchell, M. G., Montgomery, H., Holder, M., & Stuart, D. (2008). Group Investigation as a cooperative learning strategy: An integrated analysis of the literature. *Alberta Journal of Educational Research, 54*(4), 388–395.

Moreno, R. (2009). Constructing knowledge with an agent-based instructional program: A comparison of cooperative and individual meaning making. *Learning and Instruction, 19*(5), 433–444.

Morrison, C. D. (2014). From "sage on the stage" to "guide on the side": A good start. *International Journal for the Scholarship of Teaching and Learning, 8*(1), Article 4.

Ng, C.-H., & Renshaw, P. (Eds.). (2009). *Reforming learning: Concepts, issues and practice in the Asia-Pacific region.* London, England: Springer.

O'Donnell, A. M. (1996). Effects of explicit incentives on scripted and unscripted cooperation. *Journal of Educational Psychology, 88*(1), 74–86.

O'Donnell, A. M. (2006). The role of peers and group learning. In A. Alexander & P. H. Winne (Eds.), *Handbook of Educational Psychology* (2nd ed., pp. 781–802). Mahwah, NJ: Erlbaum.

O'Donnell, A. M., & Dansereau, D. F. (1992). Scripted cooperation in student dyads: A method for analyzing and enhancing academic learning and performance. In R. Hertz-Lazarowitz & N. Miller (Eds.), *Interaction in cooperative groups: The theoretical anatomy of group learning* (pp. 120–144). New York, NY: Cambridge University Press.

O'Donnell, A. M., & Dansereau, D. F. (2000). Interactive effects of prior knowledge and material format on cooperative teaching. *Journal of Experimental Education, 68*(2), 101–118.

Palincsar, A. S., Brown, A. L., & Martin, S. M. (1987). Peer interaction in reading comprehension instruction. *Educational Psychologist, 22*(3/4), 231–253.

Park, C. C. (2001). Learning style preferences of Armenian, African, Hispanic, Hmong, Korean, Mexican, and Anglo students in American secondary schools. *Learning Environments Research, 4*(2), 175–191.

Pham, T. T. H., & Renshaw, P. (2015). Adapting evidence-based pedagy to local cultural contexts: A design research study of policy borrowing in Vietnam. *Pedagogies: An International Journal, 10*(3), 256–274.

Phuong-Mai, N., Terlouw, C., & Pilot, A. (2005). Cooperative learning vs Confucian heritage culture's collectivism: Confrontation to reveal some cultural conflicts and mismatch. *Asia Europe Journal, 3*(3), 403–419.

Piaget, J. (1926). *The language and thought of the child.* New York, NY: Harcourt Brace.

Psaltis, C., & Duveen, G. (2006). Social relations and cognitive development: The influence of conversation type and representations of gender. *European Journal of Social Psychology, 36*(3), 407–430.

Psaltis, C., & Duveen, G. (2007). Conservation and conversation types: Forms of recognition and cognitive development. *British Journal of Developmental Psychology, 25*(1), 79–102.

Quint, J., Zhu, P., Balu, R., Rappaport, S., & DeLaurentis, M. (2015). *Scaling up the Success for All model of school reform: Final report from the Investing in Innovation (i3) evaluation.* New York, NY: MDRC.

Reid, J. (1992). *The effects of cooperative learning with intergroup competition on the math achievement of seventh grade students.* (ERIC Document Reproduction Service No. ED355106)

Rohrbeck, C. A., Ginsburg-Block, M. D., Fantuzzo, J. W., & Miller, T. R. (2003). Peer-assisted learning interventions with elementary school students: A meta-analytic review. *Journal of Educational Psychology, 95*(2), 240–257.

Rosenshine, B., & Meister, C. (1994). Reciprocal Teaching: A review of the research. *Review of Educational Research, 64*(4), 479–530.

Roseth, C. J., Johnson, D. W., & Johnson, R. T. (2008). Promoting early adolescents' achievement and peer relationships: The effects of cooperative, competitive, and individualistic goal structures. *Psychological Bulletin, 134*(2), 223–246.

Ross, M. C., Seaborn, A. W., & Wilson, E. K. (2002). Is cooperative learning a valuable instructional method for teaching social studies to urban African American students? In *NAAAS Conference Proceedings.* National Association of African American Studies.

Rowan, B., Camburn, E. M., Correnti, R., & Miller, R. (2007). *How comprehensive school reform works: Insights from A Study of School Improvement.* Ann Arbor, MI: University of Michigan.

Schunk, D. H. (2012). *Learning theories: an educational perspective* (6th ed). Boston, MA: Pearson.

Sencibaugh, J. M., & Sencibaugh, A. M. (2016). An analysis of cooperative learning approaches for students with learning disabilities. *Education, 136*(3), 356–364.

Sharan, S., & Shachar, C. (1988). *Language and learning in the cooperative classroom.* New York, NY: Springer.

Sharan, Y., & Sharan, S. (1992). *Expanding cooperative learning through Group Investigation.* New York, NY: Teachers College Press.

Shi, L. (2006). The successors to Confucianism or a new generation? A questionnaire study on Chinese students' culture of learning English. *Language, Culture, and Curriculum, 19*(1), 122–147.

Sills, J., Rowse, G., & Emerson, L. -M. (2016). The role of collaboration in the cognitive development of young children: A systematic review: Collaboration and cognitive development. *Child: Care, Health, and Development, 42*(3), 313–324.

Slavin, R. E. (1983). When does cooperative learning increase student achievement? *Psychological Bulletin, 94*(3), 429–445.

Slavin, R. E. (1994). *Using Student Team Learning* (2nd Ed.). Baltimore, MD: Johns Hopkins University.

Slavin, R. E. (1995). *Cooperative learning: Theory, research, and practice* (2nd ed.). Boston, MA: Allyn and Bacon.

Slavin, R. E. (2000). Reseach on cooperative learning and achievement: What we know, what we need to know. In P. K. Smith & A. D. Pellegrini (Eds.), *Psychology of education: Major themes* (Vol. III, The school curriculum, pp. 533–561). New York, NY: Routledge.

Slavin, R. E. (2009). Cooperative learning. In G. McCulloch & D. Crook (Eds.), *International encyclopedia of education* (pp. 161–178). Abington, England: Routledge.

Slavin, R. E. (2010a). Cooperative learning. In E. Baker, P. Peterson, & B. McGaw (Eds.), *International encyclopedia of education* (3rd ed., pp. 161–178). Oxford, England: Elsevier.

Slavin, R. E. (2010b). Co-operative learning: What makes group-work work? In H. Dumont, D. Istance, & F. Benavides (Eds.), *The nature of learning: Using research to inspire practice* (pp. 161–178). Paris, France: OECD Publishing.

Slavin, R. E. (2013a). Classroom applications of cooperative learning. In S. Graham (Ed.), *APA handbook of educational psychology*. Washington, DC: American Psychological Association.

Slavin, R. E. (2013b). Cooperative learning and achievement: Theory and research. In W. Reynolds, G. Miller, & I. Weiner (Eds.), *Handbook of Psychology* (2nd ed., Vol. 7, pp. 199–212). Hoboken, NJ: Wiley.

Slavin, R. E. (2014a). Cooperative learning and academic achievement: Why does groupwork work? *Anales de Psicología, 30*(3), 785–791.

Slavin, R. E. (2014b). Making cooperative learning POWERFUL! *Educational Leadership, 72*(2), 22–26.

Slavin, R. E. (2015). Cooperative learning in elementary schools. *Education 3–13, 43*(1), 5–14.

Slavin, R. E. (2017). Instruction based on cooperative learning. In R. E. Mayer & P. A. Alexander (Eds.), *Handbook of research on learning and instruction* (2nd ed., pp. 388–404). New York, NY: Routledge.

Slavin, R. E., Cheung, A., Groff, C., & Lake, C. (2008). Effective reading programs for middle and high schools: A best-evidence synthesis. *Reading Research Quarterly, 43*(3), 290–322.

Slavin, R. E., & Karweit, N. L. (1984). Mastery learning and student teams: A factorial experiment in urban general mathematics classes. *American Educational Research Journal, 21*(4), 725–736.

Slavin, R. E., & Karweit, N. L. (1985). Effects of whole class, ability grouped, and individualized instruction on mathematics achievement. *American Educational Research Journal, 22*(3), 351–367.

Slavin, R. E., & Lake, C. (2008). Effective programs in elementary mathematics: A best-evidence synthesis. *Review of Educational Research, 78*(3), 427–515.

Slavin, R. E., Lake, C., Chambers, B., Cheung, A., & Davis, S. (2009). Effective reading programs for the elementary grades: A best-evidence synthesis. *Review of Educational Research, 79*(4), 1391–1466.

Slavin, R. E., Lake, C., & Groff, C. (2009). Effective programs in middle and high school mathematics: A best-evidence synthesis. *Review of Educational Research, 79*(2), 839–911.

Slavin, R. E., Madden, N. A., Chambers, B., & Haxby, B. (Eds.). (2009). *Two million children: Success for All.* Thousand Oaks, CA: Corwin.

Souvignier, E., & Kronenberger, J. (2007). Cooperative learning in third graders' Jigsaw groups for mathematics and science with and without questioning training. *British Journal of Educational Psychology, 77*(4), 755–771.

Spörer, N., Brunstein, J. C., & Kieschke, U. (2009). Improving students' reading comprehension skills: Effects of strategy instruction and reciprocal teaching. *Learning and Instruction, 19*(3), 272–286.

Stevens, R. J., & Durkin, S. (1992). *Using student team reading and student team writing in middle schools: Two evaluations.* Baltimore, MD: Johns Hopkins University.

Stevens, R. J., Madden, N. A., Slavin, R. E., & Farnish, A. M. (1987). Cooperative Integrated Reading and Composition: Two field experiments. *Reading Research Quarterly, 22*(4), 433–454.

Stevens, R. J., & Slavin, R. E. (1995a). Effects of a cooperative learning approach in reading and writing on academically handicapped and nonhandicapped students. *The Elementary School Journal, 95*(3), 241–262.

Stevens, R. J., & Slavin, R. E. (1995b). The cooperative elementary school: Effects on students' achievement, attitudes, and social relations. *American Educational Research Journal, 32*(2), 321–351.

Strand, P. S., Pula, K., & Downs, A. (2015). Social values and preschool behavioral adjustment: A comparative investigation of Latino and European American preschool children. *Cultural Diversity and Ethnic Minority Psychology, 21*(3), 400–408.

Tan, I. G. C., Sharan, S., & Lee, C. K. E. (2007). Group Investigation effects on achievement, motivation, and perceptions of students in Singapore. *The Journal of Educational Research, 100*(3), 142–154.

Thanh, P. T. H. (2014). *Implementing cross-culture pedagogies: Cooperative learning at Confucian heritage cultures.* New York, NY: Springer.

Thanh, P. T. H., Gillies, R., & Renshaw, P. (2008). Cooperative learning (CL) and academic achievement of Asian students: A true story. *International Education Studies, 1*(3), 82–88.

Thurston, A., Tymms, P., Merrell, C., & Conlin, N. (2012). Improving achievement across a whole district with peer tutoring. *Better: Evidence-Based Education, 4*(2), 18–19.

Van Keer, H. (2004). Fostering reading comprehension in fifth grade by explicit instruction in reading strategies and peer tutoring. *British Journal of Educational Psychology, 74*(1), 37–70.

Van Keer, H., & Verhaeghe, J. P. (2005). Comparing two teacher development programs for innovating reading comprehension instruction with regard to teachers' experiences and student outcomes. *Teaching and Teacher Education, 21*(5), 543–562.

Van Keer, H., & Verhaeghe, J. P. (2008). *Strategic reading in peer tutoring dyads in second and fifth-grade classrooms* (Unpublished report). Ghent University, Belgium.

Watkins, A. F. (2002). Learning styles of African American children: A developmental consideration. *Journal of Black Psychology, 28*(1), 3–17.

Webb, N. M. (2008a). Co-operative learning. In T. L. Good (Ed.), *21st century education: A reference handbook.* Thousand Oaks, CA: SAGE.

Webb, N. M. (2008b). Learning in small groups. In T. L. Good (Ed.), *21st Century Education: A Reference Handbook* (pp. 203–211). Los Angeles, CA: SAGE.

Webb, N. M., & Farivar, S. (1994). Promoting helping behavior in cooperative small groups in middle school mathematics. *American Educational Research Journal, 31*(2), 369–395.

Wilson-Jones, L., & Caston, M. C. (2004). Cooperative learning on academic achievement in elementary African American males. *Journal of Instructional Psychology, 31*(4), 280–284.

Wittrock, M. C. (1986). Students' thought processes. In M. C. Wittrock (Ed.), *Handbook of research on teaching* (3rd ed.). New York, NY: Macmillan.

Yang, M., Badger, R., & Yu, Z. (2006). A comparative study of peer and teacher feedback in a Chinese EFL writing class. *Journal of Second Language Writing, 15*(3), 179–200.

SECTION IV

HOW DO I REGULATE MY STUDIES,
AND WHO CAN HELP ME DO IT?

CHAPTER 12

INTEGRATION OF SOCIALIZATION INFLUENCES AND THE DEVELOPMENT OF SELF-REGULATED LEARNING SKILLS

A Social-Cognitive Perspective

Timothy J. Cleary
Anastasia Kitsantas
Stephen Pape
Jacqueline Slemp

Ms. Johnson is an Algebra I teacher in an urban district that has a high proportion of families of low socioeconomic status. Through a school district–university partnership, Ms. Johnson and her colleagues were provided with ongoing, long-term professional development to enhance their activity-based instruction facilitated through the use of an interactive technological tool, TI Navigator. This classroom connectivity technology enables teachers

Big Theories Revisited 2, pages 269–294
Copyright © 2018 by Information Age Publishing
269

to wirelessly communicate with students' graphing calculator and to dynamically project students' mathematical constructions on an interactive board. Students were asked to manipulate mathematical objects, such as the coefficients of a quadratic equation, and to learn from this activity.

Many students struggled to learn Algebra I in Ms. Johnson's class. Some struggled because of limited prior knowledge of mathematics, whereas others possessed weak motivation and strategic skills. Because many of her students exhibited a history of failure in mathematics, they developed negative beliefs, such as low self-efficacy for mathematics, and an overall low level of interest or enjoyment in mathematics. Ms. Johnson's focus within the professional development was on her efforts in modeling, providing feedback, and engaging students in collaborative exchanges to enhance their self-regulated learning. Two students, Jennifer and Desmond, are composite individuals representative of students in Ms. Johnson's classroom. Both students struggled to manage their learning of foundational middle school mathematics content.

All teachers encounter students who struggle to learn concepts taught and/ or who underperform. Although the potential causes of student learning difficulties tend to include multiple factors, (such as weak academic skills or prior knowledge; poor critical reasoning or other underdeveloped cognitive abilities; and weak social-emotional skills), researchers have increasingly focused on the influence of student motivation and self-regulated learning (SRL) skills as well as the sociocultural contexts within which these regulatory skills are developed (Cleary, Velardi, & Schnaidman, 2017; Hadwin & Oshige, 2011; McInerney & King, 2017). This upsurge in research on SRL, which can be defined as a process through which individuals purposefully and strategically manage and direct themselves in the pursuit of goals, has been fueled by several factors. SRL is highly applicable to various domains, contexts, and tasks (Artino, Cleary, Dong, Hemmer, & Durning, 2014; Cleary, 2015; Kolovelonis, Goudas, & Dermitzaki, 2010) and has shown strong linkages to achievement and performance outcomes (Cleary & Kitsantas, 2017; Schunk & Greene, 2017). This construct has also been recognized as a key mechanism for overcoming the many academic, social-emotional, and behavioral challenges that students encounter, such as transitioning between elementary, middle, and high school; establishing friendships; developing a personal identity; or engaging in vocational or post-secondary planning (Cleary, 2018; Grolnick & Raftery-Helmer, 2015).

In the original version of this chapter, Zimmerman (2004) outlined two models of SRL. The first model underscored the overall process through which individuals regulate their thoughts, actions, and learning contexts (three-phase cyclical feedback loop). The second framework informed our understanding of the acquisition and mastery of SRL competencies (four-level model of SRL development). Zimmerman also synthesized research examining the role of cultural and familial processes on the acquisition of students' self-regulatory strategies, and the influence of three socialization processes (i.e., modeling, feedback, and collaboration) on the development of SRL skills and competencies within such contexts. We build on the original chapter in several important ways.

First, although we begin the chapter by focusing on the basic tenets of social-cognitive theory (SCT), we use sociocultural principles to further understand the environment's influence, as outlined within Bandura's (1986) notion of reciprocal determinism. We also shift from a focus on familial influences to teacher influences on SRL and consider contemporary research examining the integrative effects of socialization processes (e.g., modeling, feedback, and collaboration) on student achievement and SRL skills. Of particular interest in our chapter are the different ways in which social-cognitive researchers have conceptualized and studied *emulative* or *guided practice* activities, and whether such findings are consistent across different cultures. We delineate practical applications of SCT and research, and the embedded case study illustrates this theory and research from a more practical and applied perspective. Finally, we conclude the chapter by discussing important areas for future research.

THEORETICAL FOUNDATION AND MODELS

Social-Cognitive Theory and Sociocultural Perspectives

SCT has its historical roots in the pioneering work of Albert Bandura (1986, 1997) and includes a core set of assumptions and principles such as reciprocal determinism, vicarious learning, and personal agency. At the heart of SCT is *reciprocal determinism*, which depicts human functioning as a dynamic set of reciprocal relations among personal, behavioral, and environmental determinants. This principle explains human behavior as both an outcome and causal determinant of cognitive and environmental factors. The strength and nature of the reciprocal relations are not fixed, nor are they equivalent across all situations or individuals (Bandura, 1986). In fact, two students may exhibit the same behavioral concern yet display those behaviors for different reasons. For example, Jennifer and Desmond both struggle to devote the time and effort needed to adequately prepare for an upcoming mathematics exam. However, the primary cause of Desmond's test preparation struggles involves the distractions and noise that he frequently encounters at home (i.e., environmental influence), whereas Jennifer's challenges arise from her poor sense of self-efficacy and high levels of anxiety (i.e., personal influences) resulting from a long history of struggling to learn mathematics concepts.

The importance of social contexts and interaction between individuals and their social worlds are further underscored through concepts of vicarious learning, human agency, and SRL within the context of reciprocal determinism (Bandura, 1986, 2001; Schunk, 2016). In essence, although humans can learn from watching others, they are not simply passive recipients of information nor subject to the whims of environmental influences; they possess the capacity to exercise strategic and regulatory management and influence over their own actions and their environment (Bandura, 2001). A key determinant of this agentic, regulatory approach to interacting with others and the broader social world are individuals' *self-efficacy beliefs*. In the case of Jennifer, despite extensive support from her tutor and parents, she will likely give up easily and avoid difficult schoolwork because she has an overall weak sense of self-efficacy and personal agency. In short, SCT emphasizes the reciprocal and deterministic influences between individual-oriented SRL and the social or environmental context (Bandura, 1986; Cleary & Kitsantas, 2017).

Despite the clear intersection between social and individual processes, some researchers have characterized SRL research conducted from a SCT perspective as primarily individualistic with the social context either (a) not examined, (b) separated from individual SRL, or (c) manipulated as an independent variable (Hadwin & Oshige, 2011). Zimmerman (2004) illustrated this premise in his review of research examining the influence of social variables (e.g., type of parenting style) and culture (e.g., differences in SRL due to ethnic culture) on student SRL; factors that were the focus of much research over the past few decades. Thus, research has often examined SRL as "an individual process that is influenced by social aspects" (Järneoja, Järvelä, & Malmberg, 2015, p. 206) rather than as an individual process that is influenced by the cultural context in which it is developed (McInerney & King, 2017). From our perspective, it is important for SCT researchers to devote greater attention to the role of sociocultural factors more broadly, and to consider the nature of the actual interactions that occur between individuals and the contexts in which they learn.

According to a sociocultural perspective, all learning is situated within the learner's social context (Cole, John-Steiner, Scribner, & Souberman, 1978). Specifically, all higher mental functioning, including SRL, is first developed through shared cognition and joint activity. These functions develop first on the interpsychological plane as a "more knowing other" supports and directs the activities of the learner who internalizes the ways of behaving within the cultural context (e.g., family processes, classroom contexts; Diaz, Neal, & Amaya-Williams 1990). The sociocultural perspective "commonly emphasize[s] intersubjectivity and interpersonal interaction" (Järvenoja,

Järvelä, & Malmberg, 2015, p. 206). Although we do not place primary emphasis on a sociocultural theoretical framework in this chapter, we attempt to stretch some of the traditional boundaries of the SCT perspective by emphasizing the role of culture, both in a global sense and relative to classroom contexts (see Figure 12.1), and by examining emerging research that considers the dynamic interplay between individual SRL and the sociocultural and socialization influences embedded within the different levels of SRL development. Before addressing sociocultural and socialization influences or reviewing contemporary research on SRL from a SCT perspective, we first describe the meaning of individual SRL from this perspective.

A Cyclical Process Account of SRL

The three-phase cyclical loop is defined by the specific goal that an individual chooses to pursue and consists of three interdependent, multi-process phases: *forethought, performance control,* and *self-reflection.* Forethought involves individuals' proactive attempts to prepare to learn or complete an activity such as task analysis and strategic planning (Cleary et al., 2017). Because SRL is an effortful process, engaging in forethought processes and exhibiting adaptive motivational beliefs prior to performance optimally prepares individuals to strategically and purposefully approach and successfully complete learning activities. Jennifer, our composite student, struggles to complete schoolwork effectively because she creates ambiguous goals (e.g., "to do my best"), exhibits deficient strategic planning skills, and possesses negative self-efficacy perceptions.

As students shift into the performance phase, they enlist strategies to learn or perform optimally and seek to monitor their behaviors and performance. Regulated learners typically utilize an array of strategies to optimize task performance, enhance motivation and attention, and/or enlist social resources to overcome challenges (Pressley & Harris, 2008; Weinstein & Acee, 2013). As first-generation college-bound students, Jennifer and Desmond may not have access to effective models that illustrate how strategies can be used to overcome academic challenges. Of particular concern with Desmond is that he often relies on rehearsal and other rudimentary learning strategies and struggles to motivate or direct his attention effectively.

Regulated individuals also engage in self-observation during learning to generate feedback or information about their learning progress, quality of behavior, or optimal environmental conditions (Zimmerman, 2000). Consistent with other underdeveloped SRL skills, Desmond does not pay attention to or gather information about the quality of his learning when using the TI Navigator system. His inattention results in poor self-awareness, which undermines his performance.

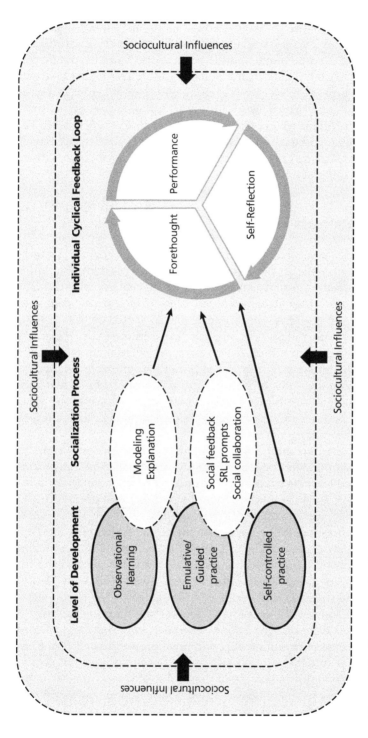

Figure 12.1   Depiction of an integrated model of sociocultural factors, socialization processes, individual-oriented SRL, and levels of SRL development. The link between socialization processes and the levels of development are indicated by the overlap between circles (primary influence) or dashed line (secondary influence) at each respective level. Sociocultural factors are assumed to influence all social and SRL processes.

Regulated students then engage in a series of self-reflection phase processes, such as self-evaluating their performance relative to pre-established goals, identifying reasons for their success or failure (i.e., attributions), and hypothesizing about the actions needed to improve performance (i.e., adaptive inferences). From a cyclical SRL perspective, engaging in self-reflection is critical because it determines whether students will adapt or change their strategic behaviors. Jennifer often gets "stuck" because she lacks sufficient feedback about her behaviors and performance and thus, engages in limited forms of reflection characterized by making debilitating ability attributions (i.e., "I failed because I am not competent") and defensive inferences (i.e., avoidance and procrastination).

SOCIOCULTURAL INFLUENCES AND SELF-REGULATION

Consistent with Figure 12.1, research supports the influence of social and cultural variables on an individual's use of SRL strategies (McInerney, 2011; Nota, Soresi, & Zimmerman, 2004). Zimmerman (2004) revealed that, although variation exists in the specific types of SRL strategies used in different cultures or regions, the importance and use of SRL strategies are emphasized across cultures. He also emphasized that family contexts and parental behaviors, such as parenting styles, modeling, encouragement, and parental involvement, influence a child's SRL abilities; a finding that more recent research has supported (Cheung & Pomerantz, 2012; Lee, Hamman, & Lee, 2007).

In addition to familial or parental influences, teacher behaviors and classroom contexts are other types of sociocultural contexts that influence student SRL development (Cobb, Boufi, McClain, & Whitenack, 1997; Cobb, Wood, & Yackel, 1993; Gresalfi, Martin, Hand, & Greeno, 2009; Perry, 1998; Reeve & Jang, 2006). Several investigations have highlighted the relationship between autonomy-supportive classroom practices and support for student SRL behaviors. In an investigation with elementary students and teachers, Perry (1998) reported that student SRL abilities were found to be higher in classrooms in which they were encouraged to be more autonomous and to evaluate their own and their peers' work, and when they felt teachers were more collaborative than managerial. More recent work has focused on the nature of teacher interactions with students and the specific teaching practices that can lead to students experiencing higher levels of autonomy. Reeve and Jang (2006) conducted research to illustrate the key practices that differentiated teachers who used an autonomy-supportive versus controlling style, and how such practices influenced student motivation. The authors reported that listening, creating time for independent work, giving students opportunities to talk, praising empowerment and mastery, encouraging effort, offering process-enabling hints, being responsive to student questions/comments, and acknowledging student experience were all positively related to student perceptions of autonomy.

The importance of autonomy-supportive classroom practices has been observed in other cultures. Sierens, Vansteenkiste, Goossens, Soenens, and Dochy (2009) examined whether Belgian student perceptions of teacher autonomy support and structure (i.e., clear expectations on student behavior, guidance in task completion to ensure goals are accomplished, and competence-relevant feedback) predicted SRL strategy use, including cognitive and metacognitive strategies. Cognitive strategies refer to those used to acquire information during the learning process (e.g., elaboration, rehearsal), whereas metacognitive strategies are used in order to direct and manage the learning process (e.g., planning, self-feedback). Autonomy support and structure were both found to be positively correlated with cognitive and metacognitive aspects of SRL. It is also of importance that structure (student-centeredness) was found to be a positive predictor of SRL, on average, in high autonomy-supportive classrooms, but not in low autonomy-supportive classrooms. For this reason, it may be most beneficial for teachers to choose to implement both autonomy support and structure in order to best facilitate student SRL development.

Similarly, perceptions of an autonomy supportive classroom were found to be positively correlated with SRL strategy use in a study including Iranian college students (Abdulhay, Rahimi, & Samigorganroodi, 2016). An autonomy supportive classroom was defined as a classroom in which the teacher instills confidence in students and encourages personal effort, as measured by a questionnaire Lin (2004) derived from Deci and Ryan's (1985) learning climate scale. The results showed that perceived autonomy support was positively correlated with self-reported SRL use. Researchers indicated that these results make sense from a motivational perspective, as classrooms with autonomy support provide students with characteristics that are necessary to engage in SRL strategies (e.g., vigor, eagerness). These results further emphasize the importance of autonomy support in the classroom.

Within the mathematics education community, the social context of the classroom has been examined for its impact on the developing mathematical competence of learners (Gresalfi et al., 2009). Early work in this field considered the development of mathematical thinking to be an apprenticeship where the classroom is considered a microculture that fosters ways of thinking based on the norms that are developed for mathematical behavior. The classroom discourse is the medium through which teachers construct social and sociomathematical norms for participation within the microculture (McClain & Cobb, 2001). Gresalfi et al. (2009) examined "the construction of systems of competence" (p. 49) to understand the development of competence as a function of the mathematical norms set for participation within the classroom. Accordingly, competence may be defined differently depending upon the demands of the classroom culture. That is, if students are rewarded for an answer, then the student who is able to generate an answer is considered competent. If students are rewarded for their explanations of their answers, then students who are able to produce cogent explanations that reveal their mathematical behavior are considered competent. These varied classroom contexts produce outcomes for mathematical thinking that varies accordingly.

SOCIALIZATION PROCESSES AND THE DEVELOPMENT OF SRL SKILLS

In addition to the influence of broad classroom factors as sociocultural determinants, SCT researchers have focused on the role of several socialization processes, such as social feedback, social modeling, and social collaboration, on the development of individual SRL. *Social modeling*, which is often referred to as observational learning, can be viewed as an umbrella term that includes more than a simple demonstration of a behavior or skill. Researchers who espouse an SCT perspective have explored the influence of *cognitive modeling* (i.e., model verbalizes thoughts and reasons for performing), *participant modeling* (i.e., model provides guided motoric assistance after an individual observes the model perform a behavior or strategy), and *coping modeling* (i.e., model initially demonstrates errors or mistakes and then self-corrects and succeeds) on students' learning and skill development (Schunk, 2016; Zimmerman, 2004). Regardless of the type of modeling, the key point is that student beliefs, behaviors, and affect can be influenced by simply watching others. It is through these models that students learn what it means to act strategically within their cultural context.

Modeling alone, however, does not typically lead to mastery of strategic skills. Students often need practice in using the skills and feedback to guide self-improvement (Cleary et al., 2017; Hattie & Timperley, 2007; Zimmerman, 2004). *Social feedback*, which is often thought of as data or information about one's level of understanding, skills, or performance, can vary in focus (e.g., outcome versus process), specificity, and effectiveness (Hattie & Timperley, 2007; Shute, 2008). For example, feedback can pertain to individuals' grades on tests or projects, behaviors or strategic processes, or overall attributes or capacities (Hattie & Timperley, 2007). As described above, we hold that this feedback conveys cultural norms for how to be strategic or competent within the culture of the classroom community (Gresalfi et al., 2009; McClain & Cobb, 2001). From a theoretical lens, it is important to recognize that all forms of feedback influence, at least to some degree, the ways in which individuals reflect (Shute, 2008). For example, if Desmond received outcome feedback from Ms. Johnson about a grade of 84 he received on a mathematics exam, he will naturally use that information to evaluate personal progress relative to a previous test or in relation to a personal goal. In contrast, if Ms. Johnson provided process feedback to Jennifer beginning with the strengths of her strategic behavior while supporting growth in effective use of strategies, Jennifer may more readily begin to reflect on ways to modify or adapt her behavior.

Social-cognitive theorists have also embraced the premise that reciprocal interactions between individuals and the social context influence student development of SRL skills (Cleary et al., 2017). Thus, the excessive amount of distraction and crowded workspace at home often adversely influence the quality of Desmond's schoolwork (i.e., social factors impact behavior). However, he also possesses the potential to exert control over and influence, at least to some degree, his home environment (i.e., behavior influences social factors). Through conversations with his parents or proactive use of regulatory strategies, such as seeking help or optimally structuring a study space at home, it may be possible for Desmond to create effective learning contexts that closely align with his individual needs. The joint effort between a social agent and students to help them develop and sustain high quality task competencies and SRL skills is labeled by social cognitive researchers as *social collaboration*, a term that roughly corresponds to what sociocultural theorists might call interactions between a "more knowing other" and the learner (Cole et al., 1978).

During a typical collaborative exchange, a social change agent works with students to help them identify areas of "challenge," coaches students to generate strategic plans to address those challenges, and supports students to evaluate their progress and learning over time. During social collaboration, the social agent asks questions, provides comments or feedback, and/or remodels key strategies to help individuals think and act in more empowered, strategic ways (Cleary et al., 2017; Harris, Graham, & Santangelo, 2013; Pape, Bell, & Yetkin-Ozdemir, 2013). Thus, social collaboration involves an integration of multiple socialization influences in a given context (i.e., modeling, feedback, prompts, and reciprocal interactions).

Although each of these three socialization influences have been shown to exhibit distinct influences on SRL processes, social-cognitive theorists have increasingly been interested in examining their collective influence across a four-level model of SRL development (Cleary et al., 2017; Pape et al., 2013; Zimmerman, 2000, 2004). In the following two sections, we provide an overview of this developmental framework and then explore how social-cognitive researchers have examined the integrative influence of multiple socialization processes within one particular developmental level, emulation.

Socialization Model of SRL Development

Zimmerman (2000) delineated the role of various socialization processes across four dynamic, complementary, and developmentally-sequenced levels: *observation, emulation, self-control,* and *self-regulation.* It is with this model that one can more readily understand the integration of multiple socialization processes and their collective influence on the development of individual SRL competencies. The four-level model was developed based on the assumption that socialization influences predominate in the early stages of learning, but that over time students learn to independently practice these skills and to use their own representations of a skill (rather than the model) to guide behavior.

Although social-cognitive theorists recognize that SRL skills can be developed in a variety of ways, they emphasize that learning often begins at the observation level. At this level, individuals learn vicariously by observing models perform strategic actions or exhibit other types of regulatory processes, such as planning, monitoring, and self-evaluating (Cleary, Zimmerman, & Keating, 2006; Pape et al., 2013; Zimmerman & Kitsantas, 1997). For example, given Jennifer's deficient strategic skills, her teacher decides to demonstrate how she can use concept maps and self-quizzing techniques to learn course content in conjunction with time management, relaxation, and self-reinforcement strategies. Extensive research has shown that models can exert positive effects on student learning and SRL skills and certain types of modeling are particularly beneficial to individuals when first learning a skill (Schunk, 1981; Schunk & Hansen, 1985; Schunk, Hansen, & Cox, 1987; Kitsantas, Zimmerman, & Cleary, 2000; Zimmerman & Kitsantas, 2002). At the emulative level, the social agent creates a structured, guided practice environment to help students use and refine their strategic and regulatory skills. As students engage in this form of collaborative practice, the social agent provides feedback, prompts, additional instruction, remodeling, and other types of collaborative supports to refine and support students' understanding and skill development (Rosenshine, 1983).

As students shift to the self-control level, the influence of socialization processes becomes less pronounced. It is at this level that students are able to proficiently display the modeled behaviors in the absence of a model. Although individuals still use their symbolic representation of the modeled behaviors to guide their self-controlled actions (Zimmerman, 2004), they are much more independent in their use and practice of regulatory skills. Despite the diminished role of socialization processes, learners still have the freedom to proactively seek out feedback, encouragement, or other social supports as needed. At the final level, the self-regulated level, learners become skilled at using personal standards of performance or authentic task outcomes as the basis for making adjustments and adaptations to their behaviors. This type of skill level typically is reached after students gain sufficient practice in using strategic or regulatory skills in unstructured, complex, or dynamic settings.

Influence of Socialization Processes During Emulation

Each of the four levels of SRL development have been examined by researchers over the past few decades (Kolovelonis et al., 2010; Pape et al., 2013; Schunk, Hansen, & Cox, 1987; Zimmerman, 2004). In recent years, however, researchers have emphasized the emulative or guided practice level, with particular emphasis placed on the collective influence of multiple socialization processes (i.e., feedback, SRL instruction, additional modeling, and collaboration; Cleary et al., 2006; Kitsantas et al., 2000; Kolovelonis et al., 2010; Zimmerman & Kitsantas, 2002). Across most of these studies, students observed a model demonstrate a particular behavior or strategy (observation level) and then received some combination of feedback, SRL instruction, and/or other forms of social collaboration as part of guided practice.

From a historical perspective, Schunk and colleagues conducted the first set of studies addressing the combined effects of modeling, feedback, and SRL instruction as part of guided practice sessions (Schunk, 1981; Schunk & Hanson, 1985; Schunk & Swartz, 1993a, 1993b). A key finding from this line of research was that combining SRL instruction with social feedback during guided practice sessions was quite beneficial to student achievement and SRL skills. Zimmerman and Kitsantas (1996, 1997, 1999) extended this work in a series of studies to investigate the role of self-recording, rather than social feedback, as the mechanism through which students gathered information. High school students were randomly assigned to one of five groups resulting from variation across two independent variables, goals (process or outcome) and self-recording (yes or no), plus a no-practice and no self-recording comparison group. Process goals and self-recording outcomes or processes during guided practice led to enhanced dart throwing skills, self-efficacy, interest, and self-reactions. In a similar study, Zimmerman and Kitsantas (1997) found that, in addition to a main effect for self-recording, those who shifted their goals from process to outcome goals performed the best, exhibited the highest efficacy beliefs, and displayed the most positive self-reactions. Zimmerman and Kitsantas (1999) reported comparable findings in a study involving a writing practice activity with high school students.

Some studies have considered the effects of multiple types of social modeling plus social feedback on student SRL and achievement outcomes. Kitsantas et al. (2000) and Kitsantas and Zimmerman (2002) used social feedback combined with different modeling conditions (coping, mastery, no model) in two contexts, dart throwing and sentence-revision writing problems, respectively. In Kitsantas et al. (2000), social feedback involved giving positive statements to students when their dart-throwing technique was correct. Zimmerman and Kitsantas (2002) emphasized a similar type of social feedback, which involved giving positive statements to students when they performed correctly each of the 12 practice sentence-revision problems. Students who received coping models tended to outperform and display more adaptive regulatory processes than students in mastery or no modeling conditions. Further, students who received feedback about their progress in using the modeled strategies exhibited higher achievement, self-efficacy, interest, and self-reactions than those who did not receive the social feedback.

Taken together, social-cognitive research has shown that modeling plus socialization processes during guided practice sessions, such as feedback and SRL prompts, can lead to positive student outcomes when social agents directly provide feedback to students during practice or when they provide SRL prompts to help students engage in more self-directed practice in their presence. In both situations, social agents serve a key role in structuring and guiding students' practice of strategic skills.

Although not extensive, the positive influence of emulation and guided practice sessions on skill development has been extended to other cultures (Kolovelonis et al., 2010; Kolovelonis, Goudas, Dermitsaki, & Kitsantas, 2013). Kolovelonis et al. (2010) randomly assigned sixth grade Greek students to 1 of 4 conditions (social feedback, process goal, and self-recording; social feedback, no process goal, and self-recording; no social feedback, process goal, and self-recording; and practice only control). Immediately following modeling of the dart-throwing technique, students practiced using this strategy over two sessions of 8 minutes each. The key finding in this study was that students who received social feedback during the initial practice and then were prompted to set process goals and to self-record their use of the dart-throwing strategy, showed higher dart-throwing performance and reported higher levels of motivational beliefs compared to other experimental and control group conditions. Thus, social feedback and self-recording can be used as complementary procedures when students are expected to engage in some activity across multiple practice sessions.

More recently, social cognitive researchers have emphasized the role that *social collaboration* can have as part of guided practice sessions or the emulation level. As mentioned previously, social collaboration reflects a joint or collaborative effort between social agents and students that often involves ongoing, reciprocal interactions and dialogue. Thus, students and other social agents can direct their learning by asking questions, providing feedback to the social agent, and/or generating their own strategies based on variations of modeled behaviors (Cleary et al., 2017; English &

Kitsantas, 2013; Pape et al., 2013; Zimmerman, Moylan, Hudesman, White, & Flugman, 2011). Of particular interest in this section are contemporary field-based studies that incorporate social feedback and social modeling processes, but that also embrace the importance of reciprocal, collaborative social exchanges between social agents and students to promoting SRL skill development during students' attempts to learn over time.

Zimmerman et al. (2011) examined the effectiveness of a comprehensive self-regulatory intervention that exposed students to coping modeling techniques where instructors taught students to detect errors and adapt their strategy accordingly while solving problems in mathematics. Instructors in the experimental group also emphasized the importance of self-reflection activities and the use of feedback about mistakes and errors to make changes to their strategic approaches to learning. Technical college students completed performance (mathematics periodic and final examination), mathematics self-efficacy, and self-evaluation measures. Participants exposed to the intervention significantly outperformed control students in the final examination and reported positive career path decisions related to other mathematics courses, though no differences were observed in self-efficacy or self-evaluation.

Further, in a teaching experiment in a seventh-grade mathematics classroom, Pape, Bell, & Yetkin (2003) supported student strategy development by creating a collaborative context in which students modeled their strategic behavior for one another. Prior to an assessment, students stated their study strategies. Prior to receiving their test results, they were asked to state again what they did to prepare for the test and to estimate their grade on the assessment. Finally, they were asked to state attributions for their results. Several times during the study, students were asked to describe, model, and classify their strategies into categories initially established by Zimmerman and Martinez-Pons (1986, 1988) and later elaborated by Pape and Wang (2003). Pape and colleagues (2003) argued that constructing a context conducive to SRL development requires "multiple representations and rich mathematical tasks, classroom discourse, environmental scaffolding of strategic behavior, and varying needs for explicitness and support" (p. 179).

Over the past decade, Cleary and colleagues have conducted a series of studies to examine the implementation and effectiveness of an applied, comprehensive intervention program called the Self-Regulation Empowerment Program (SREP; Cleary & Platten, 2013; Cleary, Platten, & Nelson, 2008; Cleary et al., 2017) on middle school and high school students' achievement and SRL processes. Across case study and experimental studies, SREP has been shown to be a potentially influential intervention for adolescent achievement and SRL skill development. For example, Cleary et al. (2017) experimentally tested the effects of SREP on middle school students' SRL skills and mathematics skills relative to a comparison condition.

The authors reported that the SREP students exhibited statistically significant changes in their strategic thinking at posttest and 2-month follow-up and a more positive trend in achievement scores over 2 years in middle school relative to the comparison condition (Cleary et al., 2017). We expand on the core components of SREP in the following section. It is there that we illustrate in more concrete terms the methods and approaches that educators can use to integrate various socialization processes as they instruct students to learn.

APPLICATIONS OF SRL DEVELOPMENT MODELS IN SCHOOL CONTEXTS

In this section, we provide a descriptive overview of SREP and an SRL-infused classroom program to illustrate how socialization processes can be infused within a broader sociocultural context. These two illustrations call attention to the importance of social feedback and social modeling within a set of reciprocal, social collaborative interactions between the social agent (teachers, SREP coach) and students in school contexts.

SRL Development in an Algebra I Classroom Context

In this section, we continue to develop the case of Ms. Johnson's Algebra I classroom and her students Jennifer and Desmond. Specifically, we focus on how Ms. Johnson implicitly infuses socialization processes within her classroom instruction, specifically within the norms of what it means to learn mathematics in her classroom. Ms. Johnson participated in a 2-year professional development program that helped her develop skills to effectively engage students in student-centered, activity-based, technology-enhanced instruction. The TI Navigator is a classroom connectivity technology that enables teachers to wirelessly communicate with students' graphing calculator and to dynamically project students' mathematical constructions on an interactive board during instruction. Students were asked to manipulate mathematical objects, such as the coefficients of a quadratic equation, using a graphing calculator and to learn from this activity (Pape, 2015).

Of particular interest in this section are the ways in which Ms. Johnson used socialization processes to support her students' participation in and regulation of their learning experiences. Video recordings of her instruction during a quadratics unit were captured across 5 days (Pape, 2015). The present description is based on an instructional model developed by Pape et al. (2013) that, similar to SREP, integrates the three-phase model of SRL and the four-level model of SRL development. In short, this model describes teacher behaviors during each of the three phases of SRL (forethought, observation, and reflection) and argues that the nature of teachers' behaviors must change in relation to their understanding of their students' levels of SRL development (i.e., observation, emulation, self-control, and self-regulation).

Instruction at the observation and emulation levels include social modeling, social feedback, and social collaboration experiences. During the observation level, teachers provide worthwhile tasks that deeply involve students in learning through their own activity, elicit students' prior knowledge, model strategy selection, and practice self-affirming statements during the forethought phase. Next, the teacher conducts a think aloud to model the use of a heuristic or coping with a mistake. Finally, the teacher models reflection as he/she thinks aloud about his/her solution.

This work began when Ms. Johnson collaborated with her mathematics department colleague to develop a series of lessons to teach their Algebra I students foundational knowledge related to quadratic equations and their associated graph, the parabola. The first lesson provided students an opportunity to manipulate the coefficients of a quadratic equation and to observe these changes to the parabola as they changed one term at a time. Students then developed a conjecture about the relationship between each coefficient and the shape, size, orientation, and position of the parabola. These tasks guided students in knowledge construction, but the students themselves were challenged to engage, notice changes, and make conjectures to represent their constructed understanding.

As the class began to engage with these activities, Ms. Johnson activated her students' knowledge of linear equations to build connections between their knowledge of the slope of a linear equation and the leading coefficient of the quadratic equation. Ms. Johnson modeled how to manipulate the leading coefficient of a quadratic equation using the technology to notice the connection between her manipulation of the quadratic equation's leading term by describing the associated changes in the parabola as she slowly changed the value of the coefficient. This focus on noticing or attending is an essential characteristic of active learning. Further, she provided social feedback as she interactively elicited students' present understandings and provided feedback on these responses to her queries. Her dynamic conversation eliciting students' statements about the mathematical activity in which they previously engaged is a form of social collaboration, as she orchestrated the social construction of knowledge with her students. Finally, the teacher engaged the students in summarizing their learning by again asking questions about the patterns of changes they observed and leading them to develop mathematical conjectures.

During the emulation phase, teachers may do some of these same behaviors, but they will begin to provide space for students to engage in structured practice as they slowly withdraw social support and students begin to take on the modeled behaviors. Emulative or guided practice sessions may include questioning to stimulate students' prior knowledge or previously used strategies before beginning the task or guided practice of a strategy (Pape et al., 2013). Following this initial activity with the leading coefficient of a quadratic equation, Ms. Johnson's students went through a similar process related to the quadratic equation's constant term. They initially worked individually but were quickly brought together in table groups to explore their initial observations. As part of social collaboration, they were asked to consolidate their "noticings" and state a conjecture about the impact of changing the constant term in a quadratic equation. Finally, students were brought back to whole-class discussion where Ms. Johnson asked students to discuss their understanding, which they collectively refined into a summary statement.

SRL Development as Part of SREP

Although SREP studies have differed in methodology (mixed model case study designs and experimental methodology), target content area (i.e., mathematics vs. biology), and context (i.e., middle school vs. high school), the basic premise is that trained SREP coaches provide modeling, feedback, and social collaboration experiences to help students learn and refine the quality of their strategic skills. Thus, in addition to providing direct instruction in strategies and SRL skill via modeling, students receive continuous feedback about their strategic skills and are afforded structured opportunities to dynamically interact with their peers and SREP coaches.

SREP is grounded in the three-phase cyclical feedback loop and the four-level model of SRL development. Thus, it emphasizes how socialization supports implemented during the observation, emulation, and self-control levels of SRL development can influence how individuals develop skills in cyclical regulatory thinking and action.

Instructional Overview

Trained coaches use a semi-structured protocol approach to administer SREP sessions to groups of four to five students one to two times per week for 30 to 45 minutes over the course of three to four months (Cleary et al., 2017; Cleary & Platten, 2013; Cleary et al., 2008). SREP instructional modules consist of three distinct, albeit overlapping activities: (a) foundational, (b) strategy learning and practice, and (c) self-reflection. The foundational modules build rapport between coaches and students, cultivate adaptive student attitudes and motivation, and introduce students to core program themes. SREP coaches then use a structured weekly instructional format (review, analysis, practice, plan, self-direction [RAPPS]) to provide modeling, feedback, and social collaboration experiences during structured practice sessions. The final broad component of SREP instruction involves a *self-reflection module.* SRL coaches administer this module after students receive performance feedback regarding an outcome of interest (e.g., mathematic test grades).

Socialization Processes Within SREP

RAPPS is an instructional format that naturally embeds aspects of the four-level model of SRL development in a weekly cycle of strategic action and reflection. It focuses on observational learning (modeling), guided practice sessions (feedback, modeling, and collaboration), and self-directed practice opportunities outside the presence of a SREP coach. During the first session in a week, the coach engages students in the *review* (R) step by "checking in" with them regarding challenges experienced when using strategies on their own, and in the *analysis* (A) step by discussing expectations and understanding of upcoming assignments or assessments as well as students' specific concerns (social collaboration). By gathering information about student successes, challenges, and areas in need of improvement, the coach is better able to provide specific feedback and encouragement to students and to structure the upcoming week's lessons on relevant strategies.

The majority of RAPPS instruction focuses on student *practice* (P); it is at this step when SREP coaches discuss and model strategies (observation level) and provide students with opportunities to practice strategies to address their individualized challenges (emulation level). Coaches overtly demonstrate the steps for using a time management worksheet or a test preparation worksheet (behavioral modeling), use think aloud techniques to reveal their thoughts during strategy use (cognitive modeling), and/or model the act of making mistakes but persisting and self-correcting (coping modeling). During these practice activities, coaches provide nuanced and specific feedback about students' use of strategies, offer encouragement and guidance, and encourage students to ask questions, generate their own ideas about potential strategies to learn, or make suggestions about focal activities during SREP, an aspect of social collaboration.

During the fourth step, *planning* (P)—that is, typically the last 5 minutes of the final SREP session each week—students create a weekly plan that specifies the strategies they intend to use when completing schoolwork. The last RAPPS step, *self-direction* (S), most closely aligns with the self-controlled level of development because it occurs outside the presence of a SREP coach. Although students still clearly rely on the representation of modeled actions as well as monitoring forms provided by SREP coaches to guide their thinking, students engage in strategic actions without receiving immediate feedback or other supports from others.

The *weekly feedback loop* is directly aligned with weekly RAPPS instruction and focuses on students' use of learning and SRL strategies. Each week, the regulatory question being addressed involves, "How well do I learn and use strategies to complete my schoolwork each week?" To illustrate, at the beginning of each week SREP coaches engage students in a reflection activity regarding their use of strategies learned during the prior weeks (R). Students and coaches then use this discussion to plan upcoming modeling and guided practice strategy sessions (A). After students practice using these strategies (P), they make another plan about which strategies to focus on when completing homework or studying for the upcoming week (P). A new cycle is created during the first SREP session the following week when the coaches and students review progress of their self-controlled practice of strategies at home (S).

Another characteristic of SREP is the use of projects from students' coursework as context for strategy choice, implementation, and monitoring. At these sessions, the SREP coach administers the self-reflection module, a structured process through which students evaluate performance outcomes relative to self-standards (e.g., prior grades, personal outcome goals), brainstorm potential reasons for their performance, and state adaptations needed prior to the next assessment or assignment. During this activity, the SREP coach attempts to steer student thinking about failure and success to variables that are controllable and most linked to success, namely their effort in using learning and regulatory strategies (Borkowski, Weyhing, & Carr, 1988) emphasized during SREP. Unlike the weekly feedback loop, the *outcome feedback loop* is designed to help students address the question, "Did my practice in using strategies over the past few weeks enable me to attain my desired performance outcome?" This broad cyclical loop subsumes several of the weekly feedback strategy-oriented feedback loops mentioned earlier.

SREP emphasizes the development of students' cyclical thinking and action by immersing them in socialization experiences that correspond to the observation, emulation, and/or self-controlled levels of instruction. Further, by guiding students to engage in the weekly feedback loops targeting the *process* of learning and the broad feedback loop focused on *performance outcomes*, students are taught that their strategic actions are linked to the outcomes they hope to attain (Cleary et al., 2017; Zimmerman & Kitsantas, 1997, 1999).

FUTURE DIRECTIONS FOR SRL RESEARCH

In this chapter, we highlighted SCT research that examined the influence of specific socialization processes (e.g., modeling, feedback, collaboration, and SRL prompts) and sociocultural factors (e.g., culture, classroom contexts) on the development of SRL skill. We also provided school-based, practical examples to illustrate how socialization processes emphasized in social-cognitive paradigms (e.g., modeling, feedback, and monitoring) can be integrated within classroom contexts. We have attempted to stretch some of the traditional boundaries of the SCT models and perspectives by considering the dynamic interplay between individual SRL and socialization influences and by providing a more detailed depiction of guided practice and social collaboration. There are some thorny questions and neglected areas, however, that should be considered in future research.

In our chapter, we indicated that guided practice activities that infuse core SCT socialization processes, such as modeling, social feedback, and social collaboration, have positive effects on U.S. students' achievement and regulatory processes. While there is evidence that socialization processes during guided practice lead to adaptive performance and regulatory outcomes with Greek students, there is a paucity of cross-cultural studies examining this issue. Further, there are even less studies conducted from a social-cognitive lens that explore how socialization processes operate and influence individual student SRL as embedded within specific sociocultural contexts. As reflected in Figure 12.1, we believe that it is important for future research to investigate how various socialization processes manifested within particular sociocultural contexts influence individual SRL.

Another issue is the use of self-report measures in research examining cultural differences in students' SRL skill use. Although these types of assessment tools are easy to administer and typically exhibit strong psychometric qualities, their use of aggregated item scores foster interpretations of SRL as a broad aptitude rather than a dynamic, fluid, and situation-specific process (Callan & Cleary, 2017). Given the increased attention that has recently been devoted to situated forms of SRL and the use of event measures, it could be fruitful for future research to utilize event forms of measurement, such as think alouds, traces, microanalytic interviews, or observations, to assess student SRL processes within authentic, cultural-specific contexts.

There have also been calls for a reconceptualization of SRL to more explicitly account for social interaction within the developmental process. For example, Volet, Vauras, and Salonen (2009) argue that changes should be made so that SRL can better account for the integrative (psychological and social) nature of SRL. In general, these researchers argue that self-regulation can be better understood by taking a combined perspective of self- and social regulation. These researchers also warn against the dangers of reductionism (only considering self-regulation), while acknowledging that co-regulation is still emerging as a field of study.

A number of researchers have attempted to differentiate between self-regulation, and co-regulation or socially shared regulation, which are considered forms of social collaboration although grounded in sociocultural theory or social constructivism (Hadwin & Oshige, 2011; Järvenoja et al., 2015). In general, SRL is defined in terms of an individual's strategic behavior to monitor and regulate one's own metacognition, motivation, and behavior. In contrast, co-regulation refers to the notion that all regulation is shared among participants in a community and early learning of SRL is frequently supported within co-regulated experiences. In these contexts, regulation is shared between the social agent and the learner, which is similar to guided practice experiences (feedback, collaborative exchanges) emphasized by SCT researchers. Socially shared regulation is frequently considered the regulation of joint activity between multiple people regulating their collective behavior as the group works toward a socially shared goal (Hadwin & Oshige, 2011). A shared approach to SRL is more cooperative where the experts, coaches, and/or instructors and the learners jointly define the task, select strategies, and evaluate progress toward the goal.

With the emergence of co-regulation and socially shared regulation, there is need for greater clarity regarding the features and components of social collaboration from a SCT perspective. Can existing SCT models and principles of SCT explain shared regulation? Future research needs to examine classroom interactions from the perspective of distinguishing constructs, such as self-regulation, co-regulation, and social regulation, to understand the relationship and areas of intersection among these related areas of self-regulation research (as self-regulation is more advanced in terms of frameworks, definitions, etc.). Similarly, Volet et al. (2009) argues that the integration of self- and social regulation is a needed area of research given the current emphasis of virtual and collaborative learning in schools. By accounting for co-regulation/social regulation, we posit that more attention is paid to the sociocultural environment (i.e., context), which can also advance the study of individual SRL (as reflected in Figure 12.1).

It is also important to note that the four-level model of SRL development emphasized in this chapter does not specify how core socialization processes intersect and mutually support the development of optimal SRL. For example, in what ways do teachers use social modeling, social feedback, or SRL prompts interactively for students in the observation stage? How are these social collaboration processes combined differently for students at the emulation level of development for a particular understanding and/or skill? Opportunities for students to practice strategic skills during the emulation phase while receiving prompts, hints, and feedback from teachers or coaches requires a high level of collaboration between students and more expert others within the environment. Perhaps the social constructivist notions of co-regulation and socially shared regulation (Hadwin & Oshige, 2011; Järvenoja et al., 2015) provide the frame for our understanding of the important interactions and interconnections between social modeling, social feedback, and social collaboration that will more powerfully explain the enculturation process.

REFERENCES

Artino, R. A., Cleary, T. J., Dong, T., Hemmer, P. A., Durning, S. (2014). Exploring clinical reasoning in novices: A self-regulated learning microanalytic assessment approach. *Medical Education, 48,* 280–291.

Abdulhay, H., Rahimi, A., & Samigorganroodi, G. (2016). The relationship between students' self-regulated learning and teacher's autonomy support. *Journal of Language and Literature Education, 18,* 53–68.

Bandura, A. (1986). *Social foundations of thought and action: A social-cognitive theory.* Englewood Cliffs, NJ: Prentice Hall.

Bandura, A. (1997). *Self-efficacy: The exercise of control.* New York, NY: W.H. Freeman and Company.

Bandura, A. (2001). Social-cognitive theory: An agentic perspective. *Annual Review of Psychology, 52,* 1–26.

Borkowski, J., Weyhing, R., & Carr, M. (1988). Effects of attributional retraining on strategy-based reading comprehension in learning-disabled students. *Journal of Educational Psychology, 80*(1), 46–53.

Callan, G. L., & Cleary, T. J. (2017). Multidimensional assessment of self-regulated learning with middle school math students. *School Psychology Quarterly.* Advance online publication. doi:10.1037/spq0000198

Cheung, C. S., & Pomerantz, E. M. (2012). Why does parents' involvement enhance children's achievement? The role of parent-oriented motivation. *Journal of Educational Psychology, 104*(3), 820–832.

Cleary, T. J. (Ed.). (2015). *Self-regulated interventions with at-risk youth: Enhancing adaptability, performance, and well-being.* Washington, DC: American Psychological Association.

Cleary, T. J. (2018). *The self-regulated learning guide: Teaching students to think in the language of strategies.* New York, NY: Routledge.

Cleary, T. J., & Kitsantas A. (2017). Motivation and self-regulated learning influences on middle school mathematics achievement. *School Psychology Review, 46*(1), 88–107.

Cleary, T. J., & Platten, P. (2013). Examining the correspondence between self-regulated learning and academic achievement: A case study analysis [Special Issue]. *Educational Research International, 2013.* doi:10.1155/2013/272560

Cleary, T. J., Platten, P., & Nelson, A. (2008). Effectiveness of the self-regulation empowerment program with urban high school students. *Journal of Advanced Academics, 20*(1), 70–107.

Cleary, T. J., Velardi, B., & Schnaidman, B. (2017). Effects of the self-regulation empowerment program (SREP) on middle school students' strategic skills, self-efficacy, and mathematics achievement. *Journal of School Psychology, 64,* 28–42.

Cleary, T. J., Zimmerman, B. J., & Keating, T. (2006). Training physical education students to self-regulate during basketball free throw practice. *Research Quarterly for Exercise and Sport, 77*(2), 251–262.

Cobb, P., Boufi, A., McClain, K., & Whitenack, J. (1997). Reflective discourse and collective reflection. *Journal for Research in Mathematics Education, 28, 258–277.*

Cobb, P., Wood, T., & Yackel, E. (1993). Discourse, mathematical thinking, and classroom practice. In E. A. Forman, N. Minick, & C. A. Stone (Eds.), *Contexts for learning: Sociocultural dynamics in children's development* (pp. 91–119). New York, NY: Oxford University Press.

Cole, M., John-Steiner, V., Scribner, S., & Souberman, E. (Eds.). (1978). *L. S. Vygotsky: Mind in society: Mind in society development of higher psychological processes.* Cambridge, MA: Harvard University Press.

Deci, E. L., & Ryan, R. M. (1985). *Intrinsic motivation and self-determination in human behaviour.* New York, NY: Plenum Press.

Diaz, R. M., Neal, C. J., & Amaya-Williams, M. (1990). The social origins of self-regulation. In L. Moll (Ed.), *Vygotsky and education: Instructional implications and applications of sociohistorical psychology* (pp. 127–154). New York, NY: Cambridge University Press.

English, M., & Kitsantas, A. (2013). Self-regulated learning in project based settings. *Interdisciplinary Journal of Problem Based Learning, 7*(2), 128–150.

Gresalfi, M., Martin, T., Hand, V., & Greeno, J. (2009). Constructing competence: Analysis of student participation in the activity systems of mathematics classrooms. *Educational Studies in Mathematics, 70,* 49–70. Retrieved from http://www.jstor.org/stable/40284558

Grolnick, W. S., & Raftery-Helmer, J. N. (2015). Contexts supporting self-regulated learning at school transitions. In T. J. Cleary (Ed.), *Self-regulated learning interventions: Enhancing adaptability, performance, and well-being* (pp. 251–276). Washington, DC: American Psychological Association.

Hadwin, A. F., & Oshige, M. (2011). Self-regulation, co-regulation, and socially shared regulation: Exploring perspectives of social in self-regulated learning theory. *Teachers College Record, 113*(2), 240–264.

Harris, K. R., Graham, S., & Santangelo, T. (2013). Self-regulated strategies development in writing: Implementation, scaling up, and relationships to the work of Barry Zimmerman. In H. Bembenutty, T. J. Cleary, & A. Kitsantas (Eds.), *Applications of self-regulated learning across diverse disciplines: A tribute to Barry J. Zimmerman* (pp. 59–87). Charlotte, NC: Information Age.

Hattie, J., & Timperley, H. (2007). The power of feedback. *Review of Educational Research, 77*(1), 81–112.

Järvenoja, H., Järvelä, S., & Malmberg, J. (2015). Understanding regulated learning in situative and contextual frameworks. *Educational Psychologist, 50*(3), 204–219.

Kitsantas, A., Zimmerman, B. J., & Cleary, T. J. (2000). The role of observation and emulation in the development of athletic self-regulation. *Journal of Educational Psychology, 92*(4), 811–817.

Kitsantas, A., & Zimmerman, B. J. (2002). Comparing self-regulatory processes among novice, non-expert, and expert volleyball players: A microanalytic study. *Journal of Applied Sport Psychology, 14*(2), 91–105.

Kolovelonis, A., Goudas, M., & Dermitzaki, I. (2010). Self-regulated learning of a motor skill through emulation and self-control levels in a physical education setting. *Journal of Applied Sport Psychology, 22*(2), 198–212.

Kolovelonis, A., Goudas, M., Dermitsaki, I., & Kitsantas, A. (2013). Self-regulated learning and performance calibration among elementary physical education students. *European Journal of Psychology of Education, 28*(3), 685–701.

Lee, P. L., Hamman, D., & Lee, C. C. (2007). The relationship of family closeness with college students' self-regulated learning and school adjustment. *College Student Journal, 41*(4), 779–788.

Lin, X.-Z. (2004). *Successful EFL learners and their self-regulation: A case study of students in advanced English program in one university motivation* (Unpublished master's dissertation). University of Ming Chuan, Taipei, Taiwan.

McClain, K., & Cobb, P. (2001). An analysis of development of sociomathematical norms in one first-grade classroom. *Journal for Research in Mathematics Education, 32,* 236–266.

McInerney, D. M. (2011). Culture and self-regulation in educational contexts. In D. H. Schunk & B. Zimmerman (Eds.), *Handbook of self-regulation of learning and performance* (pp. 441–464). New York, NY: Routledge.

McInerney, D. M., & King, R. B. (2017). Culture and self-regulation in educational contexts. In D. H. Schunk & J. A. Greene (Eds.), *Handbook of self-regulation of learning and performance* (2nd ed., pp. 485–502). New York, NY: Routledge.

Nota, L., Soresi, S., Zimmerman, B. J. (2004). Self-regulation and academic achievement and resilience: A longitudinal study. *International Journal of Educational Research, 41*(3), 198–215.

Pape, S. J. (2015). *Examining the impact of professional development to support effective use of classroom connectivity technology: Results of a two-year professional development program.* Gainesville, FL: The University of Florida Lastinger Center.

Pape, S. J., Bell, C. V., & Yetkin, I. E. (2003). Developing mathematical thinking and self-regulated learning: A teaching experiment in a seventh-grade mathematics classroom. *Educational Studies in Mathematics, 53,* 179–202.

Pape, S. J., Bell, C. V., & Yetkin-Ozdemir, I. E. (2013). Sequencing components of mathematics lessons to maximize development of self-regulation: Theory, practice, and intervention. In H. Bembenutty, T. Cleary, & A. Kitsantas (Eds.), *Applications of self-regulated learning across diverse disciplines: A tribute to Barry J. Zimmerman* (pp. 29–58). Charlotte, NC: Information Age.

Pape, S. J., & Wang, C. (2003). Middle school children's strategic behavior: Classification and relation to academic achievement and mathematical problem solving. *Instructional Science, 31,* 419–449.

Perry, N. E. (1998). Young children's self-regulated learning and contexts that support it. *Journal of Educational Psychology, 90*(4), 715–729.

Pressley, M., & Harris, K. R. (2008). Cognitive strategy instruction: From basic research to classroom application. *Journal of Education, 189,* 77–94.

Reeve, J., & Jang, H. (2006). What teachers say and do to support students' autonomy during a learning activity. *Journal of Educational Psychology, 98*(1), 209–218.

Rosenshine, B. (1983). Teaching functions in instructional programs. *The Elementary School Journal, 83*(4), 335–351.

Schunk, D. H. (1981). Modeling and attributional effects on children's achievement: A self-efficacy analysis. *Journal of Educational Psychology, 73,* 93–105.

Schunk, D. H. (2016). *Learning theories: An educational perspective.* Boston, MA: Pearson.

Schunk, D. H., & Greene, J. A. (2017). *Handbook of self-regulation of learning and performance.* New York, NY: Routledge.

Schunk, D. H., & Hanson, A. R. (1985). Peer models: Influence on children's self-efficacy and achievement. *Journal of Educational Psychology, 77,* 313–322.

Schunk, D. H., Hanson, A. R., & Cox, P. D. (1987). Peer-model attributes and children's achievement behaviors. *Journal of Educational Psychology, 79,* 54–61.

Schunk, D. H., & Swartz, C. W. (1993a). Goals and progress feedback: Effects on self-efficacy and writing achievement. *Contemporary Educational Psychology, 18*(3), 337–354.

Schunk, D. H., & Swartz, C. W. (1993b). Writing strategy instruction with gifted students: Effects of goals and feedback on self-efficacy and skills. *Roeper Review, 15*(4), 225–230.

Shute, V. J. (2008). Focus on formative feedback. *Review of Educational Research, 78*(1), 153–189.

Sierens, E., Vansteenkiste, M., Goossens, L., Soenens, B., & Dochy, F. (2009). The synergistic relationship of perceived autonomy support and structure in the prediction of self-regulated learning. *British Journal of Educational Psychology, 79,* 57–68.

Volet, S., Vauras, M., & Salonen, P. (2009). Self- and social regulation in learning contexts: An integrative perspective. *Educational Psychologist, 44*(4), 215–226.

Weinstein, C. E., & Acee, T. W. (2013). Helping college students become more strategic and self-regulated learners. In H. Bembenutty, T. J. Cleary, & A. Kitsantas (Eds.), *Applications of self-regulated learning across diverse disciplines: A tribute to Barry J. Zimmerman* (pp. 197–236). Charlotte, NC: Information Age.

Zimmerman, B. J. (2000). Attaining self-regulation: A social cognitive perspective. In M. Boekaerts, P. R. Pintrich, & M. Zeidner (Eds.), *Handbook of self-regulation* (pp. 13–39). San Diego, CA: Academic Press.

Zimmerman, B. J. (2004). Sociocultural influence and students' development of academic self-regulation: A social-cognitive perspective. In D. M. McInerney & S. Van Etten (Eds.), *Big theories revisited* (pp. 139–164). Greenwich, CT: Information Age.

Zimmerman, B. J., & Kitsantas, A. (1996). Acquiring writing revision skill: Shifting from process to outcome self-regulatory goals. *Journal of Educational Psychology, 91*(2), 241–250.

Zimmerman, B. J., & Kitsantas, A. (1997). Developmental phases in self-regulation: Shifting from process goals to outcome goals. *Journal of Educational Psychology, 89*(1), 29–36.

Zimmerman, B. J., & Kitsantas, A. (1999). Acquiring writing revision skill: Shifting from process to outcome self-regulatory goals. *Journal of Education & Psychology, 91,* 241–250.

Zimmerman, B. J., & Kitsantas, A. (2002). Acquiring writing revision and self-regulatory skill through observation and emulation. *Journal of Educational Psychology, 94*(4), 660–668.

Zimmerman, B. J., & Martinez-Pons, M. (1986). Development of a structured interview for assessing student use of self-regulated learning strategies. *American Educational Research Journal, 23,* 614–628.

Zimmerman, B. J., & Martinez-Pons, M. (1988). Construct validation of a strategy model of student self-regulated learning. *Journal of Educational Psychology, 80*(3), 284–290.

Zimmerman, B. J., Moylan, A., Hudesman, J., White, N., & Flugman, B. (2011). Enhancing self-reflection and mathematics achievement of at-risk urban technical college students. *Psychological Test and Assessment Modeling, 53*(1), 141–160.

CHAPTER 13

SUPPORTING SELF-REGULATION AND SELF-DETERMINATION IN THE CONTEXT OF MUSIC EDUCATION

Nancy E. Perry
Silvia Mazabel
Ben Dantzer
Philip H. Winne

Self-regulated and self-determined learners are deliberate and proactive. They feel *in* control and can *take* control of their learning and life circumstances. Evidence is accumulating that self-regulation (SR) and self-determination (SD) are assets that cross sociodemographic boundaries (McClelland & Wanless, 2012; McInerney & Ali, 2013) and benefit learning; social, emotional, and behavioral functioning; and general health and well-being. Theory and research in both fields increasingly emphasizes how attending to social and contextual factors can enhance understandings about students'

Big Theories Revisited 2, pages 295–318

self-regulated and self-determined learning. In this chapter, we examine how theory and research on SR and SD are evolving to integrate sociocultural perspectives on learning, and how these developments enrich and expand understandings of promoting SR and SD in complex teaching and learning environments. The chapter is divided into two main parts. First, we examine theories of SR and SD with particular attention to their absorption of recent sociocultural constructs. Second, we describe a research–practice partnership we co-created with an after school music education program. In this section, we describe the sociocultural context surrounding that program and its implications for co-constructing research and practice goals and activities. We also provide examples of how self-regulated learning (SRL) and self-determined learning (SDL) articulate within this sociocultural context. We conclude by highlighting implications for research and practice that derive from our literature review and collaboration.

THEORIES

Self-Regulated Learning Theory

Theories of SRL describe learners controlling thoughts and actions to achieve goals and respond to demands across wide ranging learning environments (Winne, 2018; Zimmerman, 2008). They focus on learners' productive engagements with tasks and activities, characterizing self-regulating learners as focused, persistent, and flexible (Blair & Razza, 2007; Diamond, 2016; McClelland & Cameron, 2012). Educational psychologists identify metacognition, motivation, and strategic action as primary drivers of SRL (Perry, Hutchinson, Yee, & Määtä, 2018; Winne, 2017, 2018), emphasizing how successfully self-regulating learners leverage their strengths for coping with challenges in academic and other tasks. These learners recognize challenge is inherent in most learning opportunities and, when tasks challenge them, draw from rich repertoires of strategies and persist to make progress and reach deeper understanding. Models of SRL describe learners engaging in cyclical processes (i.e., cycles of strategic action) to support thinking and acting before, during, and after completing a learning task (Butler & Cartier, 2004; Winne & Hadwin, 1998; Zimmerman & Campillo, 2003).

SR is developmental and much research and theorizing about SRL seeks to articulate how individual and groups of learners can be supported to improve their SRL (Butler & Schnellert, 2015; Graham & Harris, 2003; Mason & Reid, 2018). Historically (Winne, 2017) and presently (Hadwin, Jarvela, & Miller, 2018; Perry et al., 2018), theory and research emphasize how SRL trajectories are influenced not just by personal characteristics (e.g., beliefs, temperament, and cognitive abilities) but also by social, historical, and contextual experiences. In line with sociocultural perspectives on learning, Schunk and Zimmerman (1997; Schunk, 1999) emphasize a social-to-self progression in their 4-phase model of how SR develops. In the first two phases—observation and imitation—influences affecting regulation are social (e.g., significant others model SR or provide feedback about first attempts). In the third and fourth phases—self-control and SR—regulation becomes internalized through practice and learners adapt what was modeled for them to suit personal and sociocultural contexts (Usher & Schunk, 2018).

Similarly, recent models of regulating learning integrate constructs, such as co-regulation (McCaslin, 2009), socially-shared regulation (SSRL; Hadwin et al., 2018) and socially-responsible SR (SRSR; Hutchinson, 2013), which reflect elements of sociocultural theory, such as zones of proximal development, mediation, interdependence, and internalization (Vygotsky, 1978; Wertsch, Tulviste & Hagstrom, 1993). Co-regulation emphasizes the importance of instrumental interaction and activity within zones of proximal development to support SRL and SSRL. Co-regulators can be parents, teachers, peers, and tools (e.g., instructional materials, technology). Ideally, co-regulation is transitory and transitional, enabling "future regulatory uptake by the co-regulated" (Hadwin et al., 2018, p. 87). The goal of co-regulation is SRL and/or SSRL.

SSRL describes learners jointly regulating activity during interpersonal interactions or in collaborative tasks (Hadwin et al., 2018). It occurs as learners co-construct task understandings, frame shared goals and pool metacognitive, motivational, and strategic resources (Hadwin & Oshige, 2011) to achieve goals (Winne, Hadwin, & Perry, 2013). Finally, SRSR (Hutchinson, 2013) describes learners regulating themselves in pro-social, socially-competent ways to advance their own and others' learning (e.g., engaging in adaptive help seeking and giving; distributing resources fairly). SRSR facilitates self-, co-, and shared- regulation.

Self-Determination Theory

Self-determination theory (SDT) is a theory of intrinsic, or autonomous, motivation, focusing on humans' natural curiosity and desire to learn (Ryan & Deci, 2009; 2017). Like SRL theory, SDT has evolved over time to embrace the dialectical nature of human experience, how individual cognition is influenced by sociocultural environments and *vice versa* (Reeve, Ryan, & Deci, Chapter 2, this volume). *Appropriation* and *internalization* are key processes in SDT that describe how motivation progresses along a continuum from external/other regulation to internal/self regulation. The depth and quality of a learner's internalization and resultant motivation (i.e., whether more extrinsic or intrinsic) depends on how they experience interactions/transactions in their sociocultural environments (Howard,

Gagne, & Bureau, 2017; Ryan & Deci, 2017). SDT assumes that when sociocultural environments provide and model autonomy supporting strategies to expand learning and development, learners willingly accept, adopt, and internalize constructive forms of thinking and behaving. Alternatively, when learners experience external influences as controlling, their intrinsic/autonomous motivation can be undermined and their approaches to learning may become maladaptive (Reeve et al., Chapter 2, this volume; Ryan & Deci, 2009). Also, students are more likely to internalize external requests they consider personally meaningful or valuable than requests they perceive are controlling (e.g., restricting choices or demanding particular outcomes).

The goal of moving learners along the continuum from extrinsic to intrinsic motivation regulation is best achieved when socioculturally-situated factors support three *basic psychological needs* (BPNs): needs for autonomy, belonging, and competence (Howard et al., 2017; Reeve, 2015; Ryan & Deci, 2017). Autonomy refers to a child's perceived control in situations and over outcomes; it reflects feelings of agency and/or opportunities for self-endorsement. Belonging is feeling accepted and connected with others, alongside feeling like an important or integral part of a group. Competence refers to feelings of effectiveness and skill-expansion while interacting in the social environment. From an SDT viewpoint, feelings of autonomy, belonging, and competence are "universal" needs that predict subjective well-being or ill-being (Ryan & Deci, 2017). Cross-cultural research has linked BPN satisfaction with subjective well-being and BPN frustration with ill-being (Chen et al., 2015; Soenens, Park, Vansteenkiste, & Mouratidis, 2012; Wang, Pomerantz, & Chen, 2007; Taylor & Lonsdale, 2010; Tian, Chen, & Huebner, 2014).

Children's and youth's feelings of autonomy, belonging, and competence are moderated by pervasive and proximal sociocultural contexts (Ryan & Deci, 2017). Pervasive contexts include educational, political, religious, or economic cultures within which children/families develop and live. Within this larger sphere are proximal contexts such as classroom environments, familial practices, and community programs. Pervasive and proximal factors can promote or obstruct satisfaction of BPNs (Ryan & Deci, 2017). For example, controlling, unfriendly, and critical contexts can interfere with BPN satisfaction, potentially resulting in more externalized motivation or amotivation (Howard et al., 2017; Jang, Reeve, & Halusic, 2016; Reeve, 2015; Ryan, 1995; Ryan & Deci, 2017). Conversely, sociocultural contexts that appeal to learner's interests, support their sense of belonging, and make them feel capable and competent, lead to the deeper, more autonomous forms of internalization associated with intrinsic motivation and flourishing (Howard et al., 2017; Reeve & Jang, 2006; Ryan, 1995; Ryan & Deci, 2017).

Synergies Between Self-Regulation and Self-Determination Theories

Fundamentally, SR and SD theories conceptualize learners as exercising personal and collective agency in socially-responsive yet autonomous ways. Both theories position learners as decision makers acting in and reacting to environments they partially shape (Bandura, 1986; Usher & Schunk, 2018). Moreover, SR and SD theories are informed by social-cognitive and, more recently, sociocultural theories, which highlight how choices learners make are mutually determined by personal, social, cultural, and contextual factors (Bandura, 1986). Much of the research about SR and SD has foregrounded how social and contextual factors influence various aspects of the self-system, portraying a unidirectional influence of context on individuals. Classroom research presents an opportunity to highlight how human transactions influence social systems and environments, emphasizing bi- or multidirectional influences (Perry & Rahim, 2011). Research conducted *during* naturally occurring events *in* classrooms is not very common in the fields of SR and SD, but two programs of research have identified complimentary categories from their focus on qualities of classrooms that support SRL and SDL (see Perry, 2013 and Reeve, 2006 for an overview). Table 13.1 synthesizes these categories, mapping grounds for our collaboration with partners in the after school music education program, which we describe later in the chapter.

Perry and colleagues (e.g., Perry, 1998, 2013; Perry & VandeKamp, 2000) have pursued classroom research to illuminate how: (a) tasks/activities, instructional practices, and interpersonal relationships create opportunities

TABLE 13.1 Classroom Practices That Support Self-Regulated and Self-Determined Learning	
Providing Structure	Activities, routines, and participation structures enable independent and social forms of learning and accommodate student diversity
Tasks/Activities	Tasks and activities are complex by design (i.e., address multiple instructional goals, are meaningful and authentic, often extend over time, involve cognitive and metacognitive processes, engage students in aspects of the cycle of strategic action, allow for multiple products or ways to represent knowledge).
Expectations/ Instructions	Expectations and instructions are explicitly discussed and/or co-constructed with students. Instructions and expectations are clear and flexible, and explanatory rationales are provided.
Familiar Routines Participation Structures	Predictable routines for participation and norms for engagement in activities are established or co-constructed with students. Different ways of participating are valued.

(continued)

TABLE 13.1   Classroom Practices That Support Self-Regulated and Self-Determined Learning (continued)

Accommodations for Individual Differences	Tasks, activities, and assessment practices are open and flexible enough to accommodate diverse interests and abilities across students. All students can participate meaningfully.
Visual Prompts	Visual prompts cue students' engagement in productive and strategic learning.
Giving Students Influence	Students' perspectives and experiences are acknowledged and considered. They are given opportunities to take control over their learning.
Involvement in Decision Making Choice	Students take part in decision-making about what and how they learn. Choices involve higher levels of thinking (e.g., what resources to use, how to organize information).
Control Over Challenge	Modifications and/or adaptations to the level of difficulty of tasks/activities and expectations regarding its product(s) are made by students, or negotiated between teacher and students (e.g., students work at their own pace, choose resources that fit with their interests and abilities).
Self-Assessment	Students have opportunities to self-evaluate the quality of their work in progress and determine next steps/adaptations (e.g., What have I learned? How can I improve?).
Supporting, Scaffolding, Co-Regulation	Teacher/peers/tools serve as instrumental supports for learning.
Modeling/ Demonstrating	Conveying the sequence of actions needed to complete a task (through talk or action) and giving students the opportunity to practice and be successful at the task.
Questioning	Using metacognitive questions to guide learning and invite students to find solutions to problems or answers to questions on their own.
Feedback	Giving students formative, descriptive and task-specific feedback focused on the learning process so students can identify and reduce differences between progress and goals.
Metacognitive Language	Using and encouraging the use of metacognitive and strategic language to guide learning; engaging students in dialogue about thinking and learning processes.
Motivational Messages	Attributing success to effort and using effective strategies, emphasizing progress and growth, challenging students, and communicating confidence in students as learners.
Creating a Community of Learners	Fostering group cohesion through participation structures and the interpersonal tone of the classroom (i.e., students are encouraged to respect one another, share goals, and collaborate with peers); teachers and students are partners in learning and knowledge building; assessment interactions are positive and nonthreatening (e.g., emphasize growth and progress; downplay social comparisons).

for students to develop and engage in SRL; and (b) teachers and researchers, in partnership, can design tasks and structure classroom transactions to support SRL. Using case study methodology and detailed, narrative observations ("running records") has generated highly contextualized accounts of what teachers do and say to promote SRL, how they create opportunities for students to regulate learning, and how students interpret and respond to those opportunities. Consistently, students productively self-, co-, and share-regulate learning in classrooms where they engage in complex meaningful tasks and where support for autonomy affords choice, control over challenge, and opportunities to self-evaluate learning (Perry, 2013). Teachers and students in these classrooms operationalize highly effective forms of co- and socially shared regulation. These classrooms function as communities of learners in which learners feel welcome because they are part of a group, treat one another respectfully, and take responsibility for their learning while helping and seeking help from others (Perry & Drummond, 2002). Students are encouraged to share ideas and strategies. Familiar routines and participation structures support independent and social activity. Assessment practices are formative and encourage a growth mindset (Dweck, 2007).

Similarly, Reeve and colleagues have observed what teachers do and say to support students' self-determined, or autonomous, motivation in classrooms (Reeve, 2006; Reeve, Bolt, & Cai, 1999). According to Reeve's (2006) dialectical framework, students express motivations (e.g., need for autonomy, belonging, and competence; interests, values, and strivings) in response to learning opportunities and challenges. In turn, classroom activities and priorities either support or thwart students' motivations, depending on whether and how much classroom contexts align with students' needs and interests. Classroom contexts that support SDL are autonomy supporting (Jang, Reeve, & Deci, 2010; Reeve, 2006; Reeve et al., 1999; Taylor & Ntoumanis, 2007). Teachers in these classrooms demonstrate a willingness to coordinate tasks and activities with students' psychological needs, interests, and learning abilities. Learners have considerable choice and voice, but teachers also use structures, such as clarifying expectations and informative feedback to promote students' feelings of confidence and competence. Finally, teachers and students in autonomy supportive classrooms relate positively to one another (e.g., they are caring and responsive; show approval; and use gentle, inductive forms of discipline).

Researchers in the SR and SD fields need to do more to demonstrate the relevance of SRL and SDL constructs across sociodemographic groups. However, available studies indicate SR and SD are assets and predict positive outcomes for diverse learners (McClelland & Wanless, 2012; McInerney & Ali, 2013; Moffitt et al., 2011; Rutter, 2013). For example, longitudinal studies find SR predicts adjustment to and achievement in school across linguistic, cultural, and SES groups (Hutchinson, Perry, Yee, Dantzer, Lo, & Restrepo, 2015; McClelland & Wanless, 2012). Similarly, research links SD with subjective well-being, academic achievement, and school satisfaction among students with diverse cultural and ethnic backgrounds and cognitive abilities (Sheldon, Abad, & Omoile, 2009; Shogren & Shaw, 2016; Taylor & Lonsdale, 2010; Tian et al., 2014). Specific to our interests, the student-centered and flexible practices associated with supporting SRL and SDL may help diverse learners become "school literate" by helping them understand what values, norms for participation, and approaches to learning reflect a classroom's culture (Orosco & O'Connor, 2014), and creating space for teachers and students to co-construct a classroom culture suiting their community (Perry, Yee, Mazabel, Lisaingo, & Määtä, 2017). Finally, SRL and SDL promoting practices may support learners to cope with challenges/adversity in supportive environments, a key to healthy development (Rutter, 2013). Efforts to increase children's resilience parallel supports for SRL and SDL and assets associated with resilient learners and also characterize self-regulated and self-determined learners (e.g., positive self-efficacy and agency; effective regulation strategies; ability to form close, supportive relationships).

Relating Self-Regulation and Self-Determination to Music Education

Research on SRL and SDL in music learning is limited, but there are many reasons to believe both are relevant in this domain. Music learning involves hours of practice and persistence to achieve a high level of performance and, often, depends on learners' intrinsic commitment to the task— musicians have typically made the choice to study music, rather than being required to learn as part of a school curriculum (McPherson, Miksza, & Evans, 2018). McPherson and colleagues (e.g., McPherson, 2005; McPherson, Davidson, & Evans, 2016) have studied the relationship between SRL and progress in music learning. Their observations indicate learners who achieve the highest levels of performance are those who use the most sophisticated strategies for practicing their instrument. They set personal learning and performance goals to focus practice. They recruit and tailor multiple strategies to improve their musical skills, and they self-reinforce and monitor progress towards goals using personal and external feedback (McPherson et al., 2018; also see Varela, Abrami, & Upitis, 2016). These learners understand when and how to apply strategies, particularly to cope with challenging tasks.

Similarly, the most successful musicians evidence intrinsic/autonomous/self-determined sources of motivation (Evans, 2015; McPherson et al., 2018). They are driven by interest to perfect their musical skills and repertoire and this results in more effective and efficient practice. For example, Renwick and McPherson (2002, cited in McPherson et al., 2018) describe differences in a young clarinetist's practice routines across repertoires her teacher assigned and those she asked to learn. For the former, she is described as using a "play-through approach without stopping to work on errors" (McPherson et al., 2018, p. 185) For the latter, not only did she increase time spent practicing, but also she was observed adopting more strategic behaviors, such as "silently replicating the physical movements needed to play through passages, thinking carefully about upcoming measures before attempting to play them, deliberately slowing the music to grasp the actions necessary to play it, . . ." (McPherson et al., 2018, p. 185). There is also research indicating children respond better when parents and teachers focus on support for autonomy than rewards and external incentives to motivate children to learn and practice music. Children whose incentives for learning and practicing music are external (e.g., parents offering rewards, or punishment) give up their instruments earlier than those receiving "gentle reminders" and encouraging comments, which are more autonomy supportive (Davidson, Howe, Moore, & Sloboda, 1996; Faulkner, Davidson, & McPherson, 2010).

Young music learners rely on others before they can regulate interest, strategies, thoughts, actions and the music learning environment on their own, so sociocultural context is critical in the development of young musicians (McPherson & Zimmerman, 2002, 2011; Varela et al., 2016). Learners from homes where music is highly valued are more likely to value music education and set higher goals and expectations for their musical learning and performance (McPherson et al., 2018) and McPherson et al. (2018) cite research demonstrating the positive impact explicit instruction about SRL has on musicians' development. Unfortunately, research describing music education characterizes teaching in this domain as typically teacher-centered and hierarchical (e.g., master-apprentice model), which can be controlling (McPherson et al., 2018). In our personal communications with teachers, they relate that any training they received on teaching music tended to focus on music theory and performance rather than specific approaches to teaching and learning. It seems, therefore, timely for music education researchers to turn to SRL frameworks and SDT to examine music teaching and learning as multi-componential and multi-determined activities. Our review of this developing body of work suggests SR and SD have a circular relationship in music learning: Music learners whose BPNs are met in the context of a music-focused learning community are more likely to be intrinsically motivated to learn and practice their instrument or voice and self-determined motivation likely leads these learners to higher levels of SR during practice (e.g., more deliberate use of effective strategies to study/learn a musical piece).

SUPPORTING SELF-REGULATION AND SELF-DETERMINATION IN MUSIC EDUCATION

The Sociocultural Context

The music program is located in a neighborhood that has been characterized as a "community of communities" (Newnham, 2005). Close to half of its residents represent visible minority groups, including those who live and work in Chinatown, large numbers of indigenous people from across the Americas, and many new immigrants to Canada. Newnham (2005) cites an inventory of assets in the community, including considerable knowledge of diverse cultures, particularly indigenous people's perspectives; a wide range of language skills; creativity expressed through music and the arts; and an admirable capacity to care for people less fortunate than oneself. However, this is also a community that struggles with high concentrations of social problems, such as poverty, crime, substance abuse, prostitution, inadequate and insecure housing, and high rates of mental and other illness (e.g., HIV/AIDS, hepatitis, and tuberculosis; Community Directions, 2002), making it a challenging environment in which to grow up.

The music program provides free music education to school-aged children and youth living in this community. More than 200 children attend the program, which operates 5 days each week. Children in the junior program (Kindergarten to Grade 3) attend on Tuesdays and Thursdays and children/youth in the senior program (Grade 4 to 12) typically attend on Mondays, Wednesdays, and Fridays, although some students in the senior program also attend Tuesdays and Thursdays to help in the junior program and/or to provide them with a place to be after school. Students arriving after school have a meal before beginning three to four 40-minute blocks of music learning and instruction. Each child's music education includes: music theory, learning to play an instrument, and participation in orchestra and choir. Some children also receive support for exceptional learning, emotional, or behavioral needs from a certified music therapist. Most faculty are professional musicians. Some live in the community, but most do not. Most have experience teaching music in other contexts; however, the majority have no formal teacher training and, at the start of our partnership, they were feeling quite overwhelmed with the challenge of meeting the complex needs of the children in this community (i.e., children who are linguistically and culturally diverse, including immigrants and refugees;

have high abilities and disabilities; and are coping with adversities associated with living in a family and/or community with the social problems we described above).

In 2014, the development officer for the music program invited us to make a presentation to the faculty. They were becoming aware of SR as an innovation in public schools and wanted to learn more about it. At the presentation, we spoke about SRL (What is it? Why is it important? How can it be supported in educational contexts?), and we also talked about SD, particularly emphasizing the potential of supporting children's sense of autonomy, belonging, and competence to empower them as learners. We perceived the strategies for supporting autonomy and meeting BPNs were particularly relevant for these learners and bolstered Perry's SRL framework. Feedback from the faculty indicated the presentation was "eye-opening." They recognized many children attending the program were struggling with aspects of SR, such as focusing attention, coping with challenge, and adapting to complex learning and living environments. Moreover, SRL and SDL aligned with their goal of empowering learners in this context—autonomy supportive versus controlling approaches to teaching appealed to them. Subsequently we formed a research–practice partnership with three shared goals:

1. supporting children's regulation for learning;
2. enhancing their sense of SD through opportunities for regulating learning and by meeting their fundamental needs for autonomy, competence, and belonging; and
3. learning about, designing, implementing, and evaluating practices to accomplish 1 and 2.

The Framework for Our Partnership

Our partnership with faculty at the music academy was grounded in participatory approaches to research, which align with sociocultural views of learning, are collaborative in nature, and lead to designing effective and sustainable interventions in response to context-specific practical issues (Perry, Brenner, & MacPherson, 2015; Butler & Schnellert, 2012). Forming a *research-practice partnership* (RPP) is one way to operationalize participatory approaches to research (see Coburn & Penuel, 2016). Our RPP functioned as a community of practice (also a sociocultural idea) in which (a) music teachers identified priorities for themselves and their students (i.e., What does our focus need to be?), (b) researchers responded by introducing research and theoretical frameworks to inform and guide teachers' practices (e.g., SRL and SD promoting practices), and (c) educators and researchers collaborated to tailor research-based teaching strategies to suit the specific needs of the teaching and learning context (Cochran-Smith & Lytle, 2004; Halbert & Kaser, 2013; Perry et al., 2015). These iterative cycles of reflection and action have much in common with cycles of SR and previous research indicates they bring about meaningful changes in teachers' practices and positive changes in students' learning and engagement (Butler & Schnellert, 2012; Timperley, Halbert, & Kaser, 2014).

Below we offer three examples of how communities of practice functioned at three levels to support SRL and SDL at the music academy: the faculty as a community of learners (teacher–teacher support); one classroom community of learners (teacher–student support); and a cross-age peer mentoring community (student–student support).

The Faculty Learning Community

The faculty with researchers formed a community of practice, labeled "teacher learning team" (TLT). The TLT met 3 times each year for 3 years to learn and plan supports for music students' development of SRL and SDL. In addition to focusing on group goals, individual faculty members were encouraged to consider "what was going on for their learners" (i.e., the children in their music classes) and, consequently, what their personal focus needed to be. We used the *Spirals of Inquiry* (Halbert & Kaser, 2013) framework, which maps onto the cycles of inquiry and SR we have been referencing throughout this chapter, to structure teachers' inquiry (i.e., teachers found a focus, made plans, engaged in professional learning, took action, monitored progress, and made adjustments as needed). Also, we used four activities to structure our interactions at the TLT meetings. Each meeting began with a time to "check-in." This was an opportunity for teachers to reflect on and share what had happened for them and their students since the last TLT meeting ("What have you tried? What have you observed?"). Next, we would engage in a more "focused discussion." Often topics for the focused discussion were a response to previous TLT discussions. A lot of time was spent on SRL and SDL promoting practices. Typically, the researchers would facilitate the focused discussion, but often they would ask particular teachers to share their work on a particular topic (e.g., How can I get students to set realistic goals and then follow through?) or a strategy they were using to cope with a particular challenge (e.g., How can I foster a greater spirit of teamwork, cooperation, and respect in my classes?). During "work time," the TLT participants could work independently or in small groups to plan the next steps in their projects. This time was also used to complete "reflections templates" that documented individuals' questions and actions across time. These templates provided data for the researchers to use, but they also were intentionally designed to scaffold faculty members' inquiry. For this purpose, the templates were divided into four quadrants and asked faculty to respond to four questions: What did you do [between our last meeting and this meeting]? What happened? What have you learned? What will you do next? At the end of the meeting, TLT participants would report what they were planning to do next.

Over the course of the RPP, the TLT met 9 times. In addition, researchers made 60 visits to music classes, observing "what was going on" and then meeting with individual faculty members to debrief the visit. Data from reflections templates and classroom observations documented how faculty were developing and honing SRL and SDL practices and how their participation in the TLT was empowering them as teachers. For example, one teacher reflected:

> This project provided more comprehensive professional development opportunities than any other teaching initiative that I have been involved with. The opportunities that this project presented for collaboration with other teachers helped me grow as a teacher, and also provided support in managing the many challenges that would crop up in my...classroom. This project made me much more self-aware as a teacher, particularly in my techniques for motivating, disciplining, and praising students. By shifting my focus from "outcomes" to "process," I was able to successfully reach students who were previously withdrawn and fearful of participating. I emerged from this project with a deeper understanding of the different ways that students learn, and was a much more effective teacher on the other side of it as a result.

Gradually, our community of practice progressed from being mostly informed by researchers (knowledge of practice) to being informed by the knowledge teachers/practitioners gained in practice. This generated a culture of teacher to teacher support that all members in the community of practice found to be instrumental and productive. For example, one teacher reflected:

> It was a tremendous gain for me as a teacher. I didn't have teaching training, so all the information on SRL was new and so helpful. I had a place to ask questions, get ideas from other teachers, and express areas of frustration. It served the space of a staff meeting, but with expertise, which made it so helpful!

In addition to developing as individuals, the faculty as a whole advanced various program-wide initiatives (e.g., they developed a curriculum that includes learning intentions related to SRL and SDL) and teacher-to-teacher support initiatives that went beyond the TLT (e.g., creating opportunities to visit one another's classrooms, engaging in collaborative teaching, creating an online resource repository and a Facebook group). These initiatives are evidence that the benefits accrued from the partnership will continue after the researchers leave the site.

The partnership was designed to support the faculty in the ways we wanted them to support their students—the goal was to help them acquire knowledge and skills that would empower them as self-regulated and self-determined teachers. Toward this end, and as outlined in Table 13.1, we used supporting, not controlling, structures (Reeve, 2006) to guide teachers' planning, enacting, and reflecting on their practice (e.g., the *Spirals of Inquiry* framework and the TLT meeting routines). Teachers, as learners, had influence (e.g., they determined the best focus for them and their students) and support (from researchers and colleagues) in their community of practice, and these material and people resources were instruments of co-regulation (e.g., metacognitive questioning and feedback were used to scaffold faculty's development of SRL and SDL promoting practices). Below is an example of how one teacher worked through iterative cycles of planning, enacting, and reflecting that map onto cycles of SR we described earlier in the chapter (e.g., Winne & Hadwin, 1998).

One Classroom Community

"Ross's" inquiry is an example of how involvement in the faculty learning community (the TLT) impacted SRL and SDL at the classroom level. Ross is a professional musician with over 15 years of experience teaching music but has no formal teaching education. He had been teaching for a year in the music program when he joined the TLT. At first, his response to the question, "What's going on for your learners?" was that they were not working well together and not attending to his directions or rules. Therefore, Ross focused his inquiry on ways to motivate students to engage more deeply with classroom activities (i.e., giving students influence, see Table 13.1), and to foster a greater spirit of teamwork, cooperation, and respect in his classes (i.e., creating a community of learners, see Table 13.1). To accomplish this he involved students in setting classroom goals and developing activities and rules, and he made an effort at being more transparent about teaching goals and strategies, and at being clearer in outlining instructions for class activities (i.e., providing structure in Table 13.1). For example, he asked students what skills they wanted to work on in class and how they could cooperate better; he also gave students choices about how to work.

At first, students struggled to generate ideas about class rules and activities. Ross interpreted they may not have had many opportunities to give such input in the past. However, over time, Ross noticed that involving students in classroom decision making, fostering a community of learners (e.g., by establishing shared learning goals, and offering opportunities for collaboration), and providing clear and supportive structures (e.g., expectations, routines, rationales for activities) had a positive effect on students' engagement. Ross noted in one of his reflections: "Students responded very well to having choice. They sprawled out on the floor or in corners and worked very diligently, with unprecedented focus. They like having their own space and feeling ok to go at their own pace." He continued giving students input and following through on the structures they co-constructed as a classroom community, he referenced these structures often, and increased opportunities for collaboration.

However, there was one student, Zack, who despite Ross' best efforts, continued to be unwilling to participate in group activities and was disruptive to the class. Upon reflection, Ross adjusted his inquiry to focus on Zack and helping him to engage more productively in whole class and small group activities. Zack was 9 years old and beginning his 4th year in the music program. Ross described him as "very bright, energetic, imaginative, impish, vibrant, and stubborn," and said he was cooperative in one-on-one settings but struggled in groups. To scaffold Zack's development of skills that helped him feel more comfortable and cooperative in a group setting, Ross met with Zack each day before class and outlined the day's activities. Together they agreed Zack could choose to participate in class-wide activities or choose an alternative activity. In this way, Ross made accommodations for individual differences by giving Zack a choice that enabled him to control challenge (Table 13.1). Ross focused on Zack's strengths and encouraged him to take a creative role (e.g., composing rhythms, making up songs) in the singing/clapping activities that made the bulk of the music theory class and that Zack disliked. Zack welcomed the opportunity to choose and typically chose to work alone, but he did not disrupt the class any longer and he wrote a great song.

Ross chose not to abandon his goal of bringing Zack into the classroom. In a third iteration of his planning, enacting, and reflecting cycle, he reframed his approach (and standards) to consider even brief positive group interactions as a big step for Zack. He continued to encourage Zack's writing in class to take advantage of his imagination, knack for word-play and creativity. Zack gradually became more open to bringing his songs to the group and Ross guided the group in composing melodies and making musical arrangements to Zack's lyrics. Ross noticed that, as a result, Zack became more engaged and cooperative in other group activities and he "was visibly proud" to be the first student-composer to have a piece performed in the music program's concert. Zack's BPNs for autonomy, belonging, and competence were met through Ross' willingness to consider his unique needs as a learner. Subsequently, Zack expressed a strong sense of connection to the program, referring to having special friends at the program, liking his cello and the program, and feeling cool when given the opportunity to play the songs that he liked. In general, Zack and the class became more productive in their learning as they were empowered and driven by their own curiosity, interests, and values.

This example demonstrates the power of co-regulation (McCaslin, 2009) and socially-shared regulation (Hadwin et al., 2018) in the development of SRL and SDL in the context of a music classroom. It also demonstrates how one teacher honed his SRL and SDL promoting practices as he engaged in self-, co-, and shared-regulation processes. This supports previous findings that teachers engaged in supportive, action-oriented approaches to professional learning can flexibly and effectively interpret and apply theory and research to suit the specific needs of their students (Perry et al., 2015). It also suggests principles arising from SRL and SDL theory and research are robust enough to withstand adaptations that respond to specific features of sociocultural contexts.

Peer Mentoring Community

As the faculty became more confident and felt more competent supporting SRL and SDL in their classrooms, they began looking for ways to foster more student-to-student support. One of the researchers worked with the executive director and one of the teachers to design and implement a cross-age peer mentoring program (Dantzer, 2017). In this program, five older and more experienced students from the senior program mentored five younger students who were new to the junior program. Mentors formed their own community of learning, much like the TLT we described above. They participated in a "mentoring support group" to learn about SDT. During mentor meetings, they co-constructed definitions for each of the BPNs and generated "go-to statements" and "go-to strategies" to help them support their mentees' feelings of autonomy, belonging, and competence. They also engaged in iterative cycles of planning, action, and reflection. Similar to the TLT, mentor meetings provided space for mentors to reflect on their relationships with mentees, consider which strategies were working well, and identify next steps and priorities, and to receive guided and sustained support from a knowledgeable facilitator (the researcher) and each other. In one of their music classes, mentors taught mentees how to play various pieces of music, including pieces the mentees chose and one piece that mentors composed for the group. Mentors and mentees played this song at the spring concert and had it professionally recorded.

A question for the researchers was whether and to what extent the mentors, who were high school students, could acquire and apply language and strategies associated with supporting BPNs (e.g., in Table 13.1: involving their mentors in making decisions about learning, giving them choices; co-regulating their learning by asking metacognitive questions and providing informative feedback and encouraging motivational messages). In addition, would their efforts be perceived by their mentees? Audio recordings of mentoring sessions revealed ample evidence the mentors using language and strategies known to support BPNs and the mentees expressed their BPN satisfaction in the context of these relationships (e.g., in learning logs and interviews). Importantly, mentors indicated their own BPNs were met through their involvement in the program, particularly their need for developing competence.

In one relationship, Stella mentored Layla. Regarding the goal of supporting SD, Stella supported Layla's sense of autonomy by inviting her to choose songs they would learn together (i.e., giving students influence and making tasks meaningful, see Table 13.1). Layla explained the significance of this autonomy supportive move: "I got to pick our song! I wanted to learn Happy Birthday for my sister, it was our birthday a while ago! It was all good!" Stella also focused on fostering a supportive and caring relationship with Layla in an effort to make her feel connected to the academy. For example, Stella regularly took the time to ask Layla about her life outside of the classroom and disclosed information about her personal life as well (i.e., fostering a community of learners by showing interest in and respect for one another, see Table 13.1). When asked whether she felt like Stella was a friend, Layla replied, "Yes! Because she would help and she would tell me stuff! She was always kind, friendly, and happy!" Finally, Stella supported Layla's sense of competence by commenting on her effort and progress (i.e., supporting, scaffolding, and co-regulation through feedback and motivational messages, see Table 13.1). Linking effort (in this context, practice) to improvement is consistent with SDT's emphasis on helping learners to focus on those aspects of learning they have control over, which is empowering for learners (Droe, 2012; McPherson & Zimmerman, 2002; Ryan & Deci, 2017; Varela et al., 2016).

Stella experienced feelings of autonomy, belonging, and competence by acting as a role model and peer mentor. While reflecting on the sense of autonomy she gained from mentoring, Stella reported learning "...that I'm actually pretty good at leading. I don't tell myself that enough. I usually try to not lead and follow other people. But I've learned that I am actually pretty good at helping and inspiring others." According to the executive director of the program and Stella's teacher, this expression of personal agency contrasted her usual pattern of conformity and indicated her mentoring experience increased her own sense of SD. Similarly, she reported that acting as a mentor "...made me feel good! Especially when [Layla] was excited about seeing me!" When asked to reflect on how being a mentor affected her sense of competence, Stella said, "It made me feel like a teacher, like I knew what I was doing! It definitely teaches you more about yourself and your instrument."

CONCLUSIONS

Sociocultural considerations are key to understanding the relevance of SRL and SDT frameworks for diverse groups of learners. Generally, theory and research on motivation and SR involve participants from fairly mainstream, Western European and North American communities. However, a growing body of research involving learners from non-Western and marginalized communities indicates SRL and SDL are relevant for learning and living across a range of sociodemographic groups, settings, and circumstances (McClelland & Wanless, 2012; McInerney & Ali, 2013; Moffitt et al., 2011; Reeve et al., Chapter 2, this volume; Rutter, 2013). Moreover, in our experience, SRL and SDL promoting practices support teachers to implement more learner-centered and inclusive practices that align with students' experiences, interests, and abilities (Perry et al., 2017). This was a particular asset for our RPP. Children come to the music program from linguistically, ethnically, and economically diverse homes. The program includes children with high abilities and disabilities and many children in the program face extreme forms of adversity on a daily basis. Notwithstanding this potential, SRL and SDL pedagogical practices have insufficiently attended to culture or other aspects of sociodemographic diversity as explicitly as other pedagogies (e.g., aboriginal pedagogies, culturally responsive pedagogies, and pedagogies designed to promote resilience). This area needs further research to explore whether and to what extent practices promoting SRL and SDL are flexible enough to accommodate wide ranging cultural perspectives and sociodemographic experiences that likely influence learners uptake of opportunities to regulate learning in classrooms and other learning environments.

Similarly, much research about SRL and SDL focuses on mainstream subject areas (e.g., language arts, science, math, and a limited range of learning environments). We recommend expanding the scope to other subject areas and learning environments. Although fundamental drivers of SRL and SDL—metacognition, strategic action, motivation for learning, and BPN satisfaction—may be invariant across contexts, models of how they manifest or how best to support them in particular contexts would enrich theory and better support practice. For example, our partnership shed light on what it means to be a self-regulating musician and how to operationalize macro processes for supporting SRL and SDL in a music education context. Importantly, we relied on our musician-educator partners to help us understand, for example, what strategies can enhance music practice and what constitutes a complex, meaningful task in the music domain.

Finally, approaches used for studying SRL and SDL need to evolve with theories and models of these phenomena. RPPs are one example of how to align sociocultural perspectives on SRL and SDL with methods used to study them. We argue such theoretical and methodological alignment will evolve models of SRL and SDL that are more robust, socially and ecologically valid, useable, and sustainable. Our evidence for this emerged from the three examples sketched here—the TLT, Ross's community of learners, and the cross-age peer mentoring program. More evidence is needed.

REFERENCES

Bandura, A. (1986). *Social foundations of thought and action: A social-cognitive theory.* Englewood Cliffs, NJ: Prentice Hall.

Blair, C., & Razza, R. P. (2007). Relating effortful control, executive function, and false belief understanding to emerging math and literacy ability in kindergarten. *Child Development, 78,* 647–663.

Butler, D. L., & Cartier, S. (2004). *Apprendre dans différentes activités complexes: Proposition d'un modèle explicative et d'un outil d'evaluation fondés sur l'autorégulation de l'apprentissage* [Learning in varying activities: An explanatory framework and a new evaluation tool founded on a model of self-regulated learning]. Winnipeg, MB: Canadian Society for Studies in Education.

Butler, D. L., & Schnellert, L. (2012). Collaborative inquiry in teacher professional development. *Teaching and Teacher Education, 28,* 1206–1220.

Butler, D. L., & Schnellert, L. (2015). Success for students with learning disabilities: What does self-regulation have to do with it? In T. Cleary (Ed.), *Self-regulated learning interventions with at-risk youth: Enhancing adaptability, performance, and well-being* (pp. 89–112). Washington DC: APA Press.

Chen, B., Mouratidis, A., Ryan, R. M., Sheldon, K.M., Soenens, B., Van Petegem, S.,...& Matos, L. (2015). Basic psychological need satisfaction, need frustration, and need strength across four cultures. *Motivation and Emotion, 39,* 216–236.

Coburn, C. E., & Penuel, W. R. (2016). Research-practice partnerships in education: Outcomes, dynamics, and open questions. *Educational Researcher, 45*(1), 48–54.

Cochran-Smith, M., & Lytle, S. L. (2004). Practitioner inquiry, knowledge and university culture. In J. J., Loughran, M. L., Hamilton, V. K., LaBoskey, & R. L., Russell (Eds.), *International handbook of self-study of teaching and teacher education practices* (pp. 601–649). Dordrecht, Netherlands: Springer.

Community Directions. (2002). *Getting the words and the music: A guide for meaningful involvement in community-based development in Vancouver's downtown eastside Strathcona.* Vancouver, BC: Author.

Dantzer, B. (2017). Psychological well-being: Using self-determination theory to examine the reciprocal benefits of mentoring and teaching others. *International Journal of Social Science and Humanity, 7*(2), 93–101.

Davidson, J., Howe, M., Moore, D., & Sloboda, J. (1996). The role of parental influences in the development of musical ability. *British Journal of Developmental Psychology, 14,* 399–412.

Diamond, A. (2016). Why assessing and improving executive functions early in life is critical. In P. McCardle, L. Freund, & J. A. Griffin (Eds.), *Executive function in preschool-age children: Integrating measurement, neurodevelopment, and translational research* (pp.11–43). Washington, DC: American Psychological Association.

Droe, K., L. (2012). Effect of verbal praise on achievement, goal orientation, motivation, and performance attribution. *Journal of Music Teacher Education, 23*(1), 63–78.

Dweck, C. (2007). *Mindset: The new psychology of success.* New York, NY: Random House.

Evans, P. (2015). Self-determination theory: An approach to motivation in music education. *Musicae Scientiae, 19,* 65–83.

Faulkner, R., Davidson, J. W., & McPherson, G. E. (2010). The value of data mining in music education research and some findings from its application to a study of instrumental learning during childhood. *International Journal of Music Education, 28*(3), 212–230.

Graham, S., & Harris, K. R. (2003). Students with learning disabilities and the process of writing: A meta-analysis of SRSD studies. In L. Swanson, K. R. Harris, & S. Graham (Eds.), *Handbook of learning disabilities* (pp. 323–344). New York, NY: Guilford Press.

Hadwin, A., Jarvela, S., & Miller, M. (2018). Self-regulation, co-regulation, and shared regulation in collaborative learning environments. In D. H. Schunk & J. A. Greene (Eds.), *Handbook of self-regulation of learning and performance* (2nd ed., pp. 83–106). New York, NY: Routledge.

Hadwin, A., & Oshige, M. (2011). Self-regulation, co-regulation, and socially-shared regulation: Exploring perspectives of social in self-regulated learning theory. *Teachers College Record, 113*(2), 240–264.

Halbert, J., & Kaser, L. (2013). *Spirals of inquiry: For equity and quality.* Vancouver, BC: BC Principals' & Vice Principal's Association.

Howard, J. L., Gagne, M., & Bureau, J. S. (2017). Testing a continuum structure of self-determined motivation: A meta-analysis. *Psychological Bulletin, 143*(12), 1346–1377.

Hutchinson, L. R. (2013). *Young children's engagement in self-regulation at school* (Doctoral dissertation). Retrieved from https://open.library.ubc.ca/cIRcle/collections/ ubctheses/24/items/1.0073717

Hutchinson, L. R., Perry, N. E., Yee, N., Dantzer, B., Lo, D., & Restrepo, L. (2015, August). *Demographic variables in children's self-regulation.* Poster presented at the American Psychological Association, Toronto, ON, Canada.

Jang, H., Reeve, J., & Deci, E. L. (2010). Engaging students in learning activities: It is not autonomy support or structure, but autonomy support and structure. *Journal of Educational Psychology, 102,* 588–600.

Jang, H., Reeve, J., & Halusic, M. (2016). A new autonomy-supportive way of teaching that increases conceptual learning: teaching in students' preferred ways. *The Journal of Experimental Education, 84*(4), 686–701.

Mason, L. H., & Reid, R. (2018). Self-regulation: Implications for individuals with special needs. In D. H. Schunk & J. A. Greene (Eds.), *Handbook of self-regulation of learning and performance* (2nd ed., pp. 473–484). New York, NY: Routledge.

McCaslin, M. (2009). Co-regulation of student motivation and emergent identity. *Educational Psychologist, 44*(2), 137–146.

McClelland, M. M., & Cameron, C. E. (2012). Self-regulation in early childhood: Improving conceptual clarity and developing ecologically valid measures. *Child Development Perspectives, 6*(2), 136–142.

McClelland, M. M., & Wanless, S. B. (2012). Growing up with assets and risks: The importance of self-regulation for academic achievement. *Research in Human Development, 9*(4), 278–297.

McInerney, D. M., & Ali, J. (2013). Indigenous motivational profiles: Do they reflect collectivism? A cross-cultural analysis of similarities and differences between groups classified as individualist and collectivist cultures. In R. Craven, G. Bodkin-Andrews, & J. Mooney (Eds.), *Indigenous peoples* (pp. 211–232). Charlotte, NC: Information Age.

McPherson, G. E. (2005). From child to musician: Skill development during the beginning stages of learning an instrument. *Psychology of Music, 33*, 5–35.

McPherson, G. E., Davidson, J. W., & Evans, P. (2016). Playing an instrument. In G. E. McPherson (Ed.), *The child as musician: A handbook of musical development* (2nd ed., pp. 401–421). Oxford, England: Oxford University Press.

McPherson, G. E., Miksza, P., & Evans, P. (2018). Self-regulated learning in music practice and performance. In D. H. Schunk & J. A. Greene (Eds.), *Handbook of self-regulation of learning and performance* (2nd ed., 181–193). New York, NY: Routledge.

McPherson, G. E., & Zimmerman, B. J. (2002). Self-regulation of musical learning: A social cognitive perspective. In R. Colwell & C. Richardson (Eds.), *The new handbook of research on music teaching and learning* (pp. 130–175). New York, NY: Oxford University Press.

McPherson, G. E., & Zimmerman, B. J. (2011). Self-regulation of musical learning: A social cognitive perspective on developing performance skills. In R. Colwell & P. Webster (Eds.), *MENC handbook of research on music learning: Applications* (Vol. 2, pp. 130–175). New York, NY: Oxford University Press.

Moffitt, T. E., Arseneault, L., Belsky, D., Dickson, N., Hancox, R. J., Harrington, H., . . . Heckman, J. J. (2011). A gradient of childhood self-control predicts health, wealth, and public safety. *Proceedings of the National Academy of Sciences of the United States of America, 108*(7), 2693–2698.

Newnham, J. (2005). *An overview of Vancouver's downtown eastside for UBC learning exchange trek program participants.* Vancouver, BC: University of British Columbia Learning Exchange.

Orosco, M. J., & O'Connor, R. (2014). Culturally responsive instruction for English language learners with learning disabilities. *Journal of Learning Disabilities, 47*(6) 515–531.

Perry, N. E. (1998). Young children's self-regulated learning and the contexts that support it. *Journal of Educational Psychology, 90,* 715–729.

Perry, N. E. (2013). Classroom processes that support self-regulation in young children [Monograph]. *British Journal of Educational Psychology, Monograph Series II: Psychological Aspects of Education—Current Trends, 10,* 45–68.

Perry, N. E., Brenner, C. A., & MacPherson, N. (2015). Using teacher learning teams as framework for bridging theory and practice in self-regulated learning. In T. J. Cleary (Ed.), *Self-regulated learning interventions with at-risk youth: Enhancing adaptability, performance, and well-being* (pp. 229–250). Washington, DC: American Psychological Association.

Perry, N., & Drummond, L. (2002). Helping young students become self-regulated researchers and writers. *Reading Teacher, 56,* 298–310.

Perry, N. E., Hutchinson, L., Yee, N., & Määtä, E. (2018). Advances in understanding young children's self-regulation of learning. In D. H. Schunk & J. A. Greene (Eds.), *Handbook of self-regulation of learning and performance* (2nd ed., pp. 457–472). New York, NY: Routledge.

Perry, N. E., & Rahim, A. (2011). Studying self-regulated learning in classrooms. In B. Zimmerman & D. Schunk (Eds.), *Handbook of self-regulation of learning and performance* (pp. 122–136). New York, NY: Routledge.

Perry, N. E., & VandeKamp, K. O. (2000). Creating classroom contexts that support young children's development of self-regulated learning. *International Journal of Educational Research, 33,* 821–843.

Perry, N. E., Yee, N., Mazabel, S., Lisaingo, S., & Määtä, E. (2017). Using self-regulated learning as a framework for creating inclusive classrooms for ethnically and linguistically diverse learners in Canada. In N. J. Cabrera & B. Leyendecker (Eds.), *Handbook on positive development of minority children and youth* (pp. 361–384). New York, NY: Springer.

Reeve, J. (2006). Teachers as facilitators: What autonomy-supportive teachers do and why their students benefit. *Elementary School Journal, 106,* 225–236.

Reeve, J. (2015). Giving and summoning autonomy support in hierarchical relationships. *Social and Personality Psychology Compass, 9(8),* 406–418.

Reeve, J., Bolt, E., & Cai, Y. (1999). Autonomy-supportive teachers: How they teach and motivate students. *Journal of Educational Psychology, 91(3),* 537–548.

Reeve, J., & Jang, H. (2006). What teachers say and do to support students' autonomy during a learning activity. *Journal of Educational Psychology, 98,* 209–218.

Rutter, M. (2013). Annual research review: Resilience-Clinical implications. *Journal of Child Psychology and Psychiatry, 54(4),* 474–487.

Ryan, R. M. (1995). Psychological needs and the facilitation of integrative processes. *Journal of Personality, 63(3),* 397–427.

Ryan, R. M., & Deci, E. L. (2009). Promoting self-determined school engagement: Motivation, learning and well-being. In K. R. Wentzel & A. Wigfield (Eds.), *Handbook of motivation at school* (pp. 171–195). New York, NY: Routledge.

Ryan, R. M., & Deci, E. L. (2017). *Self-determination theory: Basic psychological needs in motivation development and wellness.* New York, NY: Guilford Press.

Schunk, D. H. (1999). Social-self interaction and achievement behavior. *Educational Psychologist, 34,* 219–227.

Schunk. D. H., & Zimmerman, B. J. (1997). Social origins of self-regulatory competence. *Educational Psychologist, 32*, 195–208.

Sheldon, K. M., Abad, N., & Omoile, J. (2009). Testing self-determination theory via Nigerian and Indian adolescents. *International Journal of Behavioral Development, 33*(5), 451–459.

Shogren, K. A., & Shaw, L. A. (2016). The role of autonomy, self-realization, and psychological empowerment in predicting outcomes for youth with disabilities. *Remedial and Special Education, 37*, 55–62.

Soenens, B., Park, S. Y., Vansteenkiste, M., & Mouratidis, A. (2012). Perceived parental psychological control and adolescent depressive experiences: A cross-cultural study with Belgian and South Korean adolescents. *Journal of Adolescence, 35*, 261–272.

Taylor, I. M., & Lonsdale, C. (2010). Cultural differences in the relationships among autonomy support, psychological need satisfaction, subjective vitality, and effort in British and Chinese physical education. *Journal of Sport and Exercise Psychology, 32*, 655–673.

Taylor, I. M., & Ntoumanis, N. (2007). Teacher motivational strategies and student self-determination in physical education. *Journal of Educational Psychology, 99*(4), 747–760.

Tian, L., Chen, H., & Huebner, E. S. (2014). The longitudinal relationships between basic psychological needs satisfaction at school and school-related subjective well-being in adolescents. *Social Indicators Research, 119*(1), 353–372.

Timperley, H., Kaser, L., & Halbert, J. (2014). *A framework for transforming learning in schools: Innovation and the spiral of inquiry.* Victoria, Australia: Centre for Strategic Education.

Usher, E. L., & Schunk, D. H. (2018). Social cognitive theoretical perspective of self-regulation. In D. H. Schunk & J. A. Greene (Eds.), *Handbook of self-regulation of learning and performance* (2nd ed., pp. 19–35). New York, NY: Routledge.

Varela, W., Abrami, P. C., & Upitis, R. (2016). Self-regulation and music learning: A systematic review. *Psychology of Music, 44*(1), 55–74.

Vygotsky, (1978). *Mind in society.* Cambridge, MA: Harvard University Press.

Wang, Q., Pomerantz, E. M., & Chen, H. (2007). The role of parents' control in early adolescents' psychological functioning: A longitudinal investigation of United States and China. *Child Development, 78*, 1592–1610.

Wertsch, J. V., Tulviste, P., & Hagstrom, F. (1993). A sociocultural approach to agency. In E. A. Forman, N. Minick, & C. A. Stone (Eds.), *Contexts for learning: Sociocultural dynamics in children's development* (pp. 336–356). New York, NY: Oxford University Press.

Winne, P. H. (2017). The trajectory of scholarship about self-regulated learning. *Teachers College Record, 119*(13), 1–16.

Winne, P. H. (2018). Cognition and metacognition within self-regulated learning. In D. H. Schunk & J. A. Greene (Eds.), *Handbook of self-regulation of learning and performance* (2nd ed., pp. 36–48). New York, NY: Routledge.

Winne, P. H., & Hadwin, A. (1998). Studying as self-regulated learning. In D. Hacker, J. Dunlosky, & A. Graesser (Eds.), *Metacognition in educational theory and practice* (pp. 279–306). Hillsdale, NJ: Erlbaum.

Winne, P. H., Hadwin, A., & Perry, N. E. (2013). Metacognition and computer-supported collaborative learning. In C. E. Hmelo-Silvier, C. A Chinn, C. K. K. Chan, & A. O'Donnell (Eds.), *International handbook of collaborative learning* (pp. 462–479). New York, NY: Routledge.

Zimmerman, B. J. (2008). Investigating self-regulation and motivation: Historical background, methodological developments and future prospects. *American Educational Research Journal, 45*(1), 166–183.

Zimmerman. B. J., & Campillo, M. (2003). Motivating self-regulated problem solvers. In J. E. Davidson & R. J. Sternberg (Eds.), *The psychology of problem solving* (pp. 233–262). Cambridge, England: Cambridge University Press.

CHAPTER 14

CO-REGULATION

A Model for Classroom Research in a Vygotskian Perspective

Mary McCaslin
Christine Calderon Vriesema

We have been invited to discuss work that McCaslin and colleagues have continued to engage in the Vygotskian tradition in the last decade. We are honored to do so. This chapter includes a working model of co-regulation (McCaslin, 2009) that provides a framework for how research might be conducted within a Vygostkian perspective and three illustrative streams of our research with elementary school students that are guided by it. Collectively, the research methods of each study mirror the three dominant instructional formats in classrooms: whole class, private, and small groups. Each study is discussed in the context of the co-regulation model and related scholarship. As in the original chapter (McCaslin, 2004), with each study we build a case for the importance of the individual within a sociocultural perspective; an individual whose identity is informed by changing personal capabilities in emergent interaction with historical and cultural events.

Big Theories Revisited 2, pages 319–352
Copyright © 2018 by Information Age Publishing
All rights of reproduction in any form reserved.

Emergent interaction (Wertsch & Stone, 1985) stresses reciprocal processes of mediation and internalization and highlights that both individuals and the social and cultural events of their lives change and influence each other. An essential point of a Vygotskian perspective and the co-regulation model: we are all part of a unit larger than ourselves. We begin with a short summary of Vygotskian sociocultural theory to set the foundation for our discussion of the co-regulation model and corresponding research.

A BRIEF REVIEW OF BASIC VYGOTSKIAN TENETS

In "Co-Regulation of Opportunity, Activity, and Identity in Student Motivation: Elaboration on Vygotskian Themes," McCaslin (2004) presented the influence of Marx and Engels on Vygotskian sociocultural theory. These are important considerations for understanding how Vygotsky could argue that experience is (a) *cultural* because it represents socially-structured tasks and tools, (b) *historical* because it represents the storehouse of knowledge of human kind (Luria, 1979, p. 44), and (c) *personal* because biological readiness and opportunity enable the individual to refine capacity for self-direction and thus meaningful social contribution. This perspective has three basic tenets that inform the authors' understandings of classroom research: multiple functions of language, social origins of higher psychological processes, and the integration of the affective and intellectual in human activity.

Vygotsky asserted language as the basic unit of analysis in human dynamics. Language begins in the social world: Communication from others affords communication with others and ultimately, transforms into communication (or direction) with the self. Communication with others is about transforming one's thoughts into words; self-directive language is about turning words into thoughts (Vygotsky, 1962). The multiple functions of language are consistent with the social origins of higher psychological processes: Words learned from others are transformed into thoughts guiding one's self, or what currently is known as *self-regulation*. Self-direction or regulation is about self-awareness, working toward goals, and planning solutions to problems. While behavioral outcomes might manifest differently across cultures (e.g., based on specific practices, expectations, etc.), the source of regulation remains the same. In a Vygotskian perspective, the social environment highlights the importance of opportunity and the role of culture in shaping regulation. In short, self-regulation is made possible by language learned through communication by and with others in one's environment; it is made necessary by problematic events and situations.

As the multiple functions of language suggest, one's mind is the product of social life in the Vygotskian perspective. What is originally shared by people through communication, in emergent interaction with personal development (Wertsch & Stone, 1985), becomes a form of behavior within one person (Luria, 1979). Thus, higher psychological processes begin in the social world. The foundational interpersonal role in intrapersonal understandings suggests the third tenet of a Vygotskian perspective that undergirds the work we present in this chapter: the dynamic relationship between affect and intellect. Vygotsky considered their separation a major weakness of traditional psychology: Thoughts don't think themselves; people do. People with felt concerns, believed strengths, and perceived interests; people who are engaged, with others, in living in their time and place. (For extended discussions by McCaslin of Vygotskian theoretical constructs with classroom-related research illustrations, see McCaslin, 2004, (McCaslin) Rohrkemper, 1989, McCaslin & Hickey, 2001, & McCaslin & Murdock, 1991.)

In addition to Vygotskian theory, our work also is influenced by activity sociocultural theory (e.g., Wertsch, 1985; Zinchenko, 1985). According to activity theorists, Vygotsky's focus on word meaning as the basic unit for understanding the dynamic relationship between the individual and the social world was too narrow. Instead they asserted human activity as the basic unit linking the individual and society. Activity is defined as "tool-mediated, goal-directed, action" (Wertsch, 1985, pp. 101, 76, respectively). Consistent with Vygotsky, activity theorists adhere to the social origins of these practices; however, typically they situate motives and goals in the social realm and do not consider how these social motives and goals might become properties of the individual (Kozulin, 1986; Leontiev, 1974, 1978).

Wertsch (1985) and colleagues extended activity theory to consider the emergent interaction between the interpersonal and intrapersonal planes. This approach allows for the development of personal identity consistent with a Vygotskian perspective (Penuel & Wertsch, 1995), although not studied by him. Tensions between activity theory (and recent situative approaches in learning and motivation, e.g., Nolan, Horn, & Ward, 2015), and Vygotskian perspectives are evident in considerations of individual differences among people within situations and settings, which as we discuss subsequently, are at the core of McCaslin and colleagues' work thus far.

Our research program incorporates elements from all three Vygotskian tenets. However, we foreground how students might differently mediate classroom opportunities through their activity and relationships, and what that means for their identity as students and classroom participants. The model of co-regulated learning (McCaslin, 2009) guides our work. It is one attempt to operationalize fundamental processes within a Vygotskian perspective, which we believe is useful for cross-national, cross-cultural considerations. We live in a time of considerable international challenges and changes, turmoil not unlike the era in which Vygotsky lived and came to understand the dynamic tensions among cultural, historical, and personal influences upon individuals and their societies. Thus, this perspective seems especially useful to capture moments of change and possibility in the current global landscape. The Vygotskian assertion of social origins of higher psychological processes suggests as well that these dynamics are universal dynamics across cultures, languages, and individuals. They are fundamental dynamics during times of cultural flux and continuity. Cultural differences manifest in the products of social origins and internalization dynamics (e.g., whether you speak a given language, adhere to [or resist] a given set of SRGs [standards, rules, and goals], reside in heavily populated cities or remote settings). The social origins assertions, however, claim that the surface-level manifestations adhere to the same foundational processes. For example, cultures may differ in the value they place on self-regulation; indeed, a major goal of our work is to counter the prevailing U.S. adherence to the model of the independent, self-regulating, individual. We seek to go "outside the body" and situate the individual in a unit larger than him or herself. We use the term *co-regulation* to express this relationship of the individual with other persons, opportunities, and artifacts. The basic Vygotskian point, however, is that the social, cultural, and historical influences, which are in a dynamic reciprocal relationship with the developing person, are the origins of those capabilities, beliefs, and values (SRGs).

A MODEL OF CO-REGULATED LEARNING

McCaslin (2009) represented the dynamic relationship between the interpersonal and intrapersonal realms through the construct of co-regulation. The influences of Vygotskian constructs are evident. Co-regulation (McCaslin, 2009) posits individuals who are social by nature and nurture, have a basic need for interpersonal participation and validation (McCaslin & Burross, 2008), and differ in how and what they participate—their adaptation (McCaslin & Burross, 2011; McCaslin & Vega, 2013; McCaslin, Vriesema, & Burggraf, 2016; McCaslin, Vriesema, & Vega, 2015). We foreground co-regulation in the social realm (e.g., the role of opportunity and interpersonal relationships in students' activity and adaptation in the classroom), and what that means for students' personal potential, emergent interaction, and identity dynamics.

Model Components and Processes

Figure 14.1 presents the co-regulation model that frames research on how individual differences among learners and contexts emerge. It locates three broad sources of influence: cultural (societal), social, and personal, which are well represented in the social sciences literatures. The model also

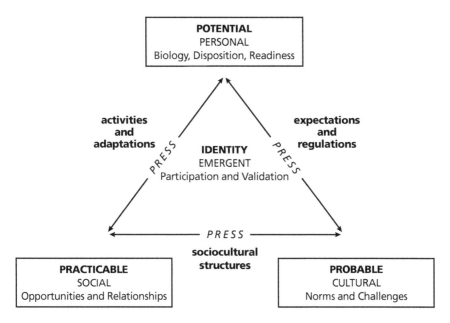

Figure 14.1   Co-regulation model of student motivation and emergent identity. *Source:* McCaslin (2009).

stresses the reciprocal presses among them, which are less-readily studied. In this model, it is the reciprocal presses among these sources of influence that co-regulate emergent identity. Reciprocal presses, for example, yield potential challenges, conflicts, and affirmations that afford learning how to struggle, negotiate, compromise, and strive as well as thrive.

Briefly, *cultural* sources of influence represent the norms and challenges that are associated with the culture (or nation or society). There is an assertion of probable, or what is most likely or desirable to happen, through cultural expectations and regulations; however, probable is not inevitable. Personal and social sources of influence can resist and press back upon cultural expectations; witness the dynamics of current cultural and political events around the globe.

Social sources of influence represent the practicable, those opportunities and relationships that can and do influence what happens in the everydayness of one's life. Schools are sociocultural institutions that negotiate the press between cultural expectations and practicable opportunities. For example, nations look to their schools to deal with cultural challenges (e.g., attenuate the impacts of poverty in the United States; facilitate migration in the European Union).

Personal sources of influence represent individual potential, including biology, readiness, language, and dispositions, all of which are in emergent interaction with the social world—including both social and cultural influences. The press between the personal and social within classrooms—how activities and adaptations are negotiated—is a major focus of the studies we subsequently present. However, each study acknowledges the press of cultural-personal dynamics in this process; each includes students who attend schools that serve families who live in poverty in the United States. Thus, each study embraces the potential malleability of cultural expectations through the workings of the public school.

Together, cultural, social, and personal influences co-regulate—challenge, shape, and guide—student identity. Students differ—in what they bring to a situation, in what and how they participate, and what that means for their time and place. Importantly, none of the sources of influence—personal, social, cultural—are equally distributed; nor are opportunities for personally-meaningful, socially-validated, and culturally-valued engagement. It is not a level playing field. Consistent with a Vygotskian approach, the co-regulation model serves as both a vehicle for understanding cultural-social-personal dynamics and a call to action.

A common misunderstanding of this perspective arises from its Vygotskian roots; namely, the co-regulation construct is often equated with the Zone of Proximal Development (ZPD). Vygotsky defined the ZPD as the "gap" between what a person can accomplish on his/her own as compared with accomplishments achieved with the assistance of a more capable other. It is reasonable to assume that a Vygotskian-influenced perspective, like this one, adheres to top-down socialization dyads and, as such, is restricted to internalization dynamics that ultimately render the learner more capable through scaffolded assistance. However, this interpretation does not capture the essence or breadth of the co-regulation perspective. Rather, co-regulation builds on the notion of relationship, the essential construct of the ZPD. Relationships between and among co-participants mutually regulate all participants in some way (Yowell & Smylie, 1999). Relationship is the essential and fundamental unit that undergirds ZPD and co-regulation. ZPD is an exemplar of this fundamental relationship not the definition of it. Co-regulation dynamics are not restricted to top-down dyadic socialization or instructional dynamics; rather, co-regulation embraces mutual regulation among cultural, social, and personal sources of influence. In the best-case scenario, each source is enriched; however, that is not necessarily the typical scenario.

Personal History

Central to the co-regulation model is the assertion that students are historical beings; they have a personal history that is part of their adaptation in both the present and expectations for their future. Thus, we assert individual differences in student experience and activity—their mediation of and adaptation to contexts, opportunities, and relationships. These individual differences are expressed in the present but they are saturated with a history of felt experiences and beliefs about the future. Experience and expectations are interpreted within developing cognitive capabilities, and remembered within a cognitive capacity that may differ over time. Thus, in the co-regulation perspective all sources of influence—personal, cultural, and social—are historical (in contrast to situative perspectives in learning and motivation; e.g., Turner & Nolan, 2015; Greeno, 1998). Finally, students' experiences—their mediation and adaptation—involve the fusion of the affective and intellectual, which also is consistent with a Vygotskian perspective on human functioning. Recently, we have termed this constellation, *emotional adaptation*, to more clearly represent our intent; in this chapter, we elaborate on this construct in the context of research on making mistakes.

Distinction From Other Types of Regulation

To summarize, co-regulation captures the dynamic interplay between personal, social, and cultural sources of influence. Together with students' personal histories, these forces shape individual student identity and the ways in which students approach learning tasks. Scholars in the United States and other countries—particularly those who study the regulation dynamics of individuals in groups or in interaction with others—increasingly share our assertion that the individual is part of a larger unit than him/herself. However, in spite of the shared assertion, researchers do not use similar vocabulary or even agree on essential constructs. A review of the literature reveals constructs such as co-regulation, social-regulation, shared-regulation, socially-shared regulation, socially-shared metacognition, and other-regulation; each of which is linked in one way or another to self-regulation. Several scholars have worked to capture the variation and commonalities, as well as the inaccuracies, among these constructs in an attempt to bring order to and empirically examine their usefulness (e.g., Adams Forsyth, Dollarhide, Miskell, & Ware, 2015; Järvelä & Järvenoja, 2011; Volet & Mansfield, 2006).

We present two examples of extensive reviews of the regulation literature. Hadwin, Järvelä, and Miller (2018), scholars from Canada and Finland, differentiated between self-regulation, shared regulation, and co-regulation. They organize these constructs by asserting co-regulation as the mediational mechanism shaping how students engage learning tasks individually (self-regulation) and with others (shared regulation), expanding upon the Winne and Hadwin COPES (Conditions, Operations, Products,

Evaluations, Standards) model of self-regulation. While self- and shared-regulation both consider students' goals, metacognition, task enactment, and so on, self-regulation reflects the practices of an individual person whereas shared regulation captures the practices of an entire group. In both cases, cultural, social, and personal influences shape the particular behaviors that students enact.

In comparison, Moreno, Sanabria, and López (2016), scholars from Columbia, trace the evolution of co-regulation of learning to earlier research on cooperative/collaborative learning. Like Hadwin and colleagues, these scholars also tackle a lack of conceptual and theoretical clarity in the co-regulation literature. They distinguish the theoretical foundations among the various regulation constructs: co-regulation (Vygotskian tradition); social or socio-cognitive regulation (Bandura's triadic reciprocal determinism); and the systemic position based in situative perspectives (Greeno, 1998), which posits groups as emergent self- and co-regulation social systems (Volet & Vauras, 2013). Like Hadwin and colleagues, Moreno et al. view co-regulation as a fundamental process; the issue of concern being more about in what context, with whom, and for what purpose (e.g., transitional support, maintenance of joint activity). They conclude their review endorsing the shared regulation construct as the most effective mode of co-regulation; that is, the monitoring of joint activity or interdependent processes in the service of a shared goal.

Clarity and precision are clearly important to theoretical and empirical advancement of regulation constructs; however, so too is evidence that theoretical efforts illuminate real-world, real-time practices and events. Toward that goal, we briefly present three international research examples that address co-regulation dynamics in day care, higher education, and vocational work settings. The array of ages and contexts demonstrates the utility of the co-regulation family of constructs.

Research conducted by Kurki, Järvenoja, Järvela, and Mykkänen (2017) featured social components of individual regulation dynamics. Kurki et al. examined the co-regulation of 30 children during challenging situations in a Finnish day care setting. Using video analysis, researchers coded the strategies that the students used and indicated whether or not the teacher intervened. Among other findings, Kurki and colleagues found that day care students developed strategies for challenging situations when the teacher was not present; however, the behaviors reflected simple strategies, such as using verbal utterances or physical behaviors (e.g., stealing toys from other children). While the simple strategies reflected attempts to regulate emotion, they were not necessarily effective at addressing the challenges. In contrast, when the teacher was present, children were more likely to use redirecting as a strategy. Moreover, after the teacher became involved, sequential analyses indicated that children subsequently redirected their activity or attention even after the teacher the left.

The research by Kurki et al. (2017) highlights the relationship between personal and social presses within the context of a Finnish day care center. In particular, the communication afforded by key relationships in the environment (social press) supported students' expression and development of regulatory strategies that extended the behaviors that students engaged on their own (personal press). This research underscores an important component of the co-regulation model regarding the role of interaction in shaping students' regulation. Namely, the research exemplifies co-regulation within the ZPD of self- and other-regulation strategies because of the shared influence of social context (in this case, the student–teacher interactions) and personal influences (e.g., student age, disposition, etc.) on student behavior in challenging interactions with peers.

Bakhtiar, Webster, and Hadwin (2017) also considered regulation dynamics in challenging situations in their study of the quality of emotion regulation among Canadian higher education undergraduates in computer-supported collaborative learning. This study extensively examined the interactions of two groups of four students, each group representing a positive or negative group climate. Even in a context of limited duration (one 90-minute session), these researchers identified the importance of initial conditions (appropriately setting the scaffold) and regulation of emotion (especially in the give-and-take of real time) and found that negative emotions constrained shared adaptations in the context of learning challenges. In comparison, encouragement and motivational statements supported positive group climate. The authors discussed their findings in terms of the interplay among self-regulated learning (SRL) and socially shared regulation of learning (SSRL). They conclude, "Hence, support tools in collaborative contexts should not only be geared towards supporting the collective group, but should also support individual work within the group" (Bakhtiar, Webster, & Hadwin, 2017, n.p.).

Finally, Motta, Cattaneo, and Gurlner (2017) studied apprentice chefs in work settings in Switzerland. Their focus was on the acquisition of content and specific professional skills among 3rd year chef apprentices, ages 17–35. Motta and colleagues elaborated upon the theoretical position of Volet and colleagues (2009) and the empirical work of Rogat and Linnenbrink-Garcia (2011). In contrast to Bakhtair and colleagues (2017), Motta et al. did not find linkages between positive and negative social emotional interactions and the quality of group interaction. Rather, their findings highlighted the role of tentativeness in question-asking and explanation-giving in initiating and maintaining high-level content co-regulation episodes. Tentativeness may function as an invitation to think.

In sum, scholars agree that the area of co-regulation and related social constructs in the manifestation of "self"-regulation is burgeoning and lacking in precision. We agree that clarification work is needed. Even so, the three international research examples we briefly described (conducted in Finland, Canada, and Switzerland, respectively) suggest the utility of the co-regulation perspective, broadly defined, across ages and contexts. Selected examples also suggest the difficulty in capturing these regulation dynamics; the rigor of each study, however, should go far to increase precision in the research that follows.

Three Studies of Student Co-Regulation in Elementary School

We now describe three studies we conducted within the co-regulation framework hypothesized by McCaslin (2009) that is guided by a Vygotskian perspective. Each study incorporated specific aspects of the model and used the framework to guide the relevant research questions. With an understanding that McCaslin and her colleagues aimed to address educational policy and practice within their particular cultural context, the three studies were situated in the United States and focused on socioeconomic conditions, specifically poverty, related to schooling. However, we argue that the tenets of the theory can extend beyond this particular region and can be used to describe the relationships between cultural, social, and personal presses in other cultures as well. Portrayal of the experiencing student—what it means to *be that student*—is a primary goal of each study. In the first, we focus on the most common classroom instructional format in the United States, whole class instruction, and ask how students might differentially mediate and internalize the learning opportunities this instructional format affords. Cultural presses upon students include their exposure to the stresses of family poverty and mobility and societal demands for improvements in their test score achievement.

In the second illustration, we examine how students reportedly mediate and cope with three social/instructional formats in classrooms: private, whole-class, and small learning groups. Our emphasis shifts from student mediation of perceived learning opportunities to the emotional experiences that each format affords. We examine students' reported self-conscious emotions and coping behavior in the context of each instructional format and (a) examine how students reportedly experience and cope within each, and (b) consider how their attempts to care for the self might protect or undermine their relationships with others. We also look more closely at scarcity of resources (in the cultural and personal arenas) as potential presses upon student reported emotion and coping—their emotional adaptation. Participating students attend schools that serve families exposed to the cultural presses of relatively high or moderate poverty density; students also differ in their relative readiness to learn.

In the third illustration, we more directly examine how students' reported emotional adaptation informs their real-time interpersonal relationships in small group learning contexts. This study combines the self-report instrumentation of Studies 1 and 2 and includes systematic coding of students' interactions with peers, their "table talk," in small group learning in mathematics. We also examine potential cultural presses on students who attend schools that serve relatively affluent families (higher socio-economic status or SES) as well as those who serve families with fewer financial resources (lower SES). Unlike studies one and two that focused only on students whose families live in relative poverty, this final study allows us to consider how students who live with the press of relatively more and less cultural capital might differentially mediate and adapt to challenges of learning in classrooms; specifically, in how they co-regulate the stresses of small group learning.

STUDENTS IN TEACHER-CENTERED WHOLE-CLASS INSTRUCTION

Comprehensive School Reform (CSR) was one federal program in the United States aimed at improving the teaching and test performance of students attending schools identified as needing improvement. Given the covariation of financial resources and student achievement in the United States, most schools identified as needing improvement are Title I schools that primarily serve students whose families live in poverty. Cultural demands for improvement required identified schools to adopt a government-approved, research-based, school-wide program. Consequences were imposed if student achievement, defined as performance on standardized tests, did not improve. Students could be retained in grade and principals fired. Subsequent versions of federal reforms changed the accountability press to include teachers as well. For example, Race to the Top legislation, enacted on February 17, 2009, targeted teachers. One constant among them: cultural demands that schools ameliorate poverty.

Tom Good and Mary McCaslin (McCaslin & Good, 2008) led a multi-year investigation of the implementation of CSR programs in Grades 3–5 classrooms in Arizona, a state known for its meager financial investment in the people—teachers and students—who work in the public schools. Part of that research involved systematic observation of classroom teaching practices (McCaslin et al, 2006). Results indicated that classroom practices primarily involved teacher-centered instruction in well-managed and friendly classrooms in which most students were on task most of the time. In the main, students were doing what they were asked to do.

McCaslin and Burross (2011) subsequently examined how teachers and their students might mutually adapt to the press of school improvement demands. A subgroup of classrooms from the original sample participated. The sample included teachers ($N = 33$) in Grades 3–5 in schools ($N = 5$) implementing school reform and their students ($N = 439$, with parent consent and student assent). McCaslin and Burross asked the following research question: Do students in these classrooms differ in non-observed ways and, if so, how do these differences relate to instructional opportunity, classroom tasks, and test performance? In terms of the co-regulation model, the study was grounded in the cultural press upon schools to improve the test performance of children living in poverty. In the foreground are the teacher-facilitated practicable opportunities and relationships within classrooms and the self-reported adaptations of their students.

Instructional Opportunities

The systematic observation protocol (McCaslin et al., 2006) catalogued instructional practices and curricular opportunities, student activity, and classroom relationships. Instructional practices data (including curriculum task features) were subjected to exploratory factor analysis procedures that yielded four independent representations of the timing and function of teacher scaffolding within teacher-centered instruction. Each instructional approach has been well-represented in curriculum/instructional literatures for some time: (a) guided elaboration (teachers use guidance and question-asking to encourage student thinking beyond the given information); (b) direct instruction (teachers promote student acquisition of basic facts and skills in an instructional press for correctness); (c) structured problem-solving (teacher aligns task demands focused on student thinking/reasoning with teacher question-asking that targets task managerial/procedural knowledge); and (d) review (teachers ask task managerial/procedural and correctness questions to assess student retention).

Observed Student Adaptation

Observation data suggested that students behaved similarly (i.e., mostly on task and productive) in the diverse instructional opportunities. However, students sought more teacher support in the structured problem solving instructional approach, which required relatively more abstract thinking. End of year test performance revealed that instructional opportunities were differentially related to student performance on the standardized SAT9 subtests. Direct instruction (DI) was the only instructional opportunity positively correlated with student test performance. This suggests that DI (of basic facts and skills) best negotiated the press between these students' potential (e.g., readiness, participation) and sociocultural demands for increasing their performance on mandated tests.

Student Reported Mediation and Adaptation

Student mediation was measured with a pencil-and-paper self-monitoring instrument ("How I Was in Class") consisting of 20 sentences that students were to underline if it described their behavior in class. Sentences comprised three scales: (a) enhancing (student behavior positively contributes to own and potentially others' learning, e.g., "I was doing my part."); (b) interfering/withdrawn (student behavior is withdrawn, limiting one's own and not contributing to others' learning, e.g., "My head hurt."); and (c) neutral (behavior that is not supportive or withdrawn, e.g., "I was sitting."). Sentences were read aloud to the students to control for reading readiness and inflection. Reports were obtained at mid-year and in spring of the school year.

Individual Differences

"How I Was in Class" reports suggested that students differed in their reported adaptations to learning in classrooms. Exploratory factor analyses identified five independent student mediation profiles: anxious and withdrawn, good worker, engaged learner, disengaged and distracting, and struggling and persistent. Table 14.1 includes three example items in each factor with the highest loadings obtained in mid-year and illustrates how the profiles differ.

Thus, while students "looked" similar to observers, on task and doing what they were asked to do, their mediation reports suggested they differ in important ways in the quality of their adaptation. As the factor items suggest, they also differ in salience; some profiles may be more apparent to teachers than others. Thus, some students' needs may be more readily recognized and met. Differences among students also likely enhance (e.g., good worker, engaged learner, struggling, and persistent) or detract (e.g., anxious and withdrawn, disengaged and distracting) from others in their learning community. Individual differences were somewhat stable over the school year, especially among the less optimal anxious and withdrawn and disengaged and distracting students. Results also suggested that good worker and engaged learner adaptations mesh well with an achievement press.

Relationships With Test Performance

Student performance (by grade level due to federal FERPA restrictions) on the required SAT9 subtests at the end of the school year was significantly

TABLE 14.1   Individual Differences in Students' Approach to Self-Monitoring at Time 1: Factor Labels, Sample Items, and Loadings (N = 439)

Self-Monitoring Time 1 Factors	Sample Items	Loadings
1. Anxious and Withdrawn	My stomach felt funny.	.676
	My mouth was dry.	.597
	My head hurt.	.544
2. Good Worker	I was listening.	.661
	I was working.	.602
	I was ready.	.580
3. Engaged Learner	I was smiling.	.636
	I was helping.	.635
	I was getting help.	.496
4. Disengaged and Distracting	I was talking.	.812
	I was looking around.	.627
	I was tired.	.459
5. Struggling and Persistent	I kept getting stuck.	.756
	I was getting help.	.512
	My hands were shaky.	.431

Source: McCaslin & Burross (2011).

related to three student self-monitoring factors. Anxious and withdrawn was negatively correlated, and struggling and persistent was positively correlated, with each SAT9 subtest. Disengaged and distracting also was positively correlated with performances in the math and reading subtests. These findings suggest meaningful individual differences among students in how they adapt to classroom demands that are not readily observed and that co-regulate students' adaptive learning (Rohrkemper & Corno, 1988). McCaslin and Burross (2011) noted that challenge/skill ratios that are sensitive to students' level of readiness and characteristic adaptations may help teachers understand how student adaptation to instructional opportunities might differ. It is one thing to struggle yet optimistically persist, quite another to struggle in the context of insecurity and frustration. The former can support eventual success; failures now and then teach how to stay with it, try another tactic, or reformulate the goal. The ultimate successful result reinforces the whole scenario. In the latter case, the stress of chronic difficulties in which students are admonished to "grit and bear it" do little to promote the enhancement of students' adaptive learning and much to fuel anxiety and a sense of personal futility. What about capable students who disengage? These students may seek distraction in the here and now but can miss out on important self-regulation opportunities along the way, as we explore subsequently.

Teacher and Student Adaptation to Instructional Opportunity

Our original study design invited consideration of how a given teacher-centered instructional opportunity differentially presses upon individual students. Study findings, however, invited consideration of reciprocal press: how teacher instructional practices might be co-regulated by the press of student adaptation. Instructional opportunities might signify an array of teacher adaptations to students to maintain their efforts to learn. Thanks to good discussion and critical feedback (Corno, 2008; T. Good, personal communication, October 2006), McCaslin & Burross (2011) noted:

> . . . teachers may well devote relatively more time to Direct Instruction and Review in part because two of the more "visible" differences in student adaptation difficulty, Anxious and Withdrawn and Disengaged and Distracting, appear to profit from them. An alternative perspective on the relationships between instructional opportunity and the Struggling and Persistent student, for example, might explore the extent to which teachers diagnostically alternate Guided Elaboration with Review to keep effortful yet struggling students on track in demanding learning. On track in their learning and on track in their motivation: Review clarifies and reinforces prior learning and prior learning attempts. Review reassures even as it provides a respite from the frustration of difficulty. How, when, and why teachers decide to alternate instructional approaches within teacher-centered instruction and how those changing opportunities are mediated by students . . . seems an especially important area for research on co-regulation of classroom learning. (p. 344)

This quote illustrates the power and blinder of old habits: an implicit belief about teacher-centered instruction includes a narrow sense of who is "in charge" and engaged in active learning. Many of us would not consider the possibility of shared power—the co-regulation—with students embedded in teacher-centered instruction. It appears that student self-monitoring reports can provide useful information for teachers' instructional decisions.

STUDENTS MAKE MISTAKES

Earlier we stressed that the tensions—the press—between and among sources of influence in the co-regulation model afford learning to struggle, negotiate, and compromise as well as thrive. The second stream of research we now discuss considers students' emotion and coping when confronted with difficulty, mistakes, and failures. Following Rohrkemper and Corno (1988), we suggest that learning to cope with the frustrations of difficulty and failure and the tedium of too-readily earned and uninformative success is central to adaptive learning and personal well-being. Adaptive learning requires opportunity. It is not necessarily a good thing when everything comes easily, just as it is not necessarily a good thing when everything comes hard.

In the United States, elite colleges are coming to recognize the academic scholarship showing the fragility of students whose history of experience with social and cultural expectations and activities has been one of smooth participation and recognition (*New York Times*, 6/25/17). There can be real personal risks in being "the smart one" or "the best athlete" that can undermine trying out new and potentially difficult opportunities, seeking help, and figuring out that others still like and love you even if you can't do something, everything, well. Students can be highly successful in meeting social and cultural presses upon their performance and aspirations yet have missed an important aspect of personal growth and potential: learning how to cope with mistakes and setbacks, grieve lost and missed opportunities, risk failure to try again, and trust yourself when facing the not-yet-known. As noted, failure, particularly chronic failure, can be detrimental. However, failure can also be constructive, an opportunity for learning about how to garner one's resources, meet challenges, and appreciate the commitment that learning from failure requires. Constructive failure is an important part of a constellation of life skills Rohrkemper and Corno (1988) called *adaptive learning*. Adaptive learning conceptualized learner, tasks, and situations as malleable. It is about acting on yourself and your situation to better meet your goals.

Emotional Adaptation

The adaptive learning construct has always been rooted in emotional experience. More recently, however, the emotional dynamics of adaptive learning have assumed a more expanded role in co-regulation work. One result is research on *emotional adaptation*—how students think, feel, and cope in classrooms—and how this might influence their peer relationships. Emotional adaptation includes emotion regulation in the present, but it also considers how personal concerns or interests are formed. This development includes the events or situations that "get" or trigger personal attention and appraisal (Frijda, 2008), how they are acted upon, and if they become characteristic of personal potential. Thus, in addition to situational or context concerns that many individuals similarly experience, we assert that individual differences can emerge in the dynamics of emotional adaptation. Our approach is consistent with researchers who include cognitive appraisals in the experience of emotion (e.g., Weiner, 2005), consider how personal concerns might mediate situational experiences (e.g., Frijda, 1988; 2008), *and* examine the interplay of emotion generation and regulation (e.g., Gross, Sheppes, Urry, 2011). We also consider the interpersonal benefits and costs of intrapersonal emotional experience.

We emphasize that emotional adaptation is learned and that during the elementary school grades it can become habitual or characteristic of students. In the co-regulation perspective, emotional adaptation is a "nonability" determinant of achievement that also is essential to understanding student learning, well-being, and classroom relationships. We view emotional adaptation as a fusion of affective and intellectual dynamics that are co-regulated by evolving social opportunities and relationships, personal concerns, and cultural expectations.

Emotional Adaptation in Classrooms: Social and Cultural Contexts

Learning in classrooms presents two primary tasks for students, and how they go about meeting each has serious implications for their present and future well-being. First, students are to master the academic demands of schooling competently, in ways that positively influence their confidence in the learners they are and wish to become. Second, students are to navigate and negotiate relationships with others in ways that mutually support a sense of shared purpose and place, a sense of valued participation. There is potential for conflicts between these two primary tasks. Coping with competence demands can undermine relationships with peers and vice versa. The costs of caring about meeting each task demand can be considerable. We now present research that explores these potential costs from the student perspective.

Co-Regulation Design
We implemented a pre-post design study within a school year (November–May) with students ($N = 415$) in Grades 4 through 6.

Social Opportunities and Relationships
Practicable social opportunities and relationships were represented by three instructional format opportunities in classrooms: private, whole class, and small group and assessed with the school situations (SS; Burggraf, 1993) inventory. SS consists of 12 vignettes representing commonly experienced classroom events. Nine vignettes describe student mistakes, failure, and setbacks; three describe student successes. Students respond to items

representing 5 scales that examine self-conscious emotions (shame, guilt, pride) and coping strategies (normalize [to make something less salient or extraordinary], and externalize [blame someone or something else]). The SS inventory allows consideration of both personal dispositions (e.g., "she is shame-prone") and contextual affordances (e.g., small groups are emotionally difficult for students). Social-personal press expectations were consistent with the coping literatures in which students differentially cope with peer and learning difficulties (see Band & Weisz, 1988; Skinner & Zimmer-Gembeck, 2007; Sotardi, 2016). Thus, we expected the most varied and aggressive reported coping strategies in small-group instructional formats and the least in private contexts.

Cultural Norms and Challenges

Cultural norms and challenges that define *probable* expectations were represented by poverty and poverty density of the families served by participating schools. Cultural-personal press expectations were consistent with the psychobiological perspective of Blair and Raver (2012), who argue that children who live in poverty continually confront the adversity of scarce resources and chronic stress. Chronic stress ultimately results in acquired tendencies to be more reactive to events. One behavioral result of that reactivity is hypervigilance for cues that signal threat followed by a decisive and over-response. We examined two levels of school poverty density, defined by percentage of students receiving free or reduced lunch: relatively "moderate" (mean = 70%) and relatively "high" (mean = 90%). We expected responses of students who attended high-poverty density schools to be more reactive to vignettes depicting personal struggle and failure than the responses of their peers who attended moderate-poverty density schools.

Selected Findings

In brief, context matters in students' self-conscious emotions and reported coping strategies when confronting routine events within classroom social/instructional contexts.

Social-Personal Press

Figure 14.2 displays how classroom instructional contexts differentially challenge students. All pretest and posttest context models are similar and significant at $p < .001$. Of the three formats, private contexts are associated with the most reported pride and the least negative emotions and related coping strategies. Small group contexts are associated with the most reported guilt and shame, least pride and externalization (perhaps suggesting that neither is wise in these contexts), and moderate endorsement of normalizing coping strategies. Finally, whole class contexts are particularly notable for the endorsement of normalization coping strategies ("everyone

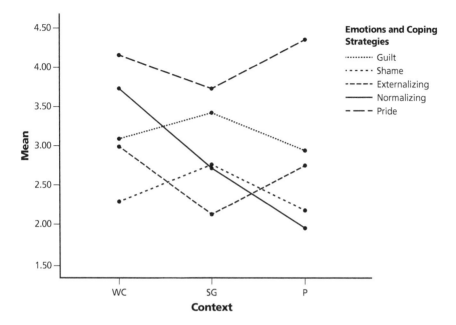

Figure 14.2 Context effects in students' emotional adaptation. Source: McCaslin, et al. (2016).

is loud sometimes"), suggesting one source of students' "thick skin" in classrooms, and the relative reduction of expressed shame.

Cultural-Personal Press

There were no achievement differences between students who attended relatively high-poverty density or moderate-poverty density schools; however, there were differences in self-conscious emotions and coping. Students who attended high-poverty density schools reported more externalizing and negative emotions and less pride than did students who attended moderate-poverty density schools. We expected the increased reactivity findings; however, we were taken aback at the reduction in these students' endorsement of pride upon success.

In sum, context matters in how students' experience and cope with "self"-conscious emotions. Social influences—the practicable everyday opportunities and relationships in classrooms that students commonly experience—that we examined with a self-report inventory suggested that classroom instructional formats differentially challenge and support students' emotional adaptation dynamics. Differential cultural influences on students also were expressed in classrooms, in ways that demand further attention. We view self conscious emotions (e.g., Tangney, 2002) as not only social (e.g., Baumeister, Stillwell, & Heatherton, 1995) but as co-regulated by the interplay of cultural, social, and personal sources of influence, which we now consider.

Emotional Adaptation in Classrooms: Student Negotiation of Personal Potential

Self-conscious emotions and coping strategies can be considered as discrete contributions to students' emotional adaptation. Our primary interest, however, is in what students "do" with their emotions—how emotion generation and regulation might co-occur in students' coping with making mistakes, to what extent these emotional adaptations are stable over the school year, and their implications for peer relationships.

Individual Differences in Coping With Emotion

Exploratory factor analysis procedures were applied to student reports. This resulted in five emotional adaptation profiles, displayed in Table 14.2, which includes a brief profile description and the three highest items and loadings.

Each of the five factors includes items from more than one scale and forms a unique pattern of responses. Unique factors suggest that how students cope with emotion is a key aspect of their emotional experience. For example, *distance* and *displace* includes 10 items from the shame, normalizing, and externalizing scales. The distance component captures attempts to withdraw from the situation to take care of the self; the displace component refers to attempts to blame someone or something else to find relief from the negative emotion. In comparison, *regret* and *repair* includes 12 items from the guilt and normalizing scales. The factor merges attempts to repair or "fix" the problem situation with attempts to "normalize" the event, making it less extraordinary and troublesome, to care for the self. It is important to consider as well what each profile might mean for peer relationships: Distance and displace invites isolation and peer resistance, aggression, or rejection. In contrast, regret and repair invites forgiveness, participation, and new beginnings. Distance and displace not only does not solve the competence task of classroom learning, it also can render the relationship task much more problematic. In contrast, regret and repair has the potential to salvage and possibly enrich each (see McCaslin, Vriesema, & Burggraf, 2016 for extended discussion).

Do emotional adaptation profiles matter? Yes. Only two of the five profiles, regret and repair and proud and modest, are desirable and possibly optimal for students and their classmates. Regret and repair attempts to restore relationships and improve situations; proud and modest likely prevents

TABLE 14.2 Making Mistakes: Student Emotional Adaptation Profiles
1. **Distance and Displace.** The student attempts to withdraw from a difficult situation to care for the self ("distance") and/or blame others or things ("displace") to find relief from negative feelings. i. You are angry with your group for being so silly. (.64) ii.   You pretend you didn't hear and wish they would stop laughing. (.61) iii. You feel like asking the teacher if you can change groups. You don't, but it's hard to forget about it. (.59)
2. **Regret and Repair.** The student attempts to normalize the event (e.g., 'everyone is loud sometimes') to care for the self and repair or fix the difficult situation to find relief from feelings of guilt. i. You think about why you got so confused and decide to think about your answer first next time. (.64) ii.   You remember this happens to other kids, too. (.60) iii. You worry about your best friend who worked hard, too. (.56)
3. **Inadequate and Exposed.** The student assumes responsibility and blame for mistakes and difficulty without engaging in strategies to care for the self in response to feelings of shame. i. You feel like a total jerk. (.64) ii.   You wish you could disappear. (.54) iii. You feel really embarrassed and wish you could go home now. (.53)
4. **Proud and Modest.** The student acknowledges success and tempers feelings of pride with humility. i. You feel proud of yourself. (.67) ii.   You are proud of how smart you are (.65) iii. You think: "I was really lucky!" (.62)
5. **Minimize and Move On.** The student adopts a "just keep going, do not dwell, look beyond it" response to "escape" mistakes and difficult situations. i. You think, it's no big deal, it was just one math lesson. (.51) ii.   You think: "She'll get over it." (.50) iii. You feel like the teacher is making a big deal out of nothing. (.50)

Source: McCaslin, Vriesema, & Burggraf (2016).

potential problematic peer dynamics linked to envy, anger, or competition from escalating. Emotional adaptation matters in the here-and-now, for individual students and their classmates, and as habits-in-the-making. Stability (correlational) analyses were considerable (range = .40–.58). Considerable is not inevitable. Emotional adaptation habits are malleable; however, they reside outside the formal school curriculum, emerging idiosyncratically amongst the challenges of varied social and instructional contexts, cultural influences, and personal concerns. Without deliberate co-regulation by their teachers—instruction, guidance, and support—students' emotional adaptation can interfere with their personal well-being and meeting the competence and relationship tasks of learning in classrooms. Students with fewer personal resources are particularly vulnerable.

Individual Differences in Readiness to Learn

We created three relative levels of student readiness to learn based upon pretest percentile rank; actual learning estimates were based upon pretest to posttest change in percentage correct scores. Learning estimates were subjected to ANOVA and Cohen's d procedures for each level of readiness. Change scores significantly differed across groups; $d = 1.15$ for students in the low readiness group, $d = 0.48$ for the moderate group, and $d = 0.05$ for students in the high readiness group. Achievement gains between test administrations, however, did not alter group membership in relative readiness levels. Notably, students who were relatively less ready to learn were nonetheless engaged in learning.

Student readiness to learn and final test score performance were related to their emotional adaptation profiles. Students higher in readiness and final test scores were more likely to endorse regret and repair and the proud and modest profiles. In comparison, students lower in relative readiness and final test scores were more likely to endorse distance and displace and minimize and move on emotional adaptation profiles. Minimize and move on is an escape strategy fueled by trivializing others and situations. Like distance and displace, minimize and move on may serve to escape the immediate threat to self, but it does not solve the immediate problem and can contribute to individual isolation and rejection by others. Students with less readiness—fewer resources—to learn likely have developed sensitivities to making mistakes and failure: their personal concerns are rooted in a learning history where no matter how much you actually learn, you still are the learner who doesn't meet the competence demands of classroom learning that others do. These dynamics seem much more nuanced and complicated than admonitions to "try harder" or "have the right mindset" suggest.

STUDENTS IN SMALL LEARNING GROUPS

Students' responses to the SS inventory suggested that small group formats were difficult social/instructional contexts for students to engage. This is not surprising given that small group learning formats fuse the two primary classroom tasks for students: developing a sense of competence and maintaining mutually positive and supportive relationships with peers. Individual differences in students' reports further suggested that attempts to cope with frustration linked to classroom learning demands (e.g., distance and displace) can cause difficulties with peers. Small group contexts in particular were likely to trigger these personal concerns. In this final study, we consider how students' actual small-group experiences are influenced by the individual differences in reported emotional adaptation and anxiety of their group members. We integrate the "How I was in Class" instrumentation used in McCaslin and Burross (2011) and the SS inventory used in McCaslin, Vriesema, & Burggraf (2016) with systematic coding of students' recorded table talk (McCaslin & Vega, 2013) in small-group learning. Participating students (N =101) were in Grades 3 and 5, and assigned to one of 24 small learning groups for six lessons in mathematics. Students attended schools that served students of families living either in relative affluence or conditions of scarcity. The larger study was conducted in October–January of the school year.

Systematic Coding of Small Group Interaction

Two complementary systematic coding systems were applied to the transcribed table talk records of students' small group interactions for three (beginning, middle, end) of the six study lessons (see McCaslin et al., 2011; McCaslin & Vega, 2013; Vega, 2014; and McCaslin, Vriesema, & Vega, 2015 for full descriptions of transcription procedures, coding systems development, revisions, and reliability). The group behavior checklist (GBC) is a low-inference system that captures a range of on- and off-task behaviors that students display in small groups. There are a total of 51 GBC variables that are applied in 30-second intervals for the entire table talk transcript. This study used four GBC variable domains: (a) planning, (b) problem-solving, (c) help-seeking, and (d) feedback. The group environment summary (GES) is a higher-inference system that captures students' interpersonal and affective dynamics and expressed coping strategies. There are a total of 22 GES variables that are applied twice, at the midpoint and end of each table talk. GES variables include group affective climate and four domains of coping behavior: (a) aggressive, (b) protective, (c) regressive/escape, and (d) somatic. In addition, we applied a word analysis program (Pennebaker, Booth, & Francis, 2007) to assess students' language precision, no matter their topic of conversation.

Student Co-Regulation Dynamics in Small-Groups

Data from GBC and GES were subjected to principal components analyses. Results yielded five independent factors that we consider distinct co-regulation dynamics that students engage when in small groups. Table 14.3 includes representative items. In order of magnitude the factors were: conflict and control, working together, resource drain, edgy compliance, and scuffle and confusion. These factors represent dynamic behavior patterns, they do not represent particular groups of students; all groups engaged in these co-regulation dynamics.

TABLE 14.3 Real-Time Co-Regulation Dynamics

Factor (% variance)	Example Items	Loading
1. Conflict and Control (25.96%)	Students are indifferent/non-cohesive/within group coalitions exist	.84
	Students display unidirectional aggression – off-task	.84
	Students display reciprocal aggression – off-task	.77
	Task participation is structured in multiple ways	.77
	Students redirect/distract other students away from a source of tension	.72
	Students tattle on each other	.71
	Students defend themselves or others	.69
2. Working Together (11.62%)	Students offer explanations	.67
	Students express disagreement	.66
	Students ask procedural questions	.64
	Students offer suggestions	.60
	Students repeat/echo others' contributions	.57
	Students ask explanation questions	.57
	Students blame others	−.55
3. Resource Drain (9.34%)	Students make excuses	.81
	Students make request for an audience	.66
	Students make request for materials	.66
	Students ask information questions	.61
	Some students are sick	.59
	Students act infantile	.58
	Students are off-task	.53
4. Edgy Compliance (7.81%)	Students giggle/laugh	.74
	Students brag	.67
	Students refuse others' further participation/contributions	.62
	Some students are in pain	.58
	Task participation is structured around turn-taking/task-taking	.53
	Some students are tired	.51
	Students are playful	.45
5. Scuffle and Confusion (7.20%)	The source of task participation structure is not identifiable	.93
	Task participation structure is not identifiable	.74
	Students are argumentative	.66
	Task participation structure is determined by the group and teacher	.65
	Task participation structure is determined by the group	−.53

Note: Total n = 18 for Conflict and Control; n = 11 for Working Together; n = 7 for Resource Drain; n = 9 for Edgy Compliance; and n = 5 for Scuffle and Confusion. All coefficients below .45 were excluded from the final factor structure.

Source: McCaslin, Vriesema, & Vega. (2015).

Relative Focus of Joint Activity

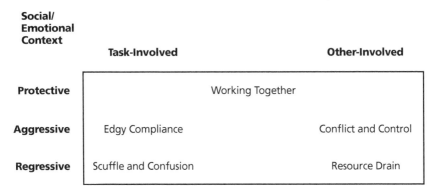

Social/ Emotional Context	Task-Involved	Other-Involved
Protective	Working Together	
Aggressive	Edgy Compliance	Conflict and Control
Regressive	Scuffle and Confusion	Resource Drain

Figure 14.3 Small group co-regulation foci. Source: McCaslin et al. (2015).

Small group dynamics can be organized into relatively task-focused (the competence demand), other-focused (the relationship demand), or the fusion of the two perspectives (e.g., small-group ideal). In addition, we can consider how coping behavior constructs, typically associated with individual behavior—aggressive, protective, and regressive—emerge as a feature of small group co-regulation dynamics. As Figure 14.3 illustrates, only the working together dynamic, in which the competence demands of the task and the relationship demands of supportively working with peers, are optimally met. In this dynamic group members can ask for help, disagree, and offer suggestions and solutions in an arena of personal safety. Not so for the remaining co-regulation dynamics. Findings suggest that small-groups are not for the faint-hearted. Nor are they for those who need clarity; a full 60% of students' table talk consisted of function words (e.g., "they," "those"). Function words are those rather vague contributions that can make a point if the listener has enough social skill or prior knowledge to correctly interpret them. Sixty percent is a lot of vague in the mix with a lot of challenging group co-regulation dynamics. It is useful to consider how personal concerns and students' emotional adaptation might be involved.

The Press of Personal Potential on Small Group Dynamics

Within each group, we averaged individual member's math readiness, disposition toward anxiety, and characteristic emotional adaptation reports. These averages represented the group composition for each variable. None of the group composition variables were related to function word use; imprecise language is a given. Averaged math readiness and emotional adaptation profiles were the only group features that related to group interaction. First, groups higher in math readiness were more likely to engage task-involved co-regulation dynamics—the protective working together or the aggressive edgy compliance. In contrast, groups with less math readiness were more likely to engage the task-involved but regressive scuffle and confusion dynamic—the only co-regulation dynamic related (negatively) to group performance on assigned tasks.

Second, 3 of the 5 group-level emotional adaptation profiles—inadequate and exposed, distance and displace, and proud and modest—were related to real-time small group co-regulation dynamics. Group-averaged endorsement of inadequate and exposed was positively related to working together; distance and displace with resource drain dynamics; and proud and modest (negatively) with edgy compliance. These findings suggest that student small group learning dynamics can be fueled by a collective fear of failure as much as hope for success.

Third, systematic observation of small groups suggests student-reported emotional adaptation is an important consideration in student's own personal well-being and, through their interactions with peers, in peer well-being. Who is in your small group matters—for them and for you. Are students aware of this as well? Group-averaged "How I Was in Class" reports suggests they are. For example, observed working together dynamics were positively correlated with group-averaged enhancing behavior reports and negatively correlated with group-averaged interfering/withdrawn behavior reports. Observed resource drain dynamics were positively correlated with group-averaged enhancing behavior reports and the averaged interfering/withdrawn behavior reports.

Students' reports are consistent with our coding of small-group interaction and illustrate the complementarity of within-group dynamics. For example, resource drain dynamics includes both those who need, yet are not able or willing to contribute to group resources (as captured by the interfering/withdrawn scale) and those who can and do contribute (as captured by the enhancing scale). Collectively, results suggest the complexity of small-group learning, the demands on self and other awareness, and the considerable skill they require.

The Press of Cultural Norms and Challenges on Small Group Dynamics

We examined the potential press of cultural norms and challenges in shaping students' small-group experiences. Our goal was to determine whether there were patterns in students' personal potential (e.g., emotional adaptation profiles at the individual level) and social relationships and activities (e.g., small-group interaction patterns) based on their particular cultural context. In this study, one aspect of cultural press is reflected in schools that serve families who are relatively affluent (relatively high SES) or financially struggle (relatively low SES).

Overall, students from both contexts were similar in their achievement, disposition toward anxiety, and the ways in which the students communicated with one another. Students attending lower-SES schools used more words in their small-groups than students attending higher SES schools. However, both groups engaged in conversation around the mathematics lessons with similar levels of (non)specificity. Cultural influences played a larger role in shaping students' emotional adaptation and small-group interaction experiences.

Relatively Low SES Contexts

The results surrounding students' SES indicated potential interactions between personal and social presses within given environments. Students who attended schools that served families with limited resources reported both greater use of distance and displace emotional adaptation strategies for coping with mistakes and difficulty and described their behavior in class at higher levels of interfering/withdrawn behaviors than did students who attended more affluent schools. Interfering/withdrawn behaviors are those characterized by withdrawing from the situation, limiting one's own learning and not contributing to the learning of others.

Student reports are consistent with our coding of small group interaction. Students in lower resourced schools engaged in more conflict and control and edgy compliance interactions than did students in more affluent schools. Thus, feeling withdrawn and reporting a greater tendency to distance and displace—to both withdraw (distance) and externalize (displace) to cope with feelings of shame—may yield interaction patterns with peers that are tenser, antagonize, and invite more peer resistance and rejection than they might in different settings

It appears that students' coping strategies help to alleviate the tension experienced on a personal level; however, the strategies students select may be more or less effective in terms of how these strategies impact others in their learning environments. For example, students who attend schools serving families with relatively less cultural capital are more likely to endorse emotional adaptation strategies in response to difficulty and failure that strongly respond (distance and displace) to the situation. As Blair and Raver (2012) predict, these students also are more likely to engage in small-group dynamics that enact more of the same: decisive over-response within an aggressive press. Their emergent interaction dynamic is one that is mutually sustaining: it is a hostile world that requires fast and strong responses—that trigger hostility. We note that these students' self-monitoring reports only recorded the distance or withdrawal aspects of these dynamics.

This is not an issue of student lack of self-awareness or veracity; the "How I Was in Class" instrumentation did not contain any opportunities to report aggressive or strongly reactive behavior.

Relatively High SES Contexts

Students who attended more affluent schools reported higher levels of inadequate and exposed emotional adaptation and engaged in more working together interactions throughout the lessons. In the inadequate and exposed emotional adaption the student accepts full responsibility for failure and does not engage any strategies to care for the self or attenuate feelings of shame. These students apparently hide their feelings of inadequacy in working together co-regulation dynamics that are protective and task-focused. On the one hand, this is a productive strategy: Working with others may well improve student learning and understanding of the material. On the other hand, this is potentially problematic. Hiding in plain sight does not afford learning from failure and how to trust and take care of yourself in the face of the unknown; valuable life skills as we have discussed.

Summary

In brief, cultural presses in both SES contexts upon students are challenging and can be limiting. They call for mindful and deliberate co-regulation to help students optimize their negotiation of classroom learning and relationship demands.

DISCUSSION

An essential point of a Vygotskian perspective is that we are all part of a unit larger than ourselves. The co-regulation model is one attempt to operationalize this position and guide research on how cultural, social, and personal influences press upon and co-regulate—challenge, shape, and guide—personal identity. The press among influences invites learning to struggle, strive, negotiate, and compromise as well as thrive. We noted that none of the sources of influence are equally distributed; nor are opportunities for personally-meaningful, socially-validated, and culturally-valued engagement. Each study we discussed included schools whose students confronted stresses associated with family poverty and mobility. One goal was to identify the array of opportunities and relationships in classrooms that support more and less productive student adaptations and personal well-being within these sociocultural contexts.

Study 1 illustrated that direct instruction opportunities in teacher-centered whole class instruction cast a wide safety- and learning-net for students. Nonetheless, students differed in expressed adaptations. Good worker, engaged learner, and struggling and persistent students suggest an array of productive learning adaptations. In contrast, anxious and withdrawn and disengaged and distracting students remind us that students can mediate instructional opportunities nonproductively. These students are classmates. How they adapt to instructional opportunity and cultural expectations for achievement is not a private matter and this can be a good thing, signaling to teachers a need for a change in instructional support.

Study 2 closely examined student self-knowledge; their personal awareness of the feelings and actions they experience in the trifecta of classroom learning formats: whole class, private, and small group. The opportunities and relationships embedded in each format differentially organized student responses and, for some students, personal concerns dominated. Student reports suggested that small group learning contexts that fuse the competence and relationship demands of classrooms were especially difficult to navigate. We identified two emotional adaptation profiles we thought could serve students and their peers well—regret and repair and proud and modest. Remaining emotional adaptation profiles, particularly distance and displace, seemed problematic because they did not solve the competence problem at hand and had the potential to interfere with the peer relationship demands of classrooms.

Study 3 directly examined the possibility that small groups are difficult instructional opportunities for most students, and particularly threatening for some. The variations among students' reported emotional adaptation profiles replicated those found in Study 2. We linked the personal concerns and emotional adaptation profiles of individual students with the other members of their small group and examined how their collective affective concerns and adaptations informed group-interaction dynamics. Group composition matters. Students bring individual differences in personal concerns and characteristic emotional adaptations that can and do co-regulate small-group activity. Study 3 included students who attended schools that serve families of relative affluence as well as those whose families financially struggle. There was some indication of a cumulative effect of differential cultural presses on students' emotional adaptation. Namely, students in schools that served families with fewer resources were relatively more reactive and antagonistic in reported emotional adaptation and in actual small group interactions. In comparison, students in schools that served families with more resources were relatively less hardy to individual disappointments and failures. In the first case, student stress and distress are more apparent and interventions by teacher or other peers are possible. In the latter case, inadequate and exposed students can stay under the radar, their apparent joint attention in the optimal working together dynamic in their small group a camouflage for personal stress.

Collectively, these studies support our call for reflection and research on differing demands of classroom social/instructional formats on student adaptation. For example, we agree with Kuhn (2015), that when students are placed in small learning groups, educators need to ask if the small group format is a means to an end (e.g., learning mathematics) or an end in itself (e.g., learning how to function in collaborative groups is a 21st century skill). Both are high priorities in the U.S. culture and there is considerable press upon schools to pursue each goal; perhaps not both at the same time. Our data also firmly illustrate the need for more nuanced language in describing the cultural contexts that students negotiate. For example, in Study 2 all students attended schools that primarily served families living in poverty. However, students who attended schools with higher concentrations of poverty density reportedly felt notably more negative and less positive emotions than did students who attended schools with somewhat lower concentration of poverty density.

Studies also support recognition of student self-knowledge and self-awareness of their adaptations in classrooms. Studies 1 and 3 included independent classroom observation of student behavior. Each validated the veracity of students' behavioral reports. Students' mediation reports contributed to enriched understanding of what it means to be *that* student in the classroom. Students' personal concerns and emotional adaptations are part of classrooms and warrant deliberate co-regulation through inclusion in the formal school curriculum and teachers' instructional practices.

Finally, we have made a case for the utility of a co-regulation model for studying individual differences in students' personal potential and concerns within a Vygotskian sociocultural perspective. Students have a personal history and they differ in what they bring to a situation, in what and how they participate, and what that means for their time and place and self-story. This suggests the futility of asserting "the" student perspective or ignoring it altogether. Rather, it calls for a better understanding of "that student's" perspectives. Individual differences among students are rooted in emergent interaction with cultural, social, and personal sources of influence, none of which are equitably distributed. It is not a level playing field but nor is it an inevitable one. We repeat: Consistent with a Vygotskian perspective, the co-regulation model serves as both a vehicle for research on cultural-social-personal dynamics and a call to action.

ACKNOWLEDGMENT

Much of this work has been engaged with colleagues Susan Burggraf, Heidi Legg Burross, Tom Good, and Ruby Inez Vega. We also acknowledge the good work of the observation and coding teams of the Comprehensive

School Reform and the Small Group Learning Projects. Our colleagues' collective good thinking and challenging perspectives are evident in the evolution of the constructs presented in this chapter. Continuing limitations are our own.

REFERENCES

Adams, C. M., Forsyth, P. B., Dollarhide, E., Miskell, R., & Ware, J. (2015). Self-regulatory climate: A social resource for student regulation and achievement. *Teachers College Record, 117*(2), 1–28.

Bakhtiar, A., Webster, E. A., & Hadwin, A. F. (2017). Regulation and socio-emotional interactions in a positive and a negative group climate. *Metacognition and Learning, 13*(1), 57–90.

Band, E. B., & Weisz, J. R. (1988). How to feel better when it feels bad: Children's perspectives on coping with everyday stress. *Developmental Psychology, 24,* 247–253.

Baumeister, R. F., Stillwell, A. M., & Heatherton, T. F. (1995). Interpersonal aspects of guilt: Evidence from narrative studies. In J. P. Tangney & K. W. Fischer (Eds.), *Self-conscious emotions: The psychology of shame, guilt, embarrassment and pride* (pp. 255–273). New York, NY: Guilford Press.

Blair, C., & Raver, C. C. (2012). Child development in the context of adversity: Experiential canalization of brain and behavior. *American Psychologist, 67*(4), 309–318.

Burggraf, S. A. (1993). *School situations.* Unpublished manuscript, Bryn Mawr College, Bryn Mawr, PA.

Corno, L. (2008). On teaching adaptively. *Educational Psychologist, 43*(3), 161–173.

Frijda, N. H. (1988). The laws of emotion. *American Psychologist, 43*(5), 349–358.

Frijda, N. H. (2008). The psychologists' point of view. In M. Lewis, J. M. Haviland-Jones, & L. F. Barrett (Eds.), *Handbook of emotions* (3rd ed., pp. 68–87). New York, NY: Guilford Press.

Greeno, J. (1998). The situativity of knowing, learning, and research. *American Psychologist, 53,*5–26.

Gross, J. J., Sheppes, G., & Urry, H. L. (2011). Cognition and emotion lecture at the 2010 SPSP emotion preconference: Emotion generation and emotion regulation: A distinction we should make (carefully). *Cognition and Emotion, 25*(5), 765–781.

Hadwin, A., Järvelä, S., & Miller, M. (2018). Shared regulation in collaborative learning environments. In D. H. Schunk & J. A. Greene (Eds.), *Handbook of self-regulation of learning and performance* (2nd ed., pp. 83–106). New York, NY: Routledge.

Järvelä, S., & Järvenoja, H. (2011). Socially-constructed self-regulated learning and motivation regulation in collaborative learning groups. *Teachers College Record, 113*(2), 350–374.

Kozulin, A. (1986). The concept of activity in Soviet psychology: Vygotsky, his disciples, and critics. *American Psychologist, 41,* 264–274.

Kuhn, D. (2015). Thinking together and alone. *Educational Researcher, 44*(1), 46–53.

Kurki, K., Järvenoja, H., Järvelä, S., & Mykkanen, A. (2017). Young children's use of emotion and behavior regulation strategies in socio-emotionally challenging day-care situations. *Early Childhood Research Quarterly, 41*, 50–62.

Leontiev, A. N. (1974). The problem of activity in Soviet psychology. *Soviet Psychology, 13*(2), 4–33.

Leontiev, A. N. (1978). *Activity, consciousness, and personality.* Englewood Cliffs, NJ: Prentice Hall.

Luria, A. R. (1979). The meaning of mind: A personal account of Soviet psychology. M. Cole & S. Cold (Eds.). Cambridge, MA: Harvard University Press.

McCaslin, M. (2004). Co-regulation of opportunity, activity, and identity in student motivation: Elaboration on Vygotskian themes. In D. M. McInerney & S. Van Etten (Eds.), *Big theories revisited* (Vol. 4, pp. 249–274). Greenwich, CT: Information Age.

McCaslin, M. (2009). Co-regulation of student motivation and emergent identity. *Educational Psychologist, 44*(2), 137–146.

McCaslin, M., & Burross, H. (2008). Student motivational dynamics. *Teachers College Record, 110*(11), 2319–2340.

McCaslin, M., & Burross, H. (2011). Research on individual differences within a sociocultural perspective: Co-regulation and adaptive learning. *Teachers College Record, 113*(2), 325–349.

McCaslin, M., & Good, T. L. (2008). A study of comprehensive school reform progress in Arizona. *Teachers College Record: Special Issue: School Reform Matters, 110*(11), 2319–2340.

McCaslin, M., Good, T. L., Nichols, S., Zhang, J., Hummel, C., Bozack, A. R., ... & Cuizon-Garcia, R. (2006). Comprehensive school reform: An observational study of teaching in grades 3 to 5. *Elementary School Journal, 106*, 313–331.

McCaslin, M., & Hickey, D. T. (2001). Educational psychology, social constructivism, and educational practice: A Case of emergent identity. *Educational Psychologist, 36*, 133–140.

McCaslin, M., & Murdock, T. B. (1991). The emergent interaction of home and school in the development of students' adaptive learning. In M. Maehr & P. Pintrich (Eds.), *Advances in motivation and achievement* (Vol. 7, pp. 213–259). Greenwich, CT: JAI Press.

McCaslin, M., & Vega, R. I. (2013). Peer co-regulated learning, emotion, and coping in small-group learning. In S. Phillipson, K. Y. L. Ku, & S. N. Phillipson (Eds.), *Constructing educational achievement: A sociocultural perspective* (pp. 118–135). New York, NY: Routledge.

McCaslin, M., Vega, R. I., Anderson, E. E., Calderon, C. N., & Labistre, A. M. (2011). Tabletalk: Navigating and negotiating in small-group learning. In D. M. McInerney, R. Walker, & G. A. D. Liem (Eds.), *Sociocultural theories of learning and motivation: Looking back, looking forward* (pp. 191–222). Charlotte, NC: Information Age.

McCaslin, M., Vriesema, C. C., & Burggraf, S. (2016). Making mistakes: Emotional adaptation and classroom learning. *Teachers College Record, 118*(2), 1–46.

McCaslin, M., Vriesema, C.C., & Vega, R. I. (2015, August). Co-regulation of elementary students' motivation and emotion in small group learning. Presentation as part of the *Variations in regulation of collaboration—Focus on group's cognitive, motivational and socioemotional processes* symposium at the biennial meetings of The European Association of Learning and Instruction. Limossol, Cyprus.

Moreno, J., Sanabria, L., & López, O. (2016). Theoretical and conceptual approaches to co-regulation: A theoretical review. *Psychology, 7*, 1587–1607.

Motta, E., Cataneo, A., & Gurtner, J. (2017). Co-regulations of learning in small groups of chef apprentices: When do they appear and what influences them? *Empirical Research in Vocational Education and Training, 9*(15), 1–20.

Nolen, S. B., Horn, I. S., & Ward, C. J. (2015). Situating motivation. *Educational Psychologist, 50*(3), 234–247.

Pennebaker, J. W., Booth, R. J., & Francis, M. E. (2007). *Linguistic inquiry and word count: LIWC2007.* Austin, TX: LIWC.net.

Penuel, W. R., & Wertsch, J. V. (1995). Vygotsky and identity information: A sociocultural approach. *Educational Psychologist, 30*, 215–234.

Rohrkemper, M. McCaslin (1989). Self-regulated learning and academic achievement: A Vygotskian view. In B. Zimmerman & D. Schunk (Eds.), *Self-regulated learning and academic achievement: Theory, research, and practice* (pp. 143–168). New York, NY: Springer-Verlag.

Rohrkemper, M., & Corno, L. (1988). Success and failure on classroom tasks: Adaptive learning and classroom teaching. *Elementary School Journal, 88*, 299–312.

Rogat, T. K., & Linnenbrink-Garcia, L. (2011). Socially shared regulation in collaborative groups: An analysis of the interplay between quality of social regulation and group processes. *Cognition and Instruction, 29*(4), 375–415.

Skinner, E. A., & Zimmer-Gemback, M. J. (2007). The development of coping. *Annual Review of Psychology, 58*, 119–144.

Sotardi, V. A. (2016). Understanding student stress and coping in elementary school: A mixed-method, longitudinal study. *Psychology in the Schools.* Retrieved from *http://onlinelibrary.wiley.com/doi/10.1002/pits.21938/full*

Tangney, J. P. (2002). Self-conscious emotions: The self as a moral guide. In A. Tesser, D. A. Stapel, & V. Wood (Eds.), *Self and motivation: Emerging psychological perspectives* (pp. 97–117). Washington, DC: American Psychological Association.

Turner, J. C., & Nolen, S. B. (2015). Introduction: The relevance of the situative perspective in educational psychology. *Educational Psychologist, 50*(3), 167–172.

Vega, R. I. (2014). *The role of student coping in the socially shared regulation of learning in small groups* (Unpublished Doctoral Dissertation, University of Arizona).

Volet, S., & Mansfield, C. (2006). Group work at university: Significance of personal goals in the regulation strategies of students with positive and negative appraisals. *Higher Education Research & Development, 25*, 341–356.

Volet, S., Summers, M., & Thurman, J. (2009). High-level co-regulation in collaborative learning: How does it emerge and how is it sustained? *Learning and Instruction, 19*(2), 128–143.

Volet, S., & Vauras, M. (2013). *Interpersonal regulation of learning and motivation: Methodological advances.* New York, NY: Routledge.

Vygotsky, L. S. (1962). *Thought and language.* Cambridge, MA: MIT Press.

Weiner, B. (2005). Motivation from an attributional perspective and the social psychology of competence. In A. J. Elliot & C. S. Dweck (Eds.), *Handbook of competence and motivation* (pp. 73–84). New York, NY: Guilford Press.

Wertsch, J. (Ed.). (1985). *Culture, communication, and cognition: Vygotskian perspectives*. New York, NY: Cambridge University Press.

Wertsch, J., & Stone, C. (1985). The concept of internalization in Vygotsky's account of the genesis of higher mental functions. In J. Wertsch (Ed.), *Culture, communication, and cognition: Vygotskian perspectives* (pp. 162–181). New York, NY: Cambridge University Press.

Yowell, C. M., & Smylie, M. A. (1999). Self-regulation in democratic communities. *Elementary School Journal, 99*(5), 469–490.

Zinchenko, V. P. (1985). Vygotsky's ideas about units for the analysis of mind. In J. Wertsch (Ed.), *Culture, communication, and cognition: Vygotskian perspectives* (pp. 94–118). New York, NY: Cambridge University Press.

CHAPTER 15

MOTIVATING ENGAGED PARTICIPATION AND GENERATIVE LEARNING IN FULLY ONLINE COURSE CONTEXTS

Daniel T. Hickey
Christopher D. Andrews

This chapter makes four arguments that are inspired by four developments since the earlier edition of *Big Theories Revisited* (McInerney & Van Etten, 2004) was published more than a decade ago. The first development is that the *situative* theories of knowing and learning explored in Hickey and Granade's chapter in that volume have become much more widely appreciated. These theories and related sociocultural theories assume that knowledge is strongly rooted (i.e., situated) in the material and social context in which it is learned and used. Most scholars affiliated with the learning sciences, educational psychology, and instructional systems technology are familiar with situative theories; many now embrace them and/or related

Big Theories Revisited 2, pages 353–377
Copyright © 2018 by Information Age Publishing

sociocultural theories as a primary orientation (e.g., Hughes & Holmes, 2005; Penuel, Cole, & O'Neill, 2016; Turner & Nolen, 2015). These developments continue a trend among cognitive psychologists towards more domain-specific forms of *disciplinary* learning (e.g., Glaser, 1984) and towards concern over sociocultural backgrounds of learners relative to the sociocultural context where learning takes place (e.g., Gutiérrez, Rymes, & Larson, 1995).

While situative and sociocultural theories and methods are still not widely embraced by motivation researchers, there is now a clearly discernible strand of motivational researchers using constructs and methods based on these perspectives. These include the *practice-grounded approach* (e.g., Dohn, 2016), *socially-shared regulation* (Hadwin, Järvelä, & Miller, 2011), *engaged participation* (Hickey & Zuiker, 2005), *co-regulated learning* (McCaslin, 2009), and *identity* (e.g., Nolen, Horn, & Ward, 2015; Oyserman, 2014). These scholars are looking beyond the influence of sociocultural factors on conventional individually-oriented aspects of motivation to derive entirely new theories of motivation. These newer theories do not reject individually-oriented constructs such as *self-efficacy* and *goal-orientation*. Rather, these newer theories generally assume that communally-oriented characterizations provide a more complete and useful approach to understanding and enhancing motivation to learn. Building on the title of Hickey and Granade (2004), our first argument is that the influence of sociocultural theories on our theories of motivation has been noteworthy.

The second important development since 2004 that inspires this chapter is the steady advance of online, open, and networked learning. The development of modern learning management systems such as Canvas has made fully online and "hybrid" instruction ubiquitous. Meanwhile, the explosion of massively open online courses (MOOCs) has allowed over hundreds of universities to offer over thousands of online courses for free (or nearly free) to tens of millions of learners. In addition to MOOCs, any individual with a smartphone now has access to a continually expanding pool of free educational online videos posted by organizations (e.g., Khan Academy and TED) and by individuals (typically on YouTube). Related developments including web-enabled digital badges (Gibson, Ostashewski, Flintoff, Grant, & Knight, 2015) and socially networked endorsements of such badges (Everhart, Derryberry, Knight, & Lee, 2016) or other displays of competencies (e.g., skills at LinkedIn) mean that recognition of learning is increasingly *crowdsourced*. In light of this development, our second argument is that situative theories of motivation are ideal (if not essential) for fully understanding and motivating engagement in these new Web 2.0 learning contexts.

The third important development since 2004 is the broad embrace of *design-based research* (DBR). With a central role in the establishment of the learning sciences as a distinct discipline (i.e., Brown, 1992), DBR has become widely known and used in the ensuing decades (e.g., Barab & Squire, 2004; McKenny & Reeves, 2013; Sandoval & Bell, 2004). DBR transcends the traditional dichotomy between *basic* and *applied* research that defines educational psychology and most motivation research. Instead, DBR builds "local" theories, typically in the form of *design principles*. Rather than testing hypotheses or demonstrating broad relevance, DBR principles are shared out along with important features of the context in which they were developed. This enables others to use those principles and further extend and refine them in other contexts. This chapter illustrates how one promising DBR framework for assessment was advanced by combining it with a theoretically coherent set of design principles from another program of DBR for engagement. This chapter argues that DBR is ideally suited for using situative theories to fully exploit new opportunities for accessing, assessing, and recognizing learning offered by digital knowledge networks.

The fourth important development since 2004 is the expanded consideration of issues of equity and social justice within the learning sciences. The discipline has embraced the broad realization that learning is not inherently positive and that some forms of learning (e.g., racism, sexism, heterosexism) are inherently negative (The Politics of Learning Writing Collective, 2017). This development is evidenced by new theories and methods for addressing these issues in recent edited volumes (Esmonde & Booker, 2017) and special issues of leading journals (Bang & Vossoughi, 2016; Tabak & Radinsky, 2014). Along these lines, this chapter argues that the *expansive framing* of learning within contemporary situative theories of learning (e.g., Engle, Lam, Meyer, & Nix, 2012) holds particular promise for motivating productive forms of engagement among diverse learners. As will be shown, the idea of expansive framing leads to specific design principles that leverage diverse orientations (to disciplines, professions, culture, race, gender, etc.) to enhance the engagement with disciplinary knowledge; doing so also serves to expand our understanding of what constitutes disciplinary knowledge, practices, and contexts. The approach presented here aims to pragmatically accommodate the very real constraints of formal courses and degrees, while also working towards a vision of education that "conceptualizes the heterogeneity of human cultural practices as fundamental to learning, not as a problem to be solved but as foundational in conceptualizing learning and in designing learning environments" (Rosebery, Oganowski, DiSchino, & Warren, 2010, p. 323)

This chapter supports these four arguments by reviewing an extended program of DBR carried out across multiple technology-based learning environments. The chapter first reviews some foundational ideas about situative approaches to motivation that were excluded from Hickey and Granade (2004) due to space limitations. The chapter then retrospectively describes the evolution of a situative DBR framework for engagement and assessment that appears particularly promising for motivating networked learning among diverse learners. The chapter then describes the current version of that framework along with specific features used to enact it in conventional online graduate education courses. The chapter concludes by imagining how the current framework might be further refined to better address concerns over educational equity and social justice.

Motivation and Situative Theories of Knowing and Learning

Sociocultural theories of knowing and learning can be traced back to the philosophy of Hegel (1991) and the theories of the early Soviet psychologist Vygotsky (1962). A significant advance in the development of the situative strand of these theories was the establishment of the Institute for Research on Learning in Palo Alto (California) in 1986 by John Seely Brown and James Greeno. One of their very first publications hinted at a new way of thinking about motivation. In the context of the then-raging debate over competition and "extrinsic" incentives, Collins, Brown, and Newman (1989) argued that *exploiting competition* was a "critical characteristic" of their nascent educational framework known as *cognitive apprenticeship:*

> One of the important effects of competition is that it provides a focus for students' attention and efforts for improvement by revealing the sources of strengths and weaknesses. However, for competition to be effective for this purpose, *comparisons must be made not between the products of student problem solving, but between the processes,* and this is rarely the case. (p. 24, emphasis added)

This represented a significant break from the prevailing assumption that competition was antithetical to intrinsic motivation and cooperative learning (two other critical characteristics of cognitive apprenticeship).

The fundamental argument made by Collins et al. (1989) was that the focus on end products in traditional classrooms (i.e., grades and test scores), rather than the processes of learning, was responsible for the negative effects of competition:

> Another factor that makes competition seem problematic is that under many forms of teaching, *students lack the means, in the form of an understanding of the underlying processes, strategies, and heuristics involved in solving problems,* for improving their performance. In these cases, the motivation to improve that might be engendered by competition is blocked, leaving students inevitably frustrated and discouraged. (p. 24, emphasis added)

To this end, cognitive apprenticeship offered new ways for helping students learn these strategies, by drawing on the assumption that they were closely bound to the disciplinary, material, and social context where they were learned and used. Hence the first two critical characteristics of cognitive apprenticeship were *situated learning* and *a culture of expert practice*.

Another important early contribution to situative theory that pointed to new theories of motivation was Pea's (1993) discussion of *distributed intelligence*. Pea described how the refinement of technological and material resources over centuries made humans more intelligent than they would be otherwise. One of several "major concepts" that Pea advanced for distributed intelligences was *desires*. Pea argued that desires shape the way individuals interpret social and material resources and (therefore) how they use them. He argued that:

> Resources of the world offer potential relationships, constrained by their affordances that may not at all be mentally represented prior to a situational perception of their meaning. Their functional roles as components of a configuration of distributed intelligence may arise only in the course of desire-driven initiatives by an actor. (p. 55)

This suggests that the desires that people bring to situations in which they might use resources (and the intelligence they contain) is a central factor in motivating people to learn to use those resources. For Pea (1993), this characterization of motivated activity suggested that researchers needed to look beyond individual's goals and interests in order to motivate learning:

> We need to understand more fully the genesis of human *desires*, because people create, invent, and innovate as they create or act in designs for distributed intelligence. They do not simply act in habitual, static ways. The interpretation, relevance, and meaning of resources available for activity are shaped by the desires with which people come to situations. (p. 55, emphasis added)

Pea (1993) went on to introduce an initial taxonomy of desires, including *task* desires (to accomplish a specific action or task), *mapping* desires (to identify ways, or map, the opportunities presented by a particular resource can help accomplish a particular task), *circumstantial* desires (desires that arise opportunistically when one of the properties of a resource reveal new potential uses), and *habitual* desires (to use deeply familiar resources in routine ways).

While the ideas in the preceding paragraphs were not discussed in Hickey and Granade (2004), that chapter focused on parallel ideas found in Greeno's (1998) notion of engaged participation. In particular the 2004 chapter explored whether Greeno's *situative synthesis* might resolve enduring tensions that have emerged between classical behavioral/associationist theories of learning and modern cognitive/constructivist theories. The most obvious manifestation of this tension between these antithetical perspectives is the debate over the consequences of extrinsic incentives for intrinsically motivated learning. A related but less obvious tension explored in the 2004 chapter concerned educational assessment and testing. The assessment debates that pit multiple-choice achievement tests against open-ended performance and portfolio assessments are rooted in these same tensions. Whereas the former tests are assumed to capture relatively specific associations, the latter assessments are often assumed to capture higher order conceptual knowledge and problem solving ability. What follows is a summary of an extended program of DBR that used situative theories to address both tensions.

A New "Multi-Level" Approach to Assessment and Motivation

The ideas explored in Hickey and Granade (2004) had emerged across several DBR cycles using the constructionist GenScope computer program for learning introductory inheritance, developed by Paul Horwitz of the Concord Consortium. As described in Hickey, Kindfield, Horwitz, and Christie (2003), this research was initiated because of disappointing learning outcomes on a sophisticated performance assessment administered in early GenScope classrooms. On one hand, it was possible that the performance assessment was simply too removed from the GenScope computer environment (a cognitive transfer argument). A more situative explanation was that students had only been engaging with variant properties of GenScope (i.e., breeding fanciful dragons) but not the invariant properties (the underlying rules of inheritance).

This situative explanation of failure to transfer learning was supported empirically when those same students performed only slightly better on a new version of the performance assessment that presented the same inheritance problems using the familiar GenScope dragons and traits. In response, the researchers developed formative assessments and discussion-based feedback conversations (following Duschl & Gitomer, 1997). These were specifically designed to support and motivate discourse around the invariant properties of the GenScope activities. These assessments supported more disciplinary forms of engagement that resulted in dramatically increased learning outcomes, with gains ultimately reaching 3.0 SD (vs. 1.0 SD in comparison classes, Hickey et al., 2003).

Subsequent annual cycles of DBR added an achievement test created with randomly-selected SAT II Biology items that were unlike any of the formative assessments. Further iterative refinements of the formative assessments resulted in gains on the performance assessment that were "echoed" in further achievement gains; the GenScope achievement gains very similar to the achievement test items. This research resulted in a multi-level assessment framework where learning was motivated and iteratively aligned across (a) informal "discursive" assessments at the *close* level, (b) semi-formal classroom performance assessments at the *proximal* level, and (c) formal external achievement tests at the *distal* level (Hickey & Zuiker, 2012).

This new multi-level assessment framework was further refined in a subsequent NSF-funded collaboration involving the Quest Atlantis educational videogame, which had been explicitly designed and refined using situative and sociocultural theories of knowing and learning. This was important because this orientation helped reveal more specific strategies for motivating disciplinary engagement at the *immediate* level. These refinements focused on the moment-to-moment interactions of learners with the virtual resources in the videogame and with their peers and their teacher (as characters in the game).

As detailed in Barab et al. (2007), Quest Atlantis was refined across multiple DBR cycles that focused on players' use of scientific *formalisms* (e.g., *turbidity* and *eutrophication*). Many of these refinements concerned the resources provided to students within the game to help them use these formalisms more appropriately when interacting in the game and when preparing brief field reports. These virtual documents had to be approved by one of the leading game characters (played by the teacher) in order for each player to advance in the game. As reported in Hickey, Ingram-Goble, and Jameson (2009), these refinements were directly reflected in progressively larger gains on the performance assessment; these performance gains were again echoed with similar (but smaller) gains on the achievement test. Referencing Collins et al. (1989) above, this and other research (e.g., Siyahhan, Barab, & Downton, 2010) provided compelling evidence that Quest Atlantis was ultimately successful in providing players with the understanding of the underlying processes, strategies, and heuristics involved in solving problems.

An Empirical Study of Situativity and Motivation

Quest Atlantis provided an ideal opportunity to explore whether a networked learning environment that had been designed and refined using situative principles of engagement could reverse the negative consequences of competition and extrinsic incentives. As reported in Filsecker and Hickey (2014), this question was explored in a study of over 100 sixth grade students across four matched classes taught by one experienced teacher. In two of the classes, students were offered "extrinsic" incentives (badges for their game avatars that gave special abilities) and were encouraged to compete both to earn high appraisals on their field reports and display their progress in the game on a leaderboard. In the other two classes, the competitive elements and incentives were replaced with appeals to challenge curiosity, fantasy, and interest (consistent with Lepper & Malone, 1987). Results showed that students in the incentivized classes displayed higher levels of engagement with disciplinary resources (as indicated by increased and more appropriate use of disciplinary formalisms in their field reports), slightly higher levels of self-reported intrinsic motivation when completing those reports, and slightly more positive changes in self-reported personal interest in learning to solve these kinds of scientific problems. The incentivized students also showed statistically larger gains in conceptual understanding on the performance assessment and larger gains in achievement.

In addition to testing the explicit hypothesis regarding the impact of incentives and competition in this new class of situated learning environments, this study was also an initial application of Greeno's (1998) situative synthesis to the study of motivation. Specifically, the study explored whether a situative perspective could provide a coherent framework for refining and documenting potentially conflicting practices for motivating learning. Such a synthesis is established by treating all forms of individual activity (i.e., the way individuals behave in response to stimuli and the way humans appear to process information) as "special cases" of socially-situated activity. In theoretical terms, this means that the incentives and achievement tests (that are more consistent with behavioral/associationist perspectives) *and* the intrinsically motivated engagement and performance assessment (that are more consistent with cognitive/constructivist perspectives) are all understood as special cases of social participation in disciplinary discourse.

In practice, this means focusing primarily on engaged participation in disciplinary discourse when iteratively refining the learning environment; this means secondarily considering the "residue" that this discourse leaves behind in the form of individual understanding, achievement, behavior, motivation, and interests. Arguably, this demonstration that competition and extrinsic incentives can positively impact intrinsic motivation and personal interest provided an initial example of the usefulness of the situative synthesis. Additional support for this synthesis is found in the manner in which focusing primarily on participation in disciplinary discourse addresses concerns over *construct irrelevant easiness* (Messick, 1995; essentially "teaching to the test"). Construct irrelevant easiness occurs when refinements that focus primarily on individual activity are then represented on subsequent individual assessments and measures which can undermine the validity of the assessment scores. The results from Filsecker and Hickey (2014) showed how the situative synthesis could address the issue of construct irrelevant easiness by attending to characterizations of engagement that are represented on subsequent measures of motivation. Because the iterative refinements focused on improving participation in social discourse, the improvements in self-reported intrinsic motivation and personal interest are more convincing than would be the case if the refinements had focused directly on improving intrinsic motivation and personal interest. In support of our second argument above, we believe that gains in individual-level outcomes are more convincing when they are residual outcomes of socially-oriented interventions, when compared to individual gains that are the result of individually oriented interventions.

Critiques of the Initial Multi-Level Framework

Alongside the Quest Atlantis research, other collaborative design-based studies were carried out using this new multi-level framework. These included studies of elementary fractions (Hickey, 2011), multi-media NASA-funded STEM curricula (summarized in Hickey, Taasoobshirazi, & Cross, 2012), and secondary new media literacies curricula (Hickey, Honeyford, & McWilliams, 2013). Looking across all of these projects revealed a more general design framework organized around four increasingly formal levels of outcomes (Hickey & Filsecker, 2012; Hickey & Jameson, 2012).

This new framework was delivering dramatically larger gains in conceptual understanding and achievement in most (but not all) of the contexts where it was used. But the framework had yet to address critiques from two esteemed colleagues. The first critique was Lobato's (2003) concerns about the framework's tacit assumptions about knowledge transfer. Lobato argued that that the initial GenScope work had employed a traditional transfer paradigm based on conventional cognitive models of learning. From her perspective, this meant that the iterative design cycles were:

> not informed by data regarding the specific generalizations that students may have formed and how the instructional environment may have afforded those connections. Attempts to revise the curriculum in the absence of such information could have undermined the overall effort to produce measures of the generalization of learning. Because of the close alignment of the instruction with the transfer tasks, the gains on the transfer measures may have been due to a training effect. (p. 18)

This "training effect" (i.e., teaching to the test) was empirically addressed in later studies by the introduction of distal achievement tests. But that did not address Lobato's more fundamental argument that those efforts to foster productive forms of discourse had been carried out from an *expert* (i.e., an observer's) perspective rather than the *learners'* (i.e., the actor's) perspective. In response, Lobato proposed using an explicitly situative approach known as *actor-oriented transfer* in iterative refinements. Rather than simply looking for evidence of increased knowledge transfer across expert-designed assessments (as the GenScope project had done), Lobato suggested that design researchers "look for the influence of prior activity on current activity and how actors construe situations as similar" and "acknowledge that what experts consider a surface feature may be structurally substantive for a learner" (p. 20).

The second critique of the initial multi-level framework came more privately. The linguist James Gee, an advisor on the elementary mathematics project, concluded that the earlier framework lacked "a theory of talk" (e.g., Gee, 2004). Specifically, Gee (2004) argued that the two environments where the nascent design framework failed to increase understanding and achievement (elementary fractions and one of the three NASA curricula) did not offer learners readily accessible opportunities to engage in disciplinary discourse. In contrast, GenScope, the other NASA curricula, and the new media literacies curricula all presented learners with relatively accessible opportunities to participate in disciplinary discourse.

From Gee's (2004) perspective, the environments where the framework was successful all presented disciplinary knowledge in the context of concrete and meaningful disciplinary practices. This meant that students could more readily "try out" those practices and "try on" the identity associated with increasingly expert participation in that discourse. In contrast, elementary fractions did not naturally lend itself to new disciplinary discourse beyond recitation of the steps used to solve mathematical problems. Similarly, one of the three NASA curricula had been organized around an abstract simulation that was weakly contextualized. Put differently, the multi-level framework was insufficient to support engagement in disciplinary discourse above and beyond the original curricula.

Put in anthropological terms, the original multi-level framework implicitly embraced an *etic* approach that employed an objective outsider/expert view of learning and motivation. Returning to Pea's (1993) notion of desires helped to frame this shortcoming of that framework as a need for a more *emic* approach that embraced a more subjective insider/novice perspective. In the curricular environments where the original framework had been successful, the various desires that individual learners brought with them were sufficient to motivate students to participate in using the disciplinary course resources in ways that helped them use similar resources more successfully in the subsequent assessment and testing contexts. The etic approach in the earlier model had overlooked more emic strategies for socially constructing desires that could further motivate students to engage in disciplinary discourse above and beyond desires that they brought into the courses. As shown next, these critiques led to an extended search for new course features and design principles for supporting the engagement of a wider range of learners.

Participatory Learning and Assessment in Fully Online Course Contexts

An opportunity to formally address the concerns discussed above was presented when the first author began transforming two graduate education courses into fully online courses in 2008. One course, Learning and Cognition, primarily served practicing teachers completing their master's degrees, but also included doctoral students from various programs. It had been challenging to motivate disciplinary engagement in the face-to-face (FTF) version of the class. Many students perceived the core course concepts (e.g., *working memory, long-term memory, encoding,* and *retrieval*) to be quite removed from the everyday practices of teaching; many of the students were taking multiple courses while teaching full time and some were also raising families. Prior refinements to the multi-level assessment framework in the FTF course had resulted in reasonably robust classroom discussions and adequate levels of achievement. But the engagement strategies drew on students' prior experiences as both students and educators in FTF contexts. These strategies did not map readily to the online version of the course, and it seemed unlikely that that experiences and desires that students brought with them were sufficient to motivate productive engagement in the (then-new) online context. Meanwhile, the concerns raised by Lobato and Gee (decribed above) loomed large.

As summarized next, Randi Engle's work provided inspiration for a response to the concerns. Building on doctoral studies with James Greeno, Engle and Conant (2002) advanced the notion of *productive disciplinary engagement* (PDE). PDE drew on the situative distinction between disciplinary *knowledge* and disciplinary *practices* introduced above. The former is what disciplinary experts "know" independent of context, while the latter is what disciplinary experts "do" in the specific disciplinary contexts in which expertise is typically acknowledged. Engle and Conant argued that disciplinary engagement was most productive when learners made numerous connections between disciplinary knowledge and their own nascent disciplinary practices.

As described next, Engle's design principles for fostering PDE were embedded within the existing multi-level framework. This resulted in a new, more comprehensive framework called *participatory learning and assessment* (PLA; Hickey, 2015). What follows is a description of five design principles that now make up the PLA framework, as exemplified by current features that emerged across perhaps a dozen iterative refinements of the learning and cognition course described above.

Problematize Content

Engle and Conant's (2002) first design principle for fostering PDE is *problematize content from the students' perspective*. Consistent with Lobato's (2003) notion of actor-oriented transfer, this means that:

[p]reviously accepted facts can be treated as examinable claims, common explanatory accounts as needing evidence, and standard procedures as needing explanation for their functionality. Thus, problems do not need to be open from the perspective of experts in a discipline, but rather open from the perspective of students interpreting them, using their available knowledge and resources. (Engle & Conant, 2002, p. 404)

As described in Hickey and Rehak (2013), this was accomplished by having students first articulate a personalized educational goal in a public (to the class) "wikifolio." These are easily editable web pages that allow threaded comments directly on them. The first assignment has students define a goal that embodies their *prior* experiences, *current* interests, and *future* aspirations. The first assignment also has students identify which of five networking groups they prefer to join. These networking groups corresponded to the last five chapters in the textbook that discussed learning and cognition in five academic disciplines (*literacy, comprehension, writing, math,* and *science*). Students then use that goal to consider the relative relevance of the ideas in each textbook chapter for that goal. Specifically, the wikifolio assignments have students rank the relevance of the roughly five *implications for education* presented in each chapter. Each week students are asked to reframe (not just cut and paste) their personalized goal, as their understanding of that goal expands alongside their disciplinary knowledge of learning and cognition. Each week, students are also asked to identify the five "most relevant specifics" by examining each bolded term in the chapter well enough to consider its relevance to their instructional goal; most of the assignments extended or modified the basic engagement routine to explore specific aspects of each chapter.

Give Authority

Publically problematizing course content in the wikifolio assignments helped enact Engle and Conant's (2002) second PDE design principle: *Give students authority.* This means positioning students as stakeholders by "publically identifying them with the claims, approaches, explanations, designs, and other responses to problems that they pursue," and assigning activities that "encourage students to be authors and producers of knowledge, with ownership over it, rather than mere consumers of it" (p. 404). In the online class, this means that there are no "known answer" questions anywhere in the public space of the class. Every student is positioned as the ultimate authority regarding the relative relevance of the disciplinary knowledge in the textbook with the real or imagined disciplinary practices associated with their personalized instructional goal. In searching for justifications of their rankings (particularly for the "least relevant" implication), students are pushed to make connections between the disciplinary knowledge in the textbook and their own disciplinary practices. Of course, all of the textbook implications are ultimately relevant to every instructional goal; many of the instructors' comments (and subsequently many of the peer comments) point to unrecognized relevance among the lowest ranked implications. Rather than a rebuke, recipients of such comments typically reacted quite favorably, sometimes rearranging their rankings in response.

During the last 5 weeks, each of the networking groups collaboratively prepares an extended group wiki where group members negotiate an exemplary problem and take a position on one of the central pedagogical debates detailed in their chapter. The students in the other groups engage in extended threaded discussion on the groupwiki; the students in the other groups also create an individual wikifolio where they search for the relevance of that chapter for their own instructional goal and academic discipline. The members of the lead group each week then share and demonstrate their newly developed authority on that topic by systematically examining all of the other wikifolios to help those peers identify unseen relevance.

Thus, the first design principle in the PLA framework combines Engle and Conant's (2002) first two PDE principles while acknowledging the public and persistent discourse that is unique to online networks: *use public contexts to give meaning to knowledge tools.* By having each student contextualize their engagement in light of their own orientation to the disciplinary knowledge and avoiding any known answer questions in the public course, the framework is intended to promote diversity and privilege divergent perspectives from the outset. Emphasizing the way that each student's unique experience, interests, and aspirations give meaning to the disciplinary knowledge contained in the textbook chapters is presumed to help "level" the course by not advantaging students who bring more of that abstract knowledge.

Hold Students Accountable

The public interactions in the online course create a context for enacting Engle and Conant's (2002) third design principle: *Hold students accountable to others and disciplinary norms.* This means that "teachers and other members of the learning community foster students' responsibility for ensuring that their intellectual work is responsive to content and practices established by intellectual stakeholders inside and outside of their immediate learning environment" (p. 405). As Hall and Rubin (1998) pointed out, public contexts in and of themselves support a form of accountability because students naturally do not want to publically reference disciplinary knowledge or practices in ways peers or the instructor recognize as intellectually impoverished or dishonest. Notably, there are no length requirements for the student wikifolios and their contents are never formally evaluated or graded. Nonetheless, the informal, personalized, and public nature of the activity (and other features described below) consistently motivate all students to write hundreds of words each week; the context manages to motivate some of them to regularly write thousands of words some weeks.

Hall and Rubin (1998) also pointed out that public contexts support "local" interaction between individuals that can be observed (and possibly scrutinized) by peers and instructors. The weekly assignments instruct students to post questions to their peers and instructor (as comments), read and comment on peer wikifolios, and participate in threaded discussions on peer wikifolios. However, there is no specific requirement for doing so, and students are not penalized if they choose not to. Nonetheless, individual wikifolios typically gain 5–7 comments (typically including one or two threads), and the comments clearly show that peers are reading the wikifolios quite closely. Meanwhile, the groupwikis typically garner from 25–40 comments, inevitably featuring extended threads that get quite detailed. Technically speaking, commenting is required during the groupwiki period, but it is not formally enforced or associated with specific points. Rather than holding students accountable for their disciplinary knowledge, all of these features are intended to hold students accountable for their disciplinary *engagement.* Together, these features are intended to foster what Jenkins, Purushotma, Weigel, Clinton, and Robinson (2009) characterized as a *participatory culture,* where "not every member must contribute, but all must believe that they are free to contribute when ready and that what they contribute will be appropriately valued" (p. 7).

Provide Resources

Engle and Conant's (2002) fourth PDE design principle is simply: *Provide resources.* This principle highlighted Gee's concerns described above that the initial multi-level framework did not include specific curricular resources for fostering productive forms of disciplinary engagement and then holding students accountable for that engagement. The intentions of the new curricular resources for motivating PDE (described above) were rather tacit, but another feature for fostering PDE was more explicitly motivational: *PDE stamps.* PDE stamps are simply comments that start with a distinctive string of characters (e.g., "&&&") and recognized noteworthy examples of PDE. Importantly, students are instructed to include an explanation of why the wikifolio entry or comment was "both disciplinary and particularly productive" when awarding stamps. These are introduced in the third week, after students have had enough experience to appreciate the difference between disciplinary knowledge and disciplinary practices. By this time, the instructor has posted numerous comments on student artifacts commending compelling examples of PDE, with a particular emphasis on ones that use diverse and unique experiences to make the disciplinary knowledge meaningful.

An analysis reported in Hickey, Rehak, and Smith (2014) found that nearly all of the hundreds of stamps awarded in one class were appropriately warranted and many of the warrants themselves represented engagement that was also disciplinary and productive.[1] Reflecting an explicitly motivational implementation of Engle and Conant's (2002) first two design principles, these principles are combined into the second PLA design principle: *Publically reward productive disciplinary engagement.*

Grade Artifacts Through Local Reflections

Across the various online courses, the first two PLA principles have been quite successful at generating extensive student artifacts each week and extensive discussion of those artifacts in peer and instructor comments. This presents the obvious question of how all that work is graded. In perhaps one of the most appealing aspects of PLA to online educators (who are often overwhelmed with privately evaluating posts and papers), the actual content of the wikifolios and comments are never formally evaluated or graded. Instead, an extension of the multi-level assessment framework provides a simple alternative for assigning points towards the grades that students usually expect (and that most schools require), while further fostering student accountability to disciplinary norms. Students finish each weekly activity by adding three brief reflections to their wikifolio. These reflections are the only part of the assignment that is actually graded. If the students post all of the parts of the wikifolio by the deadline and post three "coherent and convincing" reflections on their prior engagement they are awarded all of their points. Typically, each of the 14 weekly wikifolios is awarded 5 points out of 100 total possible points for the entire class. The first prompt asks students to reflect on the relationship between their personalized instructional goal and the disciplinary knowledge of the particular textbook chapter:

> *Contextual engagement.* How suitable was your curricular aim and educational context for learning the ideas this week? Did your classmates have goals where these implications were more directly relevant? You are not being asked to criticize your understanding or your work; rather you are critiquing the suitability of your curricular aim and experience for learning to use this specific knowledge of cognition and learning in the chapter.

The second prompt is intended to motivate students to help each other by letting peers acknowledge and reward that work in their reflection:

> *Collaborative engagement.* Review the comments from your classmates and reflect on any insights that emerged in the discussions, anything particularly useful or interesting. Single out the classmates that have been particularly helpful in your thinking, both in their comments and from reading their wikifolios.

The third prompt is more general and asks students to reflect on the more general consequences of their prior engagement:

Consequential engagement. What are the consequences of what you learned this week for your curricular aim and in general? How should we teach or instruct differently at a general level? What are the real-world consequences of these ideas? Be specific in your examples but general in your thinking.

This third prompt builds directly on the notion of consequential engagement introduced in Gresalfi, Barab, Siyahhan, and Christensen (2009). Such engagement "goes well beyond procedural and conceptual engagement" by "using tools in order to have impact on situations" and "interrogating the usefulness and impact of the selection of particular tools on outcomes" (p. 23).

The intended function of these prompts illustrates a core situative assumption about assessment: all assessments should serve both summative and formative functions, but can only do so effectively when these functions address different forms of knowing (Hickey & Pellegrino, 2005). On one hand, the reflections are intended to serve as a summative assessment of students' prior engagement. It turns out that it is quite difficult to write a coherent and plausible response to these prompts without having engaged in these practices. In this way, these prompts are intended to *proleptically* (Cole, 1993) shape prior engagement. Because students learn that they will have to reflect on these three types of engagement, the prompts are presumed to motivate students to habitually engage that way in the first place.

On the other hand, these prompts serve as formative assessments of each student's understanding of (a) the disciplinary knowledge in the chapter, (b) their own disciplinary practices and the practices of their peers, and (c) the relationship between that knowledge and those practices. This balance of summative assessment of engagement and formative assessment of understanding via simple reflections forms the basis of the third design principle in the PLA framework: *Grade artifacts through local reflections.*

In light of this chapter's fourth argument concerning diversity, it is worth noting that the engagement supported by the first three PLA principles (the vast majority of engagement in the course) has *not* been organized around known answer questions about disciplinary knowledge. Rather, they aim to collectively provide the expansive framing described in Engle et al. (2012). Specifically, the first three PLA principles are intended to (a) encourage learners to draw on their prior experiences, (b) create links between learning and transfer contexts, (c) foster an expectation that learners will continue to use what they learned in later transfer contexts, (d) promote authorship as a practice where students generate unique solutions to new problems, and (e) hold learners accountable for the content that they authored. While expansive framing has primarily been studied in terms of knowledge transfer, it seems to have profound implications for motivating disciplinary engagement among diverse learners. Our initial assumption is that expansive framing allows all students to benefit from heterogeneous disciplinary orientations, while attenuating the disciplinary authority of the instructor. Both aspects of this framing are presumed to help all students find their own disciplinary voice (e.g., Harris, 2017), which is likely to have profound consequences for disciplinary engagement and for all conventional characterizations of motivation.

Assessment Resources to Motivate Engagement and Support Accountability

At this point, the PLA framework extends entirely beyond Engle and Conant's (2002) PDE framework into the prior multi-level assessment framework. As shown next, doing so makes it possible to (a) exploit the motivational, pedagogical, and evidential affordance of the original multi-level assessment framework; and (b) systematically employ the situative synthesis introduced above to organize DBR cycles.

Ungraded Formative Self-Assessments

Each weekly wikifolio assignment concludes with an ungraded self-assessment featuring roughly six open-ended constructed-response items. These known answer items are drawn from the textbook item bank and focus primarily on disciplinary knowledge (i.e., they do not really ask about disciplinary practices). Students must enter something into the online response space in order to see an elaborated explanation of the correct answer. The instructions for the self-assessments reminds students that if they are unable to answer most or all of the items from memory that they are likely unprepared for that part of the module exam (described next). The self-assessment instructions further encourage students to (a) attempt to answer each item from memory, (b) search out information in the text and wikifolios to provide responses on items they could not answer from memory, and (c) further review the textbook sections for the items that they struggled with. The optional and private nature of the self-assessments is represented by the choice of words in the fourth PLA design principle: *Let students self-assess their disciplinary knowledge privately.*

Timed Multiple-Choice Achievement Tests

The final course resource discussed here and the final PLA principle represent a pragmatic departure from the frameworks presented by both Engle and Conant (2002) and Hall and Rubin (1998). This feature and this principle embrace an aspect of the multi-level assessment framework that has proven rather controversial, while helping illustrate the value of the situative synthesis. At the conclusion of each of the three modules that make up the course, students complete a time-limited multiple-choice exam consisting of 25 items selected from the textbook item bank. Students are given just 60 minutes to complete the exam. The exam features items that are difficult to look up quickly (because the item format requires searching for the meaning of all four possible responses) or impossible to look up (because they are "best answer" items that require a thorough understanding of the topic). The exams have been refined over the years to ensure that (a) items that are too easy or behave unreliably are replaced, (b) just one or two students gets a perfect score, and (c) the average score is around 80%.

This practice is represented by the fifth PLA principle: *Measure achievement discreetly*. This principle adds "discreet" to Hall and Rubin's (1998) three forms of interaction to highlight the assumption that such "distal" assessments of knowledge should not be prominently featured in a curriculum and should never be directly taught to. But such tests are useful for helping motivate prior engagement (partly because they can be machine-scored immediately) and essential for efficiently and objectively comparing learning in the aggregate across different sections of the same course (i.e., across different instructors such as adjuncts). Each of the three exams is only worth 10 points out of the 100 points possible for the course. Thus, a student who gets an average score on an exam only loses about 2 out of 100 possible points.

From a situative perspective, multiple-choice items have little formative value beyond helping students recognize the correct answer to that specific item. Because of this, and to maintain a reasonable level of test security, students are only shown their overall score on the exam (but not the correct answers to each item). The exams provide a unique form of evidence that is quite useful for course design and evaluation, and provides an extra layer of accountability that helps motivate busy students to engage each week. In particular, the exams are presumed to encourage students to engage with the entire textbook chapter, and not just the implications presented in the chapter summaries. The overall performance on the exams, given the challenging nature of the items, provides initial evidence that this is effective. Importantly, a situative synthesis helps reconcile the usefulness and (likely) persistence of such formal accountability tools with the belief that multiple-choice tests represent a peculiar (if not bizarre) form of disciplinary discourse. Put differently, this situative synthesis makes it possible to frame achievement tests as a very specific disciplinary practice that is uniquely but narrowly useful in formal course contexts.

Summary, Extensions, and Next Steps

This chapter has argued that situative models of motivation and DBR are useful for fostering engagement and learning in online and networked educational contexts. Together, they can yield course design principles and features that leverage diverse orientations to foster productive engagement with disciplinary knowledge and generative learning of that knowledge. The resulting PLA framework has been used and further refined in a range of other settings. Additional insights for this approach emerged when the first author's online Assessment in Schools course was scaled up and offered to hundreds of learners in a Google-funded Big Open Online Course (BOOC; Hickey & Uttamchandani, 2017). The "Assessment BOOC" used an extensively customized version of Google's CourseBuilder platform to streamline and automate many of the course features described above. That project yielded insights for using this approach in self-paced courses using open educational resources, as did an extended partnership with online secondary school teachers (Itow & Hickey, 2016). Meanwhile, further refinements are being made to the Learning and Cognition course partnership with the adjunct instructors who have taken over teaching the course.

While much work remains to be done to formally validate the PLA framework, it seems like a promising approach for motivating learning in networked learning environments and prevailing online educational contexts. One near term goal is to systematically analyze course interactions using the analysis of generative learning in Engle (2006). Doing so would analyze and frame student interactions in terms of both *content* and *context*. The content analysis would examine learners' participation in the construction of content knowledge that fostered transfer (by construction of *common ground* and embracing *differential trajectories of participation* in constructing content knowledge). The context analysis would look at how the learning and transfer contexts are framed to create *intercontextuality*. Intercontextuality is established by framing the learning context in terms of *time* (building on the past in hopes of contributing to the future) and *participation* (positioning learners as authors within a larger community). In particular, such an analysis should shed new light on the controversies and questions raised by the use of self-assessment and achievement tests in the PLA framework. Such an analysis would also help explore the assumption that generative learning and expansive framing helps advance broader goals of educational equity.

Medium term goals include building external apps that streamline and automate some of the course features with a standard learning management system, and further supporting self-paced learning. Such tools, along with insights from the aforementioned Assessment BOOC, point to a radically different future of participatory learning that transcends the prevailing course-based models of education. Perhaps the most pressing medium-term goal is a critical examination of the PLA framework in light of current considerations with educational equity and social justice. It should be noted that the term *participatory* in the PLA label was drawn from Greeno's (1998) notion of engaged participation and the corresponding model of achievement motivation (Hickey, 2003). A more far-reaching vision of participation has been advanced within *participatory design research* (PDR; Bang & Vossoughi, 2016). Building from 25 years of DBR, the PDR framework "links both structural critiques of normative hierarchies of power and imagined possible futures" while simultaneously "being committed to consequential impacts in the here and now" (Bang & Vossoughi, 2016, p. 174). As such, the PDR framework raises fundamental questions about the participatory assumptions presented in this chapter. For example, it seems possible that using a (relatively normative) *professional* lens (i.e., the orientation used to problematize content) to problematize disciplinary knowledge and expansively frame learning may discourage the use of less-normative lenses that introduce heterogeneity and encourage emic forms of engagement, such as learners' personal experience with disciplinary knowledge through the lenses of gender and race. Likewise, PLA's pragmatic-but-discreet use of conventional tests and sharp distinction between disciplinary knowledge and disciplinary practice may well be reinforcing educational inequities and undermining goals of social justice.

While acknowledging the manner in which DBR has allowed innovators to envision new educational possibilities, Bang and Vossoughi (2016) argue that:

> DBR has tended to maintain, either explicitly or implicitly, normative hierarchically-powered decision-making structures and related assumptions of objectivity, paying little attention to the positionality of researchers or their social identities in the unfolding of work. (p. 174)

Of course, the design of a formal online course like Learning and Cognition is constrained by the broader graduate degree programs it serves and the process by which those programs are reviewed and approved by third party accrediting organizations. The rapid update of innovations like MOOCs, open learning, and digital badges in recent years suggests that prevailing models of measuring, credentialing, and accrediting *achievement* will ultimately yield to new models of capturing, recognizing, and validating *learning* (see Gallagher, 2016). Just as the move to online courses provided an opportunity to expand an initial design framework, it is expected that PDR and other related developments will reveal new design principles and research methods for supporting these radically broadened notions of participation.

ACKNOWLEDGMENTS

The research described here was supported by grants from Google, the MacArthur Foundation, the U.S. National Sciences Foundation, NASA, and

Indiana University. Suraj Uttamchandani contributed directly to key ideas described here and to the writing of this chapter.

NOTE

1. These were originally referred to as "badges" but were labeled "stamps" following the introduction of open digital badges in 2012. Given the topic of the course, it seemed appropriate to characterize them specifically in terms of PDE. As described in Hickey and Uttamchandani (2017), the same technique is in an open online course on Educational Assessment. In that case, they were called "peer promotions" and students were allowed to promote one (and only one) peer wikifolio each week for being "exemplary" and students were required to add a justification in order to make the award.

REFERENCES

Bang, M., & Vossoughi, S. (2016). Participatory design research and educational justice: Studying learning and relations within social change making. *Cognition and Instruction, 34*(3), 173–193.

Barab, S. A., & Squire, K. (Eds.). (2004). Design-Based Research [Special issue]. *The Journal of the Learning Sciences, 13*(1).

Barab, S., Zuiker, S., Warren, S., Hickey, D., Ingram-Goble, A., Kwon, E-J., ... Herring, S. C. (2007). Situationally embodied curriculum: Relating formalisms and contexts. *Science Education, 91*(5), 750–782.

Brown, A. L. (1992). Design experiments: Theoretical and methodological challenges in creating complex interventions in classroom settings. *The Journal of the Learning Sciences, 2*(2), 141–178.

Cole, M. (1993). Remembering the future. In G. Harman (Ed.), *Conceptions of the human mind: Essays in honor of George A. Miller* (pp. 247–265). Hillsdale, NJ: Erlbaum.

Collins, A., Brown, J. S., & Newman, S. E. (1989). Cognitive apprenticeship: Teaching the craft of reading, writing, and mathematics. In L. B. Resnick (Ed.), *Cognition and instruction: Issues and agendas* (pp. 32–42). Hillsdale, NJ: Erlbaum.

Dohn, N. B. (2016). A practice-grounded approach to 'engagement' and 'motivation' in networked learning. In T. Ryberg, C. Sinclair, S. Bayne, & M. de Laat (Eds.), *Research, boundaries, and policy in networked learning* (pp. 145–164). Switzerland: Springer International.

Duschl, R. A., & Gitomer, D. H. (1997). Strategies and challenges to changing the focus of assessment and instruction in science classrooms. *Educational Assessment, 4*(1), 37–73.

Engle, R. A. (2006). Framing interactions to foster generative learning: A situative explanation of transfer in a community of learners classroom. *The Journal of the Learning Sciences, 15*(4), 451–498.

Engle, R. A., & Conant, F. R. (2002). Guiding principles for fostering productive disciplinary engagement: Explaining an emergent argument in a community of learners classroom. *Cognition and Instruction, 20*(4), 399–483.

Engle, R. A., Lam, D. P., Meyer, X. S., & Nix, S. E. (2012). How does expansive framing promote transfer? Several proposed explanations and a research agenda for investigating them. *Educational Psychologist, 47*(3), 215–231.

Everhart, D., Derryberry, A., Knight, E., & Lee, S. (2016). The role of endorsement in open badges ecosystems. In D. Ifenthaler, N. Bellin-Mularski, & D. Mah (Eds.), *Foundation of digital badges and micro-credentials: Demonstrating and recognizing knowledge and competencies* (pp. 221–235). New York, NY: Springer.

Esmonde, I., & Booker, A. N. (Eds.). (2017). *Power and privilege in the learning sciences: Critical and sociocultural theories of learning.* New York, NY: Routledge.

Filsecker, M., & Hickey, D. T. (2014). A multilevel analysis of the effects of external rewards on elementary students' motivation, engagement and learning in an educational game. *Computers & Education, 75*, 136–148.

Gallagher, S. R. (2016). *The future of university credentials: New developments at the intersection of higher education and hiring.* Cambridge, MA: Harvard Education Press.

Gee, J. P. (2004). *Situated language and learning: A critique of traditional schooling.* New York, NY: Routledge.

Gibson, D., Ostashewski, N., Flintoff, K., Grant, S., & Knight, E. (2015). Digital badges in education. *Education and Information Technologies, 20*(2), 403–410.

Glaser, R. (1984). Education and thinking: The role of knowledge. *American Psychologist, 39*(2), 93–104.

Greeno, J. G., & Middle School Mathematics Through Applications Project Group. (1998). The situativity of knowing, learning, and research. *American Psychologist, 53*(1), 5–26.

Gresalfi, M., Barab, S. A., Siyahhan, S., & Christensen, T. (2009). Virtual worlds, conceptual understanding, and me: Designing for consequential engagement. *On the Horizon 17*(1), 21–34.

Gutiérrez, K., Rymes, B., & Larson, J. (1995). Script, counterscript, and underlife in the classroom: James Brown versus Brown v. Board of Education. *Harvard Educational Review, 65*(3), 445–472.

Hadwin, A. F., Järvelä, S., & Miller, M. (2011). Self-regulated, co-regulated, and socially shared regulation of learning. In B. Zimmerman & D. Schunk (Eds.), *Handbook of self-regulation of learning and performance* (pp. 65–84). New York, NY: Routledge.

Hall, R., & Rubin, A. (1998). There's five little notches in here: Dilemmas in teaching and learning the conventional structure of rate. In J. G. Greeno & S. V. Goldman (Eds.), *Thinking practices in mathematics and science learning* (pp. 189–235). Mahwah, NJ: Erlbaum.

Harris, E. M. (2017). *Examining teacher framing, student reasoning, and student agency in school-based citizen science* (Doctoral dissertation). Retrieved from ProQuest https://search.proquest.com/docview/1970386480

Hegel, G. W. F. (1991). *Hegel: Elements of the philosophy of right* (A. E. Wood, Trans.). Cambridge, MA: Cambridge University Press. (Original work published in 1821)

Hickey, D. T. (2011). A gentle critique of formative assessment and a participatory alternative. In P. Noyce & D. T. Hickey (Eds.), *New frontiers in formative assessment* (pp. 207–222). Cambridge, MA: Harvard Education Press.

Hickey, D. T. (2015). A situative response to the conundrum of formative assessment. *Assessment in Education: Principles, Policy & Practice, 22*(2), 202–223.

Hickey, D. T., & Filsecker, M. K. (2012). Participatory assessment for organizing inquiry in educational videogames and beyond. In K. Littleton, E. Scanlon, & M. Sharples (Eds.), *Orchestrating inquiry learning* (pp. 146–174). London, England: Taylor and Francis.

Hickey, D. T., & Granade, J. B. (2004). The influence of sociocultural theory on our theories of engagement and motivation. In D. M. McInerney & S. Van Etten (Eds.), *Big theories revisited: Theories of engagement and motivation* (pp. 200–223). Greenwich, CT: Information Age.

Hickey, D. T., Honeyford, M. A., & McWilliams, J. C. (2013). Participatory assessment in a climate of accountability. In H. Jenkins & W. Kelly (Eds.), *Reading in a participatory culture: Remixing* Moby-Dick *in the English classroom* (pp. 169–184). New York, NY: Teachers College Press.

Hickey, D. T., Ingram-Goble, A. A., & Jameson, E. M. (2009). Designing assessments and assessing designs in virtual educational environments. *Journal of Science Education and Technology, 18,* 187–208.

Hickey, D. T., & Jameson, E. (2012). Designing for participation in immersive educational video games. In D. Ifenthaler, D. Eseryel, & X. Ge (Eds.), *Assessment in game-based learning: Foundations, innovations, and perspectives* (pp. 401–430). New York, NY: Springer.

Hickey, D. T., Kindfield, A. C. H., Horwitz, P., & Christie, M. A. (2003). Integrating curriculum, instruction, assessment, and evaluation in a technology-supported genetics environment. *American Educational Research Journal, 40*(2) 495–538.

Hickey, D. T., & Pellegrino, J. W. (2005). Theory, level, and function: Three dimensions for understanding the connections between transfer and student assessment. In J. Mestre (Ed.), *Transfer of learning from a modern multidisciplinary perspective* (pp. 251–273). Greenwich, CT: Information Age.

Hickey, D. T., & Rehak, A. (2013). Wikifolios and participatory assessment for engagement, understanding, and achievement in online courses. *Journal of Educational Media and Hypermedia, 22*(4), 229–263.

Hickey, D. T., Rehak, A., & Smith, L. (2014, April 5). *Peer-awarded merit badges for encouraging and recognizing disciplinary engagement in online courses.* Paper presented at the annual meeting of the American Educational Research Association, Philadelphia, PA.

Hickey, D. T., Taasoobshirazi, G., Cross, D. (2012). Assessment *as* learning: Enhancing discourse, understanding, and achievement in innovative science curricula. *Journal of Research in Science Teaching, 49,* 1240–1270.

Hickey, D. T., & Uttamchandani, S. L. (2017). Beyond hype, hyperbole, myths, and paradoxes: Scaling up participatory learning in a big open online course. In L. Losh (Ed.), *MOOCs and their afterlives: Experiments in scale and access in higher education* (pp. 13–35). Chicago, IL: The University of Chicago Press.

Hickey, D. T., & Zuiker, S. J. (2005). Engaged participation: A sociocultural model of motivation with implications for educational assessment. *Educational Assessment, 10*(3), 277–305.

Hickey, D. T., & Zuiker, S. J. (2012). Multi-level assessment for discourse, understanding, and achievement in innovative learning contexts. *The Journal of the Learning Sciences, 22*(4), 1–65.

Hughes, J. E., & Holmes, A. (Eds.). (2005). Situated technology professional development programs [Special issue]. *Journal of Educational Computing Research, 32*(4).

Itow, R. C., & Hickey, D. T. (2016). When digital badges work: It's not about the badges, it's about learning ecosystems. In D. Ifenthaler, N. Bellin-Mularski, & D-K. Mah (Eds.), *Foundation of digital badges and micro-credentials: Demonstrating and recognizing knowledge and competencies* (pp. 411–420). New York, NY: Springer.

Jenkins, H., Purushotma, R., Weigel, M., Clinton, K., & Robison, A. J. (2009). *Confronting the challenges of participatory culture: Media education for the 21st century.* Cambridge, MA: MIT Press.

Lepper, M. R., & Malone, T. W. (1987). Intrinsic motivation and instructional effectiveness in computer-based education. *Aptitude, Learning, and Instruction, 3*, 255–286.

Lobato, J. (2003). How design experiments can inform a rethinking of transfer and vice versa. *Educational Researcher, 32*(1), 17–20.

McCaslin, M. (2009). Co-regulation of student motivation and emergent identity. *Educational Psychologist, 44*(2), 137–146.

Messick, S. (1995). Validity of psychological assessment: Validation of inferences from persons' responses and performances as scientific inquiry into score meaning. *American Psychologist, 50*(9), 741–749.

McInerney, D. M., & Van Etten, S. (Eds.). (2004). *Big theories revisited.* Charlotte, NC: Information Age.

Nolen, S. B., Horn, I. S., & Ward, C. J. (2015). Situating motivation. *Educational Psychologist, 50*(3), 234–247.

Oyserman, D. (2014). Identity-based motivation: Core processes and intervention examples. In S. A. Karabenick & T. C. Urdan (Eds.), *Motivational interventions: Advances in Motivation and Achievement* (Vol. 18, pp. 213–242). Bingley, England: Emerald.

Pea, R. D. (1993). Practices of distributed intelligence and designs for education. In G. Salomon (Ed.), *Distributed cognitions: Psychological and educational considerations* (pp. 47–87). Cambridge, England: Cambridge University Press.

Penuel, W. R., Cole, M., & O'Neill, K. (Eds.). (2016). Cultural-historical activity theory approaches to design-based research [Special issue]. *Journal of the Learning Sciences, 4*(3).

Politics of Learning Writing Collective. (2017). The learning sciences in a new era of U.S. nationalism. *Cognition & Instruction 35*(2), 91–102.

Rosebery, A. S., Ogonowski, M., DiSchino, M., & Warren, B. (2010). "The coat traps all your body heat": Heterogeneity as fundamental to learning. *The Journal of the Learning Sciences, 19*(3), 322–357.

Sandoval, W. A., & Bell, P. (Eds.). (2004). Design-based research [Special issue]. *Educational Psychologist, 39*(4).

Siyahhan, S., Barab, S. A., & Downton, M. P. (2010). Using activity theory to understand intergenerational play: The case of family quest. *International Journal of Computer-Supported Collaborative Learning, 5*(4), 415–432.

Tabak, I., & Radinsky, J. (Eds.). (2014). Social justice research in the learning sciences [Special issue]. *Journal of the Learning Sciences, 23*(3).

Turner, J. C., & Nolen, S. B. (Eds.). (2015). The relevance of the situated perspective in Educational Psychology [Special issue]. *Educational Psychologist, 50*(3).

Vygotsky, L. S. (1962). *Thought and Language.* Cambridge, MA: MIT Press. (Original work published in 1934)

SECTION V

ARE MY PEERS AND I MORE ALIKE, OR DIFFERENT,
IN OUR SCHOOL MOTIVATION AND LEARNING?

CHAPTER 16

THE NEED FOR POSITIVE FEEDBACK

Sociocultural Consideration of Self-Evaluative Motives in Education

Constantine Sedikides

Feedback is the currency through which the social world informs, rewards, or punishes its occupants. This currency is supplied frequently and on many occasions: in schools, organizations, sports, relationships, or transient social interactions. It is dispatched not only by authority figures (e.g., teachers, managers, coaches), but also by equals (e.g., fellow students, friends, social interactants). And it is intended to influence.

Sometimes feedback does influence, as examples from education demonstrate (Hattie, 2012; Hattie & Timperley, 2007). Yet, feedback is often less impactful than is meant to be (Kluger & DeNisi, 1996; Kulhavy, 1977). As a recent article in *The Guardian* concluded, "There is remarkably little high-quality, relevant research evidence to suggest that detailed or extensive marking has any significant impact on pupils' learning" (Aubrey, 2016, para. 1).

A good deal of factors determine the extent to which feedback will be influential (Sutton, Hornsey, & Douglas, 2012). This chapter focuses on

Big Theories Revisited 2, pages 381–400
Copyright © 2018 by Information Age Publishing

the role of the self in the feedback-giving process among university students (Sedikides & Gregg, 2003; Sedikides & Strube, 1997). It is assumed, in particular, that feedback is fundamentally a self-related phenomenon, and so its effectiveness is contingent upon self-dynamics (Anseel, Beatty, Shen, Lievens, & Sackett, 2015; Hepper & Sedikides, 2012). Self-dynamics is exemplified in terms of self-evaluation motives, and specifically self-enhancement, self-protection, self-assessment, and self-improvement. What follows is a discussion of the role of these self-evaluation motives—jointly or interactively—in the feedback process, and a consideration of the relevance of culture.

SELF-EVALUATION MOTIVES

We define self-enhancement as the motive to secure, sustain, or augment the positivity of the self, and self-protection as the motive to avoid, repair, or diminish the negativity of the self (Alicke & Sedikides, 2011; Sedikides & Gregg, 2008). Although these motives often work in tandem (Alicke & Sedikides, 2009), self-enhancement tends to operate routinely (i.e., being on the look-out for self-serving opportunities), whereas self-protection tends to operate situationally (i.e., propelling into action in response to self-threat).

We define self-assessment as the motive to sustain or increase the veridicality of the self (i.e., accurate self-knowledge; Trope, 1980, 1986) and self-improvement as the motive to ameliorate aspects of the self (i.e., increase knowledge or aptitude on important self-domains; Sedikides & Hepper, 2009; Taylor, Neter, & Wayment, 1995). These two motives also work in tandem (Gregg, Hepper, & Sedikides, 2011), although self-assessment may precede, and under some circumstances precipitate, self-improvement.

SELF-EVALUATION MOTIVES AND FEEDBACK

This section is concerned with what kind of feedback students want, how they remember it, how they react to it, and how they may group in their minds feedback-processing strategies.

What Sort of Feedback Do Students Want?

Do students want and pursue predominantly positive feedback (reflecting the strength of the self-enhancement/self-protection motives), accurate feedback (reflecting the strength of the self-assessment motive), or improving feedback (reflecting the strength of the self-improvement motive)?

We will first describe research among students in Western cultures before extending the findings to students in Eastern cultures.

Feedback Desire

In theory, students could desire unequivocally accurate feedback, that is, objective input based on external standards. Such feedback, however, might entail taking on board uncomplimentary, negative, or hurtful information about the self (Gregg, Sedikides, & Gebauer, 2011; Vangelisti & Hampel, 2012). Indeed, how many students have stepped up to their undergraduate or graduate mentor asking them directly what they truly think of them? Research by Hepper, Hart, Gregg, and Sedikides (2011) showed that students desire positive feedback. In Study 1, the more positive the feedback students expected to be, the more they desired it. In Study 2, students reported that they expected to receive more positive feedback than their peers. In Study 3, the stronger the self-enhancement motive was (i.e., the higher students' level of self-esteem or narcissism), the more positive the feedback expectations were. Study 4 manipulated the strength of the self-enhancement motive via a bogus newspaper article that described the findings of a groundbreaking longitudinal investigation. In the experimental condition, students learned that people who overestimate and display their knowledge or skills (i.e., "self-enhancers") have better prospects for success in life. In the control condition, students learned that people who underestimate and underplay their knowledge or skills (i.e., "modests") have better prospects for success in life. Next, students indicated what kind of feedback (ranging from very negative to very positive) they expected to receive from both close persons (i.e., friends, family, peers) and non-close persons (i.e., academics, employers/supervisors, shop assistants). Students in the experimental condition expressed a stronger preference for positive feedback, regardless of closeness to feedback-givers, than those in the control condition. A temporarily strengthened self-enhancement motive led to rosier feedback expectations.

Feedback Solicitation

In theory, students could also pursue obstinately accurate feedback. However, they do not. Instead, they pursue positive feedback. In experiments by Gregg, Hepper, and Sedikides (2011), students engaged in a problem-solving task for 30 minutes, attempting in pairs to build a bridge with only newspaper and adhesive tape. They were then offered the opportunity to solicit feedback about their task performance. The feedback (never actually provided) was purported to be either accurate or positive. Students solicited positive, not accurate, feedback.

It is not that students are indifferent to truthful feedback. Indeed, some research indicates that the self-assessment motive can overpower the self-enhancement motive. For example, Trope (1986) showed that students chose feedback more on the basis of its diagnosticity (i.e., its potential to inform reliably whether they possessed the relevant aptitude) than its positivity. This choice, however, is contingent upon the centrality of the aptitude or trait for the self. It was William James (1907) who first formulated the *self-centrality breeds self-enhancement* principle. He wrote, "I, who for the time have staked my all on being a psychologist, am mortified if others know much more psychology than I. But I am contended to wallow in the grossest ignorance of Greek" (p. 31). The principle has a venerable tradition in psychology (Crocker & Wolfe, 2001; Greenberg, Solomon, & Pyszczynski, 1997; Tesser, 2000). In the current context, the self-centrality breeds self-enhancement principle would suggest that the self-enhancement/self-protection motives are particularly influential in personally important domains.

The principle was put to the test in research involving solicitation of feedback about one's personality traits (Sedikides, 1993). Students received a set of questions that they could ask, in a quiet and private moment of self-reflection, to find out who they truly were (note that these instructions, in essence, activated the self-assessment motive). The questions pertained to various traits varying on the extent to which they were central or peripheral to students' self-definition and on whether they were positive or negative. In particular, some traits were pretested to be central and positive (e.g., friendly, trustworthy), some peripheral and positive (e.g., predictable, uncomplaining), some central and negative (e.g., unfriendly, untrustworthy), and some peripheral and negative (e.g., unpredictable, complaining). Importantly, the questions were pretested to vary in diagnosticity, that is, their potential to reveal truly what kind of person the student was. For example, the high diagnosticity question—"Would I introduce a new classmate to my friends?"—could tell whether the student was friendly, whereas the low diagnosticity question—"Do I interrupt my professor in class?"— could not. Likewise, the high diagnosticity question— "Do I constantly inform others about my problems or ailments?"—could reveal whether the student was complaining, whereas the low diagnosticity question—"Do I like my class?"—could not. Support for the self-assessment motive would be obtained, if students were equally likely to choose high diagnosticity questions to find out if they possessed central negative traits and positive central traits; in this case, students would not be afraid of the truth even if it hurt (i.e., even if they risked drawing the inference that they were untrustworthy or unkind). On the other hand, support for the self-enhancement motive would be obtained, if students were less likely to choose high diagnosticity questions to find out if they had negative central traits than positive central traits. Here, students would avoid potentially hurtful self-knowledge, opting for comfort over truth. This pattern, though, would

not emerge in the case of peripheral traits, as knowledge about one's negative peripheral traits does not present a self-threat.

Across six experiments, students selected lower diagnosticity questions
when self-reflecting on their central negative traits as opposed to their central positive traits (although they did not differ in the diagnosticity of the
selected questions when self-reflecting on their peripheral negative and
peripheral positive traits). Students bypassed the opportunity for accurate
knowledge about their negative central traits even when they were explicitly
instructed to conduct the self-reflection process the way a scientist would
(Experiment 5) and even when they generated their own questions to test
the central and peripheral traits that they listed as having (Experiment 3).
Finally, students did so only when they were attempting to figure out what
kind of person *they* were; when they tried to figure out what kind of person an acquaintance was, they selected high diagnosticity questions for this
person's central negative traits, not central positive traits (Experiment 6).
Accuracy is important for others, whereas positivity is important for the self.

Feedback Satisfaction and Usefulness

The abovementioned experiments pitted the self-enhancement against
the self-assessment motive. But how about self-improvement? Sedikides,
Luke, and Hepper (2016) assessed whether students perceive positive and
improving feedback as more satisfying than useful. From a self-enhancement
perspective, students would desire positive rather than improving feedback,
and so they would (a) perceive positive feedback as more satisfying than
improving feedback, (b) judge positive feedback as more satisfying than
useful, and (c) be influenced more by positive feedback than improving
feedback. However, from a self-improvement perspective, students would
desire improving than positive feedback, and so they would (a) perceive improving feedback as more useful than positive feedback, (b) judge improving feedback as more useful than satisfying, and (c) be influenced more by
improving feedback than positive feedback. Across four testing sessions, the
authors provided either steadily positive feedback (percentile rankings of
92, 90, 91, and 92) or improving feedback (percentile rankings of 59, 68, 81,
and 92), which they dispatched either sequentially (at each testing juncture)
or cumulatively (at the conclusion of the testing session). Lastly, the authors
assessed—sequentially or cumulatively—perceptions of feedback (satisfying
vs. useful), psychological consequences of it (optimism about task performance), and behavioral consequences (task persistence intentions).

More concretely, the authors simulated a naturalistic setting (e.g., classroom) in each of three experiments. In Experiment 1, they gave feedback
(on multiple aptitude domains, such as analytical ability or creativity) sequentially, but assessed its perceptions cumulatively. In Experiment 2,
they gave feedback (also on multiple aptitude domains) sequentially, and

assessed its perceptions and psychological consequences sequentially. In Experiment 3, they gave feedback (on a single aptitude domain, cognitive flexibility) both sequentially and cumulatively, and assessed all dependent measures sequentially and cumulatively. When feedback was assessed cumulatively, the results signaled the operation of the self-enhancement motive. Students considered positive (vs. improving) feedback as more satisfying and useful, and regarded positive feedback as more satisfying than useful. In addition, positive (relative to improving) feedback led to higher satisfaction, more optimism about future performance, and stronger intentions to persist. When feedback was assessed sequentially, however, the results were nuanced. Students considered positive (vs. improving) feedback as more satisfying and useful in the short-term, but not long-term. Further, they perceived positive feedback as less satisfying and less useful over time (i.e., in the long-term than short-term). Yet, they deemed improving feedback as more satisfying, but not more useful, over time. On balance, these findings attested to the strength of the self-enhancement motive, as positive feedback was desired more, and was more impactful both psychologically and behaviorally, at least in the short-run.

Cultural Context

What is the role of culture on the kind of feedback that students want or solicit? Gaertner, Sedikides, and Cai (2012) addressed this issue by testing samples of American and Chinese students. These researchers included not only positive feedback, but also improving feedback and effacing feedback (as well as a no-feedback control), given that some studies had suggested East-Asian students value self-improvement (Heine et al., 2001) and self-effacement (Heine, Kitayama, & Lehman, 2001; Kitayama, Markus, Matsumoto, & Norasakkunkit, 1997; but see Yik, Bond, & Paulhus, 1998, for nuanced findings) rather than valuing self-enhancement or self-protection.

In particular, American and Chinese students rated the degree to which they desired positive, improving, or effacing feedback (vs. no-feedback) from multiple sources (teachers, classmates, friends, parents). To illustrate the feedback format, the items pertaining to teachers as a source of feedback were: "I want my teachers to tell me (a) I am a great student (*positive*), (b) how to be a better student (*improving*), (c) I am an average student (*effacing*), and (d) nothing about the kind of student I am (*no feedback*)." The researchers operationalized self-effacement as per the suggestion that, for East-Asians, "self-effacement, in the form of seeing oneself as average ... would more likely serve the cultural mandate of maintaining interpersonal harmony" (Heine & Lehman, 1995, p. 596). Both Chinese and American students expressed a desire for positive and improving feedback compared to effacing feedback or no feedback; in fact, neither cultural group wanted effacing feedback, which they perceived as undesirable as no feedback.

Taken together, the self-enhancement motive was equally strong among Chinese and American students, and so was the self-improvement motive.

How Do Students Remember Feedback?

Students seem to desire positive feedback (Hepper et al., 2011), and solicit positive rather than negative feedback (Gregg et al., 2011), regardless of how accurate the feedback is (Sedikides, 1993). But what do students remember, or, for that matter, forget? For example, when they receive positive and negative feedback in equal measure, which sort of feedback are they more likely to forget? Again, we will discuss findings in Western cultures first, followed by those in Eastern cultures.

Recall as the Signature of Self-Protection or Self-Assessment

The operation of the self-protection motive would be reflected in a pattern where students selectively forget feedback that (a) pertains to their negative central attributes as opposed to their positive central attributes (especially when feedback behaviors are high rather than low in diagnosticity), and (b) refers to them personally instead of a hypothetical peer. In all, student would process shallowly and thus recall poorly feedback that threatens the self (i.e., negative central, self-referent, high diagnosticity). By contrast, the operation of the self-assessment motive would be reflected in a pattern where students are equally likely to remember feedback: (a) about their negative central and positive central attributes, (b) especially when it refers to them (given that the peer is a hypothetical acquaintance), and (c) especially when it is high than low in diagnosticity. In all, student would process deeply and recall well both negative and positive feedback—especially accurate one—that refers to the self, as they are unafraid to pursue true self-knowledge.

The contours of the experimental paradigm are as follows (Sedikides, Green, Saunders, Skowronski, & Zengel, 2016). Students take a bogus personality questionnaire, and subsequently receive feedback in the form of behaviors they are likely to enact. The behaviors portray students' central negative traits (e.g., unkind, untrustworthy) or central positive traits (e.g., kind, trustworthy). Sample behaviors are: "You are the kind of person who would refuse to lend classnotes to a friend who was ill" (unkind) or "A teacher would leave me alone in a room while taking a test and not be afraid that I would cheat" (trustworthy). For half of students, the behaviors refer to the self; for the other half, they refer to Chris, the hypothetical peer (e.g., "Chris is the kind of person who would refuse to lend class notes to a friend who was ill," or "a teacher would leave Chris alone in a room while taking a test and not be afraid that Chris would cheat."). Following feedback delivery, students work for a few minutes on an unrelated task (e.g., name as many states of the United States as possible) and then, in a surprise move, are asked to recall all feedback behaviors in any order they come to mind. Students recall a low percentage of negative central behaviors (compared to positive central behaviors), when these behaviors refer to them rather than Chris. Further, this recall pattern is augmented when the behaviors are high rather than low in diagnosticity. In conclusion, feedback recall is in the service of the self-protection motive: Students are more concerned with defending their self-image than acquiring valid self-knowledge. This conclusion is reinforced by studies on autobiographical memory in laboratory or naturalistic settings (Ritchie, Sedikides, & Skowronski, 2017; Skowronski, 2011).

The self-improvement motive, however, when activated, can mitigate the potency of the self-protection motive. Green, Sedikides, Pinter, and Van Tongeren (2009, Experiment 1) activated the self-improvement motive via a sentence-completion (language fluency) task comprising 20 sets of 4–6 words each. In the experimental condition, 16 word sets were related to improvement (e.g., aspirations, raises, improved), whereas the remaining four word sets were fillers. In the control condition, only one word set was related to improvement. Then, students completed a bogus personality questionnaire and received feedback in the form of behaviors they were likely to perform. Recall followed. In the control condition, students manifested selective forgetting: They recalled a lower percentage of negative central behaviors than positive central behaviors. This pattern, however, was cancelled out in the experimental condition. Under the influence of the self-improvement motive, students were equally likely to recall feedback about their substantive follies and strengths.

Cultural Context

Selecting amnesia of one's shortfalls is also observed in East-Asian culture (Tan, Newman, & Zhang, 2014). More generally, self-protective recall is observed panculturally. The fading affect bias (FAB) is a case in point. According to it, negative affect associated with autobiographical events fades faster than the positive affect associated with these events. Put otherwise, the FAB serves to promote the retention of positive emotions. The FAB has been found in samples from 10 cultures (Ritchie et al., 2015).

In fact, it is likely that the self-protection motive is more prevalent in East-Asian than Western culture. Assuming that the self-protection motive is a specific case of avoidance motivation (Elliot & Mapes, 2005), avoidance goals are more potent in East-Asian than Western culture (Elliot, Chirkov, Sheldon, & Kim, 2001; Elliot et al., 2012). Also, compared to Western culture, prevention focus is more potent than promotion focus in East-Asian culture (Hepper, Sedikides, & Cai, 2013; Lalwani, Shrum, & Chiu, 2009). In addition, East-Asian culture is purported to be relatively high on collectivism or interdependence (Markus & Kitayama, 1991; Triandis, 1995), and these dimensions entail not only harmony seeking, but also avoidance (Hashimoto & Yamagishi, 2013). Moreover, members of East-Asian cultures are excessively concerned with embarrassment avoidance or face saving (Ho, 1976; Hwang, 1987) and display conformity in an attempt to eschew a negative reputation (Yamagishi, Hashimoto, & Schug, 2008). Lastly, East-Asians, compared to Westerners, are more likely to dispute having negative traits than claim they have positive traits (Kim, Chiu, Peng, Cai, & Tov, 2010).

How Do Students React to Feedback?

Students recruit a panoply of strategies in reacting to negative feedback (Sedikides, 2012). The self-serving bias is an example of such strategies. We consider research in Western cultural context before incorporating East-Asian cultural context.

The Self-Serving Bias
This refers to readily accepting responsibility for success (by attributing it to one's ability or effort), but equally readily displacing blaming for failure on others or the situation (e.g., luck). In the typical experimental protocol (Sedikides, Campbell, Reeder, & Elliot, 1998, Experiment 1), students engage in a personally important task (e.g., creativity) with a co-worker. As part of the task, they generate solutions to a problem, such as uses for a spoon or a brick. The outcome of the task is interdependent; that is, feedback about success or failure is directed at the dyad, not at the individual. After completing the task, students receive randomly determined feedback. When the feedback is positive, students attribute the success more to themselves than their co-worker; however, when the feedback is negative, students attribute the failure more to their co-worker than the self. The self-serving bias has been documented extensively (Mezulis, Abramson, Hyde, & Hankin, 2004; Sedikides & Alicke, 2012), and its strength is rising as perceived self-threat rises (Campbell & Sedikides, 1999), reflecting the signature of the self-protection motive.

Cultural Context
The self-serving bias is pervasive in East-Asian culture as well (Mezulis et al., 2004; Sedikides & Alicke, 2012). Occasionally, though, it takes on a more intricate expression. In particular, the modesty norm is relatively restrictive in East-Asia (Chiu & Hong, 2006; Yamaguchi, Lin, & Aoki, 2006). It is when this norm is relaxed, that the self-serving bias will be more pronounced. For example, Chinese students make external—luck—attributions for their successes

in the presence of a close other, but make internal—ability or effort—attributions for their successes in the presence of an acquaintance (when, presumably, the modesty norm is eased; Han, 2010). Also, Japanese students took more credit for their successes than their failures when self-presentational concerns are removed (i.e., when they are assured of the anonymity and confidentiality of their responses; Kudo & Numazaki, 2003). Finally, Chinese students make internal (ability or effort) attributions for their academic accomplishments in a competitive setting, but make external (luck) attributions for the same accomplishments in a cooperative setting (Chou, 2002).

How Do Students Cognitively Organize Feedback-Processing Strategies?

Organization of Feedback-Processing Strategies in the West

Following a review of the literature, Hepper, Gramzow, and Sedikides (2010) identified 60 manifestations of the self-enhancement and self-protection motives in Western culture. Next, these authors presented a sample of students with these manifestations (or strategies) and asked them to judge how characteristic each was for them. As an example, for "self-serving bias," students first imagined, "When you achieve success or really good grades, thinking it was due to your ability," and then indicated how characteristic this strategy was for them. Similarly, for "better-than-average beliefs," students thought of themselves "as generally possessing positive traits or abilities to a greater extent than most people do," and subsequently rated how characteristic this strategy was of them. Through multivariate (i.e., factor analytic) techniques, Hepper et al. distilled these 60 strategies into four groups, all of which implicated feedback.

One group was *positivity embracement* (comprising 10 strategies), which referred to the acquisition or retention of positive feedback, or the maximization of anticipated success. Strategies included the self-serving bias, remembering selectively positive feedback, and presenting oneself favorable to others so as to elicit positive feedback. The second group, *favorable construals* comprised six strategies implicated in interpreting feedback creatively in ways that would optimize self-enhancement and self-protection strivings. Examples of these strategies are construals of ambiguous feedback as positive, comparative optimism, and positive illusions. The third group was *defensiveness*, consisting of 18 strategies that targeted protection from self-threatening feedback. Such strategies included self-handicapping, defensive pessimism, and self-serving attributions for failure. The fourth and final group was *self-affirming reflections*. It consisted of six strategies oriented toward the attainment of favorable outcomes or self-views in the face of negative feedback. Examples of such strategies are downward counterfactual thinking, temporal comparison, or focusing on one's psychological assets. In all, this research demonstrated the plethora of self-enhancement or self-protection strategies that students can deploy to cope with an ever-changing, and often threatening, social world.

Cultural Context

The abovementioned strategies were identified in Western culture (i.e., United Kingdom, United States), as mentioned above. Follow-up research examined their relevance in East-Asian culture. In particular, Hepper et al. (2013) presented Chinese students with an abbreviated list of 20 self-enhancement/self-protection strategies. The list consisted of the five strategies that had loaded most highly on each of positivity embracement, favorable construals, defensiveness, and self-affirming reflections in the Hepper et al. (2010) study. The results demonstrated that Chinese students organized those strategies in a very similar manner to those of Western students, that is, in terms of the four groupings of positivity embracement, favorable construals, defensiveness, and self-affirming reflections.

LINGERING ISSUES

Further Thoughts About Culture

The reviewed literature indicated that the self-enhancement and self-protection motives have a strong influence on feedback-related processes in both Western and East-Asian culture (albeit the self-improvement motive is also influential), situational complexity aside (Liem, McInerney, & Yeung, 2015; Pavlova, Lechner, & Silbereisen, 2017). The argument for cultural similarity needs to be qualified. It states that, although the two motives are fundamental in both cultures, their expression differs. Work by Sedikides, Gaertner, and Toguchi (2003; see also Sedikides, Gaertner, & Vevea, 2005) illustrates this principle. These authors theorized that, in the case of social comparison, the personal importance of the evaluative domain would diverge across cultures. Individualism would be more personally important (or central) for Westerners than East-Asians, whereas collectivism would be more personally important (or central) for East-Asians than Westerners. Relying on the self-centrality breeds self-enhancement principle (James, 1907) the authors hypothesized that Westerners would self-enhance on individualistic attributes, whereas Easterners would self-enhance on collectivistic attributes. Indeed, American students rated themselves as superior to their coworkers on individualistic traits (e.g., independent, self-reliant) and behaviors (e.g., trust your own instincts rather than your group's instincts, desert your group when the group does not represent you anymore), whereas Japanese students rated themselves as superior to their coworkers on collectivistic traits (e.g., compromising, loyal) and behaviors (e.g., conform to your group's decisions, avoid conflict with your group at any cost). By implication, Westerners and East-Asians may appear to react differently to negative (or positive) feedback on individualistic versus collectivistic dimensions, but the difference can be explained in terms of the importance the two groups ascribe to each dimension; that is, controlling for importance, the feedback reactions would be indistinguishable.

The domain of feedback elicitation provides another illustration of the self-centrality breeds self-enhancement principle. Both Westerners and Easterners value receiving compliments or self-praise, given the universality of self-esteem (Schmitt & Allik, 2005; Sedikides Gaertner, & Cai, 2015), but they do so differently. Westerners appreciate self-praise and are comfortable with it (Leary, 2005; Sedikides et al., 2015). East-Asians also value it (Spencer-Oatey & Ng, 2001), but, in conformity with the modesty norm (Chen, 1993), express it indirectly. The gist of the following conversational script typifies the process (Wu, 2011). The speaker praises herself (by directing the listener's attention to an important attribute of hers), but instantaneously qualifies or retracts the self-praise (saving face or decreasing the need to back it up). Instead, the speaker proceeds to praise herself as second best (rather than best), although she skillfully chooses an extreme comparison group. Finally, the speaker humblebrags (Steinmetz, Sezer, & Sedikides, 2017): She raises a complaint, but only en route to showcasing her strength. For feedback, then, to be more receptive among East-Asian students, it will have to comply to the modesty norm or to a script such as this.

The effectiveness of feedback among East-Asian recipients may also increase via other-mediation. Theorists speculated that East-Asians self-enhance indirectly, that is, through close others (Kuwayama, 1992; Yum, 1985). Muramoto (2003) provided evidence for this speculation. Japanese students thought of a situation where they had either succeeded or failed, attributed the outcome to various causes, and reported how their family, friends, peers, and strangers might attribute this outcome. Students expected that their family and friends would exhibit the self-serving bias on their behalf; that is, their close others would give students credit for successes and blame situations for their failures. As another example of indirect self-enhancement, Dalsky, Gohm, Noguchi, and Shiomura (2008) found that Japanese engage in "mutual self-enhancement," where they exchange praise with close others.

Can Students Open Up to Negative Feedback?

The potency of the self-protection motive is understandable: Negative feedback is aversive or hurtful (Sedikides, 2012; Vangelisti & Hampel,

2012). Of course, negative feedback can likewise be useful. It may, for example, be high in diagnosticity (accurate) and hence likely to prompt efforts toward improvement. If so, it is worth examining circumstances under which students are amenable to negative feedback.

One such circumstance involves armoring the self prior to receiving the negative feedback. For example, self-affirmation (writing about one's cardinal values; Sherman & Cohen, 2006), positive mood (Aspinwall, 1998), and a sense of control (Trope, Gervey, & Bolger, 2003), all make negative feedback more palatable. So does bringing to mind a close other. In a study by Kumashiro and Sedikides (2005), students completed an intellectually demanding task and then visualized a close positive other (e.g., friend, partner), a close negative other (e.g., mother-in-law, former friend), or a neutral other (e.g., public transportation worker, checkout clerk). All students received false negative feedback about their task performance. Following that, students expressed their level of interest in receiving feedback that focused on their liabilities and skill limitations at the relevant performance domain. Students who visualized a close positive other (vs. controls) declared the strongest interest in receiving liability-focused feedback.

The role of close relationships in increasing receptiveness to negative feedback was also demonstrated by Sedikides et al. (1998, Experiment 2; see also Sedikides, Campbell, Reeder, & Elliot, 2002). Students worked on an interdependent outcomes task (i.e., creativity) either with a stranger or a close other. Upon reception of feedback, students manifested the self-serving bias (e.g., blaming the coworker for the dyadic failure), when their partner was a stranger, but not when their partner was a close other. Takata (2003) reported similar findings with Japanese students. They self-enhanced when they learned that they outperformed a stranger, but self-effaced when they learned that they outperformed a close other.

In addition, close relationships influence memory for negative feedback. Green et al. (2009, Experiment 2) examined whether selective forgetting will be cancelled out when the feedback is given by a close other as opposed to a stranger (i.e., the experimenter). In the case of close other, the feedback might be interpreted as a helpful attempt toward improvement rather than as an evaluation. This was indeed the case. Students remembered the negative central behaviors equally well with their positive central behaviors, when the feedback was dispatched from a close other (a friend) rather than a distant other.

Besides self-affirmation and relational closeness, other circumstances that might conduce to the receptiveness of negative feedback involve introspection and accountability. It has been shown that introspection (i.e., reflecting on whether and why one might have negative traits and positive traits) increases endorsement of negative characteristics while decreasing endorsement of positive characteristics (Sedikides, Horton, & Gregg,

2007). Also, accountability (i.e., having to explain and justify the way one thinks about themselves) curtails the positivity of one's self-views (Sedikides, Herbst, Hardin, & Dardis, 2002).

CONCLUDING REMARKS

This chapter addressed the role of self-evaluation motives in the feedback process. It emphasized the influence of the self-enhancement and self-protection motives (and, secondarily, the influence of the self-improvement motive) among students in both Western and East-Asian cultures. It is not that accurate feedback is irrelevant or unimportant. Rather, positive feedback is what students want and solicit, even if they have to compromise on its veracity.

The evidence indicates that the self-protection motive is more prevalent in East-Asian than Western cultures (Sedikides et al., 2015). It is not clear what the implications of this finding are. One could argue that negative feedback is more likely to optimize performance for East-Asian than Western students. We doubt, however, that this would be the case. Concern with protecting the self may be more widespread in East-Asian than Western cultures, but this does not mean that the consequences of negative feedback (i.e., hurt, aversive feelings, drop in self-esteem) are any less impactful for one cultural group over another; in fact, research demonstrates that East-Asian students are as undesirous of negative feedback as Western students are (Gaertner et al., 2012). On the other hand, it could be that the incentive to avoid receiving negative feedback is more energizing for East-Asian than Western students. Perhaps it is to the extent that East-Asians avoid negativity that they are motivated toward self-improvement. Corresponding, it may be to the extent that Western students pursue positivity that they are motivated toward improvement.

Relatedly, East-Asians show a weaker self-serving bias than Westerners (Mezulis et al., 2004), as modesty norms are more strongly internalized in the East than the West. This findings has pedagogical implications. For example, dyadic or group-based projects may be more functional in East-Asian cultures, as the feedback process may contribute toward maintaining healthier relationships among members of the dyad or the group. Students will be less likely to alienate others by attributing project failure to them or by claiming disproportionate responsibility for project successes.

We focused almost exclusively on East-Asian versus Western cultures, and on individualism versus collectivism (or on independence vs. interdependence). A task for future research would be to understand better how feedback is perceived, desired, remembered, or reacted upon across the entire span of cultures. Research by Vignoles et al. (2016) in 55 cultural groups and 33 nations has already taken steps in that direction. The cultural groups endorse different aspects of independence or interdependence, as a function of not only individualism-collectivism, but also religious heritage and country-based socioeconomic development. In fact, seven dimensions emerged: difference versus similarity, self-containment versus connection to others, self-direction versus receptiveness to influence, self-reliance versus dependence on others, consistency versus variability, self-expression versus harmony, and self-interest versus commitment to others. This multifaceted approach promises to refine the feedback-receiving and feedback-giving process.

REFERENCES

Alicke, M. D., & Sedikides, C. (2009). Self-enhancement and self-protection: What they are and what they do. *European Review of Social Psychology, 20,* 1–48.

Alicke, M. D., & Sedikides, C. (Eds.). (2011). *Handbook of self-enhancement and self-protection.* New York, NY: Guilford Press.

Anseel, F., Beatty, A., Shen, W., Lievens, F., & Sackett, P. R. (2015). How are we doing after 30 years? A meta-analytic review of antecedents and outcomes of feedback-seeking behavior. *Journal of Management, 41,* 318–348.

Aspinwall, L. G. (1998). Rethinking the role of positive affect in self-regulation. *Motivation and Emotion, 22,* 1–32.

Aubrey, E. (2016, November 29). It's official: Your school's marking policy is probably wrong. *The Guardian.* Retrieved from https://www.theguardian.com/teacher-network/2016/nov/29/teacher-schools-marking-policy-students-work?CMP=fb_gu

Campbell, K. W., & Sedikides, C. (1999). Self-threat magnifies the self-serving bias: A meta-analytic integration. *Review of General Psychology, 3,* 23–43.

Chen, R. (1993). Responding to compliments: A contrastive study of politeness strategies between American English and Chinese speakers. *Journal of Pragmatics, 20,* 49–75.

Chiu, C.-Y., & Hong, Y.-Y. (2006). *Social psychology of culture.* New York, NY: Psychology Press.

Chou, S. H. (2002). *Attribution patterns in situations of interpersonal competition and harmony* (Unpublished master's thesis). National Taiwan University, Taipei City, Taiwan.

Crocker, J., & Wolfe, C. T. (2001). Contingencies of self-worth. *Psychological Review, 108,* 593–623.

Dalsky, D. J., Gohm, C. L., Noguchi, K., & Shiomura, K. (2008). Mutual self-enhancement in Japan and the United States. *Journal of Cross-Cultural Psychology, 39,* 215–223.

Elliot, A. J., & Mapes, R. R. (2005). Approach-avoidance motivation and self-concept evaluation. In A. Tesser, J. Wood, & D. Stapel (Eds.), *On building, defending, and regulating the self: A psychological perspective* (pp. 171–196). Washington, DC: Psychological Press.

Elliot, A. J., Chirkov, V. I., Sheldon, K. M., & Kim, Y. (2001). A cross-cultural analysis of avoidance (relative to approach) personal goals. *Psychological Science, 12,* 505–510.

Elliot, A. J., Sedikides, C., Murayama, K., Tanaka, A., Thrash, T. M., & Mapes, R. R. (2012). Cross-cultural generality and specificity in self-regulation: Avoidance personal goals and multiple aspects of wellbeing in the U.S. and Japan. *Emotion, 12,* 1031–1040.

Gaertner, L., Sedikides, C., & Cai, H. (2012). Wanting to be great and better but not average: On the pancultural desire for self-enhancing and self-improving feedback. *Journal of Cross-Cultural Psychology, 43,* 521–526.

Green, J. D., Sedikides, C., Pinter, B., & Van Tongeren, D. R. (2009). Two sides to self-protection: Self-improvement strivings and feedback from close relationships eliminate mnemic neglect. *Self and Identity, 8,* 233–250.

Greenberg, J., Solomon, S., & Pyszczynski, T. (1997). Terror management theory of self-esteem and cultural worldviews: Empirical assessments and conceptual refinements. *Advances in Experimental Social Psychology, 29,* 61–139.

Gregg, A. P., Hepper, E. G. D., & Sedikides, C. (2011). Quantifying self-motives: Functional links between dispositional desires. *European Journal of Social Psychology, 41,* 840–852.

Gregg, A. P., Sedikides, C., & Gebauer, J. E. (2011). Dynamics of identity: Between self-enhancement and self-assessment. In S. J. Schwartz, K. Luyckx, & V. L. Vignoles (Eds.), *Handbook of identity theory and research* (Vol. 1, pp. 305–327). New York, NY: Springer.

Han, K.-H. (2010). The study of Chinese interpersonal attribution style and motivations for achievement. *Journal of Social Sciences and Philosophy, 22,* 41–76.

Hashimoto, H., & Yamagishi, T. (2013). Two faces of interdependence: Harmony seeking and rejection avoidance. *Asian Journal of Social Psychology, 16,* 142–151.

Hattie, J. (2012). Feedback in schools. In R. M. Sutton, M. J. Hornsey, & K. M. Douglas (Eds.), *Feedback: The communication of praise, criticism, and advice* (pp. 265–277). New York, NY: Peter Lang.

Hattie, J., & Timperley, H. (2007). The power of feedback. *Review of Education Research, 77,* 81–112.

Heine, S. J., Kitayama, S., & Lehman, D. R. (2001). Cultural differences in self-evaluation: Japanese readily accept negative self-relevant information. *Journal of Cross-Cultural Psychology, 32,* 434–443.

Heine, S. J., Kitayama, S., Lehman, D. R., Takata, T., Ide, E., Leung, C., & Matsumoto, H. (2001). Divergent consequences of success and failure in Japan and North America. An investigation of self-improving motivations and malleable selves. *Journal of Personality and Social Psychology, 81,* 599–615.

Heine, S. J., & Lehman, D. R. (1995). Cultural variation in unrealistic optimism: Does the West feel more vulnerable than the East? *Journal of Personality and Social Psychology, 68,* 595–607.

Hepper, E. G., Gramzow, R. H., & Sedikides, C. (2010). Individual differences in self-enhancement and self-protection strategies: An integrative analysis. *Journal of Personality, 78,* 781–814.

Hepper, E. G., Hart, C. M., Gregg, A. P., & Sedikides, C. (2011). Motivated expectations of positive feedback in social interactions. *The Journal of Social Psychology, 151*, 455–477.

Hepper, E. G., Sedikides, C., & Cai, H. (2013). Self-enhancement and self-protection strategies in China: Cultural expressions of a fundamental human motive. *Journal of Cross-Cultural Psychology, 44*, 5–23.

Hepper, E. G., & Sedikides, C. (2012). Self-enhancing feedback. In R. M. Sutton, M. J. Hornsey, & K. M. Douglas (Eds.), *Feedback: The communication of praise, criticism, and advice* (pp. 43–56). New York, NY: Peter Lang.

Ho, D. Y. F. (1976). On the concept of face. *American Journal of Sociology, 81*, 867e890.

Hwang, K. K. (1987). Face and favor: The Chinese power game. *American Journal of Sociology, 92*, 944–974.

James, W. (1907). *The principles of psychology* (Vol. 1). New York, NY: Holt.

Kim, Y.-H., Chiu, C.-Y., Peng, S., Cai, H., & Tov, W. (2010). Explaining East-West differences in the likelihood of making favorable self-evaluations. *Journal of Cross-Cultural Psychology, 41*, 62–75.

Kitayama, S., Markus, H. R., Matsumoto, H., & Norasakkunkit, V. (1997). Individual and collective processes in the construction of the self: Self-enhancement in the United States and self-criticism in Japan. *Journal of Personality and Social Psychology, 72*, 1245–1267.

Kluger, A. N., & DeNisi, A. (1996). The effects of feedback interventions on performance: A historical review, a meta-analysis, and a preliminary feedback intervention theory. *Psychological Bulletin, 119*, 254–284.

Kudo, E., & Numazaki, M. (2003). Explicit and direct self-serving bias in Japan: Reexamination of self-serving bias for success and failure. *Journal of Cross-Cultural Psychology, 34*, 511–521.

Kulhavy, R. W. (1977). Feedback in written instruction. *Review of Educational Research, 47*, 211–232.

Kumashiro, M., & Sedikides, C. (2005). Taking on board liability-focused feedback: Close positive relationships as a self-bolstering resource. *Psychological Science, 16*, 732–739.

Kuwayama, T. (1992). The reference other orientation. In N. R. Rosenberger (Ed.), *Japanese sense of self* (pp. 121–151). Cambridge, England: Cambridge University Press.

Lalwani, A. K., Shrum, L. J., & Chiu, C.-Y. (2009). Motivated response styles: The role of cultural values, regulatory focus, and self-consciousness in socially desirable responding. *Journal of Personality and Social Psychology, 96*, 870–882.

Leary, M. R. (1995). *Self-presentation: Impression management and interpersonal behavior.* Boulder, CO: Westview.

Liem, G. A. D., McInerney, D. M., & Yeung, A. S. (2015). Academic self-concepts in ability streams: Considering domain specificity and same-stream peers. *The Journal of Experimental Education, 83*, 83–109.

Markus, H. R., & Kitayama, S. (1991). Culture and the self: Implications for cognition, emotion, and motivation. *Psychological Review, 98*, 224–253.

Mezulis, A. H., Abramson, L. Y., Hyde, J. S., & Hankin, B. L. (2004). Is there a universal positivity bias in attributions? A meta-analytic review of individual, developmental, and cultural differences in the self-serving attribution bias. *Psychological Bulletin, 130,* 711–747.

Muramoto, Y. (2003). An indirect self-enhancement in relationship among Japanese. *Journal of Cross-Cultural Psychology, 34,* 552–566.

Pavlova, M. K., Lechner, S. M., & Silbereisen, R. K. (2017). Social comparison in coping with occupational uncertainty: Self-improvement, self-enhancement, and the regional context. *Journal of Personality, 81,* 76–86.

Ritchie, T. D., Batteson, T. J., Bohn, A., Crawford, M. T., Ferguson, G. V., Schrauf, . . . & Walker, W. R. (2015). A pancultural perspective on the fading affect bias in autobiographical memory. *Memory, 23,* 278–290.

Ritchie, T. D., Sedikides, C., & Skowronski, J. J. (2017). Does a person selectively remember the good or the bad from their personal past? It depends on the recall target and the person's favorability of self-views. *Memory, 25,* 934–944.

Schmitt, D. P., & Allik, J. (2005). Simultaneous administration of the Rosenberg self-esteem scale in 53 nations: Exploring the universal and culture-specific features of global self-esteem. *Journal of Personality and Social Psychology, 89,* 623–642.

Sedikides, C. (1993). Assessment, enhancement, and verification determinants of the self-evaluation process. *Journal of Personality and Social Psychology, 65,* 317–338.

Sedikides, C. (2012). Self-protection. In M. R. Leary & J. P. Tangney (Eds.), *Handbook of self and identity* (2nd ed., pp. 327–353). New York, NY: Guilford Press.

Sedikides, C., & Alicke, M. D. (2012). Self-enhancement and self-protection motives. In R. M. Ryan (Ed.), *Oxford handbook of motivation* (pp. 303–322). New York, NY: Oxford University Press.

Sedikides, C., Campbell, W. K., Reeder, G., & Elliot, A. J. (1998). The self-serving bias in relational context. *Journal of Personality and Social Psychology, 74,* 378–386.

Sedikides, C., Campbell, W. K., Reeder, G., & Elliot, A. J. (2002). The self in relationships: Whether, how, and when close others put the self "in its place." *European Review of Social Psychology, 12,* 237–265.

Sedikides, C., Gaertner, L., & Cai, H. (2015). On the panculturality of self-enhancement and self-protection motivation: The case for the universality of self-esteem. *Advances in Motivation Science, 2,* 185–241.

Sedikides, C., Gaertner, L., & Toguchi, Y. (2003). Pancultural self-enhancement. *Journal of Personality and Social Psychology, 84,* 60–70.

Sedikides, C., Gaertner, L., & Vevea, J. L. (2005). Pancultural self-enhancement reloaded: A meta-analytic reply to Heine (2005). *Journal of Personality and Social Psychology, 89,* 539–551.

Sedikides, C., Green, J. D., Saunders, J., Skowronski, J. J., & Zengel, B. (2016). Mnemic neglect: Selective amnesia of one's faults. *European Review of Social Psychology, 27,* 1–62.

Sedikides, C., & Gregg, A. P. (2003). Portraits of the self. In M. A. Hogg & J. Cooper (Eds.), *SAGE handbook of social psychology* (pp. 110–138). London, England: SAGE.

Sedikides, C., & Gregg, A. P. (2008). Self-enhancement: Food for thought. *Perspectives on Psychological Science, 3,* 102–116.

Sedikides, C., & Hepper, E. G. D. (2009). Self-improvement. *Social and Personality Psychology Compass, 3,* 899–917.

Sedikides, C., Herbst, K. C., Hardin, D. P., & Dardis, G. J. (2002). Accountability as a deterrent to self-enhancement: The search for mechanisms. *Journal of Personality and Social Psychology, 83,* 592–605.

Sedikides, C., Horton, R. S., & Gregg, A. P. (2007). The why's the limit: Curtailing self-enhancement with explanatory introspection. *Journal of Personality, 75,* 783–824.

Sedikides, C., Luke, M. A., & Hepper, E. G. (2016). Enhancing feedback and improving feedback: Subjective perceptions, psychological consequences, behavioral outcomes. *Journal of Applied Social Psychology, 46,* 687–700.

Sedikides, C., & Strube, M. J. (1997). Self-evaluation: To thine own self be good, to thine own self be sure, to thine own self be true, and to thine own self be better. *Advances in Experimental Social Psychology, 29,* 209–269.

Sherman, D. K., & Cohen, G. L. (2006). The psychology of self-defense: Self- affirmation theory. *Advances in Experimental Social Psychology, 38,* 183–242.

Steinmetz, J., Sezer, O., & Sedikides, C. (2017). Impression mismanagement: People as inept self-presenters. *Social and Personality Psychology Compass, 11*(6). Retrieved from https://www.researchgate.net/publication/317488264_Impression_mismanagement_People_as_inept_self-presenters

Skowronski, J. J. (2011). The positivity bias and the fading affect bias in autobiographical memory: A self-motives perspective. In C. Sedikides & M. D. Alicke (Eds.), *Handbook of self-enhancement and self-protection* (pp. 211–231). New York, NY: Guilford Press.

Spencer-Oatey, H., & Ng, P. (2001). Reconsidering Chinese modesty: Hong Kong and Mainland Chinese evaluative judgments of compliment responses. *Journal of Asian Pacific Communication, 11,* 181–201.

Sutton, R. M., Hornsey, M. J., & Douglas, K. M. (Eds.). (2012). *Feedback: The communication of praise, criticism, and advice.* New York, NY: Peter Lang.

Takata, T. (2003). Self-enhancement and self-criticism in Japanese culture: An experimental analysis. *Journal of Cross-Cultural Psychology, 34,* 542–551.

Tan, M., Newman, L. S., & Zhang, B. (2014, February). *A cross-cultural investigation of the processing of self-threatening information.* Poster presented at the annual meeting of the Society for Personality and Social Psychology, Austin, TX.

Taylor, S. E., Neter, E., & Wayment, H. A. (1995). Self evaluation processes. *Personality and Social Psychology Bulletin, 21,* 1278–1287.

Tesser, A. (2000). On the confluence of self-esteem maintenance mechanisms. *Personality and Social Psychology Review, 4,* 290–299.

Triandis, H. C. (1995). *Individualism and collectivism.* Boulder, CO: Westview Press.

Trope, Y. (1980). Self-assessment, self-enhancement, and task preference. *Journal of Experimental Social Psychology, 16,* 116–129.

Trope, Y. (1986). Self-assessment and self-enhancement in achievement motivation. In R. M. Sorrentino & E. T. Higgins (Eds.), *Handbook of motivation and cognition: Foundations of social behavior* (Vol 1, pp. 350–378). New York, NY: Guilford Press.

Trope, Y., Gervey, B., & Bolger, N. (2003). The role of perceived control in overcoming defensive self-evaluation. *Journal of Experimental Social Psychology, 39,* 407–419.

Wu, R.-J. R. (2011). A conversational analysis of self-praising in everyday Mandarin interaction. *Journal of Pragmatics, 43,* 3152–3176.

Vangelisti, A. L., & Hampel, A. D. (2012). Hurtful interactions as feedback. In R. M. Sutton, M. J. Hornsey, & K. M. Douglas (Eds.), *Feedback: The communication of praise, criticism, and advice* (pp. 153–168). New York, NY: Peter Lang.

Vignoles, V. L., Owe, E., Becker, M., Smith, P. B., Easterbrook, N. J., Brown, R., . . . & Bond, M. H. (2016). Beyond the 'East-West' dichotomy: Global variation in cultural models of selfhood. *Journal of Experimental Psychology: General, 145,* 966–1000.

Yamaguchi, S., Lin, C., & Aoki, S. (2006). Self-esteem in cultural context: The case of the Japanese. In Q. Jing, M. R. Rosenzweig, G. d'Ydewalle, H. Zhang, C. H.-C. Chen, & K. Z. Zhang (Eds.), *Progress in psychological science around the world* (Vol. 2, pp. 319–330). New York, NY: Psychology Press.

Yik, M. S. M., Bond, M. H., & Paulhus, D. L. (1998). Do Chinese self-enhance or self-efface? It's a matter of domain. *Personality and Social Psychology Bulletin, 24,* 399–406.

Yum, J. O. (1985). The impact of Confucianism on interpersonal relationships and communication patterns in East Asia. *Communication Monographs, 55,* 374–388.

CHAPTER 17

EVOLUTIONARY PSYCHOLOGY AND THE CLASSROOM

Implications for Theory, Research, and Practice in Motivation, Learning, Achievement, and Instruction

Andrew J. Martin

EVOLUTIONARY PSYCHOLOGY AND EVOLUTIONARY EDUCATIONAL PSYCHOLOGY

Evolutionary psychology emanates from classic evolutionary concepts to consider evolution in terms of the psychological mechanisms that are needed to survive, with the mind viewed in terms of the domains or modules relevant to meeting environmental challenges (Buss, 2005; Cosmides & Tooby, 1994; Dunbar & Barrett, 2007; Geary, 2008a, 2008b, 2012; Tooby & Cosmides, 1992). From an evolutionary psychology perspective, the mind is comprised of psychological adaptations and predisposed mechanisms for learning that survive because they solve context-relevant problems that help

Big Theories Revisited 2, pages 401–427
Copyright © 2018 by Information Age Publishing
All rights of reproduction in any form reserved.

individuals survive (Buss, 2005; Gergely & Csibra, 2003; Kanazawa, 2010; Pinker, 1994; Schaller, Park, & Kenrick, 2007; Schaller, Simpson, & Kenrick, 2006; Sweller, 2004)—although the specificity of this predisposition and the precise nature of these psychological modules have been the subject of debate (e.g., Karmiloff-Smith, 1997; Pinker, 2002).

Evolutionary Educational Psychology

Of the various perspectives and contributions under the evolutionary psychology banner, the one most directly informing academic achievement seems to be that proposed by evolutionary educational psychology (Geary, 2005, 2008a, 2008b, 2012; Sweller, 2007, 2008). Evolutionary educational psychology seeks to explain how evolved biases in learning and motivation influence students' capacity and motivation to learn academic subject matter and academic skills. According to Geary,

> ... by framing educational goals and research on educational practices within an evolutionary perspective, we can narrow the problem space associated with determining the most effective ways to instruct children, better understand their interest and motivational biases, and more effectively grapple with the issue of individual differences. (pp. 181–182)

Evolutionary educational psychology is rapidly gaining increasing attention in the psycho-educational domain (Geary, 2012) as it integrates seminal notions of human and academic development. Indeed, it is also being applied to other seminal educational psychology theories such as cognitive load theory (Sweller, 2012) and motivational dynamics (Martin, 2016) to help explain cognitive phenomena in the teaching and learning context.

Evolutionary educational psychology proposes two psychological systems. Biologically primary (folk) psychological systems have an evolutionary basis and involve processing information related to self, others, and group dynamics (Geary, 2008a, 2008b, 2012). Biologically secondary psychological systems are acquired through individuals' interactions with their environment. Secondary systems are typically what underpin performance environments such as school in which culturally relevant skills and knowledge are taught and learnt (Geary, 2008a, 2008b, 2012).

Geary's (2005, 2008a, 2008b, 2012) is a predominantly cognitive framework involving "conscious-psychological simulations, and working memory and controlled problem solving" (2008a, p. 182). Although recognition is given to the evolutionary bases of situated and inter-individual motivation and learning, Geary (2005) argues that classrooms and schools are not adaptively aligned with social evolutionary processes and phenomena—thus hampering achievement: "The contrast between evolved motivational biases and the activities needed for secondary learning has very important implications for children's motivation to learn in school" (pp. 9–10). According to Geary (2005), students' preference for peer relationships is not necessarily consistent with learning in the academic context. Geary (2005) states that evolved "behavioral (e.g., preference for peer activities over mathematics homework) biases will often need to be inhibited before secondary learning will occur" (p. 57). Although he recognizes that social modes may facilitate academic learning, this would generally be limited to young children in the transition to school. Further, although Geary (2005) has recognized social factors and processes relevant to cognition, these are more related to hominid brain development than classroom achievement and learning.

Evolutionary Educational Psychology and Perspectives From Other "Big" Theories

Responses to evolutionary conceptualizing such as Geary's (2005; including those from sociocultural perspectives) point to the need to more fully consider inter-individual, social, and context-relevant aspects of motivation, learning, achievement, and instruction. Berch (2007; see also Bjorkland, 2007), for example, introduced recent sociocultural perspectives on learning (i.e., situated cognition, cognition in context, and distributed cognition; see also McInerney, Hinkley, Dowson, & Van Etten, 1998; Nerressian, 2005; Walker & Horsley, 2006) and cooperation (e.g., Ladyshewsky, 2006) as possible interfaces between evolutionary educational psychology and learning and instruction. Halpern (2008) suggested Geary does not sufficiently link cooperative and group dynamics to school learning and asked, "How do cooperation and social skills figure in evolutionary perspectives on schooling?" (p. 204; see also Buss, 2009, on the broader issue of evolved mechanisms for cooperation, helping, and altruism). Keil (2008) noted that knowledge acquisition is dependent on others and that "one role of education may be to make such networks of dependency more salient and, if the education is of the right sort, more accessible" (p. 199). Indeed, Keil (2008) suggests that human learning and school are compatible: "[H]umans seem exquisitely tuned to the intentions of others in ways that make social learning and pedagogy uniquely human activities" (p. 200). Ellis (2008) also emphasized the role of social factors in evolutionary educational psychology, in fact suggesting that Geary's primary (folk) psychological systems are socially—more than genetically—derived. Martin (2016) did not query evolutionary educational psychology, but did identify potential links between it and instructional approaches relevant to social processes related to promoting motivation and engagement as articulated by expectancy-value theory (Wigfield & Eccles, 2000), goal theory (Elliot, 2005), self-determination theory (Deci & Ryan, 2012), and self-worth motivation theory (Covington, 2000).

The role of culture is another key element of sociocultural perspectives. Here, it might be suggested that evolutionary educational psychology is also relevant and informative. The biologically primary (folk) psychological factors and processes identified earlier refer to pan-human phenomena such as social interaction, communication, physical movement, and so on (Geary, 2008a, 2008b, 2012). All cultures function around these phenomena. On the other hand, biologically secondary psychological systems are developed through interactions with one's own culture and tend to be more socially and culturally constructed (Geary, 2008a, 2008b, 2012). As relevant to school, these include factors such as curriculum-based skill and knowledge. Thus, evolutionary educational psychology accommodates factors and processes that generalize across culture and factors and processes that are culture-specific. Indeed, differences in biologically primary and secondary knowledge have implications for learning in different cultures. For example, whereas biologically primary knowledge such as physical movement may be highly integrated with learning in some cultures, it may not be so central in other cultures that emphasize more sedentary learning and assessment contexts. To the extent that this is the case, evolutionary psychology applied to the classroom integrates both *etic* (universal) and *emic* (culture-specific) principles to inform how students learn and achieve.

Numerous reviews of evolutionary educational psychology have therefore emphasized the sociocultural, inter-individual and social dimensions of motivation, learning, achievement, and instruction—dimensions not extensively addressed by evolutionary educational psychology. Arising from these reviews a major question is this: From an evolutionary-based perspective, to what extent can sociocultural and inter-individual processes and factors account for motivation, learning, and achievement in classroom and school contexts? Although responses to Geary's framework argued for a greater need to consider inter-individual and social elements of classroom learning and achievement, none directly wrestled with sociocultural issues from an evolutionary perspective. This is the purpose of the present discussion. Specifically, this discussion explores the extent to which evolutionary concepts and theorizing can further contribute to an understanding of the factors facilitating and impeding learning and motivation in the socially-based context of the classroom. In so doing, the present account can be positioned as an inter-individual and social elaboration on classic evolutionary and evolutionary educational psychology theory, with particular emphasis on classroom factors and processes.1

The suggested educational yields of this approach to evolutionary educational psychology are multifold. First, it has potential to address recent criticisms of evolutionary educational psychology by seeking to account for sociocultural, inter-individual, and social processes relevant to the exigencies of classroom life. Second, harnessing evolutionary concepts relevant to "situated" achievement holds possible implications for why some students experience difficulty being optimally motivated and engaged—and what to do about this. Third, considering factors and processes that have helped humans adapt in the past has the potential to inform ways educators can enhance students' capacity to function in the ever-changing world of the future (Collie, Holliman, & Martin, 2017; Collie & Martin, 2016; Martin, 2012, 2017; Martin, Nejad, Colmar, & Liem, 2012, 2013). Fourth, revisiting classic theorizing in evolutionary and educational psychology allows new conceptual insights and directions for future considerations of students' academic development.

EVOLUTION, INTRA-GROUP UNITY, AND CLASSROOM PROCESSES AND OUTCOMES

The first theme explored here relates to intra-group unity and classic evolutionary theories and concepts that inform it. Classroom life is considered in terms of evolutionary perspectives on cooperation, mutualism, fitness, reciprocity, and connectedness. In this section, alignments between educational and evolutionary theories and concepts are explored; in a following section, qualifications, limitations and tensions relevant to these alignments are discussed.

Cooperation in the Classroom

For organisms to co-exist over time, they must balance individual interests with the interests of the groups to which they belong. This has led to the recognition that organisms are cooperative at key points in development (Barrett, Dunbar, & Lycett, 2002; Buss, 2009; Hamilton, 1964; Maynard Smith, 1982; Trivers, 1971; Wyman & Tomasello, 2007). So, too, in the classroom, students must typically co-exist as part of a group—or, if they are involved in individual achievement pursuits, they will invariably require some assistance from others to achieve to potential—a notion well-established in educational and sociocultural theorizing (e.g., see Dewey, 1916; Johnson & Johnson, 1989, 2008; Roseth, Johnson, & Johnson, 2008; Vygotsky, 1978). Thus, students must often balance or "manage" their own interests alongside the interests of the classroom (Johnson & Johnson, 1989). This holds direct implications for student and classroom achievement: if students and the classrooms to which they belong cannot successfully align, then their capacity to effectively function may be diminished. From an evolutionary perspective, then, unity and adaptive intra-group synergies are proposed as core elements underpinning student and classroom achievement. Indeed, research has demonstrated the neural and genetic bases of cooperation (Harbaugh, Mayr, & Burghart, 2007; Sanfey, 2007; Yamasue et al., 2008).

Direct and Indirect Achievement Fitness

The fact that organisms engage in cooperative behavior is perhaps surprising when considered in the context of the competing self-interest for reproductive success and fitness. Why would organisms cooperate when they must compete to secure resources for survival and fitness? To answer this, early work by Hamilton (1964; see also Maynard Smith, 1982) suggested that organisms do not need to produce their own offspring to increase their fitness. In fact, they can assist others to produce offspring that share their genes (Hamilton's Rule). Thus, there is *direct fitness* (producing one's own offspring) and *indirect fitness* (helping others to produce offspring that share one's genes) that come together to determine *inclusive fitness*.

Applying this idea to the classroom, it may be that this concept also applies to educational development. That is, students achieve by dint of their own efforts (direct achievement fitness). However, they may also help other students achieve. In so doing, they may lift the group to a higher level of aggregate achievement that, through enhanced collective efficacy and group effectiveness, might in turn assist their own capacity to achieve (indirect achievement fitness). If this were the case, inclusive achievement fitness would be posited as the result of students striving to work towards their own potential whilst also assisting others in the class to do the same. This establishes a potential evolutionary educational psychology basis for cooperative behavior in the classroom.

Connectedness and Cooperation Within Groups

Hamilton (1964) also argued that the more members in the group are related or connected to each other (referred to as the *coefficient of relatedness*), the less the benefits need to be for cooperative behavior to occur. Put another way, the more unrelated or disconnected members are from each other, the less cooperation is likely to take place. This poses a challenge in classroom contexts where student achievement striving is valued but class members are not connected to each other or are competitively motivated. From an evolutionary perspective, in such cases, cooperative behavior is less likely. Thus, the more students are connected to each other and the higher the quality of peer relationships in the classroom, the more cooperation is likely to occur.

Indeed, a body of writing on competitive contexts and recent research developments in social interdependence theory (Johnson & Johnson, 2008; Roseth et al., 2008) attest to the potentially aversive consequences of competitively-dominant educational environments (e.g., Covington, 2000; Johnson & Johnson, 1989; Johnson, Maruyama, Johnson, Nelson, & Skon, 1981; Nicholls, 1989; Roseth et al., 2008). Ultimately this may reduce the classroom's coefficient of relatedness, compromise group-level achievement fitness, and set in train problematic achievement and motivational dynamics that may impede academic development (Covington, 2000; Martin & Marsh, 2003; Martin, Marsh, & Debus, 2001a, 2001b, 2003; Martin, Marsh, Williamson, & Debus, 2003; Middleton & Midgley, 1997).

This suggests a need to decrease classroom competition and increase the coefficient of relatedness within the class to best support student and class-level achievement. Improving interpersonal relationships in the classroom can be an effective way of doing this. Indeed, numerous "big" sociocultural and educational psychology theories emphasize the centrality of interpersonal relatedness (e.g., Baumeiester & Leary, 1995; Deci & Ryan, 2012; Furrer & Skinner, 2003; Martin & Dowson, 2009; Wentzel, 1999; Nolen & Ward, 2008; Walker, 2010; Walker, Pressick-Kilborn, Arnold, & Sainsbury, 2004). Empirical data confirm the link between quality interpersonal relatedness and positive educational outcomes (e.g., Boaler, 2008; Deci & Ryan, 2012; Furrer & Skinner, 2003; La Guardia & Ryan, 2002; Martin & Dowson, 2009; Martin, Marsh, McInerney, & Green, 2009; Martin, Marsh, McInerney, Green, & Dowson, 2007; Patrick, Ryan, & Kaplan, 2007; Reeve, Deci, & Ryan, 2004; Slavin, 1996; Wentzel, 1999). There are many ways to enhance relatedness and classroom cohesion, including: shared values around mutual respect, help-giving, participation, diverse forms of success, acceptance of diversity and difference, and recognition of individual student and class strengths (Boaler, 2008; Martin, 2004; see also Wyman & Tomasello, 2007). Following from this, the concept of "mutualism" may also be relevant. This is where each student receives benefit from their shared efforts with others (see Clutton-Brock, 2009), serving to further increase the coefficient of relatedness within the classroom.

Resolving Sociocultural and Other Differences: Reciprocal Altruism and Helping Giving

Notwithstanding educators' efforts to promote intra-class cohesion, the reality is that the coefficient of relatedness will be constrained by individual differences between students. For example, even in educational environments where students are selected on the basis of a particular attribute (e.g., ability or gender), a good deal of diversity will remain on a host of other factors. For example, educational research has demonstrated sociocultural differences in educational processes and outcomes as a function of gender (Marsh, Martin, & Cheng, 2008; Martin, 2007, 2009), age or stage of schooling (Roeser, Eccles, & Sameroff, 2000), ethnicity (Ma & Kishor, 1997), and socio-economic status (Sirin, 2005). In fact, on numerous educational dimensions (e.g., motivation, engagement, self-concept), researchers have demonstrated significant variance between students—oftentimes more than between classes and schools (Martin, Bobis, Anderson, Way, & Vellar, 2011; Marsh, Martin, et al., 2008; Martin & Marsh, 2005, 2008a).

It is here that the evolutionary concept of *reciprocal altruism* (Trivers, 1971) may be relevant. In situations where there are salient differences (e.g., sociocultural) between students and where students are less connected to each other (e.g., where there is significant student-level variance), help-giving and cooperation can occur if there is a reasonable chance the individual will receive returned help or cooperation at a later point. In the classroom context, for example, students may help each other if they anticipate returned assistance from other students at some stage in the future. This reflects the concept of mutualism (Clutton-Brock, 2009): over time there are cost-benefit trade-offs that students make that assist the class and the individual students belonging to the class. Importantly, Ladyshewsky (2006) suggested that simply grouping individuals together in learning activities does not guarantee positive outcomes, rather, it is important that learners understand that to achieve one's own goals, they must help the class achieve its goals. This again raises the issue of mutualism, in that each student receives benefit from their efforts in assisting the class (Clutton-Brock, 2009).

Frequency of Interaction: Nurturing Relationships Over Time

Of course, there is also the possibility that a student's cooperation will not be returned and this might motivate students away from cooperation. This dilemma is a familiar one in game theory (e.g., see Maynard Smith, 1982) which proposes that all things being equal, refusing to help or cooperate with others can be in the best interests of the individual and the individual's survival. Importantly, however, in most contexts (including classroom contexts) things are rarely equal and one factor that moderates individuals' cooperative behavior is the frequency with which they interact (Trivers, 1971; Wyman & Tomasello, 2007). Thus, the more students interact, the more it makes sense to cooperate and assist. Indeed, nurturing interpersonal relationships over time will also be important. In the classroom context, students interact day-by-day, week-by-week, and (often) year-by-year and so cooperation and help-giving are in the best interests of one and all (see also early work by Homans, 1950).

Summary of Evolution, Unity, and the Classroom

Thus far, the chapter has explored themes around intra-group unity and classic evolutionary theories and concepts that inform it. It is evident that classroom life and sociocultural phenomena (and differences) can be considered in terms of classic evolutionary and psycho-educational perspectives on cooperation, mutualism, fitness, reciprocity, and connectedness. Figure 17. 1 and Table 17.1 summarize key ideas.

EVOLUTION, INTRA-GROUP DIVERSITY, AND CLASSROOM PROCESSES AND OUTCOMES

Although cooperative behavior plays an important role in supporting student and classroom achievement, there remains the very real challenge posed by conflict amongst students to compete for a relatively finite number of achievements. In most educational systems competition is a highly salient phenomenon and relative assessment is a dominant mode of measuring students' academic development. Under such systems, zero-sum approaches are common (for one student to rank highly, another student must rank lower) and this poses motivational barriers to learning—extensively and robustly articulated by classic theories of achievement motivation (Covington, 2000). How does evolutionary conceptualizing respond to this reality of group instruction and assessment?

Figure 17.1 Evolutionary-aligned perspectives on classroom motivation, learning, achievement, and instruction.

TABLE 17.1   Key Elements, Concepts, and Processes Underpinning Evolutionary-Aligned Perspectives on Classroom Motivation, Learning, Achievement, and Instruction

Key Elements	Key Concepts and Processes
The Classroom and UNITY	• Cooperation and mutualism are important for student and classroom functioning in a changing world. • The greater the classroom cohesion and the greater frequency with which students interact, the more cooperation and mutualism are likely to occur. • Hence, fostering interpersonal connectedness in the classroom has educational yields. • Student and classroom educational outcomes can also benefit from "reciprocal altruism."
The Classroom and DIVERSITY	• Intra-class diversity—effectively managed—can reduce intra-class conflict, provide students greater access to various forms of educational success, and more effectively map onto the diverse needs and roles relevant to an ever-changing world. • Homogeneous (uniform) classroom contexts—ineffectively managed—can increase intra-class conflict and may also fail to map onto the diverse needs and roles relevant to an ever-changing world. • Effectively managing the context-specific mix between uniformity and diversity can resolve tensions characteristic of many competitive classroom settings.

One evolutionary-based response is to harness the potentially adaptive properties of intra-group diversity. Diversity amongst group members can reduce competition for finite resources because different members compete for different resources and allows for greater chance of survival of the lineage in diverse and unpredictable environments (Darwin, 1859/1968). To what extent does diversity have similar potential in the classroom context? In this section, educational and evolutionary concepts relevant to this question are explored; in a following section, qualifications, limitations, and tensions relevant to intra-group diversity are discussed.

Niche Partitioning: Each Student Has Unique Strengths

The potential for diversity to enhance student and classroom achievement is suggested in "niche partitioning," a term addressing the diverse roles and expertise of group members (Sulloway, 2007). In the classroom context, niche partitioning suggests a need to optimally utilize students' different strengths and roles to reduce intra-class competition and to increase the fitness of the class. For example, from a sociocultural perspective, niche partitioning might entail structuring academic tasks and challenges in a way that allows for meaningful and valued contributions from all students based on their preferred learning styles, individual skills and interests, cultural background and ethnicity, life experiences and so on. In these ways, educators are best placed to counter what has been referred to as the *unidimensional classroom* (Rosenholtz & Simpson, 1984) in which there exists a narrow focus (often academic ability) on what is valued and used to assess students.

Importantly, harnessing unique student strengths would also be aimed at offsetting potentially maladaptive niche partitioning. For example, if teacher attention or investment can only be gained by way of high ability or a particular learning style, then students who do not fit this profile may look to other niches to gain the teacher's attention or approval. Misbehavior might be one such example of maladaptive niche partitioning in the achievement context (see Brophy, 1996, for further commentaries on misbehavior). That is, students gain the teacher's attention (a resource of value to students) by misbehaving.

The potential for these ideas to resolve (or reduce) conflict and promote achievement is encouraging. First, it points to the importance of recognizing and shaping the classroom context with an eye to students' different strengths, skills, and interests (see also positive psychology and asset-oriented contributions to this notion; Bandura, 2006; Coleman & Hagell, 2007; Csikszentmihalyi, 1990; Fredrickson, 2001; Martin & Marsh, 2006, 2008a, 2008b, 2009; Parker & Martin, 2009; Seligman, 2002). Second, it explicitly accommodates sociocultural phenomena and differences in the classroom. For example, differences as a function of gender, ethnicity, and socio-economic background underpin a rich heterogeneous environment that allow for authentic valuing and acceptance of individual students. Third, it suggests the need for diverse forms of investment in students—for example, directing qualitatively distinct and nuanced attention and resources to students based on their needs (i.e., student centered)—or making available a diversity of achievement forms that allow for expression of students' different strengths and abilities (Cohen & Lotan, 1995; Martin, 2007). For example, teachers may not only value achievement, but also personal progress, effort, and participation. Having a diversity of success indicators gives students greater access to success. Fourth, it implies that to enhance students' capacity to survive in a varying and unpredictable world, nurturing diversity has the potential to be an adaptive pursuit (Workman & Reader, 2004).

Taken together, in the classroom context, these arguments point to the need for accommodating diverse skills, interests, and academic orientations; the need to individualize teacher attention as appropriate for different students; the need for differential instruction; the need for student-centered pedagogy; and the need for diverse (and genuine) modes and forms of achievement to give students greater access to success in the classroom.

Of course, all this is seen as good teaching (Hattie, 2009; Martin, 2006b, 2010; Martin & Dowson, 2009; Marzano, 2003), but important here is the potential alignment with evolutionary principles that can inform education and are relevant to achievement-relevant survival and fitness.

Heterogeneous Environments: Diverse and Comprehensive Classrooms

From a biological fitness perspective, the issue of diversity might at first appear counterintuitive: Would not the cumulative selection of some genes over others lead to less rather than more genetic variability? It turns out this is not necessarily the case. It may be good for the organism's survival to produce offspring that differ on various traits. This reduces intra-group competition for the same resources and better ensures survival of the genetic lineage in environments characterized by change and variability (Barrett et al., 2002; Darwin, 1859/1969; Workman & Reader, 2004). Similarly, in classroom contexts, diversity has the potential to result in less intra-group conflict and competition and better ensure that students are equipped to deal with the diverse and fluid challenges characteristic of a changing world.

Schools and classrooms that comprise a more comprehensive mix of students may evince less intra-group conflict because there are fewer students competing for the same spoils (or more students striving for a diversity of spoils), greater subsequent potential for peer cooperation, and an enhanced potential to map onto the environmental/societal variability facing students when they complete school (see Marsh, Cheng, & Martin, 2008; Marsh & Hau, 2003; Slavin, 1987; Vinson, 2002). Indeed, early work suggested that at distinct points in group processes, different people possessing different attributes are needed to resolve the challenges that are distinct to each phase of the group process, thus, the realities of effective group functioning elicit different contributions from its various members (for seminal work, see Bales & Strodtbeck, 1951).

Summary of Evolution, Diversity, and the Classroom

Following the section on intra-group unity (and cooperation), this section has explored themes around intra-group diversity and classic evolutionary theories and concepts that inform it. It is evident that classroom life and sociocultural phenomena (and differences) in the classroom can be considered in terms of classic evolutionary perspectives on diversity. Major ideas are summarized in Figure 17.1 and Table 17.1.

QUALIFICATIONS, LIMITATIONS, AND TENSIONS RELEVANT TO EVOLUTIONARY APPLICATIONS IN CLASSROOM SETTINGS

The preceding discussion has been a somewhat uncritical formulation exploring the extent to which evolutionary concepts shed light on inter-individual and social bases of motivation, learning, achievement, and instruction. However, it is also important to address tensions inherent in the argument. Some of these are now discussed.

Tension Between Unity and Diversity

The issue of unity and diversity in educational settings is contested terrain. For example, Gottfredson (2004) argues that diverse classrooms are difficult to teach and homogeneous ability grouping allows for more effective and targeted instruction. Indeed, even researchers who generally argue for comprehensive educational settings point out that for some students (e.g., students with disabilities), homogeneous learning environments can also be effective (Marsh, Tracey, & Craven, 2006). Recent meta-analysis of ability grouping reflects similar complexity: It appears that students benefit from within-class grouping, cross-grade subject grouping, and special grouping for the gifted, but do not benefit from between-class grouping (Steenbergen-Hu, Makel, & Olszewski-Kubilius, 2016). Thus, there is tension between the various yields and realities of diversity and unity.

Tension between unity and diversity is also seen in biological evolution. For example, organisms that are uniformly well-adapted to a particular environment can be very successful. However, when the environment changes, as it often does (Martin, 2012, 2017; Martin et al., 2012, 2013), uniformity can make it difficult for organisms to survive. Similarly, from an achievement perspective, uniform groups that are well matched to the performance domain and its requirements are likely to do well; however, if the performance domain or its requirements change, intra-group breadth might be more effective.

Further, as post-school (e.g., workplace) roles become increasingly specialized, how does intra-group diversity align with this? On the one hand, it could be argued that helping different students to co-exist and recognizing diverse ways students can succeed in the classroom might lend well to specialized roles in post-school life. On the other hand, some may argue that diversity impedes the deep learning and expertise needed for specialized roles. There is also a distinction needed between diversity at the student level and diversity at the classroom level. Hence, it might be reasonable to have a class of diverse students, each with their unique set of specialized skills and strengths, provided the range of specialized skills covered all the requirements of effectiveness at the classroom level.

Managing Classroom and Individual Student Interests

Inevitably there will also be some dissonance between classroom unity and cohesion on the one hand and an individual student's opportunity to strive to his/her personal potential on the other. Thus, whilst promoting effective group functioning, another challenge concerns the opportunities for individual students to express themselves and realize personal potential. This is not a straightforward issue; for cooperation (and to some extent, mutualism) to benefit the class as a whole, some students may pay a higher than average cost to benefit the class—a position articulated under *multilevel selection theory* (Wilson & Wilson, 2008). In the classroom, for example, individual student striving will disproportionately benefit some students and to have them work under cooperative conditions requires them to disproportionately sacrifice personal interest for group interest. According to O'Gorman, Wilson, and Sheldon (2008), individuals are more prepared to make such personal sacrifices when competition between groups (e.g., classrooms) is greater than competition between individuals (students), but escalating inter-class competition poses yet another set of tensions in the educational system.

One possible way around this is to harness the value of friendship and interpersonal connections between students. Although some students may make disproportionate academic sacrifices under cooperative systems, non-achievement benefits through good interpersonal relationships over the course of a school year (and beyond) may outweigh these costs. Thus, competition between classrooms may not be the only way to render intra-class cooperation beneficial for all students; numerous intra-personal benefits derived through inter-personal connectedness may suffice. A substantial body of research demonstrates the impact of positive interpersonal relationships on valued and valuable personal outcomes. As summarized in a review by Martin and Dowson (2009), relationships in childhood and youth are a major source of happiness, a buffer against stress, the source of emotional support in daily life, and important for social and emotional development. Another benefit, perhaps tied to motivation, lies in the effect of mutual "struggle." For example, Schoenfeld (1985) found one advantage of solving difficult math problems in groups was that members were able to see each other's progress and realized they were not the only ones experiencing difficulty.

It is also the case that maladaptive classroom and individual student processes must be managed for effective achievement and achievement motivation. For example, educators need to address disruptive and distracting behaviors by some students and also be mindful of known group pitfalls such as *social loafing* (Berch, 2007). There is also the potential for problematic modes of dominance and hierarchies within classrooms and schools. Ethologists, for example, point to social dominance and social hierarchies that are established through individuals' differential ability to acquire (limited) resources. In the classroom context, students' capacity to acquire status (e.g., popularity, academic rank) will determine their place in the group (Hawley, 1999). It is possible that some students will seek to acquire status through maladaptive modes of dominance (e.g., bullying, manipulation; Hawley, 1999) and to the extent that this is the case, the academic development of others may suffer.

Nuanced Approaches to Student, Classroom, and Sociocultural Processes

Following from much of the above discussion, there is a need for research that seeks to understand the best mix of uniformity and diversity as relevant to motivation, learning, and achievement (see Berch, 2007; Slavin, 1996 for some suggested directions). There is also a need to assess this on a domain specific basis. For example, a sporting team relatively homogeneous in skill and interest will uniformly strive towards inter-group achievement (e.g., victory over other teams in a competition). On the other hand, students in classrooms tend to competitively strive towards similar achievements (e.g., GPA), potentially leading to an environment that is a constant sifting of winners and losers, haves and have-nots (see Covington, 2000; Martin & Marsh, 2003).

Research might also investigate the appropriate unit at which achievement is best facilitated. In a classroom, for example, maximizing achievement might be best realized through small group work. In small groups, students are typically better placed for cooperation, mutualism, and common purpose. In such cases, the optimal balance of unity and diversity is again vital. According to Dunbar (2000), two conditions under which cooperative and group processes are ineffective include when (a) group members are from very similar backgrounds (often holding identical goals), and (b) members are from excessively diverse backgrounds (holding goals that are overly discordant). From a sociocultural perspective, this speaks to the importance of exploring and harnessing shared human and personal values that may integrate classes comprising students that significantly differ as a function of factors such as ethnicity and socio-economic status. In so doing, students are able to retain their unique cultural foundations whilst also identifying common ground that demonstrates the shared humanity and respect underlying these differences (Martin, 2006a).

Indeed, Hamilton (1975) has suggested that inclusive fitness also poses challenges. It can result in greater conflict between groups (particularly diverse groups). Thus, whilst promoting intra-group unity, educators must guard against competition that this may promote between, for example, classrooms. Similarly, reciprocal altruism (Trivers, 1971) comprises challenges. Whereas reciprocal altruism is not difficult to foster in dyadic relationships, it becomes progressively more difficult to operationalize across multiple relationships, such as in classrooms. Again, the need to adaptively calibrate intra-class unity and diversity is evident. It may be the case that equally distributed reciprocal altruism and cost-free cooperation are not literally possible (just as the classroom is not a literal case of evolutionary human development), but efforts to foster and sustain cooperation, mutualism, and altruism have potential to assist dynamics to positive student and class effect. Along similar lines, it might also be worth considering research and theorizing that explores the evolutionary bases of compassion. This has been hypothesized as an affective state that motivates individuals (including non-kin) to assist the welfare of others at some expense to themselves (Goetz, Keltner, & Simon-Thomas, 2010) with a view to initiating, sustaining, and regulating mutually beneficial relationships (Gintis, 2000; Goetz et al., 2010; Trivers, 1971).

Taken together, this all suggests a need for adaptively managing student and classroom interests and individual (including sociocultural) differences within classrooms. For example, infusing diversely comprised classrooms with unifying mechanisms such as cooperation, mutualism, reciprocity, and interpersonal connectedness may have the potential to benefit from the evolutionary-based merits of uniformity and diversity. Indeed, according to Halpern (2008), "we need deliberate instruction in group cohesion skills, a subject missing from the curricula of most contemporary schools" (p. 204). In a sense, then, inter-individual and social elaborations on evolutionary educational psychology are about effectively harnessing the inherent "push-and-pull" between individual and sociocultural processes—tensions that underpin evolution in the biological world as well.

Student-Level Variance on Many Psychoeducational Constructs

Developments in statistical modeling (see Goldstein, 2003; Raudenbush & Bryk, 2002) enabled researchers to more accurately estimate the relative contribution of student-, class-/teacher-, and school-level effects in motivation, learning, and achievement. Findings of this multilevel research indicate that a substantial portion of the variance resides at the student level on numerous psycho-educational factors (Marsh, Martin, et al., 2008; Martin, Bobis, Anderson, Way, & Vellar, 2011; Martin & Marsh, 2005); that is, on many factors there is greater variation from student-to-student than from class-to-class or school-to-school. It will be recalled that Hamilton (1964) proposed that the more members in the group are connected to each other (i.e., the coefficient of relatedness), the less the benefits need to be for cooperative behavior to occur. Conversely, the more disconnected members are from each other, the less cooperation is likely to take place. With a bulk of variance on numerous psycho-educational constructs residing at the student level, the coefficient of relatedness is compromised.

Martin (2010; see also Martin & Dowson, 2009) recognized this substantial student-level variance and its inherent challenges in classroom contexts and proposed *connective instruction* as a means by which educators can facilitate each individual student's connection to teaching and learning (even though that individual is taught in the group setting). According to Martin, the more an individual student can personally connect to the teaching and teacher, the more motivated and engaged he or she is proposed to be. He further detailed connective instruction as that which connects to the individual student in three ways: (a) by way of substance and subject matter ("what" the teacher teaches), (b) by way of pedagogy ("how" the teacher teaches), and (c) by way of interpersonal connection ("who" the teacher personally connects with). Hence, although originally developed to deal with the significant proportion of student-level variance in the classroom context, connective instruction may also align with considerations relevant to inter-individual and social perspectives on evolutionary educational psychology.

Summary of Evolutionary Tensions in the Classroom

The first part of this chapter presented a somewhat uncritical perspective on evolutionary concepts on inter-individual and social bases of motivation, learning, achievement, and instruction. This section has identified some of the inherent tensions inherent in the argument as well as some qualifications important for theory, research, and practice going forward. Figure 17.1 and Table 17.1 present main ideas.

BACK TO THE CLASSROOM

One of the key contributions of evolutionary educational psychology (Geary, 2005, 2008a, 2008b, 2012; Sweller, 2004, 2007) relates to evolutionary-based insights into why students do not learn or are not optimally motivated and engaged in the academic setting. Evolutionary educational psychology proposes two psychological systems: primary (folk) and secondary systems. Primary psychological systems have an evolutionary basis and involve processing information related to self, others, and group dynamics (Geary, 2008a, 2008b, 2012). Secondary psychological systems are acquired through individuals' interactions with their environment. Secondary systems are typically what underpin performance environments such as school in which culturally-relevant skills and knowledge are taught and learnt (Geary, 2008a, 2008b, 2012). According to Geary (2008a, 2008b, 2012), schools and classroom tasks and activities are more directed at secondary than primary psychological systems. Hence, they are not aligned with psychological systems that have an evolutionary basis, and by implication, this is why students will find learning and achievement in these environments challenging. Geary further argues that classrooms and schools are not aligned well with the evolutionary-based social biases of children and young people and this further hampers their capacity to learn and achieve.

In contrast, the present discussion has explored evolutionary-based alignments with sociocultural, social, and inter-individual perspectives on motivation, learning, and achievement and ways that educators can harness social biases to assist these outcomes. These elaborations on seminal evolutionary educational psychology theory argue for the need of educators to directly address intra-group conflict, competition for limited resources (e.g., teacher attention), competition for narrowly defined forms of achievement, and poor interpersonal relations. At the same time, evolutionary-based inter-individual and social perspectives suggest educators should seek to activate unifying mechanisms such as cooperation, mutualism, compassion, help-giving and reciprocity to most effectively harness the diverse skills, interests, experiences, and strengths of students within the classroom. Figure 17.1 and Table 17.1 summarize key elements of this approach.

Encouragingly, unifying mechanisms such as cooperation and the like are socially-based phenomena that would be considered biologically primary (folk) knowledge and skill that humans are evolutionarily situated to acquire (Geary, 2008a, 2008b, 2012). Moreover, this being the case, they are considered pan-human processes that apply across cultures. Certainly, these basic evolutionary phenomena are put to culturally-specific uses (e.g., there are different applications of communication, cooperation, and reciprocity depending on the cultural demands of curriculum, etc.), but it is important to recognize that students are organically well-placed to acquire them. Thus, students across all cultures have a "natural" capacity to develop social skills—biologically primary (folk) knowledge. Then, in each culture they need to learn appropriate domain-specific application of these skills—biologically secondary knowledge. For example, whereas communication is biologically primary knowledge, reading and writing (and their specific forms and formats) are culture-specific (biologically secondary knowledge). Thus, in efforts to teach reading and writing, educators in all cultures can rely on the pan-human motivation to communicate.

Efforts to engage students will also rely on evolutionary pan-human processes and culture-specific processes. For example, positive peer and teacher-student relationships are well known to be conducive to academic engagement (Furrer & Skinner, 2003; Martin & Dowson, 2009) and these are heavily based on biologically primary social skills. However, there will be cultural differences in social mores, values, and customs in how interpersonal relationships are best operationalized. Again, in efforts to engage students, teachers can rely on fundamental evolutionary biases in the form of social motivations, but will need to harness these basic social motivations in culturally-specific and appropriate ways to optimize academic outcomes.

Taken together, in the classroom, there are pan-human (primary) and culture-specific (secondary) evolutionary knowledge and skills that operate to shape students' learning. Moreover, there are evolutionary biases based on primary knowledge and skills that teachers can harness to motivate students to acquire culture-specific secondary knowledge and skills. To the extent that this is the case, evolutionary educational psychology integrates both etic (universal) principles and emic (culture-specific) principles that inform how students engage, learn, and achieve.

CONCLUSION

The present discussion has explored inter-individual and social evolutionary-based perspectives to shed additional light on sociocultural, classroom, and student processes relevant to educational outcomes. This inter-individual and socially-oriented elaboration on evolutionary educational psychology emphasizes classic evolutionary concepts alongside effective mobilization of intra-class unity and adaptive harnessing of intra-class diversity. Counter to arguments that classrooms and learning are not compatible with evolutionary-based social and sociocultural biases, this chapter's inter-individual perspective on evolutionary educational psychology suggests that academic development can align with important concepts and processes articulated under classic evolutionary and educational psychology frameworks. It also provides further perspectives on why students do not achieve to potential and how to effectively address this through individual- and group-level instruction, intervention, guidance, and support.

ACKOWLEDGEMENT

The author would like to thank (in alphabetical order) Ray Debus, M'lane Field, Paul Ginns, John Sweller, and Tony Vinson for their valued and valuable feedback on previous drafts of this article.

NOTE

1. In exploring these ideas, it is important to recognize that academic development in classrooms and schools are not a replica of the evolutionary history of human development. For example, social groups in our evolutionary history are comprised of individuals who were typically genetically related, competitively vied for mates, and were focused on seeking survival resources such as shelter, food and safety. In literal terms, this is clearly not the case in classrooms that have different aims and objectives, different investments, different needs, and members who (predominantly) are not genetically related. However, there are processes and roles analogous to and in synergy with human evolutionary concepts and classroom life that might offer useful insights into factors relevant to motivation, learning, achievement, and instruction.

REFERENCES

Bales, R. F., & Strodtbeck, F. L. (1951). Phases in group problem-solving. *Journal of Abnormal and Social Psychology, 46*, 485–495.

Bandura, A. (2006). Adolescent development from an agentic perspective. In F. Pajares & T. Urdan (Eds). *Self-efficacy beliefs.* Greenwich, CT: Information Age.

Barrett, L., Dunbar, R., & Lycett, J. (2002). *Human evolutionary psychology.* New York, NY: Palgrave.

Baumeister, R. F., & Leary, M. R. (1995). The need to belong: Desire for interpersonal attachments as a fundamental human motivation. *Psychological Bulletin, 117*, 497–529.

Berch, D. B. (2007). Instructing evolved minds: Pedagogically primary strategies for promoting biologically secondary learning. In J. S. Carlson & J. R. Levin (Eds.), *Educating the evolved mind: Conceptual foundations for an evolutionary educational psychology* (pp. 109–118). Charlotte, NC: Information Age.

Bjorklund, D. F. (2007). The most educable of animals. In J. S. Carlson & J. R. Levin (Eds.), *Educating the evolved mind: Conceptual foundations for an evolutionary educational psychology* (pp. 119–130). Charlotte, NC: Information Age.

Boaler, J. (2008). Promoting 'relational equity' and high mathematics achievement through an innovative mixed-ability approach. *British Journal of Educational Research, 34*, 167–194.

Brophy, J. E. (1996). *Teaching problem students.* New York, NY: Guilford.

Buss, D. M. (2005). *Handbook of evolutionary psychology.* Hoboken, NJ: Wiley.

Buss, D. M. (2009). The great struggles of life: Darwin and the emergence of evolutionary psychology. *American Psychologist, 64*, 140–148.

Clutton-Brock, T. (2009). Cooperation between non-kin in animal societies. *Nature, 462*, 51–57.

Cohen, E. G., & Lotan, R. A. (1995). Producing equal-status interaction in the heterogeneous classroom. *American Educational Research Journal, 32*, 99–120.

Coleman, J., & Hagell, A. (Eds.). (2007). *Adolescence, risk, and resilience: Against the odds.* London, England: Wiley.

Collie, R. J., & Martin, A. J. (2016). Adaptability: An important capacity for effective teachers. *Educational Practice and Theory, 38*, 27–39.

Collie, R. J., Holliman, A. J., & Martin, A. J. (2017). Adaptability, engagement, and academic achievement at university. *Educational Psychology, 37*, 632–647.

Cosmides, L., & Tooby, J. (1994). Origins of domain specificity: The evolution of functional organization. In L. A. Hirscfeld & S. A. Gelman (Eds.), *Mapping the mind: Domain specificity in cognition and culture* (pp. 85–116). Cambridge, England: Cambridge University Press. Retrieved from https://doi.org/10.1017/CBO9780511752902.005

Covington, M. V. (2000). Goal theory, motivation, and school achievement: An integrative review. *Annual Review of Psychology, 51*, 171–200. Retrieved from https://doi.org/10.1146/annurev.psych.51.1.171

Csikszentmihalyi, M. (1990). *Flow: The psychology of optimal experience.* New York, NY: Harper & Row.

Darwin, C. (1968). *The origin of species.* London, England: Penguin. (Original work published 1859)

Deci, E. L., & Ryan, R. M. (2012). Motivation, personality, and development within embedded social contexts: An overview of self-determination theory. In R. M. Ryan (Ed.), *The Oxford handbook of human motivation* (pp. 85–110). New York, NY: Oxford University Press.

Dewey, J. (1916). *Democracy and education.* New York, NY: Macmillan.

Dunbar, K. (2000). How scientists think in the real world: Implications for science education. *Journal of Applied Developmental Psychology, 21*, 49–58.

Dunbar, R. I. M., & Barrett, L. (2007). Evolutionary psychology in the round. In R. I. M. Dunbar & L. Barrett (Eds.), *Oxford handbook of evolutionary psychology* (pp. 3–9). Oxford, England: Oxford University Press.

Elliot, A. J. (2005). A conceptual history of the achievement goal construct. In A. J. Elliot & C. S. Dweck (Eds.), *Handbook of competence and motivation* (pp. 52–72). New York, NY: Guildford.

Ellis, G. F. R. (2008). Commentary on "an evolutionarily informed education science" by David C. Geary. *Educational Psychologist, 43*, 206–213.

Fredrickson, B. L. (2001). The role of positive emotions in positive psychology. *American Psychologist, 56*, 218–226.

Furrer, C., & Skinner, E. (2003). Sense of relatedness as a factor in children's academic engagement and performance. *Journal of Educational Psychology, 95*, 148–162.

Geary, D. C. (2005). *The origin of mind: Evolution of brain, cognition, and general intelligence.* Washington, DC: American Psychological Association.

Geary, D. C. (2008a). An evolutionarily informed education science. *Educational Psychologist, 43*, 179–195.

Geary, D. C. (2008b). Whither evolutionary educational psychology? *Educational Psychologist, 43*, 217–226.

Geary, D. C. (2012). Evolutionary educational psychology. In K. Harris, S. Graham, & T. Urdan (Eds.), *APA educational psychology handbook* (pp. 597–621). Washington, DC: American Psychological Association.

Gergely, G., & Csibra, G. (2003). Teleological reasoning in infancy: The naive theory of rational action. *Trends in Cognitive Science, 7*, 287–292.

Gintis, H. (2000). Strong reciprocity and human sociality. *Journal of Theoretical Biology, 206,* 169–179.

Goetz, J. L., Keltner, D., & Simon-Thomas, E. (2010). Compassion: An evolutionary analysis and empirical review. *Psychological Bulletin, 136,* 351–374.

Goldstein, H. (2003). *Multilevel statistical models* (3rd ed.). London, England: Hodder Arnold.

Gottfredson, L. S. (2004). Schools and the g factor. *The Wilson Quarterly, Summer,* 35–45.

Halpern, D. F. (2008). How much can evolutionary psychology inform the educational sciences? *Educational Psychologist, 43,* 203–205.

Hamilton, W. D. (1964). The genetical evolution of social behavior. I and II. *Journal of Theoretical Biology, 7,* 1–52.

Hamilton, W. D. (1975). Innate social aptitudes of man: An approach from evolutionary genetics. In R. Fox (Ed.), *Biosocial anthropology* (pp. 133–153). London, England: Malaby Press.

Harbaugh, W. T., Mayr, U., & Burghart, D. R. (2007). Neural responses to taxation and voluntary giving reveal motives for charitable donations. *Science, 316,* 1622–1625.

Hattie, J. (2009). *Visible learning.* Oxford, England: Routledge.

Hawley, P. H. (1999). The ontogenesis of social dominance: A strategy-based evolutionary perspective. *Developmental Review 19,* 97–132.

Homans, G. C. (1950). *The human group.* New York, NY: Harcourt Brace.

Johnson, D. W., & Johnson, R. T. (1989). *Cooperation and competition: Theory and research.* Edina, MN: Interaction.

Johnson, D. W., & Johnson, R. T. (2008). Social interdependence theory and cooperative learning: The teacher's role. In R. M. Gillies, A. Ashman, & J. Terwel (Eds.), *The teacher's role in implementing cooperative learning in the classroom* (pp. 9–36). New York, NY: Springer.

Johnson, D. W., Maruyama, G., Johnson, R. T., Nelson, D., & Skon, L. (1981). Effects of cooperative, competitive, and individualistic goal structures on achievement: A meta-analysis. *Psychological Bulletin, 89,* 47–62.

Kanazawa, S. (2010). Evolutionary psychology and intelligence research. *American Psychologist, 65,* 279–289.

Karmiloff-Smith, A. (1997). Crucial differences between developmental cognitive neuroscience and adult neuropsychology. *Developmental Neuropsychology, 13,* 513–524.

Keil, F. C. (2008). Adapted minds and evolved schools. *Educational Psychologist, 43,* 196–202.

La Guardia, J. G., & Ryan, R. M. (2002). What adolescents need: A self-determination theory perspective on development within families, school, and society, In F. Pajares & T. Urdan (Eds.), *Academic motivation of adolescents.* Greenwich, CT: Information Age.

Ladyshewsky, R. K. (2006). Building cooperation in peer coaching relationships: Understanding the relationships between reward structure, learner preparedness, coaching skill, and learning engagement. *Physiotherapy, 92,* 4–10.

Ma, X., & Kishor, N. (1997). Assessing the relationship between attitude toward mathematics and achievement in mathematics: A meta-analysis. *Journal for Research in Mathematics, 28,* 26–47.

Marsh, H. W., & Hau, K. (2003). Big-Fish—Little-Pond effect on academic self-concept: A cross-cultural (26-country) test of the negative effects of academically selective schools. *American Psychologist, 58,* 364–376.

Marsh, H. W., Cheng, J., & Martin, A. J. (2008). How we judge ourselves from different perspectives: Contextual influences on self-concept formation. In M. Maehr., T. Urdan., & S. Karabenick (Eds.), *Advances in motivation and achievement.* New York, NY: Elsevier.

Marsh, H. W., Martin, A. J., & Cheng, J. (2008). A multilevel perspective on gender in classroom motivation and climate: Potential benefits of male teachers for boys? *Journal of Educational Psychology, 100,* 78–95.

Marsh, H. W., Tracey, D. K., Craven, R. G. (2006). Multidimensional self-concept structure for preadolescents with mild intellectual disabilities: A hybrid multigroup-mimic approach to factorial invariance and latent mean differences. *Educational and Psychological Measurement, 66,* 795–818.

Martin, A. J. (2004). The role of positive psychology in enhancing satisfaction, motivation, and productivity in the workplace. *Journal of Organizational Behavior Management, 24,* 113–133.

Martin, A. J. (2006a). A motivational psychology for the education of Indigenous students. *Australian Journal of Indigenous Education, 35,* 30–43.

Martin, A. J. (2006b). The relationship between teachers' perceptions of student motivation and engagement and teachers' enjoyment of and confidence in teaching. *Asia-Pacific Journal of Teacher Education, 34,* 73–93.

Martin, A. J. (2007). Examining a multidimensional model of student motivation and engagement using a construct validation approach. *British Journal of Educational Psychology, 77,* 413–440.

Martin, A. J. (2009). Motivation and engagement across the academic lifespan: A developmental construct validity study of elementary school, high school, and university/college students. *Educational and Psychological Measurement, 69,* 794–824.

Martin, A. J. (2010). *Building classroom success: Eliminating academic fear and failure.* London, England: Continuum.

Martin, A. J. (2012). Adaptability and learning. In N. M. Seel (Ed.), *Encyclopedia of the Sciences of Learning* (pp. 90–92). New York, NY: Springer.

Martin, A. J. (2016). *Using Load Reduction Instruction (LRI) to boost motivation and engagement.* Leicester, England: British Psychological Society.

Martin, A. J. (2017). Adaptability—What it is and what it is not: Comment on Chandra and Leong (2016). *American Psychologist, 72*(7), 696–698.

Martin, A. J., Bobis, J., Anderson, J., Way, J., & Vellar, R. (2011). Patterns of multilevel variance in psycho-educational phenomena: Exploring motivation, engagement, climate, teacher, and achievement factors. *German Journal of Educational Psychology/Zeitschrift für Pädagogische Psychologie, 25,* 49–61.

Martin, A. J. Marsh, H. W., & Debus, R. L. (2003). Self-handicapping and defensive pessimism: A model of self-protection from a longitudinal perspective. *Contemporary Educational Psychology, 28,* 1–36.

Martin, A. J., & Dowson, M. (2009). Interpersonal relationships, motivation, engagement, and achievement: Yields for theory, current issues, and practice. *Review of Educational Research, 79*, 327–365.

Martin, A. J., & Marsh, H. W. (2003). Fear of failure: Friend or foe? *Australian Psychologist, 38*, 31–38.

Martin, A. J., & Marsh, H. W. (2005). Motivating boys and motivating girls: Does teacher gender really make a difference? *Australian Journal of Education, 49*, 320–334.

Martin, A. J., & Marsh, H. W. (2006). Academic resilience and its psychological and educational correlates: A construct validity approach. *Psychology in the Schools, 43*, 267–282.

Martin, A. J., & Marsh, H. W. (2008a). Academic buoyancy: Towards an understanding of students' everyday academic resilience. *Journal of School Psychology, 46*, 53–83.

Martin, A.J., & Marsh, H.W. (2008b). Workplace and academic buoyancy: Psychometric assessment and construct validity amongst school personnel and students. *Journal of Psychoeducational Assessment, 26*, 168–184.

Martin, A. J. Marsh, H. W., & Debus, R. L. (2001a). A quadripolar need achievement representation of self-handicapping and defensive pessimism. *American Educational Research Journal, 38*, 583–610.

Martin, A. J., Marsh, H. W., & Debus, R. L. (2001b). Self-handicapping and defensive pessimism: Exploring a model of predictors and outcomes from a self-protection perspective. *Journal of Educational Psychology, 93*, 87–102.

Martin, A. J., Marsh, H. W., McInerney, D. M., & Green, J. (2009). Young people's interpersonal relationships and academic and non-academic outcomes: The relative salience of teachers, parents, same-sex peers, and opposite-sex peers. *Teachers College Record*. Retrieved from http://www.tcrecord.org

Martin, A. J., Marsh, H. W., McInerney, D. M., Green, J., & Dowson, M. (2007). Getting along with teachers and parents: The yields of good relationships for students' achievement motivation and self-esteem. *Australian Journal of Guidance and Counselling, 17*, 109–125.

Martin, A. J., Marsh, H. W., Williamson, A., & Debus, R. L. (2003). Self-handicapping, defensive pessimism, and goal orientation: A qualitative study of university students. *Journal of Educational Psychology, 95*, 617–628.

Martin, A. J., Nejad, H., Colmar, S., & Liem, G. A. D. (2012). Adaptability: Conceptual and empirical perspectives on responses to change, novelty and uncertainty. *Australian Journal of Guidance and Counselling, 22*, 58–81.

Martin, A. J., Nejad, H. G., Colmar, S., & Liem, G. A. D. (2013). Adaptability: How students' responses to uncertainty and novelty predict their academic and non-academic outcomes. *Journal of Educational Psychology, 105*, 728–746.

Marzano, R. (2003). *What works in schools*. Alexandria, VA: ASCD.

Maynard Smith, J. (1982). *Evolution and the theory of games*. Cambridge, England: Cambridge University Press.

McInerney, D. M., Hinkley, J., Dowson, M., & Van Etten, S. (1998). Children's beliefs about success in the classroom: Are there cultural differences? *Journal of Educational Psychology, 90*, 621–629.

Middleton, M. J., & Midgley, C. (1997). Avoiding the demonstration of lack of ability: An unexplored aspect of goal theory. *Journal of Educational Psychology, 89,* 710–718.

Nerressian, N. J. (2005). Interpreting scientific and engineering practices: Integrating the cognitive, social, and cultural dimensions. In M. E. Gorman, R. D. Tweney, D. C. Gooding, & A. Kincannon (Eds.), *Scientific and technological thinking* (pp. 17–56). Mahwah, NJ: Erlbaum.

Nicholls, J. G. (1989). *The competitive ethos and democratic education.* Cambridge, MA: Harvard University Press.

Nolen, S. B., & Ward, C. J. (2008). Sociocultural and situative approaches to studying motivation. In M. L. Maehr, S. A. Karabenick, & T. C. Urdan (Eds.), *Advances in motivation and achievement* (pp. 425–460). Bingley, England: JAI Press.

O'Gorman, R., Wilson, D. S., & Sheldon, K. M. (2008). For the good of the group? Exploring group-level evolutionary adaptations using multilevel selection theory. *Group Dynamics-Theory Research and Practice, 12,* 17–26.

Parker, P. D., & Martin, A. J. (2009). Coping and buoyancy in the workplace: Understanding their effects on teachers' work-related well-being and engagement. *Teaching and Teacher Education, 25,* 68–75.

Patrick, H., Ryan, A. M., & Kaplan, A. (2007). Early adolescents' perceptions of the classroom social environment, motivational beliefs, and engagement. *Journal of Educational Psychology, 99,* 83–98.

Pinker, S. (1994). *The language instinct: How the mind creates language.* London, England: Penguin.

Pinker, S. (2002). *The blank slate: The modern denial of human nature.* London, England: Allen Lane.

Raudenbush, S. W., & Bryk, A. S. (2002). *Hierarchical linear models: Applications and data analysis methods* (2nd ed.). Thousand Oaks, CA: SAGE.

Reeve, J., Deci, E. L., & Ryan, R. M. (2004). Self-determination theory: A dialectical framework for understanding sociocultural influences on student motivation. In D. McInerney & S. Van Etten (Eds.), *Big theories revisited.* Greenwich, CT: Information Age.

Roeser, R., Eccles, J. S., & Sameroff, A. J. (2000). School as a context of early adolescents' academic and social-emotional development: A summary of research findings. *Elementary School Journal, 100,* 443–471.

Rosenholtz, R. S., & Simpson, C. (1984). Classroom organization and student stratification. *Elementary School Journal, 85,* 1–17.

Roseth, C. J., Johnson, D. W., & Johnson, R. T. (2008). Promoting early adolescents' achievement and peer relationships: The effects of cooperative, competitive, and individualistic goal structures. *Psychological Bulletin, 134,* 223–246.

Sanfey, A. G. (2007). Social decision-making: Insights from game theory and neuroscience. *Science, 318,* 598–602.

Schaller, M., Park, J. H., & Kenrick, D. T. (2007). Human evolution and social cognition. In R. I. M Dunbar & L. Barrett (Eds.), *Oxford handbook of evolutionary psychology* (pp. 491–504). Oxford, England: Oxford University Press. Retrieved from https://doi.org/10.1093/oxfordhb/9780198568308.013.0033

Schaller, M., Simpson, J., & Kenrick, D. (2006). *Evolution and social psychology.* London, England: Psychology Press.

Schoenfeld, A. H. (1985). *Mathematical problem solving*. New York, NY: Academic Press.

Seligman, M. E. P. (2002). *Authentic happiness*. New York, NY: Free Press.

Sirin, S. R. (2005). Socioeconomic status and academic achievement: A meta-analytic review of research. *Review of Educational Research, 75*, 417–453.

Slavin, R. E. (1987). Ability grouping and student achievement in elementary schools: A best-evidence synthesis. *Review of Educational Research, 57*, 293–336.

Slavin, R. E. (1996). Research on cooperative learning and achievement: What we know, what we need to know. *Contemporary Educational Psychology, 21*, 43–69.

Steenbergen-Hu, S., Makel, M. C., & Olszewski-Kubilius, P. (2016). What one hundred years of research says about the effects of ability grouping and acceleration on K–12 students' academic achievement: Findings of two second-order meta-analyses. *Review of Educational Research, 86*, 849–899.

Sulloway, F. J. (2007). Birth order and sibling competition, In R. I. M. Dunbar & L. Barrett (Eds.), *Oxford handbook of evolutionary psychology* (pp. 297–311). Oxford, England: Oxford University Press.

Sweller, J. (2004). Instructional design consequences of an analogy between evolution by natural selection and human cognitive architecture. *Instructional Science, 32*, 9–31.

Sweller, J. (2007). Evolutionary biology and educational psychology. In J. S. Carlson & J. R. Levin (Eds.), *Educating the evolved mind: Conceptual foundations for an evolutionary educational psychology* (pp. 165–175). Charlotte, NC: Information Age.

Sweller, J. (2008). Instructional implications of David C. Geary's evolutionary educational psychology. *Educational Psychologist, 43*, 214–216.

Sweller, J. (2012). Human cognitive architecture: Why some instructional procedures work and others do not. In K. R. Harris., S. Graham., & T. Urdan (Eds.), *APA educational psychology handbook* (pp. 295–325). Washington, DC: American Psychological Association. Retrieved from https://doi.org/10.1037/13273-011

Tooby, J., & Cosmides, L. (1992). The psychological foundations of culture. In J. Barkow., L. Cosmides., & J. Tooby. (Eds.), *The adapted mind: Evolutionary psychology and the generation of culture* (pp. 19–136). New York, NY: Oxford University Press.

Trivers, R. L. (1971). The evolution of reciprocal altruism. *Quarterly Review of Biology, 46*, 35–57.

Vinson, T. (2002). *Inquiry into the provision of public education*. Sydney, Australia: Pluto Press.

Vygotsky, L. S. (1978). *Mind in society: The development of higher psychological processes*. M. Cole., V. John-Steiner., S. Scribner., & E. Souberman (Eds.). Cambridge, MA: Harvard University Press.

Walker, R. A. (2010). Sociocultural issues in motivation. In E. Baker, B. McGaw, & P. Peterson (Eds.), *International Encyclopedia of Education* (pp. 712–717). Amsterdam, Netherlands: Elsevier.

Walker, R. A., Pressick-Kilborn, K., Arnold, L., & Sainsbury, E. J. (2004). Investigating motivation in context: Developing sociocultural perspectives. *European Psychologist, 9*, 245–256.

Walker, R. A., & Horsley, M. (2006). Textbook pedagogy: A sociocultural analysis of effective teaching and learning, In D. M. McInerney., M. Dowson., & S. Van Etten (Eds.), *Effective schools* (Vol. 6, pp. 105–133). Greenwich, CT: Information Age.

Wentzel, K. R. (1999). Social-motivational processes and interpersonal relationships: Implications for understanding motivation at school. *Journal of Educational Psychology, 91,* 76–97.

Wigfield, A., & Eccles, J. S. (2000). Expectancy-value theory of motivation. *Contemporary Educational Psychology, 25,* 68–81.

Wilson, D. S., & Wilson, E. O. (2008). Evolution 'for the good of the group'. *American Scientist, 96,* 380–389.

Workman, L., & Reader, W. (2004). *Evolutionary psychology.* New York, NY: Cambridge University Press.

Wyman, E., & Tomasello, M. (2007). The ontogenetic origins of human cooperation. In R. I. M. Dunbar & L. Barrett (Eds.), *Oxford handbook of evolutionary psychology* (pp. 227–236). Oxford, England: Oxford University Press.

Yamasue, H., Abe, O., Suga. M., Yamada, H., Rogers, M. A., Aoki, A., Kato, N., & Kasai, K. (2008). Sex-linked neuroanatomical basis of human altruistic cooperativeness. *Cerebral Cortex, 18,* 2331–2340.

ABOUT THE CONTRIBUTORS

Christopher D. Andrews is currently a PhD student in the Learning Sciences program at Indiana University. His research interests include teacher assessment practices and participatory approaches to teaching and learning in technology-rich environments. He is currently teaching an undergraduate learning theory course for pre-service teachers. Prior to doctoral studies, he was a high school teacher for 7 years, during which time he served as a department chair and peer-leader, and was voted teacher of the year by his colleagues. He earned a master's degree in teacher education from Brigham Young University, publishing a thesis exploring teachers' definitions, reasons, and beliefs surrounding student self-assessment.

Timothy J. Cleary is an associate professor and chair of the Department of Applied Psychology in the Graduate School of Applied and Professional Psychology (GSAPP) at Rutgers, The State University of New Jersey. His primary research interests include the development and application of self-regulated learning (SRL) and motivation assessment and intervention practices across academic, athletic, and clinical contexts. He has published extensively on SRL issues in top-tier journals in school psychology, educational psychology, and medical education. He has also edited two SRL books and is currently publishing a book for K–12 teachers regarding SRL applications to classroom-based contexts. Dr. Cleary teaches graduate level classes in academic interventions, learning theory, and learning disabilities; and routinely provides professional development training to researchers, teachers, administrators, psychologists, and counselors regarding best practices in SRL assessment and interventions.

Big Theories Revisited 2, pages 429–439
Copyright © 2018 by Information Age Publishing
All rights of reproduction in any form reserved.

Jesus Alfonso D. Datu is an incoming assistant professor in the Department of Special Education and Counseling at the Education University of Hong Kong and a graduating PhD in Educational Psychology student in the Division of Learning, Development, and Diversity of the Faculty of Education at The University of Hong Kong. He is a recipient of the Lee Shau Kee University Postgraduate Fellowship. He completed his MA in Counseling at De La Salle University, Manila, Philippines (April 2014) and BS in Psychology degree (*Magna Cum Laude*) at Colegio de San Juan de Letran—Manila, Philippines (March 2011). He has published papers on how positive traits, states, and social factors may be linked to well-being and academic outcomes in reputable journals like *Journal of School Psychology, Contemporary Educational Psychology, Journal of Happiness Studies, Journal of Positive Psychology,* and *Personality and Individual Differences.* His present research interests revolve around positive psychology and educational psychology.

Maria K. DiBenedetto is an expert on self-regulated learning (SRL) and has published on self-efficacy, SRL, and microanalytic methodology. She coauthored a book on SRL and common core state standards to teach English Language Arts (Grades K–12), which is based on Zimmerman and Schunk's model of SRL. She is editing a book where each chapter is coauthored by exemplary high school teachers and scholars who analyze the teachers' lessons using a SRL framework. She has served as a consultant across the United States for students, and elementary and high school educators. In 2015–2016 she was chair of the American Educational Research Association's special interest group: Studying and Self-Regulated Learning. She is currently chair of the high school science department where she teaches, along with teaching as an adjunct in local colleges. She also volunteers at a therapeutic horseback riding ranch for people with disabilities and mentors/tutors homeless children.

Jacquelynne S. Eccles is the Distinguished Professor of Education at the University of California, Irvine and the McKeachie/Pintrich Distinguished University Professor Emeritus of psychology and education at the University of Michigan. Her research focuses on achievement, motivation, personal and social identities, gender, and family and school influences on student motivation. Her expectancy-value theory of motivated choices and her concept of stage-environment have greatly influenced research in the educational and developmental sciences. She has edited for *Developmental Psychology, Journal for Research on Adolescence, Psychological Bulletin, American Psychologist, AERA OPEN,* and *Child Development.* She is past president of Divisions 7 and 35 of APA, the Society for Research on Adolescence (SRA) and has served on the faculty at Smith College, the University of Colorado, the University of Michigan, and the University of California, Irvine.

Andrew J. Elliot is professor of psychology at the University of Rochester. He has held visiting professor positions at Cambridge University, King Abdulaziz University, Oxford University, and the University of Munich, and has been a visiting fellow at Churchill College (Cambridge) and Jesus College (Oxford). He received his PhD from the University of Wisconsin-Madison in 1994. His research focuses on achievement motivation and approach-avoidance motivation. He is currently editor of *Advances in Motivation Science*, and has over 200 scholarly publications. He has received multiple awards for his teaching and research contributions to both educational and social-personality psychology. He has given keynote or university addresses in more than 20 different countries, and his lab regularly hosts professors, postdocs, and graduate students from around the globe.

Benjamin Dantzer is a doctoral student in the Human Development, Learning, and Culture (HDLC) program at the university of British Columbia, Canada. His master's thesis explored how children and youth from impoverished neighborhoods can strengthen their communities and support one another's self-determination. While conducting this research, he discovered an interest in supporting children and youth who are "at-risk" to strengthen their own developmental and educational outcomes.

Edward L. Deci is the Helen F. and Fred H. Gowen Professor in the Social Sciences at the University of Rochester, with secondary appointments in the University College of Southeast Norway and Australian Catholic University. He is co-founder of self-determination theory, and has published nine books and over 100 journal articles. Dr. Deci is a fellow of the Association for Psychological Science, the American Psychological Association, and the Society for Personality and Social Psychology, among other associations. His numerous honors include a distinguished scholar award from the Society for Personality and Social Psychology, a lifetime achievement award from the International Society for Self and Identity, and a distinguished scientific contribution award from the Positive Psychology Network. He was named honorary president of the Canadian Psychological Association and is a recipient of a James McKeen Cattell Fund Sabbatical Award.

Daniel T. Hickey is a professor and program coordinator with the Learning Sciences program at Indiana University. He has published over 80 articles in refereed journals and edited volumes and has served as principal investigator or co-investigator on over $7,000,000 external research grants from the U.S. National Science Foundation, the MacArthur Foundation, and the U.S. Department of Education. His research primarily explores the use of situative theories of learning to uncover new approaches to capturing, recognizing, validating, and endorsing evidence of learning, primarily in online and other technology-based contexts. In recent years his research has focused particular attention on digital badges and other approaches to digital credentialing.

Amanda Inns is a doctoral student at Johns Hopkins University in the School of Education. She received her BA in Psychology from Northwestern University in 2004, and her MEd in Elementary Education from Vanderbilt University in 2009. She previously taught in elementary schools and served as a Peace Corps volunteer in South Africa, working to bring educational reforms to rural schools. She is currently writing a dissertation examining the implementation of enhanced school-based vision services. Additionally, she works on systematic reviews of reading programs. Her research interests include evaluation and implementation research as well as meta-analysis.

Ronnel B. King is an assistant professor in the Department of Curriculum and Instruction at The Education University of Hong Kong. Prior to this, he worked as a research scientist in the Learning Sciences Lab at the National Institute of Education, Nanyang Technological University, Singapore. He obtained his PhD from The University of Hong Kong in 2012 (educational psychology) and his doctoral dissertation was awarded the Highly Commended Dissertation Award by the Global SELF Research Network. He is interested in understanding student motivation, engagement, and well-being. He has recently guest edited a special issue in the *British Journal of Educational Psychology* ("Culture and Motivation," 2016) together with Prof. Dennis McInerney. He was also the lead guest editor for the special issue "Positive Education in Asia" in *The Asia Pacific Education Researcher* (2016). He has recently co-edited (with Allan Bernardo) *The Psychology of Asian Learners: A Festschrift in Honor of David Watkins* (Springer, 2016).

Anastasia Kitsantas is professor of educational psychology in the College of Education and Human Development at George Mason University. Her research interests focus on the development of self-regulated learning (SRL) and student motivational beliefs across diverse areas of functioning including academic learning, athletics, and health. She has also studied the role of learning technologies in supporting student SRL. This work has resulted in more than 100 publications and has made an important contribution towards the understanding of how people learn to self-regulate their academic, athletic, and health related learning while enhancing people's abilities to improve in these areas. She is a fellow of the American Psychological Association, Division 15, Educational Psychology and has been a active participant in many international student and scholarly groups.

Gregory Arief D. Liem is an associate professor at the National Institute of Education, Nanyang Technological University, Singapore. He currently serves as an associate editor for *Educational Psychology: An International Jour-*

nal of Experimental Educational Psychology, School Psychology International, and *the Asia Pacific Journal of Education.* He is also a member of the editorial boards of *Measurement and Evaluation in Counseling and Development, Journal of Psychologists and Counsellors in Schools,* and *the Asia-Pacific Education Researcher.* He is the editor of this book series *Research on Sociocultural Influences on Learning and Motivation* (Information Age Publishing).

Andrew Martin, BA (Hons), MEd (Hons), PhD, is a scientia professor, professor of educational psychology, and co-chair of the Educational Psychology Research Group in the School of Education at the University of New South Wales, Australia. He specializes in motivation, engagement, achievement, and quantitative research methods. He is also honorary research fellow in the Department of Education at the University of Oxford, honorary professor in the School of Education and Social Work at the University of Sydney, fellow of the American Psychological Association, fellow of the American Educational Research Association, fellow of the Academy of the Social Sciences in Australia, and president of the International Association of Applied Psychology's Division 5 Educational and School Psychology.

Silvia Mazabel is a doctoral candidate in the Department of Educational and Counselling Psychology, and Special Education in the University of British Columbia, Canada. She is the project manager for Perry's project: Promoting Positive Life Outcomes for Children and Youth. Her research and professional interests include the promotion of SRL in post-secondary settings, with a particular focus on classroom wide teaching practices that support students' engagement and active learning.

Mary McCaslin is professor and head of the Department of Educational Psychology at the University of Arizona. Her scholarship focuses on the press among cultural, social, and personal sources of influence that co-regulate student emotional adaptation and emergent identity.

Dennis M. McInerney is an honorary professor at The Education University of Hong Kong and The Australian Catholic University. He has published extensively in refereed journals and is the author of numerous books including *Educational Psychology: Constructing Learning (6th ed)* (Sydney: Pearson) and *Developmental and Educational Psychology for Teachers* (London, England: Routledge; with Dave Putwain). Major areas of research are cross-cultural studies of learning and motivation, self-processes (such as self-regulation and self-concept), and instrument design and validation. Dennis is the founding editor of this book series *Research on Sociocultural Influences on Learning and Motivation* (Information Age Publishing).

Stephen Pape is a professor of education and director of the Johns Hopkins University Doctor of Education program. Dr. Pape received his doctorate in educational psychology with a focus in learning and instruction from the City University of New York following service as a middle school mathematics and science teacher in New York City. His research focuses on technology-enhanced classroom contexts that foster mathematical understanding and the development of strategic behaviors. His IES-funded projects include a national randomized control trial that examined the impact of classroom connectivity technology on Algebra I achievement and classroom interactions. He also served as co-PI for an online professional development program, for Grades 3–5 general and special education faculty. He is presently serving as chair and member of the National Council of Teachers of Mathematics Research Committee.

Reinhard Pekrun is professor for personality and educational psychology at the University of Munich and professorial fellow at the Australian Catholic University. His research areas include achievement emotion and motivation, personality development, and educational assessment. He pioneered research on emotions in education and originated the control-value theory of achievement emotions. Pekrun is a highly cited researcher who has authored 24 books and more than 250 articles and chapters. He is a fellow of the International Academy of Education, of the American Educational Research Association, and of the Association for Psychological Science, and the recipient of the Diefenbaker Award 2015 and of the Sylvia Scribner Award 2017. He served as president of the Stress and Anxiety Research Society and vice-president for research at the University of Munich. In an advisory capacity, Pekrun is active in policy development and implementation in education.

Nancy E. Perry is professor in the Department of Educational and Counselling Psychology, and Special Education at the University of British Columbia, Canada. Her research seeks to understand how: (a) classroom processes are implicated in children's development of self-regulated learning (SRL), and (b) working with teachers to design activities and structure interactions with students that can support SRL. She currently holds the Dorothy Lam Chair in Special Education in UBC's Faculty of Education. She is past president of Division 15, Educational Psychology, in the American Psychological Association and the Canadian Association for Educational Psychology; and a former associate editor of the *Journal of Learning and Instruction.*

Johnmarshall Reeve is a professor in the Department of Education at Korea University in Seoul, South Korea. He has published 50 journal articles and three books, including *Understanding Motivation and Emotion.* He received his PhD from Texas Christian University and completed postdoctoral work at the University of Rochester. Professor Reeve's research interests center on the empirical study of all aspects of human motivation and emotion with particular emphasis on teachers' motivating styles, students' engagement, and the neuroscience of intrinsic motivation. For his work on teachers' motivating styles, he received the Thomas N. Urban Research Award given by the FINE (First in the Nation in Education) Foundation and the paper of the year from the *Journal of Sport and Exercise Psychology*. He has twice received the Distinguished Researcher Award from Korea University. Since 2011, Prof. Reeve has served as editor-in-chief of *Motivation and Emotion*.

Christine Rubie-Davies is a professor of education in the Faculty of Education and Social Work at the University of Auckland in New Zealand. She has published six books and over 100 articles, chapters, and conference proceedings. Christine has editorial roles with six journals including *Review of Educational Research* and *Contemporary Educational Psychology* and has been awarded Outstanding Reviewer by the American Educational Research Association in 2013, 2015, and 2017. She has received several research grants including a Marsden Fast Start Grant in 2010 which enabled Christine to conduct the first-ever experimental teacher expectation project designed to change teacher practices to emulate those of high expectation teachers. In addition, she won a National Tertiary Teaching Excellence Award in 2007. Christine's primary research interests are teacher expectations and beliefs that moderate expectancy effects. She particularly focuses on teacher expectation effects for ethnic minority and disadvantaged groups.

Richard M. Ryan is a professor at the Institute for Positive Psychology & Education at the Australian Catholic University and research professor in Psychology at the University of Rochester in New York. Dr. Ryan is a clinical psychologist and co-developer of Self-Determination Theory. He has published seven books and over 200 journal articles. He has lectured in more than 80 universities worldwide, consulted with numerous organizations, and has received distinguished career awards from the International Society for Self and Identity, a Shavelson Distinguished Researcher award, among many other honors. He is a fellow of the American Psychological Association, the American Educational Research Association, and an honorary member of the German Psychological Society. He has held numerous editorial posts, including editor-in-chief of *Motivation & Emotion*. He has also been a James McKeen Cattell and Leverhulme Fellow, and a visiting scientist at the National Institute of Education in Singapore, the University of Bath, and the Max Planck Institute.

Dale Schunk is a professor and former dean of the School of Education, The University of North Carolina at Greensboro. He received his PhD in Educational Psychology from Stanford University. Previously he was on the faculty at the University of Houston and the University of North Carolina at Chapel Hill, and head of the department of educational studies at Purdue University. His research focuses on the effects of social and instructional factors on students' cognitive processes, learning, self-regulation, and motivation. He teaches courses in learning, motivation, self-regulation, and educational psychology. He has published over 120 articles and chapters, and is author and editor of several books. His awards include the Barry J. Zimmerman Award for Outstanding Contributions from the American Educational Research Association Studying and Self-Regulated Learning Special Interest Group, and the Senior Distinguished Research Scholar Award from The University of North Carolina at Greensboro School of Education.

Constantine Sedikides is currently a professor of psychology and director of Center for Research on Self and Identity, University of Southampton, United Kingdom. Constantine has published more than 350 articles and chapters, as well as 15 edited volumes or journal special issues. His research has been funded from various national and international agencies, such as Economic and Social Research Council, The Templeton Foundation, and National Institute of Health. He has received numerous awards, including the Distinguished Lifetime Career Award (International Society for Self and Identity), Kurt Lewin Medal for Outstanding Scientific Contribution (European Association of Social Psychology), and The President's Award for Distinguished Contributions to Psychological Knowledge (The British Psychological Society). His major areas of research interest are self-evaluation (role of self-motives), narcissism, mental time travel (nostalgia, in particular), and authenticity.

Robert Slavin is currently director of the Center for Research and Reform in Education at Johns Hopkins University and Chairman of the Success for All Foundation. He received his BA in Psychology from Reed College in 1972, and his PhD in Social Relations in 1975 from Johns Hopkins University. Dr. Slavin has authored or co-authored more than 300 articles and 24 books. He received the American Educational Research Association's Raymond B. Cattell Early Career Award for Programmatic Research in 1986, the Palmer O. Johnson award for the best article in an AERA journal in 1988, the Charles A. Dana award in 1994, the James Bryant Conant Award from the Education Commission of the States in 1998, the Distinguished Services Award from the Council of Chief State School Officers in 2000, the AERA Review of Research Award in 2009, the Palmer O. Johnson Award for the best article in an AERA journal in 2008, and was appointed as an AERA Fellow in 2010. In 2017 he was awarded the E. L. Thorndike Career Achievement Award by the American Psychological Association.

Jacqueline Slemp is currently pursuing her doctorate in school psychology at the Graduate School of Applied and Professional Psychology at Rutgers, The State University of New Jersey. She received a bachelor's degree in psychological sciences and Spanish with a minor in neuroscience from the University of Connecticut in 2012. Ms. Slemp's broad interests include self-regulated learning in home and school contexts, student motivation, and student achievement from primary through postsecondary education. As an undergraduate, Ms. Slemp worked one-on-one with students to promote academic success and personal development. Since beginning her graduate education, Ms. Slemp has gained practical experience through fieldwork at a local high school and community clinic and has worked to further refine her research interests through involvement in Dr. Timothy Cleary's lab.

Hana Turner (**Ngāti Ranginui**) is a PhD student at the Faculty of Education and Social Work at the University of Auckland in New Zealand. Her PhD research focuses on the schooling experiences of high achieving Māori and non-Māori senior secondary school students and investigates Māori student success, teacher expectations, and the disparities in educational achievement between Māori and non-Māori students.

Stephen M. Tonks is an associate professor in the Department of Leadership, Educational Psychology & Foundations at Northern Illinois University. His research focuses on reading motivation and engagement, the interplay of culture and motivation, and ways to increase students' motivation in the classroom. He has co-authored articles and chapters on classroom engagement, academic and reading motivation, and has a strong interest in Japanese culture and education.

Christine Calderon Vriesema is a postdoctoral scholar at the University of California, Santa Barbara. Christine's research interests primarily emphasize motivation, self-regulation, and emotion among teachers and students. While centered in education contexts, her research also integrates perspectives from other areas of psychology (i.e., social, developmental, and industrial and organizational). Across all areas of her research, Christine aims to understand how context shapes motivation and action.

Ellen L. Usher is an associate professor of educational psychology in the Department of Educational, School, and Counseling Psychology at the University of Kentucky, where she is director of the P20 Motivation and Learning Lab (http://p20motivationlab.org). Her research focuses on the sources and effects of beliefs of personal efficacy in diverse contexts. In 2010, Ellen received the Early Career Award from Division 15 of the American Psychological Association. She serves as chair of the Motivation in Education Special Interest Group of the American Educational Research Association and as associate editor of the *British Journal of Educational Psychology*. She is an editorial board member of the *Journal of Educational Psychology* and *Contemporary Educational Psychology*.

Melinda Webber is an associate professor and research director of The Starpath Project in the Faculty of Education at the University of Auckland, New Zealand. She is a former Fulbright/Nga Pae o te Maramatanga Indigenous Scholar who has published widely on the nature of ethnic identity development, examining the ways race, ethnicity, culture, and identity impact the lives of young people particularly Māori students. In 2016, Melinda was awarded an esteemed Marsden Fast-Start grant to undertake a research project examining the distinctive identity traits of Ngāpuhi, New Zealand's largest iwi. In 2017, Melinda was awarded a prestigious Rutherford Discovery Fellowship to tackle an important question facing educators—"How can we foster cultural pride and academic aspiration among Māori students?"—using culturally informed and iwi-determined research methods. Melinda had a sole-authored book published in 2008 by New Zealand Council of Educational Research titled *Walking the Space Between: Maori/Pakeha Identity* and recently co-edited a book titled *Sociocultural Realities: Exploring New Horizons* in 2015.

Brianna L. Weidner is a master's student in the educational psychology program at the University of Kentucky. She graduated *Suma Cum Laude* from the University of Kentucky in the Spring of 2016 with a BA in Psychology and minors in Spanish and photography. Her research interests include the development of self-efficacy in understudied contexts and her thesis work examines math self-efficacy and its sources in urban and rural settings. She has presented her work at several national and international conferences and served as a research assistant in the P20 Motivation and Learning lab for 4 years. She hopes to use the knowledge gained from her studies to better understand the educational needs of children in the state care system.

Kathryn R. Wentzel is professor of human development at the University of Maryland, College Park. Dr. Wentzel studies the nature of teacher–student and peer relationships and how these relationships support young adolescents' goal pursuit, prosocial behavior, and academic performance. Dr. Wentzel has published over 100 articles and book chapters based on this work and has published volumes on social development, *Handbook of Social Influences in School Contexts (2016)*, and achievement motivation, *Social Motivation: Understanding Children's School Adjustment* (1996), *Handbook of Motivation at School* (2016), and *Motivating Students to Learn (2013)*. She is currently editor of *Educational Psychologist* and past editor of the *Journal of Applied Developmental Psychology*. Dr. Wentzel is past vice-president of Division E (Counseling and Human Development, AERA) and a fellow of the

American Psychological Association, Division 15, and of the American Educational Research Association, Division E.

Allan Wigfield is professor in the Department of Human Development and Quantitative Methodology, distinguished scholar-teacher, and University Honors Faculty Fellow at the University of Maryland. He was appointed in 2015 as an honorary professor of psychology at the University of Heidelberg. His research focuses on how children's motivation develops across the school years in different areas, and also on developing interventions to improve children's motivation. In his intervention work he has focused primarily on children's reading motivation and comprehension.

Philip H. Winne is professor in the Faculty of Education at Simon Fraser University, Canada. He previously held a 2-term Tier I Canada Research Chair. He researches self-regulated learning, metacognition and learning analytics; and leads a team developing software technologies to support learners and research those topics. His research is published in more than 170 scholarly books, articles, book chapters, and refereed proceedings. Winne was honored with the Robbie Case Memorial Award for outstanding contributions to educational psychology in Canada, the Barry J. Zimmerman Award for exceptional theoretical and empirical scholarship in research on studying and self-regulated learning, and the Mentorship Award from the Canadian Society for the Study of Education for his support of graduate students. He is a fellow of the Canadian Psychological Association, the American Educational Research Association, the American Psychological Association, and the Association for Psychological Science.

CPSIA information can be obtained
at www.ICGtesting.com
Printed in the USA
BVHW06s1428240418
514223BV00007B/28/P